AN ILLUSTRATED HISTORY OF
Ships
EDITED BY E.L. CORNWELL

AN ILLUSTRATED HISTORY OF Ships

EDITED BY E.L. CORNWELL

NEW ENGLISH LIBRARY
TIMES MIRROR

This edition published in 1979 by
New English Library Limited
Barnard's Inn
Holborn
London EC1N 2JR
England

Printed by Fratelli Spada, Ciampino,
Rome, Italy

450 04133 6

Illustrations:

Page 1 : The Argentinian ship 'Libertade' in Sydney Harbour. *B P Singer Features Inc*

Pages 2-3 : A model frigate used in filming. *Associated British*

Page 4 : The SA 'Vaal' (ex 'Transvaal Castle') at Southampton in 1970. *A Crisp*

Contents

A drawing by Holbein of Henry VIII's Great Ship. *Mary Evans Picture Library*

Introduction

In its broadest sense the history of ships – that is, the use of buoyant craft to provide transport for people and materials on water, or to further aggressive or defensive intentions against known or supposed enemies – is almost as old as the history of mankind himself. Moreover, just as water covers the greater part of the earth's surface, so maritime events have filled many more pages of the world's history than land-based activities.

A study of history reveals a very significant fact. It is that peoples who have developed a positive maritime economy or strategy and gained control of the sea or a considerable part of it have always emerged eventual winners of any conflict in which they engaged, and without exception those who have achieved such a capability and then relinquished it for any reason have soon gone into decline. Throughout history many battles have been won on land, but, until recent times, most or all major wars have been lost at sea.

With around 6000 years of history to draw on for its material, any book that attempts to follow mankind's long progress from the floating tree-trunk and coracle to the luxury cruise liner and nuclear-powered aircraft carrier must be a work of massive compression. The aim in this book has been to present a balanced illustrated history by selecting a number of the major aspects of mankind's association with the sea and in each of those areas to trace the significant line or lines of development in roughly chronological order.

For most of maritime history sails formed the only non-manual means of propelling a vessel. The sail using the power of the wind is in fact one of man's earliest inventions – boats with sails are depicted in Nile Valley rock carvings and on early Egyptian vases – and to many people today sailing ships have a special fascination, partly because of their great historical importance, and partly because sailing boats is such a popular recreation. As sailing craft figure prominently throughout history, so they are featured extensively in this book not only in the early sections devoted to evolution from the simple lugsail to the intricate magnificence of the fully rigged ship, but in due place in many other sections.

In contrast to the gentle pace of the progress of sail through nearly six thousand years, development of mechanical propulsion has been explosively rapid. Not until the 19th century did Symington's *Charlotte Dundas* puff and chuff its way along the Forth & Clyde Canal in Scotland, and it was not until halfway through that century that the steam engine started to be taken seriously for ocean-going ships.

The breathtaking series of technological advances that took the ship from the clanking steam piston engine to the smoothness and silence of the steam turbine and the economy of the diesel engine is covered fully in section 10. So also are the recent developments of the convenient gas turbine now coming to be preferred for warship propulsion and the astonishing nuclear plant that provides steam to propel a mighty seagoing airfield displacing nearly 100,000 tons at speeds approaching 40mph without the need to refuel for a decade or more.

Man is by nature militant and much of history is primarily of warfare. That sad fact is acknowledged throughout the book and the history of ships is found to be very much a history of conflict and, as mentioned above, the peoples who controlled the sea were frequently the history makers. The development of ships and weapons of war, short histories of the world's principal navies and the major sea battles fought down the ages are covered in separate sections and, inevitably it seems, warlike actions feature in several other sections.

But by no means all noteworthy maritime events have had to do with conflict and the achievements of courageous navigators and discoverers, the founding of maritime travel and commerce, activities of inventors and scientists who have contributed to safety and efficiency at sea, examples of the dangers that exist at sea and the notable endeavours to reduce or eradicate those dangers are all given due weight.

The final section, appropriately, sketches in a glimpse or two of the pomp and circumstance which from time immemorial have been a strong feature of mankind's association with the sea, and rounds off what we hope the reader will find is an absorbing presentation of the fascinating history of ships.

1. Beginnings

Papyrus Balsa and Dugout

LONG BEFORE THE DAWN of history, primitive man was solving the problem of how he could venture upon water. A floating log by the bank of a river or a lake or the sea might tempt him to straddle it and then to discover the way to steer it with a makeshift paddle.

In time, some inventive minds hit on the idea of hollowing out a tree-trunk by burning it or by laboriously chopping away with flint axes and knives until it had become what is really a dug-out canoe. Many similar ones are still in use today in parts of the East Indies and Polynesia, while ancient fragments have been excavated from the swamps and bogs of the British Isles, from Stone Age lake dwellings of Switzerland and from down the east and west coasts of North America.

Some researchers believe that Stone Age folk probably also used the small circular coracle which can be carried on a man's back, although light and handy enough to take his weight in the water. Originally of basket-work made water-tight with skins, and now partly of more modern materials, coracles can still be seen in the hands of fishermen on Welsh rivers. They might look rather precarious, but their behaviour can be mastered after very little practice with their short paddles.

Another type of craft of unknown age is the balsa raft of South America. Although extremely light, lighter even than cork, balsa wood continues to be used for river work as rafts, but it is a sappy timber with the disadvantage that it slowly absorbs water and gains weight. Its good qualities, however, were triumphantly shown by the Norwegian Thor Heyerdahl in 1947, when he sailed his *Kon-Tiki* across the Pacific from Peru, having built her of balsa without iron nails or wire ropes.

He made another experimental voyage some years later. From the Mediterranean he sailed across the North Atlantic to the West Indies, this time in a replica of a prehistoric papyrus boat of Ancient Egypt. The material of which it was built, *Cyperus Papyrus*, was a sedge-like plant growing in great profusion in Ancient Egypt although the variety is now extinct there. Its stems were not only made into paper, giving it the name papyrus, but for long it was the chief material used for building serviceable boats. Since Egypt had no timber except for stunted acacia, sycamore-fig and tamarisk trees, all of which made only short lengths, she concentrated on developing her papyrus craft.

Actually, as they had no keel or stem and sternposts, they were nearer to rafts than to boats. They were built by wrapping the papyrus stems together and tying them in bundles that were then lashed tightly round to form a long slim shape, with high up-turned ends curved nearly at right angles. To prevent them from hogging—arching up in the middle—a strong rope, known as the hogging truss, was stretched from end to end and strained taut over crutches above the heads of the crew.

In some early period, the boat was given a simple sail which was loose-footed, or free along the bottom. The sail and its cordage also were made of papyrus stems. Sometimes a mast was contrived of twin spars that were fixed on each side of the boat and tied together at the top, making a tall triangle. On this, or on a single pole-mast, a smaller spar, a yard, was slung crossways to carry the sail.

Later, as a protection against spray, a rectangular screen was added, well aft and to one side. Among other improvements, the sail was given a second spar, a lower-yard, at the foot, and to take the strain of a larger sail, a web of cords was spread from the mast like outstretched fingers fanwise down to the lower-yard.

The first known picture of any sailing craft comes from Egypt on a painted vase of about 3100 BC, much the same date as that on which the historical period began in Egypt with her invention of the science of of writing and the start of the dynasties. The Nile, of course, was Egypt's life-blood and the great highway of the country. Boats were a vital necessity and the river traffic, both of passengers and cargoes, was enormous. Though the boats were mainly of papyrus, there was always an increasing number of others of wood, closely copying their spoon shape. They had their short lengths of timber skilfully scarfed together and secured with mortises and tenons. Their imitation of the papyrus build even ran to their being painted in the same green of the fresh reed.

Facing page top: A sailing surfboat of primitive design dwarfed by its large sail, off the coast of Elmina, Ghana, in November 1972. *Peter Fraenkel*

Facing page below: A nearly completed dugout canoe carved out of a single log of wood, near Accra, Ghana. *Peter Fraenkel*

This page top: Modern canoes built to a simple and primitive design on the banks of the River Niger near Gao in Mali. *Peter Fraenkel*

Above: A collection of raffia reed boats drying out in the sun after having been used for lake fishing at Oristano, Sardinia. *A. Crisp*

For the building of the pyramids and the other great monuments, the heavy loads of stone were transported on huge rafts of papyrus. They were aided by the Nile itself, for since the wind in Egypt blows from the north on nearly every day in the year, vessels can sail up-river with the wind and then be carried down by the current, or vice versa. In fact this was so much a part of Egyptian life that the words for 'Go South' were shown in the hieroglyphic script as a boat with a sail and 'Go North' was represented as a boat without one.

Egypt was largely self-supporting except for timber. Already in pre-dynastic times she was trading with her neighbours, exporting gold and metal-work for timber, especially Lebanon cedar, and farther afield for spices, aromatic gums and lapis lazuli.

In all this the papyrus boat must have played some part. In 2613 BC, however, the great 4th Dynasty started with Sneferu, the shipbuilding Pharaoh, and among his achievements was 'the bringing of 40 ships filled with cedar wood', though no doubt at least some of those 40 ships were of wood themselves.

As if in confirmation, in the tomb of the next Pharaoh, Cheops, the builder of the Great Pyramid, was found a large wooden boat. Over 160 feet in length and 20 feet in beam, it had been carefully stripped down to its component parts, nearly all of them intact. They make into a shapely decked vessel not intended for sailing and with more than a hint of papyrus form. In the hermetically sealed tomb, a slight scent still lingered—the scent of the cedar-wood with which the boat was made.

Yet the papyrus boats were still to be seen on the Nile for many years and nearly 2000 year later, the Prophet Isaiah spoke of Egyptian ambassadors arriving 'by the sea even in vessels of bulrushes upon the water'.

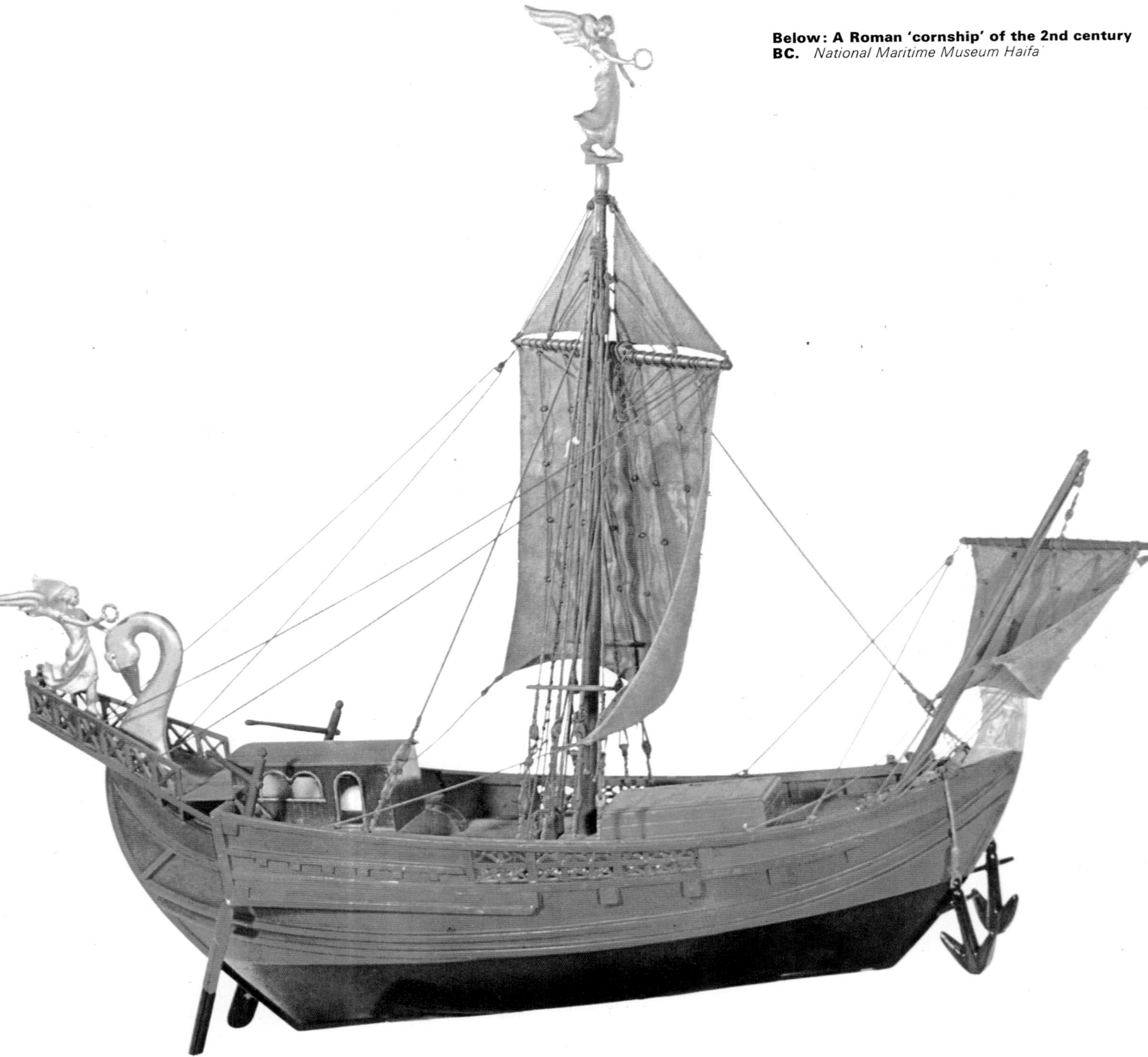

Below: A Roman 'cornship' of the 2nd century BC. *National Maritime Museum Haifa*

Early Ships of the Mediterranean

THE SHIPS OF EGYPT, the first to become seaworthy, continued to dominate the trade of the eastern Mediterranean during part of the Middle Kingdom. They dealt with Crete and Cyprus but for the all-important cedarwood, the main supply port was Byblus, on the coast of Lebanon, which at that time was the home of the Canaanites, later renamed Phoenicians by the Greeks.

Second only to Egypt's vessels were those of Minoan Crete in the Bronze Age of that area in the period 2000-1400 BC. Yet little is known of them, for the Minoans have left no record except for some cryptic scratches on stone.

In contrast, in the tomb of the redoubtable Queen Hatshepsut (1503 BC) there are excellent bas-reliefs of her ships. Five of them are sailing to the mysterious land of Punt, somewhere to the southward. The other five, with furled sails, are loading cargo. The ships were about 70ft long and, in the absence of large local timber, were probably constructed from short planks dovetailed together with wedges. This form of construction was deficient in longitudinal strength and to prevent the overhanging bow and stern sagging, a rope truss was fitted over the length of the vessel. They had rowers manning 15 oars a side and a sail of large size. The cargo shown is romantically exotic; it includes incense, sandal-wood and ebony, giraffes and baboons. The ships were probably built on the Nile, taken to pieces for transport to the Red Sea and then rebuilt for the voyage to Punt.

It was probably in the 13th century BC that Egypt started to build ships for two distinct purposes, namely, fighting and trading. One was the warship, with a stout metal ram at her bows, and the other, the trading vessel, broader and deeper in the water with a square hold for cargo.

The idea spread throughout the Mediterranean. From about the same period, the Phoenicians, that great race of seamen, have left us the earliest known impression of one of their war-galleys. It is a model in terracotta which was found in Byblus. Unlike the Egyptian ships, the Phoenician and Greek galleys probably developed from the dug-out made from a large tree trunk.

A much later artist, in 701 BC, has pictured in a bas-relief King Luli of Sidon escaping with his fleet to Tyre. His ships are biremes, that is, rowed by two banks of oarsmen, with one bank apparently staggered above the other. The rowers of Phoenicia were free men, not slaves, and their ships carried the universal large square sail of the Mediterranean auxiliary to the oarsmen. The relief also shows the warships distinct from the merchant ships.

Many decorative pictures come on vases and in wall paintings from Egypt and Greece, such as a horse's head as a figure-head and a sternpost shaped like a fish tail, but more practical are some round tops or 'crows nests' reached by ladders on the mast.

The ships of Assyria look much the same as those of Phoenicia, but the Etruscans, of whom so little is known, have left one surprise. A wall-painting found in a newly opened tomb, in 1954, dating from about 470 BC, clearly shows a two-masted ship, although it had been believed that no vessel had more than a single sail for a number of centuries. The ship's second mast, of no great length, was stepped well forward of her mainmast, with a smallish sail spread on it, apparently as an aid to ship handling rather than driving. She had a deep hull and bulwarks like many a later vessel.

That was the period of the great battle of Salamis. By then the Greek shipbuilders were largely following their own ideas. They strengthened the none-too-stout narrow hull of the war-galley with thick planks along the sides from end to end of the ship. The huge pointed ram was supported throughout her length, and unmistakably Greek was the large eye painted on each bow. At both bow and stern was built a solid deck and linking them, there was a light decking fore and aft, covering the rowers.

The merchant ship had a rounded hull with definite stem and stern. Her mast, stepped amidships, was steadied by one shroud on each side and the sail halyard was led aft to act as a backstay. She had developed into a sailing ship rather than a galley, being deeper and broader in the beam, but oars (or sweeps) still remained the more important.

A larger ship, the trireme, with three banks of oars, appeared after the bireme. How her oars were arranged is a puzzle which has caused much argument. It is clear, at least, that if the oarsmen sat in three rows, one above another, the oars of those in the uppermost tier would have had to be too long and too steeply angled to be handled at all. One theory is simply that three rowers sat side by side working at the same oar. Still another suggestion is of an outrigger running along both the ship's sides to provide the leverage for one bank, which sat just clear of the other two rows. A third theory is that, sitting together at the same level, they had separate oars of differing length, the longer ones being those inboard.

Top: Egyptian ocean-going ship of the 28th century BC. *National Maritime Museum Haifa*

Above: An Egyptian shipyard of the Old Kingdom, on the Nile, taken from an ancient relief. *Photo Lalance*

The problem becomes even more complicated with the still larger ships, the quinqueremes and the hepteremes, with five and six banks of oars; they remain one of the unsolved mysteries of the classical world.

Greek vessels engaged in many and various kinds of trading, but the most regular traffic was with the cargoes of the large corn-ships which kept Rome adequately fed. In time, the distinction between Greek and Roman merchant ships grew thin. They both adopted as a decoration for their sterns a great carving of a swan with down-curved neck. Round it, thrusting out over the water, was a light stern-walk or gallery. But it appears to have been a Roman who devised the tiny headsail called the artemon, which was spread beyond the ship's bows on a short spar that was canted well forward with the object of aiding the helmsman with his steering. It was completely forgotten after the fall of Rome and did not come into use again until the early Middle Ages.

Leif Ericsson

Top: 'The landing of Leif Ericsson in the New World', by Moran.
Courtesy US Naval Academy Museum

Above: The recovered Oseberg ship now in the Viking Ship Museum, Oslo. *Paul Popper Ltd*

Right: Carved figurehead typical of those used on Viking ships, but now believed to predate the Vikings by 200 or 300 years.
Scheepvaartmuseum Antwerp

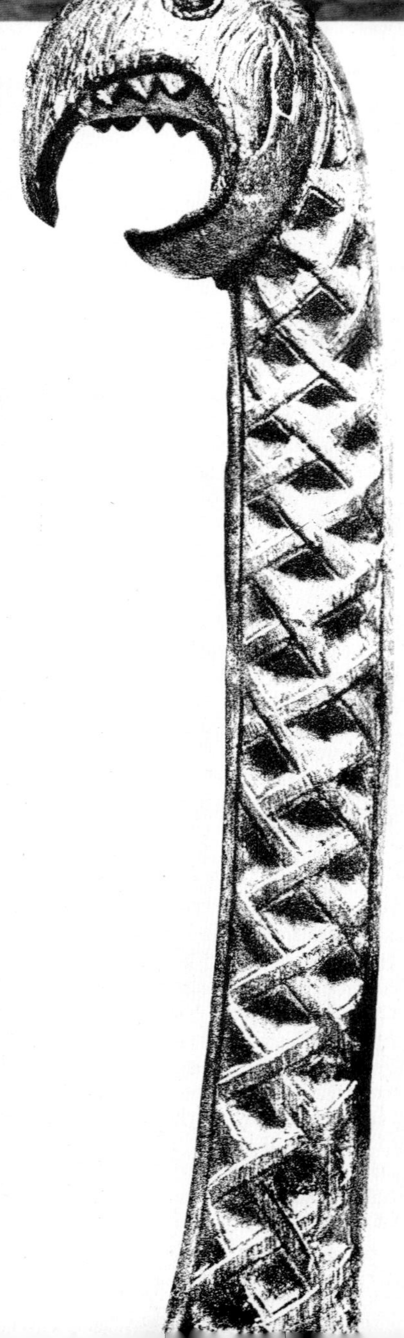

'DOWN AT GREENWICH for slaves and tin, the tall Phoenician ships stole in.' So wrote Rudyard Kipling, although the notion that the Phoenicians came to trade even in Cornwall is only a tradition. Just a few very late coins have been found in Britain bearing a Phoenician inscription and they alone could hardly be accepted as evidence. Yet, skilled seamen and navigators as they were, they had taught seamanship to the Greeks who had named their discovery, the Pole Star, after them. And what was probably their greatest feat of adventure is recorded in the annals of Egypt.

It was between 610 and 595 BC when Pharaoh Necho decided to reopen a canal long silted up, linking the Nile and the Red Sea. The Pharaoh suggested that a Phoenician ship should sail down it to explore, and away accordingly the ship went, to be lost to sight for three years. When she was about half-way through the voyage, the crew made an astonishing discovery. They suddenly noticed that when they were facing forward the sun was beginning to rise over their right shoulders instead of over the left. Unknowingly, they found that they had begun to circumnavigate the continent of Africa.

Not only Phoenician but also Egyptian ships are believed in India to have traded with ports in Kerala, on her south-western coast and it is thought that the present village of Puvar could be the mysterious Ophir.

Quite extraordinary voyages were made in the 5th century by Irish priests and monks to the northern Scottish islands and as far as the Faroes and Iceland. Their boats were the curraghs, feather-light craft of skins stretched on osier frames; far too light they seem for any but calm waters and certainly not for the savage northern seas.

Of much greater scope were the incredibly long ocean voyages made by two races of people in the course of their migrations to the islands of Polynesia and to Hawaii and New Zealand, perhaps in the first 500 years AD. Some covered hundreds of miles, relying only on systems of navigation by sun and stars that had been built up by successive generations and committed to memory.

By comparison, the voyage made by Leif Ericsson was brief and fully recorded. Of Norwegian Viking blood, he was the son of Eric the Red, the first settler in Greenland. Leif had been converted to Christianity in Norway by King Olaf, who had sent him back to Greenland to do the same for the settlers.

On his arrival, he heard a great deal of talk about Bjarni Herjulfsson's discovery of a wooded country. This Bjarni, a trader with his own boat, had been carried off course and had come upon Helluland and Markland, or Baffin Island and Labrador, as they are now called. He had not gone ashore in the unknown territory but sailed away and eventually made a good landfall on the Greenland coast.

At the prospect of bringing cargoes of timber to treeless Greenland, Leif was all eagerness. According to a chronicler, he was a big strapping fellow, handsome to look at, thoughtful and temperate in all things. He bought Bjarni's boat, a large beamy craft called a Knarr, got together a crew of 35 men and set off in the summer of 1001.

He found Bjarni's island and land, but carried on until he saw a still better coast with a fresh-water stream, plenty of timber for building and an abundance of salmon. Also there were masses of wild berries, which led him to name the country Vinland, or Wineland, from Vimber, a wine-berry or

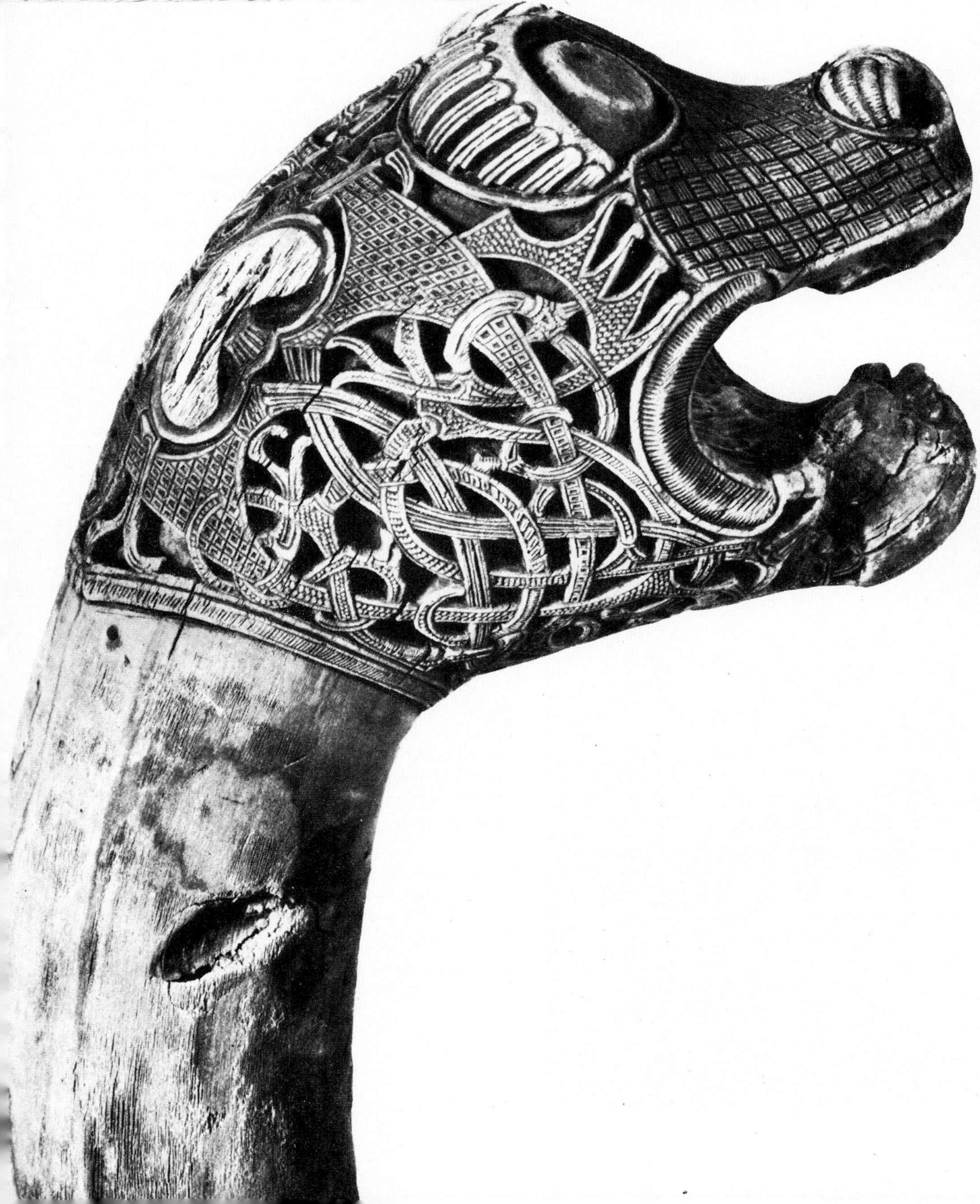

Top: A fleet of Viking warships headed by the Danish 'Raven', from an A E Wood engraving.
Mary Evans Picture Library

Left: One of the ornate carved figureheads of the 9th-century Norwegian Oseberg ship.
Copyright University Museum of Antiquities, Oslo, Norway

Above: Viking life depicted in the village museum at Hjerl Hede, Jutland, Denmark.
Mrs E Preston

grape. He was perhaps copying his father, who had called his new country Green Land to entice fresh settlers to that forbidding land.

Leif and his men cut down trees to make temporary huts while they were building a large house to hold them all. They spent the winter, a mild season, in collecting berries and felling the precious timber to take back with them in the ship in the spring. They had a triumphant return to Greenland and ever afterwards Leif was known as Leif the Lucky.

There were several more expeditions, but each had to return, partly because of shortage of food and partly to avoid the antagonism of the skraelings, as the Norsemen called either the Red Indians or the Eskimos. In the largest attempt, three ships carried 250 men and women with cattle and other livestock; a most uncomfortable and noisome voyage, one would think. It was in that voyage that a baby was born to the leaders, Thorfinn Karlsefni and his wife Gutrid, the first European child to be born in North America.

The last recorded attempt to colonise was in 1013 in two ships; it was ruined by a woman named Freydis, Leif's half-sister. By lying and cheating, she incited her husband to kill all the men who were not of her crew while she murdered the women. She herself survived to return to Greenland, where she seems to have suffered little or no retribution.

In Greenland, one of the Norse settlements, the one in the west, vanished completely in some unknown period, apparently destroyed by the Eskimos. The eastern one was long supported by a ship which was fairly regularly sent with supplies from Norway. Then, because of a war in Scandinavia, no ship arrived and the colony was eventually forgotten. It seems to have lingered on, gradually weakening from semi-starvation and inbreeding until the last of them died. The crew of a ship which went in for shelter on some date between 1406 and 1410 could find no people; only cattle running wild. Bodies were, however, discovered in the 1920s preserved in the ice of Greenland, still wearing the clothes of a long-gone century.

As to the whereabouts of Vinland, many have been the sites suggested. New England has been the most favoured, but in 1960, a Norwegian archaeologist located a site which seemed to fit the description in the sagas. It was at L'Anse aux Meadows in northern Newfoundland and excavations gave good promise that there was Leif's settlement. Two great houses were found; the biggest was 70 feet long and 55 feet wide, with walls of turf and the roof covered with sods. There was a fireplace in the centre and benches of turf along each wall. All of the several smaller houses found also had central fireplaces. The charred roof timber gave a carbon date of 1000 AD, with a possible error of 100 years each way, which is what one would expect.

Only two Viking articles were found; a soapstone spindle whorl and a bronze pin. But it is enough; there can be little doubt that Leif discovered the New World 500 years before Columbus.

Above left: Engravings showing a recovered Viking ship, how it probably looked when in service and some of the ship's gear.
Mary Evans Picture Library

Left: The preserved Gokstad ship in the Viking Ship Museum, Oslo. *Paul Popper Ltd*

A dhow under construction at Bahrain in the Persian Gulf. *D Mackenzie*

The Dhow & Half Decking

ONE SMALL MYSTERY of the sea is the name dhow. It has long been applied by Europeans to nearly all Arab ships and it had a special significance in the days of piracy and of the slave trade. Yet it is not an Arabic nor a European word; nor is it used by Arabs, who have their own names for their different types of ships, big and small. Possibly it came from some ports of call in India or, less likely, from the East African coast; no-one can say.

Another unsolved mystery surrounds the origin of the lateen sail. Whether or not it had been a purely Arab invention, it arrived in company with the dhow and it did not spread far outside the Mediterranean for many years.

It was during the 2nd century when the sight of some strange rakish vessels with sails of queer shape and incredible height first surprised onlookers in the Mediterranean. Such craft were few at first, but they were in fact the forerunners of a long-threatening storm. When the Arab armies had conquered the old Phoenician cities, they grasped the value of sea power. They built dockyards and naval bases in Syria and Crete, obtaining crews for their new warships by a form of conscription, and then waged a continuous struggle against the Byzantine Greeks. In 829 AD, they completely destroyed a Greek fleet off Thasos and from then onward the Mediterranean was their domain and a hunting ground for the unwary infidel.

With the aid of Syrian and Egyptian shipwrights, the dhow proper took lasting shape. That shape, at least below the waterline, has been described as being near perfection. It was modelled on the whale. 'To make them', the 14th-century Arab historian Ibn Khaldûn wrote; 'one must study the way in which this fish moves along by means of its fins and chest for cutting through the water'. None the less, the Arab warships were large vessels, fully capable of matching the Greeks.

The smaller dhows were going through an outstanding period of development from open boats into decked or half-decked craft. It resulted in them being planked as a permanent fixture either all over, or sometimes only at bow and stern with a 'midships well in between, which served as a cargo hold.

As used throughout the Arabian Sea, they were usually vessels of between 150 and 200 tons burden, with the stem rising from the water in a long slant; generally, they carried one mast with a yard of enormous length. They were regularly engaged in coastal trading, though in the main they were very busy in the slave trade.

Of the many types of dhows in the 19th century, only ten or so seem to be still in use. Among them, the small but very speedy Zarook of the Red Sea built up a special reputation for her less-respectable exploits such as gun running, slave carrying and smuggling. In Victorian times, the Royal Navy maintained patrols in the Red Sea in open boats, each lasting two weeks at a time, trying to put a stop to such activities, although generally the midshipmen in charge found the Arab seamen to be difficult to catch.

The medium-sized dhows are lightly built and are scarcely stout enough to meet heavy weather in the open sea. For ocean sailing, there are the Boom and the Baghla, both fully decked from stem to stern and both two-masted. The Boom, the smaller of the two, appears to be superseding the picturesque Baghla, which has intricately carved ends and five decorative stern windows.

Dhows in general can be divided into two main groups; the double-ended, and those with a flat transom stern. The rig is practically the same for each one—a long yard, the length of the vessel herself, slung on a mast which is raked well forward. The Arabs had found early that height above the waterline has much to do with the efficiency of a sail and they had adopted a new type, one that could be set on a yard and hoisted high above the masthead. The lateen sail, of the same family as the lugsail or the leg-of-mutton, is called a fore-and-aft sail. When set, it is more-or-less parallel to the centre line of the ship, unlike the square sail, which can only be set at right angles.

Instead of being secured to the mast, the lateen is laced to the yard and the mast is

Above: The Matapa boat of the Northern rivers, one of the vessels used in the Zanzibar slave trade in the latter half of the 19th century. *Illustrated London News*

Left: A 20th century trading dhow in modern Zanzibar. *Tourist Photo Library (P Fraenkel)*

Left below: A model of an Arab dhow featuring the magnificent lateen sail. *Science Museum London*

canted just short of the point of balance in order that the great weight of yard and sail can be readily handled when being raised or lowered. The handling of this rig is fascinating to watch. Tacking in the smaller craft involves bringing the yard upright and some of the crew running round the fore part of the ship with the sheet (the master rope controlling the sail) while others swing the yard round so that yard and sail have been reversed. On the other hand, the large fully decked vessel usually does not tack but wears ship, that is, turns her stern round the opposite way, to avoid the danger of being caught flat aback.

In 1938, Commander Alan Villiers spent a year sailing with the Arabs in their dhows. His book *Sons of Sinbad* was the result and in it he describes the Boom dhow *The Triumph of Righteousness.* She was nearly 100ft long, her beam was 29ft and the mast was 90ft above the sea. Her enormous yard was made of the trunks of three trees lashed together.

'It was a happy ship, well run,' he states, 'in spite of the fish-oil'. Sometimes she carried over 200 people with their luggage and the trading stock, which included the traditional amount allowed to each member of the crew. There were ships stores and frequently live stock; how they managed to handle the ship at all with the crowded deck was always a wonder to him. He even saw a small dhow so packed with bodies on the deck tnat the crew had to run over their backs in order to tack.

Dhows are still being built, mainly in India, but types are becoming fewer and there is an indication of European influence in the Indian vessels. Nevertheless, the Arab dhow, which is often still a sailing vessel pure and simple, using the wind alone, is probably the last survivor from the remote past.

A modern replica of a traditional Viking ship built by Norwegian Boy Scouts.
Royal Viking Line

The Maori War Canoe

THE DUGOUT CANOE can be found, wherever suitable trees are available, throughout the world. They vary in size according to the timber available and to their particular purpose. Dugouts found in Britain range in length from about 6ft up to the 48½ft vessel found at Brigg, Lincolnshire. The Indians of British Columbia used the huge cedar trees of that country for war canoes more than 70ft long.

Dugouts also varied greatly in shape, from the simple hollowed-out log to more-elaborate craft with added side planks and built-up bows and sterns. The great war canoes of the Maoris have been described as the most elegant of all dugouts.

The Maoris are believed to have arrived in New Zealand from the Society Islands during the 13th and 14th centuries AD. By tradition, the migration was a premeditated colonisation, but it would seem likely that drift voyaging played a part in the movements of these people.

It is probable that the voyages of about 2000 miles from the Society Islands, via Rarotonga to New Zealand were made in double canoes consisting of two dugouts joined together with a number of cross pieces, on which a platform with a shelter was erected. Without the use of these double canoes, specially fitted out for deep-sea voyaging, Polynesian migration and settlement could not have been so widespread, with movement of the people from Hawaii in the north to New Zealand in the south and eastward to Easter Island. Large numbers of these double canoes were still in use in the Society Islands in the 18th century; a contemporary account of a naval review at Tahiti in 1774 relates that 160 large and 170 smaller double canoes took part, and were manned by more than 7000 men.

However, after the Maoris had settled in New Zealand, the availability of very large timber and the decline of oceanic voyaging led to the replacement of the double canoe by the single canoe, which was suitable for coastal work.

The great war canoe was the largest and most elaborately decorated canoe used by the Maoris. These canoes were made from the finest timber available and were usually 60 to 70ft in length, with some more than a 100ft long.

When a war canoe was to be constructed, the tree—probably a Kauri pine with a diameter of more than 8ft—was carefully selected. Only stone tools were available to the Maoris and fire was used to char the wood during the felling. The stone adze and fire were also used for the preliminary shaping and hollowing-out operations. The final shaping of the hull was left until the trunk had been hauled near to the sea. Any

damage which occurred to the hull during transport could then be removed by very skilled men using light stone tools. As timber of sufficient length and girth out of which to hew a complete dugout was not always available, an extra section was sometimes added at one end or at both ends. These additions to the main hull were fixed in place by a large mortise-and-tenon joint and the parts were lashed—or perhaps sewn would be a better description—together through holes pierced at intervals in the adjoining edges.

The sides of the dugout were heightened by the addition of long planks—washstrakes. The washstrake, fitted on each side, was about 12in deep in the middle part, decreasing towards the ends so as to fit the sheer of the dugout and provide a horizontal gunwale line in the finished canoe. The washstrakes were lashed to the dugout and the seams were made watertight by caulking with dried bulrush stems. The joints were then covered, inside and outside, by narrow battens held in place by lashings through holes in the hull. Numerous thwarts for the paddlers were fitted to the gunwales and a floor grating, formed of light rods laid longitudinally on a series of cross bars, was fitted a little above the bottom of the dugout. This flooring was covered with rush mats, but a number of spaces were left in the grating to serve as bailing wells.

After the washstrakes had been fitted, a richly carved figurehead was added which also served as a forward breakwater, as its after end was made into a vertical board, filling the space between the open ends of the washstrakes. One of the favourite designs for the figurehead was a carved pattern of two large double-spiral scrolls on the vertical board and in the front was carved, in the round, a highly conventionalised human figure, with a large and hideous face, the eyes of mother-of-pearl and the tongue protruding in insult to the

Top left: An engraving of one type of Maori canoe. *Mary Evans Picture Library*

Top: Maori canoes now in a museum in Wellington. *Paul Popper Ltd*

Above: Maori Chief standing beside the carved stern of his war canoe. *Mary Evans Picture Library*

Above right: Huge Maori war canoe accommodating 120 warriors, fashioned from the trunk of a Kauri tree, preserved at Waitangi. *Paul Popper Ltd*

Right: Massive work of carving on the prow of a Maori boat. *High Commissioner for New Zealand, London*

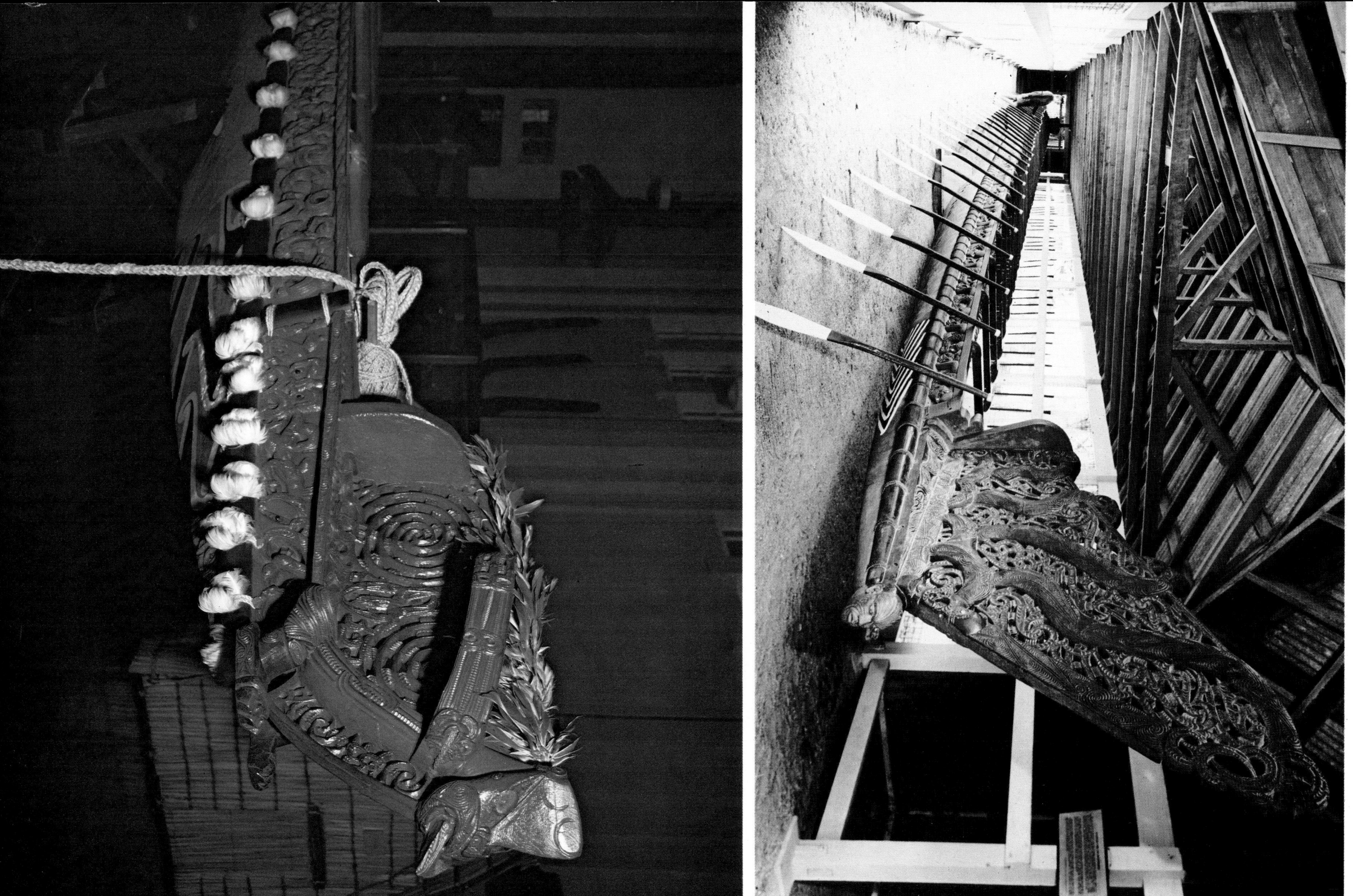

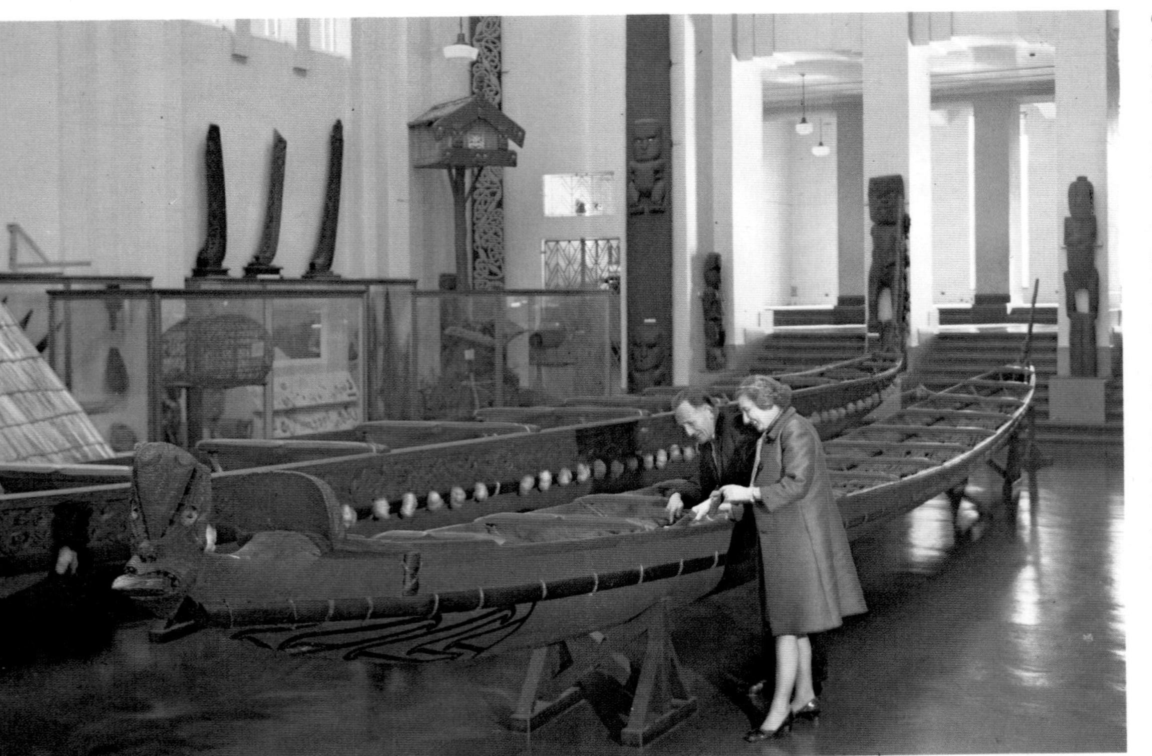

Above: Maori fishing canoe with a war canoe in the background at the Dominion Museum, Wellington, New Zealand.
High Commissioner for New Zealand, London

Left: A Maori double canoe turned over to unwarlike occupation in 1972 at the Polynesian Culture Centre, Oahu, Hawaii.
D J Kingston

Below: An engraving of a Maori canoe packed with warriors. *Mary Evans Picture Library*

enemy. Another pattern for the figurehead was a perforated complex of double and reversed spiral scrolls supported by sinuous ribs which were elaborately carved.

At the stern of the dugout a very tall upright fretted stern-piece was added. This stern-piece, usually about 18ft high and 18in wide, was carved into a perforated design of double spirals, while a small grotesque human figure was carved at the base on the forward side. The outer side of each washstrake was also ornamented with carvings embellished with shell decoration.

The narrow battens covering the washstrake seams were painted black, with tufts of the white feathers of the albatross attached at intervals by their quills to the lashing securing the batten in position. A pair of long black feather streamers were usually attached to the top of the stern piece and feather fringes outlined the carvings at the bow and stern.

The vessel was painted with red ochre, with some details blackened with a composition made from the soot of burnt wood. When a war canoe was put into commission, the figurehead was further ornamented with two long and curving antennae consisting of a pair of thin wands projecting forward, one on each side of the grotesque face of the figurehead. At short spacing, bunches of feathers were tied along the wands, with a very fine feather ornament at the tip of each wand, on which the heart of a slain enemy was transfixed.

The war canoe was usually paddled, but sometimes a V-shaped sail of matting was used. It was laced along the two long sides to a mast and spar with the apex of the triangle stepped on the floor of the dugout.

The various steps in the construction of the war canoe, and the launching ceremony were accompanied by traditional rituals in which chanting Maori priests took part.

An artist's impression of a Danish medieval craft. *Maritime Museum Kronborg*

the Bayeux Tapestry

THE BAYEUX TAPESTRY stands alone. There is nothing quite like it the world over. It is at once a historical record of a great event and a great English tragedy stitched into a magnificent work of art. With its bright colours, it is hard to believe that it is nine hundred years old. In addition to answering many questions on such matters as early armour, weapons, costume and social behaviour, it pictures the construction of 11th-century ships, their rig and their build.

Yet in spite of its name, it is actually not a tapestry but a close imitation of one in woollen embroidery. And, strangely enough, although its purpose appears to be the glorification of William the Conqueror, it was embroidered in England by English women. Now it hangs in its own museum opposite the cathedral on the Normandy coast.

The story it tells is of how Earl Harold sailed to France and, landing at St Valery at the mouth of the Somme, was taken prisoner by the local magnate, Count Guy of Ponthieu, who sent the news of his capture to Duke William of Normandy, his overlord. William gave orders for him to be escorted to his castle and received him graciously in person. Harold, so the tapestry has it, had come from King Edward the Confessor solely to promise the English throne on his death to William. The tapestry shows Harold confirming this by swearing a solemn oath on a breviary and accepting a knighthood and arms from William in acknowledgement that he was William's vassal.

The English version is very different. The Anglo-Saxon Chronicle views Harold as the true and legitimate heir to the throne who had been publicly chosen by King Edward. All that had happened, so it states, was that Harold had gone sailing on a pleasure trip and had been caught in a sudden storm. After his ship had been blown ashore and wrecked, he had been hospitably treated by William. The Chronicle, it is clear, does not believe the story of Harold breaking his oath and committing perjury.

Whatever the truth, in January of 1066, when Edward the Confessor died, Harold was crowned in Westminster Abbey on the following day. William, however, was determined to become King of England and when the news reached him he put in hand a colossal task, the building of a great fleet of ships for the very large army that he considered would be needed for an invasion. The Bayeux Tapestry shows the carpenters and shipwrights hard at work felling the trees and shaping the hulls.

The ships they built for transporting both men and horses across the Channel were modelled on the Viking Knarr type, large and rather beamy, of clinker build and double ended, with high stem and stern posts, often embellished with a ferocious figurehead. They were flat-bottomed enough to be manhandled up a gently sloping beach, such as the one at Pevensey which William chose. The heavy steering-oars show up clearly in the tapestry, as do their big iron anchors, looking surprisingly modern in shape. Other familiar nautical items are a seaman taking a sounding, perhaps with a lead, and a party hauling a ship down to the sea with the aid of a pulley-block and tackle, while others unstep a mast. Some of the vessels have as many as three stays or shrouds, rather surprisingly for that date.

There are at least two novelties. One is a long tube of some lightweight material very similar to a wind-sock of an airfield today in shape, which was made fast overhead as a recognition signal. The other is the appearance on two of the ships of a couple of shield-like objects hanging either separately over bow and stern or else together over the bow. In his book *The Bayeux Tapestry*, Mr C H Gibbs-Smith states that they are badly drawn anti-ramming devices derived from the ancient Greek aphlaston.

The tapestry itself is 231 feet long and 19½ inches wide, and is apparently less than three feet short of its original length, in spite of its great age. It was originally embroidered on coarse linen, but was later mounted on fresh material, while a number of repairs and restorations have been made from time to time. The actual work is thought to have been completed within twenty years, and perhaps less than ten, after the Battle of Hastings and to have taken not much more than two years to complete.

Except for a brief mention in a 15th-century inventory in Bayeux Cathedral, the tapestry disappeared from sight and memory until three hundred years later, when it was discovered in a side-chapel of the cathedral After being found, it was displayed on special occasions as a regular custom round the nave. However, its shape made the display there scarcely satisfactory; it would seem to have been intended for permanent hanging in some chateau.

It has twice travelled to Paris. The first journey was when it was sent for by Napoleon Bonaparte. The second was during the 1939-45 war in order to remove it from the danger zone of the Normandy landings. A few small fragments somehow made their way once into London's Victoria and Albert

Three scenes from the Bayeux Tapestry: Above left: The Norman fleet setting sail; above right: the fleet crossing the Channel; left: Harold arriving on the French coast.
All Michael Halford Library

Museum and they were generously returned to France.

Quite probably the tapestry owes its existence to that unpleasant character Bishop Odo, one of William's half-brothers, who was given the See of Bayeux at the age of 14. After the conquest of England, William bestowed on him the Earldom of Kent and appointed him joint regent with his brother during a temporary absence from England in 1067. Odo, who figures as one of the chief characters in the tapestry, dealt with the Saxons with a heavy hand even for that cruel period and he acquired vast riches in the process. In 1083 he was imprisoned for attempting to become Pope by intrigue. Released on William's death, he conspired against William Rufus in the following year with the result that he was expelled from the country with the loss of all his wealth. But most of that came later.

There is no mention in the tapestry of Harold watching and waiting for the coming of William. But before word came of the sighting of his fleet, there was news of an insurrection in the North. His rebellious brother Tostig with the sea-rover Harold Hardraga were plundering and ravaging York. Harold, with his household troops, at once rushed northward, gathering fighting-men on his way. He fought and won a battle at Stamford Bridge, destroying his enemies and then speedily dashed south again. He found that the Normans were at Pevensey before him. William had already hauled up his ships, unloaded his horses and built a strongpoint. He was ready and waiting.

Harold took up his position a little way inland on the rising ground of Senlac Hill, surrounded by his famous shield-wall of closely ordered axe-men and spear-men all on foot. Both sides were in armour of similar pattern and armed with similar weapons; the spear and the sword. In addition the English had their great two-handed axes while some of the Normans on foot and on horseback, had small bows. With the English shouting 'Out! Out!' and the Normans 'God aides! God aides!', they engaged in a ferocious struggle. It was fought as closely as ever battle could be fought; twice the Norman horsemen charged up the hill and twice they were beaten back leaving behind a welter of dead and dying men and horses.

The light was fading and men were growing weary. Suddenly the left wing of mounted Normans broke and galloped off the field in disarray. At the sight the English left their ranks to charge down in triumph. Harold, desperately trying to close up again the shield-wall, was struck by an arrow and he fell. It was the end; lack of discipline lost the English their King and many of them their homes and their land. But for a hair's breadth, William and his men could have been driven back into the sea and England would not have received that infusion of French blood into its Norse strain—whether to England's gain or loss, who can say?

The barquentine (or barkentine) had from three to six masts, all fore-and-aft rigged except the foremast, which was square rigged. It became popular towards the end of the sailing-ship era often being a cut-down former ship or barque, because the barquentine rig was cheaper and easier to manage yet retained much of the good running quality of the ship and barque.

The picture shows the preserved three-masted barquentine 'Regina Maris' in Sydney Harbour, Australia, during a voyage run by the Thomas Cook Adventure Club. *V Hayes*

2. Evolution of the Sailing Ship

THE DEVELOPMENT OF SHIP FORMS

THE GREAT FLEET which King Richard Coeur-de-Lion collected for his voyage to the Holy Land in 1191 to join the Third Crusade – gay with banners and pennons – must have been a brave sight. The ships made up a total of well over 100, with hired vessels added to the nucleus of the King's ships, including 39 galleys and a few of a larger and heavier new type of round ship called a cog.

Their voyage down to the Strait of Gibraltar and into the Mediterranean seems to have been without much incident, until Richard turned aside on the way and conquered Cyprus. Off the coast of Syria, however, they fell in with a monster; an enormous ship with no fewer than three tall masts and packed with hundreds of fierce Saracens. Richard's ships attacked the stranger from all sides but without making much impression against her height. Then the galleys were ordered in. They dashed at her with their rams, holed her sides and sank her.

The galleys, low and slim and chiefly dependent on their oars, formed a class of vessel by themselves, but the bulk of the other ships had a strong family resemblance to those of the Vikings of the past. Although they relied almost entirely on their sails, they were still clinker-built, with overlapped planking, and they had high curved ends and a single mast stepped amidships.

The vessels of the Mediterranean came of a different tradition to that of the North. A large number of them, all carvel-built, with planks edge to edge, were hired or bought from the shipyards in the southern ports, especially in Venice and Genoa, by Crusaders who had journeyed overland. One series of 12th-century drawings shows single-masted ships under both sail and oars, also with a long ram jutting out from the bow.

Different again were the later two-masted ships that King Louis of France ordered from Venice in 1268. They were to have keels 27 metres long and stem and stern posts nearly nine metres high. In addition to having two complete decks from end to end of the ship, they had a half-deck extending from the bow to amidships and extra decking at the stern to provide cabins. Similar ships were ordered from Genoa and although they were rather smaller, it is mentioned that the mainyard, the spar which carried the larger sail, was of greater length than the ship's hull.

In spite of all the variations in design of ships in general, there was a basic underwater form of hull which accords with the 8th-century Arab's maxim that it should imitate the shape of the whale. (Now, at last, that long-held tenet has lapsed in the technology of the 20th century.) The results of the Crusades from the maritime point of view did not include only the opening up of the Mediterranean to trade with the North but also the fusion, to some extent, of shipbuilding ideas. It might be more than a coincidence that the final Crusade was coming to its end just at the time of the most important development in the history of seafaring. Some nautical genius invented the stern-rudder, which had a direct effect on the shape of the hull.

For thousands of years every kind of sailing craft, from the papyrus boat of Ancient Egypt to the majestic quinqueremes of Greece or the longships of the Norsemen, had used some form of steering-oar worked over the vessel's quarter(s). The number of them varied; once the Ancient Egyptians had tried using as many as six of the oars, three on each quarter, and Mediterranean ships in general used two oars for centuries, one on each quarter, but no arrangement could be really satisfactory. The steering-oar worked well enough in vessels that were sailing with a following wind; the difficulty came with the discovery of how to tack and to make use of a wind on the beam when the ship was heeling over.

Above: Detail from a painting by Guilo Romano of the naval victory of Leone IV over the Saracens off Ostia in 849.
Mauro Pucciarelli

Right: Miniature from the chronicles of Froissart showing ships at the battle of Sluis (Ecluse) of 1340.
National Library Paris (Mauro Pucciarelli)

Quant le roy dan
gleterre & ses ma
reschaulx eurent
ordonnees leurs
batailles et leurs navires
moult richement & sagement
Ilz firent tendre et traire
les voiles contremont et vin
drent au vent de quartier
sur dextre pour avoir lavantaige
du souleil qui en venant
leur estoit ou visaige. Si
sauserent que ce seigneur vouloit
trop mynre et detyrerent vng

peu et tournoyerent tant qu'ilz
eurent a leur voulente. Les
normans qui les veoient
tourner sesmerveilloient
pourquoy ilz le faisoient &
disoient ilz resongnent et
recullent Car ilz ne sont
pas gens pour combattre a
nous. Bien veoient les nor
mans par les banieres que le
roy dangleterre y estoit per
sonnelement. Si myrent
leurs vaisseaulx en bon estat
Car ilz estoient saiges en

A cog of the type in use between the 13th and 16th centuries shown on a contemporary seal. *Mauro Pucciarelli*

A two-masted cog from a miniature from a handwritten 15th-century book, in the Riccardi Library, Florence. *Mary Evans Picture Library*

Representation of late 15th-century ship, based on a drawing from the Earl of Warwick's manuscript of 1485.

The new-fangled stern-rudder was probably the result of much experiment before it came to be hung in its most effective position on a vertical, or nearly vertical, sternpost. Then, in addition to simplifying matters for the helmsman, it also made possible a number of improvements, not least in the form of the hull, in designing ships.

It is fairly safe to assume that the Chinese had already developed their own type of rudder hung at the stern in their own way, but in Europe, the first indication of one in place and functioning is on the civic seal of the town of Elbing in Germany, in 1242. In English waters it did not appear until the 14th century, according to the evidence of the civic seals of several seaport towns. The Dover seal, for instance, dated as late as 1284, shows a vessel still using a steering-oar; incidentally, the artist has pictured it incorrectly on the port and not the starboard quarter.

There is a surprising point in both the Dover seal and one from Sandwich of 1238. Their ships have a bowsprit, which was then a sprit for holding the bow line, and in addition, both have considerably more than their fair share of shrouds and stays supporting the masts.

The era of the 14th-15th centuries, for the nautical mind, turned into a lively period of upheaval and change.

In 1340, Edward III wrote to the Black Prince to describe his victory at Sluys 'from our ship *Cogge Thomas*'. With the straight stern, the rudder had made it possible for the new-style cog to be built larger and of an altered shape, giving her more stowage room both for trade purposes and for war. She was shortened and widened in the hull, ultimately reducing her length from five times the width of beam down to three times the beam, a proportion that was carried on for years, while the size of most ships continued to grow. The deck at the forward end of the cog had become nearly triangular but in spite of all that was being done to bring her up to date, she could not reign supreme for ever in the face of the swelling demand for bigger and bigger vessels.

It was evident that clinker would have to give way to the Southern carvel style before long, and around the shipyards, there was talk of the coming of ships with two masts and even with three. King Henry V, it was said, had started to build a great vessel at Bayonne which would be 186 feet long from stem to stern as early as 1419! Who knew what the next few years would bring?

Above Centre: Ferdinand I's galleys attacking the Turks, from a 15th century engraving by J Callot in the Naval Museum at Genoa. *Mauro Pucciarelli*

Above: An engraving of a Venetian galley of the 14th century. *Mary Evans Picture Library*

A model of the barque 'Semplice', in the Naval Museum at Genoa-Pegli. *Mauro Pucciarelli*

Development of Masts and Rigs

THROUGH MANY a year, ships' masts with their sails and rigging have fascinated the layman and the landlubber. There has been much to puzzle him, starting with models from Egyptian tombs, scratches on stone, and engravings on coins and civic seals. Then there are pictures on papyri, in illustrated manuscripts, in stained-glass windows of some churches and embroidered or worked in tapestry of a past age.

In Northern European waters there is no evidence of the existence of ships with more than one mast before 1400 AD. The mast was provided with stout supporting ropes, or stays, to take the strain off the mast when the ship was pitching and plunging head into the sea. The main stay reached from the head of the mast to the ship's stem and lateral support was given by ropes, called shrouds, leading from the mast down to each side of the ship.

The shrouds also served quite a different purpose. At one time a wooden ladder was lashed to the shrouds to enable men to go aloft. Then at last someone hit on the idea of hitching short lengths of line, called ratlines, across the shrouds on both sides of the ship to make rope-ladders to the masthead All such stays and shrouds come under the name of standing rigging, in contrast to running rigging, which applies only to the ropes that are used for hauling and to control movements of the sails.

The *Grace Dieu* built for Henry V in 1418 is recorded as having a great mast, two bowsprits, six sails and 11 bonnets, though some of them were probably spares. The bonnets were extra pieces of canvas which were laced to the foot of the sail to increase the sail area. A narrow strip of canvas, the drabler, could be laced along the foot of the bonnet to gain a still greater spread of canvas.

As ships became larger, an additional mast and sail were added to the rig. The two-masted rig was not efficient for the size and type of hull in use, and by about 1460 the three-masted ship was in service in Northern waters. The bowsprit, which in single-masted ships had only been used to extend the bowlines of the square sail, then had a different part to play. It was much longer and heavier, and canted up at an angle for the forestay, or stays, to be extended to it in order to gain a stronger pull on the mast.

The masts in a two-masted vessel are named foremast and mainmast. In a ship with three masts, the after one is called mizen, a name that might have been taken from the Arabic mesan, meaning balance. The owners or captains of the few 15th-century four-masted ships probably had some difficulty in coining a name for the fourth mast, which eventually became the bonaventure mizen. So it remained until a less poetic age renamed it the jigger.

Ships became larger still and required even more power to drive them; first topmasts and then topgallant masts were added to the lower masts. The bowsprit was further extended and secured by ropes, called gammoning, which passed round it and through a hole in the stem. Later it was further secured by bobstays which led downward to the stem.

The earlier three-masted vessels set a tiny square sail on the foremast, a large square sail and a top sail on the mainmast, and a fore-and-aft lateen sail on the mizen mast.

The little fore sail was set well forward in

order that the helmsman could keep the ship off the wind. A better idea that appeared before long was the addition of the sprit sail—the artemon of ancient Rome, brought into existence again after having been lost for many centuries. The new artemon was made fast to a light spar and slung forward under the bowsprit. As a result, the foremast was stepped farther aft and the foresail, made larger, became more of a driving sail than a rather inefficient head sail.

The transformation, from the simple rig of a single mast and sail of the early cog and buss to the three-masted carrack, completely square-rigged except for a lateen mizen sail, took place in the hundred years from 1400 to 1500. The improvement in masts and sails made it possible for ships to make some progress against an adverse wind and thus made possible the long ocean voyages which resulted in Columbus's discovery of America, and Vasco da Gama's opening of the trade route to India.

With further developments of head sails —stay sails and jibs—in the 17th, 18th and 19th centuries, the progress continued and the foremast was moved farther aft.

Early in the 17th century, it was realised that more effective sail power aft could be obtained by increasing the size of the mizenmast rather than by fitting a bonaventure mizen, and the use of four masts was discontinued until the 19th century, when the increased size of sailing ships made possible the fitting of four or more masts.

The simple arrangement of six sails—courses and top sails on foremasts and mainmasts, lateen sail on the mizen and a sprit sail under the bowsprit—generally fitted to ships in the 16th century was gradually improved with the introduction of topgallant sails, royals, jibs, stay sails, studding sails and the substitution of a gaff sail for the lateen sail, until, by the end of the 18th century, no fewer than 37 sails formed the sail plan of even a small merchant ship.

Top left: Model of an Egyptian ship dating from the times of Queen Hatshepsut.
Marine Museum Lisbon

Above left: A 20th-century replica of the 'Hugin' Viking barge, at Ebbsfleet in Kent.
Barnabys Picture Library (Mrs E Preston)

This picture: A model of a Roman trireme, in the Naval Museum at La Spezia.
M Pucciarelli

From a painting by Van de Velde, the first-rate battleship HMS 'Royal Sovereign' of 1701. She probably represented the height of extravagant decoration on large warships in a century or more when ship design stagnated. The florid carving applied to all four tiers of the stern galleries can be seen, and for good measure the matching interior decoration was rounded off with painted murals in the admiral's state cabin.
National Maritime Museum London

MARCO POLO & THE JUNK

MARCO POLO, that unforgettable traveller, was 17 years old when, in 1271, he accompanied his father and uncle to Peking to visit the Great Khan of China. They were merchants of an aristocratic Venetian family. The three of them sailed as far as Ormuz, at the southern end of the Persian Gulf, before continuing overland. With young Marco taking mental note of all the wonders he saw or was told about and storing them in his memory, they safely reached Peking after four years.

Kublai Khan, the ruler of nearly half the known world (the Kubla Khan of Coleridge), received them warmly and was so impressed by Marco that he began sending him on various missions, eventually extended to Tibet, Burma and India.

The Khan wanted to keep all three travellers, refusing to allow them to return home, but after a long 17 years an opportunity came. Three emissaries arrived, with a splendid train, from the Khan of Persia. He had lost his favourite wife and was asking Kublai to send him a beautiful maiden from the same Mongol family to take her place.

Kublai chose a lovely princess 17 years of age and ordered a fleet to be made ready with ample provisions and stores to escort her. Then the emissaries persuaded the reluctant Kublai to permit the three Venetians, as skilled navigators, to leave his service and take her in their charge.

The fleet took the better part of two years to reach Persia and it arrived after the Khan had died. However, his brother had succeeded him and gave the Princess to his own son as his bride, which must have been a pleasant surprise for her. The Venetians said their farewells and started for home, travelling partly by land and partly by sea, arriving in 1295, three years after leaving the Chinese fleet.

Marco states that the fleet numbered '14 ships each having four masts and capable of being navigated with nine sails'. Although unusual, the dispatch of so many vessels was quite credible. China had been sending junks on trading voyages to India and beyond from the 7th century onward as a regular practice. Under the Ming dynasty, one fleet, said to number more than 60 ships in one account, sailed to India. Within the following 20 years, seven fleets visited various ports, from Aden to the east coast of Africa, and in fact China was dominating the Indian Ocean. Then, at the end of the 15th century, there was a change of policy

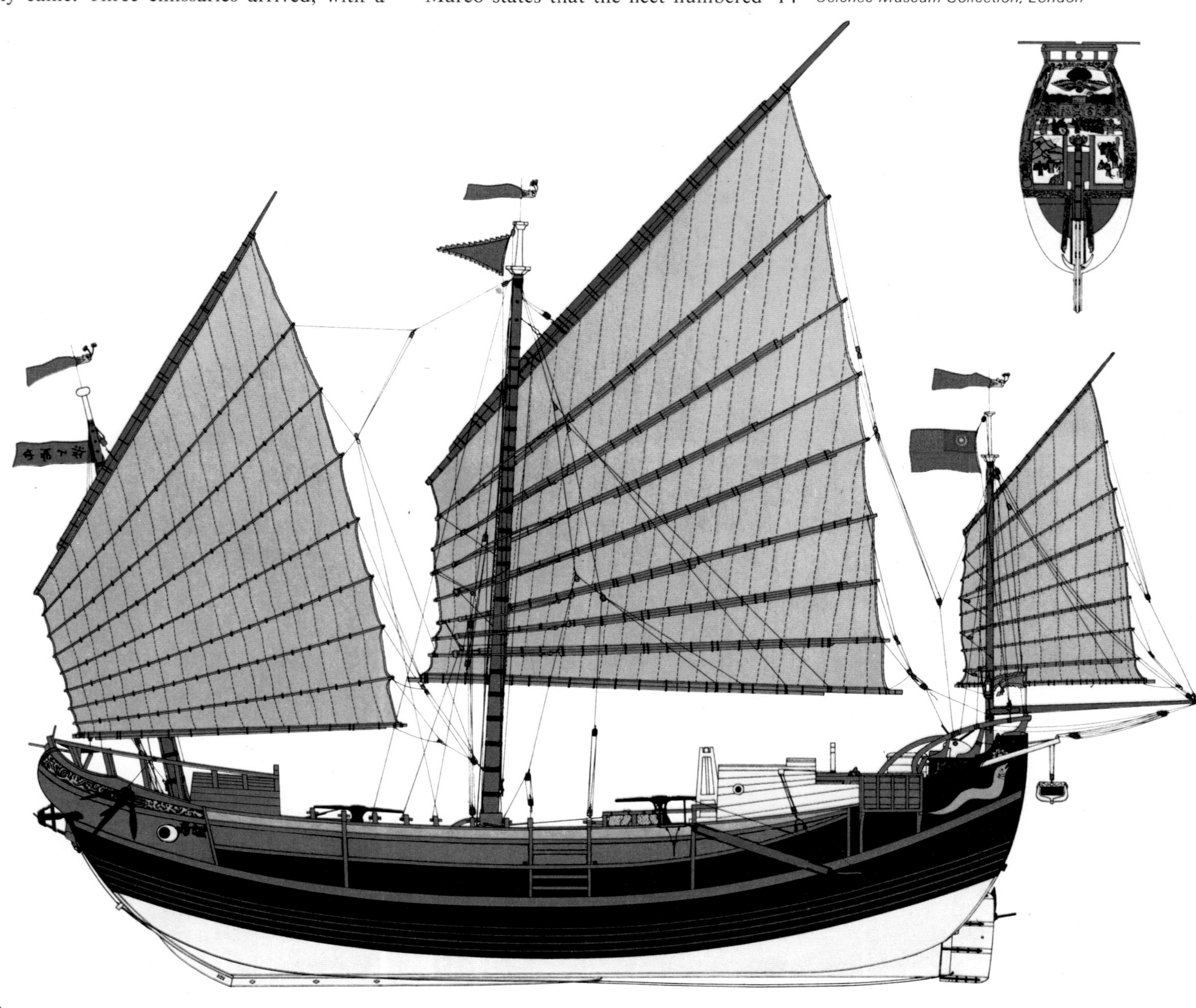

Below: The colourful carvel-built Foochow junk, a sea-going trading vessel which showed little European influence in its design, and remained virtually unchanged for 500 years.
Science Museum Collection, London

Top: An engraving by N Parr Sculp of Chinese Barks in 1752. *Mary Evans Picture Library*

Above: Another Chinese junk of the type used primarily for trade and suitable for sailing in the open sea. *Mary Evans Picture Library*

Above right: A model of a rudderless crooked-stern junk showing the stern section. *Science Museum London*

Right: The highly decorated stern of a Foochow junk; the painted emblems are traditional symbols for the vessel's welfare. *Science Museum London*

in Peking and the ocean trading came to a sudden end.

Those ocean-going junks, top-heavy and almost ludicrous as they might appear, were actually remarkably efficient vessels. One, the *Keying*, showed her seaworthiness in March 1848 when she came up the Thames after crossing the Atlantic via the Cape of Good Hope and New York.

Until recently, there were more than 70 different types of junks, including those at work on the rivers. The North China junks had bluff bows and flat bottoms; those from South China had sharp bows and deep draught. They varied in many other characteristics, although the basic principles were the same or similar for all. Usually, they had forward-thrusting bows and high sterns. It was on the larger areas of the Foochow junks' oval-shaped transoms that the artists, who spent much time and bright paint in decorating the rest of the vessel, let themselves go in a bewildering medley of characters and scenes, leaving very little space untouched.

The junks were carvel-built, with long and heavy planks fastened to the frames, the body timbers, and to the bulkheads which divided the hull into watertight compartments. A massive stern-rudder was enclosed in a trunk casing and it could be hoisted up or lowered when necessary to clear the bottom in shallow conditions, and perhaps also to act as a kind of drop-keel or leeboard, to prevent the junk from being carried to leeward when sailing on a wind. With the stern-rudder, dating from the 4th century, the watertight compartments and the number of masts, from two up to five, the junk was far ahead of Western shipping until at least the 15th century.

In addition to the vessel herself, there was the factor of the sails. Described by one eminent authority as the ultimate in aerodynamic efficiency, they were a form of square lugsail made of linen or bamboo matting. They consisted of oblong panels stiffened by battens of bamboo and working rather on the same principle as a Venetian blind. There were no stays or shrouds, but each panel had its own parrel, or collar, round the mast and its own rope leading to the master-rope, the mainsheet, so that each and every panel could be spread or shut at one pull on its rope, making reefing in heavy conditions a simple business. An indication of the value of this type of rig is given by the fact that it was chosen by Commander King for his voyage round the world which ended triumphantly in May 1973.

The Japanese junks differed from those of China in many respects. They had little claim to be picturesque and they were apt to be unhandy in a seaway. Their sails had no bamboo panels but were squares of cloth or matting set on yards. Another contrast to the Chinese junk was that the rudder, although it could be lowered or hoisted, was not enclosed but worked in a well open to the sea.

The Chinese had already learnt how to navigate by sun and stars long before 1090, when they developed the navigational compass. At first, it was a piece of lodestone rotating in a bronze bowl but later the magnetised needle came into use.

Marco Polo, even after he had come, famous and wealthy, to the end of his travels, was not allowed to settle down in peace. A year afterwards, when war broke out with Venice's old rival, Genoa, Marco had to take command of a war-galley. The Genoese won and he was captured. He was in prison for three years and it was there that he dictated his book to a fellow prisoner, a Frenchman; surely it is one of the greatest stories of travel and stout-hearted adventure known to the world.

Top: A model of an 18th-century Chinese junk with rather tattered sails.
Maritime Museum Gothenburg

Above: Another model of a Chinese junk in the Naval Museum at La Spezia.
Mauro Pucciarelli

Ships' Castles & Defences

THE ARABIAN FLEET, locked in a long-drawn-out war with the Greeks of Constantinople in the 8th century, had two main classes of fighting-ships. Their historian tells of the difference between those that were 'castellated' and the others that were not, meaning the castellated ones had battlemented little castles or castle-like contrivances fitted half-way up the masts. He describes them as having been in the nature of wooden boxes from which large stones or arrows could be thrown or shot at enemy ships, or, in a form of attack not unlike some aspects of modern warfare, as a vantage point for the flinging of 'white naphtha' down-wind at the enemy.

The historian goes on to give an illuminating, if somewhat highly coloured, picture of the Moslem fleets: 'Their ships regularly sailed in the Mediterranean and pounced upon the Christians as a lion seizes his prey. The whole sea was full of Moslem ships, whilst the Christians could no longer float a plank on it'.

The use of some form of fort, strong-point or castle on board ship was an adaptation of a very old idea, much older than is generally thought, and it came early to Europe. Even in the latter days of the Vikings, the larger vessels had a fighting platform at the bows. The use of the ship's castle that succeeded it was widespread in English waters in the activities of the Cinque Ports during the four centuries after the Norman Conquest.

When the Confederation of the Cinque Ports had taken shape as the defender of the south-east coast—the keeper of the gateway of England, so to speak, the individual ports undertook in return for their special privileges equally special obligations. The so-called Barons of the Ports undertook to furnish the King once a year, whenever called upon, with 20 ships for a period of 15 days and with a crew of 21 men in each vessel. In order to fulfil that duty, the 'Portsmen' usually had to take ships and their crews off their normal occupation of fishing and coastal trading.

If the ships were needed to swell the King's fleet in time of war, as was likely to be the case, they would have to be suitably equipped for immediate service by their owners. At first, temporary fighting platforms were added to the bows and the stern for the use of the knights and men-at-arms who might be taken on board. Then a round or square fighting-top, originally made of wicker-work and then of wood, which was secured to the mast, though not half-way up in the old Arabian style but at the masthead.

The evidence of ships in civic seals is generally apt to be a little suspect in matters of detail, since the artist, faced with the problem of fitting the length of a vessel into a circular frame, was apparently inclined to express his feelings by indulging his fancy (as some marine artists are tempted to do today). Nonetheless, a number of English seals of the 13th century concur in representing both the fore- and after-castles as square boxes. They are often elaborately carved and painted, without roofing or covering, and are raised high above the level of the deck with their inboard sides supported by stout posts.

After the vessel had completed her term of duty, such additions were removed before she returned to peacetime work. But as time went on, they were enlarged and improved until, when the ship was in use, they became prominent features. From giving the impression of large boxes open to the sky, they were roofed over, probably with coloured fabrics, giving a greater decorative effect in tune with the rich array of the banners and pennons of nobles and knights.

At last the castles became too unwieldy to be carried on board and fitted into place in sockets, so they ended by being built in as a permanent part of the ship. This was probably felt to be a welcome move by the Portsmen, who were carrying on a sanguinary and seemingly endless feud with the men of Yarmouth. Not content with that, they, with Dutch, Irish and Gascon allies, once fought a private battle against Normans, Frenchmen and Genoese at a prearranged meeting-place in the Channel.

Top left: A 19th-century reproduction showing olden-time 'Shyppes', the central subject having an occupied masthead castle. *Mary Evans Picture Library*

Top right: Model of Columbus's 'Santa Maria' with lateen-rigged mizen mast. *Marine Museum Paris*

Below: Model of a 13th-century ship with small forecastle and extensive decorated aftercastle. *Marine Museum Lisbon*

Above: Model of a late-16th-century warship with aftercastle grown into a high multi-tiered stern. *Royal Scottish Museum Edinburgh*

Right: Model of a Roman warship with midship castle. *Marine Museum Lisbon*

In the later period, the forecastle was heightened in order to achieve a good level for hand-to-hand fighting and its name is perpetuated in the modern foc's'le. The aftercastle at the stern, the summer castle, as it used to be known, was also made higher, though not to the same extent. It had begun to prove its value for cabins and cabin-space. The fighting-top, on the mast, had also developed a dual purpose, as a crow's nest for the lookout in time of peace and for the dropping of missiles and pouring down Greek fire when the ship was in action.

The time came when the ship's castles lost their usefulness in the great outburst of building larger and larger ships. Decks were raised ever higher and higher until, in a matter of only a few years, the era of multi-decks and triple masts had arrived.

Manueline Ships

IN THE LATE 1490s, after the decline of Venice as a great trading power with an almost unequalled command of the sea for commercial purposes, Portugal, under the guidance of King Emanuel I, became a flourishing maritime nation. Indeed, Portugal was the first European country to attain great heights in voyages of discovery and adventure; its sailors developed a lucrative trade with the East which in previous times had been monopolised by Venetian galleys.

The Portuguese empire was founded between 1499 and 1580 and the painting overleaf depicts ships built during the reign of King Emanuel I, around the first quarter of the 16th century. The best-known name in the field of Portuguese exploration was that of Prince Henry the Navigator. Under his direction, example and influence great voyages were made and many new territories were discovered. In 1500 Brazil was claimed by Pedro Cabral, a Portuguese who sailed for India but came upon the South American coast more or less by accident. Ascension Island, St Helena and Tristan da Cunha were all discovered by Portuguese mariners in the early years of the 16th century.

The African coast was explored and many small states were conquered by the Portuguese; others became allies of Portugal and some were totally destroyed. A Portuguese African settlement which was considered remarkable in its early formation, the West African colony of Angola, is still in existence today although many of its formerly Portuguese-dominated neighbours have long since shaken off the yoke of colonisation.

The period of Portuguese art coinciding with the reign of King Emanuel I, also called the Manueline period, was one of the richest and most flamboyant, on canvas as well as in sculpture and architecture. It aptly coincided with the growth of the nation as a maritime power, many relics of which are to be seen in the Naval Museum in Lisbon which houses the painting overleaf.

Below: The 'Saõ Gabriel', a similar ship to that used by Vasco da Gama in his search for a sea route to India in the 1490s. *Marine Museum Lisbon*

Bottom left: A portrait of Vasco da Gama by Lopez in 1524; the painting now hangs in a Lisbon museum. *M Pucciarelli*

Bottom right: The first voyage in 1497 of Vasco da Gama's fleet to India as depicted in an early naval book. *M Pucciarelli*

Picture overleaf: *M Pucciarelli*

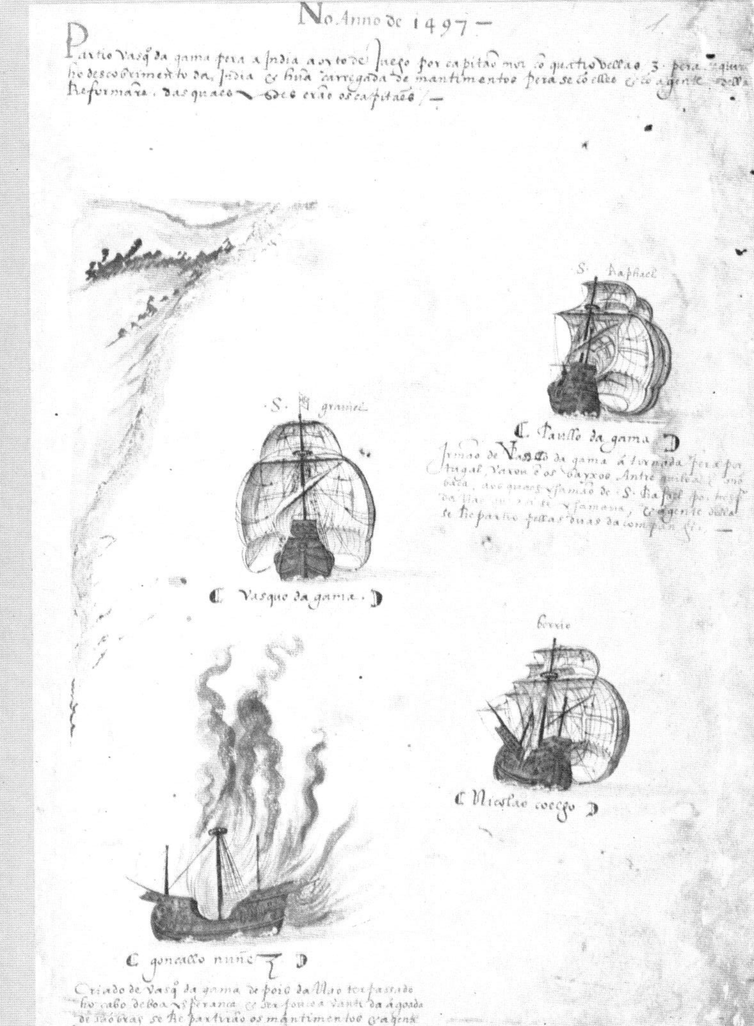

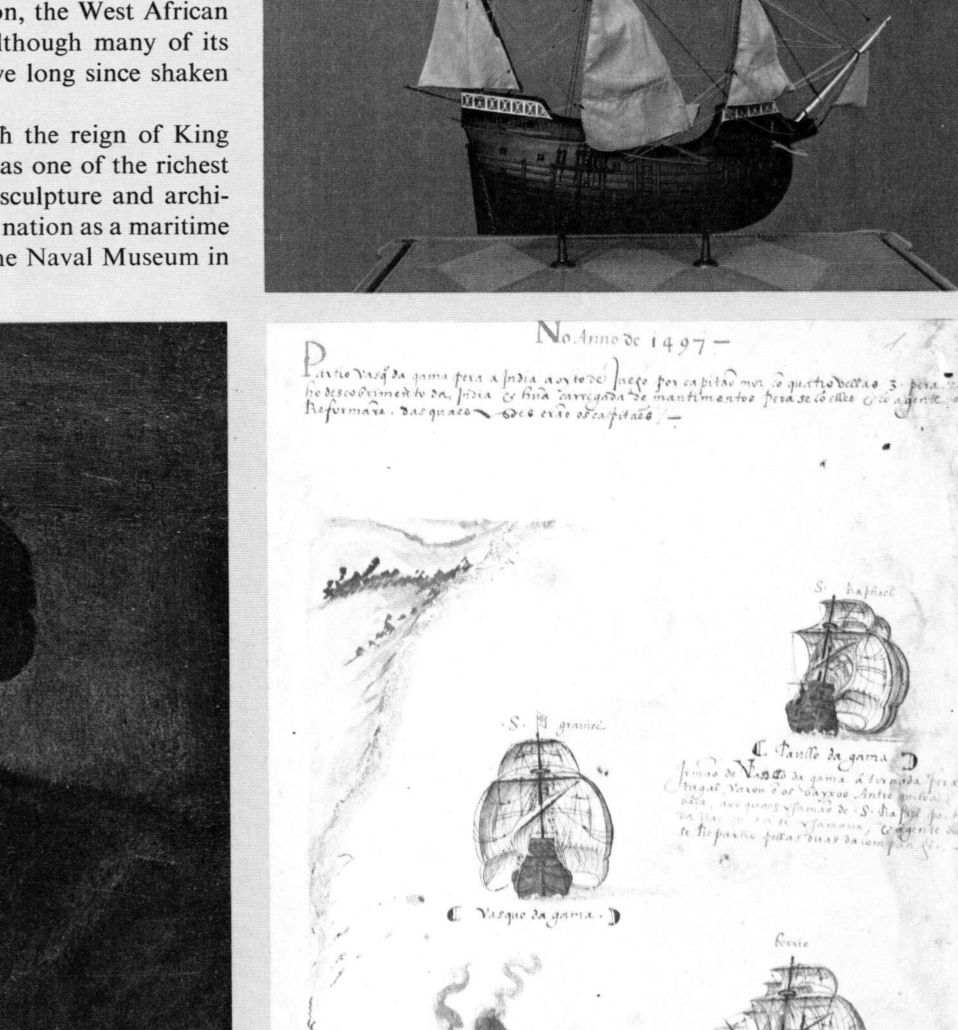

THE FLUYT

THE NAMES GIVEN to different types of ships and small craft have been many and various since man first put to sea. A name might suddenly have appeared, to be widely used across the oceans for two or three generations and then, just as suddenly, have disappeared. Sometimes the same type of vessel has had several different names and sometimes a single name has served for several different types.

The name of Fluyt applied to a ship, for example, has two different origins. One came from the French term 'en flute', which was used to describe a warship that had some of the guns taken out to convert it into a transport vessel. Apparently the rows of empty gunports along the sides when the gunports were open suggested to some musical person the holes in a musician's flute. The type of ship itself soon came to be called a flute without the French en.

Of far greater usage was the Dutch Vlieboot, which in time was adopted in English as flyboat, fliebote or plain flute, according to taste. The vlieboot was originally nothing more than a small boat that was in use on the great channel, the vlie, or 'sleeve', running into the Zuyder Zee. Over the years the type was developed and much increased in size until it had become large enough to be rigged with three masts—the same rig as that of a bark but with bigger spread of sail. It came into prominence in the great period of expansion of the 16th and 17th centuries, when the number of Dutch merchantmen of different types and classes multiplied enormously.

The fluyts were round-sterned flat-bottomed ships, with sides sloping sharply inward, and fairly narrow. Of between 400 and 600 tons burden, they had a squarish box-shaped cabin set above a rounded hull. Until the year 1700 or later, the Dutch flutes had a curious feature in that the sides of the cabin were covered with rough clinched planks set horizontally. The stern was exceptionally high and its after part overhung the water.

Employed as a merchantman in time of peace and regularly as a troop-transport or storeship in war, the type was so popular with Dutch seamen that it found its way down into the East Indies as well as into the Baltic and the Mediterranean. It was the high rounded stern, a survival from the past of the Low Countries, and the high pinched poop above, that distinguished the flutes, or flyboats, in English eyes. In England vlie was taken to mean not sleeve but flying or speedy and, having larger crews and a bigger spread of canvas, they were generally faster than their Dutch counterparts of equal size. The English versions, however, appear to have had a

much wider range, varying from as little as 20 to 150 tons burden. A 16th-century owner, who seems to have had some experience of sea fights, described his flute as having been built 'to take and leave when the skirmish is too hot for him to tarry'.

Quite a number of fly-boats were built in English shipyards for gentlemen adventurers and privateers, among them Sir Walter Raleigh and his half-brother Sir Humphrey Gilbert. Raleigh's vessel, named the *Roebuck*, from his family crest, made a couple of voyages to the New World in the attempt to found the colony of Virginia. In order to pay the expenses of the enterprise, he sent his captain of the *Roebuck*, John Clarke, on privateering cruises from Plymouth. Captain Clarke made at least three good hauls, capturing a Dutchman, the *Waterhound*, laden with wine, a second Dutch ship, the *Angel Gabriel*, with a Spanish cargo, and a French vessel laden with linen. Raleigh ordered the *Waterhound's* master with her pilot and several of her seamen to be kept on board the *Roebuck* and the unfortunates had to sail in her, when the time came, to America and back, not returning home until three years later.

Left: A representation, 'a hieroglyphic of Britain', used as the frontispiece of John Dee's 'Arte of Navigation' of 1577.
Illustrated London News

Below: A selection of Dutch ships of the late 17th century depicted on tiles.
Handels-OG Sofartsmuseet Kronborg

Right: Painting of a typical Dutch Fluyt, by M J Barton.

Below right: Engraving of Sir Walter Raleigh, by H Robinson. *Illustrated London News*

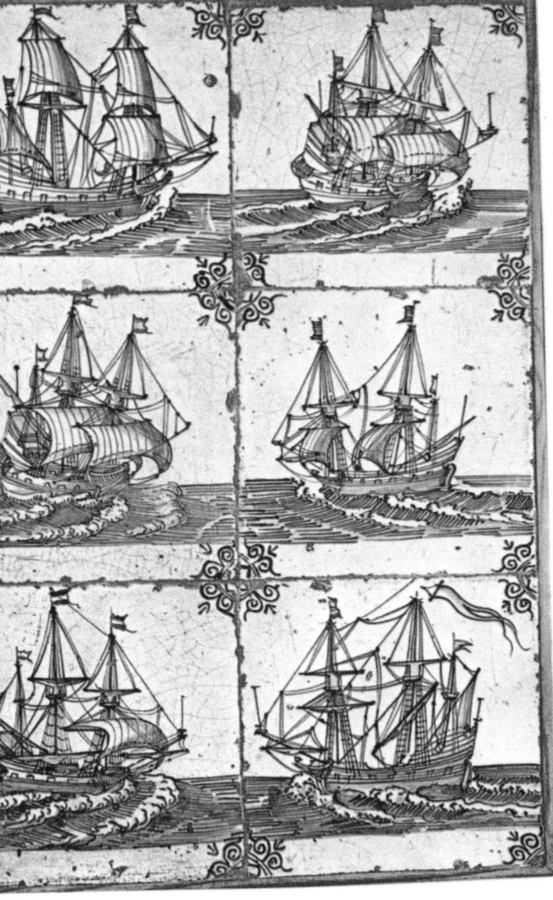

ARCHITECTURA NAVALIS MERCATO

NAVIUM varii generis *MERCATORIARUM CAPULICARUM, CURSOR* *ALIARUMQUE*, cujuscunque conditionis vel molis formas et rationes exemplis ære incisis, Demonstrationibus denique Dimensionibus calculisque accuratissimis illustr Autore *FRIDERICO HENR. CHAPMAN*

HOLMIÆ. Aº MDCCLXVIII.

HENRIK AF CHAPMAN

Above: The frontispiece of af Chapman's 'Architectura Navalis Mercatoria' is this drawing of shipping in Stockholm harbour, executed by af Chapman himself. *John R Freeman & Co*

Right: A painting by J Hagg of the Swedish fleet leaving Revel after engaging a Russian squadron in May 1790. *Maritime Museum Stockholm*

Above right: Portrait of Fredrik af Chapman from his book 'Försök till en Theoretisk' of 1806. *John R Freeman & Co*

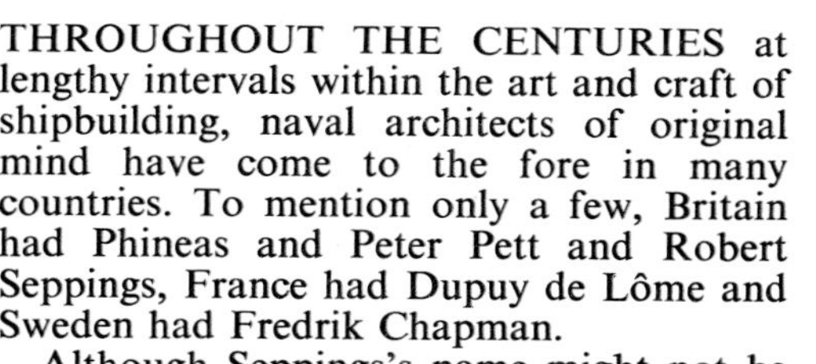

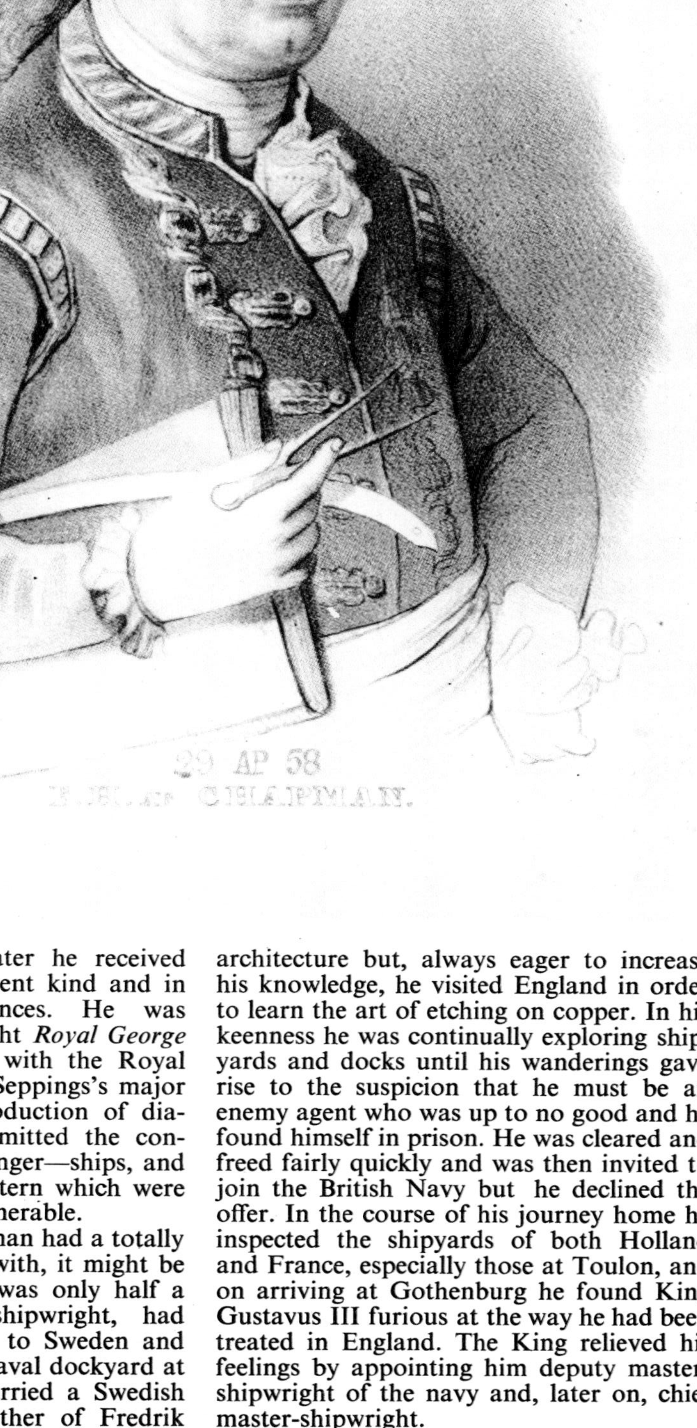

THROUGHOUT THE CENTURIES at lengthy intervals within the art and craft of shipbuilding, naval architects of original mind have come to the fore in many countries. To mention only a few, Britain had Phineas and Peter Pett and Robert Seppings, France had Dupuy de Lôme and Sweden had Fredrik Chapman.

Although Seppings's name might not be generally known, he was a pioneer of shipbuilding methods and an inventor of genius. He was born in 1767 in Norfolk, about eight miles from the birthplace of Nelson, the son of a cattle breeder who was so unsuccessful that young Robert, to earn money in his early days, had to carry letters to the neighbouring town on a mule.

On the death of his father he was adopted by an uncle, a retired captain of the Royal Navy in Plymouth, who apprenticed him at the age of 15 to a working shipwright in Plymouth Dockyard. The uncle also adopted two nieces from another family branch and one of the girls eventually married Robert. As a result of other marriages the family acquired a strong naval flavour with no fewer than three admirals added to the captain as relations of one kind or another.

In 1804 Robert Seppings became the Master Shipwright at Chatham and one of his inventions, a lifting mechanism called Seppings Blocks, so pleased the Board of Admiralty that he was granted a monetary reward of £1000, a most unusual gift for those days. Five years later he received another reward of a different kind and in most unusual circumstances. He was knighted on board the yacht *Royal George* while she was under sail with the Royal Standard aloft. However, Seppings's major achievement was the introduction of diagonal framing, which permitted the construction of stiffer—and longer—ships, and a new type of bows and stern which were much stronger and less vulnerable.

Fredrik Henrik af Chapman had a totally different history. To start with, it might be argued that by blood he was only half a Swede. His father, a shipwright, had emigrated from Yorkshire to Sweden and had been taken on in the naval dockyard at Gothenburg. There he married a Swedish girl, who became the mother of Fredrik Chapman in 1721. As a boy he was apprenticed in the Gothenburg dockyard, but he also worked in other Swedish yards in order to gain wider experience. He was so enthusiastic that in 1741 he went to London to work as a ship's carpenter for a couple of years. After further study in Sweden, in 1750 he returned to London to work as a student under Thomas Simpson, the celebrated mathematician. He was the founder of the method of calculating the area of irregular curvilinear figures which, as Simpson's Rule, is still in use in dockyards.

By that time Chapman was becoming recognised as a great authority on naval architecture but, always eager to increase his knowledge, he visited England in order to learn the art of etching on copper. In his keenness he was continually exploring shipyards and docks until his wanderings gave rise to the suspicion that he must be an enemy agent who was up to no good and he found himself in prison. He was cleared and freed fairly quickly and was then invited to join the British Navy but he declined the offer. In the course of his journey home he inspected the shipyards of both Holland and France, especially those at Toulon, and on arriving at Gothenburg he found King Gustavus III furious at the way he had been treated in England. The King relieved his feelings by appointing him deputy master-shipwright of the navy and, later on, chief master-shipwright.

In 1777-8, promoted to the rank of colonel (a little strangely to English ears) as well as being a member of the Admiralty Board, he sat on various committees and commissions which had as their object the improvement of the Swedish Navy. He also designed two big ships, the *Prins Adolf Fredrik* of 62 guns and the *Wasa* of 60 guns (not the ill-fated *Wasa* which sank on her maiden voyage in 1628 at Stockholm but her later namesake).

Among his collection of titles and ranks, he was appointed works manager of the navy in 1781 and was clearly a very active one who saw to it that his workmen were also very active. The admiral who was commander-in-chief of the fleet reported to King Gustavus in November 1782, 'Yesterday morning at 8 o'clock 60-gun ship *Konung Adolf Fredrik* and the frigate *Bellona*, 40 guns, were launched after four months. On the same day at 1 o'clock in the afternoon the keels were laid and the stem and stern posts erected of the 60-gun *Faderneslandel* and the 40-gun *Minerva*. All ribs and other timber for these vessels were sawn and bent within four months. These are quite apart from the fact that costs are much lower than ever which have happened at your Royal Majesty's Dockyard'.

Between 1782 and 1785 Chapman planned and launched 10 60-gun ships and 10 40-gun frigates and in that period was promoted to rear-admiral. In 1881 he became a vice-admiral. As relations between Sweden and Russia were growing strained, he drew up extensive plans for heavy ships which would be able to hold their own against the three-decked Russian fleet. His projected ships were to have been armed with 66, 74, 80, 94 and 110 guns, according to size. Unfortunately the programme had to be dropped through lack of funds and only one of the long list of vessels was built, the *Gustav Adolf* of 76 guns and 50 tons displacement.

Chapman devoted considerable time to various experiments, which included 2000 model tests to establish the degree of resistance in the water of different forms or shapes of ships. He started to develop tests of their after lines, but reverted to older methods after tests he made with the 40-gun frigate *af Chapman*. With that vessel which carried his name he himself sailed at the age of 82. He died in his 88th year.

His fame rests today largely on his *Architectura Navalis Mercatoria*, a monumental tome which, first published in 1768, has appeared in many editions. It contains a very large number of line drawings of the various types of merchantmen and warships. They are delicately and clearly drawn but are without any captions or explanatory text. The frontispiece is a fascinating panorama or double-page print of the shipping in the port of Stockholm.

In a companion volume there is another double-page display of vessels and small craft. They have a wide variety of rig, encompassing hog-boats and cat-boats, Venetian gondolas, English herring-busses, a royal yacht and an Algerian dhow. The companion volume was published by Chapman in 1775, under the name of *Tract om Skepps Byggeriet*. It is really a treatise on various aspects of naval architecture and the building of ships with all kinds of related and ancillary topics. They range from the different methods of launching ships in France, England and Holland to the necessary precautions that should be taken to ensure stability against the possibility of the ship heeling over.

Chapman declares that, with all three topsails and topgallants, the spanker, fore-topmast staysail and jib set, a ship sailing six points off the wind must heel no more than seven degrees, and adds advice on how to obtain good performance on all points of sailing. Dealing with the hull shape, he states that all ships should have their greatest depth a little before the middle and they should be leaner aft than forward. Those designed as vessels of burden ought to be fuller in the middle and all ships, he declares, should have their centre of gravity just 'before the middle of their length'.

He decided that the cause of the vast number of different ship types lay in factors such as the climate, the varying depths of the seas and the location of those built in Europe, similar though they might be. As to the debated question of proportion in ships, the breadth should be between one-third and one-quarter of the length. He gave a mass of helpful information under appropriate headings, such as the measurements of tonnage and stowage and the proportion needed for provisions, the proportions of masts and yards for merchant ships and, strangely enough, the proper proportions of privateers.

The *Tract om Skepps Byggeriet* was translated into several other languages, and into English in 1813 by the Reverend James Inman. To celebrate the bicentenary of the *Architectura Navalis Mercatoria*, it has been published with selections from Inman's translation of the *Tract* in the form of a single composite volume by Adlard Coles. It is an impressive tribute to the memory of one of the world's greatest naval architects, who, among all the rest, produced some very interesting hybrid warships for operations in the Finnish archipelago against the Russians.

Above: Engraving of a convoy of ships at about the time that af Chapman designs were widespread in Europe, from the book 'History of a Ship'. *K Fenwick*

Above right: Drawing by af Chapman of frame timbers or ribs. *John R Freeman*

Right: The Chapman-designed 60-gun 'Wasa' of 1788 painted by J Hagg under sail off Gothenburg. *Maritime Museum Stockholm*

Evolution of the Square Rig

THE SQUARE RIG derives its name not from the shape of its sails but from the fact that they can be set square to the centreline of the ship, as opposed to the fore-and-aft rig where the sails can be sheeted fore and aft along the centreline.

Medieval ships, such as cogs, had a single square sail. As ships increased in size, one and then two additional masts appeared (the mizen and the fore masts). The flagpole above the top (the fighting platform on top of the mast) was converted to carry a small upper square sail—the topsail, which first appeared on the late 15th-century carracks. The flagpole thus became the top mast; it was stepped on the lower mast trestle-trees because a single pole mast could not be made strong enough. Even so, the big lower masts had often to be made by assembling many baulks of timber, which were clamped together by rope bands, the wooldings. Each mast—the lower and top masts—had its own standing rigging of forestays, shrouds and backstays.

By a similar evolution, the topmast and topsail were surmounted by a topgallant (pronounced t'gal'nt) mast and sail. They first appeared on galleons during the first decade of the 16th century. Then came the royal mast and sail (first seen on the *Sovereign of the Seas* of 1637). The royal

Top: The square rig of the brig 'Royalist' in August 1972. *A Greenway*

Left: An oil painting by Peter Wood of the 1875 barque 'Alastor'.

Left: The French topsail schooner 'L'Etoile' wearing the square sail on the foremast; she is pictured off Portsmouth during the Tall Ships Race in August 1972. *A Greenway*

Top: A silhouette of the brig 'Unicorn' in the Solent in May 1973. *A Greenway*

Above centre: The Russian four-masted barque 'Kruzenstern' off Cowes in August 1974. *A Greenway*

Above: An 1814 pen-and-wash drawing of the square-rigged warship HMS 'Aboukir'. *National Maritime Museum London Crown copyright (K Fenwick Collection)*

mast eventually became a single spar with the topgallant mast so that ships of the 18th century onwards usually had masts made up of three sections, despite the adding of yet another sail—the skysail—which came into use around 1812.

Above the skysail, a few freakish East Indiamen and extreme clippers would set flying handkerchieves known as skyscrapers, moonrakers (or moonsails) and stardusters (or star gazers) Those fancy kites were not worth their extra weight in rigging aloft as they were so small compared with the lower sail (the course) or the topsail. On the other hand, the lateral 'wings', or studding sails (pronounced stuns'ls), set from booms run out from the yards, gave quite an improvement in speed in light winds from abaft the beam.

As the ships kept growing in size and as labour costs increased, the labour-saving device of splitting the topsail into two separate sails (the lower and upper topsail) appeared in the 1850s. Topgallants followed the same trend, with double topgallant above double topsails. Further labour-reducing trends included the disappearance of skysails and studding sails. The latter were rendered obsolete by the introduction of the much stronger steel yards and rigging so that the modern sails were proportionally much wider than the original pattern. Finally even the royals were dispensed with, and that rig is known as the stump-topgallant rig or the bald-headed rig. It was also nicknamed jubilee rig because it appeared the year of Queen Victoria's jubilee. The stump-topgallant rig carries in fact the same number of yards as the classical skysail rig but the staying arrangement is quite different.

Prior to the 19th century, sailing vessels were named mainly according to their trades and uses, to their hull types or to local practice. Thus we had the pink, the flyboat, the hulk, the cat-bark, the Baltimore clipper, the frigate, the sloop-of-war and many other types of vessel. The standardisation of rig nomenclature was a relatively late development. The square-riggers of the 19th and 20th centuries are classified as follows:

The ship is a sailing vessel with three or more masts all completely square rigged. Because the ship rig was the standard rig, the name has almost become a synonym for vessel. The largest and only five-masted ship ever built was the German *Preussen* of 1902. One four-masted ship still afloat is the *Falls of Clyde;* she is in the process of restoration as a museum-ship in Honolulu.

The barque (or bark) has three or more masts, all fully square rigged except for the sternmost one, which is fore-and-aft rigged. The rig appeared toward the beginning of the 19th century but it only became common after 1860. There were barques with up to five masts and several four-masters still survive, some in commission, such as the Russian *Kruzenstern,* which participated in the 1974 Tall Ships Race.

The barquentine (or barkentine) has three to six masts, all schooner rigged (fore-and-aft) . except the foremast, which is square rigged. Apart from an experimental model built in 1803, barquentine rig first appeared in the 1840s. It became popular towards the twilight of sail, as it involves smaller expenses than a barque, yet keeps some of the running capabilities of the latter. Many barquentines were in fact ships or barques cut down for economy. The *Regina Maris,* a picture of which appears on page 26, which also competed in the 1974 Tall Ships Race, is a good example of a three-masted barquentine.

The jackass barques are square-riggers with three or more masts and any sail combination that falls somewhere between a barque and a barquentine. A three-masted jackass barque might have a fully rigged foremast, a main with a large gaff sail surmounted by square sails and a mizen mast like a barque's. A four-masted jackass barque usually has square-rigged fore and main masts and schooner-rigged mizens and jigger masts. Jackass rigs were never very common so that their different types never got a proper name beyond the deprecatory blanket name given by traditionally minded sailors. The Swedish *Meta av Bixelkrok* presently plying the Mediterranean has a gaff sail on the lower main and fore masts and with those sails set, she is a jackass barque, although she can also set regular courses and assume the configuration of an ordinary barque.

The brig has only two masts (main and fore masts) both fully square rigged, although brigs seldom set a main course in front of the gaff mainsail (which is comparable to the spanker of a ship). The brig was a successful coastal and deep-sea trader during the 18th and 19th centuries, as she could economically call at small ports offering too small a cargo to fill the holds of her larger sisters. There are only two examples of the brig still sailing; they are the British Sea Cadet Corps' *Royalist,* which was launched in 1971, and the *Unicorn,* which was converted from a Baltic trading ship in 1973.

The snow is a brig on which the gaff mainsail is hooped on a small trysail mast stepped on deck just abaft the mainmast, its cap lodging in the main top. The arrangement allows a bigger hoist of the mainsail, above the crane holding the main yard. There are no snows in existence today.

The brigantine was an infrequent rig akin to the brig but with a much taller gaff mainsail surmounted by a square topsail and a topgallant carried on a pole mast (in one piece with the topmast). Also the main mast did not have a top (the decked platform) and was in effect identical to the main mast of a main-topsail schooner (see below).

The hermaphrodite brig, often also called brigantine, was much more common than the true brigantine. Her foremast was that of a brig and her main that of a schooner, hence the hermaphrodite. It is a handy and handsome rig for vessels in the 60- to 120-foot range. The largest hermaphrodite brig in commission is the 115-foot *Wilhelm Pieck* from East Germany.

The bilander was a coasting vessel (by-land-er) much in vogue from the 17th until the early 19th century. Bilanders were similar to the two types of brigantines, except that they had a lug mainsail and either a lug topsail or a square topsail and topgallant.

The polacca is a Mediterranean three-masted vessel in which at least the main mast is square rigged, the others being either square rigged or lateen rigged. The square-rigged masts of such vessels are made of a single pole stayed only above the lower yard and at the truck. Thus the topsail, topgallant and royal yards can be lowered to just above the lower yard; such an arrangement is referred to as a polacca rig. There were also brigs and brigantines with such a rig, such as the British hermaphrodite polacca brig *Marquese.* The Sicilian **velocera** of the 18th and 19th centuries can be described as a barquentine with a foremast polacca rigged and the main and mizen masts each carrying a single large lateen sail.

To complete the list of ships with at least one mast purely square rigged, we should mention the **Humber keel,** with a single mast fitted with a deep square mainsail and with a very short square topsail. Many of her rigging aspects are a direct legacy of the Norse ships and cogs.

Many fore-and-aft vessels also carried, and sometimes still carry, one or more running square sails. **The topsail schooner** is a schooner carrying one or more square sails on the foremast. The foretopmast usually carries one topsail (such as is the case with the French Navy's *Belle Poule* and *Etoile*) or a double topsail (such as the Sail Training Association's *Sir Winston Churchill* and *Malcolm Miller*).

If a fourth yard is also carried, extra stays are added making it a topgallant yard. An example of the **topgallant schooner** rig is the British vessel *Captain Scott*, built by a Scottish yard and launched in 1971. The lower yard of topsail schooners often carries a deep-running square sail which travels like a curtain along a rod fitted under the spar, and which brails against the mast. Some schooners only cross a single yard fitted with the sail just described, such as the brand new Dutch training vessel *Eendracht,* and it is sometimes topped with a triangular 'square' topsail (known as a raffee), such as can be seen in the schooner *Westward*, a vessel built in Germany in 1961 and used as an American school of oceanography.

The two-topsail schooner is a schooner with one or more square topsails on two separate masts and not a schooner with double topsails. In that category are mainly two-masted schooners such as the Baltimore clippers, which are also referred to as **main-topsail schooners,** but the five-masted Vinnen sister-schooners (1827 tons) also belong to the same group. They carried double topsails and a topgallant on the fore and mizen masts, while the main, jigger and spanker masts had gaff topsails. Every possible transition has been seen between topsail schooners and hermaphrodite brigs or barquentines.

The topsail ketch is a ketch carrying one or more yards on the main mast. Because they remind us of topsail schooners, they are sometimes called schooner-ketches, which is barbarous, and it should be remembered that the original ketch was square rigged on both masts.

There is not a single square-rigger left trading; all are either training ships, yachts, museum-ships or hulks. However, the new environmental awareness, the big increase in bunker fuel cost and the depletion of oil reserves might provide the impetus necessary to build a prototype Dynaship. Designed by a German engineer, Herr Prölss, the Dynaship is a revolutionary square-rigger. The yards are aerofoil-shaped and are rigidly fixed to the mast column. There are no stays or braces; to trim the sails, the whole column is rotated. Wind tunnel experiments and computer simulations show that such a ship would be as fast on the average as a fast freighter and, although fully automatic, her power requirement would only be one-twentieth of a similar-displacement motor vessel.

Until the square dyna airfoils cross the seas, square sails will continue to be worked as they were a century ago. The standing rigging of stays and shrouds is quite similar on square-riggers to the ordinary fore-and-aft vessels and the modern yachtsman will understand it readily enough, but even he will feel like a meat ball in a spaghetti dish when confronted with the maze of running rigging to be found on a square-rigger in commission. Although there is not the space here to describe the leads and belaying points of the hundreds of running ropes, we can explain the use and function of the lines that control a square sail.

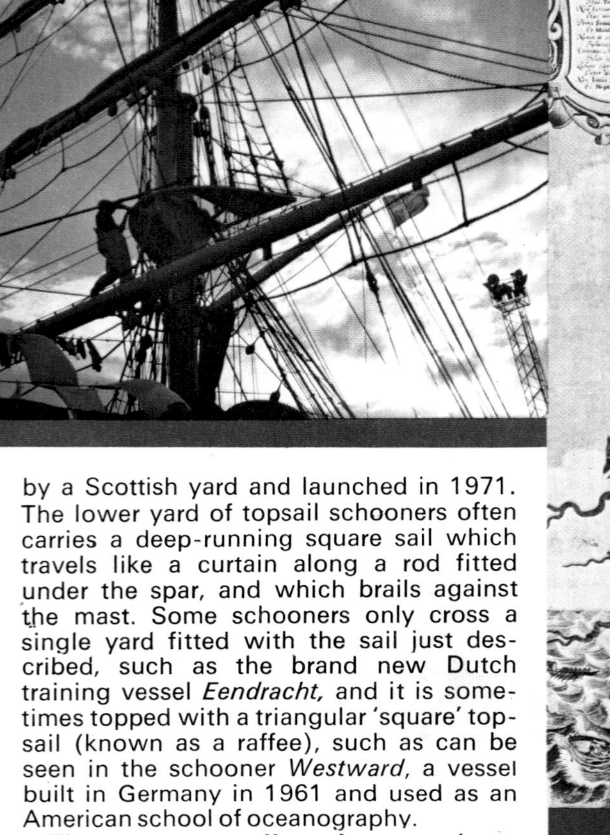

Since about 1800 the top or head of the sail is not attached or bent directly to the yard, but to a rod, the jackstay, which runs like a rail just above the yard to which it is screwed. The two lower corners of the sail or clews are brought down to a sheave in the yardarm, or extremity of the yard, below by means of a sheet. The rope then travels below that yard to its centre where it reeves through another sheave and leads down to the deck. The courses do not have a yard to stretch their feet and therefore the sheets lead directly to a block on the side of the deck abaft the sail.

It is desirable, for increased stability and for ease of working aloft, to lower the yards when the sails are not in use. There are two types of yards, those that can be lowered and those that cannot. Standing yards always remain at the same level on the mast. Course yards are left standing because they would clutter the deck if they were lowered and in the case of double topsail and double topgallant rigs, the lower topsail and lower topgallant yards are also standing because they are as low as they can go on their respective masts. Upper topsails, upper topgallants, or single topsail and single topgallant yards and all the higher yards are hoisting

Top: The brig 'Royalist' leading the hermaphrodite brigantine 'Black Pearl' in the Solent in August 1972. *C E Abranson*

Above left: The mizen top of the 1935 square-rigger 'George Stage' *P M Wood*

Above: 'Sovereign of the Seas' of 1637, the first ship to carry royals.
National Maritime Museum London

Above right: Drawing showing the general arrangement of various square rigs.
C E Abranson

Right: The Polish fully rigged ship 'Dar Pomorza' in the Tall Ships Race in August 1972. *A Greenway*

yards and when they are not in use they are lowered on their mast section as far as they will go.

The sails are trimmed by rotating the yards by means of braces which are ropes attached to the yardarms. The weather clew of a course is hauled forward by a tack which therefore works in the opposite direction to the sheet. Whereas the braces swing the yard in the horizontal plane, the vertical trim is achieved by way of lifts which lead from the yardarms to a block on the mast above, and hence down to the deck. The lifts always remain taut on standing yards and they help to relieve the weight on the crane hingeing the latter against the mast. The hoisting-yard lifts are also taut when the yard is in the lowered position and they are left slack when the yard is hoisted for setting sail. In harbour the slings are often used to cant the yards to clear warehouses or other vessels alongside, or so that the yard can be used as a derrick. Canted yards (which are said to be a'cockbill) are also used as a sign of mourning.

The vertical sides of a square sail are called leeches and, as the head and foot sides, they are reinforced by a boltrope sewn on the canvas. The hemp boltropes of the leeches would stretch and the windward leech (the luff) would shake badly when working to windward. To improve the set of the sail a bridle fixed to the luff would be hauled forward by a rope known as a bowline. Bowlines disappeared when non-stretch wire boltropes came into use during the second half of the 19th century.

In order to furl a sail it is first necessary to draw it up against its yard to spill the wind. If the yard is of the hoisting type, it is lowered at the same time, so in effect the yard is drawn down to the folds of the canvas. The ropes used for gathering the sails are generically known as brails and on square sails there are three types of brails—the buntlines which haul up the foot of the sail, the leech lines which haul up and gather in the sides of the sail and the clewlines which bring up the lower corners of the sail to its yard.

Buntlines and leechlines are bent on the boltrope and lead up to the yard by passing in front of the sail, whereas the clewlines pass behind the sail. When dealing with the courses, clewlines are referred to as clew garnets. All the ropes mentioned lead to the pinrails on the deck but once the sail is clewed up (gathered), it is necessary to go aloft and walk along the yard, using the footrope that hangs beneath it, in order to roll the canvas in a tight bundle balanced on top of the yard and to lash it securely with gaskets.

Topgallants and higher sails never carried reefing gear; when it was blowing too hard for those sails, they were simply brought in. Topsails had up to three rows of reef points on merchantmen and four on men-of-war. Courses carry one or two rows. As for conventional reefing in sloops or ketches, a reefing tackle is used, but instead of drawing the leech down to the boom, it draws it up to the yardarm. The reef points can then be passed around the yard or the jackstay and when the row is all made fast the tackle is slacked and the reefed sail is trimmed.

The theory is simple but doing the job on an ice-sheathed topsail in a Cape Horn snorter called for real seamanship and many broken nails. Reefing is probably the most arduous work on a square-rigger and today the great majority of square-rigged school-ships either do not carry reef points at all or do not use them, preferring to hand the sail completely and to switch on if need be the 'iron topsail'.

Brigs, Barques & Schooners

IT WOULD NOT be too much to say that any sailing vessel ever built was the result of several forms of compromise. Not only had the opposing claims of seaworthiness and speed to be reconciled but there were other problems besides those of the design and depth of hull.

If she was to be a man-of-war the problems multiplied. How many guns was she to carry? Where should they be mounted in order to balance the ship? And since the guns would have to be laid, loaded and fired, where could all the hands for the gun crews be packed? Crammed would be a better word; few warships were built for comfort.

One example of what conditions could be like in a small ship came from Admiral Cochrane (Lord Dundonald) when he, a tall man, was in command of a small vessel in the early 1800s. Her deckhead was so low that in calm weather he made a practice of standing in his cabin, with arms and face protruding through an open skylight up into the daylight, and shaving himself.

Leaving hull-forms and guns aside, the compromise in the rig of the sailing vessel of any size is plain for all to see; the compromise between the speed of the square-rigger sailing free or before the wind, and the ability of the fore-and-after to sail on a wind or close-hauled. Notable exceptions are the big modern racing schooners with their emphasis on speed.

The early three-masted ship carried square sails on two of her masts, the fore and main. At the beginning of the 18th century, she set triangular fore-and-aft headsails—the jibs and staysails—with more staysails between the masts. Up to about the middle of the 18th century she set a lateen on a lengthy and heavy traverse yard pointing skyward. Then, rather late in the day, the lower leading edge of the lateen was found to be useless and was cut away, leaving the remainder of it to be laced to the mast. Still later, a gaff with its jaws gripping the mast came into play and eventually, after about 30 years, superseded the lateen yard.

The gaff mizen sail became known as the driver in the Royal Navy and the spanker in merchantmen. A square topsail and topgallant sail were then set on the mizen mast above the fore-and-aft driver.

One full-rigged ship, the German *Preussen*, actually had five masts and was the only full-rigger ever built with that number, although there were a few five-masted barques. A steel ship 433 feet long with a beam of 54 feet, she could set 30 square sails and up to 18 more fore-and-afters. Her end came in a collision in the English Channel eight years after she had been launched.

While we are on the subject of sails, the East Indiaman *Essex* can be mentioned for she could, and did on occasion, set no fewer than 63 sails, most of them fair-weather and studding sails with enticing fancy names.

The tea clippers, like the Indiamen, were for the most part square rigged but built on very different lines, with speed as the chief object. Though copied from American models, their English builders went farther with their narrow proportions which, with the *Thermopylae* and the *Cutty Sark*, gave them a length of 5.9 times their beam. But the era of the tea clippers was brief indeed; it is difficult to realise that their reign did not last for much longer than a quarter of a century.

As the longer-lasting bulk-carrier ships and barques increased in size, it became obvious that a fourth mast would be needed. Some vessels were built with a square-rigged additional mast named the jigger, but generally they were barques with the fourth mast carrying a fore-and-aft spanker and jigger topsail. The biggest example was the

Above: A painting by Peter Wood of the four-masted barque 'Archibald Russell' of 1905.

Right: A view of the deck of the sail trainer 'Libertad' looking forward from the poop.
P M Wood

American *Great Republic*, which was launched in 1853 and was, in fact, the largest wooden vessel ever to be launched.

The term barque came originally from the Latin barca, through the Danish bark, and initially meant a small ship, although the barques of the turn of the last century were certainly not small. Both the barques and the full-rigged ships fell wholesale victims to the advance of steam and the use of iron for shipbuilding. A few survivors managed to carry on for a decade or two by bringing wool and grain to Europe from Australia but nowadays there is hardly a square-rigger afloat except for a fair number of school ships, chiefly Scandinavian and Russian, successfully training youngsters as seamen. Perhaps there might also be one or more brigs still sailing about the world for pleasure.

Strictly speaking, the barquentine, whose name came from the French, was more or less an adaptation of the barque and was not a square-rigged vessel, although she set square sails on the foremast; the mainmast and mizen carried fore-and-afters. It was a labour-saving and money-saving rig that came into its own in the later days of sail. So that crews could be kept down to a minimum, vessels of barquentine type were built with multiple masts—four, five and even six of them.

It was similar with brig and brigantine, which were at one time practically interchangeable names; brig was simply a shortened version of the same word for two-masted vessels, until the day came eventually for them to be more strictly defined. The brig became solely the name for vessels that were square-rigged on both the fore and main masts whereas the brigantine was generally square-rigged on the foremast only and had fore-and-aft sails on main mast. Both types could be very handy craft. In the Victorian era the Royal Navy had a special training squadron of brigs for teaching

Below left: Another Peter Wood painting; the US clipper of 1851, 'Flying Cloud'.

Below: Stern of the training ship 'Royalist'. *E C Abranson*

Bottom: The double-spanker rig of the sail trainer 'Gorch Fock' as displayed in the Solent in August 1972. *E C Abranson*

newly joined lads practical seamanship and the scheme gave remarkably effective results.

In a still earlier day, the era of the pirate and buccaneer, the rover captain who needed a fast vessel would seldom be content until he had captured a brigantine for his trade. Incidentally and quite without any connection of pirates, it is of interest to note that the *Mary Celeste*, the American vessel of the great unsolved sea mystery, was a brigantine.

Almost forgotten today, a very close relation to the brig was the snow, which came from the Dutch. She differed from the brig in having a small trysail mast abaft the main mast. The pink, also a borrowing from the Dutch and a lost memory to English seamen, was something of a curiosity. The shape of her hull was strange, very curved and rounded to meet a tightly narrow stern which narrowed still more as it rose. The pink seems usually to have had three masts, two of them with square sails and topsails and the third with a lateen.

Yet another adoption, one that is very obviously Dutch in origin from the mere sound of the name, is the schooner. It started as a yacht in its native waters but soon changed after wider application. Basically fore-and-aft rigged, the schooner developed all kinds of variations in rig and number of masts. The older type, the topsail schooner, had square topsails and a fore-and-aft topgallant sail. A schooner carrying square and fore-and-aft sails on both masts was known as a hermaphrodite. One of the type, an American privateer named the *Prince de Neutchatel*, created havoc among shipping in the English Channel in the War of 1812, capturing an unheard of number of prizes. She set a second sail, a topgallant, above the topsail on the foremast. Her great speed, which no British ship could match, stemmed largely from an exceptional spread of canvas that was her undoing in the end. Three British men-of-war sighted her and gave chase in a stiff breeze that was too much for her straining masts and she sprang them both, to become a prize herself.

Since the start of the present century more than a few schooners have sailed under four, five or six masts; there was a single vessel with seven, the *Thomas W Lawson* launched in 1902. Her masts were all of the same height, each 135 feet of steel topped by 58 feet of pine. With that vast towering array, she was worked by a mere handful of men, no more than 16 of them for a crew. She had steam winches for hoisting and lowering the sails but no unbiased eye could see her as beautiful. Her life was short; she mysteriously turned turtle off the Scillies, leaving only one survivor.

Sadly, the era of the large sailing-vessel has ended. Yet, scattered about the world, there are still cruising or trading brigs, barquentines and schooners. The schooner has found a new role as the modern yacht while surprisingly, in the shipyards here and there a new windjammer is coming to life.

Below: Scott's auxiliary barque 'Discovery' when she was moored on the Thames Embankment and served as headquarters of the Sea Scouts and Sea Cadet Training Corps. She is about to undergo extensive rehabilitation under the auspices of the Maritime Trust. *D J Kingston*

Bottom: French sail training schooners 'La Belle Poule' and 'L'Etoile'. *P M Wood*

16th CENTURY PRESTIGE SHIPS

A drawing by Holbein of Henry VIII's Great Ship. *Mary Evans Picture Library*

JAMES IV OF SCOTLAND sent his friend and naval adviser Andrew Barton allegedly to hunt Flemish pirates, but in 1511 the English merchants were complaining that Barton was worse than the Flemings. Henry VIII of England encouraged the Earl of Surrey to fit out two ships to search for the two under Barton. After a desperate fight Barton was killed and his captured ships were brought into the Thames. James was furious and prepared for war with England.

Among his preparations was the ordering of a giant four-masted carrack which was to be the largest and most powerful ship in the world. Two or three carracks of more moderate size would have cost no more and would have been a better bargain; but the great ship began a fashion in Europe for abnormally large carracks that was to bedevil naval architecture for the next 23 years. It produced a brood of monsters more suitable for displaying the prodigality of their royal owners than as serious fighting ships.

For her time James's *Great Michael* was a wonderful achievement. A Frenchman, Jacques Tarrat, was engaged to supervise her construction, for a ship of her size would have to be carvel-built and Scottish shipwrights used the clinker method. Much of the oak for her construction was imported because the forests of Scotland could provide only a fraction of what was needed. Even so, the timber for her building 'wasted all the woods of Fife'. Her dimensions as given by contemporaries seem incredible for the date. She was 240 feet long, 36 feet 'within the walls' (internal beam), and to protect her against gunfire her sides were 10 feet thick, giving her a total beam of 56 feet. It is little wonder that she 'cumbered all Scotland to get her to sea'. The £40,000 she was said to have cost was then an immense sum.

She mounted 315 guns, mostly very light pieces for use against men, but she also had three basilisks which fired 200lb shot. There were 120 master-gunners, 300 seamen and 1000 soldiers in her crew. Her 'principal/captain' was Andrew Wood and Barton's brother Robert was 'master skipper'.

When she was afloat the king had her protection tested by ordering a cannon to be fired at her and the shot did not pierce her side. He was extremely proud of her and 'took great pleasure every day to come down and see her, and would dine and sup in her sundry times, and be showing his lords of her order and munitions'.

Henry VIII was then at war with France and in a battle off Camaret Bay on August 10, 1512, his largest and finest ship, the *Regent*, grappled the largest and most powerful ship owned by Louis XIII, the *Marie la Cordelière*. After a terrific fight the English boarded the enemy, but she burst into flames (rumour had it that a French gunner 'being desperate, put fire in the gunpowder') and both ships were burnt as they lay lashed together. Henry required a replacement for the *Regent* and at the same time he was jealous of the prestige the *Great Michael* was bringing to Scotland, so he decided to go one better than King James. His new ship was laid down by Master Shipwright William Bond in September 1512 to the design of Robert Brygandine.

Named the *Henry Grâce à Dieu*, she was a carrack and similar to the *Great Michael* in appearance, but measurement comparisons are lacking. A total of 3739 tons of timber was used in her construction and as Henry's Tudor thrift forbade him to spend more of his own money than he could help, his lords and gentlemen were required to contribute materials to build her. More than half the timber was acquired in that way so she cost Henry only £8708 5s 3d. She was launched and 'hallowed' (Henry was still a Catholic) in June 1514 in the presence of Henry and Queen Catherine of Aragon as well as 'the lords and prelates of the Kingdom, who all dined on board at the King's charge'. The ambassadors of his allies, the Pope, the Emperor Charles V and the Republic of Venice, were also there. She was not, however, completed for sea until 1515.

Regarded as a wonder of the world, by Tudor reckoning her tonnage was 1500. The methods of estimating tonnage then in use cannot be equated to those of today, which would certainly make her very much larger than 1500 tons—perhaps two or three times as much. She had four masts with topgallant sails on the fore, main and mizen masts and a topsail on the bonaventure mast, all sails on the two last-named masts being lateens. No other ship of the time is known to have had three tiers of canvas on more than one mast; but it is unlikely that they could be used very much at sea, if at all, and they were probably really for show and to make the ship look taller and more majestic. Even the *Great Michael* had a topgallant on the main only and nothing above a topsail on the fore mast or above the lateen sails on the mizen and bonaventure.

The *Great Harry*, as she was generally called, must indeed have been a very remarkable ship, if Sir William Fitzwilliam was not merely trying to please her royal owner when he wrote, with perhaps more enthusiasm than seems to be entirely genuine, from her in the Downs on June 4, 1522, that she sailed better than any other ship in the fleet and could weather them all except the *Mary Rose*. That a normal, high-built carrack magnified to abnormal proportions could be a fast sailer and weatherly is surprising, to say the least. It is worth noting that when she was rebuilt in 1539 she was reduced in size and her Tudor tonnage became only 1000.

She had eight decks and originally carried 184 guns, 43 of them heavy pieces, namely eight 'long' and 35 'short' guns. Some were old-style breech-loaders and a few were the powerful bronze muzzle-loaders then coming into use and which were little inferior to guns still in service three centuries later. The Anthony Anthony drawing at Cambridge shows her after rebuilding, when her armament was reduced to 122 guns. She then also carried 500 yew bows, 10 gross of bowstrings, 200 morris pikes, 200 bills, 10 dozen lime pots (unslaked lime was sometimes used to blind an enemy down-wind), as well as 'great stocks' of arrows and darts.

She had 301 seamen, 50 gunners and 349 soldiers. All her men were assigned to stations and her quarter-bill is the earliest known. The colours used for her decoration in 1514 were yellow ochre, vermilion, crimson lake, brown, green, and varnish, also red and white lead for 'painting of tops, sails and images', so she may have had images of saints on board, like the ships of other Catholic countries, or possibly decorative carvings are meant.

Like the other giant carracks of her time she was a white elephant, better suited to display the wealth and pomp of her country in peaceful summer seas than for serious war service. Indeed until well into the 18th century large men-of-war of all nations were laid up during the winter months and fitted out again in the spring for the summer campaigning season, while smaller and handier ships kept the sea all through the year. In the 16th century the largest ships went to sea only on special occasions; in the course of her 38 years' service the *Great Harry* was only once in battle, at Spithead in 1545.

The *Great Michael* also saw little service. She was in the Scottish fleet that was assembled when war with England broke out in 1513. James spent a few days in her to encourage his seamen before he marched off with his army towards his death in battle. The rest of the fleet comprised a galley of 30 oars which acted as tender to the *Great Michael* and 13 'great ships of war' as well as some smaller craft which would be privately owned merchantmen in peace time. The Earl of Arran was admiral with his flag in the *Great Michael*. James ordered him to sail for France and join their allies but he disobeyed and went instead to Ireland, sacking and burning Carrickfergus, then returning to Ayr to sell the plunder. James was annoyed and ordered Sir Andrew Wood to supersede him but it was too late—the fleet had sailed for France before the message reached it.

While the *Great Harry* was still building James fell at Flodden, leaving his fleet in French waters. Louis died in 1515 but his successor Francis I saw a chance to replace the *Marie la Cordelière* easily and cheaply. He offered 40,000 francs for the *Great Michael* and in 1516 she became his and was known as *la Grande Nef d'Ecosse*. The rest of the Scottish fleet went with her but Francis had little use of any of them, although the *Grande Nef* remained in the French Navy List until 1527, she took part in no operations and might never have gone to sea. The other Scottish ships disappeared quickly from the list and are believed to have been broken up for the timber in them or to have rotted away in French harbours.

Henry also very soon found that giant ships were more of a nuisance than an asset, for the *Great Harry* was too big for most harbours, which were small and shallow although adequate for normal ships of the time. Indeed, the trouble of the *Great Harry's* size began with her building and led to the foundation of the first permanent English dockyard for the building and repair of ships of war. An open space near Erith had been chosen for her construction and, to protect her construction materials from the weather, storehouses were built on the site, then quarters and messes for the shipwrights and labourers were added. Thus what had been intended to be the normal temporary site for the building of one ship became permanent. It proved to be such an advance on the old haphazard system that other dockyards were established at Deptford and Portsmouth, the rest following in later reigns.

When Henry went to meet Francis in June 1520 at the Field of Cloth of Gold his prestige ship drew too much water for the harbours of Dover and Calais, so he had to use a smaller ship, the *Katherine Plesaunce*, of 100 Tudor tons. The artist (believed to be Vincent Volpe) who painted the Hampton Court picture of Henry's departure from Dover did his best to preserve Henry's prestige for posterity by magnifying the ships, giving the largest—the one with Henry on board—cloth of gold sails and the topgallants carried only by the *Great Harry*, which was not there. In fact, at the time when Henry most wished to make an impression with his largest ship he was unable to use her. He never built another ship of more than 450 Tudor tons, apart from rebuilds and repairs of old ships.

If Henry was disillusioned with large ships, some foreign powers were not, and as they had less money to spend than he had, it suited him well enough to see them expending it on prestige ships of less service value than ones of modest dimensions. In the second and third decades of the century the fashion begun by the *Great Michael* flourished and produced some interesting, although not very effective, monster men-of-war.

In 1523 the Knights of Malta had the *Santa Anna* built at Nice. The Mediter-

Left: Painting by Norman Wilkinson of Henry VIII's 'Henri Grâce à Dieu', launched in 1514.
M Muir Collection

Top: Portuguese ships of the 16th century with the 'São João' of 1535 in the foreground, as depicted on Madrid Tapestries.
R K S Fenwick Collection

Above: The ex-French and ex-Scottish vessel 'Unicorn' of 1537. *RKS Fenwick Collection*

Right: Colour print of the 'Henri Grâce à Dieu'.
The Parker Gallery

ranean shipwrights had more experience of building large ships than their North European colleagues and the *Santa Anna* was an outstanding example of the culmination of the carrack type which was soon to be replaced by the lower-built and more-weatherly galleon. She was visited in 1533 by the Spanish chronicler Friar Don Juan de Funes, and he enthuses about her wonders. He declares that she was not only a great ship of war but that she was sometimes used to carry 900 tons of wheat from Sicily or Spain to Malta. She had six decks, the two below the waterline being covered with lead and fastened by bronze nails, as was also the outside of her lower hull.

So strongly was she constructed that her sides could not be penetrated by shot and even a whole fleet would be unable to sink her. A chapel on board was dedicated to Saint Anne, and her armoury had equipment for 500 soldiers. The great cabin for the officers had butteries and serving rooms, and she even had a garden of shrubs and flowers growing in boxes of earth in her stern galleries. Her company had freshly baked bread instead of ship biscuits, for she had a windmill and ovens. There was a forge for three blacksmiths or armourers, and she mounted 50 heavy guns and numerous light pieces. He adds that she sailed and handled well despite being so lofty that her somercastle was 'three palms' higher out of the water than the masts of a galley, and she was so sound that any water entering her came from above. Her first captain was an English Knight of Malta, Sir Thomas Weston.

Gustavus Wasa of Sweden followed fashion with the *Elefant* (also called the *Stora Krafveln*) in 1532. She was 174 feet long and 40 feet in beam, being referred to as the great carvel, which probably means no more than that she was carvel built, which was still a novelty in a Swedish ship.

Not to be outdone, Francis I decided to replace the *Grande Nef d'Ecosse* by an even bigger ship, a colossal five-masted carrack named the *Francoise*. She was built at his new port Francisopolis (later Le Havre) but when they tried to get her to sea in September 1533 she grounded on the bar and blocked the entrance. Refloated with much difficulty, she was towed back to her berth, where she still was on November 14 when a north-easterly gale capsized her; for a long time her wreck obstructed the harbour. Eventually she was broken up and her timbers used to build houses in the St Francois quarter of the town.

Portugal produced her own giant, the *São João* of 1534. She carried 336 guns but was unlike the others in not being a carrack. She was something new and an early example of a galleon type. Both the Maltese *Santa Anna* and the *São João* served in Charles V's successful Tunis expedition of 1535, and the former's sides were said never to have been penetrated by shot from the shore batteries during the fighting. Two artists went with the expedition and were responsible for the designs of the Madrid Tapestries which commemorated the event.

Among the ships represented are the two named above and the portraits give the impression of being true ones. The *Santa Anna* is shown with four heavy guns each side about halfway down the hull, three tiers of lighter guns in the very high somercastle and two more tiers in the forecastle. She is full-bodied, with a big tumblehome and a carrack head with a beakhead and figurehead below it. Lower still she has a spur, evidently intended for use against galleys.

The *São João* is very different and plainly shows the influence of galleasses then being developed by the Venetians. Her forecastle is low for the time and there is no carrack head, instead she carries a deadly-looking spur. With a long waist, she has a moderately high somercastle without the steep sheer found in carracks, and she shows five heavy guns a side very close to the water, with two tiers of lighter pieces in the somercastle and forecastle. Her chief interest is that she made a complete break with the old carrack tradition and foreshadowed future ship development on galleon lines.

All the giants except the unlucky *Francoise* saw some war service but they collected few battle honours. Essentially show-ships intended to impress beholders with their size and majesty, they were much less formidable as fighting ships than they looked.

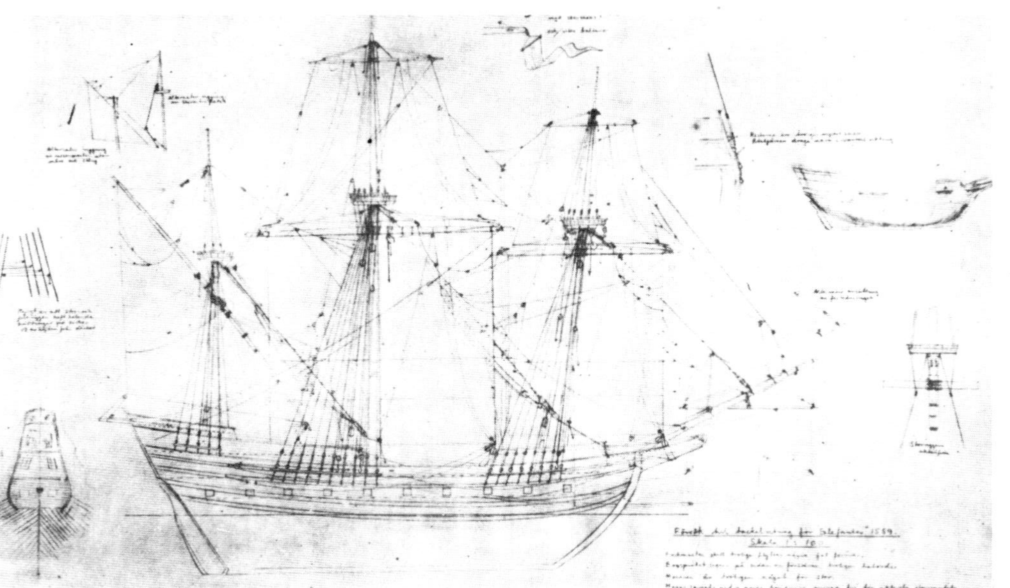

Below: James IV of Scotland (1473-1513). From an engraving in the Wellcome Institute. *Courtesy of the Wellcome Trustees*

Right: The rigging plan of the 'Elefant', a Swedish ship built for Gustavus Wasa in 1532. *Marine Museum Paris*

Below right: The 'Henri Grâce à Dieu', from an illustration in Anthony's 'Declaration of the Royal Navy' of 1546. *Mary Evans Picture Library*

Facing page: A model of one of the yachts owned by King Charles II, founder of the title Royal Navy when be abolished Cromwell's 'Peoples Ships' after the Restoration. The new king was presented with the first Royal Stuart Yacht by the Dutch and he quickly added a second which was named 'Katherine'. It was probably in one of them that he reviewed the Fleet in 1665 when it was mobilising for the second Dutch War. *M Osborn Collection*

Erikson's Steel Barques

ONE EARLY MORNING in April 1936 a splendid vessel was sailing up the English Channel under the white and pale blue of the Finnish flag, bound for Ipswich. She was the *Herzogin Cecilie*, a steel four-masted barque (square-rigged on three masts and fore-and-aft on the jigger) which had been built for the German Norddeutscher-Lloyd Line, had been handed over to the French after the 1914-18 war and then sold. Her master, Captain Sven Eriksson, had with him on board his English bride on a honeymoon trip and all the signs promised a pleasant voyage. There was only a moderate sea and a light breeze with a mist that was becoming just dense enough to warrant fog-signals.

Suddenly, something loomed darkly out of the dimness and, before she could turn, the barque was among rocks and was holed. It happened near Bolt Head, on the Cornish coast, miles off course, though how or why has never been decided. No lives were lost and in fact everybody was able to get on shore without injury.

The *Herzogin Cecilie* was a pathetic sight with her bunched canvas and sagging rigging; two tugs managed to tow her clear of the rocks and there were high hopes of seeing her trim and seaworthy again. Then the weather took a hand, interrupting the repair work and, worse still, the sodden grain in her cargo gave off a toxic gas that settled her fate.

She was a big loss to her owner both physically and financially. Gustaf Erikson (no relation to his namesake, Sven), who owned the largest fleet of steel barques in the world, headed by the *Herzogin Cecilie*. He was not only a passionate admirer of square-rigged ships but also had a keen eye for business.

He had gone to sea as the ship's boy when only nine years old and was promoted to mate at 18, altogether spending 11 years as mate and master. In 15 years he had seen his home only five times but when he reached 41 years of age he gave up command for ownership, in the port of Mariehamn on his native island of Åland.

The Åland island group, 25 miles off the coast of Sweden, was seized by Peter the Great in 1714 but the people retained close ties with Sweden, including the language. In 1917 Finland declared her independence from Russia and the Ålanders tried to rejoin Sweden but the League of Nations in a peculiar judgment decreed that the islanders should be autonomous while remaining part of Finland. Gustaf Erikson therefore was technically a Finn.

In 1913 he bought his first big ship, the Scottish-built *Renee Rickmers* which he renamed *Aland*. On her initial voyage in wartime she struck a reef and was lost. A second British-built vessel, the elderly *Borrowdale*, was also lost during the war. In neither case could the insurance be recovered but although hard hit, Erikson managed to carry on with his purchases and sales. During the next few years he bought the steel full-rigged ship *Grace Harwar*, and the steel barque *Professor Koch* of Scottish build, and just after the war the steel four-masted barque *Lawhill*.

Then came the period of the great shipping slump. In harbours and estuaries not just sailing ships but even steamships lay idle, in rows waiting with empty holds. Yet despite all the warnings against such folly, Erikson continued to buy ships.

After the war the Versailles Treaty had obliged Germany to cede to the Allied nations all merchant ships of 1600 tons and over. Every square-rigged ship was covered by that order and Herr Ferdinand Laeisz, the owner of the great line of sailing vessels which had each been given names that

Facing page above: A Peter Wood painting of Erickson's barque 'Lalla Rookh' discharging timber; she earlier served British, Norwegian and Finnish owners under different names.

Facing page below: The 'Herzogin Cecilie' finally stranded at Bolt Head, Devonshire; she was scrapped on the spot. *L·Dunn*

Above: The 1905 Greenock-built four-masted barque 'Archibald Russell', bought by Erikson in 1924, from a painting by Peter Wood.

Right: Another picture of the 'Herzogin Cecilie' painted by Peter Wood with a tug in attendance.

Below: The 1876 Glasgow-built iron barque 'Loch Linnhe' about to enter London River, painted by Peter Wood.

started with a P, had to part with them all. Splendid tall ships were being sold almost at scrap prices as several recipient countries, not knowing what to do with them, passed them on for any sum they would fetch.

That was the opportunity for sea-minded Ålanders and Finns, and above all for Captain Gustaf Erikson. His purchases included the steel four-masted barques *Herzogin Cecilie* and *Pommern*, both purchased in 1922, the *Carradale* purchased in 1923, and the *Olivebank* and *Archibald Russell* bought in 1924. The steel barques *Penang* (ex-*Albert Rickmers*), *Killoran* and *Carmen* were also added to the Erikson fleet in 1923-24, while the four-masted barque *Hougomont* was bought in 1925.

Under the German flag the *Herzogin Cecilie* had a complement of 88, a total which included two schoolmasters and 65 cadets. After the war, flying Erikson's houseflag, she sailed in 1928 with a crew of 26, including six apprentices. Later on, in 1932, the total had risen to 32, comprised of three mates, cook, steward, donkeyman, carpenter, three able seamen, 10 ordinary seamen, 10 apprentices and a ship's boy. Gustaf Erikson believed in spreading the apprentices thinly among his ships and usually they totalled about 100.

Top left: Postcard presentation of the 'Pommern' off Falmouth; she is preserved near Erikson's home at Mariehamn.
L Dunn Collection

Above left: The steel barque 'Lawhill' bought by Erikson just after World War I.
L Dunn Collection

Left: The three-masted barque 'Winterhude', 1980grt, built in 1898. *L Dunn*

Below: A Peter Wood painting of the 'Grace Harwar' of 1877, bought by Erikson in 1917.

Then there was the *Hougomont*, a barque always a byword for trouble. In 1902 when sailing from San Francisco to Liverpool, she drove on shore in Solway Firth. She had her hatches stove in and looked a wreck but was well repaired and refitted. Then, three months after leaving one west coast South American port for another, she was posted missing at Lloyds and eventually arrived at Sydney in Australia, having been a victim of adverse winds. Her next exploit was to run ashore outside New York, though she was successfully refloated.

Captain Erikson bought her in 1925 and she seems to have kept clear of further misbehaviour until three years later, when she lost her spars off the coast of Portugal. Back in English waters, she sailed downriver from Gravesend on December 31 but did not get much farther than Start Point, in Devon. The winter gales had kept her beating about the North Sea, a session that was followed by a collision in the Channel.

A vessel with such a record must have had specially good qualities or she would not have remained for long with Erikson. He could buy and sell ships without any touch of sentiment interfering. It was business just as the handling of cargo, from guano to canned meat or grain to machinery, was business.

In the years from 1929 to 1935 Erikson's purchases included seven steel four-masted barques—the *Melbourne*, *Viking*, *Ponape*, *Pamir*, *L'Avenir*, *Passat* and *Moshulu*. In addition to the large steel ships the Erikson fleet included a number of smaller sailing vessels such as the wooden barques *Warma* and *Elakoon*, both built in Finland during the early 1920s and bought by Erikson in 1933. His fleet usually numbered about 20 ships until the 1939-45 war came and spoiled it all.

At the end, his ships had dwindled to three. He died at the age of 74 in his home at Mariehamn, where the graceful lines and towering spars and rigging of the retired barque *Pommern* makes a lasting and fitting memorial to a determined old seaman.

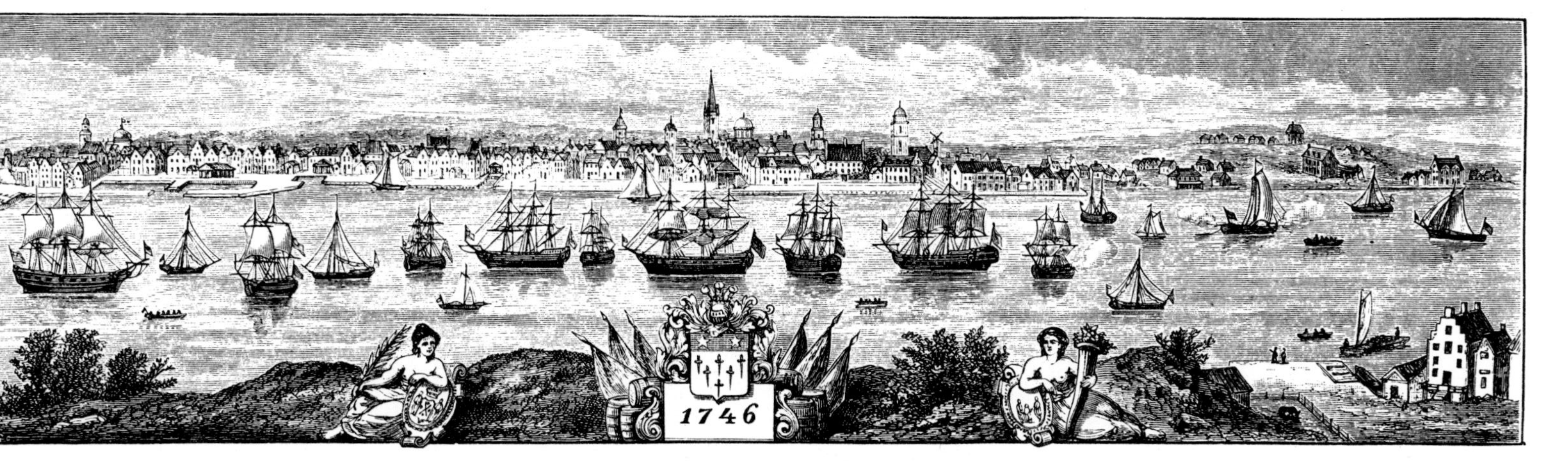

AMERICAN SAIL

SHIPBUILDING in North America started at a very early date, the first ship being the *Virginia*, a two-master of unspecified rig which was built in 1607 on the Kennebec River, Maine. From 1640 onwards even large ships for the period (90-100ft long and of 400 tons) were being built in the American colonies for the West Indian trade and even for owners abroad. The Colonial vessels were identical to contemporary English-built vessels; they were ships, barques, brigantines, ketches, sloops, pinks and shallops. Schooners (fore-and-aft or with square topsails), brigs and snows made their appearance in the early 1700s; some of the schooners built in the southern Colonies were used for smuggling to and from the West Indies and were sleek and fast vessels for the times. The King's Navy bought or ordered some vessels from American yards, the first being the fourth-rate *Falkland* built at Portsmouth, New Hampshire, in 1690; however, no seagoing naval units larger than schooners were built for the Royal Navy after 1749.

The first armed vessels commissioned by the Rebels during the American Revolution were converted merchantmen, such as the 26-gun ship *Alfred*, first vessel of the United States Navy, and the eight-gun sloop *Providence*, a fibreglass reconstitution of which is now sailing from Newport, Rhode Island. The Continentals purchased from France two frigates and four East-Indiamen (merchant vessels eminently suitable for man-o'-war conversion), one of which, the *Bonhomme Richard*, made history with her capture of HBMS *Serapis* off Yorkshire in 1779. The *Bonhomme Richard* sank as a result of the action; her wreckage has been located and investigation by divers was planned for 1979.

The Continental Navy ordered 16 frigates of 32, 28 and 24 guns – from scattered American yards and three ship-rigged sloops of 18 guns. These ships were slightly old-fashioned, with a beakhead bulkhead, but those that were captured intact by the English were usually recommissioned in the Royal Navy – a mark of approval, although their durability proved to be poor as they had been built in an emergency with improperly seasoned timber. Only one ship-of-the-line, the *America*, was built in America (at Portsmouth) during the Revolution but she was handed over to France before commissioning. The State navies were mainly made up of converted merchantmen and of shallow-draught 'radeaux' and galleys for harbour defence; however, they included a few home-built or foreign-purchased frigates and brigs-of-war.

The Revolution was the occasion for the fitting out of large numbers of privateers. At the beginning these were also hastily converted merchantmen but they were soon replaced by purpose-built vessels. By far the most popular rig was the schooner and the average size was small; the largest American privateer was a 120ft fore-and-main-topsail schooner. The 1937-built topsail schooner *Swift of Ipswich* (69ft hull), which sails out of Santa Barbara, California, gives a fair idea of the appearance of a Revolutionary War privateer. Brigantines, brigs and snows were also used; few privateers were ship-rigged. Of the latter, the *Rattlesnake*, 89ft on deck, was a little beauty and her lines, if applied to a larger hull, would have produced a clipper of the 1840s.

After Independence the American shipowners discovered that they no longer benefited from the moral and effective protection of the Royal Navy – and the Continental Navy, or what remained of it, had been disbanded. American merchantmen were fair prey for any privateer, pirate or corsair. The only protection for undermanned and undergunned merchantmen is speed: this thoroughly started the process of fast-ship design that culminated with the clipper ships of the mid-1800s.

By 1790 the schooner had become the most popular rig in America, the combined schooner tonnage far exceeding that of all square-riggers under the Stars and Stripes.

Top: A view of East Side, New York, in 1746. *Peter Newark's Western Americana*

Above, centre: San Francisco, as seen from the bay, in 1868. *Illustrated London News, 7 November 1868.*

Above: The Baltimore brig HMS 'Blackjoke', left, used in the fight against the slavers was itself a captured slaver, 'Henriquetta'. *RKS Fenwick Collection*

The popularity of the schooner was due to its potential speed and weatherliness, to its small manning requirements and to its handiness in narrow waters, although many also undertook long ocean voyages. Innovations first appeared in the small pilot schooners, 40 to 60ft long, where experimentation was less expensive. The hulls were characterised by much deadrise (V-section) in the mid-section, by long bow and stern overhangs, by a considerable drag (angle of the keel so that the draught aft is

The 'Bonhomme Richard' and HMS 'Serapis' as depicted in an oil painting by Dominic Serres. *Courtesy US Naval Academy Museum*

greater than forward) and low freeboard without bulwarks and often without even an open rail. The scantlings were light to reduce displacement. The masts had a very pronounced rake (backward lean) and carried a fantastic spread of canvas.

After the Revolution the commonly boomed foresail was superseded by an overlapping loose-footed sail. Only fishing schooners and the smallest coastal schooners were pure fore-and-afters; all others carried at least one square fore-topsail, and, quite often, a square main-topsail as well. Except on the larger units the yards were lowered to the deck when not in use, to reduce top-hamper and windage. A few three-masted schooners were built prior to 1812 but they were rather oddities.

Among the most extreme schooners were the Revenue 'cutters'. In the English Revenue service cutter-rigged vessels were the norm and the term cutter is adopted in America to the present day in connection with any Revenue vessel, regardless of type. Revenue cutters had to be faster and more weatherly than the opposition, had to be seaworthy and be able to stay at sea for long cruises in all sorts of weather and had to be shoal-draughted to patrol inshore bays. Their average size before the War of 1812 was 56 to 110ft on deck, with a beam one-quarter of the length. Every possible intermediary rig between the schooner and the brig was to be found and all made lovely vessels.

Unlike the schooners, the square-rigged merchantmen of the period up to 1812 were built, as a rule, with more of an eye on cargo capacity than on speed. Being large vessels, they were too expensive to venture in high-risk trades and they were engaged in the European packet trade, the East India and the China trades. These ships were moderately fast to slow and were not significantly different from their English counterparts.

Despite the anti-militarist opinion that prevailed during the early years of the new nation, it soon became painfully apparent that if America intended to have a maritime commerce, she would need a navy to protect it. The prime source of aggravation came from the Barbary corsairs operating from small Muslim principalities in North Africa whose incomes derived from piracy. In 1794 Congress passed the legislation for the creation of the Navy of United States and for the building of men-o'-war. The young country did not have the money or the manpower to build and maintain a fleet of ships-of-the-line in the same way as European naval powers. The initial appropriation was for six frigates which were designed to be more powerful than any faster opponent and faster than any more-powerful enemy.

Three of these six frigates were rated at 44 guns; the *United States* (launched at Philadelphia in 1797), *Constitution* (Boston, 1797) and *President* (New York, 1800). They measured 175ft on the gundeck and were 23ft longer and 13ft wider than the improved British forty-fours. The advantages of a larger ship for a given number of guns are greater speed, more space to handle the guns and gunport sills higher above the waterline, allowing the guns to be used in sea or heeling conditions that would prevent the use of the guns of a smaller ship. British ships were notoriously overgunned and this also strained their hulls.

One of the major innovations which greatly increased the firepower of the American frigates was the flush spardeck which almost made them into miniature two-decker ships-of-the-line; the gangways linking the quarterdeck to the fo'c'sle were made very large, leaving only a narrow well in the centre for use as a hatchway. These gangways were not strong enough to carry a full armament and the waist was unarmed; however, the lengthened fo'c'sle and quarterdeck were heavily armed. The forty-fours carried 30 long 24-pounders on the gundeck, two bow chasers and 20 to 22 42-pounder carronades on the upper deck (except for the *Constitution* which had 32-pounder carronades).

Two of the original frigates, the *Constellation* and the *Congress*, were rated at 36 guns (but actually carried 28 long 18-pounders and 20 32-pounder carronades) and measured 164ft on deck. The *Constitution* is preserved at Boston but the *Constellation* that can be seen at Baltimore is not, despite popular belief, the 1797 frigate, but an 1854 sloop-of-war. The sixth frigate, the *Chesapeake*, was originally intended to be a forty-four but was finished in 1799 as a thirty-eight.

These original six frigates made history, both in terms of ship design and naval actions. Between 1796 and 1814, with the Quasi-War with France, the wars against the Barbary corsairs and the War of 1812, 15 other frigates, eight ship-sloops, six brigs and 13 large schooners were built for the US Navy. In 1814 four 74-gun liners were laid down but were completed after peace had been signed. These liners were failures; they had an insufficient displacement for their batteries and they rolled violently.

The War of 1812 brought the commissioning of a large number of privateers, nearly all schooners. They were very fast and handsome vessels and, with the large American frigates, they made the international reputation of the US ship designers and builders. One of the most famous privateers was the schooner *Prince de Neufchatel*, 108ft, built at New York in 1812-13. She carried 18 carriage guns and an amazing press of canvas. She was rigged as a hermaphrodite schooner, that is, like a modern brigantine but with a loose-footed gaff spencer on the lower foremast instead of the main-staysail. She was a very successful privateer and was extremely fast – she made good 17 escapes from British men-o'-war and she had the same speed-length ratio as the fastest clipper ships of the 1850s; her lines were used for some of the most famous opium clippers.

After the Napoleonic Wars the Revenue cutters assisted the US and Royal Navies in repressing piracy in the Caribbean. The post-war cutters were of pilot-boat (schooner) design with lengths ranging from 48 to 70ft and they were followed by larger cutters rather similar to the naval schooners of 1800. New Revenue cutters were ordered in 1848, including a square-rigger and the *Joe Lane*, a 114ft topgallant schooner of advanced clipper model; the beautiful charter yacht *Shenandoah*, built in 1964 and based at Vineyard Haven, Massachusetts, is built along the lines of the *Joe Lane*.

Slaving had been practised for a long time by American shipowners, since the *Desire* built in 1636 at Marblehead, Massachusetts. The early slavers were mainly sloops, brigantines and schooners in the 50 to 70-ton range but they were not specifically built for the trade and were only as fast as required by balancing the extra expense for more speed against the higher cargo wastage during slow 'middle' passages. When the trade was declared illegal and naval patrols began to chase slavers after the Napoleonic Wars, the slave traders evolved purpose-built vessels designed to evade the embargo; these had fast hulls of 60-100ft length improved from the Baltimore clipper privateer lines. The rigs were, in order of popularity, topsail schooners, brigantines and brigs.

No fully-rigged ships or barques were designed for the trade although a few were entered by 'amateurs'. The armament was usually a single gun or carronade mounted on a pivot amidships, which could be traversed across a wide angle. This was sufficient to fight off wild natives and highjackers; no attempt was made to fight it out with naval cruisers. Many of the successful cruisers were captured slavers as the slavers were often faster than the naval-built vessels. Such were the Baltimore brig HMS *Black Joke* ex-*Henriquetta* and the Baltimore schooner HMS *Fair Rosamond* ex-*Dos Amigos*. Slaving voyages died hard despite their assimilation to piracy in US courts in 1820. The *Wanderer*, a luxury yacht flying the respectable burgee of the New York Yacht Club, was caught red-handed in 1858 and in 1860 the clipper ship *Emanuela* was captured with a cargo of 600 negros and the ship *Erie* was caught with 890 slaves on board.

The Baltimore clipper type reached its peak from 1814 to the 1850s and the 1977-built replica *Pride of Baltimore*, at Baltimore, gives a good idea of the grace of those vessels, which were copied in Europe and which influenced other types of vessel, from fishing boats to fully-rigged ships.

The early New England fishing boats were mainly inshore 'Chebacco-boats' with a pink stern and 'dogbodies' with a square stern; both types were cat-schooner rigged. without bowsprit or jib. During the 1820s they were replaced respectively by 'pinkies' and 'jiggers', which had bowsprits. These boats were in turn succeeded, from 1846 onward, by fast Baltimore clipper models with excessively shoal draughts that provoked many capsizes – the draught was increased from 1884 and the round stem or spoon bow appeared in the late 1890s.

The coasting trade was almost monopolised by schooners from 1800 onwards. Until 1850 these were full-ended models. The three-masted schooners appeared in earnest in the 1850s as a result of increasing size. After the Civil War the three-masted fore-and-aft rig became preponderant and the hulls were either shoal-draught with centreboard or deep-draught; both types later merged into a deep centreboard model. The first four-poster was the *William L. White* built at Bath, Maine, in 1880. She was followed by others and by five- and six-masted schooners. The only seven-masted schooner ever built, the *Thomas W. Lawson*, was launched in 1902 at Quincy, Massachusetts. Unlike most other large US schooners, she was built of steel. She was 385ft long and measured 5218 tons gross; she was one of the three largest sailing ships ever built, with the five-masted barque *France II* and the five-masted ship *Preussen*. The *Thomas W. Lawson* was reputed to handle like a cow.

Meanwhile shipbuilding had appeared on the West Coast, starting with two-masted keel schooners for the lumber trade. The Pacific Coast vessels were mainly built and manned by Norwegian immigrants but were inspired by East Coast models. The Alaskan sealing schooners introduced the

Below, left: A coloured engraving of the first stages of the 'Chesapeake'-'Shannon' duel.
Courtesy the New Brunswick Museum

Below, right: Water colour by Peter M Wood of a Banks schooner.

Bottom: Model of the seven-masted steel-built vessel 'Thomas W Lawson'.
Science Museum London (photo D Rudkin)

rather ugly leg-o'-mutton mainsail that became a distinctive West Coast feature, along with the oddly shaped triangular topsail clewed to the boom-end, and the fore-course brailing against the lower mast. During the late 1890s three-, four- and five-masted schooners became common. Two three-masters of the period survive – the 1895 *C. A. Thayer* preserved at San Francisco and the 1897 bald-headed *Wavona* preserved at Seattle.

The deep-sea square-rigged merchantmen of the post-1812 period carried on, in the main, the cargo-capacity priority of earlier years. Competition for passengers and the latter's preference for short passages did put some pressure for fast ships in the Atlantic packet trade and by 1825 the packet ships were sharper than previously and built on the frigate model. The demand for fresh tea that had not spent endless months becoming stale in the holds of slow wagons gave rise to the fast China packets that first appeared as schooners and grew to brigs and ships of the large Baltimore clipper model. An extreme model of that description was the 1833 ship-rigged *Ann McKim* – but a ship-rigged Baltimore clipper was no novelty; the merchantman *Hannibal* of 1811 was such a vessel.

The trend for speed produced in 1844-45 the remarkable China packet *Rainbow* which in turn prompted the design of the *Sea Witch* in 1846. The *Sea Witch* is often described as the 'first real clipper ship'; she was however the result of a continuous evolution and it is quite impossible to define technically the clipper ship in opposition to non-clipper ships – the only criterion for the clipper label is an unquantified but excessive sacrificing of capacity for speed. The craze for speed was sharply enhanced by the California gold rush of '49 and collapsed at the first trade recession. However, even if the clippers are now fashionably discounted as a short-lived fad for speed, after having been overglorified and romanticised, they were undoubtably extraordinarily beautiful thoroughbreds. They were also all too often hellships, for part of their speed was due to the reckless and brutal driving of their crews by bully masters and bucko mates, a type of officer that unfortunately outlived the clippers and carried on in many of the later Down-Easters.

Whereas many of the pre-clipper packet ships still carried the beakhead and head rails inherited from the frigates, the clippers brought up their planking to the stem and discarded the rails, retaining only a small ornamental trailboard. The clean bows and the rounded stern of the clippers were adopted by the packets, producing the 'medium clipper' type which followed the heady but short-lived years of the extreme clipper. The more mundane medium clippers (such as the English *Cutty Sark* which is preserved at Greenwich in London, England) were more adapted to a variety of trades and cargoes, combining good speed with reasonable capacity.

In America most of these vessels were built 'Down East' – in Maine – and were known as Down-Easters. Such was the ship *St Mary* which was built in 1890 and wrecked on her maiden voyage in the Falkland Islands. A mid-section of her hull was retrieved in 1978 and is exhibited at the Maine State Museum at Augusta. Few steel square-riggers were ever built in the States and these were near-copies of the British steel windjammers; by then the merchant maritime pre-eminence of America had faded away.

The barque rig already existed in small European vessels of the late 18th century but it did not become common before the 1850s and it was really only in the large European steel windjammers that it gained popularity. The Boston clipper *Great Republic*, built in 1853, was rigged, before the fire that ravaged her, as a four-masted barque. She was the first four-masted square-rigger and the largest wooden hull (4555 tons register, 325ft) ever built.

The barquentine rig was an effort to combine the low labour requirements, cheapness and weatherliness of the schooner rig with the superior performance of the square rig for ocean passages. The barquentine became popular in the 1880s in the States as a substitute for the large three- and four-masted schooner rig; barquentines with up to six masts were produced.

One cannot conclude even a brief survey of American sail without mentioning a special type of ship which contributed much to the growth and prosperity of the nation – the whaleship. Whaling had been practised since early colonial times, starting with inshore whaling with sloops; the whales were towed back to the beach for flensing (cutting up) and trying (melting out). The inshore stock was soon exhausted and bigger ships were built to pursue the whales relentlessly offshore; the right whale population decreased and the whalermen turned their attentions to the sperm whale.

By 1760 tryworks – the brick furnace and cauldrons for trying the blubber – were built on the decks of whaleships, abaft the foremast. After a decline during the Revolutionary War, whaling increased again but the ships had to go farther afield to seek their quarry, to the South Atlantic. They hailed primarily from Nantucket, New Bedford, Mystic and Boston. It was English whalermen who discovered the rich South Sea grounds in 1788 and the Japan grounds in 1819 but the New Englanders were by far the greatest whale hunters in the 19th century. In 1842 there were no fewer than 594 Yankee whaleships at sea. Hunting methods might have been crude and inefficient compared to those of today but the sheer number of sailing whaleships (not all of them American) did lead to the near-extinction of the hunted species, in particular the right whale. The Yankee whaling heyday lasted from 1835 to 1860. The discovery of petroleum oil in 1858 and Confederate raiders during the Civil War combined with the depletion of the stocks to make American whaling a thing of the past although it lingered on until the 1920s.

During the period 1760-1860 whaleships were mainly ships (or barques in the later years) in the 200 to 400-ton range. With voyages lasting from three to five years or more they needed the size to carry the provisions and bring back an economic cargo. Speed was not an essential feature but seaworthiness and seakindliness were. The hulls were usually bluff and with sharp floors and easy bilges so that they would roll down easily when flensing a whale lashed alongside. Whaleships were often converted merchantmen of the ordinary packet model and some were purpose-built, after 1855, on the medium clipper model; they were not all heavy tubs. During the last years of American whaling schooners of the Bank's type were also used.

The only sailing whaleship in existence today is the *Charles W. Morgan* (314 tons, 105½ft) which is preserved afloat at Mystic, Connecticut. She was built for the trade at New Bedford in 1841 and went whaling until 1921; she has logged more miles and caught more whales (more than 2500) than any other whaleship. She is now preserved under her original rig, that of a ship with single topsails, but for a number of years she was rigged as a barque with double topsails. She displays many whaleship characteristics; the heavy wooden davits on which the whaleboats were kept at the ready, the tryworks, the hinged cutting stage on the starboard side and skids above the deck to carry spare boats. The hull is black with a white band with painted gunports. The stern is square, with small windows and a gold American eagle.

The main and fore-royal polemasts each carry two padded hoops in which the lookouts steadied and braced themselves. The poop-deck is typically New English with its 'round house' consisting of two deckhouses on each side of the deck, right aft, in which are the galley, the bosun's locker and the companionway to the cabin. These two houses are joined by a common flat roof that spans and shelters the helmsman's position. The steering is also typical; it is done by a wheel fixed to the tiller and which moves with the latter, the steering rope being rove round the wheel's drum, and the ends made fast to the ship's timbers.

Left: Another Peter Wood painting: the US clipper 'Flying Cloud' of 1851.

3. Navigators and Discoverers

ROUNDING the CAPE

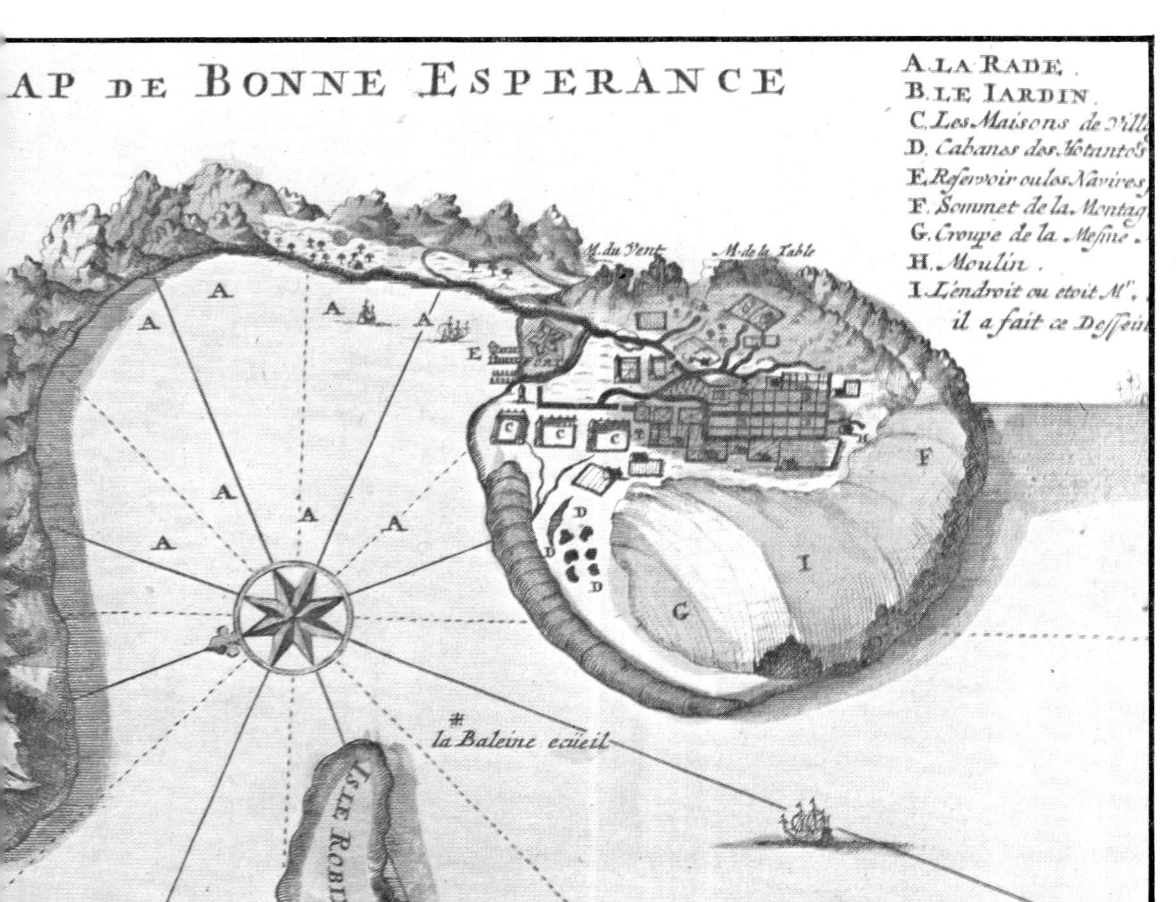

PRINCE HENRY the Navigator stands alone in the annals of the sea. No other man could claim to have been responsible, directly or indirectly, for the discovery of half the world in a single century. That is the Prince's unique distinction.

Born of an English mother—the daughter of John of Gaunt, with the King of Portugal as his father, he won his spurs at the age of 20 fighting against the Moors at the siege of Ceuta in 1415. In 1419 he was made governor of the Algarve and later resided at the town of Sagres, near Cape St Vincent, where he studied navigation. While his brother Pedro toured Europe for nautical books and charts, he gathered round him a number of would-be explorers, teaching and advising them, and filling them with enthusiasm.

The time was ripe and the prospect bright for voyages of discovery. Portugal was in a rare interlude of peace at a time when Prince Henry and his companions could handle improved navigational instruments and new charts at their leisure. Below them they might see against the blue of the Atlantic the pictured sails of the latest type of light caravel—square-sterned, seaworthy and capable of sailing within five points of the compass, fit surely for long voyaging.

Those were the exciting days when the old-style cartographer would fill blank areas on his chart with pictures of ferocious beasts that never were on sea or land. He

Above left: Sixteenth-century map of the central Atlantic and coast of Brazil attributed to Lopo Homen, in the French National Library. *M Pucciarelli*

Below left: A Mortier colour engraving of 1700 of the Cape of Good Hope. *M Pucciarelli*

Above: Representation of Vasco da Gama's fleet for his third voyage to India in 1524, from the Portuguese Navy Ministry 'Book of the Navy'. *M Pucciarelli*

Above right: Model of a 15th-century Portuguese caravela. *Maritime Museum Lisbon*

might lure the explorer with fish-tailed beauties and some such statement as, 'Here be mermaydens which some do call syrens'. Then there was the magic Island of the Seven Cities to find, somewhere out in the Atlantic, and the lone isle of Antilia, though the hunt for the latter was to go on for centuries.

Prince Henry must have felt the excitement but he had no intention himself of leaving his quiet Sagres for the open sea, although he nursed an ambition to make contact with the semi-mythical Prester John, the Christian ruler among African mountains. The Prince appears to have thought it his duty to remain on shore, developing his religious and commercial plans while encouraging and financing fresh expeditions. He spent the greater part of his life studying the possibilities of the uncharted world and of overseeing the creation of new trade routes. It was under his direction that the lost Azores were rediscovered, but still more promising was the rounding of the Moroccan Cape Bojador in 1434. The first cargo of West African slaves and gold reached Portugal in 1441 and from then on his captains worked their way farther down the West African coast, bringing back more unhappy slaves to develop the barren soil of the southern province of Alga.

Then, in 1461, came the tragedy of Prince Henry's death. By one year he had missed the triumph of hearing the report of a Portuguese ship sailing into the Gulf of Guinea. An interval of some years was followed by the successful voyage of one Diego Cam, who found the mouth of the Congo River and set up a pillar to mark his progress. He made a second voyage along the coast, setting up another pillar and collecting more negroes for slavery on the way. In all, he explored 1450 miles of West African coastline.

Barthelommeo Diaz was next on the scene. In 1487 he sailed from Lisbon with two ships in an attempt to find Prester John. The currents inshore proved so troublesome, however, that he stood well out to sea and sailed far to the southward. Looking in vain for land, he altered course and steered eastward, perhaps wondering what grim mystery might lie ahead. Without knowing it he had achieved fame for all time by doubling the Cape of Good Hope, the first European to do so. His crews were growing mutinous, however, after their exertions, so he was forced to turn for home.

The currents that had beset him on his outward voyage gave him little difficulty and he had a fair wind for much of the way, except while rounding the Cape. He named it the Cape of Storms but his King later renamed it to give a hint of welcome.

Following in the wake of Diaz went Vasco Da Gama. He was a mariner of much experience who had also fought as a soldier. Born in 1460 of an aristocratic family, he is described by a contemporary as being 'very disdainful, ready to anger and very rash'. He had equipped himself for an ambitious voyage to discover a sea route to India with all the latest information in books and charts and with the best navigational instruments, while, of the four ships he took, two had been specially built for the voyage. Diaz had given him much sound advice from his own experience, which, rather suprisingly, Da Gama took. He was recommended to build square-rigged vessels of broad beam and light draught instead of caravels, which had insufficient space for stores. Diaz also advised an offshore route to avoid calms and fierce local storms.

As a result, Da Gama took the new *Sao Raphael* and *Sao Gabriel* with a small vessel and a big storeship. On a July day in 1497 all officers and crews attended a religious ceremony in the presence of the King and his court immediately before they set sail from the Tagus to prepare for the coming perils. The weather was fine and remained fine, although there was a sad lack of wind. Thomas Stevens, an Englishman on board the flagship, who wrote a good letter, described how 'sometime the ship standeth still sometime she goeth but in such order that it was almost as good to stand still'.

However, at last, she and her consorts arrived at the Cape, doubling it without mishap, and followed the coast northward. At Mossel Bay, near Georgetown, the natives entertained the ships' companies with music and dancing 'in the style of negroes'. Sailing on, they passed the last pillar Diaz had set up and reached Melinda, North of Zanzibar, where Da Gama had the good fortune to obtain from some Moorish merchants an Indian pilot, who brought his ships to Calicut. There, he was not welcomed, largely owing to some more Moorish merchants who forcibly resented any competition and stirred up the natives. Da Gama himself was caught by Indians

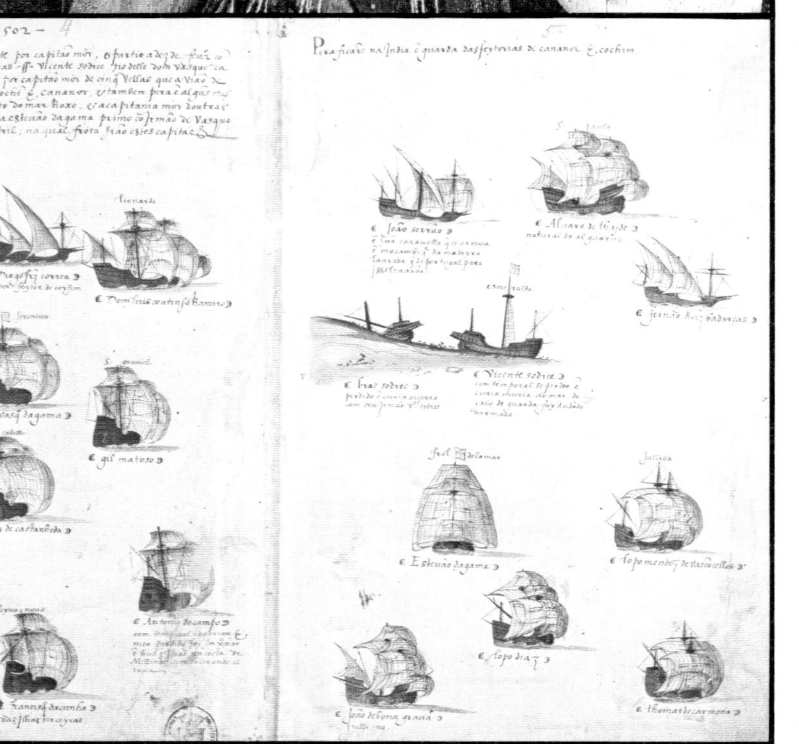

Left: Detail from the 'St Vincent Panels' showing Prince Henry the Navigator (1394-1460), in the Portuguese Museum of Ancient Arts, Lisbon. *M Pucciarelli*

Below left: Portuguese Navy Ministry's 'Book of the Navy' illustration of da Gama's fleet on the second voyage to India in 1502. *M Pucciarelli*

Above: Portrait of Pedro Alvarez Cabral, from Sousa Macedo's 'Retratos e Elogios', in the Academy of Sciences Library Lisbon. *M Pucciarelli*

and had to fight his way out of imprisonment and out of the harbour. He decided to return to Portugal.

He had to discard his smallest vessel at Mozambique as his crews, depleted by illness and accident, were not enough to man the ships even though the storeship had been scuttled, having outlived her usefulness. Otherwise there is little to record of the homeward voyage, which took three months. With the outward passage, it had covered 24,000 nautical miles.

At Lisbon Da Gama was greeted as the triumphant hero, the creator of new greatness and wealth-to-be for Portugal. King Manuel ennobled him and ordered the holding of great fétes in all the principal cities in his honour.

In order to take early advantage of Da Gama's achievement, a fleet of 13 ships was made ready to sail to India. It was commanded by Pedros Alvares Cabral, a navigator born in 1467, with a distinguished record. His fleet sailed from Lisbon in 1499, the year after Da Gama returned.

For some reason he led his ships too far to the south-west. He might perhaps have been anxious to avoid the calms of the Gulf of Guinea or to carry out instructions from King Manuel. The King might have wanted to make sure that the newly born sea route via the Cape did not run foul of the Treaty of Tordesilla, which, in 1494, had laid down the respective spheres of Portugal and Spain under the aegis of the Pope. Whatever the reason, there was no mistaking the fact that one morning the lookouts sighted the crest of a most intrusive mountain where no mountain should be. Cabral by accident had discovered Brazil. Actually he was not the first European discoverer, although he did not know it. In the previous year a Spaniard, Vincent Yanez Pincon, a companion of Columbus, had happened upon the country and he had taken possession in his Sovereign's name. Cabral, in blissful ignorance, also took possession in his King's name.

From Brazil he started off again for India, but on a voyage that was dogged by misfortune. One of his ships came to grief near the Cape Verde Islands, four others were sunk by storms in the South Atlantic and one went hopelessly astray. To add to the list, a crew mutinied and as a result the ship and her rich cargo were lost. With the remaining six ships of his fleet, Cabral managed to arrive at Calicut, where he built a factory, with another at Cochin, to the south. He left a sufficient staff and sailed away. Almost at once the natives rose and massacred every person he had left behind.

When the news reached the King, he at once ordered a fleet to be fitted out to take punitive action and appointed Cabral to take command. Da Gama, however, intervened and begged for the command, so that he could avenge his own personal insults. In consequence, he sailed off with a fleet of 20 ships to Calicut and bombarded the town immediately on arrival. He did not deal gently with the townsfolk.

On his return to Lisbon with his vessels laden with gold and rich treasures, for the second time he was given a hero's welcome by the King and created 'Admiral of the Ships for Ever'. But great as his achievements were, his reputation is marred, even in the violence current at the time, by stories that were quite horrific; tales of Portuguese women being flogged through the streets of Calicut watched by the Indians, of tortures with boiling oil and worse.

As for the unfortunate Cabral, the run of ill luck that had latterly clouded his successes remained with him to the end. In 1520, while on a voyage in the North Atlantic, his ship was overwhelmed in a storm and sank with all hands.

But the fact remains, Da Gama, Cabral, Prince Henry the Navigator and Bartholemmeo Diaz, four men widely different, between them opened up the world for the generations to come.

WHO DISCOVERED AMERICA?

JUST AFTER DAWN on October 12, 1492, a Genoese admiral waded ashore on a Caribbean island, sank to his knees in the soft sand of what he thought was an outlying part of Asia, and claimed it in the name of his sponsors, the King and Queen of Spain. For Christopher Columbus, it was the triumphant culmination of 16 years of hawking round the royal courts of Europe the idea that the riches of the East could be reached by sailing westward. For the great majority of people since, the scene signifies his discovery of America.

It is not surprising that the events of 1492 and after have overshadowed the fact that, long before Columbus, America was probably discovered not once, but many times. None of the other claimants to discovery—they include Arabs, French, Japanese, Romans, Turks—enjoyed Columbus's advantages. His voyage was meticulously documented; other accounts are incomplete, confused or fanciful. Some claimants rely only on a piece of evidence here, a piece there, some on historical detective work. No other discoverers saturated America with colonists as the Spaniards who followed Columbus did. There is therefore no living proof of settlement before 1492 to match that of the Spanish-speaking Americans of today. Most important of all, with the discovery in 1500-1 that America was a continent, the exact nature of the land Columbus reached was known and recorded for later ages to note.

The unbroken connection between America as Columbus discovered it and America as we know it now owed its existence to the fact that in 1492, Europe was emerging from the violence, ignorance and insecurity of the Middle Ages into the clearer, more curious and more venturesome light of the Renaissance. It was

Above: The departure of John Sebastian Cabot from Bristol in 1497. He made a landfall at Cape Breton Island, now part of Nova Scotia, which had been colonised by Norsemen 500 years earlier. *City Art Gallery Bristol*

Left: A sandglass in the National Maritime Museum, London, such as was the seaman's means of measuring time in the days of Columbus. *National Maritime Museum London*

LANDING OF COLUMBUS AT GUANAHANI (BAHAMA ISLANDS) OCT. 12, 1492.

WRECK OF THE CARAVEL SANTA MARIA, COLUMBUS'S SHIP, ON THE COAST OF HISPANIOLA, DEC. 24, 1492

during the Renaissance that much of the knowledge and thought of the ancient Greeks and Romans was rediscovered, including their ideas of the geography of the Earth. Among the ideas lay an imperfect but unmistakable notion that something like the continent of America existed. In 380 BC Greek philosophers believed that there was 'an island of immense extent' beyond the ocean then thought to surround Europe, Asia and Africa; at about the same time the poet Plato was writing of the 'Island Continent of Atlantis'.

Such clues, and much else, became forgotten and precious writings and records became mislaid or lost during the long period of chaos that followed the fall of the Roman Empire in about 476 AD. During that atavistic age, when barbarians ran wild across Europe, creating conditions in which physical survival was the prime aim in life, what learning and culture managed to persist generally did so only when it was in the care of scholarly monks in remote monasteries.

Ireland, on the fringes of the European Continent, was one of the last places to feel the savage surge of the barbarian hordes, and this made it a crucible of culture long after the deep shadow of the so-called Dark Ages had blanketed the rest of Europe. Barbarian pressure could, however, be felt in Ireland in the 6th century AD and, with the possible approach of anarchy, the Irish began to look westwards for a place where they might in better safety preserve their civilisation, with its fine arts and devout religion.

Irish monk-sailors sought sanctuary in the Orkneys and Shetlands, the Hebrides and Iceland and, in about 570 AD, one of them, it seems, crossed the Atlantic and found America. The evidence lies in *Navigatio Sancti Brendani,* which tells in fanciful fashion how St Brendan meandered all over the ocean, touching Greenland, the Canaries, the Bahamas and Chesapeake Bay. Yet, among tall stories of heavenly choirs and apocalyptic visions, there are descriptions which fit the American scene too closely to be entirely ignored.

There was, for example, the calm area into which the saintly seaman sailed where the sea resembled 'a thick curdled mass'—an apt description of the Sargasso Sea, that still seaweed-strewn tract of the Atlantic off the American coast. One port of call for St Brendan was an island with flat terrain, surrounded by water so calm and clear that he could see to the bottom of the seabed. The description might fit the Bahamas, the low-lying Caribbean islands set in the transparent lagoons of the only coral sea in the Atlantic.

According to *Navigatio,* one of St Brendan's crew stayed behind in the Bahamas to convert the natives to Christianity, and in that the Irish discovery claim is backed by circumstantial evidence. In 1519, when the Spaniards conquered Mexico, they discovered that the pagan Aztecs worshipped a white-skinned god called Quetzalcoatl, whose sign was a cross and whose mother was a virgin. Like Christ, Quetzalcoatl preached peace and charity, principles quite opposite to the rest of the Aztec creed, which normally required blood and violence to appease its gods.

Where could the obviously foreign idea of a Christ-like god have come from? If it did not travel west to Mexico from the Bahamas, it could have filtered southwards from Newfoundland where, according to one of the Norse sagas, the 11th-century Viking Thorfinn Karlesfni learned of the presence of the Irish from a group of Skraelings, or Red Indians. 'They said there was a land nearby which was inhabited by people who wore white garments . . . and carried poles before them to which cloths were attached. People believed this must have been Hvitrammannaland, or Ireland the Great.'

If it was true, then America would have been the fourth new land, after the Färoes, Iceland and Greenland, where the Vikings arrived to find the Irish had preceded them.

The Norse Sagas, however, also propose the Vikings as discoverers of America, if only discoverers by accident. In 986 AD, according to one Saga, Bjarne Hergulfsson set sail from Iceland for the new Viking colony in Greenland. After a few days, Bjarne and his crew were lost in unfamiliar waters, surrounded by fog and driven before strong winds. When the fog finally cleared, they had completely lost their bearings.

The Vikings had probably drifted southward well past the southern tip of Greenland, for when Bjarne eventually hoisted

Facing page: A page from an October 1892 issue of 'The Illustrated London News' reproducing illustrations of Columbus's 1492 voyage.
Illustrated London News

Above left: Christopher Columbus, from an early portrait. *Illustrated London News*

Bottom: Portrayal of the death of Columbus by F Ortego. *Mansell Collection*

Below: An early colour print of St Brendan and his monks at sea, from a manuscript in the Bodleian Library. *The Queen's College Oxford*

sail and pointed his prow westward, he reached a country not unlike Newfoundland. Where he should have seen mountains and glaciers, Bjarne saw instead the thick forests of the warmer south. Mystified, he sailed northward up the coast, only to find more forests fringing the coastline. Still farther north, somewhere along the coast of Baffin Island, Bjarne turned eastward and sailed on until at last he sighted the great black mountains and glittering masses of ice he knew to be Greenland.

Nearly 15 years passed before a second Viking voyage to America took place. In AD 1000 Leif Ericsson set sail with 35 men reached Baffin Island and from there followed Bjarne's course in reverse, to land finally on the coast of Newfoundland. The Vikings were fascinated by the rich grassland, the plump salmon and trout of lake and river, the thousands of caribou and great forests with their birch trees reaching heights nearing 100 feet. Greenland had nothing like it, nor did it have the abundance of wild grapes that led Leif to call the unknown country Vinland. The Vikings, who presumed it to be a westward extension of the continent of Europe, spent the winter in Vinland and returned to Greenland the following spring, their ship laden with timber and vines.

The obvious riches of Vinland led, naturally, to an attempt at colonisation. In the spring of 1003 AD a party of Vikings under Thorfinn Karlsefni left Greenland, crossed the narrow Davis Strait and sailed southward, to land on the northern tip of Newfoundland. Conditions in that second Vinland seemed ideal at first, but within two years the savage Newfoundland winters and the hostility of the Skraelings put an end to the colony. In 1005 the Vikings returned to Greenland, taking with them a valuable cargo of vines, furs and timber.

It appears, however, that the Vinlanders left evidence behind them, for in the 1960s, excavations at Cape Bauld, the extreme northern point of Newfoundland, revealed the foundations of seven Viking-type turf buildings, as well as metalworking tools, anvils, spindles and whorls. Tests have shown them to date from the 10th century. In addition, certain cartographical evidence exists of a pre-Columbian, probably Viking, discovery of America. In 1300, 1424, 1434 and 1436, European maps and globes showed a land far west of the Atlantic called, variously, Antilia or Isola Nova Scoperta. The Vikings were not themselves cartographers. It was an art which flourished much farther south, particularly in Germany and Italy.

However, it is not difficult to see some of the ways in which the mapmakers' information could have spread southward from Viking Scandinavia. Soon after they returned from Vinland, Gudrid, wife of Thorfinn Karlsefni, went to Rome. She was, of course, well qualified to speak at first hand of the Vikings' American discoveries and doubtless did so. The Vikings had by that time been converted to Christianity and for them, as for all Christians in western Europe, Rome was the cosmopolitan hub of the continent, the city from which information was disseminated to all parts of the Christian world.

News of land to the west might also have travelled south with the reports of Tyrker, a German member of Leif Ericsson's party, who apparently returned home soon after the first Vinland expedition. Europeans in the continent's northern ports also knew of the regular trading voyages the Vikings made to America until the 14th century and of the rich cargoes they brought back, cargoes which included turkey, a bird then peculiar to North America. So, in various ways, a large body of knowledge seems to have been created by the 15th century which, despite gross inaccuracies and serious misconceptions, contained the important fact that land lay across the Atlantic.

The Europeans who probably knew more about it than anyone else were the Portuguese, the finest and most experienced sailors of the time. In the course of wide-ranging expeditions west and south into the Atlantic, the Portuguese explored and colonised the west coast of Africa and, in 1427, discovered the Azores. Then, in 1452, they encountered the edge of the Sargasso Sea which, to their trained observant eyes strongly indicated land to the west. On that voyage the Portuguese ranged as far east as the vicinity of Cape Clear, in south-west Ireland, and there they found another clue; though winds blew strongly in the area, the sea was found on that occasion to be calm, a feature which they considered to mean that it must be sheltered by a vast land mass to the west.

Intriguing as it was, Atlantic exploration westward was not a priority with the Portuguese at that time. Until about 1460, when it proved larger than they had expected, their main efforts were directed at reaching the East by sailing round Africa. Then, between 1460 and 1480, the Portuguese turned their attention westward once more, and in those two decades several navigators were sent to find 'Antilia and other islands in the Atlantic'. In the course of the new search one of them found something so important that, in 1480, the Portuguese imposed the death penalty for anyone who betrayed the secrets of their Atlantic expeditions.

The secret which the Portuguese were so ruthlessly intent upon keeping might well have been the existence of America, which their explorations by 1480 had indicated was of great size. That it appeared so great as completely to block

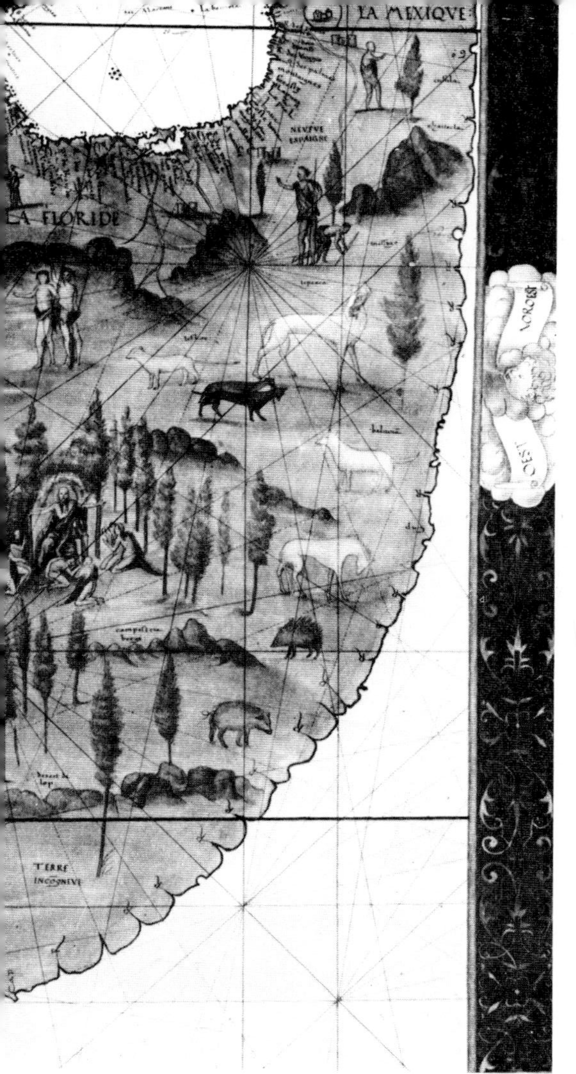

Top: Detail from a world map made for King Henry II of France (1547-1559), showing North America. *Mansell Collection*

Above left: A representation of Amerigo Vespucci using an astrolabe, used to illustrate a book of the writings of the 13th-century Florentine poet Dante. *Mansell Collection*

Left: Prince Henry the Navigator, a detail from the bigger painting 'St Vincent' by Goncalves. *Mansell Collection*

Above: From a portrait of Vespucci in the National Gallery, Naples. *Mansell Collection*

the westward route to the East is perhaps corroborated by Portuguese resumption of the round-Africa voyages in 1481, which consequently would seem the only way for them to reach Asia. Knowledge of America could explain, too, the cryptic refusal in 1484 of King John II of Portugal to sponsor Christopher Columbus. He had, he said, 'information regarding the western lands more positive than the visions of the Genoese'.

King John was, however, a realist. When the frustrated Columbus left Portugal in 1485 to try his luck in Spain, John knew he must act quickly to stop his Spanish rivals exploiting America. Accordingly, in 1486, John granted a charter to Fernão Dulmo, ordering him to colonise 'the islands and mainland in the West'. Dulmo, who had to bear the greater part of the cost himself, ran into financial difficulties and possibly his venture never materialised.

This is the last that is known of Portuguese intentions regarding America before 1492 and it leaves the unanswered question which Portuguese navigator landed in what part of America and when. Favourites among some historians, not all of whom are Portuguese, are João Vaz Corte-Real and his sons Miguel and Caspar who, some time before 1472, are believed to have discovered Labrador, Newfoundland and the Hudson and St Lawrence rivers. Who were the Corte-Reals? Although his sons made minor names for themselves in the history of American exploration, the father, João, was the humblest of people—a porter in a Duke's household. Yet, in 1474, this lowly servant was given the governorship of the richest province in the Azores. Surely only a truly remarkable feat could have raised such a man to such a position.

'About the time the governship of Terceyra became vacant,' Cordeiro's *History of the Azores* records, 'there landed two gentlemen who had recently returned from Stockfishland (Newfoundland), which they had gone to discover by order of the Portuguese king. One of these gentlemen was João Vaz Corte-Real . . . and he petitioned that he might have the governship in reward for his services'.

There is independent evidence that João might have been accompanied by three Danes, namely Johannes Sclovus, a pilot, Hans Porthorst and Diderik Pining. Co-operation between the Danes and Portuguese, whose royal houses were connected by marriage, might explain why the 1472 expedition made for Newfoundland and the area explored by the Danes' ancestors, the Vikings. In Newfoundland, of course, the Portuguese found the lucrative fisheries which they later exploited to the tune of £1 million a year.

Keeping the fisheries secret from their Spanish rivals was feasible, but America as an entity was far too huge to remain perpetually unknown, as the Portuguese might have hoped. After Columbus claimed it on behalf of Spain, the Spaniards built there a gold- and silver-rich empire that became the envy of 16th-century Europe. Envy was particularly strong in England, whose Welsh Tudor queen, Elizabeth I, longed to break the Spanish monopoly in America. Among the means she employed to do so was promotion of the story that in 1170 America was discovered by a Welsh prince called Madoc, who was, by inference, one of Elizabeth's ancestors.

The basic information came from innumerable old Welsh poems and ballads which made of Madoc a legendary hero who left his homeland for a life on the ocean because of quarrels among his royal relatives. Madoc, according to the Welsh bards, sailed southwestward from the north Welsh coast, turned west south of the Azores, touched the edge of the Sargasso Sea and the Bahamas, skirted the southernmost tip of Florida and landed at the spot where Mobile, Alabama, now stands. There is also a 13th-century narrative of Madoc's voyage which includes a description of what might well have been the Sargasso Sea. The author, Willem the Minstrel, called it 'a treacherous garden . . . which no storm could ever dissipate and which swallowed up ships'.

Evidence of Madoc's possible landfall in Alabama came to light 200 years after Elizabeth had tried to use it as a political pawn against Spain. In 1782 Governor Sievers of Tennessee discovered some very ancient fortifications in Cherokee country. The aged Cherokee chief, Oconostota, told Sievers how he had heard his father and grandfather say they were built by people called Welsh, and that they had 'crossed the Great Water and landed near . . . Mobile'. Sievers also encountered a Frenchman who had lived with the Cherokee and had traded with a 'Welsh tribe'. The Frenchman found they spoke 'much of the Welsh dialect . . . many of them were very fair and white and frequently told him they had sprung from a nation of white people . . .'.

These so-called Welsh Indians, the Mandans, aroused a great deal of interest and in 1792 a young Welshman, John Evans, set out for America to investigate. At that point the Spanish governor of New Orleans, seriously concerned, wrote 'It is in the interests of his Catholic Majesty that reports of British Indians in Mandan country be denied once and for all'. Such reports were not news to the Spaniards. In 1493, Columbus returned to Europe to report that 'the nations of Virginia and Guatemala celebrate the memory of an ancient hero whom they call Matec', a name not all that different from that of the Welsh prince.

Also, in 1598, a history of Spain had been written which recorded that the inhabitants of Mexico believed 'a son of the Prince of Wales, called Madoc, in the year 1170 sailed into the West Indies and inhabited the country of Mexico'. A 1599 translation of the history was, perhaps, part of the evidence which prompted John Evans's trip to America. His activities were regarded by the Spaniards with deep suspicion, but he spent six months among the Mandans before they arrested him and charged him with being a British spy.

When Evans was eventually released, it was soon clear that he had been offered an irresistible bribe to stop his researches. He headed a party of Spaniards to a Mandan village, made speeches praising the Spanish king, tore down a Union Jack left there by British traders and ran up the Spanish flag in its place. Evans then received his reward—a large cash payment and a job as a land surveyor.

All this, one might argue, is hardly positive evidence on which to base a claim to the discovery of America, and with the possible exception of that of the Vikings, much the same could apply to the other claims. In any historical controversy spurious theories, ambiguous evidence and what has been called 'the silence of history' obscure the argument. The only certain thing is that historical habit dies hard. Widespread belief in Columbus's claim to have discovered America in 1492 will undoubtedly be transmitted to future generations, where, just as surely, dissidents will disagree and try as hard as they do now to substitute their own rival candidates.

NEW

WAYS TO THE EAST

THE MYSTIC LANDS of Cathay and Cipango, old China and Japan, called to the bravest navigators for centuries. Their search for the north-west passage, that fabled short-cut to the wonders of the East, cost many lives and ships.

There was John Cabot, an Italian and 'a very good mariner' who came to live in Bristol in his early forties with his wife and sons in 1495. He approached Henry VII with a proposal to fetch spices (pepper, cloves and nutmegs) cheaply from the Indies by way of the passage. The King, much interested, granted him letters patent to sail with five ships to discover 'regions or provinces of the heathen and infidels'.

All Cabot could obtain was one small vessel, the *Matthew*, with a crew numbering 18 hands, including a Genoese barber. Cabot sailed from Bristol in May 1497 and using rather a primitive method of navigation, made a good landfall in late June near Cape Degat on the northern tip of Newfoundland, his 'New Found Land'. There, he was only a bare five miles away from the site of a colony founded by Leif Ericsson 500 years before.

Cabot landed and took possession of the country in the King's name. Seeing few signs of natives, he sailed on through the Strait of Belle Isle, which separates Labrador from Newfoundland, into the Gulf of St Lawrence. He found a depth of more than 100 fathoms in the Gulf and, deciding it was the north-west passage, he thought it best to return home to mount a full-scale expedition.

The homeward voyage caused no trouble and he was soon on his way to London to report to the King. Henry rewarded him with a present of £20 and an annuity of £20 but, not to be outdone, Cabot's elder son Sebastian somehow talked himself into a royal gift of £6; his name has confused the story of John Cabot ever since.

In the spring of 1498 John was authorised to sail to Japan. He was to set up a trading station there which would give English merchants wonderful opportunities. The King lent him a ship, complete with crew and supplies, while Bristol merchants produced four others laden with trade goods. They sailed in May though one vessel got into difficulties and had to return. The other four carried on with their voyage and were never seen again, having vanished without trace.

The next attempt to find the passage was made by a 'gentleman explorer', Giovanni Verrazano, of Florence, who was living in Dieppe. He borrowed from the French Navy, a ship named *La Dauphine* and crossed the Atlantic to North America in 1524. He concentrated at first on the coastline from Florida to Maine, which entailed some very skilful seamanship. Then, sailing north-eastward, he missed much of Nova Scotia but landed for water on the Newfoundland coast. Food, however, was short and he returned directly to France, dropping anchor on July 8, 1524, at Dieppe just two weeks later.

His second American voyage was to Brazil, but in 1528 he sailed in the ship *La Flamenque* with his brother Girolamo, the map-maker, to the Caribbean, anchoring off Guadeloupe. There, leaving the ship's boat with his brother on board clear of the breakers, he waded ashore to speak to some natives on the beach. Too late he saw that they were not friendly Indians but Caribs and to the horror of Girolamo, who could give no help, the great navigator fell to cannibals.

Another expedition that started from France was led by Jacques Cartier, who was born in 1491 at St Malo. He had spent most of his youth at sea and at the age of 38 he was presented by the Abbot of Mont-St Michel to the King as the master mariner to find lands in the New World for France. As a result he was granted from the Royal treasury 6000 livres for equipping two ships, each with a crew of 61, and after some difficulty in manning, he sailed on April 20, 1534.

He sighted land by moonlight at Cape Bonavista, Newfoundland, on May 10, meeting much trouble with drifting ice until a breeze blew it clear. As he explored up the coast it grew plain that no-one would starve, what with the great auks, the gannets and wildfowl and once, a swimming bear 'as big as a cow and white as a swan'.

Sailing through the Belle Isle Strait, Cartier explored the southern shore of Labrador and the mouth of the St Lawrence River, completing a circuit of its gulf. The ships met Indians 'untamed and savage' and others who came to meet them in two fleets of 40-50 canoes full of dancing natives yelling and holding up furs to trade for trinkets. The season was then far advanced, so Cartier decided to return home before the weather broke; in spite of foul weather he arrived home safely just under four months later.

For a second voyage, in the following year the French navy loaned him three ships and the King contributed 3000 livres towards the cost. His flagship was *La Grande Hermine* (the *Big Weasel*) of 12 guns, with *La Petite Hermine* of four guns and *L'Emerillon* (the *Sparrowhawk*) two guns. Among the total 112 combined crews were 12 of Cartier's relations. There were also seven carpenters, one barber-surgeon, an apothecary and a trumpeter.

They started on May 19, 1535, but made little headway for a month owing to bad weather but arrived eventually and passed through the Belle Isle Strait to investigate the St Lawrence by boat. After much effort, Cartier penetrated as far as the site of present-day Montreal. In order to spend the winter in Canada his men built a fort below the Rock of Quebec. There they endured snow four feet deep and ice two fathoms thick on the river, with the ships frozen in until mid-April. In February, an epidemic of scurvy struck Frenchmen and natives alike and many died before the Indians produced a very effective remedy.

Cartier had not found the passage but at least he had discovered the great river highway of Canada. And then he developed ambitions in another direction. A friendly Huron chief named Donnaconna possessed of a vivid imagination had invented, to please him, a Kingdom of Saguenay full of gold and rubies and wonders greater than those of Cathay. Cartier kidnapped him so that he could tell it all to the French King and he also took 10 other Indians, adults and children, none of whom ever saw Canada again.

When he sailed for St Malo, in June, he had to leave the hull of *La Petite Hermine* to the natives, since he no longer had enough men to crew her. The King, however, received him warmly and was impressed by the samples from Saguenay of iron pyrites and fragments of sparkling rock which did duty for gold and diamonds. He gave Cartier 3500 livres for his expenses and 100 more for the Hurons, with a pension for Donnaconna.

It was five years before Cartier sailed on his third voyage, supposedly under the orders of the Sieur de Roberval, a Protestant nobleman who arranged to follow him. With five ships he arrived at his old anchorage after a month in Newfoundland. He found the natives had become hostile through contacts with Europeans and, sending two ships back to France, he camped farther away in Camp Rouge, nearer the Ottawa River. He made sorties to find the route to Sanguenay but general misery and lack of manpower for defence against the natives forced him to strike camp in June 1542. Finding Roberval at St John's, Newfound-

Top far left: Jacques Cartier, the French master mariner who explored Canada in the 16th century. *Mary Evans Picture Library*

Top right: An engraving of Cartier's ship exploring the icy mouth of the River St Charles in 1535. *Mary Evans Picture Library*

Left: The Italian explorer Giovanni Verrazano's ship 'La Dauphine' in Newport harbour in 1524. *Mary Evans Picture Library*

Inset: An engraving of John Cabot's son, Sebastian, explaining voyages of discovery to Henry VII. *Mary Evans Picture Library*

Above: A portrait of perhaps the best known seeker of the north west passage, Henry Hudson. *Mary Evans Picture Library*

land, he defied orders to return to his camp and sailed home, to receive a rapturous welcome.

Among the aristocratic colonists in Roberval's ship was his own niece, Marguerite, and when he, a strict Calvinist found that she had a lover, he was horrified. He took her with her nurse, some food, guns and ammunition and marooned them on an island in the Gulf of St Lawrence in the summer of 1542. As the ships sailed off, Marguerite's gallant jumped overboard and swam ashore with more guns and ammunition. He built a cabin but he died before the end of the winter and she kept his body with her until the ice melted and she could bury him. She bore a child; it died and then, a year later, the nurse died.

Marguerite lived on through the bitter winters and even managed to shoot three bears. After more than two years French fishermen saw smoke. They landed and found her emaciated and in rags, but alive. They took her back to France, where she became a school-teacher. Her story reached Queen Marguerite of Navarre, who used it in her Heptameron and held her up as a splendid example to all women.

The story of Henry Hudson is probably the most poignant of all. He is first heard of as the skipper of the bark *Hopeful* trying to discover the North Pole and the North-West Passage for the Muscovy Company. With a crew of 10 and a boy he sailed from Gravesend in April 1607 in an attempt to locate the passage round the North of Greenland but finding it impossible, he returned to the Thames. In the following year he tried again with the same result, so the Muscovy Company lost interest.

In 1608, still hopeful, he successfully tried the Dutch East India Company and sailed from Amsterdam in the vessel *Half-Moon* to cross the Atlantic and reach Nova Scotia. After exploring the river that bears his name, he returned to England in September. In April 1610 he again started out, that time in the 55-ton bark *Discovery*, privately fitted out, to search for the passage. By the end of June he had felt his way into the strait named after him and in the next three months he explored the great bay beyond; 'a labrinth without end' he described it.

His crew hauled *Discovery* ashore in James Bay, to find themselves frozen in. As food became short quarrels broke out and when the ice thawed 'a dissolute moneyed fellow named Green' led a mutiny. Hudson was trussed up and, with his son John and eight others, was thrust into the ship's boat and set adrift. Some mutineers then landed to kill deer and were themselves killed by Eskimos but an ex-mate, Robert Bylot, sailed *Discovery* back to England with only three surviving out of eight. They were tried for mutiny but found not guilty.

Bylot afterwards made two voyages to the Far North in *Discovery*. Ironically, on the second attempt he found and named Lancaster Sound, off Baffin Bay. Though he was never to know it, he had discovered the gateway to the North-West Passage.

Top: Henry Hudson's famous exploration ship, the 'Half Moon'. *Mary Evans Picture Library*

Above: Sebastian Cabot, a navigator and explorer in the style of his father John Cabot. *Mary Evans Picture Library*

Right: A painting by Peter Wood of a model of Hudson's ship 'Half Moon' of 1609. *P M Wood*

MAGELLAN STRAIT

THE SOUTHERNMOST reaches of America are bleak regions of desolation and death where the elements are engaged in a desperate struggle. The tortured land, thrown up by the internal fire and by the crumpling of the earth's crust, is carved by the gales and blizzards of the Howling Fifties, by ice and glaciers and by the relentless swell and tides of the Southern Ocean which invade it through countless fjords and channels.

Barren islands to windward of the Magellan Strait, sombre and lifeless forests in the middle reaches, and rocks, bogs and tussock grass to the east discourage land travel while currents, eddies, fog, sleet and williwaws are nightmares to the mariner. Even the albatross, the penguins, the skuas and the sea lions find it a difficult place, yet a few Indian tribes had been living there for ages unknown, eking out a wretched and primitive existence. Those desolate lands and windswept waters were to prove just as mean and inhospitable to European seamen.

In 1914 the Treaty of Tordesillas shared the world between Portugal and Spain. Everything to the west of 46deg 37min W was Spanish; all lands to the east were Portuguese. For Spain, it was a matter of reaching the Spice Islands by the western route, and Columbus had not solved that problem. Ferdinand Magellan, a Portuguese navigator snubbed by his king, was to be Spain's instrument of discovery. He knew some Portuguese secrets which hinted at a passage south of America into the South Sea—the maps of Behaim and of Schoner, and the reconnaissance journey of João de Lisboa in 1514. There was also the voyage in 1515 of the Spaniard Juan Diaz de Solis, who spoke of a strait.

Magellan set sail from San Lucar on September 20, 1519, as captain-general of about 250 men and five ships led by the flagship *Trinidad*. Despite a stormy and mutinous passage, Magellan discovered the Strait of Patagonia (it was named Magellan Strait in 1534) and sailed on to meet his death in the Philippines in 1521.

In 1525, Garcia de Loaysa and del Cano went on another expedition to the Moluccas by way of the strait. Whereas Magellan was favoured by the weather when he navigated his strait, the real character of the place was only revealed on the later voyage. They traversed it, but met a bad end at destination and a relief expedition was sent out in 1527 under Alvaro de Saavedra; he inaugurated the safer Spanish route to the East—following the trade winds to Mexico, thence overland to the Pacific and following the trades to the Orient. The overland route was seen to be the obvious way after several other expeditions got mauled in or near the strait.

In 1540, Don Alonso de Camargo reached Peru from Spain by the strait, also at a high cost in ships and men; overland by the Panama Isthmus was the better way to and from Peru. So it happened that the Magellan Strait was almost forgotten by the Spaniards when Valparaiso was sacked by pirates who came out of the blue in 1578.

On September 15, 1577, Francis Drake made sail for a pretended voyage to Alexandria, but his real aim was to sail through the strait and to plunder the fat

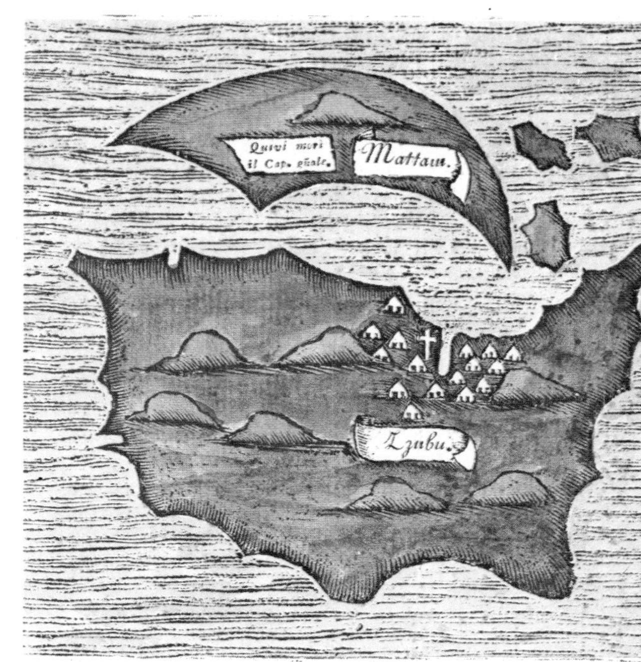

Top left: Engraving by Jules Noel showing the ships 'Astrolabe' and 'Zélée' among the ice in the Antarctic seas.
Mary Evans Picture Library

Top: An engraving specially done for 'Moore's Voyages and Travels' depicting Commodore Byron in company with Patagonian natives.
John R Freeman & Co

Above: A map from the diary of Antonio Pigafetta (Magellan's Italian secretary) of Mactan island, near the Philippines, where Ferdinand Magellan was killed by natives.
M Pucciarelli

Spanish possessions on the Pacific. There were many parallels with Magellan's journey but a major deviation led to his discovery of what later came to be named Cape Horn.

Taken by surprise, the incensed Spaniards, unaware of Drake Strait (the Cape Horn route), decided that the Magellan Strait needed fortifying to prevent further raids. Pedro Sarmiento de Gambóa was sent with two ships from Peru to assess the military and colonial possibilities of the strait. It took him three months to reach the western entrance and on the way his consort deserted back to Callao. The strait was crossed in a mere three weeks and three native 'interpreters' were kidnapped on the way, sowing the seeds of the future hostility of the Indians.

Sarmiento sailed on to Spain, where he fitted out an expedition of 23 ships but the command was given to an incapable court favourite, Diego Flores. On September 15, 1581, 3000 souls embarked—mariners, friars, soldiers, colonists with wives and children, blacksmiths, masons, stone-cutters and even trumpeters. Five ships were lost before even leaving the coast of Spain and many more Spaniards died of a plague during the crossing of the Atlantic and the lengthy stop in Brazil. On the way to Argentina three worm-eaten ships foundered and intelligence was gathered about the passing of new English privateers; the race for the strait appeared to be lost and there were arguments about the suitability of pushing on.

They did push on and after hideous hardships the remnants of the expedition eventually reached the target in the narrows of the strait and the fort of Don Felipe was built and seeds were planted. A settlement was also started at Nombre de Jesus. Thomas Cavendish, who left Plymouth in July 1586 for Magellan Strait, passed Nombre de Jesus and found it a ghost town. He also called at Don Felipe to salvage the guns; because of the starved bodies littering the place he called it Port Famine—a name which has stuck.

By the end of the 16th century, Holland, having shaken off the Spanish yoke, was becoming an international power with interests in the East. She sent two expeditions by way of the Magellan Strait in 1598, under Simon de Cordes and Oliver van Noort. They met the usual lot of gales, starvation and mutinies and only one ship limped back to tell the tale without even making a profit.

France was still out of the picture, but a private Frenchman, Malherbe, sailed

Facing page left: Figurehead of Commodore Anson, the British circumnavigator. *R Westwood*

Facing page top: Inhospitable natives of Otaheite (Tahiti) attacking Captain Wallis, who discovered their island. *Mary Evans Picture Library*

Below left: A portrayal by O W Brierly in 'The Illustrated London News' of May 24, 1873, of the discovery of the Strait of Magellan in 1520. *Illustrated London News*

Left: Bleak scenery observed by mariners in Antarctic waters since Magellan's discovery, and sketched for 'The Illustrated London News' in 1875 by an officer of the 'Valorous'. *Illustrated London News*

through the strait in the early 17th century on a round-the-world voyage—mostly overland—which took him 25 years.

In 1614-1617 a Dutch East India Company expedition under Joris Spilbergen sailed round the world, through the strait, at last achieving a success. The Dutch East India Company monopolised the eastern trade, forbidding any other Dutchman to use either the way of Good Hope or of Magellan (Drake Strait still remaining an unused English secret). But there were interlopers intent on beating the monopoly; in 1616 Cornelius Schouten and le Maire discovered the loophole—Cape Horn. That route was not a great improvement on the strait; the weather was just as bad, the sea worse, and one could not water or stock up with salt penguins as in the strait; but there was more sea room.

In 1669-1671, Narborough and Wood surveyed the strait in greater detail than their predecessors. In 1714, Legentil Labartinais, a French merchant and privateer, navigated the strait from east to west. In 1740, England and Spain were at war again and Commodore Anson was sent to the Pacific. He chose the Cape Horn way and his expedition was successful, as told in detail on pages 95–9 of this book. In 1764 Commodore Byron was sent out to discover new lands thought to lie to the south (the myth of the Southern Continent lasted until Cook). After claiming the Falklands for England he sailed through the strait. The quest for 'Terra Australis' went on; Wallis and Carteret left Plymouth in 1766 and spent four miserable months in the strait with winds, rain and scurvy. The ships became separated on the Pacific side and made independent returns, Wallis discovering Tahiti on the way. The Frenchman Bougainville, on the same quest, entered the strait on December 2, 1767, with two ships and experienced the usual rains, fogs and currents. He had friendly contacts with the Indians but they ended in grief.

After Bougainville, Cape Horn was preferred by the explorers, Cook and Lapérouse. The Spaniards' last exploratory effort was then made by Cordoba, who updated the chart of the strait but still left all the side channels in blank—gaps that were filled by the British survey ships *Adventure* and *Beagle* in 1828. The captain of HMS *Beagle*, Prengles Stokes, became a victim of the curse of the strait; the storm-swept solitudes he was surveying combined with the loneliness inherent in his rank drove him out of his mind and he committed suicide. His grave can still be seen near Port Famine.

He was suceeded by Robert FitzRoy, who completed the expedition and who led the next surveying journey. The *Beagle* returned in 1832 to chart the Fuegian Archipelago, so that the naturalist Darwin, who was aboard, skirted the strait proper, but many of his observations on the Fuegian natural history and Indians also apply to the strait. It is an irony of fate that Darwin, the greatest proponent of the theory of evolution, was specifically taken on the *Beagle* by FitzRoy (who was a strict believer in the scriptures) to help dispel the 'unholy' ideas which were already emerging; at the time Darwin was considering entering the Church. That disappointment of FitzRoy was instrumental in his own death; he cut his throat in 1865. The *Beagle* seems to have had a jinx for her commanders.

The last great expedition to sail through the strait was that of Dumont d' Urville, in 1837, on his way to outline the coast of Antarctica. But that was the age of the Cape Horn trade; the faster ships did not need to stop midway on their journeys to water and they preferred sea room, so the strait saw little merchant shipping. The strait town of Punta Arenas was founded in 1849, after a short abortive settlement at Puerto Bulnes. It was used as a coaling station for the few steamers which ventured around South America, but the economics of wind and coal still favoured the Cape Horn windjammers. They, however, suffered severe casualties and in 1906 it was suggested that steam tugs be based at Punta Arenas to tow the sailing ships

Il Capitano Wallis afsalito dagli Otaitiani

Above far left: Engraving showing Magellan making use of navigational instruments during his voyages of exploration.
Mary Evans Picture Library

Above: Coloured engraving from 'The Voyages of Captain Cook' showing Captain Wallis's poor reception at Tahiti.
M Pucciarelli

Far left: Charles Darwin, the naturalist, whose studies included researches into the indigenous life of the Fuegian Archipelago.
Mary Evans Picture Library

Left: The giant Patagonian Indian chief of 1570, Quoniambec, from an engraving in the Wellcome Institute.
Courtesy of the Wellcome Trustees

through the strait. But a single day's tow would have cost as much as two weeks under sail off the Horn.

In those days the Royal Navy was often seen in the strait; in 1881 HMS *Doterel* blew up in Punta Arenas harbour with the loss of 143 crew (there were only 12 survivors). In the early 1880s the harbour was used as a base for the French hydrographical naval survey of the *Romanche,* under Capitaine Martial. The first proper navigational markers were erected in the strait in the early 1860s and the first lighthouses were built at the end of the century. A famous lighthouse is the one perched on the Evangelistas Island in the middle of the Pacific entrance. It was built in 1896 by the British engineer Slaight and is manned by five men. It is exposed to every westerly gale and the relief is done by a tender which sometimes has to wait for up to 40 days for amenable conditions, during which time the tender shelters by a landward island in a cove named Forty Day Harbour. Even then, getting on the lighthouse is a perilous matter, as it must be done by jumping from a boat to a rope ladder and the swell is always huge.

Punta Arenas became a whaling port in 1894 when Chileans of Norwegian origin started the Magellan Whaling Society. In those days whales were to be found in the strait, but soon the whalers had to range farther afield. Whaling activities were pursued up to well after the second world war.

In 1896 the strait was navigated by a gallant small sloop—the *Spray,* from Boston. Her skipper, Captain Joshua Slocum, a real seaman with salt water and Stockholm tar in his veins, was accomplishing the first solo circumnavigation. He got a true Magellanic greeting just as he had rounded Cape Virgins, on February 11, and finally reached Punta Arenas.

The next historical event was during the 1914-18 war. Admiral von Spee's Far East Squadron had smashed a British squadron under Rear-Admiral Cradock at Coronel, off the Chilean coast. Admiral Sturdee was quickly dispatched with a new fleet consisting of the battleship *Canopus,* the battlecruisers *Invincible* and *Inflexible,* the cruisers *Carnarvon, Cornwall, Kent* and *Macedonia,* the light cruisers *Bristol* and *Glasgow* and the armed merchantman *Orama,* with the mission to patrol both ends of the Magellan and Drake Straits. While the squadron was preparing for the blockade by refuelling at Port Stanley on East Falkland island, von Spee's ships inadvertently bumped into the English force and the chase was on (December 8, 1914). The Falkland battle resulted in the sinking of all the German ships except the cruiser *Dresden,* which succeeded in getting away and making Punta Arenas.

Under the laws of neutrality, she left within 24 hours and thereafter for many months played a game of hide-and-seek with the *Glasgow, Carnarvon* and *Kent.* She hid in various inlets and bays (such as Sepulveda's Bay and the Dresden's Inlet near Cape Horn) and was victualled during that time from Punta Arenas by a German national, Captain Pagels, who owned a tug used in peace time for ferrying passengers to and from their ships anchored off Punta Arenas. The British consul offered a large sum of money to Pagels if he was willing to disclose the whereabouts of the *Dresden,* but he refused to do so. Eventually the *Dresden* was caught by the *Kent* and *Glasgow* at Cumberland Bay in Juan Fernandez Island (of Robinson Crusoe—Alexander Selkirk fame). After a brief exchange of fire the German master scuttled his ship by blowing her up, and the wreck may still be seen.

Meanwhile another drama was being enacted far to the south. The expedition led by Ernest Shackleton had sailed to the Antarctic on the *Endurance* in 1914; the ship got caught in the ice in the Weddel Sea and was eventually crushed on October 27, 1915. The 28 men of the party took to camping on the ice after unsuccessful attempts to sledge the boats, but they were drifting with the pack. They finally managed to jury-sail and pull the boats to Elephant Island, where the best boat—a 22-foot whaler—was jury-rigged and Shackleton and five other men sailed her across 800 miles of the most miserable sea in the world to South Georgia, a distance they covered in 25 days—a most extraordinary feat of seamanship and endurance.

After crossing the island overland (which has only been done once since by well-equipped mountaineers), Shackleton reached the whaling station of Stromness on May 20, 1916. He unsuccessfully tried to reach Elephant Island with a Stromness trawler, and again on a Uruguayan fisheries vessel, from the Falklands. He finally went to Punta Arenas, where the British colony and some Chileans chartered the schooner *Emma,* which was also beaten back by the ice and weather. Then the Chilean Navy provided the Punta Arenas ocean-going tug *Yelcho,* which left on August 25, reached Elephant Island on the 30th, picked up the shipwrecked colony and landed them at Punta Arenas on September 3. The most remarkable fact is that all the *Endurance's* crew survived.

The Chilean Navy at Punta Arenas has many times since been involved in Antarctic rescues (as well as expeditions and surveys), the latest being two evacuations of scientific parties on Deception Island when it erupted in the late 1960s, and the picking up of the tourist passengers of the *Linblad Explorer,* which recently ran aground on an Antarctic island.

The opening of the Panama Canal in 1914 rang the death knell of the square-riggers and depressed the bunkering activities of Punta Arenas. However, the town has grown to 70,000 inhabitants, who live mainly from the export of wool and mutton, primarily to Britain. It is the administrative capital city of Chile's province of Magallanes and it is also a naval base. The town has a shipyard and is the centre for mining operations (lignite and gold) and for oil exploration in Tierra del Fuego. Oilfields are in production near Manantiales and a new oil port has been built at Caleta Clarence on Gente Grande Bay, Tierra del Fuego, providing about a third of Chile's requirements.

The increase in the size of merchant ships, particularly of tankers, means a renewed traffic through the strait or round the Horn of those vessels too big for the Panama Canal. During the southern summer cruise ships on round-the-world tours call at Punta Arenas and visit the fjords.

The strait is now well charted, and has an excellent buoyage and beaconage; there are about 100 lighthouses in the waterway and adjacent canals. Even so, the weather is the same as of old; Puntarenians still have to fight frequent 'panteoneros' blowing at 100 knots or more (the Panteon is the town's cemetery), and the fogs, blizzards and williwaws can be just as dangerous in those narrow waters nowadays as they were in the days of sail. The tidal range at Dungeness Point Lighthouse (near Cape Virgins) reaches 11 metres and the first and second narrows can have spring-tide currents of nine knots; there are many races and also maelstroms where the Pacific and Atlantic tides meet. There is no need to ask why the Magellan Strait is such a graveyard of ships, both old windjammers and modern steamers.

However, safety has been greatly improved by the navigational aids and the introduction of compulsory pilotage organised by Chile (even though the strait is considered an international waterway). For west-bound ships the pilots are picked up off Dungeness Point and are carried all the way to Talcahuano or Valparaiso—the north-bound shipping now follows the more protected inland route of interlocking fjords and channels which link the strait to 'Middle' Chile. The weather is so unpredictable near the Evangelistas that pilots are flown to Australia or New Zealand to board east-bound ships. Since it takes more than a day to cross the strait, two pilots are carried so that there is always one on the bridge; even today mariners tackle the strait with a healthy respect.

Waghenaer and CHARTING

THE EARLIEST nautical maps, or charts, are things of mystery to the modern man. It is very difficult to make head or tail of them, especially the Arabic ones, and when the old cartographers have let their imaginations take charge, the task of reading them seems almost impossible. Even so, sailors apparently managed with them for a considerable time, until 1569, before the great advance of the Fleming, Gerard Mercator appeared. His new approach represented the earth's surface as if on a cylinder but spread out flat. Mercator's projection was later amended and perfected by an Englishman, Edward Wright, whose name is now nearly forgotten.

The great era of eager exploration of the sea, during the latter part of the 16th century, created the need for proper records of navigational hazards in strange waters. Soon the explorer and the pilot on their voyagings began to take written notes of shoals and tidal flows, of soundings and anchorages and the stars, instead of relying solely on experience and memory.

One can imagine them sitting over their schnapps or ale in harbour with their mates exchanging information that gradually grew into a stock of nautical lore. By 1550 a few small books, mainly Dutch or Flemish, appeared, giving sailing directions for stretches of the northern seas between Iceland and Cadiz, which usually were the limits of sailing for the ordinary mariner. The directions were almost entirely restricted to harbour and tidal information, illustrated with little sketches of churches and other landmarks along the coast.

The first to collect hydrographic material giving coastal navigation and sailing directions, known as 'rutters', was a Dutch pilot, Lucas Jabszoon Waghenaer, of Enkhuizen. In 1584-85 he published the first part of a book, *Der Spieghel Zeevaerdt*, containing an atlas of charts and directions charting a wide area east and west of the Zuider Zee, which he knew well. The book was a success with Dutch mariners and it was followed in the next year by a second and equally successful part. Each was at once popular and went through several editions and translations into many languages.

The English edition, entitled *The Mariners Mirrour*, was produced with re-engraved script in 1588 by Anthony Ashley, the Clerk to the Privy Council, who was commissioned to undertake it by Sir Christopher Hatton. It is indeed a sumptuous volume, large and heavy, with a splendidly coloured frontispiece surrounded with drawings of navigational instruments to introduce the wealth of tables in the following pages.

Starting with the declination of the sun, the phases of the moon and the tidal movements, it goes on to instructions in the handling of astrolabe and quadrant. There are lists of fixed stars and their uses, followed by an ingenious cut-out star compass. A table of distances by sea between the chief Continental ports leads to another for traversing degrees of latitude and different angles. Then come the charts, each with details of landmarks and depths of moorings in the various harbours shown and charted.

Originally the charts were uncoloured, but unknown hands tinted all of them some time in the 17th century and a few have been recoloured. Quite a number are magnificent. Between them, they extend from the north of Europe into part of the Mediterranean; Britain has been specially favoured, with a series of large-scale charts of sectors of the coastline. England has been well done but Scotland ends sadly decapitated and mangled in the northern counties.

Nearly every chart is decorated with fascinating pictures of spouting whales, here and there in tandem, and equally fascinating ships are scattered about the sea. The vessels are not mere copies and often differ in various ways in their size and rig.

In two separate charts of Portuguese waters ships are shown firing broadsides on both sides simultaneously, in mighty billows of smoke, one of them from her lower gundeck with apparently five guns. Two Spanish ships have square sails and lateens in differing combinations. Then there is a fine carrack of Portugal with high ends, and several other large and small vessels with high poops.

Referring again to the British coast, a four-masted ship-of-war with two tiers of guns, is shown heading down-Channel under a spread spritsail, foresail and mainsail, and a main topsail and a furled topgallant. She has lateen mizen and bonaventure mizen both drawing well.

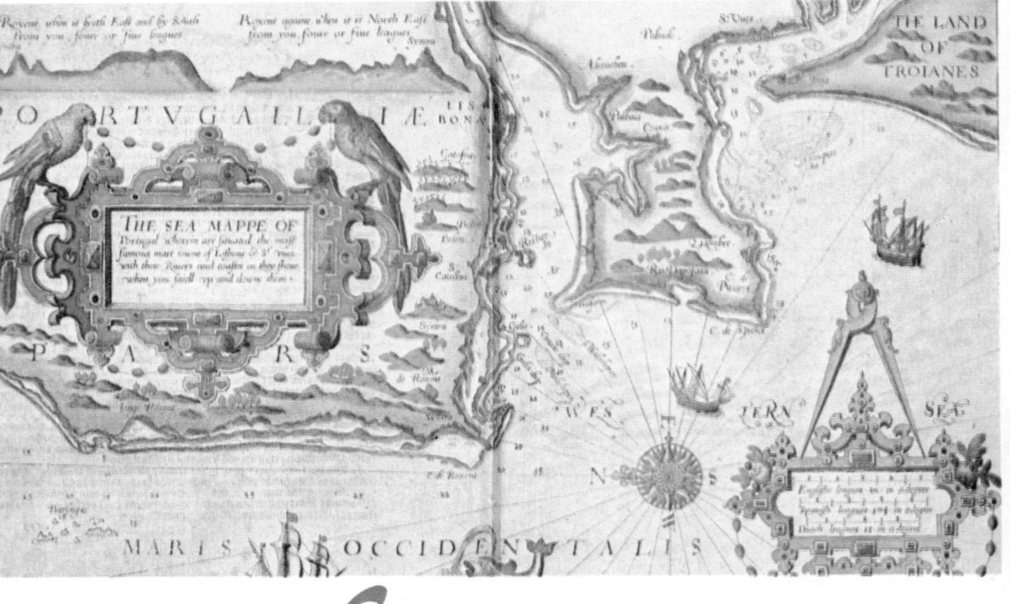

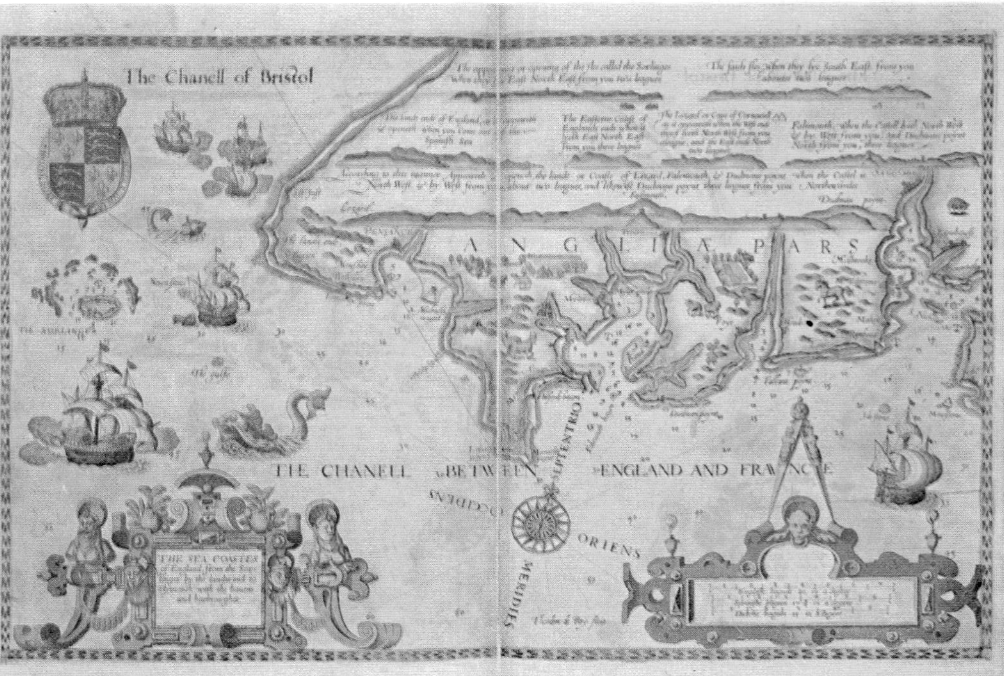

Top: A sea map of Portugal from 'The Mariners Mirrour'. *By permission of the British Library*

Above: A map of the sea coasts of Britain (showing the south coast and the English Channel) from 'The Mariners Mirrour'. *By permission of the British Library*

Right: A chart of the Atlantic from the Catalan Atlas of 1339, one of the first complete world atlases. *By permission of the British Library*

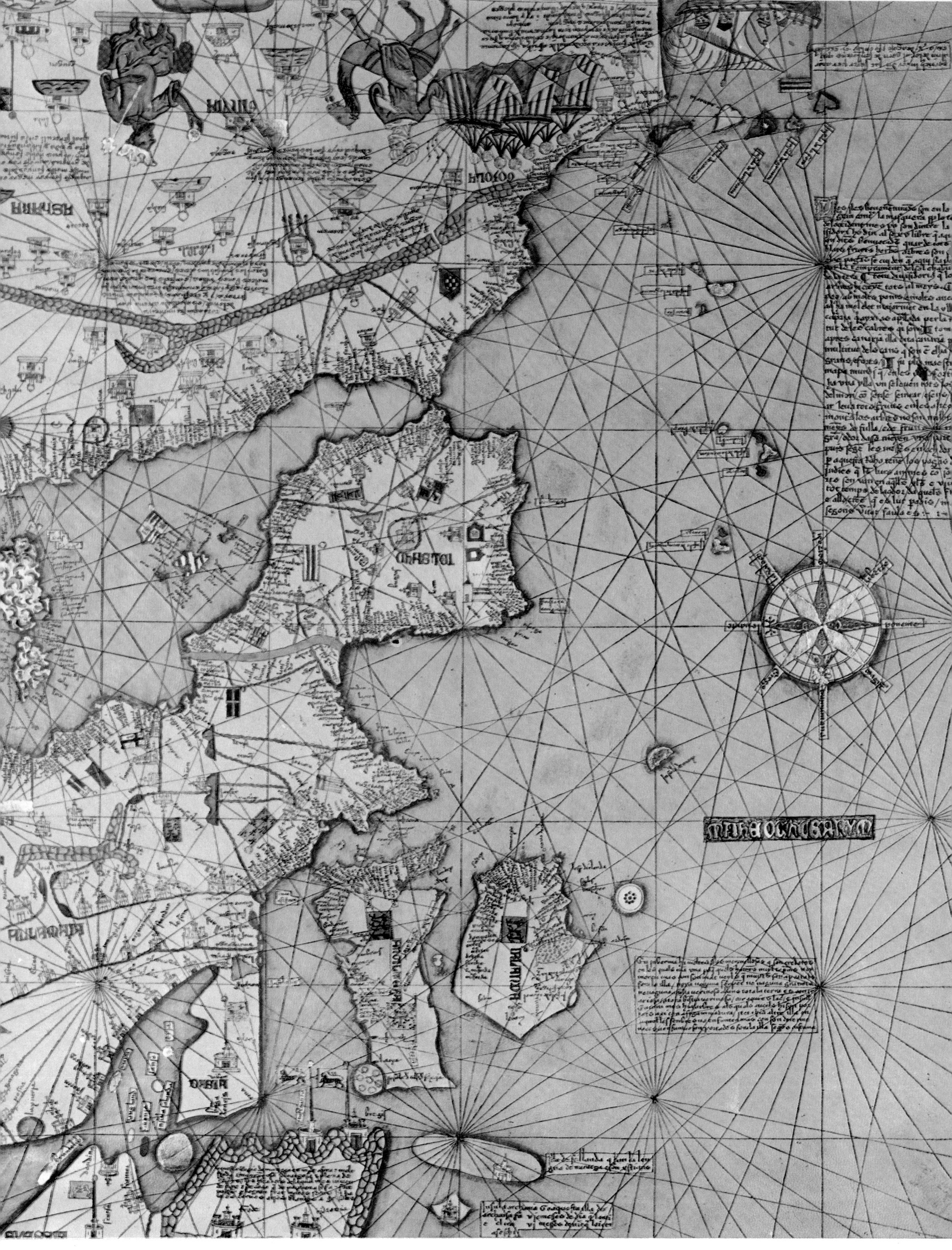

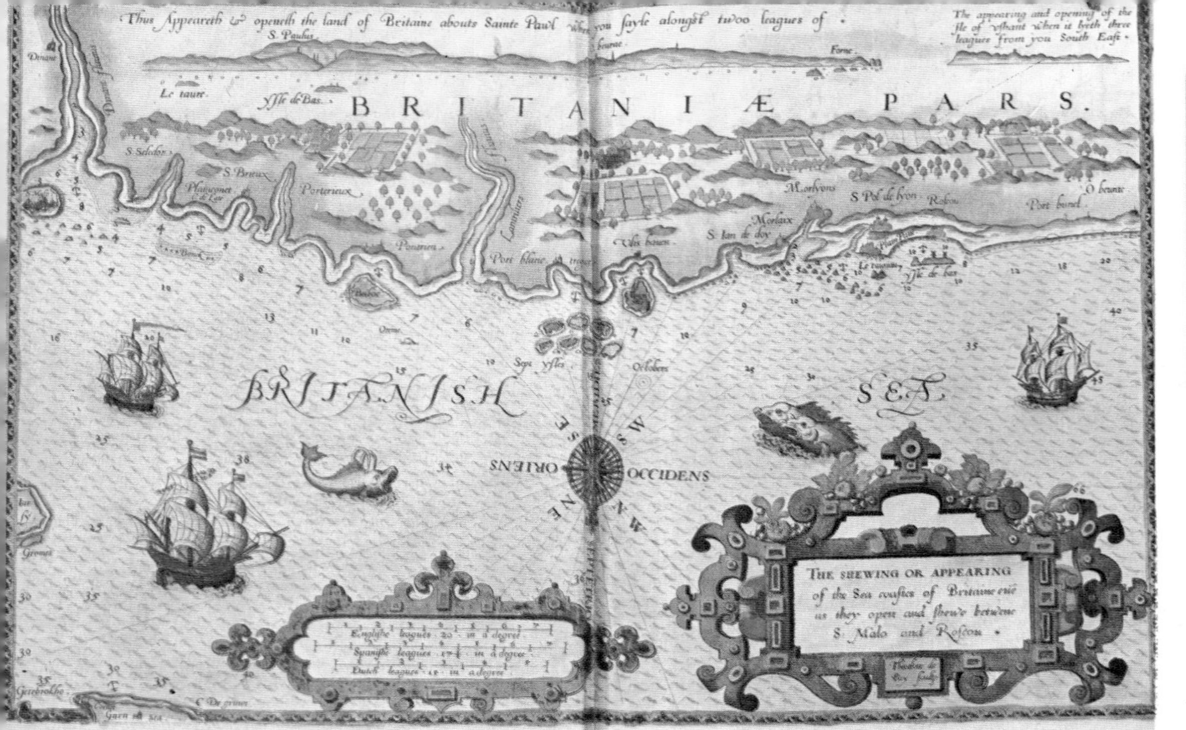

Above: The Bay of Biscay between Rio de Sella and Auiles, from 'The Mariners Mirrour'. *By permission of the British Library*

Left: The coast of Britanny between St Malo and beyond the port of Roscoff, from 'The Mariners Mirrour'. *By permission of the British Library*

Below left: A map showing the discovery of the Gulf of Guinea, promoted by Fernao Gomes. *Lisbon Academy of Sciences*

Bottom left: A map of the coasts of Flanders and Picardy, from 'The Mariners Mirrour'. *By permission of the British Library*

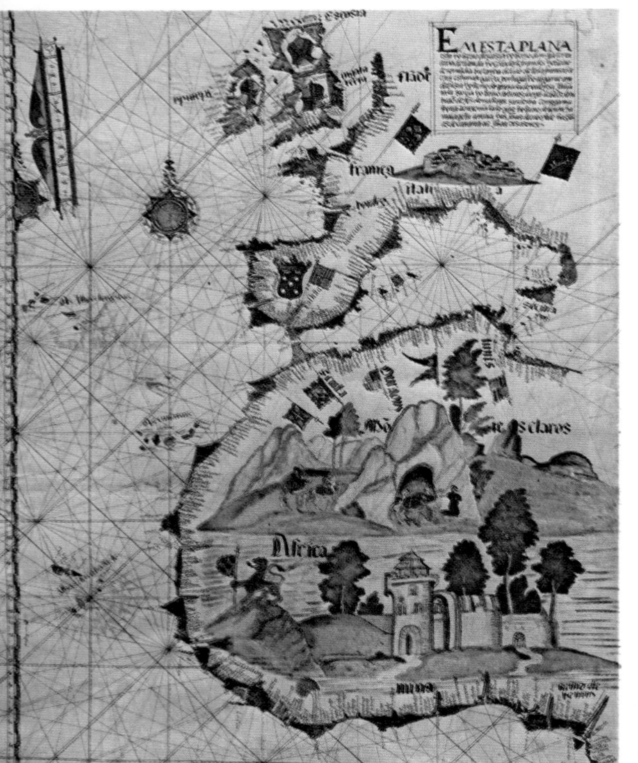

More interesting still are the fishing-boats in English waters. The sea off Hartlepool is thronged with tiny inquiring fishes breaking surface, while fishermen are overhauling their nets. The tall main masts of their boats are unshipped and lying out over the bows, although the mizen masts are still stepped and held by the stays.

In addition to the whales and a sea-serpent or two, with one solitary flying-fish that has somehow found its way into the Bay of Biscay, Waghenaer has livened up his charts with appropriate animals here and there along the coastline. From wolves and a reindeer in Norway to farm-stock and horses, they go south to pairs of parrots mounting sentinel over Spanish or Italian waters.

There is a German translation of *The Mariners Mirrour* in the British Museum with a facsimile of the text, but the quality of the colourings does not compare with the tinting in the original volume. In 1592 Waghenaer published another volume under the title of *Thresoor der Zeevaert;* it was similar to his first book, with the text re-written and expanded and charts on a much smaller scale, but showing the coastline with greater accuracy.

During the following 14 years, six Dutch and three French editions of *Thresoor der Zeevaert* were published and although there was demand for them, the issues seem to have been rather scanty. Copies of it are now few and far between, but one copy, in French, dated 1601, is in the British Museum. There are engravings in the book by an Englishman, Benjamin Wright. It appears to have been published in Amsterdam and the translation into French is not very good. However, it contains 25 double-page charts finely engraved in copper and a number of woodcuts in the text.

At the end of the volume there is a general statement of the growing interest being developed by the Dutch in the East Indies, thereby foreshadowing the formation of the Dutch East India Company in 1602. There are instructions for sailing round Africa, notes on the ports and trade in commodities of India, of the East Indies and even of China, together with a treatise on the five possible routes from England to the Far East. They are listed as:

1 By the Cape of Good Hope, sailing Eastwards.
2 By the Strait of Magellan sailing Westwards.
3 By Forbusscher's North-West Passage (which Waghenaer cheerfully admits had not then been explored).
4 By Barentzoon's North-East Passage (which also seems a non-starter since it had been explored only in part).
5 By going straight across over the North Pole.

There is no doubt, however, that the imaginative work of Waghenaer has been intensely valuable. His application of nautical science overtook the slow and tedious rule-of-thumb methods of many maritime adventurers.

Rule-of-thumb navigation nonetheless lingered on here and there almost into our present-day technical triumphs. In the 1940s, for instance, there flourished a hard-bitten coaster skipper who more often than not worked his way down the east coast ports of England and Scotland. Not the most literate of men, just how he managed to pass his Master's examination was his own secret, but he knew how to handle his ship. When challenged, he would recite the names of every lighthouse and lightship between Aberdeen and Newhaven, with light-buoys thrown in for good measure, giving their correct sequence and the class of light, whether occulting, fixed or flashing, and stating the colour of each. He never hesitated or made a slip. Lucas Waghenaer could have talked to that skipper.

Quest for the
NORTHEAST PASSAGE

ON MAY 10, 1553, the day three ships left Radcliffe Dock, Stepney, there was great excitement on the banks of London's river. As the vessels passed Greenwich, where young King Edward VI lay dying, 'courtiers came running out and the common people flocked together, standing very thick upon the shore . . .' To quote Richard Hakluyt, chronicler of English voyages of exploration, 'it was a very triumph in all respects to the beholders'.

For some, though, the departure of the ships for unknown and uncharted seas meant more than just another romantic river spectacle. For several years, demand for woollen cloth—England's chief export—had been declining, and it was becoming more and more necessary to find new markets. England's merchants were also growing impatient of the monopoly that the Hanseatic League of German merchants enjoyed in northern Europe, a monopoly which bound the English to trade only through Hansa agents.

Those facts were among the inspirations behind the audacious spirit which first stirred in the 1550s, and later exploded in that blaze of maritime enterprise characterised by the exploits of John Hawkins, Francis Drake, John Davis, Martin Frobisher and others. An older inspiration was the lure of the supposedly treasure-laden East. Ever since the 13th century, when Marco Polo had so temptingly described them, European imagination had been titillated by the gold-roofed cities of Cipangu (Japan) and the spices of Cathay (China).

In trying to reach that eastern Eldorado, Columbus, sailing westwards in the service of Spain, had stumbled on America, while the Portuguese were pioneering a route to the East round the coast of Africa. Excluded by the Iberian monopoly from the obvious routes, north Europeans began to seek the East through a northwest passage along the north coast of America. Only when that eluded them did attention focus in the opposite direction, on a route along the Arctic coast of Asia. It was to find a Northeast Passage, as well as to establish in the colder countries along the way new markets for English cloth, that a Merchant Venturers company was formed in 1552. The sum of £6000 was raised to equip a fleet, and the company appointed Sir Hugh Willoughby to lead the expedition. By a unanimous vote, Bristol-born Richard Chancellor was picked as pilot-general.

An engraving after the contemporary portrait by N Ntkin of Ivan the Terrible in the Book of Titles. *Russian State Archives*

Little is known about Chancellor and even less about Willoughby, a tall, well-born gentleman who might have fought in King Henry VIII's Scottish wars. Of the two, the merchants thought more of Chancellor, whom they regarded as 'a man of great estimation . . . in whom alone great hope for the performance of this business rested'. Such confidence was well founded. Sebastian Cabot, governor of the company, had seen Chancellor's capabilities on a voyage to the Levant, and John Dee, another driving force behind the expedition, knew of his skill in tackling problems of navigation and in improving navigational instruments.

The vessel *Bona Esperanza* (120 tons) was given to Willoughby and Chancellor was put in command of *Edward Bonaventure* (160 tons). The captain of the 90-ton *Bona Confidentia* was Cornelius Durfoorth. In all, 108 men and 11 merchants went with the ships, which carried provisions for 18 months.

The preparations went ahead in a mood of high confidence, for the merchants never seriously doubted that the expedition would reach Cathay. That view was apparently shared by the authorities, for King Edward provided letters addressed, grandiosely, to the 'Kings, Princes and other Potentates inhabiting the northeast parts of the world toward the mighty Empire of Cathay'. Such optimism derived from the gross inaccuracy which characterised geographical knowledge at that time. There was a widespread belief in the theories that the northern coast of Asia sloped steadily southeastwards from the North Cape to China, and that, somewhere in the Arctic ice lay a channel of temperate water through which ships could pass unhindered. To prepare for what was envisaged as a voyage through near-tropical seas, the bottoms of the ships were sheathed in lead. Sheathing was a precaution common in Spain, used to thwart the marine worms which thrived in the tropics and could bore through the toughest wood.

One person who had a different view was Sir Henry Sidney, father of Sir Philip, and patron of Richard Chancellor. Loth to part with his protegé, he told the merchants, 'How many perils for your sakes . . . Chancellor is now to run . . . He shall seek strange and unknown kingdoms . . . commit his safety to barbarous and cruel people . . . hazard his life among the monstrous and terrible beasts of the sea . . .'

Such dangers were doubtless in the minds of those seamen who wept to see familiar shores slip from sight on the day the ships cleared Orford Ness and struck northeastwards for Norway. Sighting the Norwegian coast at latitude 66 degrees, the ships turned north and sailed towards the Lofoten Islands. There, Willoughby, Chancellor and Durfoorth agreed that, should a storm scatter the fleet, each was to make his way independently to Vardo. It was a prophetic arrangement. Hours later, a violent storm blew up. As the tiny ships were tossed about on heavy seas, Willoughby bellowed to Chancellor to keep close. Almost in the same moment, Willoughby's *Bona Esperanza* began to draw away, and with *Bona Confidentia,* disappeared from sight in the poor visibility.

Chancellor, left alone, steered *Edward Bonaventure* on a difficult course to Vardo, which he reached safely to find that nothing was known of the other two ships. For an anxious week, Chancellor waited in Vardo, little knowing that Willoughby and Durfoorth were hundreds of miles away, having been blown past the North Cape towards Novaya Zemlya. Without Chancellor, they were utterly lost. For weeks, they scoured the inhospitable coastline but, as Willoughby plaintively put it, 'the land lay not as the Globe made mention', and Vardo eluded him. It was, by then, early September, and with winter fast approaching, Willoughby gave up the search and anchored on the east Lapland coast near the mouth of the Arzina River. There, he decided to spend the winter.

By that time Chancellor was well on his way towards a totally unexpected adventure. Despairing of a rendezvous with Willoughby, Chancellor had left Vardo to sail northeastwards across 'a huge and mighty sea' in the last of the perpetual sunlight the Arctic summer had to offer. Then, turning south, he entered a great bay called, as he learned from some fishermen, the Bay of St Nicholas. He had sailed into the White Sea, and late in August anchored at the mouth of Dvina River, in a remote corner of the land then ruled by the Czar who became known to history as Ivan the Terrible.

Chancellor and his crew had arrived in a country which many Englishmen believed implicitly to be inhabited by barbarians and cannibals, whose behaviour had hardly improved since the days of their savage Tartar ancestors. Even the venturesome Chancellor was extremely wary when, on September 2, he went ashore at the point where Archangel now stands. His suspicions deepened when, despite initial friendliness, the Russians refused to trade or do more than send a message to Czar Ivan about the English ship's arrival. For days, the authorities demurred while Chancellor grew more and more impatient at the delay. Finally, after forcing the Russians to give him sledges and guides, he set out to travel the 1500 snow-covered miles to Moscow. He was not many days out, however, before he met the Czar's messengers, who were speeding northwards with Ivan's express command to bring the visitors to the Russian capital immediately.

The sanction of their Czar was what the Russians had been waiting for. Their attitude changed completely, and they began to fight among themselves to be of service to the Englishmen, who arrived in Moscow to find a welcome hardly less overwhelming. Chancellor was summoned into Ivan's presence, to find the Czar seated in splendour, wearing a 'long garment of beaten gold, an imperial crown upon his head, a staff of crystal and gold in his right hand . . .'

Chancellor presented to Ivan King Edward's letters requesting 'free passage, help and trade for these our servants' and two hours later received a singular mark of honour for so complete a stranger—Ivan's invitation to dinner. It was there that the Englishman saw the pomp of the Russian court in full display, as 140 servants in gold livery waited on 200 richly robed nobles. As he ate roast swan off solid gold plates and drank wine from a massive gold cup, Chancellor also observed that, however uncouth his nobles seemed, the Czar himself was no barbarian. It was on Ivan's qualities of statesmanship and intelligence that Chancellor worked during the long winter he passed at the Kremlin.

Chancellor's arrival had been fortuitous, for he had come at a time when Ivan was anxious to extend contacts with the West, and it was only the influence of Western civilisation, he felt, that could help raise his country from its depths of barbarity and backwardness. When Chancellor left Moscow in February 1554, he carried

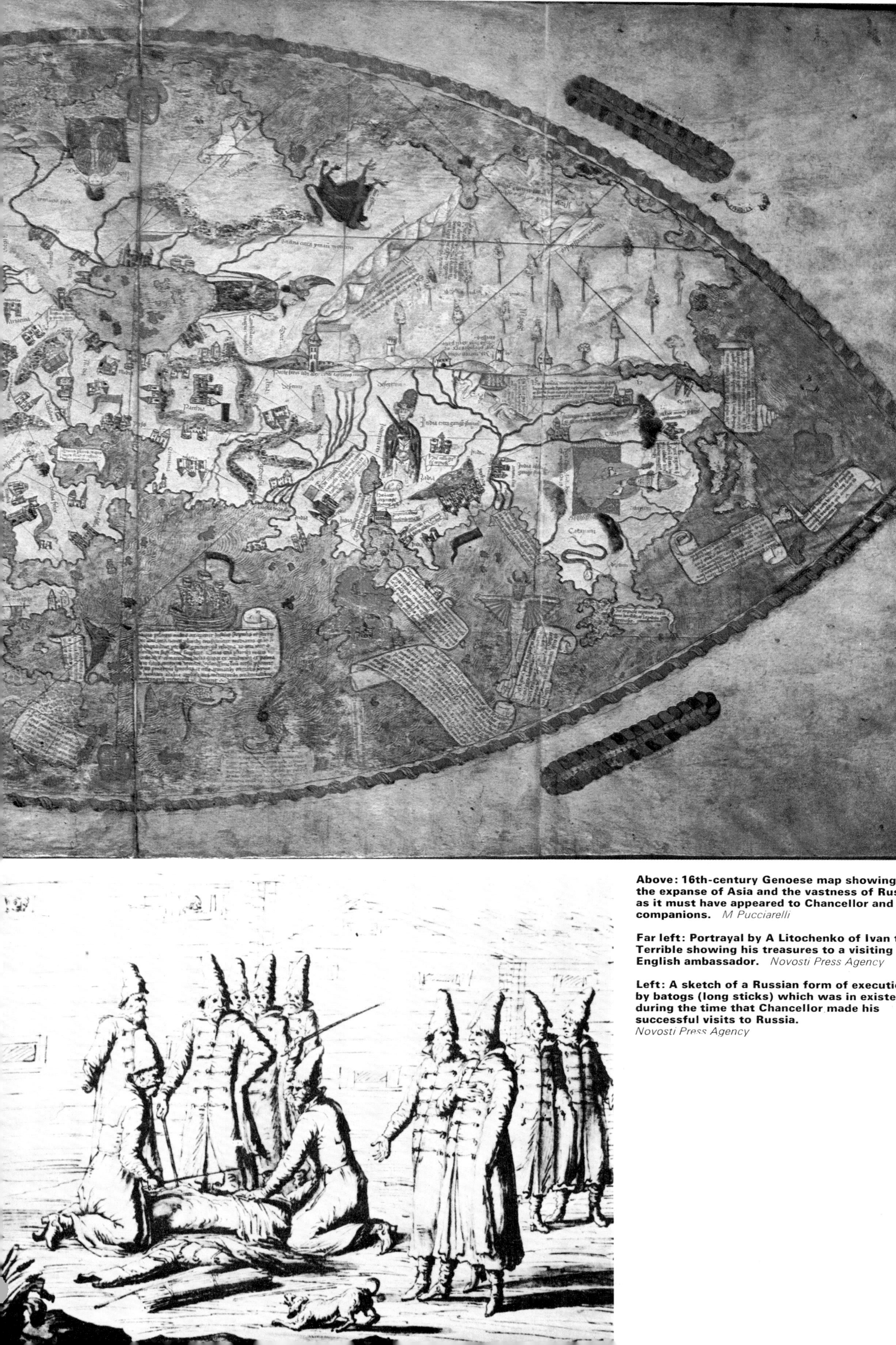

Above: 16th-century Genoese map showing the expanse of Asia and the vastness of Russia as it must have appeared to Chancellor and his companions. *M Pucciarelli*

Far left: Portrayal by A Litochenko of Ivan the Terrible showing his treasures to a visiting English ambassador. *Novosti Press Agency*

Left: A sketch of a Russian form of execution by batogs (long sticks) which was in existence during the time that Chancellor made his successful visits to Russia. *Novosti Press Agency*

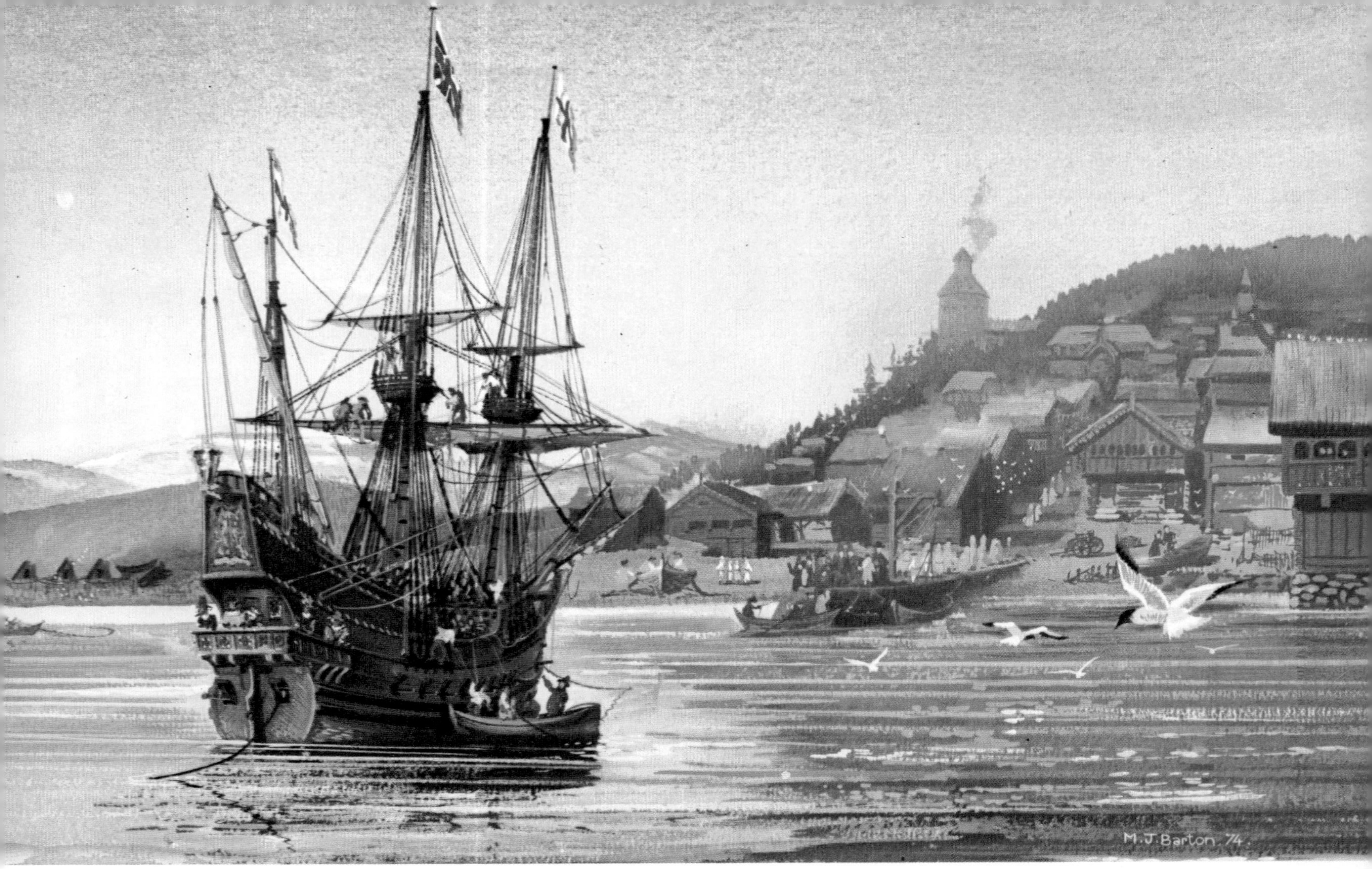
M.J.Barton.74.

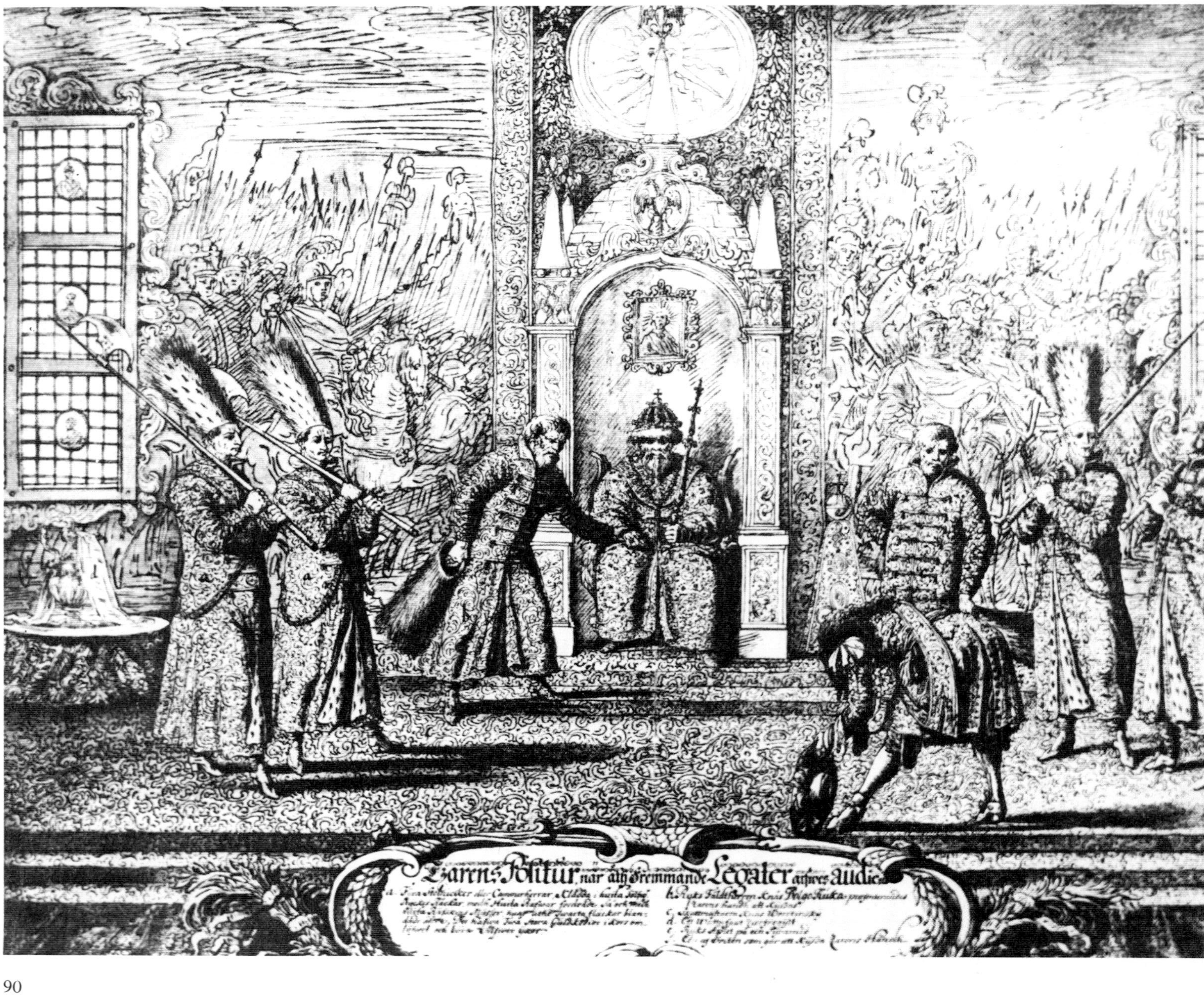
Zarens Positur när ath fremmande Legater athöres audie

with him letters from the Czar requesting King Edward to send a member of his council to conclude a formal trade agreement. However, unknown to Chancellor, King Edward VI had been dead for seven months, and England was now ruled by his half-sister, Queen Mary. Also unknown to Chancellor was the fate of Willoughby and his companions who, with their ships imprisoned in the ice, had frozen to death in the fearsome Arctic cold by January 1554.

Although he had failed to find the northeast passage to Cathay, the news Chancellor brought home to London in the late summer of 1554 aroused considerable excitement. His discovery of the new direct and potentially fruitful Russian market more than compensated the merchants for their thwarted dreams of Eastern treasure. The Merchant Venturers reformed as the Muscovy Company, and were granted a monopoly of the Russian trade by Queen Mary and her Spanish husband Philip. Quickly, a second fleet was organised and equipped, and on May 1, 1555, Chancellor sailed with two ships, *Edward Bonaventure* and *Philip and Mary*, taking with him a cargo of sugar and cloth as well as two Muscovy Company agents.

Chancellor's brief for the voyage included orders to find Willoughby, as well as to 'learn by all ways and means possible how men may pass from Russia either by land or sea to Cathay . . .' The merchants doubtless hoped that Willoughby had already found his way there, for a two-year silence like his was not unusual in that age of slow communications. However, such hope did not long survive the arrival of *Edward Bonaventure* and *Philip and Mary* in Vardo, for by the summer of 1555, Russian fishermen had already found Willoughby's ships locked in the ice, their ill-clad emaciated crews dead and decomposed.

Leaving her companion ship at Vardo, *Edward Bonaventure* sailed alone to the Dvina River, where Chancellor and a trading party disembarked to make their way to Vologda, 550 miles from Moscow. After 17 days at Vologda, where they warehoused their goods, Chancellor, George Killingworth and three others continued to Moscow, which they reached on October 4. Six days later, when the Englishmen presented to him their letters from Mary and Philip, there was no doubt that Czar Ivan was immensely pleased to see them. As Killingworth later wrote, 'His Grace did ask how our Queen's Grace did, calling her cousin, saying he was glad we were come in health to his realm . . . And we went one by one unto him, and took him by the hand, and then his Grace did bid us go in health and come to dinner . . .'

At a banquet as dazzling as the one Chancellor had attended in 1553, the Englishmen sat in the place of honour, in the centre of the hall, and though warned by some Italians to beware whom they trusted, they soon found that Russian friendliness was no façade. On November 20, they concluded a trading agreement with the Czar which granted English merchants free use of Russian ports, free trade within the country, and freedom to be ruled by their own laws. Three trading centres were to be set up—at Colmogro, Vologda and Moscow—and Ivan even guaranteed reparations should any English ship engaged in the Russian trade be set upon and robbed by pirates.

While those negotiations were going on, *Edward Bonaventure* and *Philip and Mary* had sailed back to England, taking with them the bodies of Willoughby and his companions. Within hours of their arrival, in early November 1555, grisly versions of the Lapland tragedy were current in London. The merchants of the Muscovy Company were, however, too hard-headed to pay attention to tales of the weird attitudes in which Willoughby and his men had been found frozen, and within five months, had organised and equipped a third fleet. On April 23, 1556, *Edward Bonaventure* and *Philip and Mary* sailed from Radcliffe Dock, carrying extra crews to man Willoughby's ships. Accompanying them was the tiny 10-man pinnace *Serchthrift*. While *Philip and Mary* sailed to Lapland to recover Willoughby's ships, the other vessels headed for the White Sea where, in early June, they parted. To the thunder of farewell salvoes, *Serchthrift* set off alone to follow instructions to find the still-elusive passage to Cathay.

On July 20, Chancellor left Moscow accompanied by Osep Nepea, the Czar's ambassador, and his suite of 16 attendants. Together, they travelled towards the Dvina River, where *Edward Bonaventure* had anchored to await them. When the ship had been loaded with a cargo of train oil, tallow, furs, felt and yarn, she set sail for England accompanied by *Bona Esperanza* and *Bona Confidentia* and their new crews, and also by *Philip and Mary*. However, as they skirted the coast of Norway, the four ships ran into a raging storm which only *Edward Bonaventure* managed to ride out. *Bona Confidentia* was shattered to pieces on the rocky coast, and the other ships were driven ashore at Trondheim. *Philip and Mary* survived to reach London, but *Bona Esperanza* disappeared and was never seen again.

Four months passed before Chancellor was able to struggle within sight of home, but even when, in mid-November 1556, he arrived off Pitsligo Bay, it was to meet violent winds and heavy seas which dragged his ship towards the rocks. Ground tackles were laid, but the cables snapped. With a hideous smashing of timbers, *Edward Bonaventure* disintegrated on the rocky shore. As she did so, Chancellor made a desperate effort to save the Russian ambassador. He launched a small boat, and with Nepea and his suite aboard, tried to row for the shore. But the craft capsized and Chancellor, together with seven Russians, was thrown into the swirling waters to drown.

Ambassador Nepea was saved by some Scots, who looted the wrecked ship and held the Russian prisoner for about four months. When he was eventually released, and entered London on March 26, 1557, he was the first Russian ambassador to be seen there. The trade he came to cement lasted for more than 30 years, to the immense profit of English merchants, who had to wait far longer to reap similar riches in Cathay.

Facing page top: Painting by M Barton of Richard Chancellor's ship 'Edward Bonaventure' arriving in Vardo en route for Russia.

Facing page below: An engraving depicting the manner in which foreign ambassadors were received by the Czar in the Granoritaya Chamber of the Kremlin.
State Historical Museum Moscow (Novosti Press Agency)

Top left: Ivan the Terrible. *Novosti Press Agency*

Above left: A watercolour by L Lissner of Czar Ivan inspecting the work of Russia's first printer Ivan Fedorov. *Novosti Press Agency*

Left: The fur trimmed cap first used to crown the Russian Czars in 1547.
Novosti Press Agency

DRAKE

'DRAKE he was a Devon man and ruled the Devon Seas', wrote Newbolt, but Drake sailed farther than the seas of Devon. He was eight years old when, to escape religious fanatics, his father took him in 1541 from his native Tavistock to live in an old hulk at Chatham, on the River Medway, in Kent. There, where the river flows into the Thames estuary, he spent his boyhood among boats and shipping.

Having Sir John Hawkins as his kinsman meant that young Francis Drake went to sea as a matter of course as soon as he was old enough. A description of him runs, 'Low in stature, of strong limbs, broad breast, round-heade, well-favoured face and of good countenance'. He was apprenticed to the skipper of an old coaster, a rough and hard school but one well qualified to teach seamanship.

When he was first in command of a ship, with Hawkins in 1568, he had his early brush with Spain. At San Jean De Ulua, in spite of binding promises to the contrary, the Spaniards suddenly attacked in overwhelming force. Three ships, one of them belonging to the Queen, were lost and the knowledge of the treatment Spaniards meted out to the captured 'heretic' sailors gave Drake an undying hatred of Spain.

At Plymouth, he fitted out two small ships, with pinnaces on deck for inshore work, and sailed westward again. Aided by another ship which came to join him, he took and sacked the chief Spanish port of Nombre de Dios, on the Isthmus of Panama, where the silver was brought from the mines for shipment to Spain. Then he crossed the isthmus, guided by friendly local Indians. He stopped on the way to climb a tall tree and looked out over the glittering sheet of the Pacific. There and then he made a vow to sail the first English ship on that ocean and went on to create havoc among the shipping at Panama.

It took only three weeks for his ships to recross the Atlantic and they were back sailing up Plymouth Sound on a Sunday morning, giving the parsons barely time to preach their sermons. His ships, flamboyantly strung with streamers and flags, gave tongue with their guns. Sermons or no sermons, the people poured out of the churches as fast as people could run; it was not every day that Francis Drake came home to Devon, and with a bar or two of solid silver to show. The Queen sent for him and made much of him and the Earl of Essex asked for his help in patrolling the Irish Sea.

However, five years passed before he was able to realise his ambition to sail the Pacific and by then he had reached the age of forty. He suffered at times with two wounds caused by Spaniards—a ball in his leg and an arrow-wound in his thigh—but they had not cost him his sense of humour. The preparations for his new voyage could not be kept secret, though whispers were spread of Alexandria being the intended destination in order to allay Spanish suspicions. Theoretically at least, all that Drake proposed to do was to sail through the Strait of Magellan into the South Sea. On that basis he was given support and encouragement by Queen Elizabeth and backed by her financial interest in the enterprise.

Five vessels were to take part, with a ship of about 18 guns as his flagship. Her name was the *Pelican* at the start but it was changed to *Golden Hind* by Drake during the voyage. Accompanying her were a ship of two-thirds her size, the *Elizabeth*, two sloops, a pinnace too small to have a name, and other pinnaces on deck in sections. Presented by the Queen with perfumed water and sweetmeats, Drake set sail from Plymouth halfway through November 1577.

Facing page top: Engraving by Jodocus Hondius depicting the circumnavigations of Drake (1577-80) and Cavendish (1586-88). *By permission of the British Library*

Facing page bottom: Anonymous engraving depicting Drake, inserted in the Lumley copy of Hakluyt in 1939. *John R Freeman & Co Ltd*

Left: Portrait by an unknown artist of Sir Francis Drake. *National Portrait Gallery*

Above: Replica of Drake's 'Golden Hind' built at Appledore, Devon, awaiting her mainmast in 1973. *Courtesy Golden Hind Ltd*

Below: A drawing of the actual 'Golden Hind', which started life (and Drake's epic voyage) as the 'Pelican'. *National Maritime Museum London*

ROUND THE WORLD

Off the Cape Verde Islands, more or less in mid-Atlantic, he had the good fortune to capture, probably illegally, the laden Portuguese ship *Maria*. She was a valuable prize, not only because of her stock of provisions but even more because of her pilot, Nuno da Silva, who was of great help to Drake and became his staunch friend.

After making a quick passage with the north-east trade winds, they sighted the Brazilian coast and sailed southward to Port St Julian in Patagonia. There Drake dealt with Doughty, the mystery-man of the fleet. Thomas Doughty, who had been a friend of Drake and captain of a ship, was loose of tongue, suspected of fomenting mutiny and of dealing in sorcery. Drake would have none of it; it was wrecking the voyage. He had Doughty tried by a jury of captains, who found him guilty, and he sentenced him to death. On the shore of the same little harbour where, strangely enough, Magellan had hanged his mutineer 50 years earlier, Doughty was beheaded after he and Drake had taken Holy Communion together. Afterwards, Drake mustered the ships' companies and made a speech. 'I will have the gentlemen to pull with the sailors', he said. It was to be the keynote of their life together.

At St Julian, he stripped and sank the two least seaworthy of the ships and the prize-ship *Maria*, spreading their crews among the other three vessels to fill the many gaps caused by illness and accidents. The ships were careened (turned on their sides) to have their bottoms scraped and cleansed of marine growths, thoroughly overhauled and refitted, before they sailed into Magellan's Strait. Drake had no chart of the strait, merely his skill and experience, but 'by guess and by God', as the old phrase goes, after a fortnight of effort, endurance and sheer determination, all three ships won through. They were in the Pacific, Drake's 'South Sea'.

A hurricane wind took charge and drove the *Pelican* under bare poles first to the north and then far to the southward. It whisked away the one little sloop, which was never seen again. The *Elizabeth*, after managing to anchor, was forced back into the strait and there she stayed for several weeks waiting in vain for Drake. Finally, she made her way back to England.

Drake gave her up and, with his single ship, followed the coasts of Chile and Peru, capturing Spanish ships, sacking towns and creating panic, until his mere name terrified Spanish ears. His richest prize, the *Neustra Senora de la Concepcion*, caught after a long chase, was laden with gold and silver. In a generous mood, he gave the Portuguese captain valuable presents, and money and clothes to all the crew. Drake loved display and pomp. He had his gilded silver tableware, and a trumpeter and music, always at his meals. And his men adored it all as they adored his hearty wit and his occasional bellow.

At last he decided that it was time for the homeward voyage. In September of 1579, he careened his ship, then renamed *Golden Hind*, once more, and, after calling for water in the Philippines, sailed for the Moluccas, where he had a warm welcome from the Sultan. They made a treaty together while the crew packed the ship with spices in every possible stowage space.

Sailing on, they came to an uninhabited but pleasant island where, after building a fort, they spent an idle month. But as she was getting under way again, the *Golden Hind* ran hard on to a reef and Drake had to get her off by jettisoning eight of his guns and half the precious spices.

In mid-June he doubled the Cape of Good Hope, and at the end of nearly three years he arrived at Plymouth, the fifth navigator to have circumnavigated the globe. He brought back with him only 57 men but plenty of gold and silver, certainly enough to please the eyes of Queen Elizabeth.

Her Majesty came down to Deptford to see the *Golden Hind* and there, defying Philip of Spain and all that he could do, on board his own ship and with his own sword, she knighted Sir Francis Drake. By the Queen's order, the *Hind* was preserved in dry dock for posterity, though she lasted little longer than a century.

Drake married twice, in 1569 to his Plymouth sweetheart Mary Newman, and again three years after her death, in 1585 to Elizabeth Sydenham of a landed family.

At the beginning of open war with Spain in 1585, he commanded a fleet which sailed to the Caribbean and captured four cities, including Cartagena. He was destined to die in those waters, in Nombre de Dios Bay, though much was to happen before then. It was in 1587 that he singed the King of Spain's beard at Lisbon, but that is really part of the story of the defeat of the 'invincible' Armada.

Below left: A portrait by an unknown artist of Queen Elizabeth I. *National Portrait Gallery*

Bottom: A drawing by G H Davis showing a typical 500-ton ship of the Elizabethan fleet at the time of the Armada. 'Golden Hind' was a little over 100 tons.
London Electrotype Agency

Anson's Epic Voyage

IN JANUARY 1740, the British Admiralty commissioned a squadron under Commodore George Anson to attack Spanish commerce in the Pacific. As well as preying on Spanish shipping, it was intended that he should capture Valdivia in Chile, and link up with an expedition under Admiral Vernon to be sent to attack the Spanish settlements in the West Indies, with a view to taking Panama and the Isthmus, key to all the treasure of Peru.

Anson had manning problems. He was 300 sailors short, and had been promised them and the replacement of all his old men and boys by fit experienced able seamen. But he was told that none of them could be spared, and sailed without them. He had also been promised Colonel Bland's regiment and three independent companies of 100 men each as a land force. This arrangement was cancelled on the eve of sailing, and he was allotted 500 old out-pensioners of Chelsea College, men worn out from wounds, sickness and long service. As it was, only 259 came on board. All those who could walk out of Portsmouth had deserted. In their place Anson was given 210 raw marine recruits.

For forty days, Anson's eight ships groaned and laboured in the Solent, waiting for favourable weather. Then, with the gleam of Peruvian silver fading in his eye, the Commodore could wait no longer, and on September 18, 1740, he weighed from St Helens in the teeth of a contrary wind, with his shakily manned squadron, comprising the five men-of-war *Centurion* (flagship, 60 guns), *Gloucester* (50), *Severn* (50), *Pearl* (40), and *Wager* (28), as well as the sloop *Tryal* (eight guns) and the two victualling ships *Anna* and *Industry*.

They had adverse winds and took 37 days to reach Madeira, a passage often done in 10 or 12 days. Captain Norris of the *Gloucester* returned home for his health, and the rest drowned their forebodings in Madeira wine, with which they filled many of the water casks. The Commodore was in a hurry, having heard that a Spanish squadron of seven or eight ships under Admiral Pizarro was in the offing, and on November 3, he sailed on the long haul south to Santa Catarina Island off the southern coast of Brazil. On November 19, the *Industry* left them. The ships were so deeply loaded that their lower ports could not be opened, and the increasing foulness of the air between decks contributed to the sharply rising sickness rate. Anson ordered six extra air scuttles cut in each ship, but many men, subsisting on crackerhash (a mess of ship's biscuit and water) and rancid salt pork, were dying, and many more groaning and sweating in their hammocks with the raging temperatures and terrible stomach pains of sea fever.

Above left: Sailors of Anson's time, relaxing on shore. *National Trust Shugborough*

Above: Anson's flagship 'Centurion' engaging 'Nuestra Senora de Cabadonga' from Acapulco. *Mary Evans Picture Library*

It was with joy and relief that the coast of Brazil was sighted on December 16. On the 20th, the squadron anchored in the bay of Bon Port at Santa Catarina, and Anson lost no time in having tents erected ashore for the reception of the sick, of which there were 80 from the *Centurion* alone. The decks were scraped and 'tween decks smoked and washed with vinegar, to remove the stench and kill the vermin. But neither this nor the plentiful new diet of fresh fruit and vegetables, fresh meat and sweet crystal water could rid the men of disease. The climate was close and humid, and they were plagued by 'muscatos' by day and sand flies by night.

Centurion alone buried 28 men, and her sick list increased from 80 to 96. In readiness for Cape Horn, all fit men worked at strengthening sprung masts, reeving new standing rigging and extra preventer shrouds, and striking down some of the great guns into the hold to make the ship stiffer in a wind. On January 18, 1741, the squadron weighed anchor and headed south. They did not know that the Governor of Santa Catarina had sent a fast ship ahead of them to report their movements to Pizarro, who lay at Buenos Aires with all his ships.

On the second day out, *Tryal* lost her mainmast in a violent squall, and in the full gale and thick fog which followed, *Pearl* became separated from the rest of the squadron, which battled on down the 'desart and inhospitable coast'. After a month of such, they sighted a sail and manned the guns. *Gloucester* intercepted and recognised the *Pearl,* which had news, all bad. Her Captain, Dandy Kidd, was dead, and she had narrowly avoided clashing with five Spanish men-of-war.

Right: Portrait by A Pond of Admiral Lord Anson.
National Trust Shugborough (John Rackham)

Anson put in at St Julian, last port of call before the Horn, and was delayed refitting the *Tryal.* The Commodore's chaplain, Richard Walter, marvelled at the Patagonian landscape, utterly bare of trees, but lush with grass which fed 'immense herds of cattle', slaughtered only for their hides and tallow, and the penguins like 'little children standing up in white aprons'. On February 24, 1741, the squadron left St Julian for the Horn. If the ships became separated rounding the Horn, they had a list of rendezvous points, off Valdivia, the island of Nuestra Senora del Socoro, or, failing them, the island of Juan Fernandez.

On March 6, after a night and day of violent winds, they sighted the awesome white peaks of Tierra del Fuego, and steered along its eastern shore all day. That night they lay to and bent on an entire new suit of sails. Soon after eight in the morning, they rounded Cape San Diego in fair weather and began to open the Straits of Le Maire between Tierra del Fuego and the island of Los Estados (Staten Island). In two hours they were through, helped by a brisk gale of wind and a swift tide. The sun shone, the smooth ocean before them gleamed with Chilean gold and Peruvian silver.

But before the sternmost ships, the *Wager* and *Anna,* had cleared the Straits, the sky was black, the wind veered towards the west, the tide set fiercely from the east, and *Wager* and *Anna* were almost wrecked on Los Estados. The whole squadron was thrust back into the South Atlantic. The gales and short but mountainous seas which followed shocked even the oldest and most experienced hands. Men were tossed overboard, smashed to the deck, thrown into the hold. Broken thighs and collar bones were common. For days on end the ships would lie under bare poles, then cautiously set topsails in a lull, only to have them instantly torn from the yards. Snow and sleet froze rigging and sails, which became brittle and snapped at the touch of numbed and frost-bitten fingers. Even though the wind sometimes abated, the waves did not subside, but went on hammering the ships until their frames loosened and they let in water at every seam. No one slept dry, if he slept at all.

Right through March, the elements kept up their punishment, with the squadron standing towards the south-west but making no way at all. A very violent gale of wind, hail and lashing rain on the 23rd, with 'a very great sea', which blew *Centurion's* mainsail away, seemed mild to the hurricane which followed and washed an able seaman overboard. His shipmates were 'the more grieved at his unhappy fate, as we . . . conceived from the manner in which he swam that he might continue sensible, for a considerable time longer, of the horror attending his irretrievable situation.' *Gloucester's* main yard was broken, *Tryal's* pumps could not keep pace with the leaks. After 40 days of this agony, *Centurion, Gloucester, Wager, Tryal* and *Anna,* though in bad shape, were still together, but they had lost sight of *Severn* and *Pearl,* Some time later, *Gloucester, Wager* and *Anna* also became separated from *Centurion* and *Tryal.*

The weather was not the only enemy. Almost simultaneously with the unleashing of the fury of the Cape Horn gales, the symptoms of scurvy, the disease caused by a diet of salt meat unrelieved by fresh fruit and vegetables, began to run riot among the men—the livid spots, swelling legs, putrid gums, ulcers, violent pains, shivering fits, and the deadly lethargy and morbid loss of spirit, which was so often a prelude to sudden death. In April, 43 died of scurvy aboard *Centurion,* and almost everyone was touched by it.

Doggedly, *Centurion* and *Tryal* beat to the south-west until April 22, then edged northward, battling hard gales until on the last day of the month they found themselves north of the Pacific end of the Strait of Magellan. On May 8, 1741, they arrived at Socoro Island and cruised there for several days, but the other ships did not show up. Scurvy had by then killed or disabled so many hands that there were barely enough to work the ships. They stood north for Juan Fernandez, through continuing gales, sickness and fatigue until May 22, when the worst hurricane they had yet suffered hit them. *Centurion* lost nearly all her sails and standing rigging. A giant sea snapped her shrouds and left her masts dangerously unsupported, and the ship almost went ashore on the island of Chiloe. The death rate from scurvy had then doubled, and was running at about five or six a day. At last, on June 9, they sighted Juan Fernandez. Half of *Centurion's* crew had died of scurvy, and of the 200 left, only six seamen were fit for duty. Officers, Anson himself included, servants and boys had to join in to work the ship to anchor. In *Tryal,* only the captain, his lieutenant and three men were able to stand by the sails.

The fruits, vegetables, fish and flesh on the fertile green island, where Alexander Selkirk, the real-life Robinson Crusoe, was marooned, stopped the scurvy, and a grateful Anson sowed lettuce, carrots and other vegetables for the future use of mariners, and planted plum, apricot and peach stones. Several elderly bearded goats were found wearing the tags attached to them by Selkirk 32 years before. On July 23, *Gloucester* struggled in, two-thirds of her crew dead, the remainder exhausted, sick and dying of thirst. She had sighted the island on June 21 and had taken a further month to reach it.

On August 13, a three-masted ship was sighted, which some thought to be a Spanish cruiser. It was the *Anna.* Of the other ships there was no sign, and they did not see them again. (*Severn* and *Pearl* did not persevere with the passage round Cape Horn, but put back to Brazil. *Wager* fought her way round but was wrecked on the Chilean coast. A mutinous majority of her men sailed her longboat back to Brazil, and of the remainder, six men put to sea in her barge and were never seen again, while Captain Cheap and three officers eventually returned to England, after a period as prisoners of the Spaniards.)

Anna was found to be dangerously rotten and was broken up. Then, on September 8, with all the sick out of danger and repairs made, Anson sailed. On the 12th, they took their first prize, the *Nuestra Senora del Monte Carmelo* out of Callao in Peru. Of greatest value in her cargo, mostly sugar and cloth, were trunks full of wrought plate and silver dollars weighing nearly 5000 pounds. Anson learned from Captain Zamorra that Pizarro's squadron, which had chased the *Pearl* off St Julian, had been so savagely mauled by the Cape Horn weather that two of his largest ships had sunk and the rest returned, smashed and dismasted, to the River Plate. The Spaniards also reported that Admiral Vernon's attempt to capture Cartagena had failed, and Anson decided to abandon his own attempt on Panama. The *Carmelo* was put into service, carrying the guns taken out of the *Anna.* On the evening of September 24, *Centurion* overhauled another Spaniard. Anson's gunners were about to open fire when an English voice identified her as the *Arranzazu,* prize of the *Tryal,* with £5000-worth of silver on board. *Tryal* herself was so leaky and her masts so faulty that she was destroyed and her prize manned as a substitute.

The reconstituted squadron, less *Gloucester,* which was stationed off Paita, near Callao, cruised off the normally busy port of Valparaiso, but news of their presence had reached the Viceroy, and the ocean was bare. Anson hastened north to join *Gloucester* and oppose with maximum strength any Spanish squadron which might sortie from Callao. On passage, they overhauled and captured the *Santa Teresa de Jesus.* Expecting the *Gloucester, Centurion's* lookout reported a sail which was soon identified as another Spaniard, the *Nuestra Senora del Carmin.* The wind dropped, but Lieutenant Brett ran alongside her in *Centurion's* barge, firing in the air, whereupon 'the enemy made no resistance being sufficiently frighted by the dazzling of the cutlasses, and the volley they had just received'. An Irishman in her crew told Anson that there was in the customs house at nearby Paita, where *Carmin* had provisioned, a fortune in silver which a fast ship was to take to Acapulco in Mexico to buy part of the cargo of Chinese silks and East Indian spices brought by the annual galleon from Manila in the Philippines. The Commodore determined to take Paita that very night.

In the darkness, Lieutenant Brett with 58 men landed from the ships' boats. With drums banging, the sailors yelling and cheering in joy at the release from the frustrations and miseries of the voyage and 'with the hopes of an immense pillage' advanced on the fort, and the garrison fled. Wrought plate, silver dollars and other

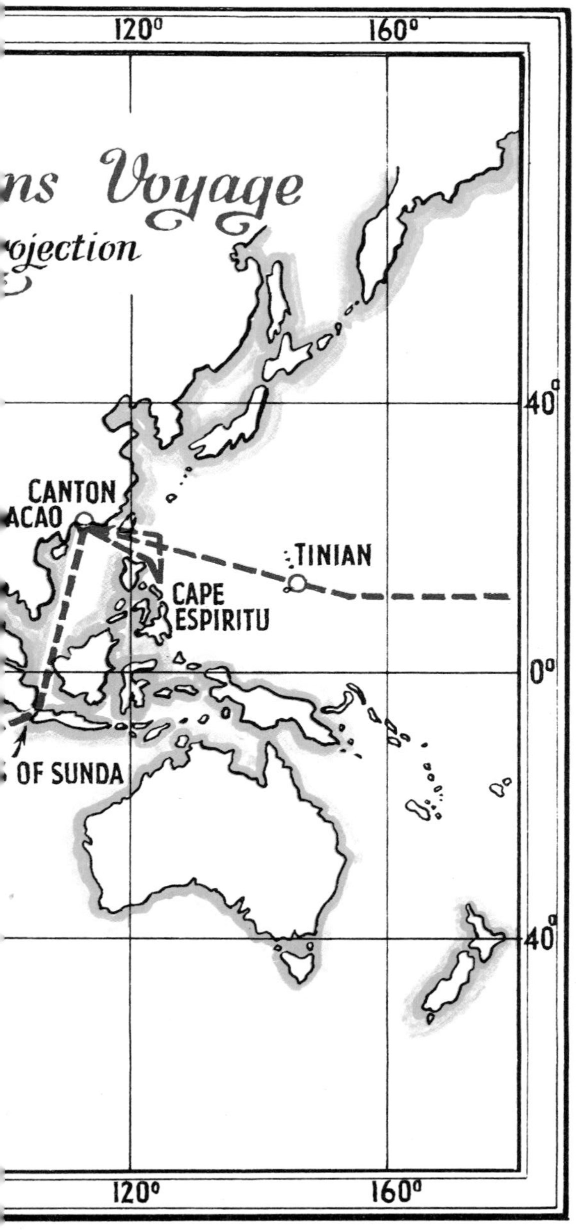

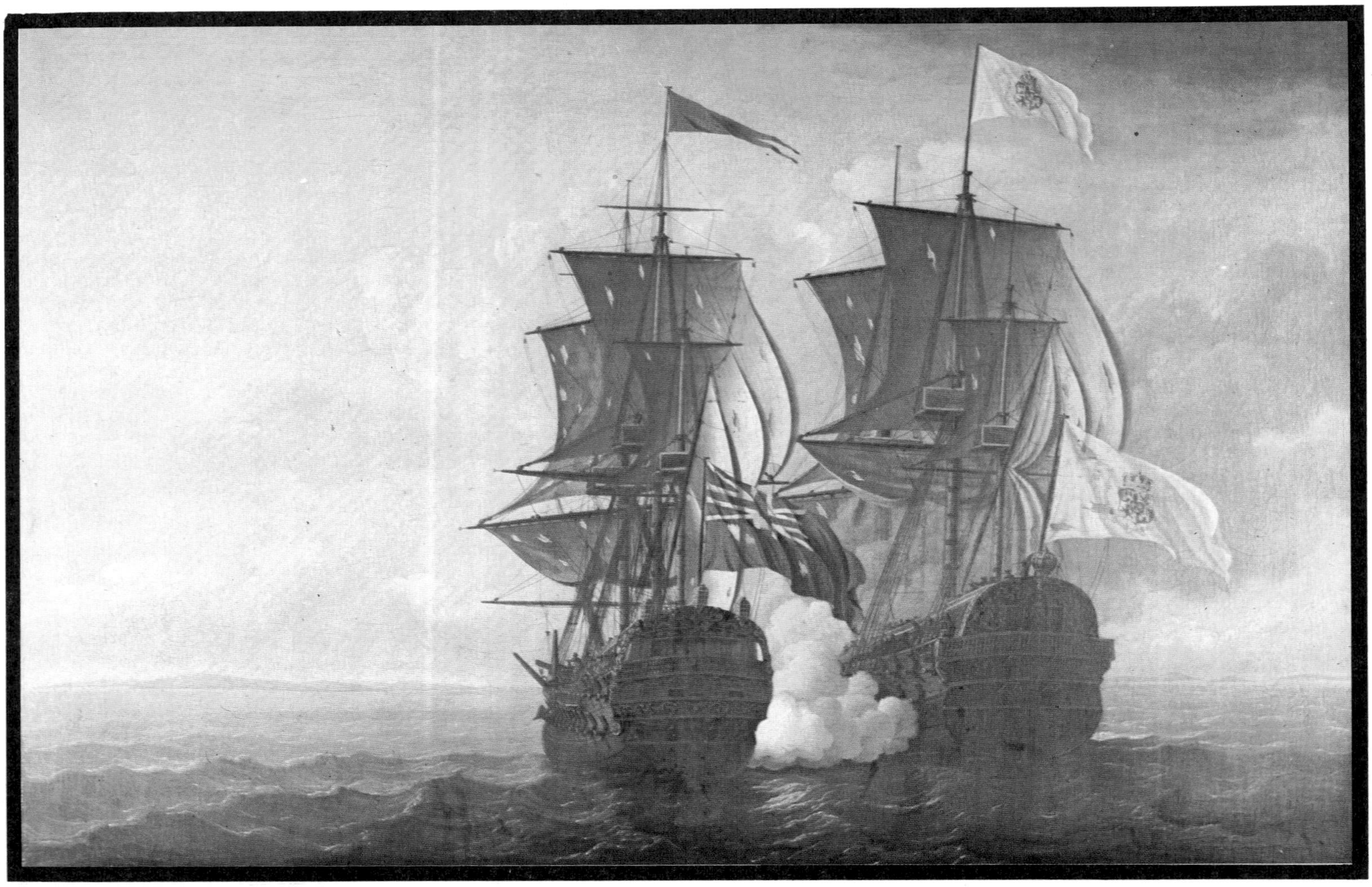

REFERENCES
Prizes taken by the Centurion
The burning of the TOWN of PA
SANTA FEE in the SOU

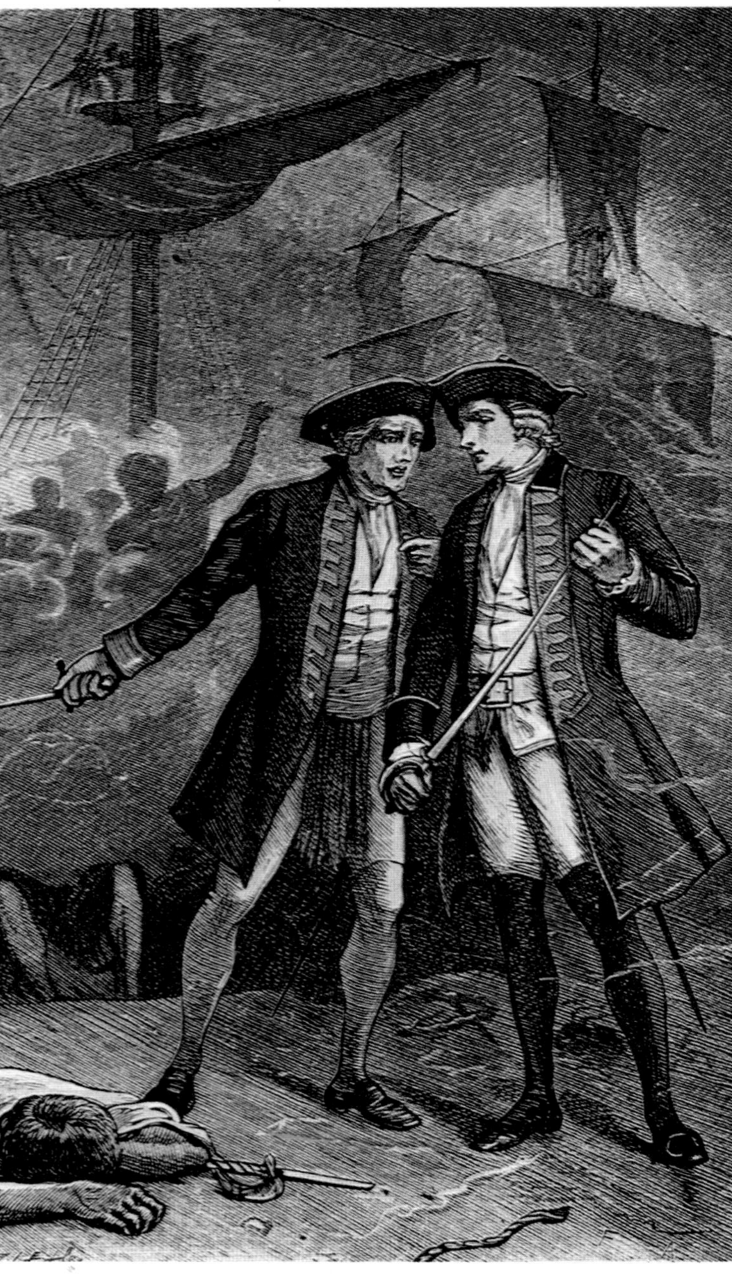

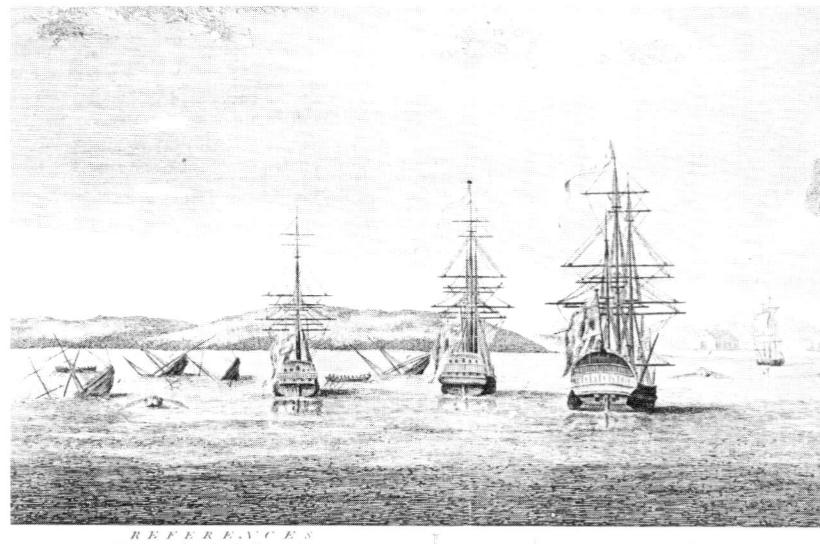

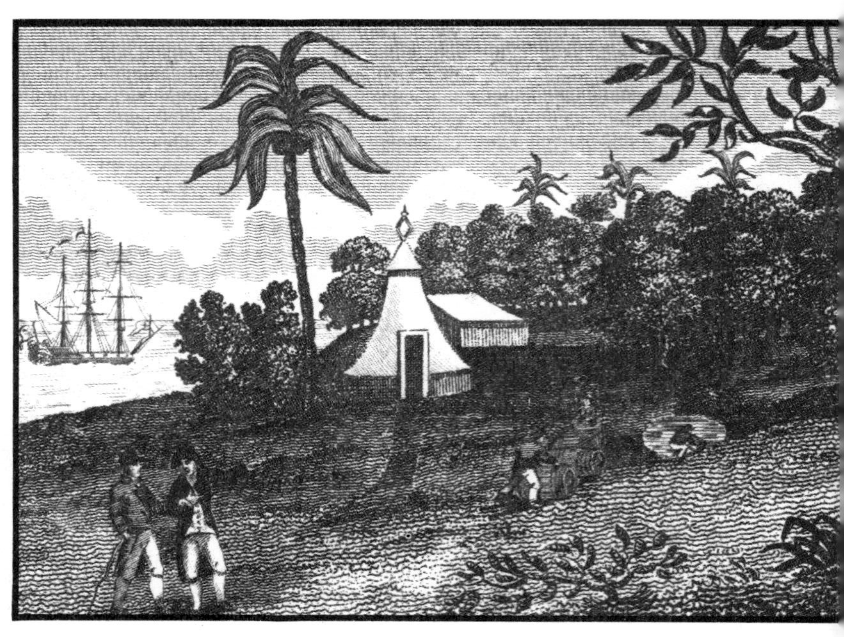

coin to the value of £30,000 were ferried out to *Centurion,* and at midnight on November 16, 1741, the squadron—*Centurion, Carmelo, Teresa, Carmin, Arranzazu* and the new prize *Solidad*—weighed and stood to the westward. Two days out *Gloucester,* towing another prize, joined them. With all his ships now in company, the Commodore sailed north for the coast of Mexico and the Manila galleon, which he knew was now at sea, bound for Acapulco.

On December 3, they sighted the island of Quibo, having stripped and burned the *Teresa* and *Solidad,* which had been slowing them down. After wooding and watering, and feasting on the meat of the green turtle, they put to sea again on December 9 and next day captured and scuttled the *Jesu Nazareno,* from Panama. For a month they suffered heavy gales from the west, dead calms and heavy rains, and it was not until January 26, 1742, that they were off Acapulco, where they cruised without result for another month. On February 19, three captured fishermen confirmed Anson's suspicions. The Manila galleon had come in on January 9. But the Viceroy of Mexico had fixed her departure, carrying all the silver paid for her cargo, as March 14.

They took station with renewed hope 15 leagues to seaward, awaiting the great ship with the royal standard of Spain at her masthead. March 14 passed with no galleon, and ten more empty days. Then Anson was forced to leave station and put into the port of Chequetan for water and the anti-scorbutic lime. As the whole squadron could not muster enough hands to man a fourth-rate man-of-war, Anson reluctantly burned *Carmelo, Carmin,* and *Arranzazu,* all well-found ships, and by Sunday May 2, was back off Acapulco with *Centurion* and *Gloucester.* But with the stormy season building up on the Mexican coast, and the westerly monsoon due on the coasts of China, where Anson intended to seek repair and replenishment, he could wait no longer. On May 6, 1742, they looked their last on the mountains of Mexico and set course across the vast Pacific for Canton River and Macao, reaching south for the favourable tradewind. There was general despondency at their failure to catch the Manila galleon, but Anson had not yet given up.

A brisk passage was anticipated, but it was seven weeks before they got into the tradewind, and the scurvy broke out again. The wind was constant from the end of June until July 26, then for four days westerly gales battered them. It was then that *Gloucester,* rotten in almost all her timbers and masts, began to break up. Her foretopmast came down, breaking her foreyard, and was with great difficulty repaired, only to collapse again. Her maintopmast followed, she leaked by her sternpost, and her hold was rapidly filling with water, covering her freshwater casks and provisions. Her handful of men and boys on deck were exhausted and sick. Anson did the only thing possible, and on August 15, she was burned. When, on August 28, the lone *Centurion* arrived at Tinian in the Marianas, she could muster only 71 semi-fit men for duty, instead of her normal 400. The Commodore, though ill himself, carried some of the sick ashore on his shoulders, and the fresh fruit, vegetables, pure water and sweet air of the island worked their cure.

On September 22, a storm blew out of the east, parting the flagship's cables and driving her out to sea, marooning Anson and many men ashore, who, seeing her suddenly gone from the lagoon, thought her sunk. Anson made plans for lengthening a small Spanish ship to carry them to China, but on October 11, battered and leaking, the flagship limped in. Ten days later they left Tinian, steering for Macao, with the weakened leaking ship labouring dangerously before a big following sea. But there was again full health and vigour aboard, and on November 12 they anchored in Macao road.

Anson's requests for stores and repair facilities had to be approved by the Chinese Viceroy of Canton. It was the beginning of April 1743, after protracted negotiations, including the entertainment of three mandarins aboard *Centurion,* before the ship was refitted and provisioned. On April 19, she weighed, made sail and stood out to sea, ostensibly for Batavia.

But that was camouflage. Anson anticipated that, as he had prevented the previous Manila ship from leaving Acapulco, there would more than likely be two vessels leaving Mexico that year; he took up station off Cape Espiritu Santo, Samar Island, where the treasure ships could be expected to make their first landfall in the Philippines some time in June. On May 31, an officer was writing in his journal, 'Exercising our men at their quarters, in great expectation of meeting with the galeons very soon . . .' and on June 11, . . . 'Begin to grow impatient at not seeing the galeons.'

At sunrise on June 20, a sail was reported in the south-east. At half-past seven she was recognisably a large Spanish galleon. To make the best use of his depleted crew against the fully manned heavily gunned Spaniard, Anson stationed two men at each gun simply to load it, while mobile parties of 10 or 12 men fired the guns as soon as they were ready. Rain squalls hid the galleon about noon but cleared to reveal her lying to, waiting for them. Towards one o'clock she was within gun shot, and Anson opened fire.

Keeping to leeward of her to prevent her escape, he lay on her bow, where, using his very wide gun ports, he could traverse almost all his guns upon the enemy, while the Spaniard could bring only some of hers to bear. Mats in the enemy's hammock nettings caught fire, hampering and demoralising her men, while *Centurion* maintained a rapid, unflagging cannonade, and sharpshooters in her tops did terrible execution on the galleon's upper decks. Finding himself close aboard her, Anson swept her decks with grape shot. Spanish gunfire dwindled as her surviving gunners deserted their quarters, and the vessel's wounded commander, General Don Jeronimo de Mentero, ordered the royal standard of Spain lowered from her main topgallant masthead. (The Spaniard had lost 67 dead from her crew of 550; Anson had two men killed. '. . . of so little consequence are the most destructive arms in untutored and unpractised hands,' reads the account.)

The long delay at Macao had caused Anson to miss the galleon's consort, which had reached Manila before *Centurion* arrived off Espiritu Santo, but the *Cabadonga,* a prize worth a million and a half dollars, was ample recompense. In her strongroom she carried 1,313,843 pieces of eight and 35,682 ounces of virgin silver, worth about £400,000, his share of which —not to mention the other booty—would make every one of *Centurion's* sailors who returned to England a rich man.

Returning to Canton, Anson took shelter there from seasonal hurricanes, spending the time by improving British links with the Viceroy, who received him in great splendour at the head of 10,000 troops. The troops were dressed in new uniforms for the occasion, but they by no means outshone the British Commodore's own small retinue of 19 sailors in scarlet jackets and blue silk waistcoats, the whole trimmed with silver buttons, with silver badges on jackets and caps. On December 15, 1743, *Centurion* got under sail for the long haul home, which was uneventful. Table Bay was reached on March 11, 1744. By June 12, the Lizard was in sight, 'and the 15th, in the evening, to their infinite joy, they came safe to an anchor at Spithead.'

Anson, dubbed 'the Father of the Navy', was created a peer in 1747, became First Lord of the Admiralty in 1751, and in 1761 was promoted Admiral of the Fleet. He died in 1762, aged sixty-five.

Left: Painting by John Clevely showing capture of the 'Nuestra Senora de Cabadonga' by 'Centurion' off the Philippines in 1743.
National Trust Shugborough (John Rackham)

Below far left: Colour engraving of Anson receiving a message that 'Centurion' is on fire.
Mary Evans Picture Library

Below: Burning by Anson's force of the town of Paita (Payta) in the South Seas.
Mary Evans Picture Library

Bottom: A view of Tinian, in the Marianas, where some of Anson's crews sought recuperation for a while.
Mary Evans Picture Library

DARWIN & THE BEAGLE

Below: Down House, Charles Darwin's residence in Kent, from a drawing in 'The Graphic' of July 1, 1882.
Illustrated London News

Right: The statue of Charles Darwin, in the Natural History Museum, London.
Illustrated London News

Far right: Drawing showing details of the 'Beagle's' construction, from Darwin's book 'A Naturalist's Voyage round the World'.
Murray

Below far right: Portrait of Robert Fitzroy.
National Maritime Museum London

HIS BRITANNIC MAJESTY'S 10-gun sloop *Beagle* was not very imposing in size. She was only 90 feet in length and of 242 tons displacement, but somehow she managed to accommodate, or rather stow, 74 or more people on board. Yet between 1831 and 1836 she sailed on a five-year voyage that has made her as famous as almost any ship in time of peace.

She owes her fame to Charles Robert Darwin who, before he sailed in her, was practically unknown. A graduate from Cambridge, he was on friendly terms with Adam Sedgwick, the professor of geology and with another professor, John Stevens Henslow, who lectured on botany. Instead of following his father's example and becoming a doctor, at the age of 23 Darwin was thinking of entering the Church, but natural history drew him and he spent some weeks with Professor Henslow in the Welsh mountains. Shortly afterwards he was surprised to get a letter saying that Henslow had recommended him as a naturalist for a voyage in the *Beagle*, which the Admiralty was sending to survey uncharted coasts in the southern hemisphere.

He wrote accepting the offer but his father persuaded him to write a second letter turning it down. However, Darwin's uncle, Josiah Wedgwood, of pottery fame, saw the advantage of the voyage and talked Charles's father into letting the young man go. So Charles Darwin wrote a third letter, again accepting; at a later interview by the captain of the *Beagle*, Robert Fitzroy, the two men, although poles apart in character and outlook, took a liking to each other on sight and he was engaged.

Joining the *Beagle*, he found on board two lieutenants, a surgeon and his assistant, the purser, one midshipman and a highly gifted artist, Augustus Earle, who came from America. There were the master and his two mates, the boatswain, the carpenter, two clerks, eight marines, 34 seamen and six boys. Also, there were four other passengers, three of them natives of Tierra del Fuego, north of Cape Horn, whom Fitzroy had taken on board in his previous voyage. In a gay moment he had named one man 'York Minster' and another, brighter and younger, 'Jeremy Buttons' while a pleasant young girl became 'Fuegian Basket'. Fitzroy had seen to their education in England and had displayed them to the King and Queen, who gave the girl a bonnet and a ring with money to buy clothes for herself. The fourth passenger was a young missionary who intended to land with them on Tierra del Fuego and remain to teach and minister to the natives in general.

The main objects of the *Beagle's* voyage were to chart the South American coast and to obtain accurate fixing of longitude by chronological reckonings. Fitzroy, a splendid navigator, was three years older than Darwin. Extremely hospitable and friendly from the first, he offered to share his cabin. That was not an unmixed blessing, as Darwin discovered only too abruptly the first night. His sleeping corner was so cramped that a drawer had to be taken out of a chest before he could stretch his legs in his hammock.

He and the captain came to know one another very well indeed. They invariably had their meals together and, for the earlier part of the voyage at least, had many an interesting talk. Darwin mentions how astonished he was to see an array of 22 chronometers so that Fitzroy could always be sure of having real accuracy.

The voyage had a belated start and it was December before the *Beagle* got under way, only to be forced back to port again twice by the weather, with Darwin suffering fierce bouts of seasickness each time. When they eventually did sail they took 63 days to cross the Atlantic and to make a landfall at Bahia, on the Brazilian coast.

Darwin had lost a little of his admiration of the captain after he had seen some Christmas roysterers among the crew sentenced by him in a sudden rage to be flogged. Fitzroy's outbursts of anger on little cause persisted throughout the voyage, interposed with long periods of cheerful conversation, though Darwin had to tread warily on any question of religion because Fitzroy proved to have a firm belief in the literal truth of every word of Holy Writ.

The *Beagle* followed the coast southward to Rio de Janeiro and there Darwin started a practice of leaving the ship to take an excursion whenever possible. With Augustus Earle he took lodgings in the town. Then with great good fortune he fell in with a party on horseback led by an Irishman bound for his plantation in the tropical forest. Soon he found himself in a strange world of beauty and wonder, continually discovering new surprises in sights and sounds and making good use of his collecting bottle.

He was horrified, however, by seeing the treatment the slaves received on the plantation. For example, one old lady he met kept thumb-screws for disciplining her female slaves by crushing their fingers. So shocked was Darwin that, on his return to the ship, he became involved in a furious argument with Fitzroy, who saw no evil in slavery. Darwin was actually on the point of walking off the *Beagle* but was stopped on deck by the first lieutenant, John Wickham, who talked him into staying.

When the ship sailed north to continue surveying, Darwin stayed at Rio for several months in company with Augustus Earle, the artist, and Midshipman King, while he spent his time collecting specimen insects and birds. The *Beagle* then collected the three of them and Fitzroy cruised south, charting the coasts of Patagonia. There at a little spot named Punta Alta, Darwin made one of his biggest discoveries in the fossilised skeletons of extinct prehistoric animals. He was delighted but they were no pleasure for the first lieutenant (the ship's husband) when the queer fragments were laid on his spotless deck, even though he had already endured slimy fish specimens thereon.

In spite of all that was said of him, Fitzroy, strangely enough, was adored by his men. The magnificent seamanship he

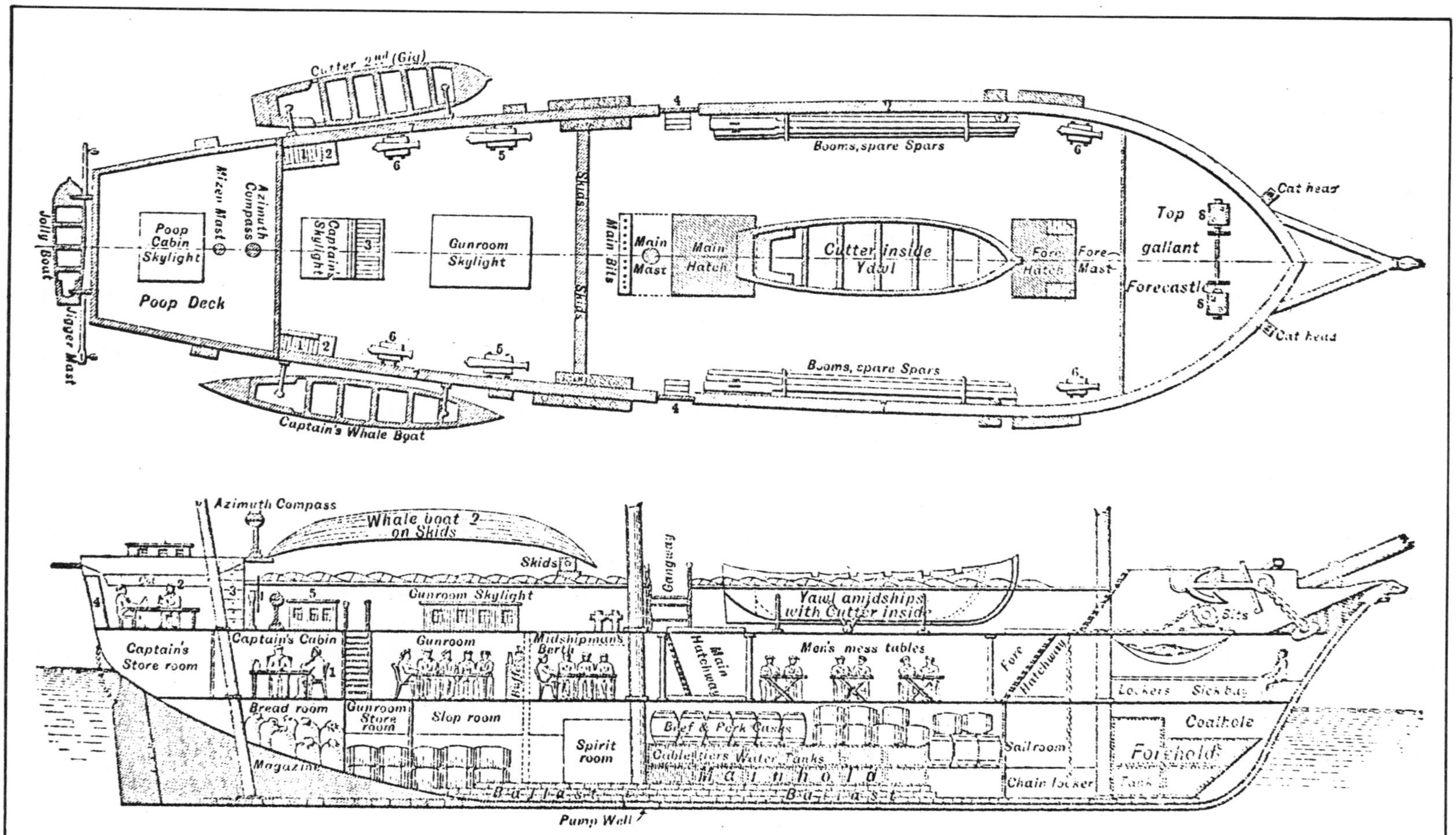

DIAGRAMS OF THE "BEAGLE."

displayed might have been a factor and it was badly needed, since the *Beagle* laboured for a month to round Cape Horn in mountainous seas which nearly swamped her again and again. Once the Horn was behind them, the three Fuegians were landed with the missionary and provided with suits of clothes, tents and all kinds of articles and gear that might be of help to their savage compatriots, who were watching them from a distance. The London Missionary Society had provided items such as tea-trays, crockery, white linen and wine-glasses.

When they had chosen a suitable place and were settled in, the *Beagle* sailed off to more charting. Ten days later she returned during one of her trips to obtain supplies and provisions, to find the camp wrecked and that the local Fuegians had stolen whatever took their fancy. Matthew, the missionary, had been knocked down and roughly treated, 'York Minster' had gone wild and even Miss 'Fuegian Basket' hid and sulked. Wisely, the missionary decided to give up and return to the ship.

A year passed before Fitzroy was able to pay another visit. 'Jeremy Buttons' was still there, friendly and giving presents but clad only in a loincloth instead of one of the splendid suits. Emaciated as he was from semi-starvation, he could not tear himself away from a new-found wife.

About that time the *Beagle's* surgeon was replaced by a younger doctor who took a keen interest in natural history. Thereby Darwin gained a fellow enthusiast always ready to lend a hand with his specimens. He was alone, however, when he was given a close demonstration of an earthquake, while walking on the southern Chilean coast. The shock was followed by three gigantic tidal waves which seem to have made him more interested than apprehensive.

Soon afterwards, in order to study geology in the mountains, he rode a distance of 500 miles from Patagonia on a mule, crossing the Cordilleras Mountains to a rendezvous with the *Beagle*. Then, as a result of the effects of a storm, Fitzroy decided that one ship was insufficient to survey the coast and he bought out of his own pocket an American sailing vessel of 170 tons, naming her *Adventure*. Leaving the ships busily charting Darwin stayed on shore for 10 weeks packing specimens of insects, fishes and mammals. One parcel alone that he sent to England held 1529 specimens. Aboard again, the ship sailed for New Zealand but the *Beagle* ran on to rocks at the mouth of the river Santa Cruz and there was considerable delay while carpenters repaired damage to the ship's bottom.

Fitzroy's temper was not improved by a letter which had eventually reached him from the Admiralty. It forcefully ordered him to dispose of the *Adventure* forthwith and to discharge the additional sailors he had taken on. It was not all loss however; he sold the *Adventure* at a slight profit.

At last the *Beagle* sailed for the Galapagos Islands. There Darwin was in a magical world. On one island alone he counted 26 species of land birds and he found that, due to the islands' isolation, the majority of the specimens were of unique species of plants, reptiles, birds, fish and shells; many species varied in some form from island to island. He had much to interpret. The giant turtles fascinated him and in high spirits he temporarily gave up natural history to ride on the back of one monster. But there was only too much evidence on the beaches that the crews of whalers looked upon the islands as a living larder and that the turtles were rapidly diminishing.

From the Galapagos the ship voyaged to Tahiti, then to New Zealand and on to Australia and various island groups where Darwin studied coral formations. Then, when all hands were looking forward to rounding the Cape of Good Hope homeward bound, the captain decreed that they must take the longer route by way of South America.

Finally they reached England after a voyage lasting nearly five years. For a long time Darwin worked feverishly sorting and classifying enormous unending collections of specimens, writing and meditating over the theory of the origin of life that was rapidly developing into conviction in his mind. There were books and articles to write and then the momentous meeting of the British Association and the clash of two opposing views, the new and the old, the latter typified by Bishop Wilberforce, unkindly known as 'Soapy Sam'. Not the least disturbing was the interruption of his old captain and one-time friend, Vice-Admiral Robert Fitzroy the fundamentalist, who expostulated 'If I had known what was in my ship . . .'; but he was mercifully shouted down.

Darwin never left England again. He moved to the fine Victorian country home at Down House, near the Kentish village of Downe. There he developed a mysterious illness and a moodiness which he tried to counter by throwing himself into his work, his writings and his amplification of the theory that had taken his name across the world. The illness and the moods had him firmly in their grasp until he died at the age of 73. But he laid the foundation of the theory of evolution that has placed him among the greatest of great pioneers.

Below: The 'Beagle' pictured in Sydney Harbour, Australia.
National Maritime Museum London

An early mariner's compass exhibited in the Naval Museum at Genoa-Pegli, Italy, probably dating from about the 16th century. The crude magnetic compass using lodestone was known to the ancient Chinese and was in use in Europe by the end of the first millenium AD. The pivot-mounted needle of magnetised iron over a compass card divided into 32 points had been introduced by about the 15th century but a precision-engineered instrument did not come into general use until the 18th century.
M Pucciarelli

THE CHALLENGER AND CHARTING

AFTER HMS *Challenger* had seen 15 years of not very notable service as a 22-gun corvette, in 1870 she underwent a transformation. She was berthed in Sheerness Dockyard, where all her guns were taken out except two, and those were left for signal purposes, not for war. Then she was given a thorough overhaul from keel to truck. Bulkheads between decks were knocked down and rearranged to make new stowage spaces and cabins.

Challenger's preparation for a new role was mainly due to the President of the Royal Society, who felt strongly that an oceanic expedition was badly needed and was in fact long overdue. He had approached the Admiralty Hydrographer, the head of the Naval Survey Service which had been formed at the turn of the century to record and index surveys made by navigators from Captain Cook onwards. The Admiralty gave its approval to the project and the hydrographer made it his business to see that the ship was suitably equipped.

The command of the ship was given to Captain George Nares, who was 39 years of age and, according to a brother officer, 'a devilish good fellow'. Born in Aberdeen, Nares had gone through the usual naval training for cadet and midshipman and had then taken part in the Arctic expedition which in 1852 tried to find Sir John Franklin. After serving in the Crimean War he had gained experience in deep-water dredging for biological specimens from two small gunboats, the *Lightning* and the *Porcupine*, and it was probably that experience that led to his being given the command.

Three days before Christmas he sailed the *Challenger* to Portsmouth. She was the first ship of the Royal Navy to be specially fitted out for oceanography and had on board thousands of fathoms of $\frac{1}{2}$-inch rope made from Italian hemp, probably the major item of her surveying equipment. At Portsmouth the civilian members of the expedition joined the ship, headed by Professor Charles Wyville Thomson, a noted maritime biologist. With his friend Dr W B Carpenter he had sailed earlier on trips in the *Lightning* and the *Porcupine* to chart the seabed between the Scottish mainland and the Faroes and had found life existing at a depth of 600 fathoms (3600 feet).

In the *Challenger* he had the company of three naturalists of various kinds. There were John Murray, Professor H N Moseley, who, forever an eager observer, was called 'a seagoing Pepys', and Rudolf van Willimoes-Suhm. In addition there was John Young Buchanan, a chemist and physicist. Unfortunately Willimoes-Suhm died after contracting an illness on the voyage.

John Wild, of Swiss nationality, went as the official artist and also acted as secretary to Dr Thomson. A fellow artist was a very gifted navigating sub-lieutenant, Herbert Swire, who kept a continual record of the interesting natives and scenes as they sailed, from birds to sunsets. The second-in-command of the ship was Commander J L P Maclear and the survey work was in the hands of the navigating lieutenant, T H Tizard. It was fortunate that Professor Thomson in particular and Captain Nares were able to work together in harmony throughout Nares's stay in the ship and, in fact, the voyage in general seems to have had a cordial atmosphere.

Before they sailed the purpose of the expedition had been set out in broad terms and approved by the Naval Survey Service. The aim was to investigate the physical condition of the deeper seas in the great ocean basins up to the southern ice barrier. Depths, temperatures, currents, circulation, specific gravity and penetration of light were all to be studied. Secondly the chemical condition of the sea water at various depths from the surface to the bottom were to be examined for organic matter in solution and particles in suspension. There were to be studies of the distribution of organic life at different depths of the ocean floors. Apparently there was no time limit for the expedition and no rigid programme.

After the *Challenger* had been at sea for a week or two and had shaken down into a routine life, training began in the work of dredging, sounding and the taking of samples. Later would come the messy business of sorting out on deck their hauls of unfamiliar fish, corals and sponges.

The ship had a twin-cylinder engine which could give her eight knots and Nares made a practice of using it for moving to fresh areas, and then disconnecting the propeller and hoisting it out of the way so that he could work on site under the steadier motion of sail.

Before starting serious work he put into Lisbon, where the King of Portugal visited the ship and wished the expedition well, making a pleasant beginning for the years ahead. Soon work started in earnest and the voyage ceased to be any kind of pleasure cruise. There was so much to do and so much to learn with all the wide oceans to cross and recross, sounding and trawling—and parting ropes until the handlers learned the trick of using them. At least they seem to have been saved the worst of the rolling and rough motion of the seas by a device designed to steady the ship when the hauling ropes were over the side. It was a contraption of wood and long ropes of rubber which is said to have been a splendid shock-absorber.

Below left: The crusader figurehead of HMS 'Challenger'. *Fleet Public Relations Officer (photo Institute of Oceanographic Sciences)*

Right: A collection of frail shells brought back from the 'Challenger's' voyage. *Institute of Oceanographic Sciences*

Below: Engraving depicting HMS 'Challenger' at sea. *Institute of Oceanographic Sciences*

From Lisbon Nares sailed to Halifax, Nova Scotia. Thereafter Bermuda, the Cape of Good Hope, Sydney and Melbourne, Fiji, the Philippines, Yokohama and Montevideo are only a few of very many ports of call. He voyaged in great sweeps across the globe with one diversion so far to the southward as to meet pack-ice and to collide at night with an iceberg, though fortunately without more damage than a broken spar. Altogether he crossed the Equator six times.

His voyaging was interrupted when he put in to Hong Kong; a letter for him arrived from the Admiralty offering him the command of the expedition which was to be formed to attempt to reach the North Pole in 1874 from HM ships *Alert* and *Discovery*. The compliment was too great for Nares to decline. He handed over command of the *Challenger* to an officer at Hong Kong, Captain Frank Tourle Thomson, for him to continue the survey.

By far the greater part of Nares's work was done. He had laid the foundations of modern oceanography and he brought home with him some of the results, including a

few charts of the deep seas. In order to obtain them, the ship had slowly voyaged a total of 68,890 nautical miles in 3½ years and in doing so had consumed 4700 tons of coal. In the course of the exacting work 144 members of the crew of her complement of 243 remained throughout. There had been seven deaths and 26 men had been invalided out of the Navy or had been left in hospital on shore; five others had gone with Captain Nares to the Arctic. The greatest depth of ocean that had been plumbed was 4500 fathoms (27,000 feet), a figure that was not to be equalled for a long time and one that was so astonishing as to be looked upon with suspicion in more than one quarter.

The ship returned to England in May 1876 by way of the Strait of Magellan, having sent on ahead in other vessels her wealth of reports on the ocean depths and their composition, the biological discoveries of new species and of the distribution, both vertical and horizontal, of the fauna.

Apart from the official reports, several accounts of the voyage were written by some of the naval officers. Sub-Lieutenant Swire both wrote and illustrated an attractive description, from which much of this article is taken. Engineer Sub-Lieutenant Spry published repeated editions of his own story and J J Wild, the artist, also produced one. Of the naturalists, there was Henry Moseley's *Notes of a Naturalist* and Sir Charles Wyville Thomson's *Voyage of the Challenger*. Sir Charles was appointed editor of the official report, which ultimately filled 50 large volumes, but unhappily he died within the first six years, due it was believed to the burden of such a work. John Murray, later Sir John, was chosen to take his place.

As to the stout ship herself, today she would probably have been preserved for future generations to admire. But with the usual lack of imagination of the period she was commissioned as a coastguard and drill-ship at Harwich in 1876 and was paid off two years later. In 1883 she was converted into a receiving-hulk for new naval entries and moored in the Medway at Chatham, unsightly but useful. In 1921 the shipbreakers had her, but at least her figurehead has survived.

Above: Natives of New Guinea fleeing from the path of the unfamiliar spectacle of the 'Challenger's' steam launch.
Cassels History of England (*K Robins Collection*)

Right: A portrait by Stephen Pearle of Captain George Nares, master of the 'Challenger'.
National Maritime Museum London

Bottom: Officers of HMS 'Challenger' assembled on her deck; the captain is seated in the front row holding a straw hat.
Trustees of British Museum (*Natural History*)

4. Ships of War

The Venetian Argosy

VENICE, for long the Queen of the Adriatic, was to become, at her peak, the most powerful state in the Western world. Closely linked to the sea as she was, her outlook and, indeed, her very life were in her fine ships. In the early days she discovered the value of her salt-pans and, never backward in any prospect of gain, she traded ever more widely with Syria, Dalmatia and other parts of the Levant, making good profit from the specially built vessels.

Soon, the Venetians had a fleet strong enough to come to the help of the Byzantine Empire. The mighty Doge, their head of government, in person led Venetian galleys to rescue the Imperial ships which had been cut off by Saracens in southern Italy. Once again, in the 11th century, Venetian galleys beat off an attack, on Constantinople itself, by Dalmatian pirates. In return for their services, the Greek Emperor gave the Venetians free access to all parts of his dominion for their trading. He also made them a gift of a Dalmatian forest, thereby saving Venice any worry over the supply of timber for shipbuilding.

A major opportunity came to Venice with the start of the Crusades in 1095. She contributed 200 galleys for the First Crusade, at a price. But her most profitable transaction was at the time of the Fourth Crusade, in 1198. The Doge, Enrico Dandolo, undertook to provide King Louis of France with sea transport for his army of Crusaders to the Holy Land on certain terms. In addition to sending 50 of her own armed galleys, Venice was to build for the French enough shipping to carry 9000 knights, 20,000 sergeants-at-arms on foot and 4500 horses. Dandolo agreed to provision them all for the period of one year. In return Venice would receive one-half of any land or other property that might be captured and would be paid the sum (which is variously estimated) of 85,000 silver marks.

When it came to the point and the ships had been built, the amount of cash proved to be beyond the capacity of the French to pay. Dandolo then suggested a compromise. If the French, before they sailed to Palestine, would turn aside and help to discipline Constantinople, which had latterly become a nuisance to Venice, then he would be ready to reconsider the terms. Constantinople, of course, was known by all to be very rich.

The French agreed and so there was perpetrated an appalling crime against humanity and Christianity at a cost of undying shame. But Venice gained half the city and also facilities for trade by sea and overland. She also annexed a number of the Aegean Islands as well as Crete and the port of Zara from Hungary. And at last she had won her 170-year struggle with her rival, Genoa, for the command of the Mediterranean. Every sea, it seemed, was hers.

By that time, the Venetian argosies, alternatively called Flanders galleys, had begun regular voyages from Venice to the Low Countries and up the Thames to London. They had been built as merchant vessels for carrying wine, spices and special cargoes such as Eastern silks and the lace and glassware for which Venice had become famous. Manned by a small crew for handling sail, they were rowed double-banked by about 80 or more unfortunate galley-slaves. They were of the usual carvel build of planks edge-to-edge, with sharp bow and stern but full body amidships to give a large stowage capacity. The two masts were lateen-rigged, as was to be expected in Mediterranean ships, and it is a possibility that their repeated arrivals in Northern Europe brought the pattern for the fore-and-aft rig used on many Dutch vessels.

For a lengthy period, the galley was the supreme ship. Indeed, it had become so long before Charles of Anjou, who was King of Naples in 1260, ordered a number of them from Venice. One record gives the measurements of the ships as 28.20 metres on the keel and 35.50 metres overall length, with beam of 3.70 metres and depth of 2.08 metres, though such a length/breadth ratio would have been more suitable to a warship than a merchantman.

After the 14th century, the power of the Venetian galleys was increased by adding to the length of their oars. The ships bought by Charles of Anjou were said to have 108 oars 7.90 metres long. The rowlocks, instead of being fixed in the gunwale, were set away from the hull on the rail of an outrigger which passed round the entire ship. In addition to the added leverage it

Below left: A painting of Venice by Canaletto: 'The Basin of S Marco on Ascension Day'. *National Gallery London*

Below: An early engraving showing shipping at Venice. *Mary Evans Picture Library*

Right: A 15th-century colour impression of a shipyard from the Marciana Library in Venice. *M Pucciarelli*

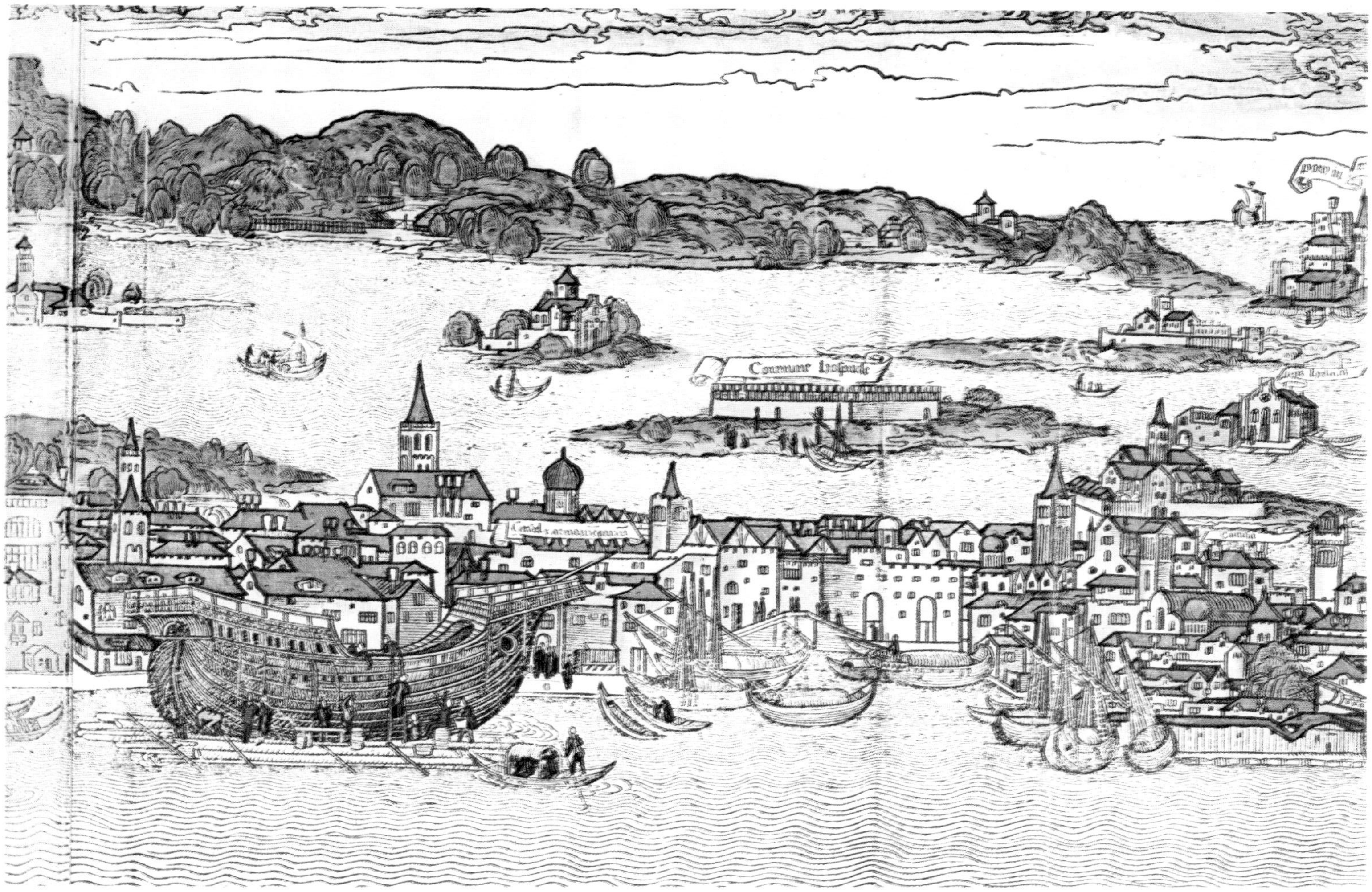

gave the oars, it served also to reduce the effect of being rammed.

The Flanders galleys were invariably escorted out of the Mediterranean and beyond by war-galleys, chiefly to ward off lurking pirates. The warships were armed with five small guns in the forecastle, the first cannon to be introduced into Italy. They fired only little stone balls but they were alarming enough for one Arab spectator, who wrote, 'You would think it the very thunder of God'. The galley of the Venetian argosy in time developed into the galleass, a larger and more powerful vessel. With three masts, the galleass relied more on sails than oars, despite the large number of rowers.

At the start of the 16th century, when she was at war with Turkey, Venice was said to employ 16,000 workmen, caulkers, carpenters, and painters—and 36,000 seamen. During one period at the Arsenal, one of the most stupendous nautical establishments in the world, a new galley was completed every morning for a hundred consecutive days.

But by then, Venice was soon to be involved in the great battle of Lepanto and, although she was on the winning side in that terrible fight, it marked the end of her triumphal progress. Gradually she began to wither, losing prestige, trade, her islands and her lands, until the Venetian argosies sailing to the northward with their rich cargoes had become only a memory of the past.

Above: A 14th-century impression of V from a manuscript in the Bodleian Libra *Mary Evans Picture Library*

Below: Model of a 16th-century Veneti trireme galley in the Naval Museum at Spezia. *M Pucciarelli*

THE GALLEON

BY THE LATE 15TH CENTURY English merchants were sending their own ships to the Mediterranean instead of depending on Italian-owned carracks and merchant galleys. This resulted in an exchange of nautical ideas and also brought English ships into conflict with the Barbary Corsairs and other enemies.

The traditional fighting ship of that sea was the long low galley driven by oars, and in the local conditions it could be a very formidable foe, well able to outmanoeuvre and board the slow tubby sail-driven northern merchantmen. The answer was powerful guns, and to be most effective against galleys they had to be close to the water. But such guns were so heavy that they needed a hull of merchant ship type to carry them. Thus far, naval guns were small and were mounted in the upperworks of carracks, and as galleys usually attacked from ahead or astern, only a few could be brought to bear and in any case they were too light to have much effect. As well as heavier guns, handier ships were needed, able to twist and turn to keep their broadsides towards the enemy.

The Italian states were experimenting with large galleys, based on their merchant galleys, with a stout timber fort armed with guns forward and a few guns along the sides above the oars; they were galleasses but they were only partially successful. Moreover, they were heavy to row and slow when compared with ordinary galleys,

Below: The galleon 'Santa Anna', from a drawing by R Morton Nance as it appeared in 'The Mariners' Mirrour' Vol 1. *K Fenwick Collection*

Bottom: Watercolour by Kenneth D Shoesmith of a 16th-century high-built Spanish galleon leaving Spain for South America. *Illustrated London News*

as well as being poor seaboats and unsuited to Atlantic or North Sea conditions. They were pure fighting ships and merely heavy reinforcements to normal galley fleets. What was really needed was some combination of the qualities of both carrack and galley, and many years passed before the compromise was found.

Two ships of novel design joined Henry VII's fleet in 1497, the *Mary Fortune* and *Sweepstake.* They were only about 80 tons in the measurement of the time but they were sea-going ships with high seaworthy hulls, yet they also had such rowing power that the *Mary Fortune* had 52 'long ores' and the *Sweepstake* 60. Their armament, however, was light, for they had only four gunners and the shot they carried was 'dyce of yron' (small shot). They were re-built and renamed in either 1511 or 1512 and remained in the lists until 1527. Towards the end of their service they were called rowbarges, a name also applied to a short-lived type of 20-ton rowing craft built by Henry VIII. The French copied them and turned the English name into roberges, saying of them that 'they were shorter and higher than galleys or galleasses and better able to encounter the waves of the ocean'. They also inspired a succession of experimental craft built by Henry VIII and called galleys, galleasses or galleons.

Henry VIII had the faults of the other Tudors, but his love of ships played an important part in the foundation of English sea power, while his taste for noise and bluster led to his deep interest in cannon of the most powerful types, which provided his ships with fighting powers hitherto unknown. He knew more about ships (at least in theory) than most kings of England and considered himself an amateur ship-master and pilot. He had a mariner's dress made of cloth-of-gold and a 'whistle' (bosun's pipe, then the insignia of a sea-officer) of 'unicorn's horn' (narwhal's tusk) which he wore on a golden chain. He claimed to be the actual designer of many of his experimental ships—which might only mean that he told his master ship-wright, James Baker, his ideas and left the practical man to carry them out. Whenever a new ship joined his fleet, or an old one had been altered, he required a full report of its sailing and other qualities, and even during his last illness he wrote to ask how the latest one 'was able to brook the seas'.

A Frenchman named Descharges was the first shipwright known to have risked weakening a ship by piercing its hull for guns; but his ports were round and small, and were closed in bad weather by sheepskin bags over both gun muzzles and portholes. In England gun ports were soon adopted for Henry's ships and improved by making them square so that lids could be fitted and the guns run in, bringing their weight farther inboard and making it possible to seal the ports more effectively than leather bags could do; the credit for the change was given to James Baker.

Carracks being well-tried, Henry retained them in his fleet and in the earlier part of his reign hired them out (like earlier sovereigns) to merchants for trading voyages. But he soon grasped the novel conception that big guns might be better

battle winners than boarders. Light guns in the castles could never be that and the few heavy guns already being mounted in ships were short-range breech-loaders which did little damage to a ship's structure except at the closest range. He had heard that bell-founders in Italy and the Low Countries were casting long-range muzzle-loading bronze guns that could take a powder charge which would blow the chamber out of a breech-loader. These guns were reputed to throw iron balls with such force that they could demolish stone walls. Henry coveted them, but they were very costly.

His father had left him rich but his Tudor thrift worried him when money was required for state purposes. However, his own pleasures were a different matter—and ships and guns were among his hobbies. In the first year of his reign he bought enough tin and brass to make one hundred bronze guns and appointed one Humphrey Walker 'Gunner at the Tower'. The following year, 1510, he commissioned 48 from the famous Hans Poppenruyter of Malines and when they were delivered he tried them on a row of houses in Hounds-ditch. Delighted at the results, he ordered another hundred; a weapon that could demolish a row of houses or breach a fortress could also pierce the sides of ships. Soon England was turning out both bronze and iron guns of high quality in large numbers, made by imported foreign experts and English craftsmen until the latter had mastered the techniques required. By the decade 1520 to 1530 English guns were in such demand abroad that Henry banned their export. He thus amassed the largest artillery park in any country and the Venetian ambassador wrote that Henry had 'enough cannon to conquer Hell'.

Henry was getting the guns he wanted,

but is was more difficult to devise the right ships to carry them. Something nimbler and more weatherly than the cumbrous carrack was needed to make the best use of them; yet only a carrack with her large cargo capacity could carry the weight of his heavy guns. He approached the problem in two ways. First, he converted ordinary carracks, for if the ships could carry cargo, he thought, they could equally well carry a similar weight of guns. Mariners and shipwrights objected that cargo below the water line and guns above it were very different things when it came to a ship's stability; but they valued their necks more than he did, so the cargoes came out of the royal ships and the guns went in.

The ships became so packed with ordnance that their seamen begged to have them lightened. As early as 1512 the lord admiral, Sir Edward Howard, complained that his ship was so 'overladen with ordnance' that she could not carry sail; and it was over-gunning that was to cause the loss of the *Mary Rose* many years later. After 1533 Henry stopped trying to hire his ships to merchants. He had destroyed their value as cargo carriers, but he was unrepentant, although his pocket was touched.

Facing page above left: Model of an Elizabethan galleon of 1600.
Science Museum London (Crown copyright)

Facing page left: The 'Anne Gallant' of 1545 as depicted in the Anthony Anthony Rolls.
K Fenwick Collection

Facing page top: Engraving of a typical 16th-century galleon.
Mary Evans Picture Library

Top: A painting by Norman Wilkinson of the 'Henri Grâce à Dieu' of 1514. *M Muir Collection*

Above left: Model of a galleon-type vessel used as a restaurant in Disneyland, California. *D J Kingston*

Left: Henry VIII's 'Great Bark' (formerly the 'Great Galley') of 1515.
K Fenwick Collection

His second approach was even more important. The French had a way of bringing galleys round from the Mediterranean for summer forays against the English coast, and he needed fast rowing craft to deal with them. In the calm weather the French chose, carracks could not get near them as they just rowed away out of gunshot. To counter them Henry built rowbarges, galleys, galleasses, galleons and barks, but those names had no real meaning (except that the ships referred to had oars) and were often all applied at different times to the same ships. Originally, galleons were a type of Mediterranean galley but Henry's rowing craft were small true ships with oars, quite unlike Mediterranean galleys. The years to 1530 were a period of experiment as type after type of rowing craft was built, tried and discarded, but all the time experience was gradually being gained.

Without his knowing it, Henry might partially have solved the problem as early as 1515. He had already built his giant carrack, the *Great Harry,* and then he wanted the largest galleass as well. The result was the *Great Galley,* a monster of 800 Tudor tons with 60 oars a side and the full four-masted rig of a large carrack. Built at Greenwich, she carried 217 guns (mostly small) and was disappointing in service. She was clinker built and too big for that method, so the hull worked alarmingly in a seaway and leaked abominably; she was described as 'the dangeroust ship under water that ever man sailed in'.

Also, she was far too heavy to row. However, she had some good qualities, for she was thought worth replanking carvel fashion in 1523 and then remained in service as a galleass for another 15 years; then, in 1538, she was still good enough for rebuilding as a pure sailing ship and was renamed the *Great Bark.* In this form she served until 1562. Unfortunately her proportions have not been preserved, nor has her performance under sail. But as she was built for both rowing and sailing, she must have had more length to beam than previous sailing ships of her size. That she sailed better than she rowed is proved by her conversion into a pure sailing ship. After her oars were discarded she might well have been the first true sailing galleon.

Meanwhile Henry called in the acknowledged experts in galley construction, Venetian shipwrights, in the hope that they could solve his problems. Francesco Bressan, the head shipwright, had invented a bastard galley with both ship and galley features and another of his family 'a most beautiful galleon' design, which might not have got beyond the model stage. Then Vettor Fausto designed a large and powerful vessel which, he claimed, could be used either for trade or war, and he called her a galleon. Launched at Venice on October 10, 1531, she was referred to only as 'The Galleon of Venice'. The French naval historian Admiral Jurien de la Gravière says of her 'this galleon, bristling from stem to stern with guns, seemed, by her vast bulk, a floating citadel, a sort of helepole, behind which the fleet of galleys could manoeuvre in safety . . . She was known as a good sailer'.

After some modifications, the vessel served against the Turks in 1537. Then on September 27, 1538, she earned undying glory at the Battle of Prevesa. Separated from the rest of the Christian fleet, she was caught while becalmed by 140 Turkish galleys. From one o'clock until sunset successive waves of them assailed her in line abreast, 15 or 20 at a time, discharging their bow guns and then

Below: Model of the 'Great Michael' of 1511, now in the Royal Scottish Museum, Edinburgh. *K Fenwick Collection*

Bottom: Painting by Charles Dixon of the 'Henri Grâce a Dieu' ('Great Harry') from the book 'The Sea Its History and Romance'. *K Fenwick Collection*

Right: Drawing from the Anthony Anthony Rolls of the 'Grand Mistress' of 1545. *Science Museum London (K Fenwick)*

Below right: The replica of the 'Golden Hind' moored in the Pool of London in April 1974. *D J Kingston*

Far right: Painting of a typical 17th-century warship by Charles Dixon. *K Fenwick Collection*

withdrawing to make way for the next wave of attackers. She ended the battle a shattered wreck but undefeated and was finally rescued by Christian galleys. The Turks had the better of the battle, but this one ship had plainly shown that the future of naval warfare lay with heavily gunned ships. Small wonder that Henry thought men from Venetian shipyards could help him.

In 1541 the Spanish ambassador told Charles V that Henry had 'sent to Italy for three shipwrights experienced in the art of constructing galleys; but I fancy he will not make much use of their science, as for some time back he has been building ships with oars to a model of which he was himself the inventor'. The ambassador was right; they could teach little except improving the English shipwrights' carvel building methods, for Henry in his restless search for the right ships to carry his guns had produced much more seaworthy rowing ships than the Mediterranean countries had done, for all their reputation and experience. They did in fact build him a Mediterranean galley, but she required more than 200 rowers, which was why galley navies used slaves; free rowers cost too much. Galley slaves were not used in England and free rowers were very difficult to recruit. Henry's English rowing ships spent most of their sea time under sail and their crews were prepared to row for short periods in calms or in and out of harbour; but full-time rowing did not appeal to them at all.

The French had copied Henry's row-barges and some of his other rowing ships. When his forces captured Leith in 1544 they brought back 'two goodly shyppes', the *Salamander* and *Unicorn*, which had been presented by Francis I to James V of Scotland. They dated from 1537 and were French versions of Henry's largest galleys. The greatest French contribution to sailing galleons were privateers, and especially those of one shipowner, Jean Ango of Dieppe, whose ships preyed on the Spanish treasure flotas. He built fast low corsairs designed for the purpose and one of them, referred to as the 'Galleon of Dieppe', was taken by the English in 1524 and might well have given Henry and his shipwrights ideas. By the 1570s French sailing galleons were so good that Drake used a ship 'of French build' for his voyage round the world (1577-1580); but it is not clear whether the *Golden Hind* was built in France or was an English copy of a French design.

In 1545 Henry launched two ships of about 450 tons that were the culmination of all efforts. While they were building the *Grand Mistress* and *Anne Gallant* were called galleons but during their service they were classed with the galleasses. They were in fact true sailing galleons and there was to be no further progress until Elizabeth's reign. Both are portrayed in the Anthony Anthony Rolls and are enlarged versions of the most successful earlier galley-ships, but if they had oars they must have worked through the gun ports as no oar ports are shown. They were lower and more weatherly than their Elizabethan successors, yet in spite of their success as fighting ships they were allowed to rot after Henry's death. By 1552 the *Grand Mistress* was unseaworthy and was sold out of the service by 1555, while the *Anne Gallant* is not in the lists after 1559.

Their story is ironic. Henry had witnessed the fight in Spithead, when the over-gunned *Mary Rose* filled and sank and the French galleys concentrated on the *Great Harry* until the English light forces came up and drove the enemy back upon their own fleet. During the two days of fighting the big ships never came to grips and only Henry's light craft, although heavily outnumbered, did very much.

Three weeks later another battle was fought, off Shoreham. The English were in three divisions, one being composed of 'the ships with oars' to act as a fast squadron, and the *Grand Mistress* and *Anne Gallant* were included, a proof that they were considered fit to act with rowing vessels. The wind was light, the sea calm at first—perfect weather for Mediterranean galleys—and the French got the weather gage. On August 15, 1545, they attacked and were very roughly handled. The lord admiral, Lord Lisle, reported that 'the *Grand Mistress* and *Anne Gallant* did so handle the (enemy's) galleys, as well with their (broad) sides as with their prows, that your great ships in a manner had little to do'. The two galleons had been more than a match for galleys, using their guns and spurs with great effect. They were helped by a change of weather, for the wind freshened and enabled them to make full use of their sail-power to outpace the galleys and then use both spurs and guns.

The new ships were what Henry had worked for throughout his reign and he did not realise it. He had not seen them in action off Shoreham and he had seen the French galleys at Spithead. So instead of more *Grand Mistresses* and *Anne Gallants* his building programme for 1546 comprised four galleasses of an inferior design to the galleons and 14 rowbarges to deal with the situation he had seen at Spithead—one which was unlikely to recur, and never did. Henry died on January 28, 1547, without knowing that he had given England ships whose successors, with little modification, would before the century ended turn England from a small island into a great power.

Galleons of the southern nations were more indebted than England's to the Mediterranean galleass, indeed the Portuguese galleon *São João* of 1534 was a galleass forward and almost a carrack aft. For many years Mediterranean galleasses had three-masted lateen rigs, but towards the end of the century some were square rigged, making them, in effect, rowing galleons.

The beginnings of Spanish galleons are even more obscure than in other countries, but were certainly on Mediterranean galleass lines. Carracks suited Spain so well that at first there was little need for change. Spain had the finest infantry in the world and carracks provided the soldiers with floating castles from which to fight in land fashion. The raids of French and English warships and privateers on the treasure routes from the Americas to Spain eventually demanded new ideas at sea. From the early 1560s Spain's great admiral, Santa Cruz (1526-1588), realised the urgent need for the new galleon type armed with heavy guns to protect the flotas. He therefore designed a class of large war galleons especially for this purpose. At first they patrolled the most vulnerable area, between Spain and the Azores, but that merely forced the raiders farther out into the Atlantic.

Pedro Menéndez de Avilés (1519-1574) was captain-general of the flotas for three separate periods, and he introduced a convoy system, using the big war galleons as escorts right across the Atlantic. But such convoys were slow, so he also designed an original, and very successful, fast but powerfully armed ship, the gallizabra, which the English called a treasure frigate. Intended for small but valuable cargoes—gold, silver and precious stones—the gallizabras sailed without escort, being fast enough to avoid big war galleons yet so heavily armed that they could fight off the smaller raiders which were fast enough to get close to them. They were, in fact, a very specialised form of galleon. Sir Richard Hawkins was so impressed by them when he was a prisoner of the Spaniards that he tried in vain to get them introduced into the English Navy. Avilés's arrangements were so effective that from 1567 to 1627 the flotas and gallizabras rarely fell prey to the corsairs.

Meanwhile Sir Richard's father, Sir John Hawkins, was building galleons for Elizabeth's fleet. They carried on where Henry VIII's galleons left off, but in one way they were retrograde, for the castles fore and aft were increased in height, although not to the degree they had reached in carracks. It made them less weatherly but was necessary to satisfy the majority of seamen who still clung to the idea of dominating an enemy from high castles. Even so, they were the best ships for war or commerce yet devised, especially after they were given sails made to measure instead of the mere wind-bags formerly used. The main difference between war and merchant galleons was the introduction of special gun decks and heavier guns in the former, but the merchantmen still carried enough guns to be valuable additions to a fleet in war time.

After the Spanish Armada fighting had shown the superiority of English galleons, the Spaniards copied them, but as much larger ships which in time blended with the Santa Cruz galleons, both for war and cargo, and made such general use of these ships that it became traditional to call all Spanish treasure ships galleons, even as late as the 18th century, by which time English seamen had corrupted the word into galloon.

GALLEYS AND GALLEASSES

THE MERE MENTION of a war-galley can conjure up visions of galley-slaves collapsing over their oars. Usually, of course, in antiquity the oars were manned by slaves and in later times either by criminals or by prisoners-of-war, when conditions were much the same. In favourable weather the shapely vessel could also travel swiftly under sail alone. Long, very long, lean and low in the water, with shallow draught, the galley was in a class by itself, changing little over the years in build and rig.

The galley was not robust, in fact, it was lightly built; but it was at home in the short choppy seas of the Mediterranean as it would never have been in the open Atlantic. From early in the 15th century onward, every state and country of any consequence in the Mediterranean basin, from Turkey to the Knights of St John, had its fleet of war-galleys, though in varying degrees of decorative magnificence.

The largest numbers of them were those of Venice and Spain, both of which could at one time muster a hundred. The Spanish galleys were based on Catagena, chiefly to protect shipping from the Turkish and Berber pirates. There, the Spaniards had started manning their craft with infantry soldiers as oarsmen but quickly found the idea to be unworkable. Then convicts or other wrongdoers took their place on the benches and, it was reported, were 'treated like volunteers'. Judging from the later reputation of the Spanish galleys, the volunteer spirit does not appear to have been at all long-lived.

In the 15th century the oars were ranged in groups of three, with one man to each, until it was found to be more efficient and simpler to have several rowers on one oar, which was made much longer and heavier. By the 17th century, French galleys at least were equipped with as many as 33 pairs for five, six, or seven men pulling together on each bench. Usually the looms, or handles, of the oars had wooden cleats nailed to them in series of six or seven handgrips. Otherwise the wretched rowers had scanty consideration. They were chained to the bench, which was about ten feet long and four wide, and there they sat, perhaps all day long with one naked foot on the stretcher and the other raised and on the bench in front. On those benches, covered with sacking and stuffed with wool, men rowed, suffered and died.

One Frenchman, Jean Marteille de Bergerac, who had the misfortune to be sentenced in 1707 to his country's galleys, for the crime of being a Protestant, so he declares, wrote an account of his experiences. He describes how, when at sea, the master of the galleys was positioned aft beside the captain to hear his orders, while two under-officers were positioned one amidships and the other at the bows. All carried and used whips for flogging the entirely nude bodies of the rowers, who had to be kept alert for the sound of a whistle which gave them various orders to be obeyed at once.

The writer states that the men, including of course himself, had to row 10, 12 and even over 20 hours at a stretch. Any rowers who collapsed were given pieces of bread soaked in wine as a stimulant, but if all efforts failed to rouse them they were flogged and thrown overboard. He adds that the galley was not as fast as he expected and he estimated her speed as being no more than four-and-a-half knots, or rather less than five miles an hour.

Another French victim has given some additional details of his short but horrible time when chained to a bench. In his case, each oar had seven rowers. He was surprised to see the large number of men there were on board in such a remarkably small space and he mentions that few of the oarsmen had room to sleep at full length. Up forward were 30 sailors on a platform which he guessed to be about ten by eight feet. They were carried chiefly to fight off an enemy at the bows and to tend the two large lateen sails, which could give some respite to the rowers from their grinding labour at the oars.

At the other end of the vessel the captain and officers lived in a cabin on the poop, where their cramped state and general conditions were not so much better than those of the seamen. They had a canopy spread overhead to give some protection from sun and spray but it had to be taken in during spells of bad weather, when the continual fling of water on board brought misery to all.

The lengthening of the galleys' oars for handling by several rowers together made it necessary to have the benches turned slightly athwartships in order not to foul the innermost rower. At about the same time the vessel was encircled by a wooden outrigger which carried tholes, or pivots, for the oars to work on, giving more-powerful leverage, and which would also help to ward off an attack. A much greater innovation however was the arrival of guns as the main weapon in place of the ferocious-looking ram-bow.

At first a gun of fairly large calibre was laid on a bed of well-filled sacks in the eyes of the vessel, in other words right forward, in the bows. Its weight rested on the end of the corsia, an upward extension of the galley's keel which, added primarily for strength, served also as a gangway along the full length of the vessel.

The gun was a great advantage, although it had limitations. It could not be trained either laterally or vertically, and otherwise only by aiming the galley itself at the target. Later on, it was joined by two smaller guns on each side of it in the bows, making a total of five chase guns, as they were called, all pointing forward.

The French had found that sentencing unwanted citizens to the galleys was an extremely handy and useful way of obtaining free labour, which perhaps explains why they finally owned one of the largest fleets in the Mediterranean and also why they continued to build galleys until 1720. Even England at one time experimented with ten of the type, but only to learn its short-comings in the Channel and letting them end their days in the role of tugs, towing ships up or down the Thames.

In spite of all they achieved, galleys were really under a severe handicap in a fight. They could attack only end-on, whether with the earlier ram or the later gun, and owing to their length they were unable to manoeuvre quickly. To turn at all meant making a wide arc and, in the process, exposing their barely protected sides to the enemy.

In a set-piece fleet battle there would, of course, be no such problem, provided that the flanks of the fleet could be effectively covered, and galleys would line up side to side with each screening the next. And they had above all the precious facility of being largely independent of the wind, having both oars and sail.

Another handicap, one that was due to their crowded state and the shortage of storage space on board, was that they were unable to stow any quantity of provisions which would allow them to keep the sea. Generally their cruises had to be of short duration.

Above: Model of a Maltese galley of the 1700s, in the Naval Museum at Genoa-Pegli.
M Pucciarelli

Left: A galleass of the 18th century from a colour engraving by Mortier of Amsterdam.
M Pucciarelli

It was perhaps thinking along these lines that set some early and unknown naval architect evolving a new idea. What was needed, he saw, was a big vessel which would have all the advantages both of the galley and of the normal ship without any of the disadvantages of either. It would be fast, capable of being rowed by a large number of oarsmen, rigged to carry three large sails, able to turn and manoeuvre without fuss, two-decked and armed with guns along the sides.

This paragon of ships was given the name of galleass. She, or more probably a later version, was about 160 feet long in the hull, 130 feet on the keel, 30 feet in the beam and had a stern-post 20 feet high. Besides lateen sails, she had 30 banks of oars, each bank composed of two oars and every oar managed by six slaves who were in chains.

Five galleasses more or less answering to that description took part among the galleys in the battle of Lepanto in 1571 and they gave a good account of themselves. But nothing could give them the grace of line that distinguishes a good ship. The profile was low and, without sails set, the galleass looked a monstrosity, an unhappy compromise.

In 1588 it was a different story from that of Lepanto. The four galleasses that were prominent in the battle of the Armada fought bravely and well but apparently no one had foreseen what would be the effect of heavy gunshot on those great splintering oars. The galleass was clearly not a success for a fleet battle, but in the hands of the Venetians it became a useful merchant ship.

Britain's Henry VIII had once had a galleass built on the Thames, but he soon had it completely rebuilt as a normal ship of war. He also at one time owned two war-galleys, the *Galley Subtle* and the *Galley Blanchard*. They had been captured from the French and with a touch of true economy they were kept manned by their own crews. The English captain who was first appointed to the *Subtle*, however, seems to have had language trouble and was replaced by a Spanish captain with a Venetian as patron, or sailing master, who were presumably linguists.

In 1638 a Spanish and a French fleet, each of 15 galleys, met and fought close inshore at Genoa. It was a strangely transitional affair, with guns firing in prelude to a savage hand-to-hand fight between men in armour using muskets and pistols, swords and daggers. At the end, the French had captured three galleys and the Spaniards two but in reality it was practically a drawn battle, which was fitting enough, as it was the last great fight between Mediterranean galleys.

While they were slowly ending their days, galleys were finding fresh life farther afield. The Swedes, guided by Henrik af Chapman, and Russians were building numbers in the Baltic on the French model. With them they made furious forays, and the galley survived for another 100 years, although they were never really popular as fighting ships.

Above: Another Mortier engraving, of a bomb ketch armed with guns along the sides.
M Pucciarelli

Below: The French galley 'Reale' from a Mortier engraving. *M Pucciarelli*

This picture: Painting by W F Mitchell of a 74-gun ship of the line circa 1794. *Photo D Rudkin*

Bottom: Guns of the First Rate HMS 'Victory' preserved at Portsmouth which was said to handle as well as a 74. *P D Hawkes*

The 74

IT IS OFTEN SAID that there was little change in warship design between the Armada and Trafalgar. That statement is true in the sense that the fundamental basis of the design of the three-masted wooden man-of-war did not change. However, even if the development of the fighting ship between 1600 and 1800 appears small, viewed in context, the developments in detail introduced during those 200 years produced a great increase in fighting power and general performance. The *Revenge* (1577) and *Sovereign of the Seas* (1637) were both outstanding in their day, but would not have had a chance against the standard fighting ship of Nelson's period, the 74-gun line-of-battleship.

With the exception of minor specialised craft like bomb ketches, warships from the Armada to the introduction of steam were built to a common pattern. At any one time all but the smallest brigs, cutters and the like had a similar layout and a three-masted rig. The main variations were in size, gunpower and fineness of lines. Generally speaking, the larger the ship the more concentration there was on the guns, and less on fineness of lines, as the large ship needed more room in her hull for the bigger crew and their stores.

As the length of a wooden hull was severely limited, the whole length of the ship had to be used to carry an adequate broadside of guns, which meant 'full ends', or in other words bluff bows and sterns. However, a big ship could carry more sail and go faster in rough conditions than a smaller ship which was speedier in light winds. So size and gunpower were linked, and were the main distinguishing features of different types of warship. The bigger ships were for fighting battles, the smaller ones for subsidiary duties, such as scouting, carrying dispatches, escorting convoys and so on. Therefore, it was logical to classify ships by the number of guns they carried.

The English fleets that fought the Armada and later the Dutch included many merchantmen, for at that stage there was little difference between a well-armed merchant ship and all but the largest warships. However, warships were growing in size, and the differences grew greater until, by the end of the third Dutch war (1674), it was obvious that there was no longer any place for the ill-armed and poorly disciplined merchant ship in the increasingly rigid line of battle. Subsequently merchantmen might be hired for subsidiary naval purposes, but not to serve as ships of the line, although there were a few exceptions. In the American War of Independence, for example, an East Indiaman was converted on the stocks to become the 74-gun line-of-battleship *Bombay Castle.*

Just as the merchant ship was eliminated from the line of battle, so were the smaller types of warship as it became obvious that at least two decks of guns and thick sides were essential for a battleship. Any ship carrying fewer than 50 guns was too weak to take part in a major battle, but arming a ship with 100 guns or more pushed the art of building wooden ships to its limits, and was very expensive in terms of money, timber and men. Because of the difficulty of building a ship longer than about 200 feet from wood by conventional methods, any ship carrying more than 80 guns needed three complete decks of guns, with a deeper hull and more freeboard and, therefore, more windage and less handiness than a two-decker. The fact that the *Victory* was a popular flagship for half a century was due to the accident that although a three-decker, she sailed as well as a 74-gunner.

The *Victory* (and all other ships of 100 guns or more) was a First Rate; ships carrying 98 to 84 guns were Second Rates, those with 80 to 64 guns Third Rates, and the 50- and 60-gun ships at the lower end of the battleship classes were Fourth Rates. The rating system was in use long before the end of the 17th century but it was some time before the best compromise between size, power, economy and handiness was found. It took a long process of trial and error before the 74 was established as the standard battleship in the three largest 18th-century navies, those of France, Spain and Great Britain. The First and Second Rates were never completely supplanted as they were useful flagships and status symbols, and powerful adversaries in battle. The 74 had a smaller sister, the 64, which was weaker but useful for outlying stations or convoy escort, and still capable of serving in the line of battle. The smaller Fourth Rates however gradually went out of use; by about 1756 50-gun ships no longer served as battleships.

Though there had been odd examples of ships carrying 74 guns being built earlier, the 74 as a type first appeared in the French and Spanish navies in the period between the Peace of Utrecht (1713) and the outbreak of war between Britain and Spain in 1739. At that period British major warships were notoriously smaller and weaker than their equivalents in the other major navies. The 70-gun ships, and even more the three-decked 80-gun ships, were both badly designed and too small for their armament. Even when the Royal Navy began to follow the example of the Spanish and the French in building 74s (the first was built in 1747), they were still inferior to foreign vessels of the same nominal force. The early British 74s had some difficulty in fighting their lower-deck guns (which were the heaviest) in a heavy sea or a fresh wind, when their French contemporaries could still keep their gun ports open, precisely because the French ships had greater beam and were stiffer.

Although British ships improved later, throughout the 18th century the French and Spanish had the reputation of building better ships. Although their reputation was not wholly deserved, it was true that the French were much further advanced in the study of theoretical naval architecture, but their more scientific attitude did not necessarily mean that the British shipwrights, working more empirically, could not build equally good ships. Certainly British ships tended to be built with more

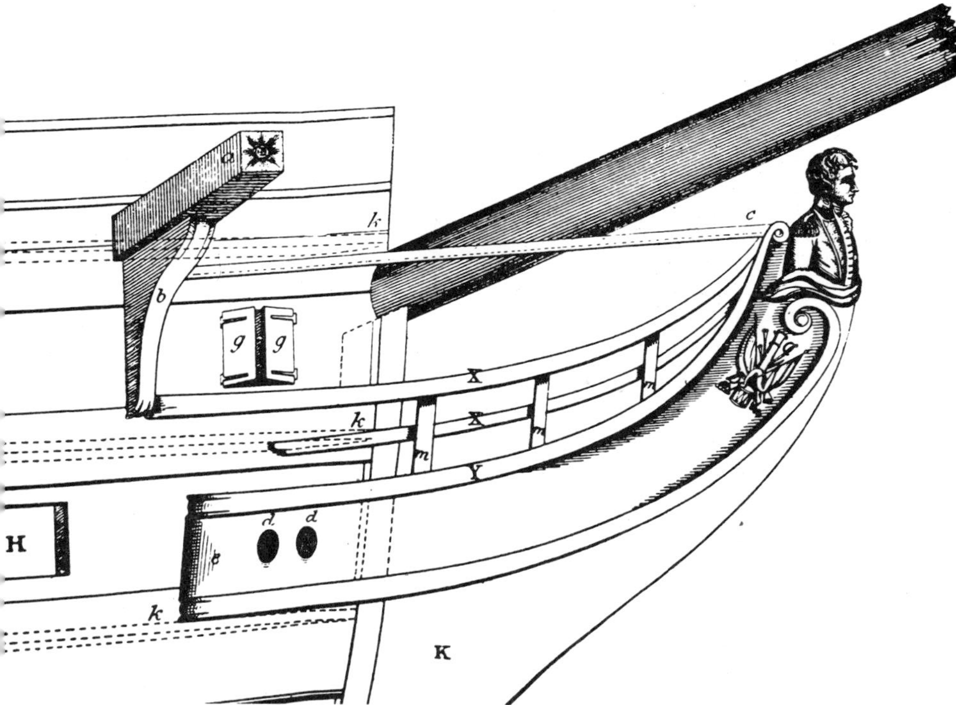

Top left: Cutaway drawing of an Elizabethan galleon, ancestor of the 74-gunner. *Illustrated London News*

Top: Model of the frigate 'Najaden' of 1811. *Naval Museum Copenhagen, Denmark*

Above: Figurehead of a 74-gun ship, as depicted in a drawing from the 1815 edition of Falconer's Dictionary. *K Fenwick*

of an eye to economy, and also usually carried more guns on a given tonnage. Undeniably the practical test of combat showed that the British ships were consistently superior as fighting machines, due almost entirely to the human factor. It meant that plenty of French and Spanish ships were captured by their supposedly inferior British contemporaries, and could then be used, and copied, by the Royal Navy.

As regards construction, the hull of a 74 was made of thick wood capable of resisting heavy punishment, and the most frequently used was oak. By the 18th century suitable trees, particularly for the great curved bow and stern timbers, were becoming rare, and many experiments were tried, the most successful being the building of a number of ships of teak at Bombay after 1800. The keel and frames of a 74 ,which were so close together that the side was nearly solid before it was planked, took up an immense amount of timber even before planking and decking had been done. A ship of that size would require between 3000 and 4000 cartloads of timber.

Other requirements were tall straight pines to make the masts; by the time the 74 appeared most masts in the Royal Navy were made, that is, constructed of several pieces of timber carefully fitted together. All ships carried spare spars to replace those lost in action or through stress of weather. The complicated network of standing and running rigging could easily be replaced by a skilled crew.

The details of rigging did not change very much during the time when the 74 flourished, though the gaff spanker replaced the old lateen mizen sail, and staysails and jibs were adopted, as was the dolphin and chain rigging. The most important change affecting mobility was the general adoption of copper sheathing by the Royal Navy during the American War of Independence. It meant that a ship could keep her speed for much longer when at sea for long periods, because the copper prevented the underwater growths that would otherwise slow her down. Coppering also stopped the depredations of the teredo worm and other marine borers which would otherwise weaken the hull, particularly in tropical waters.

The hull of a two-decker was divided by the gun deck; above it was the armament and accommodation space, below it the store rooms, magazines and bilges. Forward on the upper deck was the great stove which was used to cook for the entire ship's company. The only major pieces of machinery were the windlass used for raising the anchor, and the pumps (the chain pump was probably introduced about the same time as the 74), and the ship's wheel; everything else was done by block and tackle and manpower. The crew was the most important part of a warship; they worked the sails and the guns, and because very few ships were sunk in action in that period, finished off an enemy by boarding. About 600 men lived sometimes for years on end within the hull of a 74.

During the later 18th century there were important developments in ventilation, hygiene and diet, which meant that fewer men died, but still the death toll from disease and accident was far higher than from enemy action. The greatest dangers to a wooden sailing warship were fire and the weather; far more ships were lost by all navies to those causes than to enemy action.

Despite her primitiveness to our eyes, the 74 was the most complex artefact of her day. She was a complicated work of architecture in wood, capable of resisting the stress of storms, and carrying in her hold sufficient stores to support a large community over a long period. Her sails and rigging were a complicated and precise instrument for utilising the wind to provide propulsion. She carried more and heavier guns than an army would have in its train. Her navigating officers would use some of the most complicated instruments of their day.

The 74s, and particularly those of the Royal Navy, also played an important part in the history of their time, in the 18th century wars for overseas empire. For their last and greatest war a great naval historian put the matter in a nutshell; it was 'those far-distant storm-beaten ships upon which the Grand Army never looked' which 'stood between it and the dominion of the World'.

The main purpose of a ship of the line was to carry the largest possible broadside battery of guns. The smooth-bore muzzle-loader was not a very accurate or long-range weapon, so quantity had to replace quality. The earliest British 74s carried 28 32-pounders on the gun (or main) deck, 28 18-pounders on the upper deck and 14 9-pounders on the quarter deck and forecastle. There were, therefore, three separate deck levels for guns, but since the uppermost was not continuous, and the waist of the ship was open, the ship was called a two-decker.

The larger 74s like the *Triumph* carried a slightly heavier battery, with 30 24-pounders on the upper deck and only 16 9-pounders. During the American War of Independence a number of improvements in gunnery achieved widespread use in the Royal Navy. One of the most important was the use of a flintlock for firing the gun, much more reliable than the old slow-match, although that was kept as a standby. The other important innovation was a new type of gun, a light short-range piece called a carronade, which could fire a much heavier ball in relation to its own weight, and required a smaller crew than the conventional long guns. Carronades could be added to the armament of the poop and forecastle in the larger warship without much difficulty, and in 1779 the establishment of all 74s was increased by the addition of two 12-pounder carronades to the forecastle and six 12-pounder carronades to the poop guns.

Although 74s then carried 82 guns, they were still known under their original designation, because carronades were not carriage guns; they were mounted on slides, not on the usual truck carriage with its four little wheels, and so they did not count. By the end of the century heavier carronades were being carried—32-pounders—but in 1806 it was decided to rationalise matters.

Instead of ships carrying a mixed battery of guns of different calibre, the order went out that all 74s were to use only one size of shot. The new establishment was 24 long 24-pounders on the gun deck, 28 medium 24-pounders on the upper deck, and four medium 24-pounders and 14 24-pounder carronades on quarter deck and forecastle. The last four medium guns would be for use as chase guns, firing ahead and astern, and giving more range than the carronades. The change actually lightened the load the ship had to carry, as the guns weighed a total of 157cwt instead of 181cwt, and the weight of the broadside was only marginally less, 888lb instead of 928lb. After the Napoleonic Wars further improvements were made in ordnance, including the use of shell guns, but by then the 74 was on the way out.

While on the subject of weapons, it would not do to forget about the ship's boats of a Royal Navy 74. During the long years of blockade the Royal Navy raised the so-called cutting-out raid to a fine art; often the only way to strike at enemy coasters, warships in harbour, or small forts on shore was to send the boats in. The largest boats—the launch and the cutter—could carry small carronades and sometimes made quite extended voyages on their own. The boats greatly extended the offensive range of a warship, and it would not be unrealistic to think of a line-of-battleship as resembling a modern aircraft carrier, capable of launching strikes at otherwise inaccessible targets.

The gradual standardisation of the 74 can be seen by comparing the composition

Top: Ornate stern and quarter of a 74.
R Brown

Left: Highly gilded stern on the model of the 1649 Second Rate, 'Sophia Amalia'
Naval Museum Copenhagen, Denmark

Above: Side view of the 'Sophia Amalia' model showing the gunports.
Naval Museum Copenhagen, Denmark

of the lines of battle in a number of famous actions. For example, in 1692 the British fleet at Barfleur consisted of a medley of types, typical of a 17th-century battle, although the high proportion of 70s can be seen from Table 1.

TABLE 1 (number of ships)

100 guns (4)	96 guns (3)
90 guns (8)	82 guns (1)
74 guns (1)	72 guns (1)
70 guns (21)	66 guns (2)
64 guns (2)	62 guns (1)
60 guns (4)	54 guns (3)
50 guns (6)	48 guns (3)
44 guns (1)	

Velez Malaga was fought in 1704 between the British and Dutch on one side against the French and Spanish on the other. The British fleet showed less variety than before, unlike the enemy fleets, while the Dutch squadron demonstrated the tendency of that navy to build smaller vessels of shallow draught because of the shallow seas around Holland. The disposition at Velez Malaga is shown in Table 2.

TABLE 2

BRITISH	
96 guns (3)	90 guns (2)
80 guns (9)	76 guns (1)
70 guns (16)	66 guns (1)
50 guns (2)	
DUTCH	
90 guns (1)	72 guns (3)
64 guns (6)	54 guns (1)
52 guns (1)	
FRANCO-SPANISH	
104 guns (1)	102 guns (1)
96 guns (1)	92 guns (4)
88 guns (4)	86 guns (2)
84 guns (2)	80 guns (1)
74 guns (3)	70 guns (3)
68 guns (2)	64 guns (2)
62 guns (2)	60 guns (6)
58 guns (9)	56 guns (5)
54 guns (3)	

Half a century later, at Quiberon Bay in 1759, the 74 was already established as the most common type on the British side, as shown in Table 3; at the Saintes in 1782 there were more 74s than all other types put together in the British fleet (Table 4); and Trafalgar was fought mainly between 74s (Table 5).

TABLE 3

BRITISH	
100 guns (1)	90 guns (3)
74 guns (7)	70 guns (5)
64 guns (2)	60 guns (5)
(there were also 4 50-gun ships)	
FRENCH	
80 guns (4)	74 guns (6)
70 guns (3)	64 guns (8)

TABLE 4

BRITISH	
98 guns (4)	90 guns (1)
74 guns (20)	70 guns (1)
64 guns (11)	

TABLE 5

BRITISH	
100 guns (3)	98 guns (4)
80 guns (1)	74 guns (16)
64 guns (3)	
SPANISH	
140 guns (1)	112 guns (2)
100 guns (1)	80 guns (2)
74 guns (7)	64 guns (1)
FRENCH	
84 guns (1)	80 guns (3)
74 guns (15)	

Up to 1800 the Royal Navy operated a total of 139 74s (including ships building). Of those, 14 were ex-French, 10 ex-Spanish and one captured from the Dutch. An individual example of the copying of a foreign design was the first of a class of enlarged and improved 74s, the *Triumph* laid down in 1758 and launched in 1764. She was for long considered the best of her type, and the inspiration for the design came from a ship wrecked in the same year as she was laid down. That was the French *Invincible* captured by Admiral Anson in 1747.

In that same year the first British-built 74, the *Culloden*, had been built at Deptford. She was $161\frac{1}{2}$ft long on her gun deck, $46\frac{1}{2}$ft broad and her tonnage was 1487. The *Triumph* was longer ($171\frac{1}{4}$ft), broader ($49\frac{3}{4}$ft) and of greater tonnage (1825). A typical 74 of the Napoleonic period, the *Bulwark* of 1807, showed a further advance in dimensions (181ft 10in by $49\frac{1}{4}$ft and 1940 tons).

The early years of the 19th century produced a number of structural innovations. The old-style 'square' bow with a bulkhead running across the width of the ship had always been a weak point, very few guns could be fired from it and, especially, it was much thinner than the massive sides. In 1804 Seppings put a 'round' bow, capable of taking more guns, on the *Namur* while she was being cut down from a 90 to a 74 at Chatham. It was only a matter of time before an even weaker area, the stern with its great cabin and its windows, was given similar treatment, but that was delayed because senior naval officers naturally preferred to keep their comparatively spacious, light and airy quarters.

In 1817, however, the first round stern appeared; it was uglier but much stronger than its predecessor. Another, and more important, innovation was made at Chatham in 1805, the use of diagonal framing in the 74 *Kent*. Later the *Warspite* was entirely constructed using that system, and the *Tremendous*, when she was rebuilt even had diagonal framing used for the deck beams. The new constructional method meant that less wood had to be used; instead of making the sides of the ship thick and solid with massive frames, greater strength could be obtained by laying the main timbers diagonally fore and aft. It was a change from a transverse system to a longitudinal one, but the real significance was that the old limitation on length had been lifted.

With longer ships possible the main reason for the 74 had gone, Not many ships were built in the long years of peace after 1815, and none of them was a 74; the new ships were either larger or smaller. The number of 74s on the Navy List diminished slowly, as wooden ships can have a long life, but most were in reserve or used as training ships or hulks of one kind or another. The last 74 to see action seems to have been the *Blenheim*, off Canton in 1841 during the First Opium War.

The *Implacable*, captured from the French as the *Duguay Trouin* in 1805, served off the coast of Syria in 1841 against Mehemet Ali. She survived for a long retirement until after the 1939-45 war, when proposals were made to preserve her in dry dock at Greenwich (where the *Cutty Sark* now rests). She was badly infected with rot, and as enough money was not forthcoming, in 1949 she was towed out into the Channel, flying the white ensign and tricolour side by side, and was scuttled. Even then the last of the 74s showed her toughness. Her bottom had been blown out, but she remained afloat, and more explosive had to be used to sink her.

ENGLISH WARSHIPS were first designated by the number of guns carried at the beginning of the 17th century, and from about 1630 the English fleet was divided into six classes or Rates. Initially First Rates were ships with more than 90 guns, Second Rates those between 80 and 90 guns, Third Rates 50 to 80, Fourth Rates 38 to 50, Fifth Rates 18 to 38 and Sixth Rates those with fewer than 18 guns.

From then until well into the 19th century every ship of the Navy was listed in one of the six classes according to her size and gun-power; each had a strict complement of officers and men. However, from time to time alterations occurred in the upper and lower limits of each division of Rate. Very similar classifications were adopted for most navies. In France the classes were known as the Premier to Sixieme Range, and corresponding terms were applied in other European navies.

With the adoption, in the middle of the 17th century, of Formal Fighting Instructions and the enforcement of line ahead as the order of battle, it was necessary to ensure that a much smaller and less powerful warship was not opposed by a stronger vessel, therefore the smaller Rates of warships were excluded from the battle line, which was made up from vessels with more than 50 guns, that is, usually, the First, Second and Third Rates only, and the vessels of those Rates became known as ships-of-the-line.

The principal functions of the various Rates can be described as follows: First, Second and Third Rates—service as ships-of-the-line in general fleet actions; Fourth Rates—guard duties with convoys of merchant ships, service as cruising ships in foreign waters and on expeditions of great distance; Fifth Rates—acting as reconnaissance vessels when attached to fleets of larger warships, to repeat signals and for operating against privateers; Sixth Rates—coastal patrol duties. The above definitions are, of course, only a general indication, as the duties undertaken by individual warships of the different Rates varied considerably.

In the 18th century a large proportion of the warships with fewer than 50 guns were known by the various denominations of frigates. The name frigate was given to various types of warship at different periods, but the best known application was to the 18th-century vessel specially designed for scouting, convoy duties and attacks on enemy merchant ships, which carried its main armament on a single gun-deck.

During the first half of the 18th century the largest vessels in the Royal Navy to carry their main armament in that manner were the Sixth Rates of 24 guns. In 1757 a new class was introduced, the 32-gun frigate and by the end of the century the navy had frigates of 40, 38, 36, 32, 28, 24 and 20 guns. In the 19th century the frigate continued to be a most important and useful unit of the sailing navies and at the beginning of the century the British Navy had over 200 frigates. The increase in size continued and frigates of 50 and 60 guns came into service.

The first attempt at standardisation for warships of the Royal Navy took place in

First Rate to Sixth Rate

Left: **A Dutch Second Rate of 1670.**
Parker Gallery (D Rudkin)

Bottom left: A study by N Fielding of a Second Rate (new class) line-of-battle ship of 92 guns.
D Rudkin

Below: Model of an 18th-century Fifth Rate warship. *P M Wood*

1677, when Admiralty officers and navy shipwrights prepared the first Shipbuilding Establishment which laid down the principal dimensions of warships of each class. After the first Establishment further official rules, laying down not only the standard dimensions of each class, but also the sizes of the timbers used in their construction, were issued in 1691, 1706, 1719, and 1745, with additional proposals in 1733 and 1741.

Although the successive regulations gradually increased the size of ships—for instance, a 100-gun ship built on the Establishment of 1745 was about two feet wider on the beam and about 11 feet longer on the gun-deck than a 100-gun ship of the 1677 Establishment—the rigid specifications of the rules retarded the progress of English naval architecture and constrained the initiative of the shipwrights as it gave little scope for experiment and new forms of construction.

During the period of the Establishments, British warships were often too small for the number of guns they were intended to carry and, therefore, lay low in the water

Right: Engravings showing a cutaway section and the rigging of an English First Rate warship. *Parker Gallery (D Rudkin)*

Bottom: Another study by N Fielding depicting a First Rate (new class) line-of-battle ship of 110 guns. *R N Frost Collection (D Rudkin)*

so that lower-deck guns could not be used in rough seas, and the ships sailed and worked heavily. The ship designers and builders of other countries were free from the restrictions of standardisation and able to incorporate in their warships the result of experiments and investigations into the design of the underwater hull form of ships.

In particular, French warships were built with a greater space between each gunport in comparison with British vessels. That feature increased the length of the vessel in relation to the number of guns carried and the beam of the vessel was increased in proportion, making the ship more buoyant with the lower guns higher above the water and more space available around the weapon for the gun crew. After about 1750 British ship designers and shipwrights were allowed more freedom to experiment, to produce bigger and better warships and to copy the designs of captured vessels.

In the 17th century it was the practice to protect the underwater hull of a ship from damage by marine pests with wooden sheathing applied over a layer of tar, hair, sulphur and tallow. Experiments were also made with lead sheathing but it was unsuccessful because of corrosion caused by electrolytic action set up in salt water by the lead and iron fastenings of the hull.

In 1761 the British frigate was sheathed with sheets of copper below the waterline, but again corrosion occurred with the iron fastenings. After about 1780 copper was used instead of iron for underwater fastenings of the hull and copper sheathing was then found to be satisfactory. By the end of the century the underwater hulls of most warships were protected by copper sheathing applied in thin sheets, each about four feet long and 14 inches wide. More than 3000 such sheets were required to sheath a large warship.

THE SAILING FRIGATE

AMONG THE WELL-ARMED but slow and clumsy English men-of-war of the mid-17th century, there appeared a three-masted 'light, nimble ship, built for the purpose of sailing swiftly' of 315 tons and 30 guns named *Constant Warwick*. Fast and powerful enough to capture merchantmen and elude heavier warships, she was called a frigate, a term derived from the earlier Italian fregata, a small galleass, through the French frégate. She inspired shipwrights during the time of the Commonwealth to experiment with finer underwater lines, reduced upperworks and longer keels.

The War of The Spanish Succession of 1701-1714 showed the lack of a fast, stable, well-armed and seaworthy small warship for reconnaissance. War with France and Spain in 1739-1748 produced the British 44-gun frigates of 678-914 tons, too slow for the job, which carried all their guns on two lower decks; the second deck was useless in heavy weather.

In 1756, the Seven Years War between England and France began. The English introduced a new class of vessel in the experimental 36-gun 718-ton frigates *Brilliant* and *Pallas*, launched in 1757; they were meant to counter the new French frigates of the *Aurore* class, launched in the same year, also with 36 guns, but larger (946 tons) and better sailers. A year later the English captured the *Aurore*, renamed her HMS *Aurora*, and studied her fine lines.

By the time the American War of Independence broke out in 1775, the French were building new improved frigates, which the British Navy countered with a 32-gun class of 670-720 tons and 30 vessels of a 28-gun type of 600 tons. A good example of the latter was HMS *Ariel*, built to the design of Sir J Williams at Dover in 1785, a model of which is in the Science Museum at South Kensington. She carried all her main armament (24 9-pounders) on one main gun-deck, which became a basic feature of frigates, and a few light guns (four 3-pounders) on the long quarter-deck. The gangways joining foc'sle to quarter-deck were broader than in previous ships, but the waist, often called 'the shambles', was still wide open, exposing the 10 guns and their crews located there.

American shipyards built 13 frigates mounting from 24 to 32 guns. By 1778, all but four of them had been lost, but the American warships were active on both sides of the Atlantic, aided by their French and Spanish allies, and at times cut off all communication between the Old World and the New, capturing ships, ammunition and stores. In April 1778, the Scottish-born John Paul Jones sailed round the British Isles, spreading alarm everywhere, with a squadron composed of his flagship, the old converted French merchantman *Bonhomme Richard* of 42 guns; the *Alliance*, an American frigate of 36 guns, well built but commanded by an incompetent Frenchman; the 20-gun *Pallas* and two smaller ships. Off Flamborough Head, they met a large convoy from the Baltic protected by the frigates *Serapis*, and *Countess of Scarborough*. *Serapis* was a new fast 50-gun ship, but instead of using his superior speed and gun power, Captain Pearson overconfidently allowed the *Bonhomme Richard* to come to close quarters, where the desperate aggression of Jones beat him into surrender.

With the carronade, invented in the late 1700s, the armament of frigates advanced considerably. The carronade, or 'smasher' was a short thin-barrelled gun with a wide bore firing a ball with great penetrating power over a short range of about 100 yards or less. It was a light gun, and could safely be fitted in effective numbers on a frigate's upper decks without endangering her stability. Filled with grape shot, the smasher could clear an enemy's decks and mangle his rigging. The large 956-ton Spanish frigate *Santa Monica*, captured in 1779 by HMS *Pearl*, carried 28 long guns when taken, but was re-armed for British service with 26 12-pounders on her gun-deck, 10 6-pounders and eight 18-pounder carronades on her upper deck.

In 1793, Revolutionary France declared war on Britain. British frigates were immediately sent out to warn homeward-bound merchantmen, and to escort convoys across the Atlantic and North Sea.

Others cruised in the Channel, looking for the enemy's merchantmen and watch-

A painting by J Cartwright of HMS 'Little Belt' and US frigate 'President' off Sandy Hook, New Jersey, in May 1811.
Courtesy US Naval Academy Museum

ing for his Fleet movements. Two young frigate captains eager to enhance reputations for skill and initiative were Edward Pellew of the *Nymphe* (36 guns) and James Saumarez in *Crescent* (36). Pellew put out from Falmouth with a largely new and untrained crew which included 80 Cornish tin miners, and at daybreak on June 18, off Prawle Point, encountered the crack French frigate *Cléopatre.* The two ships ran parallel before the wind, their broadsides crashing into one another. Skilful gunnery control by Edward's younger brother Israel cleared *Cléopatre's* decks, shattered her wheel and brought down her mizen mast and Captain Mullon surrendered. 'We dished her up in 50 minutes, boarded and struck her colours,' Pellew reported.

Saumarez was cruising off Cherbourg in October watching for a French frigate which had made repeated sorties at night to catch British merchantmen. In the small hours of the 20th, the *Réunion* came out, but the wind dropped and she could not get back before *Crescent* had cut her off. The Frenchman tacked with all sail but *Crescent,* with superior seamanship and a hull clean from the dockyard, closed her, and a two-hour battle began. The French gunners shot too high, and although *Crescent* lost her foretopsail yard and foretopmast, Saumarez manoeuvred her into the coveted raking position across the enemy's stern. 'Our guns were so well served,' he reported, 'that the French ship soon became unmanageable, and enabled us to rake her fore and aft; in that situation she struck her colours.'

Repeated single-ship victories of this sort by British frigates revealed deficiencies in French seamanship and gunnery, discipline and morale, which went from bad to worse the more French ships stayed in harbour rather than risk action. But 100 British frigates were insufficient to meet the heavy demands made upon them. At Christmas 1793, a French squadron of five ships of the line attacked a Newfoundland convoy escorted only by the frigate *Castor,* capturing the frigate and many merchantmen. On June 16, 1795, Cornwallis's five ships-of-the-line and three frigates almost went the same way when they fell in with a greatly superior French force that included 12 ships-of-the-line. With the enemy overtaking fast, the frigate *Phoenix* pretended to be signalling to an imaginary British fleet just over the horizon, and the French broke off the action.

The frigates did invaluable work as 'the eyes of the Fleet.' Patrolling frigates sighted Villaret-Joyeuse's elusive fleet and enabled Lord Howe to win the victory of The Glorious First of June in 1794. In September 1798, Captain Richard Keats in the frigate *Boadicea* sighted a French squadron of one ship-of-the-line and eight frigates slipping out of Brest. Keats crowded on all sail to inform the Admiral in Torbay, and the French were intercepted off the Irish coast. In a wild five-hour chase through high seas and a rising gale, in which the British frigate *Amazon,* in the van, carried away her mizen mast, the French flagship and six frigates surrendered. Captured aboard the French ships were 3000 soldiers going to reinforce French troops in Ireland and the Irish rebel leader Wolfe Tone.

At Copenhagen in 1801, the *Amazon,* captained by Edward Riou, very efficiently piloted Nelson's division of the Fleet into the Sound and down the Outer Channel by the Swedish shore, to take the moored Danish ships by surprise from the south, having previously made a thorough check on the correct positioning of the buoys placed there to guide them. Unfortunately, she and the other four frigates present had later to be thrown in against the northern and stronger part of the enemy's line, and *Amazon* was so badly knocked about by the heavy guns of the Trekroner fort that she was forced to withdraw, and Riou was killed as she turned away.

In the evening of September 1, 1805, Captain Henry Blackwood's frigate *Euryalus,* with every scrap of sail on her, gusted into the Solent with the news that Villeneuve was in Cadiz. On September 14th, Nelson sailed from Portsmouth, arriving off Cadiz a fortnight later. Withdrawing the main body of the Fleet 50 miles out into the Atlantic, he stationed the four frigates *Euryalus, Naiad, Phoebe,* and *Sirius,* under Blackwood, close in with orders to '. . . watch all points and all winds and weathers.'

With first light on October 19, *Sirius,* the inshore frigate, signalled 'Enemy have their topsail yards hoisted.' By 09.30, Nelson had ordered 'general chase south-east.' For some hours on the 20th, the enemy ships were lost in bad visibility, but *Euryalus* picked them up again in the afternoon and held on to them. Through the night of the 20th-21st, Blackwood kept Nelson informed of Villeneuve's every movement, using signal guns, blue lights and rockets. With the daylight, Nelson steered for the enemy, and the battle of Trafalgar was joined.

Trafalgar was won, but the war went on, with British frigates continuing the wearisome grind of blockade off the French coast. One of them was HMS *Shannon,* which was one of a new class of frigates, mounting 38 18-pounder guns and 14 carronades, based on the design of the captured French frigate *Hebe.* She was constructed by Brindley's of Frinsbury, near Chatham, on the Medway, a firm which had not built frigates before, but specialised in seventy-fours and stout East Indiamen. *Shannon* had the familiar bluff bows, but fine underwater lines which gave her a good turn of speed, and a flush upper deck with waist decked in. In the spring of 1807, *Shannon,* with the frigate *Meleager,* gave protection to the British whaling fleet off Greenland, but in 1808, she was back cruising off Ushant and the Black Rocks of Brest, apprehending the occasional small brig or schooner.

She was still there two years later. 'Tough as I have been,' wrote her Captain, Philip Broke, 'I cannot last much longer. I have seen all the ships and men out two or three times . . . Many about me are yielding to the fatigue and confinement of a life which is not natural to man . . .' Broke was a captain of exceptional ability, a gunnery fanatic who had made of the *Shannon* a fighting ship of unsurpassed efficiency. His innovations included the fitting of 'dispart' sights to the guns for better aiming; scientifically graduated and notched 'quoins', or wedges, for the guns, to give a horizontal-fire reference in all attitudes of the ship, even at night; and a system of operating all the guns of a broadside in concert, involving common scales of elevation, and lines of bearing cut in the deck at each gun controlled by reference to a master compass rose on deck.

In the spring of 1811, *Shannon* sailed to join the British North American Squadron. She entered Halifax, Nova Scotia, on September 24, 1811, after a rough five-week passage, where she found the 60-gun *Africa,* the frigates *Guerrière* (38 guns), *Spartan* (38), *Belvidera* (36) and *Aeolus* (32), and six sloops.

For 10 months, *Shannon* cruised between Halifax and Bermuda in the protection of homeward-bound convoys. On the last day of June 1812, she was entering Halifax when Broke was hailed and told that the USA had declared war on Britain after the *Guerrière* had taken men out of an American ship. The American Commodore Rodgers had chased the *Belvidera* and fired on her. She lay in Halifax, her maintopmast and cross-jack yard fished with capstan bars where two 24-pound balls from the US frigate *President* had gone clean through them.

With seven frigates and 10 smaller ships, the United States Navy was taking on only that part of the might of the Royal Navy's thousand active-service ships that were not engaging the prime enemy—France. The British North American Squadron was confident, but had not studied the opposition. When the Quaker shipbuilder Joshua Humphreys of Philadelphia had been asked by Congress in 1794 to design six warships, he had concluded, 'As our navy for a considerable time will be inferior in numbers, we are to consider what size ships will be most formidable and be an overmatch for those of an enemy . . . Frigates will be the first object, and none to be built less than 150 feet keel . . .'

Three very large frigates, *Constitution, President* and *United States,* were built, over 200 feet in length, with a displacement of 2200 tons. Their long keels and especially fine lines, based on those of the speedy Baltimore clippers, made them fast and stable vessels, capable of carrying an exceptionally heavy battery, based mainly on the 24-pounders, in contrast to the 18-pounder standard in British frigates. Their gun-decks were higher than in British frigates and more efficient in bad weather. Their solidly planked upper decks were broken only by hatchways. *Constitution* carried 54 guns, comprising 30 long 24-pounders on the gun-deck, 22 32-pounder carronades and two 12-pounder bow-chasers on the upper deck. Three smaller 38-gun frigates, *Chesapeake, Constellation* and *Congress,* were built on

Above An unidentified frigate and cutter as depicted in a painting by F Butterworth. *Science Museum London*

Right: The US frigate 'Constellation' which was launched in 1797 and is now preserved at Baltimore, Maryland. *K Poolman*

similar lines, with 24 18-pounders on the gun-deck, 21 24-pounder carronades and two 18-pounders on the upper deck.

The American crews contained no pressed men, and were captained by brilliant seamen. British seamen had grown over-confident, British captains, with the exception of men like Broke, put more value on spit-and-polish than on regular drill and practical seamanship.

Young Captain Dacres of the *Guerrière* was such a captain; his ship was an old French prize, smart in her new paint but slack from lack of drill. On the afternoon of August 9, she was idling her way to Halifax when Isaac Hull in *Constitution* overtook her from windward. Dacres opened the battle with a broadside at extreme range from his starboard 18-pounders, then wore and fired his port broadside. All his shots went high, except for two glancing blows. The two ships exchanged fire for nearly an hour, Dacres wearing to fire his broadside, Hull yawing to avoid being raked.

Then Dacres gave up his unsuccessful raking tactics. With the wind dead astern, he increased sail. But the swift *Constitution* overhauled him and brought up alongside *Guerrière* to deliver a series of coolly aimed broadsides. The Americans' heavier metal and more-accurate regular fire soon told. *Guerrière's* mainmast crashed overboard to starboard and the slings of her main yard parted. Her speed dropped and the fallen mainmast in the water dragged her bow into the wind. Hull crossed her bows and raked her, wore round and raked her again. He shaved the *Guerrière's* bows so close that her bowsprit stuck in *Constitution's* mizen rigging. Both ships exchanged a murderous musket fire, then broke apart. *Guerrière's* foremast and mainmast went overboard and she surrendered.

On October 5, off the Canary Isles, Captain Stephen Decatur in the *United States* fell in with Captain John Carden in HMS *Macedonian,* a smaller but fast 38-gun frigate fresh from refit in England. Carden's notorious strictness did not extend to gun practice. Believing his opponent to be the 32-gun frigate *Essex,* which he knew to be armed chiefly with the short-range carronades, Carden kept his distance, only to suffer disastrously from Decatur's long 24-pounders. He lost his mizen topmast, and the *United States* was able to keep ahead of him, pouring in diagonal fire until *Macedonian* was forced to surrender.

In December, *Constitution* (Commodore Bainbridge) was at sea off Bahia when she sighted HMS *Java. Constitution* carried 52 guns that day, the British frigate 49. Both were fast and light on the wheel, and it was a more even match than in the previous frigate encounters.

At first both ships jockeyed for a raking position, exchanging fierce broadsides. *Constitution's* wheel was shot away and she had to be steered by relieving tackles, two decks below. Bainbridge was wounded in the hip and thigh. Then *Java* lost some of her head sails and caught in stays, so that *Constitution* was able to rake her. Captain Lambert rammed *Java's* bow into *Constitution's* quarter and led a boarding party, but murderous fire from carronades and muskets drove them back, and *Java* lost her foremast as the two ships separated. When she finally struck her colours, *Java* had lost all her spars except the lower mainmast, her crew was decimated and Captain Lambert lay mortally wounded.

On the afternoon of June 1, 1813, Captain James Lawrence brought the USS *Chesapeake,* with a crew new to the ship, out of Boston Harbour to fight the *Shannon,* a ship at peak efficiency, captained by the best gunnery officer in the Royal Navy. The American was trailed by small boats packed with Bostonians come to watch another *Guerrière.*

Lawrence, with undrilled gunners, wanted to come to close quarters. This suited Broke, who knew that the longer American 18-pounders outranged his own. As *Chesapeake* came up on *Shannon's* starboard quarter, Lawrence, instead of crossing Broke's stern and raking *Shannon,* ranged alongside. At 17.50, *Shannon* opened fire and soon both ships were pouring grape and canister, bar shot, star and chain shot into each other. Superior training had its effect. *Chesapeake* had come up with too much way on her, and as she forged ahead she lost some of her forward sails, successive helmsmen were killed, and she swung into wind, away from *Shannon.* Lawrence was mortally wounded, his sailing master dead, his sailors and marines decimated. *Shannon* now poured in a raking fire, fatally wounding *Chesapeake's* first lieutenant, captain of marines, fourth lieutenant and boatswain. *Chesapeake* gathered stern way, she ground into *Shannon's* timbers, and the rigging of both ships became enmeshed. Broke's carronades and marine muskets reduced *Chesapeake's* upper decks to a bloody shambles. There was great confusion among the now practically leaderless Americans.

Broke judged this the right time to lead a boarding party. The *Shannon* men drove the desperately resisting American marines off the upper deck, and the ship was theirs. Then with a rending of rigging the ships broke apart. Resistance flared up again. Broke was hacked down by a cutlass, but as he lay bleeding he saw British colours hoisted above the American.

With that short bloody battle, the heyday of the sailing frigate was really over. In Britain, the rush to design and build new frigates to match the great Humphreys vessels produced ships like HMS *Glasgow,* of 50 guns, built on the Thames in 1814, which took part in the bombardment of Algiers in 1816 and was at Navarino in 1827; and the *Liffey,* 1269 tons, with 40 guns, including 28 24-pounders, which served in the Burma war of 1824. That war saw the first use of a steamer on active service, and by mid-century sailing frigates were being modified with the addition of steam propulsion.

Until that time, sailing frigates did much useful work. HMS *Pique,* launched in Plymouth in 1834, operated against Carlist forces in northern Spain in 1837, and fought in the Syrian campaign of 1840. HMS *Arethusa,* 2127 tons, launched in 1849, bombarded Odessa and Sevastopol in the Crimean War, and in 1861 was fitted with a screw. The USS *Constellation* ('The Yankee Race Horse'), bottled up in Hampton Roads for most of the War of 1812, fought Algerian pirates in 1815-1817, and served in the Mediterranean throughout the American Civil War of 1861-65. She is now preserved as a public monument in Baltimore, where she was built. *Constitution* also survives, preserved at her birthplace in Boston, the finest example of the sailing frigate ever built.

Below: A painting by Edward Moran of the burning of the frigate 'Philadelphia' in Tripoli Harbour in February 1804.
Courtesy US Naval Academy Museum

The Early IRONCLADS

THE GLORY of the British Navy, the finest and largest in the world, had been built on sailing wooden warships. 'Heart of oak are our ships' was the start of a popular song, and it was also the truth. Oak forests had disappeared to build the fleet of so-called wooden walls. However, in early Victorian days, changes were looming up; steam power was increasingly challenging sail and iron was beginning to be used for shipbuilding. Tradition is very dear to the Royal Navy, even today, and there was considerable resistance to change.

Iron was already being used to build commercial craft and the navy had some iron ships, but they were not fighting ships. Britain was not at war with anyone and many ships of the fleet were laid up. There were large stocks of timber and this was the material the shipwrights were skilled in using. With the normal feelings of the need for economy while in a state of peace, there was little urge to build in new materials.

Some of the early iron was very brittle and when the navy did firing tests on the light iron-built *Ruby* in 1840, damage was worse than on a similar-sized wooden vessel. The navy built some iron craft, but they were not completed as warships. One of them was the *Birkenhead*, which was launched in 1845 and became the subject of the famous heroic tragedy in 1852, when she foundered as a troop ship off the coast of Africa. Of course, later iron, largely as a result of the process invented by Bessemer, was of much better quality and less brittle.

It was left to the French to make the first moves in the use of iron as armour. They built what were floating batteries of guns, rather than boats, for use in the Crimean War. The batteries were wooden platforms, protected by iron, so as to resist the effect of Russian shells. For their purpose they were very successful, and Britain followed France by building similar batteries; two were of wood with iron armour and three were entirely of iron. However, it was 1855 before the British batteries were ready and they were too late to prove themselves in the Crimea.

As the batteries had to get from where they were built and fitted out to the scene of action in the Crimea, they were made boat-shaped. The lower portion was in the form of a flat-bottomed pointed box, equipped with sail and screw-driven. They must have been most odd-looking craft, and indeed were found to be inefficient and unwieldy under their own power, so they had to be towed most of the way. They were not all the same, but all had armour 4in thick taken to 3ft below the waterline, which must have been a considerable weight on a platform such as one described as 186ft long and mounting 16 68-pounder muzzle-loading guns. One of the British batteries, the *Terror*, completed too late for the Crimean war, spent her days as a commissioning base at Hamilton, Bermuda, until 1903.

France was then second to Britain as a world sea power. As a result of her experience with the armoured batteries, she went ahead building armoured ironclad warships. Britain stuck to wood, of which she had plenty, and the skill to fashion it into ships. The French had a half-built warship, intended to be an all-wood two-decker. The design was altered by M Dupuy de Lome in 1858 and cut down a deck so that it could be armoured all round with iron. The vessel was launched as *La Gloire*, to become the first ironclad and to mark the start of competition between the maritime nations to build better, and usually bigger, warships armoured with iron, and later steel. Britain was forced to join in.

The mid-Victorian period was the time of great engineers and inventors, as well as the industrial revolution. British facilities and technical knowledge were ahead

Top: HMS 'Warrior' of 1860, the first British ironclad, and 'Black Prince', the last two British warships to be built with figureheads.
National Maritime Museum London

Below: A painting depicting the 1862 battle between the two ironclads, 'Monitor' and 'Merrimac' during the American Civil War.
National Maritime Museum London

Left: HMS 'Agincourt', part of the mid-19th-century British ironclad fleet. *Illustrated London News*

Below: A painting by T Buttersworth of an earlier HMS 'Warrior'. *National Maritime Museum London*

of France and the rest of the world, so Britain was in a good position to go ahead with iron shipbuilding, despite the reluctance of the Navy to move away from wood. The *Warrior* was launched on December 30, 1860; the world's first iron-built and armoured warship. She was a very different ship from any that had gone before and started a new era of warships.

At that time the naval dockyards could not cope with the construction of an iron ship of such a size and a commercial yard received the contract; the builder was the Thames Ironworks and Shipbuilding Co, at Blackwall, on the tidal Thames down-river of London, from the design prepared by Sir Isaac Watts and John Scott Russell. The *Warrior* was in use as part of an oil pipeline pier until 1979 when she became the subject of a restoration project.

The size of the *Warrior* was arrived at by the intention that there should be a battery of 15 68-pounder guns with 15ft between the guns. To the resultant dimension of the gun platform were added a fine bow and a good run aft, to provide a fast hull. Main dimensions were length 380ft, beam $58\frac{1}{2}$ft and draught 26ft, and the displacement was 9210 tons. The ship was described as a frigate, because all the guns were on one deck, although she was very different from any frigate that had preceded her.

At that time there was a distrust of steam engines and even ships fitted with engines were fully rigged for sailing, partly as a reserve source of power and as a means of economising in the consumption of coal, which needed considerable space for stowage. The *Warrior* was fully rigged, but she was given the most powerful engines fitted to a warship up to that date. The coal-fired steam engines were of the horizontal trunk-type with cylinders 104.6in in diameter and of 48in stroke. Indicated output on trials was 5470hp, giving a speed with the single propeller of 14.35 knots. Best speed under sail was about 10 knots.

At that time armour was used to protect the fighting area and not the whole ship. One reason for having all the guns on one deck was to reduce the amount of armouring needed. The only protection given to the ends of the ship was an arrangement of sub-divisions to make watertight compartments. The armour plating was iron $4\frac{1}{2}$in thick, backed by 18in of teak. The plates extended for 213ft along both sides and were 22ft deep, stretching from the upper deck to 6ft below the waterline.

Although originally designed for existing guns, better guns became available while the *Warrior* was building. The new main armament was of 110-pounder breech-loading rifled guns to fire conical shells. Eight of them were installed in the armoured area, with one each at bow and stern. They were supplemented by 26 of the 68-pounders originally intended, eight of which had to go outside the armoured area. Additionally, there were four 40-pounders on the quarter deck, but they were mainly for saluting.

When launched, the *Warrior* was the most powerful warship in the world, with guns and armour superior to all other ships; perhaps with justification, she was regarded as invincible. However, although rifled breech-loading guns eventually became accepted, those originally fitted to *Warrior* gave some trouble and were removed in 1867. They were replaced by four 8in and 28 7in rifled muzzle-loaders, which became standard in the navy until the 1880s.

Up to that time, warships had been rated according to the numbers of guns. Although *Warrior* was the most powerful warship afloat, according to the rules she was a third-rater, giving her captain a lower status (and pay) and making her complement 670 instead of the 1000 she could have carried. It was not until the 1880s that the word battleship came into use, to give a more reasonable recognition of ships of the new form.

It was a transitional period between sail and power, so even such a new conception as *Warrior* showed the influence of earlier sailing warships. She was flush-decked and had three masts, with their attendant rigging. The two funnels were between the two forward masts and each mast carried square sails and a gaff-headed fore-and-aft-sail. There could be up to three head sails on the bowsprit.

The boilers and engines were low and occupied much of the centre of the vessel. Coal bunkers were below the waterline. Accommodation for the crew came above the waterline, with the men sleeping in hammocks in every available space. The captain's cabin aft had the galleried windows around the quarter, reminiscent of the more gentlemanly and less violent days of sail.

In March 1862, in Hampton Roads, Virginia, two ironclads fought an inconclusive battle in the American Civil War. The Confederates had raised the sunken *Merrimac* and armoured it with sloping iron sides; it played havoc with Union shipping. The Union answer was the *Monitor*, also iron-cased. Both ships finished intact. Even if they had little effect on the progress of the war, they proved the ability of iron to resist the gunfire of the day.

The success of *Warrior* brought an end to the building of large wooden ships for the Royal Navy. *Victoria* was one of the last of the three-decker wooden warships. She was completed after the supremacy of ironclads had been established, yet she was sent to Malta as flagship to the Mediterranean fleet in 1864. Expert opinion was hostile and both Parliament and the press condemned the action. The official reasoning was that a roomy well-ventilated ship was needed as a headquarters. It was believed that the crowded ironclads would be unhealthy in hot climates. Conditions were not as bad as expected and the *Caledonia* took over as the first ironclad flagship of the Mediterranean Fleet in 1867.

Ironclads had their comfort improved by forced-draught ventilation, which was introduced in 1873. Newer ships were given greater weights of armour, and the ability of sails to drive them became less, so that steam became increasingly more important, although it was a long time before sails finally disappeared.

After *Warrior*, the Admiralty began to catch up on the production of ironclads, with 11 iron-built and nine wooden-hulled ironclads built during the 1860s. The *Black Prince* came first, in 1861, as a sister ship to *Warrior;* she was also built by a commercial yard. The *Achilles* was built at Chatham in 1863, as the first iron ship to be built in a naval dockyard. She was also the only British warship to be built with four masts, and had the largest sail area of any warship (44,000sq ft). At 9820 tons, she was heavier than *Warrior* and her dimensions were 380ft long, $58\frac{1}{4}$ft beam and $27\frac{1}{2}$ft draught. Her engines produced 5720hp and drove the ship at 14 knots, and she was claimed to make almost as much under sail. Later, she was reduced to three masts, but she still carried the largest sail area in the British Fleet.

Above: The 18-gun steam frigate 'Defence', which was part of the new ironclad fleet in 1862. *Illustrated London News*

Facing page above: The first sea-going ironclad, the French ship 'La Gloire' of 1859, from a lithograph by Le Breton.
National Maritime Museum London (Crown Copyright)

Facing page below: A coloured lithograph by T G Dutton of HMS 'Minotaur' (1863) which, with her sister-ship 'Shannon', carried more sail than any other ironclads.
National Maritime Museum London

The next three ships were given armour the full length of their hulls. They were the *Minotaur, Agincourt* and *Northumberland* and were all alike, with displacement of 10,700 tons, length of 400ft, beam of $59\frac{1}{2}$ft and draught of $27\frac{3}{4}$ft. They were given ram bows and were the only five-masters in any battle fleet. The 400ft of armour each side was $5\frac{3}{4}$in thick at the centre, tapering to $4\frac{1}{2}$in at the edges, on a backing of 10in of wood. Not surprisingly, the performance under sail with such a great weight to drive was poor, but speed under power was quite good, at 14 knots. All three ships became flagships.

Up to the time of *Minotaur* and her sisters, steering was still manual, that is, the rudder was turned by the steering wheel directly through cables and linkage. Despite the introduction of gearing, the effort needed to move the rudder became too much at times. Soon after the *Agincourt* came into commission, during heavy weather in the English Channel, the effort of 15 men fighting to hold her four-tier wheel was insufficient to keep her under control. As a result, the *Northumberland* was given power-assisted steering, the first ship so to be equipped; it was then fitted to the other two of the class. Increasing trust in steam propulsion was implicit in the removal of the second and fourth masts from all three ships.

Britain still had plenty of good shipbuilding timber and small craft continued to be built of wood. Some smaller warships were built as iron-cased wooden hulls, both to use up good timber and economically to maintain British supremacy at sea over the French.

The *Lord Clyde* and the *Lord Warden*, both built to use up large amounts of wood still in the dockyards at Chatham and Pembroke, were built as iron-cased frigates. They were the heaviest wooden-hulled ships, of 7750 tons and 7940 tons respectively, and were launched in 1864 and 1865 and given rigs almost the same as *Warrior.* The wooden construction was massive. The 2ft oak ribs were filled between with oak which was covered by a skin of $1\frac{1}{2}$in iron plates, followed by a further 6in layer of more oak and a belt of armour tapering from $5\frac{1}{2}$in at the centre to $4\frac{1}{2}$in towards the ends. There was a further sheath of 5in oak covered with a layer of muntz metal (as a protection against fouling and marine borers) below the waterline.

The *Lord Warden* had a comparatively uneventful honourable service of 18 years, the last six as flagship of the Mediterranean fleet. The *Lord Clyde* was a sister ship, but she had a short life full of trouble. She was given new trunk-type engines, which were the most powerful at that

time, but they wore out in two years. She was given new engines, but after six months' service she ran aground. When docked to have the damage inspected, a serious fungus attack was found on the green wood from which she had been built, so she was sold out of the Service in 1875 for a small sum.

With the realisation that sail was no longer needed there came a gunnery change. Because of the masts and rigging, guns could only be conveniently arranged to fire broadside. Any sort of swivelling gun would have only a small arc of fire, without the risk of shooting away masts or rigging. With steam engines as the only means of propulsion, a different deck layout became possible.

Turret guns with restricted movement had, however, already been tried on sailing ships. The armoured warship *Monarch* served 45 years on the effective list and can claim to have given the longest service in the armoured battle fleet. She was built in 1868 and was 8300 tons and 330ft long. She was given two turrets with restricted arcs of movement between her three masts. After a modernisation refit lasting seven years, she emerged in 1897, still with three short masts, but without sails. Engine power of 8126hp gave a maximum speed of $14\frac{3}{4}$ knots, and coal bunkerage was sufficient for a range of up to 6000 miles.

Monarch had a freeboard of 15ft and, judging from her long active service, was stable. *Captain* was a generally similar vessel, built in 1869, but had only nine feet of freeboard. While sailing with Captain Cowper Coles, her designer, on board, she heeled so far under the press of sail in a beam wind, that she did not recover but turned over completely and sank, taking with her all but 18 men.

After a fairly lengthy period of transition, in 1872 there came *Devastation*. She became the prototype sail-less battleship. She had new compound engines and a central island carrying funnels, derricks, boats and controls. The design enabled turrets to be arranged, one forward and one aft, each having a clear swing of more than 180 degrees. With the passing of sail, the term ironclad was also on the wane and steel completely replaced iron in the hulls of British warships from 1881 onwards.

The three-decker battleship HMS 'Victoria' was among the last of the type to be built. She carried 121 guns and represented the acme of development of the sailing warship, the traditional 'wooden walls'. The 'Victoria' was launched in 1859, the same year in which the French 'La Gloire', a broadside battleship heavily iron plated over wood, appeared and only a year before the British iron-hulled battleship 'Warrior' was launched. Both the French and British ironclads were powered by infant steam, though for security they retained their sailing rig. From a painting by W Fred Mitchell.

DEVASTATION TO INFLEXIBLE

IN NOVEMBER 1869 the warship of a new era was laid down in the Royal Dockyard at Portsmouth. Not only was she to be the first battleship to do without sails and the first large iron ship to be built at Portsmouth, but the massive main armament of four 35-ton muzzle-loading guns intended for her also had novel features. They were to be mounted in forward and aft turrets, with two of the monster guns in each, which would give direct fire ahead and astern and clear arcs of bearing on the beam.

The *Devastation*, as the new ship was named, was equipped to train the turrets by steam power, but the guns would still be loaded laboriously by hand. Even the training round would be far from swift; from full elevation to full depression, for instance, was an operation taking at least 13 minutes. In contrast to their size, the secondary armament was far behind, with a total of half-a-dozen 6-pounders and 14 smaller guns.

The *Devastation* was well provided with armour. Along the sides it varied in thickness from 12 down to 8½ inches and the turrets were thicker still at 14 down to 10 inches, with a backing of 18 to 16 inches; the conning-tower had armour between nine and six inches thick. The full weight of the armour was 2540 tons and to keep it down to that weight the bow and stern were left practically unprotected, a point that gave rise to controversy but was later accepted.

The ship was square in section, with the maximum beam running for two-thirds of the length, and the bottom was almost flat. The flat forecastle had no sheer and only nine feet of freeboard, the straight bow terminating under water in a prominent ram. Since steam was her sole motive power it was necessary to provide considerable capacity in her coal bunkers in the days before coaling stations existed, or perhaps had been even thought of. Having two propellers, she had an even chance of retaining mobility in the event of a major mechanical breakdown.

Although she was in several ways a big advance in naval architecture, the design advances had in fact been foreshadowed in the so-called breastwork monitors, of which the *Devastation* and her sisters were enlarged repeats. The two funnels and lack of a mast and yard, and the all-round low freeboard and great turrets roused a good deal of comment. In fact she was roundly condemned on nearly every side. Even so, when she was rammed by HMS *Resistance* in 1874, although some side plating was displaced, she did not spring a leak or incur serious damage, which says much for her stout build.

The record of the new guns was not so favourable. There was certainly one incident with the Devastation class, and possibly another, of a gun exploding during practice and killing some of its crew. It was possible apparently to reload a gun even when the previous round had failed to fire. If that happened the double-charged gun could burst at the next firing.

The *Thunderer* was built at Pembroke in 1872 as a sister ship of the *Devastation*, but there were some improvements and modifications incorporated. Her big turret guns were of two different sizes, with one pair of 35 tons and the other of 38 tons. She was of rather greater displacement than the *Devastation's* total of 9330 tons and was fitted with hydraulic gun-loading gear. Soon after being commissioned she took on board 16-inch Whitehead torpedoes for tests and experiment, an unusual employment in a battleship at that date. The *Thunderer* also had her troubles. In 1876 off Portsmouth a safety-valve failure led to a boiler explosion, causing 45 deaths and 50 injured in the ship's company. A double-charged gun explosion in 1879 resulted in 11 men killed and 30 injured.

Above: A painting of HMS 'Devastation' in the National Maritime Museum, London.
National Maritime Museum London

Accidents notwithstanding, turrets and big guns had come to stay and the next step in development was in 1876, with the *Inflexible*. She was of about 11,880 tons and was something of a phenomenon in the British fleet, probably inspired by the Italian turret ship *Duilio*. *Inflexible's* armour on the waterline was restricted to a central citadel and she had thick protected iron decks fore and aft. Her looks were strange indeed when she started life rigged as a brig and with two funnels. She had a full set of sails, amounting to 18,500 square feet of canvas, in the rather optimistic idea that she could take her place and keep station in

THE BOMBARDMENT OF
ALEXANDRIA, 11TH–12TH JULY, 1882.
De Simone, 1883.

the manoeuvres and exercises of the wooden ships of the Channel Fleet. The original rig did not last for very long. In her first refit the masts and yards were taken out and replaced by pole masts with signal yards.

The two turrets were arranged in echelon between the funnels under a 'flying bridge' and both were integral with the central citadel, a major item which measured 110 feet by 75 feet and rose $9\frac{1}{2}$ feet above water. The turrets held the heaviest guns of the British Navy—muzzle-loading giants of 80 tons. With high bulky funnels spaced widely between the masts, low freeboard and apparently no bulwarks, and with a great beam and narrow superstructure, she was certainly no beauty. But she did have one unique feature that was eventually adopted in all navies; her ends, otherwise unprotected, incorporated an armoured deck along the waterline with very full subdivision above that line in order to localise flooding.

Left: Painting by De Simone of the bombardment of Alexandria in July 1882. *The Parker Gallery*

Bottom: A gatefold from a July 1882 supplement of 'The Illustrated London News' showing the ships engaged in the bombardment of Alexandria. *Illustrated London News*

Below: Representation from a May 1876 edition of 'The Illustrated London News' of the launch of the 'Inflexible' at Portsmouth Dockyard. *Illustrated London News*

Left: The after stokehold of the 'Thunderer' showing the exploded steam boiler which killed 45 men in July 1876.
Illustrated London News

Above: The launch of an unnamed ironclad, as depicted in a Raphael Tuck book.
M Muir Collection

Below left: Painting of HMS 'Inflexible' in the National Maritime Museum, London.
National Maritime Museum London

In general, *Inflexible's* armour was thicker than any ships of her era, or indeed since. Besides that, she carried two 60-foot torpedo-boats and some newly developed torpedo equipment, including submerged tubes and a grid for launching torpedoes over the bow. In addition she had electric lighting, watertight compartments for engines and boiler, and even anti-rolling tanks.

Both the *Devastation* and the *Inflexible* were among the nine big ships that sailed to Egypt under the command of Admiral Sir Beauchamp Seymour in a time of crisis. In 1882 a notable Egyptian character and wayward rebel, Arabi Pasha, was threatening to seize the Suez Canal, which was vital to Britain, and diplomacy proved useless. Arabi, in spite of all efforts to dissuade him, persisted in building or strengthening the line of forts guarding Alexandria. When an ultimatum sent by Seymour was ignored, he ordered a bombardment of the forts.

The majority of the ships engaged were broadside ironclads, which meant that only about half their guns could be used. Although their fire was impressive and accurate, the damage it did to the forts was a good deal less than had been expected. After enduring nearly four hours of shelling, the defenders of the main fort decided that they had had enough and abandoned it, whereupon a landing-party from the *Inflexible* spiked or blew up its guns. During the afternoon one fort after another stopped firing and it was all over. The casualty-list in the fleet at the end amounted to a total of six killed and 27 wounded; a very light list considering that 75 projectiles had hit the ships.

The engagement had at the least served to show the effectiveness of the iron plating of all the ships that were under continuous shelling and cannon-ball fire. It provided a realistic proving ground, fortuitous or not, in those days of change, experiment and discovery, which covered the general replacement of the muzzle-loading gun by the breech-loader. The timber-built ships, those 'Wooden Walls of Old England', were fast vanishing and the torpedo had made its ominous appearance. There was the coming of the twin screw-propellers, and improvements in engines and boilers. Last and certainly not least, there was the reign of the all-big-gun ship that was to endure until the era of the aircraft carrier after the Pacific battles of the 1939-45 war.

THE NEW NAVY

IN 1881 when William H. Hunt accepted the office of Secretary of the Navy, the United States fleet comprised a heterogeneous assortment of wooden-hulled vessels, variously classed as screw frigates, corvettes and sloops, four iron gunboats and 14 shallow-draught monitors, each armed with a pair of 15-inch smooth-bore guns and all laid up in varying states of disrepair. In addition, there were under construction (officially classed as being 'rebuilt') five larger monitors, the iron hulls of which had been laid down in 1874.

Under the leadership of former Civil War generals the nation foresaw no external threat and with much to be done at home by way of opening up the west there was little demand for any overseas adventure. In the circumstances Congress limited the activities of the Navy to showing the flag in distant waters coupled with the provision of some degree of protection for American seaborne trade in areas where piracy was still prevalent; a policy which involved spending as little money as possible. This then was the 'Old Navy', hard worked and proud of its traditions, but obsolete and only twelfth in the numerical line-up of the world's navies – behind those of China, Chile and Denmark!

The navy was outdated and it was becoming increasingly apparent that urgent action was required if even minimum commitments were to be met. Out of that conviction, William Hunt, convinced that past inaction was due largely to a lack of appreciation of the place of the United States in a global context, appointed a working party to investigate the role of the Navy and to make recommendations concerning the strength and make-up of the fleet.

The Naval Advisory Board, headed by Rear Admiral John Rodgers, set to work but quickly became embroiled in fruitless argument centred in particular on the choice of iron or steel as a structural material. Abroad, steel was fast replacing iron for ship constructions; it was stronger than iron, of very much more consistent quality and could be produced in very much larger sizes of plate. At that time, however, there was little capacity in the United States for the production of steel and difficulties were foreseen in developing the necessary sources of supply. The opposing factions failed to agree and the Advisory Board submitted two reports of which the majority version called for the immediate construction of 38 cruisers and 25 torpedo boats, their hulls to be built of steel, which extravagant proposal was rejected out of hand. Then, in September 1881, the assassination of President Garfield brought in its wake the removal of Secretary Hunt and his replacement, as a political pay-off, by William E. Chandler.

Eventually, in 1882, Congress authorised the construction of two cruisers, although no additional financial provision was made beyond the regular Navy Department vote. Cost-conscious at all times, Congress decreed the appointment of a second Naval Advisory Board to oversee the building of the proposed cruisers. In the event, the new board, headed by Commodore Robert Shufeldt, managed some revision of the programme and the appropriation of 1,300,000 dollars for the construction of three small protected cruisers and a dispatch vessel. The bill authorising this modest beginning was signed by President Chester Arthur on March 3, 1883.

Tenders for the construction of the four vessels were invited in May 1883 and eventually, in the wake of considerable delays and alterations to plans and specifications, orders for all four were placed with John Roach of Chester, Pennsylvania. Although strictly within the law, since Roach had submitted the lowest tender, the choice proved something of a disaster. Unsatisfactory steelwork, destruction of part of the shipyard by fire and indecision on the part of the Navy Department delayed the completion of the 1485-ton dispatch vessel *Dolphin*, with the result that her initial contractor's sea trials started about two months late and ended catastrophically in

Top: United States Navy steel-built steam frigate 'Chicago' as portrayed in 'Harper's New Monthly Magazine' of June 1886.
Peter Newark's Western Americana

Above, centre: The launching of the first US Submarine Torpedo-boat 'Adder'.
Illustrated London News, 24 August 1901

Above: The US armoured cruiser 'Brooklyn' whose design was influenced by French ideas.
E. Muller

November 1884 with the fracture of her steel propeller shaft.

However, 1884 was election year once again and President Arthur's interim Republican government was swept aside by Grover Cleveland and a Democrat administration which took office in March 1885. The new Secretary of the Navy, William Whitney, in the light of the abortive *Dolphin* trials, had the contract invalidated, bringing all work to a halt not only on the *Dolphin* but also on the cruisers *Atlanta*, *Boston* and *Chicago*. Two years later John Roach was dead, leaving his shipyard in the hands of his creditors.

Since no other shipyard was willing to take over the contract, completion of the ABCD ships was put under the direction of the Navy Department and eventually in December 1885, notwithstanding her initial rejection, the *Dolphin* was commissioned without ceremony as the first ship of the 'New Navy'. The 3189-ton single-screw cruisers *Atlanta* and *Boston*, each armed with a pair of 8-inch and six 6-inch breech-loading rifled guns, followed in July 1886 and May 1887 respectively and this modest construction programme was completed with the delivery in April 1889 of the somewhat larger protected cruiser *Chicago*, a 4500-ton twin-screw vessel mounting four 8-inch, eight 6-inch and two 5-inch guns. None of these vessels carried any torpedo armament.

All-in-all, the quartet represented a tremendous step forward in United States naval design philosophy, although the choice of compound machinery reflected the contemporary limitations of US engineering practice. In 1889 the ABC cruisers and the 1710-ton steel gunboat *Yorktown*, completed in that year by William Cramp of Philadelphia, were organised under the command of Rear Admiral John G. Walker as a 'Squadron of Evolution' to provide basic training in fleet work and tactics for those who were to man the ships of the New Navy. Painted white with buff or black tops to buff funnels and with gleaming brightwork, the vessels set new standards of elegance when they visited foreign ports for the purpose of showing the flag. In 1888-89 the little dispatch vessel *Dolphin* undertook a round-the-world cruise in the course of which she steamed about 58,000 miles without incident apart from a few very minor machinery failures.

The ABCD ships had proved themselves and had brought the US Navy out of the long years of post-Civil War neglect, engendered by the prevailing isolationist spirit, back on to the world scene. Already, however, William Whitney's strictures in respect of the design of these vessels had resulted in the postponement of the construction of a further pair of protected cruisers, authorised in 1885, pending modifications to improve protection and internal layout. In the event, an order was placed in 1887 with William Cramp for the construction of a fourth cruiser, somewhat smaller than the *Chicago* and mounting a single-calibre battery of 12 6-inch guns, but once again lack of experience in steel fabrication delayed the erection and plating of her hull on the slipway and not until March 1890 was she launched as USS *Newark*. Despite the almost complete abandonment of sail by the major navies for front-line warships, the 4083-ton *Newark* carried a full three-masted barque rig which contrasted strangely with her twin screws and horizontal triple-expansion machinery.

In the meantime, the Union Iron Works of San Francisco had been awarded a contract for the construction of a fifth cruiser which, in order to expedite delivery, was to be built to plans prepared by Armstrong's of Newcastle-on-Tyne, England, for the Japanese cruiser *Naniwa*, although the intended armament was somewhat lighter.

Laid down in 1887, the 4040-ton *Charleston* carried no sails and was commissioned for service in December 1889, more than a year before the *Newark*! The *Baltimore* and *Philadelphia* built by William Cramp, again to plans prepared by Armstrong's, followed in January and July 1890 respectively and finally, in November 1890, the Union Iron Works delivered the 4083-ton *San Francisco*, a 19-knot vessel mounting 12 6-inch guns which, apart from the absence of sail, was virtually a sister of the *Newark*.

With the delivery of the *Newark* in February 1891, the front-line strength of the US Navy comprised eight protected cruisers, none more than five years old and all but the *Atlanta* and *Boston* capable of 18 or 19 knots. In addition, much had been learned about the construction of steel ships and their machinery, and necessity had given birth to a modern naval armaments industry capable of meeting the needs of the fleet. In the case of the *Atlanta*, launched in October 1884, manufacture of the forgings for her 8-inch guns proved too great an undertaking for the infant US steel industry of the day and they had to be bought in from the United Kingdom. However, the Midvale Steel Company of Philadelphia was in a position to produce the necessary forgings for guns of 6-inch calibre and less, and by 1887 the Bethlehem Iron Company had built up the necessary facilities and expertise to take on the manufacture of forgings for all large breech-loading guns.

The eventual aim, ever since the appointment of the Naval Advisory Boards, had been the construction of a balanced fleet which would be capable of looking after US overseas interests wherever and whenever the occasion might demand. For obvious reasons, however, early construction programmes made no reference to large armoured vessels and not until 1886 was it considered that the capacity and skills of the domestic steel industry were sufficiently developed to undertake such work. There still remained outstanding the question of design experience, or rather lack of it, and in the circumstances the Navy Department offered 15,000 dollars for the submission of detailed plans for a 16-knot armoured coast defence ship to be built in a US shipyard, a private or a navy yard, the development of which had been encouraged by a measure enacted by Congress in August 1886.

In the event, of 13 designs submitted, that for a second-class battleship prepared by the Naval Construction & Armament Company of Barrow, England, was accepted, the subsequent order for her construction being placed with Norfolk Navy Yard where it was laid down in 1889. Although launched in June 1892, completion was delayed by lack of experience in the fabrication of armour plate and by the late delivery of her triple-expansion machinery so that it was August 1895 before she eventually commissioned for service as USS *Texas*.

Already outdated, the 6315-ton vessel was armed with a pair of 12-inch guns in single turrets sited, in order to achieve the maximum arcs of fire, en echelon above a redoubt protected by 12-inch armour; the arrangement was similar to that in British battleships of the Ajax and Colossus classes. She mounted also six 6-inch and 12 6-pounder guns in addition to four 18-inch Whitehead torpedo tubes. The obsolete *Texas* was in a class on her own; she contributed little to subsequent US battleship design although she did in fact play a useful role during the Spanish-American War of 1898.

The *Texas* was followed in September 1895 by the 6682-ton *Maine*, initially classed as an armoured cruiser but rerated before completion as a second-class battleship. Armed with four 10-inch guns in twin turrets, again arranged en echelon, the *Maine* bore some resemblance to the *Texas* and like the latter vessel had little influence on the mainstream of US battleship development. Her destruction, possibly by internal explosion, in the course of an operational visit to Havana, Cuba, in February 1898, triggered off the Spanish-American War the outbreak of which followed in May that year.

In 1890 Congress authorised the construction of three 'seagoing coastline battleships' to be named *Indiana*, *Oregon* and *Massachusetts*. Launched in 1893, these heavily armed vessels carried four 13-inch guns in twin mountings forward and aft, eight 8-inch guns also in twin turrets and four 6-inch casemate-mounted guns, all on a normal displacement of only 10,288 tons. Powered by triple-expansion machinery driving twin screws, the Indiana class were designed for 16 knots, although it is doubtful whether that speed was ever achieved. In fact, too much had been attempted on a small displacement although, on the other hand, the trio did form the nucleus of a US

battle squadron, albeit of limited radius of action since the normal coal stowage was but 400 tons.

In the meantime, the early protected cruisers had been followed by the 5870-ton *Olympia*, completed by the Union Iron Works in 1895, and the 3213-ton sisters *Cincinnati* and *Raleigh* built respectively by the New York and Norfolk Navy Yards. The *Olympia*, mounting four 8-inch and 10 5-inch guns, with six 18-inch torpedo tubes, gained fame as Admiral Dewey's flagship at Manila Bay on May 1, 1898, and is still afloat as a naval museum at Philadelphia. At the same time the US Navy took up the armoured cruiser theme of a large fast vessel protected by an arched armoured deck supplemented by a partial vertical armoured belt. The principle had originated in France and was adopted in the design of the *Maine*, although the vessel had been reclassified as a second-class battleship.

The first true armoured cruiser built for the US Navy was the 8200-ton *New York*, a 21-knot vessel mounting six 8-inch and 12 4-inch guns, delivered by William Cramp in 1893. Designated Armoured Cruiser No 2 (the *Maine* having been classed originally as No 1), the *New York* was followed by the 9215-ton *Brooklyn* (No 3) the design of which owed much to French influence. With her raised forecastle, pronounced tumblehome and tall funnels rising 100 feet above the level of the boiler furnace grates, she was of distinctive appearance and quite unlike any other cruiser serving with the New Navy.

Small-ship design demonstrated a desire for innovation in the matter of weapon systems. The small dispatch vessel *Dolphin*, herself reclassified eventually as a gunboat, was followed in December 1889 by the even smaller *Petrel*, a barquentine-rigged screw gunboat which contrived to mount four 6-inch guns on a hull only 176 feet long on the waterline and displacing but 892 tons. With a maximum speed of only 11½ knots she was just about the slowest vessel in the US Navy of her day!

Authorised in 1885 at the same time as the *Petrel*, the 1710-ton *Yorktown* was designed as a torpedo gunboat on the lines of similar craft then in service with the major European navies but, although provided with openings, the planned six torpedo tubes were never installed and the *Yorktown*, which first commissioned for service in April 1889, was assigned to the Squadron of Evolution. In later years she was employed in keeping with the accepted gunboat concept as a small cruiser showing the flag and on general police duties, thereby maintaining an American presence in distant waters. The activities of such vessels seldom reached the newspapers but their ships' companies were probably harder worked and created more goodwill than any serving in the larger and more glamorous vessels of the fleet.

In the early 1880s a young army officer, Lieutenant Edmund Zalinski, had developed a so-called dynamite gun to fire shells charged with guncotton, a relatively unstable explosive capable of developing far more destructive energy than the conventional black powder bursting charge. Guncotton is of course sensitive to shock and heat or both and compressed air was employed as the propellant in the smoothbored gun. The dynamite gun excited considerable interest amongst investors and eventually the Pneumatic Dynamite Gun Company of New Jersey was formed to manufacture and market the weapon.

Thereafter, pressure was brought to bear on the Navy Department and in 1886 Congress approved the appropriation of 350,000 dollars for the construction of a 'dynamite gun cruiser', the order for which was placed with the Dynamite Gun Company, which subcontracted the hull and machinery to William Cramp. Launched as *Vesuvius* on April 28, 1888, this small 929-ton craft was armed with three 15-inch dynamite guns built into her forecastle structure at a fixed angle of eighteen degrees, aim being a matter of pointing the vessel at the intended target. The *Vesuvius* first commissioned for service in June 1890 but although spectacular her weapon system was doomed to failure. She ended her active career in 1918 as a gunboat armed with a single 3-inch gun.

Authorised in March 1889, the design of the armoured ram *Katahdin* was regressive rather than innovatory but there existed within US naval circles at the time a school of thought which still favoured the ram as the weapon for coastal defence. The Royal Navy had built the armoured torpedo ram *Polyphemus* with a powerful torpedo armament in 1881, but the US Navy did not introduce the torpedo as a fleet weapon until about 1894 and the 2155-ton *Katahdin* was armed only with four 6-pounder guns. Despite the arguments in favour of the ram as a weapon, it had to be admitted that experience had shown it to be more destructive in peace than in war! In the event, the *Katahdin* proved cramped, uncomfortable and of little practical use; after a year in commission she was paid off and, apart from a brief excursion during the Spanish-American War, saw no further service until eventually she was hulked as 'Ballistic Experimental Target A'. Her end came in September 1909 when she was sunk off Rappahannock Spit, Virginia.

Facing page: The 4500-ton cruiser 'Chicago' of 1889 as seen in 'The Sphere' of 11 July 1903. *Illustrated London News*

Top: USS 'Oregon', one of three powerful 'seagoing coastline battleships' authorised in 1890 and launched in 1893. *J Maber Collection*

Above: 'Kentucky', the 11,540-ton battleship, from a stereograph of 1907. *Peter Newark's Western Americana*

The coast battleships of the Indiana class with their limited capability and radius of action were followed by the 11,340-ton *Iowa*, launched by Wm Cramp in March 1896 and accepted for service in June the following year. With a higher freeboard, greater radius of action and a lighter but more-effective 12-inch gun, she was a far more formidable fighting ship than her immediate predecessors. Like the armoured cruiser *Brooklyn*, she was easily distinguished by her pronounced tumblehome and 100-

foot funnels, which put her in a class on her own where battleships were concerned.

In 1881 the Naval Advisory Board had proposed the construction of torpedo boats as an integral part of the US fleet, although it was not until August 1886 that Congress authorised funds for the first such craft. She was appropriately named *Cushing* after Lieutenant William Cushing who in October 1864, in charge of a steam launch armed with a spar torpedo, had sunk the armoured gunboat *Albemarle* in the Roanoke River. Built by Herreshoff of Bristol, Rhode Island, the galvanised steel-hulled *Cushing* displaced 105 tons and with quadruple-expansion machinery driving twin screws was capable of 22 knots. Armament comprised a fixed 18-inch torpedo tube in the bow and two pivoted torpedo tubes on deck. The *Cushing* commissioned in 1890 but she was employed mainly on experimental work to establish the basic requirements for subsequent US torpedo boat design.

Progress was in fact very slow and only in that same year, 1890, was the building of a second vessel, to be named *Ericsson*, authorised by Congress. Design problems and machinery breakdowns seriously delayed construction work and not until February 1897 was the *Ericsson* commissioned for service with the fleet. In the meantime orders for three more craft, each of 142 tons, had been placed with the Columbian Iron Works of Baltimore but by then major design problems appear to have been resolved and the *Foote*, *Rodgers* and *Winslow*, each armed with three 18-inch Whitehead torpedo tubes, were completed between August 1897 and April 1898 – with the outbreak of the Spanish-American War but a few weeks off.

In keeping with their nocturnal role, the torpedo boats were painted black but, these small craft apart, United States warships still retained their white hulls, gilt scroll work and buff, or black-topped buff, funnels. However, in the wake of the declaration of war against Spain, a uniform dark-grey livery was adopted for all but the torpedo craft.

At the turn of the century the fleet comprised five battleships, with another eight under construction, two armoured cruisers, 16 smaller protected and unarmoured (or peace) cruisers, 17 gunboats and eight torpedo boats; in all a formidable force although not yet the balanced fleet envisaged in the early days of the Naval Advisory Boards.

The 11,540-ton battleships *Kearsarge* and *Kentucky*, completed by the Newport News Shipbuilding Company respectively in February and May 1900, represented a further stage in US capital ship development, although in fact they were still classed as Coast Battleships (Nos 5 and 6). Apparently, the 12-inch gun mounted in the *Iowa* had not come up fully to expectations and the *Kearsarge* and *Kentucky* were armed with four of the earlier pattern of 13-inch guns in twin mountings forward and aft. An unusual feature was that the twin 8-inch mountings forming the secondary armament were carried atop the 13-inch gunhouses but in practice this 'superposed turret' arrangement involved the disadvantage that the 8-inch guns could not be trained independently of their parent 13-inch turrets. In other respects, however, the sisters were relatively conventional although, like the Indiana class, lack of freeboard had an adverse effect on their seakeeping qualities. Both vessels carried a tertiary battery of 14 5-inch casemate-mounted guns.

As in other navies, a need to counter the torpedo boat threat led to the development of the torpedo boat destroyer, the first such vessel for the US Navy being the 420-ton *Bainbridge* delivered by Neafie & Levy of Philadelphia in 1902. Engined with triple-expansion machinery of 8000ihp driving twin screws, the *Bainbridge* was capable of 28 knots; her offensive armament comprised two 18-inch Whitehead torpedo tubes, two 3-inch quick-firing guns and five 6-pounder guns. In all, 16 destroyers were included in this first group authorised in 1898 and it was these craft which initiated the line of development leading eventually to the successful flush-decked designs of the First World War.

For nearly 20 years the US Navy Department had been slowly feeling its way, benefiting to some extent meanwhile by the experience of foreign navies in the fields of ship design and operation, while the US shipbuilding and marine engineering industries developed the necessary skills and expertise for the construction of a modern fleet. Thus, in the development of the major warship types the US Navy lagged, at least on paper, some years behind the front-line European navies.

On the other hand, the United States was well to the forefront in the matter of submarine design, largely due to the inventive genius of an Irish migrant John P. Holland who, after many years of experiment, built as a private venture a 54-foot-long craft driven on the surface by a 45bhp petrol engine and when submerged by a battery-powered electric motor. She was armed with a single 18-inch torpedo tube and an 8-inch Zalinski-type dynamite gun, despite the fact that the dynamite gun was already considered ineffective. In April 1900 this small submersible, named *Holland*, was purchased on behalf of the US Navy and in June that same year, Congress authorised the construction of six vessels of the Adder class built to the same basic design but 64 feet long and armed with only a single 18-inch torpedo tube. A seventh craft of the same type, named *Plunger*, was built in lieu of an earlier Holland steam-driven submarine which had not been accepted by the Navy.

Battleship construction continued with the three 11,565-ton vessels of the Illinois class completed in 1900-01 which, with a higher freeboard and the abandonment for the time being of the superposed turret principle, represented a distinct improvement over their immediate predecessors of the Kearsage class. The three 12,370-ton battleships of the Maine class followed and then, in May 1906, completion of the 14,948-ton *Virginia* marked a return to the superposed turret arrangement, although it was not repeated in later classes.

By mid-1907 the United States fleet comprised 22 battleships, nine armoured cruisers, 22 smaller cruisers, 16 destroyers and seven submarines together with an assortment of torpedo boats, gunboats and supporting craft. In all, it represented the beginnings of a balanced fleet but it has to be remembered that the available strength had of necessity to be divided between two oceans, a situation which had been aggravated by the increased commitments inherited in the wake of the Spanish-American War.

In December 1907 a major part of the US battle fleet assembled in Hampton Roads; 16 battleships, a flotilla of destroyers and supporting vessels, the former painted once again in the old white-hulled livery, with black-topped buff funnels and gleaming brightwork, forming what was to become known as the Great White Fleet. The round-the-world goodwill cruise was intended not only to demonstrate that the United States was prepared to play its part in the conduct of world affairs but also to provide a training ground for those who were to command and administer the fleet in years to come. With the return of the fleet to Hampton Roads for a Presidential Review on the anniversary of George Washington's birthday in 1909, the New Navy had come of age and the groundwork had been prepared for the part the United States Navy was to play in the coming First World War.

Below: 'Kearsage', the great battleship of 1900.
'The Sphere', 11 July 1903 (Illustrated London News)

THE SUBMARINE

THE FIRST known recorded mention of a submarine, apart from devices for working under water such as diving bells, is in a book published in 1578. William Bourne's *Inventions and Devices* contains a description of a boat with bilges filled with leather bags capable of being emptied by screw presses; the boat was intended to run below the surface, and the rowers drew their air through a hollow mast.

As there is no proof that Bourne's boat was ever built, the credit for the first working submersible craft goes to the Dutchman Cornelius van Drebbel, who tested two boats on the Thames in 1620. The claims made for him were clearly overstated, but his design for an oar-propelled vessel, sealed with greased leather, did work, and even King James I is reputed to have travelled in one of them. The first mechanical submarine, however, was built by the Frenchman de Son in 1653, when he designed a catamaran driven by a clockwork engine. The idea collapsed, however, because the engine failed to move the hull, and nothing more was heard of submarines for over a century.

The Royal Navy's blockade of the rebellious American colonies drove David Bushnell to design his *Turtle* in 1776. It was a small one-man submarine driven by a hand-worked propeller, and it achieved the first military mission in submarine history. On September 6, 1776, an army sergeant attacked the 64-gun ship HMS *Eagle* off New York, but, probably owing to the copper sheathing, he failed to find a suitable place on the ship's bottom for securing the charge. After several attempts the *Turtle* and her brave occupant withdrew safely, foiled by lack of a suitable weapon.

During the French Revolution another talented American, Robert Fulton, produced a submarine known as the *Nautilus*. After several unsuccessful attempts to sell his idea, he finally interested Napoleon Bonaparte, who gave him financial backing. The *Nautilus* was built and functioned satisfactorily, but nothing came of the experiment because of haggling over money and a number of quibbles over the legal status of submarine crews. In desperation Fulton crossed the Channel to present his submarine ideas to the hated British, and built an improved *Nautilus*.

Above: The British conventionally powered submarine 'Narwhal', of the Porpoise class, at Puerto Rica in 1969. *A Greenway*

This picture: A modern German U-boat in surface trim. *German Embassy London*

But again, after some impressive experiments, professional naval opinion was able to kill the idea. In a famous comment on the subject Lord St Vincent said, 'Pitt was the greatest fool that ever existed to encourage a mode of warfare, which those who command the sea did not want, and which, if successful, would deprive them of it'. However, the submarine was still far from a workable weapon of war, and it is fair to say that the Royal Navy was quite correct in turning down the submarine at such an early stage.

Other submarines followed in the mid-19th century, with Bauer's *Plongeur Marin* used against the Danish fleet in 1850, and the French *Plongeur* designed by Captain Bourgois in 1858. But it was the Americans who once more took the lead with their 'Davids' in the Civil War of 1861-66. The term 'David' was coined because the Confederate Navy thought of itself as David tackling the Federal Goliath, but there were in fact three or four types. The first type was not a true submarine but a partially submersible torpedo-boat with a steam engine and funnel; she could trim down until only the funnel and hatchway were above water and then charge an enemy with her spar torpedo, a long pole tipped with explosive. In October 1863 one such tiny vessel inflicted severe damage on the Federal ironclad *New Ironsides,* but the blast sank the 'David'.

Another type was oar-propelled, and could be fully submerged for a limited time. In February 1864 the *H L Hunley* successfully sank the steam sloop *Housatonic* at Charleston, the first time a warship had been sunk by a submarine. Unfortunately the explosion again sank the attacking submarine, a problem which could not be avoided as long as the spar torpedo was the best weapon available.

In England several inventors tried their hand at designing submarines, but the only successful designer was the Reverend George Garrett, who built a small egg-shaped boat at Liverpool in 1878. Luckily he attracted the attention of the Swedish industrialist Nordenfelt, who heard about the success of his second submarine, the *Resurgam.* A third boat was built at Stockholm, but that time the Whitehead fish torpedo provided the weapon which had been lacking previously. The self-propelled Whitehead torpedo enabled the submarine to attack from a safe distance, changing what had been only an interesting experiment into a weapon of deadly proportion. Several boats of Garrett-Nordenfelt design were built and sold to Turkey, Greece and Russia, but as their steam propulsion system was unsuited to submarines they were little more than curiosities.

Electric power provided the only answer, and the first submarine to use that type of propulsion was one built in Spain in 1888 by Isaac Peral, a naval officer. The idea was quickly developed in France too, and in the same year the French launched the *Gymnote,* a 60-foot cigar-shaped submarine driven by an electric motor supplied with current from 564 lead-acid accumulators. She proved sufficiently successful for a much larger submarine to be ordered in 1890, and named *Gustave Zédé* in honour of the *Gymnote's* designer. The French had long been searching for a cheap weapon to offset British naval supremacy, and they saw in the submarines the way to protect their coasts against attack at a fraction of the cost of battleships and fortifications. Design followed design, and by the turn of the century the French had an unchallenged lead in submarine development.

The only country to show anything like the same enthusiasm was the United States, which organised a competition in 1893 to stimulate designers. The winner of this competition was an Irish-American, John P Holland, who had been designing submarines for years to aid Ireland in her fight for independence by destroying the Royal Navy. Holland's ideas survived a disastrous attempt by the United States to improve the design, and eventually a second boat was built in place of the first, at Holland's own expense. She was so successful that she was immediately bought, and in 1901 the British Government also bought the rights to build Holland-designed submarines for the Royal Navy.

With three of the world's major navies firmly committed to the submarine, progress was rapid. The Holland designs proved that their idea of separate propulsion for working above and below water was preferable to the French idea of all-electric propulsion. That in turn forced designers to look for something better than the petrol engine, whose inflammable fumes caused frequent explosions. The answer was found first in the heavy oil engine, using paraffin, and finally the diesel motor, which was the most economical. The first diesel-engined submarine was the French *Aigrette,* launched in 1904, followed by the Russian *Minoga,* but the British, Americans and Germans proved more conservative, the last-named waiting until 1912.

By August 1914 there were over 270 submarines in service with various navies, as shown in the table.

Distribution of submarines in navies in August 1914

	Boats in service	*Boats building*
Austria	6	6
France	45	25
Germany	29	—
Britain	77	—
Italy	18	2
Denmark	7	2
Greece	2	—
Holland	7	4
Japan	13	13
Norway	4	—
Peru	2	—
Portugal	1	—
Russia	28	2
Sweden	5	—
USA	35	6

However impressive these figures looked, the submarine had not yet seen war. But between 1914 and 1918 the submarine had not only matured into a reliable and efficient type of warship, but had also become a deadly instrument of total war which caused millions of pounds' worth of damage and almost brought Great Britain to starvation and collapse. By the end of the war the Germans had completed 390 U-boats, which sank over 11 million tons of shipping, or a total of 6520 ships, of all nationalities. A further $7\frac{1}{2}$ million tons of shipping was damaged, and the value of the ships and their cargoes is beyond computation.

Virtually nobody saw such an effect in 1914, for it was universally accepted that maritime warfare would be fought in the old-fashioned way, with submarines stopping the enemy's merchant ships, removing their crews and then sinking them or sailing them home as prizes. Neutral shipping would of course be exempt, and in any case the submarine's main role was

considered to be attacking surface warships. Several factors combined to prevent that from happening for very long. At first warships proved easy targets, as when U9 under Kapitan-leutnant Weddigen sank the British armoured cruisers *Aboukir, Cressy* and *Hogue* together in September 1914, but they became less vulnerable when they moved everywhere with an escort of destroyers.

Then the British, under the mistaken impression that the German Government had requisitioned all foodstuffs, declared that the ships carrying edible material to the German ports were liable to be seized as prizes. The German U-boats had operated under international law, but only with great difficulty, for a submarine's crew was too small to allow her to put prize crews aboard her captures. Furthermore, any loitering on the surface to stop, search and examine neutral ships for contraband increased the odds of an enemy warship catching her. The harsh application of the blockade gave the Germans an excuse to relax the restrictions on their U-boats.

As the land war dragged on the Germans looked more and more to the U-boats to bring the war to a close by halting the flow of American munitions to Great Britain and France. The declaration of a war zone around the British Isles in February 1915 allowed the U-boats to sink any merchantman on sight, and the power of the new weapon was quickly demonstrated. Losses rose from a total of 48,000 tons in January 1915 to a peak of 185,000 tons in August. At that point the Allies gained a respite, thanks to growing American alarm at the slaughter of neutral shipping and the death of Americans on the high seas. The U-boats were ordered to restrict their attacks to transports and cargo-carrying vessels, and unrestricted warfare was not resumed until January 1917.

The political risks were enormous, but so were the prizes; nothing less than total victory for Germany. Despite all the warnings of American hostility the shipping losses rose to new levels – 881,000 tons in April 1917, at which point the British Isles had only six weeks' supplies left. A negotiated and ruinous peace with Germany seemed almost inevitable, with the defeat of France to follow, but on April 5 the United States declared war on Germany and put her entire resources at the disposal of the Allies.

At long last a series of overdue countermeasures was put into effect. The greatest of them was convoy, which had the effect of making the U-boats expose themselves to attack by warships surrounding groups of merchantmen. The simplicity of convoy

Top: The British Oberon-class patrol submarine 'Otus', armed with homing torpedoes, in Chilean waters in 1969.
A Greenway

Left: The American nuclear-powered fleet submarine 'Woodrow Wilson', armed with ballistic missiles, in the Atlantic.
Naval Photo Center Washington

was the only sure means of countering the submarine's unique quality of secrecy. A giant programme of shipbuilding was begun, and by 1918 the offensive had passed to the Allies, with U-boat losses rising to unbearable heights. When the Armistice came in 1918 the U-boat arm had lost 178 submarines and over 5000 men, 40 per cent of its personnel.

Between the wars there was a number of experiments in all navies based chiefly on wartime designs produced by Germany and Britain. The main German idea that was developed was that of the cruiser submarine, with long endurance and a heavy gun armament, while the chief British contribution was the concept of submarine-borne aircraft. Neither had much influence on submarines during the 1939-45 war or on tactics, and when Germany began to build submarines in 1934 she chose the medium-sized designs which had proved themselves 16 years earlier. The Americans and Japanese, on the other hand, developed large boats for the vast distances of the Pacific, and the American boats proved particularly well designed for the job.

When war broke out in September 1939 there was no doubt on either side about how submarines would be used, and the sinking of the liner *Athenia* on the first day, although against orders, set the pattern. The British Admiralty for its part put convoy into immediate effect, but lacked the enormous numbers of escort vessels that had been available in 1917. The 'locust years' had reduced the Royal Navy to a shadow of its former strength, and the losses in 1940-41 were grievous. The entry of the United States into the war in December 1941 did little at first beyond offering the U-boats a vast number of new targets, for the US Navy had also neglected to build escort vessels during peacetime. But the major contribution of the United States was its enormous shipbuilding capacity, and in 1942 mass-produced mercantile hulls and warships began to appear.

In the Pacific, American submarines soon began to show the superiority of their design and tactics by making large inroads into Japanese shipping. By comparison Japanese submarines scored few successes, and the American campaign in the Pacific showed what catastrophic damage could be inflicted on an island nation by the destruction of its commerce. The enormous losses of oil tankers immobilised Japan's air force, and those surface ships that escaped destruction at sea were unable to put to sea for lack of fuel. The reluctance of the Japanese to adopt convoy, under the illusion that it was merely a defensive measure, was paid for in blood.

The U-boats, organised by Admiral Dönitz, himself a submariner in the 1914-18 war, improved their techniques, and Dönitz introduced the 'wolf pack', which was a co-ordinated mass attack. The first U-boat to make contact with a convoy merely shadowed it while broadcasting details to U-boat HQ which then guided others to the target. When all were in position the pack attacked on every side, and theoretically a convoy and its escorts could be swamped.

Several convoys were badly mauled in 1942-43, but no convoy was ever annihilated by U-boats, thanks to the heroic efforts of escorts and the discipline and tireless devotion of civilian crews. The first effective countermeasure was ASDIC (now called sonar), which had actually been under development in 1918; it was an underwater listening device that had been perfected by the British and kept a closely guarded secret until 1940. Then came radar which allowed escorts to detect submarines operating on the surface, and refined forms of the device could even detect periscopes. The third important device was high-frequency direction-finding (Huff-Duff for short) which enabled escorts to pinpoint U-boats which were transmitting a radio signal. The three devices can be said to have made victory over the U-boats possible, but they were in fact accompanied by a whole range of weaponry and tactics used by ships and aircraft.

Aircraft proved a tremendous help to convoys, for their presence made it even harder for U-boats to stalk convoys, but in the early years of the war aircraft lacked the range to fly across the Atlantic. Eventually a judicious blend of long-range aircraft flying from advanced bases, and small extemporised aircraft carriers, the escort carriers and merchant aircraft carriers, gave convoys air cover all the way across the Atlantic. New ideas on convoy dispositions, particularly raising the number of ships in each convoy, also enabled the escorts to match each new development by the U-boats. The crisis came in 1943, when new countermeasures were tested against the new tactics and equipment introduced by Dönitz. The Battle of the Atlantic was decided in 1943, although it did not end until 1945, for it marked the last time that Germany had any hope of sinking sufficient ships to cut communication between America and the British Isles.

Dönitz continued to develop U-boat weaponry, and two innovations stand out. The first, a Dutch idea, was the Schnorkel, an air mast that enabled submarines to recharge their batteries while running at periscope depth, and thus reduced the time necessarily spent on the surface. The second was the fast-underwater submarine with large battery capacity and streamlined hull to give greater submerged speed and endurance. From the second idea came a third, the hydrogen peroxide submarine designed by Professor Walther, with a steam turbine using oxygen released from the peroxide fuel and so needing no outside air. A drawback was the extreme instability of the fuel.

Fortunately for the Allies, very few of the new submarines were finished by 1945, and the Germans' ideas were mainly of use to the victors. The Russians, British and Americans seized as many examples of German submarine technology as they could, and during the 1950s a whole new series of fast streamlined boats appeared in all navies. Although some examples of peroxide-fuelled submarines were tested, only the British pursued the idea for very long. An American development, the nuclear propulsion reactor, showed far more promise.

The British nuclear-powered conventionally armed fleet submarine 'Valiant' pictured at night in Torbay. *A Greenway*

The main advantage of the nuclear reactor is that it can generate enough heat to provide almost unlimited steam without using any oxygen at all. On the other hand, a reactor is large and needs much shielding, so nuclear submarines have to be much larger than conventional types and are therefore less handy. They are also very expensive, and only four countries – the USA, Britain, France and the USSR – have built them so far. Their great speed and endurance make them hard to attack by conventional means, and they are the most potent of warships. Furthermore, the invention of submarine-launched ballistic missiles has given the submarine destructive power greater than all the bombers of the 1939-45 war put together.

It might seem that there is no counter to the nuclear submarine but there are various factors acting against it. For one thing it is a lone wolf, for it cannot communicate very freely while submerged and therefore operates partly blind. Then, new anti-submarine weapons have been developed; the helicopter, flying much faster than the submarine can move, can search with a suspended (dunking) sonar and drop such weapons as homing torpedoes. Standoff weapons like the American ASROC and the Anglo-Australian IKARA can reach a submarine from a distant ship. Aircraft can search the ocean using devices that can detect distortion of the earth's magnetic field caused by the metal in a submarine's hull (magnetic anomaly detection or MAD). High-speed running produces a wake and sound effects underwater that can be detected by listening sonars.

The nuclear submarine is undergoing development of hull shape, equipment and tactics all the time. It can now deploy underwater fire control, new types of torpedo and new weapons to hit back at enemies like the helicopter and specialist anti-submarine ships. The British SLAM system, for example, fires small anti-aircraft missiles from a launcher at periscope depth and the American SUBROC is fired from a torpedo tube, leaves the water and flies to its target area and then becomes a depthcharge.

Above: The US destroyer 'Maddox' which was attacked by North Vietnamese vessels in the Gulf of Tonkin in 1964. *Central Press Photos Ltd*

This picture: D73 HMS 'Cavalier', one of the Navy's C-class destroyers, pictured in 1971. *A Greenway*

THE DESTROYER

FEW REMEMBER today that the destroyer was originally the torpedo-boat destroyer; it was brought into being for the specific purpose of protecting the major units of a fleet from the small fast craft evolved to operate the newly invented automobile torpedo. The name, shortened to destroyer, continued to be applied long after the initial purpose had become but one of a number of tasks allotted to that type of ship. Nevertheless, a historical survey must begin with a brief account of the evolution of the torpedo-boat.

The first of the type were steam launches towing the explosive device known as the Harvey torpedo after its inventor; or they were fitted with a spar torpedo—a long pole projecting forward and downward from the boat with an explosive charge on the end, detonated by ramming against the target's side below the waterline. The latter were successfully used by both sides in the American Civil War. Between 1873 and 1875, the British firms of Thornycroft and Yarrow specialised in torpedo boats and built a large number for many nations. They were craft of about seven or eight tons displacement and a speed of 15 knots.

Then, the Whitehead locomotive torpedo came on the scene. First in the field to construct a sea-going craft designed to operate locomotive torpedoes were the French, in 1877, whose Torpedo Boat No 1, of 101 tons, had two axial torpedo tubes, one forward and one aft between the twin screws. Although the concept was ahead of its time, its speed of only just over 14 knots made it of little value. Meanwhile, Thornycroft had produced the *Lightning*, a little craft of 19 tons, but with a speed of 18 knots. When *Lightning* was adapted to mount a Whitehead torpedo launching gear in the bows, she became the first of a large number of such boats which were built by Thornycroft and Yarrow for several governments.

Next in the process of evolution came larger boats, the first of which was the *Batoum*, a 40-ton craft built for the Russians by Yarrow, and which achieved a speed of 22 knots. She and her successors were designated 1st Class Torpedo Boats, the smaller craft being 2nd Class. Russia and France were the chief advocates of the torpedo-boat, acquiring respectively, 115 and 50 of the first-class boats by 1884, compared with Britain's modest 19. The French in particular, under the influence of Admiral Aube and a *Jeune Ecole* among naval theorists, believed that the era of the battleship had passed. In its place should be a swarm of fast light craft for coastal defence and light cruisers for attack on an enemy's sea-borne trade, the classic *guerre-de-course* so often resorted to by them in the past. In 1886 Aube, then Minister of Marine, ordered 34 new torpedo-boats and established a Torpedo School.

By that time the British Admiralty had woken up to the threat being posed by the Royal Navy's traditional rival across the Channel. Between 1886 and 1892, they built a series of classes of ships known as torpedo-gunboats, or catchers, the last of which, the Jason class, were ships of 700 to 800 tons although with a speed still less than 20 knots. Similar ships were being built by the French. They were all too slow, unmanoeuvrable and too conspicuous to catch torpedo-boats as they made their sneak attacks by night.

The first to perceive the required design were the Spanish, who had had a ship built for them in 1884 by Thompson of Clydebank (later the John Brown shipyard). She was the aptly named *Destructor* (destroyer), of 386 tons and the first warship to be driven by twin triple-expansion engines, which gave her a speed of 22½ knots. As the speed of torpedo-boats rose, however, she was soon outmoded. Therefore, a breakthrough was necessary; at last, in 1893, it came about when Yarrow produced HMS *Havock*, the first true torpedo-boat-destroyer.

Displacing only 240 tons, and with a low silhouette, she was still able to house twin reciprocating engines and the water-tube boilers to supply them with steam for a speed of 27 knots; on her upper deck she mounted one 3-inch (12-pounder) gun and three six-pounders, and she had three torpedo tubes altogether.

The *Havock*, her sister-ship *Hornet*, and the *Daring* and *Decoy* built by Thornycroft, were so successful that 36 more similar boats were ordered by the Admiralty. The class became known as the 27-knotters (later A class). From that time onward, TBDs formed a substantial element of the British Navy, new classes following almost annually, with efforts made to improve the performance of each. Consequently, when the French produced a torpedo-boat, the *Forban* in 1895, and Yarrow built the TBD *Sokol* for Russia, each of which achieved 31 knots, the British ordered the large class of TBDs known as 30-knotters.

They were still quite small ships—300 to 400 tons—extremely wet and uncomfortable in a seaway, when their low turtle-back forecastles were constantly awash. To drive them at 30 knots, their reciprocating engines had to develop very high piston speeds and, apart from numerous breakages, few actually achieved that speed in loaded condition. Two of them, however, the *Viper* and *Cobra*, in 1899 became the first warships to make use of the marine steam turbine invented by the Hon Charles Parsons, the *Viper* achieving 36-38 knots and the *Cobra* a knot less.

Unfortunately for the progress of turbine drive in British destroyers, in pursuit of spectacular speeds *Viper* and *Cobra* were built with very light scantlings and only ¼in side plating. When the *Cobra* broke her back and foundered in rough seas, a reaction against turbines and high speeds arose. The Royal Navy, between 1903 and 1905, preferred to have instead larger (550 tons) ships, powered by reciprocating engines; they were the more seaworthy River class, slower (25½ knots), sturdier and they had a high flared forecastle (which became standard for British destroyers). At the same time they were able to mount the increased gun armament of up to four 3-inch guns compared with the single 3-inch and five six-pounders of the 30-knotters.

Turbine technique was nevertheless preserved in one of them, the *Eden*, and in 1907 turbine drive as well as boiler firing with oil fuel became standard practice with the Tribal class. Although the Tribals varied in size and armament, their performance was similar, with speeds between 33 and 35 knots, and their armament was two 18-inch torpedo tubes and either five 3-inch or two 4-inch guns.

The French, under the influence of the *Jeune Ecole*, were at first content with their large number of basically defensive torpedo-boats. Not until 1899 did they acquire their first destroyer, the *Durandal*, a 300-ton vessel built by the firm of Normand. It might be that they profited by the delay to iron out some of the problems of high-speed reciprocating engines, as the *Durandal* and her successors, some of which achieved 31 knots, attained a reliability which their British contemporaries lacked. Certainly, the French experimented exhaustively before finally adopting

Top: The guided-missile destroyer HMS 'Hampshire' in the Pacific Ocean in 1969. *A Greenway*

Above: HMS 'Fife', a County-class guided-missile destroyer in August 1973. *R Adshead*

Above centre: Federal German Navy Ships at the NATO Spithead Review in June 1970, with destroyer D183 in background. *A Greenway*

Above right: HMS 'Somali', one of the Tribal-class destroyers of World War II. *J G Steel*

oil firing or turbine drive, the first class to incorporate both concepts as well as a raised forecastle, being the 700-ton Casque class, laid down in 1909; they mounted two 3.9-inch and four nine-pounder guns and four 18-inch torpedoes. The designation *contre-torpilleur* (torpedo-boat destroyer) was temporarily abandoned by the French Navy, in favour of *torpilleur d'escadre* (fleet torpedo-boat).

The Germans, when they began to develop an Imperial Navy, built a number of torpedo-boats annually from 1887 onwards, increasing successively in size, engine power and armament until 1906, when they built the G137, the first boat to incorporate turbine drive, giving her a speed of 33.9 knots, and an armament of one 3.5-inch gun and three six-pounders. Favouring a large number of torpedo-tubes (five in this case) at the expense of gun power and, therefore, the concept of attack rather than defence, the Germans designated their boats High Seas Torpedo-Boats rather than Destroyers. By 1913, whereas the standard British destroyer, with a displacement of 1200 tons and a speed of 27-29 knots, mounted three 4-inch guns and four 21-inch torpedo tubes, the contemporary German craft of 700 tons mounted only two or three 3.5-inch guns, but up to six 19.7-inch torpedo tubes and had a speed of 32-34 knots. In other words, the Germans operated basically torpedo-boats (hunters) and the British torpedo-boat-destroyers (hunter-killers).

By that time, all navies incorporated a force of destroyers or torpedo-boats, mostly capable of 30 knots. Their task, whether called by one name or the other, was the dual one of attacking an enemy's battle fleet with their torpedoes and driving off enemy torpedo craft attempting to do the same. In the United States, where a naval renaissance was taking place, about 26 new destroyers of 700-740 tons, turbine-driven at 30 knots and mounting five 3-inch guns and six 18-inch torpedoes, joined the fleet between 1909 and 1912.

The Japanese had been the first to operate destroyers in war; they were British-built vessels of the 30-knotter type with which they had opened hostilities against Russia in 1904 by a night attack on the fleet in the Roads outside Port Arthur. They also played an active part in the three major sea battles of the Russo-Japanese War. On each occasion their achievements were less than impressive. Even at Port Arthur, where the Russian fleet was taken completely by surprise, out of 18 torpedoes fired at the anchored enemy ships only three hit, damaging, but not sinking, two battleships and a cruiser. Only in the Battle of Tsu-shima did they achieve anything further. They gave the *coup-de-grace* to the shattered and stationary battleships *Suvarov* and *Navarin*, fatally torpedoed the battleship *Sissoi Veliki* and damaged the *Admiral Nakhimoff* and the old cruiser *Vladimir Monomakh*. To gain that achievement during the annihilation of an incomparably less effective enemy fleet, well over 100 torpedoes were fired.

That disappointing performance in one of the two main roles expected of the destroyer, the torpedoing of enemy heavy units, was to repeat itself during the 1914-18 war. During the night phase of the Battle of Jutland, more than 70 British destroyers opposed the passage of the German Battle Fleet across the wake of the British Grand Fleet. In a series of encounters at point-blank range they succeeded in sinking only one battleship, the pre-dreadnought *Pommern*. On the other hand, the threat of the torpedo fired *en masse* had earlier probably done more to rob the British of a decisive victory than any other factor. Twenty-eight torpedoes fired by the German flotillas to cover the escape of their battleships from the trap sprung on them by the Grand Fleet had caused the latter to turn 45 degrees away and lose touch with its prey for the remaining period of daylight.

By the end of the 1914-18 war, the standard British destroyer was one of the very numerous V and W classes, about 1500 tons at deep displacement, mounting, after later modifications, four 4.7-inch guns and two triple clusters of 21-inch torpedo tubes, with a shaft horsepower of 27,000 driving them at 35 knots. Not until 1924 were new destroyers laid down for the Royal Navy. They could be said to be only improvements of the W class, as were all the flotillas, each of eight boats and a leader, added annually, the A to I classes, the last of which was laid down in 1936.

By that time, though destroyers were still given a powerful torpedo armament and a gun armament calculated to put them on equality with others of their type in foreign navies, their principal function had become that of screening major units —battleships, aircraft carriers and cruisers —as well as troop convoys, against submarine attack. British and American destroyers were, therefore, equipped with sonar submarine detecting devices—called Asdic by the British—and mortars and launching rails for a 'pattern' of depth-charges.

Other navies took similar building 'holidays' before beginning modernisation programmes. The French Navy then added the larger Tigre-class *contre-torpilleurs* of about 2126 tons and with an armament of five 5.1-inch guns. They were followed, between 1928 and 1934, by a further 18 ships of 2400 tons and a similar armament, but an increased speed of between 37 and 40 knots. Six later ships of the Fantasque class achieved 43-45 knots on trials. They were in reply to the Italian Navigatori class which had a speed of 40 knots.

The US Navy began its modernisation programme, so far as destroyers were concerned, by laying down in 1932 the eight ships of the Farragut class, great improvements upon the flush-decked four-funnelled destroyers of their earlier war and post-war programmes. With an armament of five of the new 5-inch 38-calibre dual-purpose guns which were to become the standard US destroyer guns, and 12 21-inch torpedo tubes in quadruple mountings, geared turbines of 42,900 horsepower and a speed of $36\frac{1}{2}$ knots, they can be said to have been prototypes of the huge number of destroyers built for the 1939-45 war.

For all the major navies, including then a reborn German navy, the lapsing of the Washington and London Naval Armament Limitation Treaties in 1936, the signing of the Anglo-German Naval Agreement and the looming of the clouds of war, led to a feverish programme of building. Included were the British J, K, L and M classes and the Tribal class. The J to M class, with a displacement of 1610 tons, generally mounted six 4.7-inch guns and two quintuple torpedo-tube mountings. One of the torpedo mounts was later removed to allow an increased anti-aircraft armament. The Tribal design, with a displacement of 1870 tons, accepted a decreasing role for the torpedo in fleet operations and, to mount eight 4.7-inch guns, the torpedo armament was from the start limited to a single quadruple mounting.

Had the British persevered with their experiment with liquid-oxygen-driven torpedoes in the 1930s to produce such weapons as the Japanese Long Lance torpedoes, which could carry a 1000lb warhead at 36 knots for 22 miles or half that distance at 49 knots, their destroyer armaments might perhaps have been different. The average Japanese destroyer from 1933 onwards, when the Long Lances were perfected, was a ship of about 2000 tons displacement, six 5-inch guns and nine 24-inch torpedo tubes, with nine reload torpedoes in upper-deck housings, and had a speed of 34 knots.

Such ships were to achieve spectacular successes in night surface actions with American forces during the Solomon Islands campaign. American destroyers of the Fletcher class, built in great numbers during the war, were of about the same size and armament, with the exception of their 21-inch torpedoes. They proved to have numerous defects which had not been rectified when, late in 1944, they were replaced by new electric torpedoes of a type copied from the German.

The primary importance of the role of convoy escort for all but the most up-to-date destroyers during the 1939-45 war led to the readoption of the classification, derived from the days of sail, of frigate for the older destroyers modified for that role. For a time, indeed, after the war, it seemed as though the anomaly of retaining the title destroyer long after it had ceased to have a contemporary meaning would cause it to disappear from the navy lists of the world. Many ships that would have otherwise been classified as destroyers became frigates in the Royal Navy, *escorteurs* or *frégates* in the French (where the term *contre-torpilleur* has again been abandoned) and *uniti scorta* in the Italian.

In the British and Italian navies, however, the name has lingered on, applied to ships immediately below the cruiser in size, such as the 5650-ton County-class guided missile destroyers of the British and the 3900-ton Impavido class of the Italians. In the United States Navy the classification of similar ships does not follow any simple or clear-cut rules; some frigates are larger than destroyers and even larger than wartime cruisers.

Ignoring the anomalies, however, it is perhaps fitting to close this historical outline of the destroyer's story by saying that today, where the name occurs, it indicates a warship of moderate size whose main weapons are missiles, either surface-to-air, ship-to-ship, or a combination of both, with the addition of a rocket-transported anti-submarine homing torpedo.

Top: 'Rostam' a Mk5 destroyer built for the Iranian Navy by Vickers of Birkenhead and pictured here in dry dock at Southampton in March 1973. *J Eastland*

Above: The US destroyer 'Purdy' taking on oil fuel. *D Mackenzie*

Right: HMS 'Fife' leading other guided-missile destroyers in August 1973. *R Adshead*

The Royal Netherlands Navy guided-missile cruiser 'De Ruyter' at a NATO naval review at Spithead in 1970. *A Greenway*

THE CRUISER

THE CRUISER is described by popular historians as the successor to the sailing frigate. That is, perhaps, rather like saying that the aeroplane is the successor to the balloon.

The principal task of the frigate was to scout for the line-of-battle ships. Its role of commerce protection and raiding grew up largely because of its usually greater speed than the battleship; its smaller crew which required less what would be termed today logistic support, and because it was more expendable. However, detached duties such as escorting convoys or attacking enemy shipping were also the tasks of a variety of other ships, for instance, corvettes, sloops, brigs and cutters. The cruiser in the second half of the last century took over the functions of many such sailing vessels.

Nevertheless, the classification of cruisers to some extent reflected the practice in the sailing navy and there were armoured, protected and light cruisers (unprotected as a rule by armour plate). In due course the cruiser category was extended to the point where it embraced ships from perhaps only 2000 tons displacement up to 14,000 tons or more.

There were further specialised subdivisions, including torpedo cruisers; cruiser-minelayers; training cruisers (usually older cruisers of conventional design adapted for the task, although a few were built for the role, such as the Argentine Navy's *La Argentina* of the 1930s); and even one or two seaplane-cruisers, of which the pre-war Swedish *Götland* was perhaps the best example.

In time of war fast merchant ships, usually passenger or cargo-passenger liners, were fitted out as armed merchant cruisers. They were employed in the war between Russia and Japan at the beginning of the present century, as well as in the two world wars. The practice of fitting out merchant ships for naval service is not, of course, of recent origin, since armed merchant ships were the first warships long before there were organised navies operating under control of the monarch or state.

The term cruiser in the Royal Navy appears to have been applied to a specific type of warship in the 1880s for the first time. Though much bigger than contemporary battleships, the first armoured warships in the Royal Navy—the *Warrior* and *Black Prince*—each of 8800 tons displacement, were officially rated as iron-frigates (later cruisers) and not as battleships. Among the leading maritime nations, the term cruiser gradually came to mean a ship capable of sustained cruising for long periods without the support of a base or depot ship. In the Royal Navy one definition used to be a ship whose crew was large enough to warrant the ship carrying their pay accounts.

Although for nations such as Britain and France, cruisers were of importance for the protection of overseas territories and trade, the original frigate requirement to scout for the battlefleet was not forgotten. The armoured cruiser was intended to take its place in the battlefleet to deal with comparable enemy ships which might attempt to distract the battleships from their task of destroying the enemy battlefleet.

The armoured cruiser concept reached its peak with the Royal Navy's 14,000-ton *Drake, Leviathan* and *King Alfred* of 1902-03. Those ships had a speed of 24 knots, which was considerably more than the speed of contemporary battleships, but it did not offer a sufficient margin over the performance of the new dreadnought battleships when they started commissioning about three or four years later. The *Minotaur, Defence* and *Shannon,* of approximately the same size as *Drake,* were completed in 1908 and were the last armoured cruisers in the Royal Navy.

The same year the first of the battle-

This picture: A triple 8-inch turret of the heavy cruiser USS 'Newport News'.
J Eastland

Left: The 'Ajax' of 1935, one of the cruisers of the Leander class. *Illustrated London News*

Below left: The 1919 cruiser 'Delhi', one of eight ships of the D class.
Illustrated London News

Below: A second-class British cruiser, HMS 'Latona', from a painting by W F Mitchell.

Bottom: HMS 'Norfolk', a County-class guided missile destroyer of the type that largely replaced the earlier conventional cruisers in the 1970s. *Barnaby's Picture Library*

cruisers, the *Invincible, Inflexible* and *Indomitable,* were completed and with their armament of eight 12in and 16 4in guns they completely outclassed the *Minotaur,* which mounted four 9.2in and 10 7.5in guns and, with a speed of 23 knots, was also two knots slower. At the Battle of Jutland in 1916 the fate of the armoured cruisers was sealed when three of them were exposed to the fire of the German High Seas Fleet and were eventually sunk with heavy loss of life.

The big armoured cruisers were not economical ships and required about as much coal as a battleship. Moreover, their crews, numbering 700 or more, were the same as those in many battleships. Consequently, the task of overseas trade protection was entrusted more to the protected cruiser, which was really the successor of the corvette and the later steam corvette. The Royal Navy's ship *Blake* was a good example of a protected cruiser, that is, a ship with an armoured deck but lacking the side armour fitted in an armoured cruiser.

She was launched at Chatham in 1889 and was of about 9000 tons displacement. She was armed with 6in guns and was the first cruiser to be powered by triple-expansion engines. Her armour protection took the form of an arched deck over engine and boiler rooms. On top, the armour was of 3in thickness and the sloping sides of the arch were covered by 6in armour. A particular feature of the *Blake* was her considerable radius of action—possibly the most vital asset of all for a cruiser in the Royal Navy. (*Blake* eventually became a destroyer depot ship.)

Powerful cruisers were also being built in the 1880s and 1890s by some of Britain's likely rivals at sea. The 6300-ton French *Dupuy de Lôme* had an armament of 7.5in and 6in guns, but having a speed of only 20 knots, she was too slow to be a successful commerce raider. The somewhat larger American *Columbia,* with 22 knots, was faster but her armament was mixed and comparatively light, consisting of only one 8in, two 6in and eight 4in guns. The Russian *Rurik* was of about 10,000 tons displacement but could only make 18 knots. Although completed four years after the *Dupuy de Lôme* and two years after the *Columbia,* she retained full sailing rig—a somewhat surprising feature for a ship completed in 1894. She was armed with four 8in, 16 6in and six 4.7in guns.

As the *Dreadnought,* completed in 1906, at a stroke made all other battleships obsolete, so the British *Powerful* and *Terrible,* displacing 14,200 tons and completed a short while before the turn of the century, were far superior to any other nation's armoured cruisers. But to attain their designed speed of 22 knots they were each fitted with 48 boilers. The provision of boiler feed water as much as coal was a consideration of great importance for cruiser design.

As to stoking in the larger armoured cruisers, as well as in battleships, the nightmare task of shovelling coal into such large numbers of boilers was slightly eased by a small 'railway line' of coal skips. They ran on a moving belt from the bunkers down one side of the boiler room and were tripped to tip their load on to the deck plate in front of the appropriate boiler. Even so, when working up to full speed, life in the boiler rooms must have been at best hot, dirty and noisy. Most boilers had upper and lower doors to the furnace and there was sometimes a tendency among the stokers to shovel more coal into the lower doors since they were easier to reach. Unless supervised closely, some stokers also tended to pile the coal in the furnace mouth rather than ensuring it was evenly distributed over the furnace floor.

Apart from at Jutland, the big armoured cruisers saw little real fighting. Some guns landed from the *Terrible* and *Powerful* in Cape Colony in the early days of the Boer War gave splendid service, while the *Kent* fought well at the Falkland Islands battle in December 1914. The light cruiser type was basically divided into two categories of second-class and third-class cruisers. Armament in the former was usually a mix of 6in and 4in guns; the latter were usually armed only with 4in and for a time were classed as scouts.

The Forward-class light cruisers really marked the evolution of the type from the protected cruiser in the Royal Navy. They displaced about 2900 tons and had a speed of 25 knots. The Gem-class light cruisers, also completed in 1905, displaced 3000 tons but had a speed of only 21.75 knots, although they had an armament of 12 4in guns compared with nine in the Forward class. By 1914 light cruisers were attaining speeds of 30 knots. Numbers of them were employed working with destroyers as senior officers' ships; in 1914 the *Amethyst,* of the Gem class was thus used in the Harwich Force, but she was too slow for the task and was soon replaced by a new light cruiser.

One elderly British light cruiser, the *Hermes* launched in 1898, was fitted out in September 1914 as a seaplane carrier. The following month she was torpedoed and sunk off Dover by a German submarine while returning from operating her aircraft in support of the army fighting the Germans in the Dunkirk area. Earlier in her career the *Hermes* had had a total boiler failure in the West Indies and for a while was under sail, which earned her the nickname of 'the three-funnelled brig'!

By 1918 the light cruiser was attaining a speed well in excess of 30 knots, and was carrying an armament of five 6in guns in the case of the later ships of the British C class. Yet tonnage had only risen to about 4000. Turbines and oil fuel made the improved performance possible. The need for cruisers able to out-gun the most powerful in the German Navy resulted in the introduction of the 7.5in gun in the British Raleigh class in the immediate post-war years. One of the class, *Vindictive,* was fitted out as a seaplane carrier but later became the Dartmouth cadet training ship. The five Raleigh-class ships were the only British cruisers to mount that size of gun in the inter-war years.

The big increase in speed in the battle-fleet and the loss of some older cruisers to submarines and more-powerful enemy surface ships in isolated sea areas meant that other tasks had to be found for some of them. A number of cruisers had their gun armament reduced to a few six-pounders and were fitted below decks with stowage and rails for mines. Three old minelayers converted from light cruisers—*Intrepid, Iphegenia* and *Thetis*—were sunk as block-ships during the 1918 raid on Zeebrugge in Belgium in an attempt to stop German submarines leaving their base at Bruges. Various other old cruisers were converted into depot and accommodation ships.

After the end of 'the war to end wars' in 1918, the major naval powers set about trying to prevent future arms races by solemn treaties. The first treaty signed in Washington limited cruisers to a maximum of 10,000 tons displacement. That was considerably larger than any British cruiser then in service but it was a limit that suited the US and Japan well because of the vast distances their navies faced in the Pacific. The Japanese fairly soon broke the treaty limits and managed to put 10 8in guns in ships only marginally above the treaty limit. France and Italy concentrated on speed at the expense of armour and range. French ships of the light cruiser/destroyer flotilla-leader type were recording 36 or 37 knots.

The first British cruisers designed to the treaty limitations were the 11 County-class ships. (Two more were built for the Australian Navy and two of a slightly modified design were built in Spain: one, *Canarias,* was still in service in 1979.) They mounted eight 8in guns, were virtually unarmoured and were officially credited with a speed of 32 knots. In the late 1920s, the Counties were followed by two slightly smaller and less expensive ships, *Exeter* and *York,* each carrying six 8in guns.

The 1930 London Treaty, and the parlous state of the national economy at the time, made the Admiralty realise that if anything approaching the agreed minimum of 70 cruisers was to be maintained for policing the trade routes and protecting overseas interests, it would be necessary to look at much smaller designs. Between 1931 and 1934 the five Leander-class cruisers were laid down. They displaced 6840 tons and were armed with eight 6in guns. However, Japan produced the far more powerful Mogami-class cruisers armed with 15 6in guns. After the war, in 1945, it was discovered that those ships had been rearmed before the war with eight 8in guns.

In 1934-36, with the Arethusa class,

Left: Guided-missile cruiser 'Albany', 13,900 tons, flagship of the Sixth US Fleet in the Mediterranean. *US Navy*

there was what amounted to a reversion to the light cruiser design of the 1912 era in the Royal Navy. The four Arethusa-class vessels before the war served mainly as senior officers' ships for destroyer flotillas. They were armed with six 6-inch guns on a maximum displacement of 5270 tons. The Arethusas and the three larger Amphions (all three were transferred to the Royal Australian Navy) were intended to replace the C-class cruisers of 1917-18 vintage, which were due to be scrapped in 1936 under the terms of the London Treaty. But some of the C-class ships converted into anti-aircraft cruisers were saved from the scrapyard. In place of their 6-inch guns they had 10 4-inch anti-aircraft guns and multiple-barrel two-pounder pom-poms.

Shortly before the outbreak of war in 1939 the Royal Navy began building the Dido-class ships which were planned to carry 10 5.25-inch guns. The Americans built the Atlanta class armed with 16 5-inch guns. In fact, two of the Dido class, the *Bonaventure* and *Scylla,* never received their intended guns; instead the guns are believed to have been used to provide high-altitude anti-aircraft defences for the approaches to London along the Thames Estuary. As a result both ships carried eight 4.5-inch guns in open mounts. Of the other ships of the class, five of an improved design mounted only eight 5.25-inch guns. In France and Italy in the late 1930s the accent was on large destroyer leaders; for example, the French Le Terrible class armed with five 5.5-inch guns and capable of a speed of 37 knots. The later Captain Romani class of the Italian Navy followed a similar concept. Neither class had a very distinguished war record.

In the early 1930s the resurrected German Navy began building what soon became known as pocket battleships of the Deutschland class. They were diesel powered, which gave them very long endurance, and were armed with six 11-inch guns. They had a speed of 26 knots and good armour protection which technically made them successors to the armoured cruiser of pre-1914 days; they were indeed classed by the Germans as *panzerschiffe*.

The late 1930s saw completion of the British Southampton-class cruisers which, with 12 6-inch guns, were to be the answer to the Japanese Mogami class. The basic design of the Southamptons had two triple 6-inch turrets superimposed fore and aft, twin funnels, an aircraft catapult and hangar between the funnels, four 4-inch gun mountings on each side just aft of the after funnel, and tripod mainmast and foremast. It became the virtually standard arrangement in the Royal Navy up to the present day.

After the eight Southampton class came two of an improved type, *Edinburgh* and *Belfast*. The main difference apart from increased size and protection were that they originally mounted four additional twin 4-inch guns and the mainmast was stepped forward of the second funnel. The *Belfast* was mined in 1943 and broke her back. When her reconstruction was completed in 1943 she emerged with large bulges along each side which were intended to strengthen her, and she lost four 4-inch guns in return for a big increase in 40mm anti-aircraft guns.

The Colony-class ships differed mainly from the Southamptons in that they had vertical instead of raked funnels. The surviving ships of both classes, with the exception of *Nigeria*, ended the war with nine 6-inch guns, X turret having been replaced by light AA guns.

The *Swiftsure, Superb* and the Canadian *Ontario,* which followed the Colony class, had only nine 6-inch guns on completion and also had no aircraft hangar or catapult. Aviation fuel fires during the war had shown the danger of having aircraft on board.

After the war the *Superb's* sister ships *Tiger, Blake* and *Lion* (launched as *Defence*) were completed to a revised design; two twin 6-inch turrets, each with a rate of fire of 20 rounds a minute per gun, replaced the original nine 6-inch guns, while six 3-inch, originally with a rate of fire of 120 rounds per gun per minute, replaced the eight 4-inch weapons. With *Tiger* and *Blake* there were further modifications in which only the 6-inch turret in A position and the 3-inch in B position were retained; a hangar and flightdeck for four anti-submarine helicopters replaced the after 6-inch turret, and two quadruple Seacat SAM launchers replaced the midship 3-inch.

The American answer to the Japanese Mogami design was the Brooklyn-class light cruiser with 15 6-inch guns. The Americans pushed ahead with completely new cruiser designs during the war, with the Baltimore class mounting nine 8-inch guns. They were followed by the Oregon City and Des Moines classes, the latter being easily the largest cruiser ever built, with a displacement of about 21,000 tons.

The Brooklyn design was succeeded by the Cleveland class mounting 12 6-inch and 12 5-inch guns. Probably the peak of light cruiser design was reached with the 15,000-ton *Roanoke* and *Worcester,* also armed with 12 6-inch guns.

Apart from the Royal Navy's Tiger-class ships, the only cruisers in the Western fleets designed since the war are the Dutch *De Zeven Provincien* and *De Ruyter*, each carrying eight 5.9-inch guns, and the French *Colbert* and *De Grasse*, each with 5-inch guns. The US Navy's nuclear-powered cruiser *Long Beach*, completed in 1961, is armed with Talos and Tartar SAM systems and a couple of 5-inch guns.

Six of the Cleveland class were reconstructed to carry twin Talos or Terrier missiles and retained one or two triple 6-inch gun turrets. Two of the Baltimore class, the *Chicago* and *Columbus*, were rebuilt with Talos and Tartar missiles replacing all guns, although later they and the similarly rebuilt *Albany* of the Oregon City class were given two 5-inch guns to counter attacks by aircraft and small surface craft. The Dutch *De Zeven Provincien* also has had four of her eight 5.9-inch guns replaced by a Terrier SAM launcher. The world's first two major missile ships were the American Baltimore-cruisers *Boston* and *Canberra*, in which the after triple 8-inch turret was replaced in the 1950s by two twin Terrier launchers; both ships are now in reserve.

Since the war the Russians alone have embarked on a large programme of building conventional cruisers and 24 Sverdlov-class ships armed with 12 6-inch and 12 3.9-inch guns were ordered, probably in the late 1940s. By 1951 14 of them had been launched. Most have since been scrapped or sold and a further four were scrapped before completion, but at least two had one turret replaced by a SAM launcher. All of the class had a considerable minelaying capacity.

Cruiser/minelayers as a separate type have vanished from the world's navies. One early purpose-built example of the type was the British *Adventure* completed in the 1920s. She was an unusual ship with a transom stern and fitted with diesel engines for economical cruising as well as steam turbines for speed, foreshadowing modern dual-propulsion schemes.

In the early 1940s four 40-knot minelayers of the Manxman class were built for the Royal Navy and two more were built later in the war. The *Manxman* remained in service until 1971, though latterly as a mine countermeasures support vessel and then as a marine engineer officer training ship. Both she and her sister *Abdiel*, later sunk, were on occasion disguised as Vichy French ships during the war to aid minelaying in hostile waters.

The cruiser as a type has all but disappeared and by 1980 the large missile frigate or destroyer leader will have replaced all but a handful of cruisers in a few minor navies. But no other type has featured so prominently in the development of the world's navies over the past century. Nor has any type of warship proved more adaptable in meeting the changing demands which technology and new tactics have placed upon it, and indeed the name is retained in the new class of specialist helicopter and S/VTOL aircraft carrier, which are called variously anti-submarine cruiser, helicopter cruiser, through-deck cruiser and command cruiser.

The Aircraft Carrier

HMS 'Ark Royal' in the English Channel in June 1972 carrying Phantom and Buccaneer aircraft. *J Eastland*

THE USE OF AIRCRAFT at sea was quickly appreciated by farsighted officers in the British, American, German and French navies within a very short time of the Wright brothers' historic flight in 1903. The first flight made by an aircraft from a ship was in 1910, when a Curtiss biplane took off from a platform rigged on the American cruiser *Birmingham*. The following year, the Americans landed a Curtiss biplane on the battleship *Pennsylvania*, but on both occasions the ships were at anchor.

In January 1912, a Short biplane successfully flew off the deck of the British battleship *Africa* and at King George V's Coronation Fleet Review at Portland the following May, a Short biplane took off from the *Africa*'s sister *Hibernia* while she was steaming at 10 knots. The experiment was repeated from the battleship *London* steaming at 12 knots a couple of months later.

Although thought was being given to the fitting of radios in naval aircraft to improve their reconnaissance capability, which was their main role, and even to their use as bombers and torpedo carriers, the gun remained the most important naval weapon. The flying-off platforms in battleships prevented the main armament being used; for that reason, it was decided to fit out the old cruiser *Hermes* as a seaplane carrier. Hydro aeroplanes, as seaplanes were initially called, seemed better suited for use at sea, since they required only hangar and workshop space on board and derricks or cranes to lower them into and recover them from the water.

Although the seaplanes operated from *Hermes* proved their value for reconnaissance during fleet exercises, the need for a seaplane tender as an integral part of the fleet was still not fully established. In 1913, *Hermes* had been paid off, but a merchant ship building at Blyth was taken over for conversion to a seaplane tender and was named *Ark Royal.*

The first occasion when ship-borne aircraft were involved in hostilities occurred in January 1914, when seaplanes from the American cruiser *Birmingham* and the battleship *Mississippi* were employed on reconnaissance duties during the war with Mexico. But by August 1914, all British naval aircraft were shore-based. France had converted the depot ship *Foudre* into a seaplane tender and Germany was concentrating almost exclusively on Zeppelin airships for use at sea.

As *Ark Royal*'s conversion could not be completed before 1915, the Admiralty commandeered three English Channel ferries, *Empress, Engadine* and *Riviera,* as seaplane tenders. They were fitted with hangars and a small platform served by derricks for handling seaplanes. Work was also put in hand to improve the aircraft handling capabilities of *Hermes* because although *Ark Royal* had a longer deck, her speed of 11 knots made her too slow to work with the fleet. To meet the need for a ship with adequate length to provide a flying-off platform and also fast enough to work with the fleet, the elderly Cunarder *Campania* was purchased in October 1914 for conversion, work on which was completed late the following spring.

The first offensive action by ship-borne aircraft took place on Christmas Day 1914, when the three former Channel ferries escorted by cruisers and destroyers steamed into the Heligoland Bight to attack German airship sheds in the Hamburg area. Fog resulted in only one seaplane reaching its target and its bombs missed; four seaplanes were lost. Similar attacks on German Zeppelins in their bases continued spas-

Facing page top: HMS 'Ark Royal' with a Buccaneer aircraft being readied for take-off on the steam catapult. *Michael Turner*

Facing page, below: An American Essex-class carrier, of which 24 were built in the 1940s and which could each operate over 100 aircraft, pictured from a light cruiser underneath its reconnaissance floatplane. *MacClancy Press*

Above: The commando cruiser HMS 'Bulwark' with Wessex helicopters on the flightdeck during exercises in 1973. *R Adshead*

Left: This picture of the early British carrier 'Furious' after her third reconstruction shows the short flying-off deck forward of the hangar below the main flightdeck. *Charles E Brown*

modically throughout the war and culminated in the highly successful Tondern raid in 1918, when aircraft from the converted battlecruiser *Furious* destroyed two Zeppelins.

In 1915, seaplanes from the *Ark Royal* attacked a Turkish battleship in the Dardanelles and a seaplane from the converted Isle of Man ferry *Ben-my-Chree* in the same area that year made history by hitting a Turkish supply ship at 300 yards with a torpedo.

The *Campania,* on joining the Grand Fleet in the summer of 1915, was found to have too small a flight deck (it measured 120ft) and by the end of the year, she had been taken in hand for further conversion. She had to stop to lower seaplanes into the water and it was ordered that they should only be launched after the enemy had been sighted by scouting cruisers. This limitation on her use was the main reason for her being ordered to return to harbour before she could join the fleet at the Battle of Jutland in May 1916. *Engadine,* working with Beatty's battlecruisers, did get one seaplane airborne during the battle and it reported the movements of some enemy light forces.

More former ferries were converted to carry seaplanes, including *Vindex, Nairana, Manxman* and *Pegasus.* The first could carry two landplanes, but they had to be assembled before they could be flown off. As none of the conversions to that date had proved entirely satisfactory, the Admiralty decided shortly after Jutland to convert two liners then under construction for Italy. In the event, only one was converted and she was named *Argus.*

In view of the time taken to convert the *Argus,* the battlecruiser *Furious* was given a flying-off deck in place of her forward 18in gun turret—despite fierce opposition from the naval gunnery world. The light cruiser *Yarmouth* was also given a flying-off platform for a single aircraft but, unlike those fitted in battleships before the war, it did not interfere with the use of the main armament. Four more cruisers were later similarly converted to give the scouting forces some means of countering German reconnaissance Zeppelins.

Towards the end of the war, *Furious* had her deck extended aft, which meant removing her other 18in gun turret. But landing wheeled aircraft was hazardous, partly because of the turbulence and smoke caused by the funnel uptakes, and because the only means of stopping an aircraft was for the flight-deck party to grab the aircraft's lower planes as it rolled on to the deck.

The successful deck landing of a Sopwith Pup on *Furious* in 1917 decided the Admiralty against ordering further seaplane carriers; in addition to fitting the after deck in *Furious,* the design of *Argus* was ordered to be modified, as was that of the new *Hermes,* which had been laid down from the keel up as an aircraft carrier. To fill the gap until those ships were ready, the new cruiser *Cavendish* (later renamed *Vindictive*) was also given a take-off and landing deck.

Because of the problems caused by the midships structures dividing the take-off and landing decks in *Furious* and *Argus,* they were further modified by moving the boiler-room uptakes over to the starboard side, to give a clear length of deck. The policy of fitting flying-off platforms in capital ships and cruisers was continued, but only in October 1918 did the *Argus* appear as the first ship with a flight deck similar to that in the carrier as it is known today.

Even without having to contend with funnel turbulence and smoke, landing on a carrier remained hazardous, as the arrester wires as first fitted were simply stretched across the deck and weighted at each end with sandbags.

By Armistice Day 1918, ship-borne aircraft had been employed in the North Sea, Mediterranean, off the coast of East Africa, and the eastern Indian Ocean where the seaplane tender *Raven II* was employed hunting for the German raider *Wolf.* In numbers of ships and aircraft, not to mention experience, the Royal Naval Air Service easily led the world at the time of its merger with the Royal Flying Corps in 1918 to form the Royal Air Force.

France and America both had seaplane tenders, while Japan had the converted merchant ship *Wakamiya* as an aircraft tender. But America particularly was to press ahead stongly with the development of carriers. In the 1919 Atlantic fleet exercises, the minelayer *Shawmut* was used as a flying-boat tender, while the battleship *Texas* had flying-off platforms for two Sopwith Camels following her service with the Grand Fleet.

The Americans' use of various warships as auxiliary flying-boat tenders was extended and in 1921, the converted collier *Langley* was commissioned as a proper aircraft carrier. The former merchant ship *Wright* had the unusual distinction of being both a seaplane tender and the Asiatic Squadron flagship. The 1922 Washington Treaty resulted in the cancellation of two new American battlecruisers and their being redesigned as the aircraft carriers *Lexington* and *Saratoga.*

In France the battleship *Bearn* was also converted in the course of construction into a carrier and completed in 1925-26. But Japan began building a carrier designed for the role from the start—the 9500-ton *Hosho.* Two more battleship and battlecruiser designs were redrawn as carriers and emerged in the mid-1920s as the *Kaga* and *Akagi.*

Italy acquired a seaplane tender, the *Giuseppe Miraglia,* which was a merchant ship conversion, like the Spanish *Dedalo* which could also carry support facilities for a small airship. Later, this ship made history when she was used to test the first rotary-wing aircraft, Cierva's Autogiro, at sea.

In Britain, the success of the *Furious* conversion resulted in a similar conversion for her original sister ships, *Courageous* and *Glorious,* while the former Chilean battleship *Almirante Cochrane,* whose construction had been suspended throughout the war, was completed as the carrier *Eagle.*

By the early 1930s the ability to carry aircraft in some form at sea became almost *de rigeur* for all but the smallest navies. The results were some interesting designs, such as the seaplane-cruiser *Gotland* in the Swedish Navy and the Australian seaplane tender *Albatross.*

It was, however, the Americans, closely followed by the Japanese, who set the pace in the development of the large aircraft carrier. Although the *Ranger* of 1933 was less than half the size of the earlier American carriers *Saratoga* and *Lexington,* she could carry 75 aircraft, compared to the earlier ships' maximum of 90. The *Enterprise* and *Yorktown,* launched three years later, were able to carry 100 aircraft on a nominal displacement of 19,900 tons, compared to the *Saratoga's* 33,000 tons.

France virtually opted out of naval aviation and built only the seaplane tender *Commandant Teste,* carrying 26 aircraft, in addition to the *Bearn,* between the wars. In Britain, successive disarmament conferences and political expediency resulted in the RAF putting the naval side of its responsibilities in a backwater in order to find funds for Lord Trenchard's 'omnipotent' bombers, while the Admiralty, also short of funds, concentrated available money mainly on keeping up cruiser strength for the protection of shipping. In Germany, work began in the late 1930s on two carriers, the *Graf Zeppelin* and *Peter Strasser,* although neither was destined ever to be completed.

Only in 1937 was the Royal Navy able to launch a new carrier, the 22,600-ton *Ark Royal.* But at least she represented about 20 years of carrier experience; by then also, hydraulic arrester wires were in service and compressed air was used for catapulting reconnaissance aircraft from battleships and cruisers.

The year of *Ark Royal's* launch saw the laying down of the new British Illustrious class carriers. Although nominally credited with an aircraft capacity of 60, they carried far fewer aircraft than contemporary American carriers such as *Enterprise,* because their strength deck was the armoured flight deck, whereas in the American carriers the hangar deck was the strength deck and the flight deck was wood planked. In addition, the British ships had enclosed forecastles, which gave them superior sea-keeping qualities, particularly when steaming fast into a head sea to launch aircraft.

Shortly before the outbreak of war, both France and Russia began constructing carriers, but in neither country did work progress very far before the war had intervened. In 1939, Britain entered the war with the *Ark Royal, Courageous, Glorious, Eagle, Hermes, Furious* and *Argus*; the last-named was assigned to a training role and at one time she had been operating 'Queen Bee' radio-controlled target aircraft. There were also two seaplane tenders, the former Australian *Albatross* and the *Pegasus,* ex-*Ark Royal.*

The first successful major action of the war using naval aircraft, that against the German cruiser *Konigsberg* at Bergen in 1940, did not involve a carrier; the forerunner of the Japanese and American Pacific carrier battles was the attack on the Italian fleet at Taranto in November 1940 by aircraft from the *Illustrious* and *Eagle.* At the time of her entry into the war, America had seven carriers, excluding the obsolescent *Langley.* Japan had ten, of which six were employed in the attack on Pearl Harbour in 1941.

Above: The first Russian aircraft carrier 'Kiev', commissioned in the mid-1970s as first of a class of three, is of the through-deck or command cruiser type designed to operate helicopters and/or aircraft that can take off and land vertically or nearly vertically, like the British Harrier. *Ministry of Defence*

Above right: A helicopter view of USS 'Nimitz', second of the US Navy's massive nuclear-powered carriers deploying about 100 aircraft, in the Mediterranean in 1977. *Inter-Air Press*

Starting with Midway in 1942, it was the great carrier battles between the Americans and Japanese which firmly established the carrier's position as the capital ship in place of the battleship. Losses on both sides initially were heavy, the Americans losing the *Lexington, Hornet, Wasp* and *Yorktown,* to be followed later by the *Princeton.* But the Japanese at the end of the war had not a single carrier left.

The Royal Navy, too, suffered. The *Courageous* was torpedoed in 1939 while on anti-submarine patrol; German surface ships sank the *Glorious* the following year off Norway; and later the *Ark Royal, Eagle* and *Hermes* were all lost.

The loss of *Courageous* ended the use of independent patrols for submarines by large carriers, but the vital need for air support against the U-boats, particularly in the gap in mid-Atlantic which shore-based aircraft supporting convoys could not reach, was keenly felt. From this need was born the escort carrier—initially a converted German merchant ship which had been captured and renamed HMS *Audacity.* Before her conversion in 1941, the old *Pegasus* had been fitted with a catapult to launch a naval Fulmar fighter and several other ships were similarly converted and equipped to give convoys a measure of immediate air protection and provide a means of destroying German long-range reconnaissance aircraft that were used to guide U-boats to the convoys.

Audacity could carry 12 Martlet fighters but had no hangar and the aircraft were parked on the 460ft deck. *Audacity,* which was later sunk, was the forerunner of about 34 escort carriers in the Royal Navy, most of them American-built converted merchant ships, and more than twice that number in the US Navy.

The Americans also converted 11 Worcester and Cleveland class cruisers during construction into light fleet carriers. One, *Princeton,* was lost and *Independence* was expended in the 1946 Bikini Atoll nuclear bomb experiments. The backbone of the American wartime carrier fleet was formed by the 24 Essex-class ships, although some were not completed until after the end of the war.

Although roughly comparable in size, as designed, to the British Illustrious class, they could carry up to 107 aircraft. Their wooden flight decks, which helped make this capacity possible, proved a liability, particularly during the closing days of the war when they were attacked by Japanese kamikaze aircraft. The *Franklin,* for example, was so severely damaged that she was never operational again.

Among the oddities the war produced were the first, and only, paddle aircraft carriers—the converted Great Lakes steamers *Sable* and *Wolverine,* which the Americans used for deck-landing training. In Britain, a new design of carrier intended also to serve as an aircraft repair ship was the *Unicorn,* completed in 1943. She was used mainly as an escort carrier in the war, but performed her repair and ferry carrier role in the Korean War in the early 1950s.

By 1944, with the elimination of most of the German surface fleet, the build-up of the Royal Navy's contribution to the American forces fighting the Japanese was under way. By VJ-Day 1945, all six of the fleet carriers, *Illustrious, Formidable, Victorious, Indomitable, Implacable* and *Indefatigable,* had played their part fighting the Japanese and several survived hits by kamikazes. Unlike the American carriers, their armoured flight decks allowed them to operate aircraft again within a matter of hours.

The end of the war saw the first of the light fleet carriers in the Pacific. They were built to Lloyds specifications up to main deck level with an eye to their post-war conversion into fast cargo ships—an option never taken up. Of 16 of the class ordered, two were converted during construction into aircraft repair ships. One of them, the *Perseus,* was fitted with a ramp for testing the new steam catapult in the 1950s, and at Rosyth dockyard had the embarrassing experience of launching a pilotless test aircraft which failed to crash into the sea as planned and instead circled Edinburgh and the dockyard for some minutes.

In 1946, the *Ocean,* of the same class, became the first British ship to land a jet fighter. *Ocean* also pioneered the use of helicopters at sea.

At the time of the Japanese surrender, eight larger carriers of the Polyphemus class were being built and they had a displacement of 18,000 tons, compared to the early light fleet carriers' 13,000 tons. Four of the former were never completed, as was also the case with the *Leviathan* of the smaller type. The end of the war also terminated construction of the 50,000-ton fleet carriers *Gibraltar, Malta* and *New Zealand.*

The light fleet carriers played their part in helping to rebuild Allied navies and the *Colossus* became the French *Arromanches,* while the *Venerable* became the Dutch *Karel Doorman,* replacing the escort carrier *Vindex* which had been on loan. The *Warrior* was lent to Canada and was replaced later by the *Magnificent* and then the *Powerful,* renamed *Bonaventure.* Australia took over the *Terrible* and *Majestic,* renaming them *Sydney* and *Melbourne.* The former, with the British *Triumph, Ocean, Glory* and *Theseus,* provided virtually all the air support the Commonwealth gave the UN forces in Korea.

In more recent years, Argentina has acquired the former *Karel Doorman,* now the *25 De Mayo,* while Brazil has the former *Vengeance,* now the *Minas Gerais.* With the sale of the *Karel Doorman,* the Dutch abandoned carriers, as did the Canadians with the scrapping of *Bonaventure.* In the Royal Navy, only one light fleet carrier remains, the *Triumph,* which is now a heavy repair ship, and the only other survivor, the *Hercules,* is now the Indian *Vikrant.*

The light fleet carriers' slow speed (about 25 knots maximum) and small capacity and flight deck length made them unsuitable for the increasingly heavy jets coming into service, although *Warrior* for a time had a rubber covering on her flight deck aft to see if jets could be landed without undercarriages on deck. The need to find some means whereby it would be unnecessary to rig a crash barrier to stop aircraft which failed to hook on to the arrestor wires aft resulted in the angled deck, which allows an aircraft to go round again if it misses the wires.

The American carrier *Antietam* was the first fitted with this British invention and the first British carrier so fitted was *Centaur,* of the Polyphemus class. But the maximum desirable angle of about $8\frac{1}{4}$ degrees could only be fitted in larger carriers such as the *Victorious,* which was totally rebuilt from 1950-58, and in the new American Forrestal-class carriers, built in the 1950s. It was later fitted in the earlier three American Midway-class carriers, as well as in the British *Ark Royal,* of 1955, and *Eagle,* of 1951.

The *Eagle* was also the first ship fitted with the mirror landing aid, which was later replaced by a system of lights designed to guide the pilot approaching the deck—at about 120 knots in the case of the American Phantom fighter, for example.

The future became clear for carriers in 1961 with the completion of the American nuclear-powered *Enterprise.*

But with the *Enterprise's* successors today costing £1000 million each even the Americans are now turning away from giant carriers. Russia showed the way in 1976 with her first carrier, the 43,000-ton *Kiev,* equipped with 12 Flogger vertical take-off ('jump jet') fighters and 20 helicopters.

Now the *Kiev* and two sister ships have been joined by Britain's first 'jump jet' carrier *Invincible,* which began trials early in 1979. This 19,500-ton ship, classed as an anti-submarine cruiser, is being followed by two more named *Illustrious* and *Ark Royal.* The Invincible class will normally carry eight Sea Harriers and nine Sea King helicopters.

India is also planning to buy the Sea Harrier for her one ageing carrier and Spain and Italy are building new carriers with Harrier operations in mind. British technological achievement with the Harrier has been matched with the *Invincible's* design, which includes an inclined 'ski-jump' ramp on the flightdeck by use of which for take-off the Harrier's load can be increased by 2000lb.

It was the Harrier's potential for development matched with the design of the *Invincible* which prompted the American Secretary of the Navy to spell out the death sentence on the big carrier. After a visit to the British ship he said America could no longer afford big carriers and that the US Navy must have aircraft like the Harrier in small carriers.

The British cruiser 'Blake' is one of a pair of Tiger-class ships of 12,500 tons that have been rebuilt and fitted out as helicopter cruisers, mainly for anti-submarine duties. They are armed with 6-inch and 3-inch guns and Seacat missiles and normally carry four Sea King helicopters. Here 'Blake' is pictured during landing and take-off trials of the VTOL Harrier.
British Aerospace

5. Naval Weaponry

LISSA
OLDEST NAVAL WEAPON

'DASH at your enemy and sink them', was the stirring signal that heralded the attack of the Austrian battle-line when the Austrians fought the Italians not far off the island of Lissa in June 1866.

Lissa, as might be expected from its position 30 miles from the Dalmatian coast, has had its fair share of early history. Even in its later days during the Napoleonic Wars, it was seized from the Austrians by the French; then, in spite of its formidable array of guns and fortifications, it fell into British hands. For five years the island was used by Britain as a base for naval operations until it reverted happily to the Austrians.

A year later, in 1866, when Italy went to war with Austria, her northern army met such a humiliating defeat by the Archduke Albrecht, with a far smaller force, that all Italy demanded revenge. As a first step, the fleet sailed for Lissa, and the commander-in-chief had orders to capture the island. He bombarded the batteries and landed some troops. The Admiral, Count Carlo Pellioni di Persano, aged 60, seems to have been a charming personality, pleasant to all but lacking in determination, and perhaps more fitted for a conference table than for the bridge of a ship. In contrast, Rear-Admiral Wilhelm von Tegetthoff, his Austrian opposite number, 20 years younger, had already given ample proof of his judgment and quick decision.

Both admirals had command of fleets which included a number of armoured ships but the Italians, in a hurry to create a powerful and up-to-date fleet, had no settled plan for the use of their vessels. They had built or bought from different sources without clear ideas. The two largest, the *Re d' Italia* and the *Re di Portogallo*, had been built in New York with unseasoned timber, which affected their strength.

The two ships were protected with iron four to seven inches thick on the waterline and at the guns. All the guns were muzzle-loaders, in imitation of the British Admiralty which reverted to them in place of breech-loaders in 1866. One new ship, the big *Affondatore*, classed as a turret-ram, had lately come from England, where she had been built, to join Persano's fleet. She had two heavy guns mounted in turrets behind five inches of iron, but the most striking feature was a mighty ram, 26 feet of it, thrusting out of the bows.

The use of the ram during the American Civil War had caught much attention; one result was the purchase by Italy of two smaller rams (as the vessels were called), the *Terribile* and the *Formidabile*. Besides the two rams, there were in the fleet seven more ships, with a turret ship and a corvette,

Far left: **Impression of a ship with prominent rams built by King Hieron of Syracuse in 280 BC.** *Illustrated London News*

Centre left: Painting in the National Maritime Museum, London, of the battle of Lissa in July 1866.
National Maritime Muesum London (photo D Rudkin)

Facing page bottom: Exaggerated ram bow, nearly 40ft long, of the French cruiser 'Dupuy de Lôme' of 1890. *Illustrated London News*

Left: A representation of the collision between HMS 'Victoria' and HMS 'Camperdown' in June 1893, in which 'Victoria 'was fatally damaged by 'Camperdown's' ram bow.
Parker Gallery

This page bottom: Athenian warship of 500 BC with ram typically in the shape of an animal. *Illustrated London News*

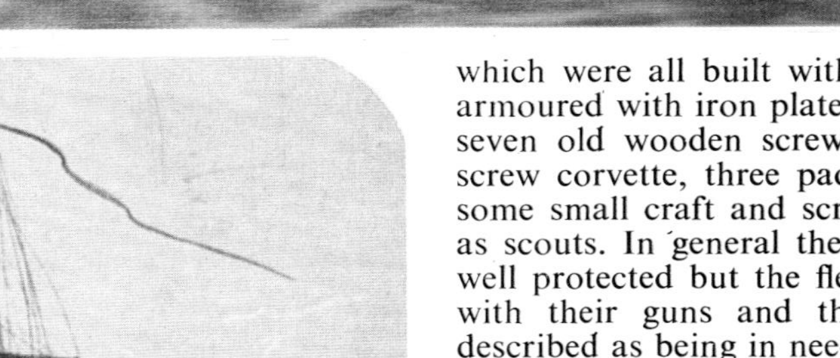

which were all built with iron frames and armoured with iron plates. There were also seven old wooden screw frigates and one screw corvette, three paddle corvettes and some small craft and screw gunboats used as scouts. In general the larger ships were well protected but the fleet lacked practice with their guns and their engineers are described as being in need of training.

Admiral Tegetthoff's fleet was less than half the size of Persano's. He flew his flag in the *Ferdinand Erzherzog*, which, with two other ships, the *Erzherzog* and *Hapsburg*, was intended to have been armed with heavy Krupp breech-loaders but owing to the war had to make shift with early smooth-bore 56-pounders of shorter range instead. Only seven of his ships were armoured and all were of timber. The seven armoured ships were protected by iron plating four-and-a-half to five inches thick, though one was without armour for the battery and was plated only on the waterline, amidships and astern. Forward, she was all wooden planking. In addition to the seven ironclads, the fleet included seven elderly wooden ships, some screw and some paddle propelled, including an old ship-of-the-line.

Admiral Tegetthoff was lying with his fleet at Pola, the main Austrian naval base at the southernmost point of Istria. He was waiting in readiness for word of the Italians when the news reached him of the bombardment of Lissa. Off he went with his ships in the early light of day and he sighted the island and the masts of ships the following morning.

He had made it clear to his captains that the order of sailing was to be the order of battle to avoid manoeuvring in face of the enemy. His fleet was divided into three divisions, each in a wedge-shaped line, led by the seven armoured vessels, with his flagship at the apex of the wedge. Astern of them came the seven unarmoured ships, followed by the third division of small craft. Tegetthoff's idea was for the old wooden ships to attack one end or the other of the enemy line as their part in what he intended to be a close and decisive battle. He wasted no time in sending unnecessary signals to men who knew his intentions. None he sent was as long as his famous order to charge.

Admiral Persano, for his part, seemed to be allowing the battle to take care of itself, so far as tactics went. What he did do was to order his ship and the next astern to stop just as the fleets opened fire. While the rest of his column sailed on in line-ahead with their guns belching smoke and flame, he had suddenly made the astonishing decision to change his flagship and go on board the *Affondatore*, the big new turret ram. It was a decision that was bound to lead to misunderstandings and lost signals when his fleet was unaware of the move.

The two ships had to stop for his transfer and this gave time for a large gap to form ahead of them, hidden by the clouds of smoke. The smoke also hid the fact that Admiral Tegetthoff was leading his armoured squadron through the gap. Then the squadron broke formation and Tegetthoff attacked the Italian van, while a Commodore Petz with the unarmoured ships dealt with the rear.

The battle dissolved into general disarray. Having passed through the Italian line, Tegetthoff made two attempts to ram and hit the *Re d'Italia* and the *Palestro*, without causing much damage, though an Austrian shell exploded in the stern of the *Palestro*, starting a serious fire. She turned out of the line in great masses of smoke to try to put out the fire while the Austrians closed round the stricken *Re d'Italia*. Tegetthoff in the *Ferdinand Max* steered for the *Re d'Italia* at a speed of 11 knots and with his ship's ram bow caught her amidships with a frightful crunch, tearing a great hole in her side. She rolled over and sank, taking several hundred men with her.

Her fate seemed to take all the fight out of the Italians and when the burning *Palestro* finally blew up with heavy casualties the battle was all but over. Persano collected his beaten and depressed fleet for his return home to Ancona to explain how he had been defeated by a far smaller force with much more modern ships. The Italian losses included 381 killed in the *Re d'Italia* and 231 in the *Palestro*. One ship was in need of major repairs and two others would never sail again.

The Austrian losses amounted to 38 killed and 138 wounded although in their armoured ships only three had been killed and 30 wounded. Most of their casualties occurred in the old wooden ship-of-the-line *Kaiser*, which had tried to ram the *Re di Portogallo;* the vessel itself, though unprotected, needed comparatively little in the way of repairs.

The strange fact about the battle of Lissa is that, while ship after ship on both sides made attempt after attempt to use their rams, only a single vessel was sunk and no others were damaged. Yet, stranger still, the navies of Europe and North and South of America accepted the ram as a major weapon, clinging to the delusion into the 20th century. It seemed to have been forgotten that the ram was not a new weapon in sea warfare but one of the oldest, dating back to and beyond the war-galleys of Ancient Greece and Phoenicia. France appears to have resuscitated it in the 1850s after it had lingered in the Mediterranean for

Right: The 'Re d'Italia' sinking after being rammed by Tegetthoff's flagship 'Ferdinand Max'. *M Muir Collection (photo D Rudkin)*

Below: Ram bow still in vogue in 1898, as this model in the Science Museum, London, of HMS 'Albion' shows. *Photo D J Kingston*

Below centre: HM torpedo ram 'Polyphemus', 1881, in dry dock gives a good view of the prominent ram. *Illustrated London News*

Bottom: The battleship 'Trafalgar' of the late 19th century had a cast-steel spur filled with teak. *Illustrated London News*

Below right: An 1872 vessel classed as a turret ram, HMS 'Glatton'. *Illustrated London News*

a period before fading away. Then it came to life again in America in various guises during the Civil War.

Britain followed the lead of France and the ram-bow soon became a standard feature of capital ships and cruisers, with a curved fore-foot reaching forward under the water. The ram-bow was responsible for the loss of the battleship *Vanguard;* in 1875 she was accidentally rammed, off the Wicklow coast, in a dense fog by another battleship, HMS *Iron Duke*. Fortunately she took some time to sink so that everyone on board was saved by ships' boats.

A far greater tragedy, the worst ever to overtake the Royal Navy in peacetime, was the collision in 1893 of the commander-in-chief's flagship HMS *Victoria* with HMS *Camperdown* during manoeuvres in the Mediterranean. Through an error of judgment by the admiral, the *Camperdown's* ram bow tore into the flagship's side, making a huge hole and heeling her over as the sea flooded in. The Admiral, conscious of his mistake, remained on the bridge as she went down and 359 officers and men went to their deaths with him.

In the two world wars quite a number of captains of ships achieved their ambition to sink an enemy submarine by ramming, willingly accepting the damage done to their own vessels' bows. But in general the vogue of the ram was only a temporary one, barely outliving the 19th century. After all it was a short-range weapon, very limited in scope in modern times. It actually accomplished little and was really a return to a primitive device that could expect little success in the face of the continuing developments in weaponry on, above and below the sea.

Sinope and explosive shot

GUNPOWDER, Shakespeare's 'villainous saltpetre', has been known for 2000 years or more in China. There, mixed in the right proportions of sulphur, saltpetre and charcoal, it has long played a great part in festivals or devil-scaring in firecrackers and small ingenious fireworks. The Chinese merchant fleets brought the components, or knowledge of them, quite early to India and Arabian traders carried them on until they reached the Mediterranean. It was left to the western world to use them for destruction.

The Arabs are known to have used gunpowder in the year 690 at the siege of Mecca, but at sea they preferred the closely related fierce incendiary material known as Greek fire, with which it is often confused. Some kind of explosive rockets are believed to have made history during the reign of the Greek Emperor in 880 but gunpowder seems to have been slow to reach western Europe. It was not until 1325 that the Moorish King of Grenada, Ismael Ben Feraz, 'had among his machines some that cast globes of fire with resounding thunders and lightning causing fearful injuries to the towers and walls of the city'.

In 1345, Edward III of England, who had some primitive cannon, left records of accounts covering the purchase of gunpowder, and 100 years later Henry V, when preparing for his invasion of France, gave orders that no gunpowder should be taken out of the country without a special licence.

As the years and the centuries went by and the guns on land and sea were being steadily improved, the solid roundshot gave way to projectiles which caused much damage; but rifled and shaped for maximum destructive effect as they had become, it was the Russians who were first to fire a naval gun charged with an explosive shell. The date was 1853.

With Britain, France, Turkey and Egypt on one side and Russia alone on the other, there was a diplomatic tangle over the question of a weakening Turkey. Tsar Nicholas I was anxious to protect the Christian Slavs of the Balkans and to win free access to the Mediterranean by occupying Constantinople. He suggested to the British Ambassador a partition of Turkish territory between England and Russia. It was hardly a policy pleasing to Turkey or to Britain, nor was it welcome to France where Napoleon III was thirsting for glory.

When in May 1853 it was learnt, through the Turkish Sultan, that Russia was intending to occupy the Danube a British fleet of seven ships-of-the-line under the command of Vice-Admiral Dundas and a French fleet of nine large ships sailed to Besika Bay, near the entrance to the Dardanelles, and anchored to await events.

Unfortunately, at that time the British Ambassador does not seem to have been the soul of diplomacy. The Sultan refused the Tsar's demand and although neither side declared war, war it was. At once the British and French fleets entered the Dardanelles by Turkish invitation and moved up to Constantinople to protect the Turks, not yet as full allies but much more than sympathetic friends.

Above: Portrayal of the Turkish fleet under attack with explosive shot at Sinope.
National Maritime Museum London

With the main Turkish fleet was a captain of the Royal Navy, Captain Adolphus Slade. He bore the name of Mushraver Pasha, with the temporary rank of rear-admiral while he was on loan to the Sultan. His opinion of the Turks as seamen was not high. In 1853 he found them half-trained or hardly trained at all and their senior captain objected to their practising reefing and handling sails while at anchor, to spare the feelings of the Sultan should a man fall from aloft. Allah, he said, was expected to make sailors.

On one occasion at sea when Slade looked round for the men presumed to be stationed at the topgallant sheets and halyards he saw them on their knees in prayer. On the other hand, they were generally lively and alert and quick to obey orders.

The Russians were reported to be at sea with a squadron of three battleships, two frigates and a steamship. Consequently it was decided to send the large frigate *Nusretie* to strengthen the Turkish squadron which had been ordered to sail to the Black Sea port of Sinope. Slade himself sailed in the *Nusretie* to Sinope and suggested that at least two battleships should be sent to Sinope as reinforcement. Instead it was agreed that the next squadron, which was to winter at Sinope, should be composed of battleships and frigates instead of frigates and corvettes as had been originally proposed. Yet when Slade returned with the first squadron to

Constantinople he found that his advice had been ignored and the decision to send a more powerful fleet had been reversed 'by the desire of the British Ambassador'. The unfortunate Vice-Admiral Osman Pasha had sailed for Sinope with no warship bigger than a frigate.

The small Black Sea port of Sinope had long enjoyed a life of peaceful trading and fishing. Once it had been a colony of Greece until it had fallen into the hands of the Tiurk – the Byzantine Turks. Ships had come and gone with their cargoes with seldom anything to disrupt the port's placid routine. Now came ships of war; nothing very big it is true but still quite exciting to see, although their crews were not in very good shape and were practically without winter clothing in bitter weather.

The excitement became rather doubtful when Russian ships, big ships some of them, came over the horizon. They gradually showed themselves to be three battleships, a frigate and one of the new-fangled steamers, but they sailed away again, to the relief of everyone watching. Then four more steamships hove into sight but to the relief of all they were flying the Turkish flag as they entered the bay and moored alongside. After a day or two, three of them steamed away, but the fourth one stayed.

The Russian ships appeared again and began sailing to and fro, clearly waiting until, nearly a week later, more vessels joined them. In command of the united Russian fleet was Vice-Admiral Nakhimov, who had the reputation of being an upright and courageous sailor. He saw that the weather was too rough for his ships to try to enter the bay and kept them to seaward for three more days. He had under his command a total of 11 ships. There were three ships-of-the-line with 120 guns each, three others of 84 guns, two of 54 and two small steam vessels in addition to the steamer that had arrived earlier in the bay.

The Turks had a good deal less than half the Russian gunpower, at least in numbers. Reports vary widely but at least the flagship of the Turkish admiral can fairly safely be listed as having 64 guns. The five frigates probably had between 42 and 45 each, the two corvettes perhaps 22 each and possibly 10 or 12 on the steamers.

On November 30 the weather moderated and the Russian ships moved into the bay and anchored in an arc before the town and near the Turkish squadron, with the battleships opposite the Turkish frigates. The Turks held their fire for a while, except for a single old-fashioned five-gun battery perched on and nearly hidden by a low cliff, which was causing some damage to the enemy. When a signalled request from the second-in-command of the squadron to open fire was disregarded the other vessels waited no longer, hopelessly outnumbered and outgunned as they were. For half an hour or so the Russian guns were fired with too much elevation, their shells passing over the frigates' bulwarks; but the aim was corrected and soon it was all at an end, except for the burning Turkish wrecks.

Sinope was not the kind of battle that is bright with glory in history books. The Turks had only out-of-date guns firing the old solid roundshot; the Russians were firing shells charged with gunpowder. Explosive shells had of course been used for years in mortars and on bomb-ketches, but conventional ships had used them only rarely since the first recorded use by the French at the bombardment of San Juan d'Ulua in November 1838.

The Sinope action (some called it a massacre) lasted for not much longer than an hour before the Turkish squadron literally ceased to exist. It had been smashed into wreckage, except for one little steamer that escaped although chased by the Russian steamers. Most of the others had been sunk or set on fire and burnt out during the battle. The Turkish admiral and three of his captains were taken prisoner and Turkish killed were estimated to have totalled 3000 or more. The Russians lost 38 killed and 240 wounded.

The Battle of Sinope was the first significant demonstration of the effect of explosive shot on wooden ships. But that was not all; shells falling in the town were said to have destroyed two-thirds of its buildings. The effect on the bewildered townsfolk of the sudden murderous bombardment must have been stupefying, as terrible as a modern bombing raid with no aircraft to be seen or heard. The story of Sinope, with additions, spread shock and horror throughout Europe, and particularly in France. Russia became a fearsome bully, an inhuman monster, and in less than two years France and Britain were to do battle with the ogre in the curious and bloody conflict that was the Crimean War – and their ships would be firing high-explosive shells.

Apart from the common shell, various new types of explosive projectile were destined soon to make their appearance in actual warfare. Among them was the shell developed (at his own expense) by Major Henry Shrapnel as far back as 1784; he eventually became a lieutenant-general and commander of artillery. Others included case-shot, designed to burst inside the gun barrel and discharge a rush of lead or iron balls; and grape-shot, which differed from case-shot only in the size of the balls. But the most lethal of breech-loading explosive shells was Shrapnel's; it was exploded by a charge set off by a time-fuse after leaving the gun and flung its spread of shot over a wide area. Its superiority was proved conclusively and has immortalised the name of its inventor.

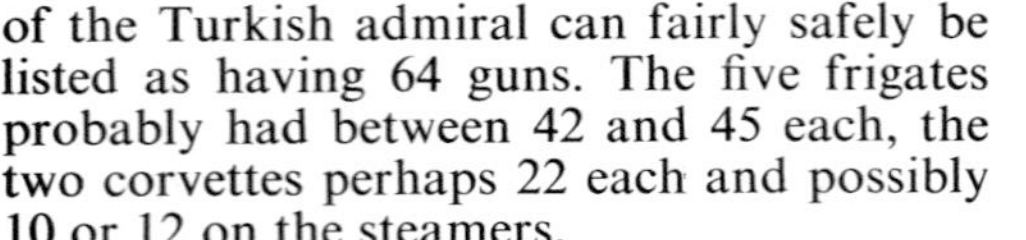

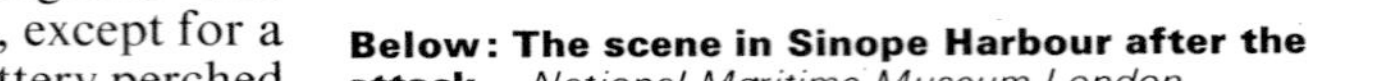

Below: The scene in Sinope Harbour after the attack. *National Maritime Museum London*

GUNS & GUNNERY

Above: A 32-pounder cannon at the side of HMS 'Victory' preserved at Portsmouth.
P D Hawkes

WHEN GUNS FIRST went to sea in the last half of the 14th century, they were little more than small-arms firing balls only a few ounces in weight. It was not until the latter part of the 15th century that weapons which we would describe today as cannons became the heavy armament of ships. These were guns built-up with longitudinal wrought-iron bars held together by shrunk-on iron hoops. They were breech-loaders with a removable chamber either screwed or wedged in position; they might be as much as nine feet long, with a calibre of eight inches and weighing about 8000 pounds; but there was a great variety of size with such names as basilisk, bombard, sling, serpentine and so on. The big guns were mounted on fixed wooden carriages and, at first, were placed so as to fire directly ahead from the fore deck.

As more of such guns became available, some were mounted on the open waist deck to fire on the beam through gaps in the bulwarks. When lofty fore- and after-castles were added, other smaller guns were mounted on their several decks, firing through gunports cut in the side planking.

So far, the hull itself was unpierced, but by the beginning of the 16th century, the practice of mounting heavy guns on the main deck on wooden carriages with two small wooden wheels or trucks on their fore end, to fire through square gunports cut in the side planking had been introduced. The extra hazard involved in piercing the ship's side had to be accepted as guns were becoming very heavy and had to be mounted lower down to preserve ship stability. The guns themselves were greatly improved, having become muzzle-loaders cast in bronze and bored out. They also became more standardised so that from their names rough indications of their sizes could be gleaned. The dimensions in the following table must nevertheless be taken only as a general guide for guns of the 16th century.

The cannon, it will be noted, was not at that time the generic name that it has since become. The main armament guns until the end of the broadside era were called the great guns. The most interesting of the table are the culverin and demi-culverin, the long-range guns introduced at the same time as the specialised fighting ship, the galleon. Developed primarily by Sir John Hawkins, Comptroller of Queen Elizabeth's navy, the design of the galleon gave it greatly improved sailing qualities compared to the existing big ships, the carracks, while the decked-in waist enabled a tier of demi-culverins and sakers to be mounted on the upper gun deck or main deck, and culverins on the lower gun deck. Thus designed and armed, galleons were

Name	*Calibre (inches)*	*Length (ft in)*	*Weight of Gun (lb)*	*Weight of Shot (lb)*	*Range (yd) Random, or Extreme*	*Point Blank*
Cannon-royal	$8\frac{1}{2}$	8-6	7000	68	1700	250
Cannon	7	10-9	6000	40	1600	250
Demi-cannon	$6\frac{1}{2}$	11-0	4500	32	1500	240
Cannon-pedro or Perier	6	10-0	3000	24 (stone)	1400	240
Culverin	$5\frac{1}{4}$	12-0	4000	18	2600	300
Demi-culverin	$4\frac{1}{4}$	11-6	3000	9	2600	300
Saker	$3\frac{1}{2}$	7-9	1800	5	1700	250
Minion	$3\frac{1}{4}$	6-6	1200	4	1600	250
Falcon	$2\frac{1}{2}$	6-0	680	2	1500	240
Robinet	1	3-0	300	1/2	1000	200

able to gain the position to windward of the old-fashioned carracks and engage at a range outside that of the fewer but heavier cannons, demi-cannons and periers carried by the latter.

The big test of their capabilities came with the arrival of the Spanish Armada in the Channel in 1588. In a series of actions over a period of six days they hovered on the outskirts of the massed defensive formation of the Armada, bombarding with impunity the clumsy carracks of which it was composed. Early results were disappointing, however; the shot fired by the culverins was not heavy enough to smash the stoutly built carrack hulls. It was not until the Battle of Gravelines, when the English galleons were taken into much closer range, that rather more damage and very heavy casualties among the massed soldiers on board the carracks were inflicted.

A new form of naval warfare had been introduced in which broadside fire by the great guns was the prime means of achieving victory, rather than the human assault by the soldiers carried in warships for that purpose, though boarding might still be necessary to subdue a stubborn enemy. The next 200 years saw little basic change in naval guns and gunnery. Cast iron came to be generally substituted for bronze in the late 16th century. By the middle of the next century, guns were mounted on wooden carriages with trucks at the four corners to facilitate running in and out to reload, which was done by means of side tackles. When the application of a slow match to the touch hole fired the gun, it recoiled on its carriage and trucks until brought up by a thick rope known as the breeching, fastened to the rear end of the gun carriage and to the ship's side.

The picturesque names had been discarded and guns were designated by the weight of the shot they fired, varying between 42-pounders and three-pounders. As ships came to be built with two, three or (by the 18th century) even four complete decks of guns, the heaviest were, naturally, mounted lowest, with nine-pounders on the upper deck. The 42-pounder gun was gradually discarded during the 18th century, the more easily managed and more quickly reloaded 32-pounder becoming the biggest of the great guns.

Besides solid iron balls, guns could be loaded with other types of shot, for example, Canister or Case—a number of small balls packed in a cylindrical metal case (for use against people); Grape—nine small shot (larger than in Case), the size varying with the calibre of the gun, in a thick canvas bag tightly corded to make a cylinder; Langridge—scrap-iron used instead of shot to destroy sails; Chain—two cannon-balls connected by a chain; and Bar-shot—two cannon-balls connected by an iron rod. Chain and bar-shot acted like a bolas to destroy rigging and masts. It was also common practice to heat solid iron balls before firing them as an effective weapon against combustible wooden ships.

Another type of gun used at sea was the mortar, a short-barrelled large-calibre weapon firing projectiles, usually explosive, at a high angle of elevation. They were most often mounted in small vessels known as bomb-ketches or simply bombs, used for bombarding shore positions.

The late 18th century saw the introduction of flint-locks in place of the primitive slow-match, with goose quills filled with powder kneaded in spirits of wine to provide the priming. Another innovation was the fitting of tackles by means of which the guns could be trained 45 degrees before or abaft the beam. A combination of these more than doubled the rate of fire. To regain the destructive power of the old cannon-royals and similar heavy guns, came the carronade, (from the Carron Iron Works in Scotland) a lightly constructed short-barrelled gun which could hurl comparatively large shot a short distance. Its effect at point-blank range of about 400 yards earned it the name smasher. Its light weight permitted 42- or even 68-pounders to be mounted on the upper deck of ships of the line in place of the less-destructive nine- or 12-pounders, giving such ships a huge advantage if action at short range could be forced.

The successes achieved by the carronade in Anglo-French fights during the American war of Independence and the Napoleonic wars led to their being mounted in an ever increasing proportion in the British Navy and to the neglect of gunnery practice at longer ranges. This was one of the causes of a series of defeats of British frigates in action with the American super-frigates in the war of 1812. A corresponding British victory, when the USS *Chesapeake* was quickly overpowered by the well-trained crew of HMS *Shannon,* led to gunnery reform in the Royal Navy and the foundation of its Gunnery School under the command of Captain Broke of the *Shannon.*

As with every other sphere of naval activity, the progress in naval guns and gunnery received a tremendous boost from the improvement in engineering skills of the Industrial Revolution during the latter half of the 19th century. The first notable innovation was that of explosive projectiles. First used in action by the Russian squadron at the Battle of Sinope in 1853, the rapid destruction of their Turkish opponents led to their general introduction in all navies. In turn, there came the introduction of iron-clad ships and, as the shells fired from smooth-bore guns could not penetrate armour, the next development in what was to become a continuing competition between guns and armour was to give the former rifled barrels to improve the ballistics of the shell.

The first steps in this direction were taken in 1846 by a Sardinian, Major Cavalli, and a Swede, Baron Wahrendorff, each of whom constructed a gun with spiral grooves machined on the inside of

Top: The guns of the USS 'Constitution' now preserved at Boston, Mass, USA. *J R Batts*

Above centre: View out through one of the open gunports. *J R Batts*

Above: The battleship HMS 'Rodney', in 1935, firing a salvo from five of her nine 16in guns, mounted in three triple turrets. *Illustrated London News*

Facing page: A painting of the huge 18in gun being fired on HMS 'Lord Clive' in 1918. *Oscar Parkes*

its barrel. Into these fitted spiral projections on the cylindrical projectiles. It was, however, a breech-loading gun devised by Mr W G Armstrong (later Lord Armstrong, and head of the famous armaments firm) that was adopted by the British Navy. Armstrong's was a built-up gun, consisting of a barrel strengthened by a number of coils or jackets shrunk on to it. The barrel was rifled with a number of shallow grooves; the cylindrical pointed projectiles were cased in lead so as to bite into the rifling. The breech incorporated a hollow screw, through which the gun was loaded and which held in place a wedge inserted to close the end of the barrel.

Unfortunately, this type of breech proved unsafe and after a number of accidents it was discarded and the Royal Navy reverted to muzzle loading for the next 20 years. In the earliest types of such guns the shells were studded. The studs were engaged in the grooves of the rifling and the shells eased awkwardly down the barrels. The French Navy, the Royal Navy's chief rival at that time, had adopted, and were to retain, the interrupted screw type of breech block which in time was to become almost universal for big guns.

The next major development was the adoption of a small number of the biggest available gun on rotatable mountings in place of batteries of guns firing on the broadside. The idea of mounting these guns on the ship's centre-line inside an armoured revolving turret was first put into practice by John Ericsson, who designed the *Monitor* for the United States in 1862 at the beginning of the Civil War to deal with the Confederate ironclad *Merrimac*. With a very low freeboard, driven by a steam engine and looking, according to contemporaries, like a Camembert cheese-box on a steam-driven raft, *Monitor* fought an indecisive duel with the *Merrimac*. But the concept of the turret had come to stay. A number of improved Monitors were built for the United States.

Such ships lacked ocean-going qualities, however. When a contemporary British designer, Captain Cowper Coles, RN, designed HMS *Captain* with a full rig of square sails as well as steam motive power, and two twin turrets mounted on the fore-and-aft line amidships, her disastrous loss in 1871 by capsizing in a sudden squall when under sail, made a convincing demonstration that the combination was an impossible one. It was the sail rig which had to go and the British *Devastation* built in 1873, with a turret forward and aft, each housing a pair of 12-inch guns, and rigged with a solitary signal mast, set a general fashion for battleships which, with minor deviations, was to persist for the next 30 years.

There were variations. Ships continued for a while to be given a square rig of sails and to be built on the central battery style, with pivot guns distributed so as to permit some of them to fire in any chosen direction. The Russians even acquired some circular coast-defence battleships (the famous Popovskas), the object being to provide a steady platform for the big guns mounted in the centre on a revolving platform. The French, favoured by their early adoption of breech-loading, mounted their big rotatable guns at the top of circular towers called barbettes, inside the armoured cover of which ammunition could be delivered.

As in other technical fields, the momentum of the Industrial Revolution during the last two decades of the 19th century brought a continuous and rapid development in design and manufacture of guns and ammunition. This, and the ever improving methods of giving ships armoured protection acted mutually to spur one another to further efforts. Guns in battleships increased in size, reaching a maximum in the monstrous 17.7-inch Armstrong muzzle-loaders mounted in the Italian battleships *Duilio* and *Dandolo* in 1876. (The biggest guns in the Royal Navy were those of 16.25-inch in the *Benbow* of 1888.)

The introduction of brown powder, an improved propellant compared with the old black powder, raised muzzle velocities, led to longer gun-barrels and the adoption by the Royal Navy of breech loading with the interrupted-screw thread type of breech block. Brown powder in turn gave way, towards the end of the century, to a comparatively smokeless powder composed of a mixture of nitro-glycerine and gun cotton, named cordite. To achieve the higher rate of fire possible with breech loading, the calibre of main armament guns

was reduced and the 12-inch finally became standard for battleships at the end of the century. Guns were mounted in barbettes and enclosed in turrets, operated and trained by hydraulic power; the whole arrangement was called at first a turret-barbette, but was later loosely called a turret. Besides the turret guns, battleships of the period, which we may anticipate by calling pre-dreadnoughts, mounted a mixture of guns between 6.2-inch and 9.2-inch on the broadside.

Cruisers also had a mixed armament with perhaps a 9-inch or 10-inch gun forward and aft and a battery of smaller guns, all breech-loaders, to fire on the broadside.

A further development in the continuous competition for dominance between guns and armour plate was the improvement in projectiles. The first step was the introduction of cast steel shells in 1881, followed by the Compound Armour Piercer in 1885 with a hardened point on a soft body. A Sheathed Projectile with a hard envelope and a soft core was developed in 1887, and the French firm, Holtzer, produced a chrome-steel shell. Cast steel was later superseded by forged steel, of which Firth and Vickers produced shells. When they were defeated by the invention of face-hardened steel armour, shells with solid soft-steel caps and later with hollow caps were devised. Up to 1895 the armour-piercing shell was not expected to carry a destructive bursting charge through the plate. But then there was produced the semi-armour-piercing shell, which carried a bursting charge of five per cent capacity; by 1914, semi-armour-piercing shells

carrying $6\frac{3}{4}$ per cent and fully armour-piercing shells with $2\frac{3}{4}$ per cent of high-explosive filling were standard.

An important development about 1888 was that of so-called quick-firing guns of comparatively large calibre (up to six inches) namely, Armstrong's invention of a type of interrupted-screw-thread breech mechanism in which a single movement of the breech lever revolved the breech-block to unlock (or lock) it, and swing it open (or shut). It was achieved primarily by making the breechblock conical instead of cylindrical so that it could be swung away on its hinges without first having to be withdrawn.

Top: A painting by Frank Wood of the original 'Dreadnought' in 1906, which had twice as many 12in guns as any ship then afloat. *National Maritime Museum London*

Left: From an 1876 picture in 'The Graphic', new 100-ton guns being lifted aboard 'Europa' at Newcastle upon Tyne. *Illustrated London News*

Below left: The 33 900-ton battleship 'Rodney', showing the unusual for'ard positioning of her armament. *Illustrated London News*

Eventually this type of breech was given to most guns of 4.7-inch calibre and above by the British and French navies. The newly emergent German navy preferred the wedge-type breechblock, as had long been in use in three- and six-pounder guns, and was later adapted to semi-automatic action (by ejecting the empty cartridge on firing) for most guns up to four inches calibre. Ships most affected by the advent of the QF gun, of course, were cruisers and below. Nevertheless, battleships also benefited in that they could mount batteries of six-inch quick-firing guns as defence against the newly developed torpedo-boat and torpedo-boat destroyer. So, at the turn of the century, navies were made up principally of battleships with four 12-inch guns in twin turrets and a mixed secondary armament of 9.2-inch and six-inch guns, armoured cruisers with eight-inch and six-inch, protected cruisers with six-inch and four-inch guns. Still almost totally lacking was any effective means of controlling the guns, particularly with mixed armaments of guns with different muzzle velocities, times of flight of projectiles and rates of fire. Action was visualised at point-blank range and few steps towards giving practice at long range had been taken.

Revolutionary developments were being gestated, however, in the minds of such innovators as the Italian designer Vittorio Cuniberti and Admiral Sir John Fisher, who advocated the adoption of a homogeneous all-big-gun armament for battleships to fight at long ranges, and of Captain Percy Scott in the British Navy and Lieutenant Commander WS Sims in the US Navy, who advocated more-ambitious fighting ranges and improved methods of training gun-layers and of controlling gunfire. It was the dynamic Fisher who was in the best position to push his concepts through; the result was the *Dreadnought* in 1905, a battleship with an armament of ten 12-inch guns in twin turrets and a secondary armament of three-inch guns, the first of a class of ship that was to become the backbone of all major navies. The same concept produced the all-big-gun battle-cruiser to take the place of previous armoured cruisers; the first to be completed was the *Inflexible*, mounting eight 12-inch guns and given a speed of 25 knots at the expense of armour protection.

To enable the heavy armaments to be effectively controlled at long range, they were fired in salvoes of at least four guns simultaneously, so that provided the shells fell right for line it was possible to see that all were over the target, all short, or some over and some short (a straddle) and range corrections could be made. At first, each turret was fired independently as the sights came on; then a director sight was mounted in a fighting top from which all guns could be fired simultaneously by a single trigger. A similar system was later provided for cruisers and eventually destroyers also. Mechanical plotting systems were installed to calculate and apply the rate of change of range and of inclination of the target.

When air attack became a feature for ships to reckon with, anti-aircraft guns, either automatic or semi-automatic, were devised with mountings which enable them to fire vertically. To provide a measure of control, they were linked to range-finders and predictors which calculated the fuse-length to be given to the high-explosive shells and the aim-off, or deflection, to be applied to the sights.

Basically, they were the sort of guns and control systems with which the 1914-18 war and a portion of the 1939-45 war were fought. The size of main armament guns had increased to 15 inches by the end of the 1914-18 conflict; during the later war, 16-inch calibre was the commonest, though the two huge Japanese ships, *Yamato* and *Musashi*, mounted 18.1-inch guns. Secondary armament similarly rose to a usual maximum of six inches. The advent of radar during the war greatly improved the accuracy with which guns could be initially laid and directed.

Since the end of that war, the rate of fire of naval guns has been enormously increased, with guns as big as eight-inch calibre being made fully automatic, which has brought other problems, such as cooling and rates of wear of barrels. Electronics and computers have increasingly been incorporated in the control systems. To a great extent, guns have been superseded by rocket-propelled missiles as the main offensive and defensive above-water armament of warships. There have been suggestions, however, that the process might have gone too far, leaving inadequate and unsuitable fire support for the disembarked troops of amphibious forces; indeed, at one period of the Vietnam war, the US Navy found it expedient to re-commission one of its battleships from reserve for the protection of landing troops.

Experiments are now being made with rocket-propelled shells. If they are successful, the big gun could well have a role still to play.

THE TORPEDO

A TORPEDO can be described as a cigar-shaped under-water weapon which carries an explosive warhead and is, or was, intended to attack enemy vessels below the surface of the sea. This was not always an accurate description; in the earlier part of its 100-year-old existence the name was freely given to several kinds of nautical explosive devices that were made to function in differing ways. Moreover, from 1885, when Nordenfeldt armed a submarine with a locomotive torpedo, the story of one has become increasingly that of the other.

A student of the American university Yale, David Bushnell, is believed to have discovered, in 1775, how a charge of gunpowder could be exploded under water. He devised the *Turtle*, a submarine magazine in the form of a large lemon-shaped submersible, deeper than its length, designed to clamp a charge on a ship's bottom which would then be set off by means of a clock mechanism. An operator sitting in the centre would drive the submersible into place by turning a propeller shaft by hand, in the dark, while he also steered and attended to buoyancy and other vital matters.

Over-optimistic as it might seem, the device had a full-scale trial. When Lord Howe arrived in American waters from England on a diplomatic mission during the War of Independence, an attempt using the contraption was made on his flagship, the 64-gun *Eagle*, by an American sergeant, Ezra Lee. However, Lee had to scuttle the *Turtle* as he was unable to pierce the metal sheathing of the *Eagle's* bottom to attach the charge. Ironically, Howe had travelled to America to try to negotiate a friendly settlement with the colonists.

Another American, Roger Fulton, during the Napoleonic Wars built the ancestor of all submarines. He had started with the avowed intention to 'deliver the French and all the world from British oppression'. Whatever his ideals, he left France and tried to promote his device in England under the name of Francis. An Admiralty Commission examined his designs for a submersible and declared it impractical. However, in a practical demonstration off Deal, in the presence of Prime Minister Pitt, Francis sank the captured French brig *Dorothea* by exploding a submarine mine under her hull.

It seemed a convincing demonstration, if only against a stationary target, but within a week the battle of Trafalgar was

Above: A Norman Wilkinson painting of sailors handling an 18-inch Whitehead torpedo. *M Muir Collection (photo D Rudkin)*

Right: A German WW2 conception at the Norwegian Navy's Torpedo Inspection School a Marder one-man submarine/torpedo once intended for large-scale production in Norway. *L Dunn*

Facing page top: Early 20th-century French submarine 'Méduse' fitted to take two torpedoes on deck and one in the tube, pictured at La Pallice in about 1910. *L Dunn Collection*

Facing page centre: Forward torpedo tubes of a British T-class submarine, built from 1937 to 1944. *L Dunn*

Far right: A 1920s picture of hoisting a torpedo on to Iron Duke-class battleship HMS 'Benbow' after a practice run, with destroyers 'Wren' and 'Wivern' in attendance. *L Dunn Collection*

fought and English interest in freakish underwater craft waned. Fulton went back to America and experimented with a new type of mine for use at sea. For the result he borrowed the French word torpillo (the cramp fish or electric eel) which in English was corrupted into torpedo. (The difference between mine and torpedo at that time was a very fine one.)

The name was quickly taken up in America, where several enthusiasts were developing the spar or outrigger torpedo—an explosive charge carried at the end of a long pole rigged in a small and speedy boat. It was supposed to be detonated by a strong thrust at a ship's side and the devoted crew of the boat, if they survived, had to rely on the confusion on board the attacked vessel to make their escape. One spar torpedo was caught and destroyed by the Royal Navy off Long Island during the American War of 1812; it appears to have been the only recorded instance at that time.

There was also an attempt to sink the British ship HMS *Ramillies* off New London by a submersible. But the one-man crew of the manually propelled boat was unable to screw the charge on to the *Ramillies* and an alert sentry spotted the craft and gave the alarm. It is quite likely that the attacking boat had been designed by Robert Fulton, who had spent some time in America experimenting with submarine craft.

Fulton returned to Paris round about 1800 and concentrated on building an impressive new submersible, 20 feet long and of five feet beam, which he named *Nautilus*. It was designed to stay under water for three hours and he and two passengers were once submerged for one hour, sitting by candlelight. On one occasion he claimed, he spent six hours under water, breathing through a lengthy tube which reached above the surface. Napoleon awarded him 10,000 francs, most of which went to pay for a refit and alteration of the *Nautilus*. One of his improvements was to fit sails, which he called wings but which in a later era would be classed as hydro-planes.

In the end Fulton changed his allegiance once again. In response to overtures from the British Government, he proposed plans for a great fleet of submarines which would attack and sink French invasion fleets in their harbours. As it turned out, he died with many of his projects unfulfilled.

In the course of the American Civil War several attempts with spar torpedoes were made on ships on the Great Lakes in 1863, but all without success. One sizeable ship, the Federation ironclad *Albemarle* was attacked, under heavy defensive fire, by a Lieutenant Cushing in a steam launch armed with a spar torpedo in Roanoke River. He blew up and sank the ship and his own boat but was able to swim clear and escape.

The most astonishing record was that of a submersible named *Hunley;* on her first trial she was swamped and sank, drowning all eight men of her crew, their captain the sole survivor. After being salvaged, on her second trial she was caught by a squall and again sank, taking six of the crew. There were still further mishaps and altogether during development trials the craft drowned a total of 35 men. But always there was someone to try again and eventually the *Hunley* was driven at the Federal 1200-ton warship *Housatonic* and in a terrific explosion both the warship and the submersible were sunk; there were no survivors from the *Hunley*.

By 1866 the British Mediterranean fleet was testing the new Whitehead torpedo, the weapon destined to revolutionise underwater warfare. Robert Whitehead was an English engineer who, after spending some time in Marseilles, France, set up in business in Italy. In Fiume, where he bought a workshop, he met a retired Austrian naval officer, Captain Giovanni Luppis, who suggested that a self-propelled under-water craft could be controlled by long lines arranged to unreel as the craft ran. The upshot, two years later, was the first Whitehead torpedo. It was 14 feet long and 14 inches in diameter, with a chamber for explosive in the nose, and was propelled and fired by compressed air. Its speed under water was six knots and the range was up to 700 yards.

In 1870 the British Admiralty, impressed by the reports on Whitehead's torpedoes, invited him to England to give a demonstration. Many people were horrified at the dastardly suggestion of waging war under water but the Admiralty was thoroughly satisfied. Whitehead was given a workshop in the arsenal at Woolwich and by 1872 he had completed a 16-inch torpedo. When he eventually left Woolwich the British Government bought the rights in the torpedoes for £15,000.

Within a few years of the Whitehead, between 1870 and 1880, two noteworthy types of torpedoes were produced in America. They were the Howell and the Bremmem, which had different novel methods of control. Neither overshadowed the Whitehead, which by 1891 had been given new means of propulsion by steam turbine or electric motor and had reached a surface speed of 29 knots and a range of up to 800 yards. The maximum diameter was now 18 inches and the original guncotton of the warhead had been replaced by TNT.

Success with the new weapon brought the days when capital ships and cruisers had to exercise in rigging out steel torpedo-nets round their hulls, to protect them from attack when at moorings, and torpedo crews were needed to overhaul and practise with the torpedo-tubes on their decks. The naval ports were continually adding to their swarms of black-painted turtle-backed torpedo-boats, or torpedo-catchers as they were called, since they were intended for the double role of attack and defence. By the end of 1895 Britain had 82 of the new fast little craft (which became a by-word for discomfort), France had amassed a total of 195 and Germany had acquired 158.

From the beginning France had taken a special interest in under-water projects and had built a long sequence of submarines of various types. Outstanding among them were the *Gymnote* of 30 tons, built in 1886, which, with 55hp, could make a submerged or surface speed of six knots. The *Morse*, a smaller boat of 1900, carried one torpedo in a tube and two more on deck. A major advance was the 1901 class, which had steam power for a speed of 12 knots on the surface and electric motors to give five knots submerged. While others had taken the torpedo-tubes inboard, on French boats they were still carried outside the hull, which is where they started. By 1901, when Britain owned only five submarines, France had already assembled a total of 23 boats. Germany at that time had none.

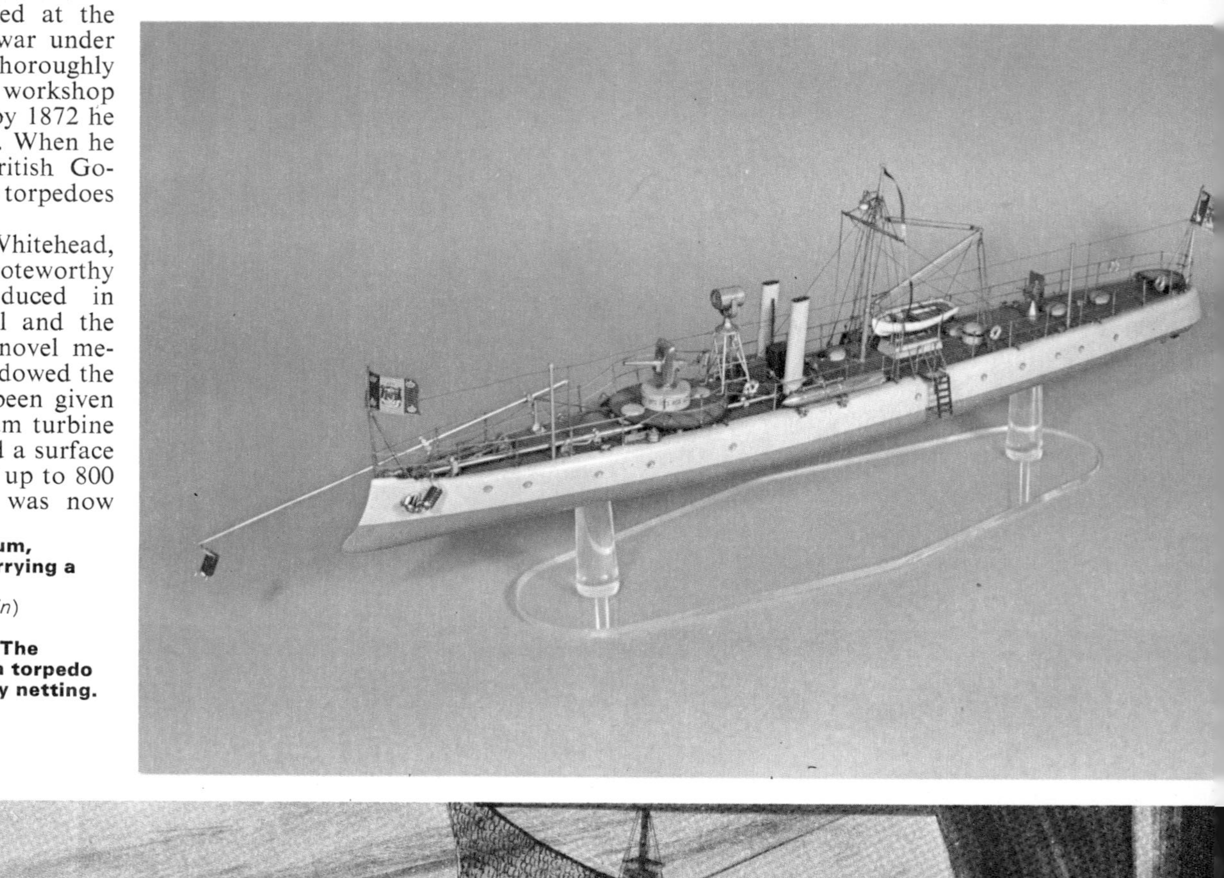

Right: A model in the Science Museum, London, of a 1906 fast steamboat carrying a long spar torpedo.
Science Museum London (photo D Rudkin)

Below: A page from a 1909 issue of 'The Illustrated London News' depicting a torpedo attack on a dreadnought protected by netting.
Illustrated London News

Top: The design of the fighting ship to serve mighty turrets fore and aft is well shown in this picture of the battlecruiser HMS 'Hood', completed in 1918 with eight 15in guns in four turrets.
National Maritime Museum (Cribb, Southsea)

Above: Pre-dreadnought battleship HMS 'Majestic' of 1895, with main armament of four 12in guns in two revolving turrets on top of fixed barbettes.
J Crosley (from an old postcard)

The Development of Turrets

EVER SINCE THE advent of the ironclad made the smooth-bore cannon firing solid projectiles ineffective against warships, armour and fire-power have contended for the mastery. On the one side, armour advanced from the early wrought iron to steel, to nickel steel and finally to face-hardened steel; on the other, guns became rifled, firing explosive shell at an ever higher muzzle velocity; they were mounted on pivots and sited on the centre-line, enabling them to fire on either beam. They also became ever larger, with a few huge long-range pieces taking the place of the numerous smaller guns of the old broadside.

The large pieces were, of course, on revolving mountings. They were served by large crews who, together with the comparatively complex machinery, were exposed to an enemy's gunfire. It was desirable, therefore, to place both under the protection of armour. Three men of inventive genius were applying their minds at much the same time to devising such an arrangement—in the United States the Swedish engineer John Ericsson, in Great Britain Captain Cowper Coles, in France Dupuy de Lôme.

Ericsson was first in the field, his concept having been accelerated at the beginning of the American Civil War in 1861 by the urgent need of the Federal Government to acquire a warship capable of challenging the Confederate steam frigate *Virginia*—she in fact was and is better known as the ex-USS *Merrimac*, which had been ingeniously converted into an ironclad. Ericsson therefore designed a ship to mount a pair of 11-inch muzzle-loading smooth-bore guns, firing solid shot, on a centre-line turntable. All but a short length of the gun barrels was surrounded by a circular structure made of eight layers of 1-inch iron, of 20 feet inside diameter and nine feet in height. Thus, the gun turret was born; the ship was to give its name to a type—the monitor.

It was somewhat ahead of its time. Although the first iron-hulled warship, HMS *Warrior*, had been launched the year before in England, no such construction methods were yet in use in America. The USS *Monitor*, therefore, was of wooden construction, encased down to the water line in five layers of 1-inch iron plate. To carry the concentrated weight of the two big guns and to withstand the shock of their discharge, the timbers were so large that their weight, with that of the armour added, immersed her so deeply as to leave less than two feet of freeboard. She looked, indeed, like nothing so much as a Camembert cheese on a steam-driven raft. As such she was barely seaworthy and only reached Hampton Roads from New York after a hazardous journey in rough seas.

The ensuing duels between the *Monitor* and the *Merrimac* were indecisive; but the turret concept had come to stay. Numerous improved versions of the monitor were built for the United States Navy and they played a commanding role in the riverine operations in the American Civil War. Across the Atlantic, meanwhile, Captain Coles and Dupuy de Lôme were each designing more seaworthy ships mounting gun turrets. For the Danish Navy, the *Rolf Krake* with two 8-inch turrets and the similar *Arminius* for the Prussian Navy were built in Britain to the former's design in 1865.

Dupuy de Lôme introduced the turret into the French Navy in the *Cerbère* in the same year, followed by the Tonnerre class, which mounted two $11\frac{1}{2}$-inch breech-loading guns worked by hydraulic power in a revolving turret similarly powered. Their equivalents and contemporaries in the Royal Navy were the coastal battleships or breastwork monitors, typical of which was the *Glatton,* which mounted a pair of 12-inch guns in a revolving turret, and *Hotspur,* which had a fixed turret with a single gun revolving inside it on a turntable.

The concept of turret-mounted guns in ocean-going battleships did not find great favour at first owing to the contemporary refusal to rely only upon steam propulsion and the continued provision of a full rig of sails as well. For such ships, the central battery of guns firing on the broadside was more suitable. Nevertheless, the British Admiralty had designed and laid down the *Monarch* with two turrets amidships. With the normal forecastle and poop preventing fire fore and aft and the maze of standing rigging restricting it on other bearings, the arrangement had few if any advantages over a central-battery ship.

Captain Coles in the meantime had designed a ship to be built by Laird's of Birkenhead for the Royal Navy which he believed would overcome the disadvantages. Though his original concept of a flush-deck ship, with no poop, or forecastle was rejected by Laird's in the interests of seaworthiness, his plan to rig her with tripod masts requiring little standing rigging and a flying deck from which the running rigging would be worked was accepted.

Unfortunately Coles's ship turned out to weigh 800 tons more than had been calculated and had a freeboard of only $6\frac{1}{2}$ feet instead of $8\frac{1}{2}$. Nevertheless, she was commissioned as HMS *Captain* and won golden opinions from all who sailed in her. But then, on a black night of storm in September 1871, caught in a sudden furious squall, the *Captain* capsized and sank, taking with her Captain Coles, as well as her commanding officer, Captain Burgoyne, and all but 18 of her crew of nearly 500.

Although, as a result of that catastrophe, ships with central batteries continued to be built for some years further, the *Captain's* fine gunnery performance had made the development of the turret inevitable. It was the sail rig that would have to be sacrificed. So in 1873 the *Devastation,* a battleship with twin turrets fore and aft and with only a solitary signal mast, joined the British fleet, the forerunner of a long line. A serious disadvantage of the turret was its great weight. In the *Devastation* it resulted in a very low freeboard (as had been the case in the *Monitor*) and the constant washing down of the upper deck in even a moderate seaway.

Two different techniques of gun mounting soon developed—in turrets or on the open-topped towers called barbettes. In the Royal Navy and other navies which relied upon the British firm of W G Armstrong for their guns and therefore continued to accept muzzle-loading after the failure of the Armstrong breech mechanism, revolving turrets were employed. While small-grained black powder was still the propellent, guns were short-barrelled and could be run back inside the turrets, there to be reloaded in the normal way. As guns got longer, however, it became necessary to provide loading tubes leading obliquely up from the deck below into the turret. Eventually guns got so long that loading had to be done with the gun muzzles protruding from the turret. To enable that to be done under cover, an armoured glacis was built so that when fully depressed the muzzles were under its cover; the loading tubes passed through the glacis.

The French avoided the difficulty. They had successfully adapted an American invention to perfect the interrupted-thread type of breech mechanism for all their large guns, which they mounted on revolving platforms, on barbettes, over the top of which they fired. It was a much lighter arrangement; the ships rode higher in the water and the crews enjoyed a better line of sight. Such barbette mountings were also to be seen in the coast-defence battleships built for the Russian Navy, the *Novgorod* and the *Vice-Admiral Popov.* Called Popoffkas, they had circular hulls driven by six propellers, the object being to provide steady gun platforms.

Barbette mountings had the disadvantage of exposing the gun crews to enemy fire and made muzzle-loading impossible, until the introduction of hydraulically operated disappearing mountings on which the guns sank behind the armour to be reloaded. The *Popov* was so fitted; so were

Right: Captain Coles's HMS 'Captain', which proved the efficacy of turrets, but had too little freeboard and capsized in a squall in 1871; from a lithograph by T G Dutton.
National Maritime Museum (Crown Copyright)

Below: Again, massive turrets carrying 18.1in guns dominate the silhouette of the Japanese battleship 'Yamato'—with her sister 'Musashi', the biggest battleships ever built.
Lt Cdr S Fukui

many French ships of the period, while the Royal Navy incorporated it in the central-battery arrangement of HMS *Téméraire* in 1877, which had two 25-ton guns so mounted.

Turrets had come to stay, nevertheless, and at that time were associated with an armoured central citadel within which they were diagonally mounted, as in the Italian *Duilio* and *Dandolo* designed by the celebrated Benedetto Brin. Their guns, four 100-ton 17.7-inch Armstrong muzzle-loaders, were the largest ever mounted until the 18.1-inch guns of the Japanese *Yamato* and *Musashi* of the 1939-45 war. The British reply, on a similar design, was the *Inflexible*, launched in 1876, mounting two twin turrets of 80-ton 16-inch guns.

Two new factors were then to lead to a revolutionary change in the design of battleships—the advent of the torpedo boat firing the locomotive torpedo, and the adoption by the British of the interrupted-thread breech mechanism which brought the abandonment of muzzle loading. Between 1882 and 1885, a class of ships named after distinguished admirals which, besides a number of 6-inch, 6-pounder and 3-pounder guns as an anti-torpedo-boat battery, mounted a pair of breech-loading guns on a barbette at each end of the citadel. The first two of the class had 12-inch guns, five had 13.5-inch, while one, the *Benbow,* had single 16.25-inch guns on each barbette.

Two last examples of ships with big guns in turrets were to be built for the Royal Navy in 1887, the *Sans Pareil* and *Victoria,* which each mounted two 110-ton 16.25-inch breech-loaders in single turrets forward. Such monstrous pieces, however, had so slow a rate of fire with the loading machinery then available that maximum gun calibres were thereafter until 1915 to be 13.5 inches. The turret system continued to be criticised on the grounds that it entailed a low freeboard and placed the guns too low over the water. When the Royal Sovereign class of eight battleships was laid down in 1889, all except one of them mounted their four 13.5-inch guns on fixed open barbettes constructed of 17-inch armour plate. The exception was the *Hood,* which incorporated turrets that showed up unfavourably compared to the barbettes in the remainder.

One final step had to be taken to bring about the system of mounting a battleship's main armament that was to become standard. The introduction of Harvey case-hardened steel enabled armour of six to eight inches to be substituted for the eight to 18 inches in, for example, the *Royal Sovereign.* The resultant saving in weight permitted the mounting of revolving turrets on top of the fixed barbettes in the Majestic class, launched between 1895 and 1896. With two twin 12-inch turrets, the Majestics became the prototype for pre-dreadnought battleships in all navies. Called originally turret-barbettes, the new mountings came eventually to be designated simply turrets.

An indication of a capital ship type of the future was provided by the two Italian ships *Italia* and *Lepanto,* which Benedetto Brin designed to follow the *Duilio* and *Dandolo* in 1883. They again mounted four 17.7-inch guns in turrets, but the armour belt was almost completely sacrificed. It was replaced by a system of cellular sub-division into numerous small compartments filled with cork or coal extended over the whole length of the ship. The saving in weight enabled 18 knots to be achieved—a speed much superior to that of contemporary capital ships. They were thus, in some ways, forerunners of the battlecruiser design inaugurated in 1906 with the *Inflexible.*

For a brief period of ten years from 1895, the pre-dreadnought battleship with a main armament of four 12-inch guns in two turret-barbettes and a secondary armament of numerous 6-inch or 8-inch guns was the standard design everywhere. Nevertheless, before the turn of the century, inventive minds were being influenced by the theories of the Italian Vittorio Cuniberti, who was advocating the advantages of a battleship armed only with big guns all of the same calibre which, by facilitating the spotting of the fall of shot, would permit effective fire at the great ranges of which guns were by then capable.

Cuniberti's ideas were rejected by his own countrymen, but they encouraged the British Commander-in-Chief Mediterranean, Sir John Fisher, in 1898 to set the Chief Constructor of Malta Dockyard, W H Gard, to design two all-big-gun ships, a battleship, which Fisher termed the *Untakeable,* and the armoured cruiser *Unapproachable.* They were to be the embryos of the revolutionary *Dreadnought* and the first battlecruiser *Inflexible.*

Another eight years were to elapse before the *Dreadnought* took the water. In the meantime, it was two fleets of pre-dreadnoughts which were to meet in combat on three major occasions in the Russo-Japanese War, actions which were clearly to demonstrate the fact that only the main armament of 12-inch guns of the battleships on each side played any significant part; and, indeed, that the smaller guns, when they were in range, only seemed to confuse the fire control picture with their shell splashes. There were no doubts, therefore, about the rightness of the decision to build the *Dreadnought* mounting ten 12-inch guns in twin turret-barbettes with an anti-torpedo-boat battery of only 3-inch guns. And when the *Dreadnought* was launched on February 10, 1906, a year and a day after being laid down, at one stroke every other existing battleship was made obsolete.

The turret ship was then entering the brief heyday during which it was believed to reign supreme. The *Dreadnought* was succeeded by the super dreadnought with 13.5-inch, and then 15-inch guns, in superimposed turret-barbettes. Armour protection, speed and size of gun all increased, class by class. Engineering technique then brought forth the 'fast battleship' with a speed of 30 knots or more, making super-dreadnoughts obsolete unless they could be modernised to a similar standard—as were a number of Japanese ships.

But all the while the ships that were to dethrone the battleship—the aircraft-carrier and the submarine—were advancing in effectiveness. And although at the end of the 1939-45 war the British and Americans had plans to build capital ships larger and more powerful even than the huge Japanese *Yamato* and *Musashi,* which each mounted nine 18.1-inch guns in three triple turrets, it was the realisation that the day of the battleship was long over as much as the desire for armament reduction that caused the abandonment of such ideas.

The turret has survived the departure of the battleship. Guns as small as 3-inch are mounted in them in modern ships. They and 6-inch guns are loaded and fired at a rate which would have classed them as machine-guns a score of years earlier. The turret is no longer the special feature of one type of ship as it was in the day of the battleship. But the modern turret is different, chiefly in that it has lost its armoured cladding and its roof is merely to keep the weather out; the guns it houses are universally automatic and the turrets are unmanned.

HMS 'Devastation' of 1873, with twin turrets fore and aft and only a single signal mast, heralded the final abandonment of sail rig. *Illustrated London News*

Director Gun Control

IT IS OFTEN SUPPOSED that director firing of a warship's guns was devised by that arrogant inventive gunnery genius, Captain (later Admiral Sir) Percy Scott, in the early years of the present century, and that it was first installed in Britain's early dreadnought battleships shortly before the 1914-18 war. In truth, it is of much earlier origin.

During the Napoleonic War period the more progressive British post-captains, notably Sir Charles Douglas, Rodney's chief of staff at the battle of the Saintes, and Sir Philip Broke, of HMS *Shannon* versus USS *Chesapeake* fame, appreciated the advantages of being able to aim all the guns of a ship-of-the-line's broadside on to the same target—especially when, though visible from the poop, it was obscured by powder smoke to those on the gun decks—and to deliver a hammer blow by firing them all together.

By the time HMS *Excellent* was brought into use as the first gunnery school ship at Portsmouth in 1830, such 'director firing' was taught there as a standard practice to be used throughout the British Fleet. It was nonetheless as primitive a method as were the guns which it controlled, the 24- and 32-pounder muzzle-loading cannon, firing solid cast-iron balls which comprised the armament of a sailing ship-of-the-line. It depended entirely on verbal orders, relayed from the 'directing' compass on the poop to each individual gun, for elevation, training and firing.

Improvements had to await the introduction of electricity, initially supplied by batteries, on board Britain's early ironclads in the second half of the 19th century. Here, for example, is Lieutenant 'Jacky' (later 'Admiral of the Fleet Lord) Fisher writing in the 1860s; 'The following appears to be a simple method of firing by electricity, from the maintop (or any other desired position) in order that the delivery of fire by the officer at the Director should be instantaneous on his sights being aligned'. But although he added that 'the arrangements made to carry out this system from the heavy guns on board HMS *Excellent* met with perfect success', it was rejected by the War Office's very conservative Ordnance Committee, which was then responsible for meeting the Admiralty's gunnery requirements, for such naïve reasons as, 'a considerable length of wire would be necessary to meet the entire range of a gun's training and would be much in the way'.

Fisher was not, however, a man likely to yield to such objections. By the 1890s, after he had been Director of Naval Ordnance and subsequently Controller at the Admiralty, Britain's pre-dreadnought battleships were equipped as thus described in *Naval Gunnery* by Captain H Garbett, RN, published in 1896; 'The Director is used to bring the fire from a turret or battery under the control of the Captain during action. It consists of a telescopic sight which can be moved up and down for elevation, and also over an arc just as a gun is trained. It is placed in the armoured conning tower, and has an electric firing key connected to every large gun. Converging stops are fitted to the guns on the bow, beam and quarter, to enable them to be rapidly trained to deliver a broadside on the same point, the necessary elevation for the range being passed to them from the director.'

Even so, this form of director firing had substantial limitations. The bearing on which the guns were to be trained, and the angle of elevation to which they were to be laid, still had to be passed verbally, albeit, by then, by means of voice pipes. Moreover, the bearings were restricted to three—45, 90 and 135 degrees from right ahead. And, having ordered the guns to be trained on one of them, the director layer had to wait before firing until either the ship made an appropriate alteration of course, or until the target's movements brought it on to the designated bearing. It was, nonetheless, a useful system at a time when it was supposed that naval battles should be fought at a maximum range of about 4000 yards (two miles), only twice that of Nelson's day—'a range at which', to quote Admiral of the Fleet Lord Cunningham writing in another context nearly fifty years later, 'even a Gunnery Officer cannot miss'.

The advent of the 20th century changed all that. First, that new underwater menace, the Whitehead torpedo, when provided with a 'heater' engine instead of one rely-

Director controlled 6-inch guns of the Peruvian cruiser 'Almirante Graü' (ex-HMS 'Newfoundland'). *A Greenway*

ing only on compressed air, achieved a range of 8000 yards, which dictated the need for gun battles to be fought outside that distance. Second, in 1905 Japan's Admiral Togo demonstrated, by his destruction of the Russian Admiral Rozhdjestvensky's Baltic Fleet at Tsushima, that naval guns could be dangerously effective at as much as 10,000 yards. So, by 1910, British battleships were accustomed to carry out their battle practice firings at ranges of that order, the gunnery officer's aim being 'hit first, hit hard and keep on hitting'.

Meantime, Scott, in particular, had realised the need to site a ship's principal gunnery control position high up on the foremast, leaving the armoured conning tower to serve only as a stand-by position in event of action damage, and to site the principal director in a lightly protected 'pill box' either immediately above or immediately below the high spotting top. At the new long ranges it was only from those positions aloft that the principal control, spotting and rate officers, and the director layer and trainer, could see an enemy ship and their own ship's fall of shot, clear of the cordite smoke expelled by their own guns, and the high white splashes thrown up by enemy shells falling short of the ship.

As important, Scott's director, in addition to high-power telescopes for its layer and trainer, incorporated electrical transmission of elevation and training from the master sight to the guns, which were no longer restricted to firing on a few specified bearings. In front of each gunlayer was a receiver on whose dial a red electrically operated pointer indicated the required elevation, and a mechanically operated black pointer indicated the actual elevation of the gun. So, too, did each gun have a dial with red and black pointers indicating the director's and the gun's angle of training. Since the receivers incorporated corrective mechanisms to allow for the differences in height and lateral distance between the gun and the director, it was only necessary for gun layers and gun trainers to keep their red and black pointers in line for the whole broadside to be correctly aimed at the target ordered by the captain through the principal control officer to the director. Not unless the electrical transmission failed was it necessary for gunlayers and gun trainers to use their own telescopic sights, through which their view of the enemy was often obscured.

As soon as each gun was loaded and its gunlayer on target, he pressed a switch which illuminated a 'gun ready' lamp in the director. And when all the lamps were burning, the director layer gripped his firing trigger, to produce a broadside whose splashes, from shots necessarily spread 200 to 400 yards apart (because of unavoidable small differences between individual guns and their cordite charges), could be spotted against a distant target as 'short' or 'over' and the necessary corrections applied to the range (for example, 'Up 400', 'Down 800' etc) to produce straddles, that is, some shots short, some over and, with luck, some hits.

The foregoing basic description of Scott's director system needs to be amplified in three respects. First, the director's crew included a sightsetter who applied the range of the target, as estimated by the spotting officer or, preferably, measured by rangefinder, to the master sight so that the necessary angle of elevation for that range was transmitted to the guns. Secondly, it was found impracticable for individual gunlayers to follow with their pointers the continuous movements of the director due to its layer chasing the roll of

110—THE ILLUSTRATED LONDON NEWS—JULY 20, 1935

ALL THAT GOES TO PRODUCE A GREAT BRITISH WARSHIP'

DRAWN BY OUR SPECIAL ART

1. THE CAPTAIN ON THE BRIDGE ISSUES HIS ORDERS BY VOICE-PIPE TO THE CONTROL TOWER.

2. THE CONTROL TOWER, SITUATED 80 FEET ABOVE SEA LEVEL.

PRINCIPAL CONTROL OFFICER.
DIRECTOR TRAINER.
DIRECTOR LAYER.
RANGE-TAKER.
OBSERVER OF FALL OF SHOT.
ASSISTANT CONTROL OFFICER.
EXPANSION TANK MACHINERY.

3. THE PRINCIPAL CONTROL OFFICER ISSU HIS FINDINGS TO THE TRANSMITTING STA

7. NOW THE RANGE-TAKERS TAKE THE RANGES & SEND THE RESULT TO THE TRANSMITTING ROOM, WHICH WORKS OUT THE MEAN RANGE & RE-TRANSMITS IT TO THE CONTROL TOWER.

RANGE-TAKER.
RANGE-FINDER.

A GREAT BRITISH BATTLESHIP WITH HE

3-16IN GUNS.
3-16IN GUNS.

9. ONE OF THE GREAT TURRETS PREPARING TO FIRE.

GUNLAYERS.
TURRET OFFICER.
GUIDES OF LOADING CAGE.
CAGE HOIST LEVER.
RANGE-TAKER.
PERISCOPE.
APPROXIMATE POSITION OF TURRET TRAINER.

10. THE TURRET TRAINER, WATCHING THE POINTER ON THE DIAL BEFORE HIM, MOVES THE TURRET ACCORDINGLY

VOICE PIPE.
POINTER.

11. THE TURRET IS NOW IN THE CORRECT POSITION. THE GUNLAYERS INDIVIDUALLY LAY THEIR GUNS ON THE TARGET.

FROM THE CAPTAIN'S QUIETLY SPOKEN ORDER TO THE PULLING OF THE PISTOL-TRIGGER PROCESSES INVOLVED IN THE GUNNERY EXERCISES SCHEDULED TO FOLLOW THE NAVAL REVIEW

This drawing is intended to illustrate, in rough outline only, and explain in simple terms the severely scientific procedure of fighting a modern battleship, where the work of killing is reduced to cold mechanics and mathematics. From the Captain on the bridge, quietly issuing his commands, goes a message to officers and men cooped up in the control tower over his head, some 80 ft. above the water line. Looking through a slit in the "upper storey" of the control tower, the Principal Control Officer, through his voice-pipe, points out the target to the transmitting station far down in the ship below the water-line. Meanwhile the Director Trainer trains the control tower on to the target and simultaneously all the main armament and the other control towers turn in the same direction. The transmitting station re-transmits the position of the target to all the stations concerned. The range-finders in the control towers and turrets take the ranges of the target, and these are sent to the transmitting station, which works out the mean ranges and passes this information back to the control tower. The mean range is set on the director sight, while the elevation and training directions

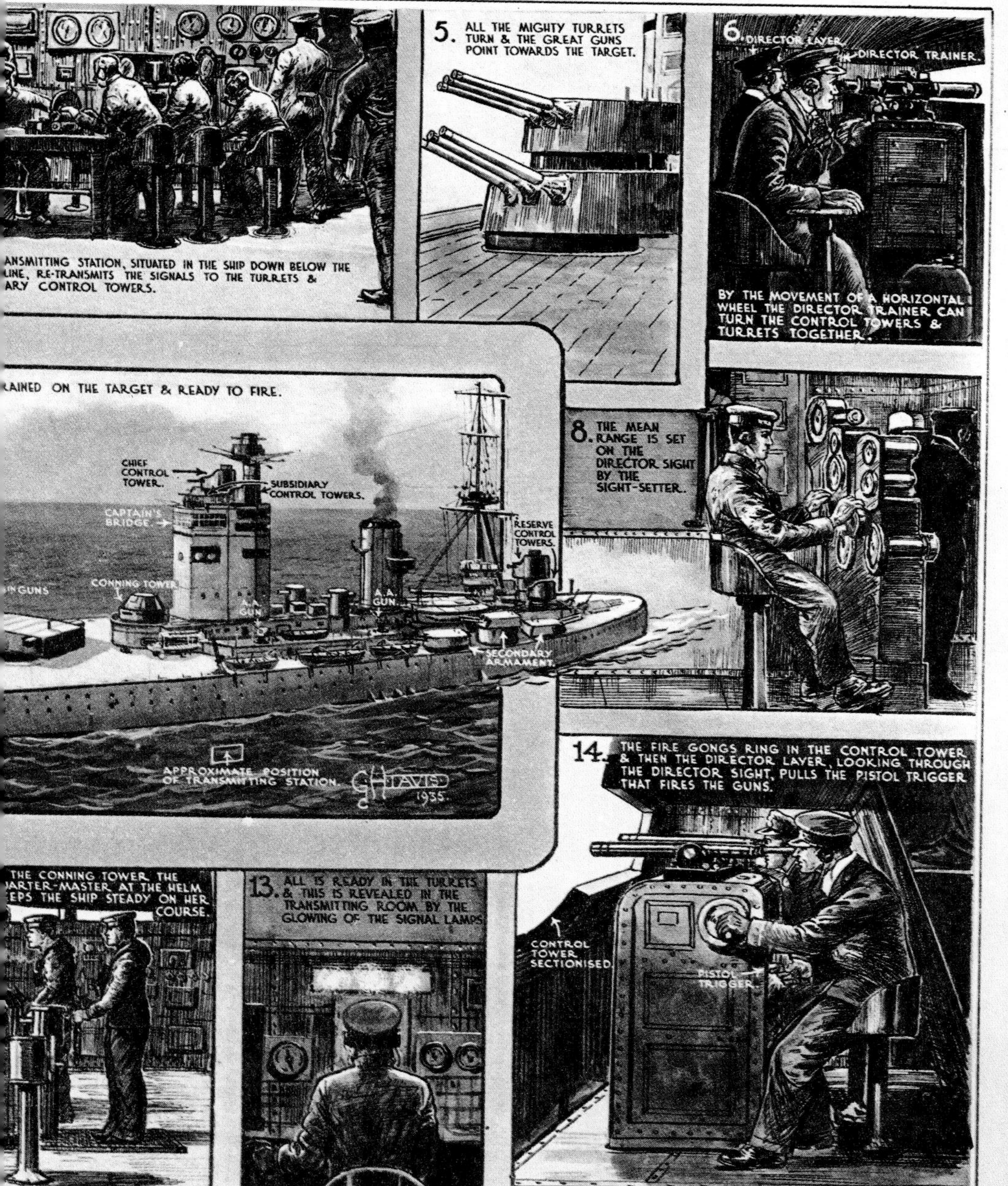
July 20, 1935—THE ILLUSTRATED LONDON NEWS—111

"...ATTLE-THUNDER": COLD SCIENCE BEHIND THE BIG GUNS.

...vis, with Official Permission.

...ansmitting station, situated in the ship down below the ...line, re-transmits the signals to the turrets & ...ary control towers.

5. All the mighty turrets turn & the great guns point towards the target.

6. Director layer. Director trainer. By the movement of a horizontal wheel the director trainer can turn the control towers & turrets together.

...rained on the target & ready to fire.

Chief control tower. Subsidiary control towers. Captain's bridge. Reserve control towers. ...guns. Conning tower. A.A. gun. A.A. gun. Secondary armament. Approximate position of transmitting station.

G. H. Davis 1935.

8. The mean range is set on the director sight by the sight-setter.

14. The fire gongs ring in the control tower & then the director layer, looking through the director sight, pulls the pistol trigger that fires the guns.

Control tower sectionised. Pistol trigger.

...the conning tower the ...arter-master at the helm ...eps the ship steady on her course.

13. All is ready in the turrets & this is revealed in the transmitting room by the glowing of the signal lamps.

...UTLINE OF SUCCESSIVE STAGES IN FIRING A SUPER-DREADNOUGHT'S 16-INCH GUNS— EXEMPLIFIED BY OUR COLOURED ILLUSTRATION OF H.M.S. "RODNEY" FIRING A BROADSIDE.

...t to the gunlayers in the turrets. The Turret Trainer, watching the ... of a dial, moves the turret and its three gigantic guns accordingly. ...rret assumes the correct position, with the officer in charge looking ... his periscope and the guns' crews busy at their tasks. In a few ... they jump clear and all is ready to fire. In the conning tower ...artermaster at the helm keeps the ship steady on her appointed ... It is "Zero Hour"! Suddenly the signal lamps in the transmitting ... glow brightly, indicating that all is ready in the turrets. Instantly the signal from this station rings the fire gongs in the control towers and turrets, and at the same moment the Director Layer, looking through his director sight, presses the trigger of the pistol grip which fires the guns, either all together in a gigantic deafening salvo, or one by one as directed. Those able to watch can see the great shells, each as heavy as a taxicab, go hurtling through space to the target, perhaps seventeen miles away. Then in the far distance great spouts of foam as high as a church steeple leap up from the riven sea and denote the "straddling" of the enemy.

a ship in a seaway. The director layer had to wait until the upward roll of the ship brought his sight 'on' before pressing the firing trigger, a limitation which not only reduced the rate of fire but which contradicted all that Scott had espoused for individual gunlayer's firings, for which he had devised his well-known Dotter device for improving their aim.

The disadvantage was not overcome until in 1917 the Henderson gyro was added to directors. By means of an internal prism the gyro stabilised a director layer's line of sight so that it was kept on target without transmitting continuous changes in the angle of elevation to the guns. It also allowed the director layer to press his trigger as soon as the gun ready lamps were burning, after which the gyro fired them automatically as the ship rolled on to target.

Thirdly, the angles of elevation and training went from the director to the guns by way of the transmitting station, which was sited in the armoured bowels of the ship. There, from own ship's known course and speed and the estimated course and speed of the enemy, an instrument called after its inventor, Lieutenant Dumaresq, calculated the deflection (that is, aim off) to be applied to the angle of training of the guns, and the rate of change of range to be applied through a range clock to their angle of elevation to match the time of flight of the shells from the guns to their target. This simple method of allowing for the relative movement of the enemy during the period of half a minute or more was

Left: A double-page spread from the July 20, 1935, edition of 'The Illustrated London News' showing the progressive stages of laying and firing a super dreadnought's 16-inch guns. *Illustrated London News*

Below left: High-angle directors aboard the German destroyer 'Bayern'. *A Greenway*

Below: The County-class guided missile destroyer HMS 'Hampshire', which employs the very latest in director control. *A Greenway*

superseded in 1913, after several years of comparative trials, by an electro-mechanical digital computer. In thus using such an instrument, the Navy was much in advance of other professions.

It was not, however, then called a computer. Its overall shape and its inventor, Lieutenant (later Admiral Sir) Frederic C Dreyer, led to it being named the Dreyer Table. (Dreyer profited from earlier experiments with an instrument devised by one Arthur Pollen.) It incorporated not only a large Dumaresq and an improved range clock, but means by which, from a continuous plot of the bearing of the target, and of its range as measured by the ship's several rangefinders—one was fitted in each turret—its true course and speed could be calculated and applied instead of only the estimated ones, which were always difficult for the spotting and rate officers to judge correctly.

The Dreyer Table also applied corrections to the angle of elevation to allow for the temperature (which affected the explosive power of the cordite charges) and to the angle of training to allow for the wind and for the spin imparted to the shells by the rifling of the guns (drift), both of which curved the trajectory of the shell in the horizontal plane.

As installed in his flagship, the armoured cruiser *Good Hope*, in 1907, Scott's extemporised director showed sufficient promise for a prototype to be fitted in the dreadnought *Thunderer* in time for extensive comparison trials with her sister ship, HMS *Orion*, in 1912. The results were conclusive; the *Thunderer* scored 36 hits out of 39 rounds fired at a mean range of 8500 yards; the *Orion* (which had no director) managed only six hits out of 27 rounds fired.

Orders were then given for all British capital ships to be so equipped and, under the impetus of war, the work was completed in all but two of those in the Grand Fleet by the time that Jutland was fought on May 31, 1916. And by the end of the war director firing had not only been applied to the secondary armaments of capital ships, but to cruisers and, in a simplified form, to destroyers. It was also copied by other navies, especially those of the Allies, including the USA which had previously rejected a comparable system conceived back in 1890 by one of its own officers, the brilliant Bradley Fiske, inventor of the telescopic gun sight. For contrast, the Imperial German Navy, though noted for its efficient gunnery, relied on a simple director only for indicating the bearing of a target. For laying and firing their warships' guns they continued to use individual gun sights.

Between the two world wars the director firing system fitted in new and modernised warships in the principal fleets was substantially improved in two respects. More sophisticated fire control tables—a change of name against which the egotistical Dreyer protested in vain—were produced, the between-decks compartment in which they were installed being more appropriately named the fire control room (FCR). Secondly, the spotting top and the director were combined into a single protected revolving tower accommodating the principal control, spotting and rate officers, a rangefinder, and the master sight with its layer, trainer and sight setter. In capital ships the principal director control tower (DCT) was mounted above the bridge structure, and the secondary one lower down abaft the mainmast, after armoured conning towers had been abolished. Additional DCTs were mounted on each side for their secondary armaments. But most cruisers and all destroyers had to be content with a single DCT above the bridge.

The early battles of the 1939-45 war were all fought between ships fitted with the 1914-18 form of director firing, or with the type just described. By chance, all four ships engaged in the River Plate action, fought on December 13, 1939, the British cruisers *Ajax*, *Achilles* and *Exeter* against the German pocket battleship *Admiral Graf Spee*, fell into the latter class. Moreover, and significantly, although it lacked the range to be of value, the *Graf Spee's* DCT mounted an early type of metric radar, an invention which was to revolutionise naval gunnery just as it transformed other fields of warfare.

Prominent fire-control director and radar mounted above the bridge of a Russian Riga-class frigate. *A Greenway*

First, it provided a means by which a DCT's master sight, and thence the guns, could be laid and trained on to an invisible target so that an enemy ship could be engaged by night without the use of self-revealing star shell or searchlight. (Equipment was soon developed to enable a prospective target to detect the searching radar pulses, becoming more subtly self-revealing since it could not be known whether the target had been alerted or not.)

Secondly, the enemy's range could be measured with greater accuracy than with the best visual rangefinder, which long experience had shown could be as much as 1000 yards in error. Thirdly, with centrimetric radar it was found to be possible to spot the fall of shot on the display tube and to measure the distance of each splash from the target, and so to apply an accurate spotting correction; it was in sharp contrast to the old 'short, over and straddle' method which was all that was possible with the human eye, notwithstanding various instruments designed to overcome the limitations.

The large aerials of the early gunnery radar sets were necessarily mounted on top of the existing DCTs, but by the end of the war, after the introduction of centrimetric radar, new ships mounted DCTs whose design included nacelles on each side to house the smaller aerials it required. The radar sets themselves – transmitters and receivers – were initially installed wherever suitable spaces could be found in individual ships, but in modern ones they are fitted in a special compartment adjacent to the fire-control room. Display tubes are provided in both DCT and FCR for accurate training, ranging and spotting.

This outline description of director firing has so far considered only low-angle firing, that is, ship versus ship gunnery. Between the two world wars it was also developed for anti-aircraft fire, ships being fitted with additional high-angle directors for their AA armament, whose control systems (HACS) included means by which the fuse of each shell could be set to a calculated length. Aerials for radars which gave greatly improved accuracy were first mounted on top of existing AA directors and subsequently were incorporated in newly designed ones. Finally, radar provided a means by which a director could be locked on, which enabled small-calibre guns to follow a fast-moving target, such as an aircraft or torpedo boat, automatically and so with much greater accuracy than had previously been possible.

Which brings us almost to the present day. Just as Sir Charles Douglas and Sir Philip Broke would not have recognised their primitive concept of director firing in Scott's system as fitted in HMS *Thunderer* in 1912, so Scott would marvel at the extent to which his relatively simple idea (though it was considered objectionably complicated by his contemporaries, who opposed its introduction for that reason) has been developed into the sophisticated equipment with which all types and sizes of naval gun are controlled in even the smallest of warships.

Today, in an age of missiles, anti-missile missiles, homing torpedoes, multi-targeted missiles, data processors, automation, electronic countermeasures and the silicon chip, all can marvel at the extent and pace of progress of technology which even now, at the touch of a button, is capable of starting an entirely automatic process that could annihilate most of the world in a matter of minutes.

6. Piracy, Mutiny and Smuggling

PIRACY and the HANSEATIC LEAGUE

PIRACY—ROBBERY on the high seas, is of ancient lineage, an occupation or calling going far back in time. If we disregard Ancient China as an unknown quantity, perhaps the first known record of piratical acts came in the 8th century BC from the Persian Gulf, where, with their knowledge of its coral reefs and dangerous shoals, the Gulf-dwellers lured ships to destruction.

It was 100 years later when the famed Sennacherib, King of Assyria, sent in his ships and troops to end the nuisance. By then, piracy, in the Mediterranean as well as in the Gulf, was becoming a recognised institution. Criminals, refugees, landless men and escaped slaves stole ships and formed colonies on the sea-coasts to prey on shipping almost in respectability.

They were flourishing when Julius Caesar, as an arrogant young man, was captured by one coterie in 78 BC during a voyage in a slow merchantman to Rhodes. He was well treated and was duly ransomed but being Caesar, his first act when freed was to borrow four war-galleys and 500 soldiers to turn the tables on his late hosts, afterwards faithfully fulfilling his promise to behead all the prisoners he took.

Early in the 2nd century AD the Emperor Trajan sailed into the Persian Gulf and dealt out retribution to the pirate fraternity there with fire and sword. Then, in the 4th century, King Shapur of Persia came with the same intention, but with added savagery. Having captured a number of Arabs, he had holes pierced through their shoulders so that they could be strung together on ropes, thereby gaining him the name among Arab historians of Lord of the Shoulders.

Piracy in the Mediterranean had its ups and downs until, in 695, the Arabs flooded in from the eastward, bringing a new threat to shipping. But whatever the nationality and status of the pirate, he had a considerable advantage in plying his trade. At that date, when there was neither chart nor compass, the shipmaster would navigate chiefly by rule of thumb, hugging the coast and steering from headland to headland, while the waiting corsair, lurking close inshore, could choose his moment to dash out and take his quarry by surprise, probably without much need for a chase.

There is a touch of irony in the mention by an Arab historian, writing in 760, of 'the dreaded pirate vessels of the people of the parts of Sind' which were encountered by Arab ships in the Indian Ocean. Before many years had passed, along the whole stretch of the Barbary coast, Arab slavers were active with their speedy craft. Of the unfortunate captives, most in demand on the slave-block in the market were the European Christians, as they had a reputation of being willing and docile.

The advent of the Crusades, making the hordes of prisoners a glut on the market, had a depressing effect on the slave trade from which it did not recover for a century and a half, when the dhows of Algiers, Tunis and Barbary came into their own. Those

were the days when hawk-like men in flowing robes sailed their outlandish craft up the English Channel to snatch a cargo of comely girls from villages on the Cornish coast, or even from the banks of the Thames itself.

Northern Europe, France and the countries of the British Isles had their share of pirates, but the North coast of Germany was particularly infested with them. Their outrages on shipping became so alarming that German merchants in a number of settlements, from Bruges to Novgorod, banded together early in the 12th century in a loose federation for mutual protection and benefit. It was eventually called the Hanseatic League, or Hansa for short. The league developed into a close corporation, with Cologne at the head, although the important city of Lübeck was refused entry.

Four so-called counting-houses were established in Novgorod, Bergen, Bruges and, not least, at the Steelyard in London, known as the Cologne Hansa. The position of the German merchants there was inclined to be a little precarious in times of international stress, but at last the English King Henry III undertook to protect them by charter. One consequence of the charter was that Lübeck was at last able to link with Hamburg, at the start of the league proper in the early 13th century.

The Hanseatic League's younger days were full of hazard. Much mercantile traffic sailed to and fro in the Baltic from France, Holland, Norway and England and though the Viking Age was on the wane, there was still, for some time, the likelihood of meeting marauding Danes or Swedes. The situation was changing, however, with the arrival in the Baltic of the Hansa ship, the cog, as she was called. With her high

Left: A gun mounting on an armed merchantman of the German Hansa towns. *A Verlag*

Below left: A pirate scene in the Gulf of Mexico, from a colour engraving by Mortier. *Mauro Pucciarelli*

Below: An engraving showing German trading ships of the Hanseatic League at sea. *Mary Evans Picture Library*

sides and fighting platforms at bow and stern, she was often able to hold her own. Unless she was set upon by more than one or two galleys in a concerted attack, she usually had little trouble in beating them off.

The cog was a new type of vessel, large, strong and heavy and eminently seaworthy. Continual development, both in the shape of the hull and in size, because of the need for greater capacity for cargo, she was becoming less and less easy prey. Oars had been discarded and she relied upon her large square sail. The steadily increasing size made it necessary for shipwrights to give up the overlapping planks of the clinker build and to adopt the edge-to-edge carvel style instead. A major step forward was the adoption of a rudder hung at the stern. At first it was shaped to fit under the curving stern, then it was tried at different slants before being pivoted more or less vertically, as is done today. In 1962, a 14th-century cog still in moderately good shape was retrieved from the mud of Bremen harbour.

The Hansa was beginning to reach its peak in the 14th century, but the geographical position of the three Scandinavian nations, holding between them the gateway to the Baltic, was a handicap not to be endured by the German merchants. Norway, in 1349, was the first Scandinavian country to have to surrender her trade and 21 years later, a series of internal disputes in Denmark gave Hansa an opportunity to intervene. By the Treaty of Stralsund, in 1370, the league acquired the whole of the lucrative Danish trade in dried and pickled cod and herring. Thus the last of the diminishing Viking trade with Russia and the Baltic states came to an end.

Hansa was then able to claim that the seas of Northern Europe were the league's by right of might; and it was enough to debar interlopers, including English and French ships, from venturing into its preserves. In the harbours of south-east England, however, the hardbitten men of the Cinque Ports had their own views on what constituted piracy, and on occasion took matters into their own hands.

Hansa was a monopoly if ever there was one. It handled, in addition to fish, tallow and flax, pine trees for masts, hemp and honey, beer in barrels, boards for shipbuilding and a host of other commodities. However, towards the end of a long period of existence, Hansa leaned more and more on the shoulders of its associates of the Teutonic Order, those grim German monk-knights who themselves took to commerce and gained great wealth.

After that, the herring altered its life-cycle and crossed the Baltic, bringing new life to the Danish fisheries and fishing fleets. Aided by Denmark, Holland came forward to carry a growing share of trade in Northern waters in fierce rivalry with England. The Hanseatic League, which had been formed 500 years before to deal with pirates, had lost its function and was fading away, while piracy continued to live.

Right: A Hanseatic League warship of the 13th century. *Mary Evans Picture Library*

Below: Mediterranean pirates tossing dice for the custody of prisoners. *Mary Evans Picture Library*

Hansa & Herrings

During the Middle Ages the herring was fiercely sought and its habitats and fishing vessels were protected from piracy. Protective activities in connection with the Baltic herring fisheries were a prime reason for the formation of the Hanseatic League. The decline of the League started when herring disappeared from the Baltic in the 18th century. The Dutch succeeded the Hansa as herring 'kings' and developed the sturdy buss, a design which survived several centuries and was copied by the English.

These pictures show models in the Science Museum, London, of English busses of (left) the 16th and (above, at back) 18th centuries, and in the foreground above an 18th-century hoy used to ferry fish from buss to port. *Photos D Rudkins*

HIGH BARBAREE

THE PIRATICAL COAST of North Africa, the coast of High Barbaree, flourished for the greater part of 16 centuries. Borrowing its name from the Berbers, it spread, in time, from Tripoli westward beyond the shore of Algiers and past the Pillars of Hercules to the coast of the Salee Rovers.

As early as 1390 Tunisian pirates had become such a menace to shipping that Genoa recruited 'a great number of lords, knights and gentlemen of France and England' under the command of Henry of Gloucester with English longbowmen to wipe them out. After besieging the pirates in a fortress on the Tunis shore for a month, disease drove the attackers to come to terms but at least they had curbed the raiding for a while.

Just a century later the flood of Moors who had been driven from Spain by Ferdinand and Isabella, and were a warlike people thirsting for revenge, found that they could recoup their losses if they took to the sea. Many had built big galleys and learnt how to handle them under sail and oar. First and foremost the Spanish coast became a hunting-ground, with stalwart male slaves manning rowing benches and comely girls to grace the harems. However, such exploits of mere raiders were overshadowed by a Greek renegade, Barbarossa, 'Red Beard'. Having adopted Mohammedanism, he had made his home in Tunisia and early made himself famous by capturing two great war-galleys, owned by the Pope, which were laden with very valuable cargoes.

Ferdinand of Spain, horrified at such deeds, made attack after attack on the coastal towns of Barbary and its shipping but in the end his forces were driven out from all but the fort at the entrance to Algiers which prevented ships from entering or leaving the harbour. Then Barbarossa acted. After he had been repulsed several times he launched a ferocious assault on the fort preceded by two weeks of heavy gunfire, whereupon the survivors of the garrison had to surrender. Barbarossa, true to his reputation, watched while the wounded governor of the fort was put to death for his stubborn defence.

The fort was at once destroyed by Barbarossa's orders and work was started on the great mole of Algiers, which is still in existence, It took thousands of Christian slaves two years to build. Two weeks after the fort had been destroyed nine Spanish ships bringing troops, unaware of the change in fortunes, with ammunition and provisions for the garrison sailed towards Algiers. Their crews were puzzling over the ruins of the fort, when they found themselves suddenly surrounded by the corsairs' galleys. They were taken prisoners and provided a total of 3000 to swell the slave-market.

In 1534 Barbarossa had 61 galleys specially built for a new departure. He led them through the Strait of Messina, stripped the harbour clear of all the ships there and took them away with the inevitable hundreds of Christian slaves. When he died a notable personage named Murad succeeded him in a working arrangement with the Sultan. Born a Christian, Murad had been captured as a child and taken to Algiers, where he was sold as a slave to a corsair of the Coast, but he himself soon became one of the most famous of all pirates. He seems to have had a special feud with the Knights of Malta and after one fight in which he captured a vessel twice the size of his own he was rowed triumphantly back to Algiers with the Knights as his galley-slaves. Appropriately enough, his death in the end came at the hands of Knights of Malta.

On the other hand the large number of European renegades who distinguished themselves as pirate leaders was surprising. For instance, in 1588 the 35 Algerian galleys had as their captains 11 Turks and no fewer than 24 Europeans. Two Englishmen at least are known by name. One was Sir Francis Verney of Buckinghamshire and the other is simply known as Ward, a naval deserter. Yet between 1569 and 1616 Algerine vessels had captured a total of 466 British ships and had sold their crews into slavery. In 1631 the British Consul at Algiers had written to the King declaring that if ransoms were not sent quickly the numbers of English slaves would soon increase.

The Barbary pirates were becoming even bolder. As many as 30 of their ships were used in abducting people from the shores of the Atlantic coast and merchant vessels were being captured in the English Channel. One pirate was even captured in the Thames. The inhabitants of the south-west became so nervous that they had the Lizard light put out of action in case 'it would conduct pirates'.

Oliver Cromwell was the first Briton to take really decisive action. He sent the redoubtable Admiral Blake with a fleet to deal with the Barbary Coast. In 1655 he took his fleet into the Bay of Tunis in two squadrons and finding the Dey insolent and

Facing page: Painting by T Whitcombe of the bombardment of Algiers by Admiral Pellew on August 27, 1816. *Parker Gallery (D Rudkin)*

Above: The French fleet, one of several punitive squadrons sent to quell the Barbary pirates. *M Muir Collection*

Left: Algerians firing a Frenchman from a mortar. *M Muir Collection*

Below left: The harbour of modern Algiers. *P Carmichael*

utterly beyond reasonable negotiation, he anchored his ships and opened fire in response to cannonading from the shore.

Blake's own squadron engaged the main fort at musket range while the smaller ships attacked the Dey's nine big vessels moored inshore. So deadly was the gunfire of his fleet in reply to the Dey's artillerymen that soon the harbour forts were in ruin, the guns dismounted and the moles cleared of men. Then when the fire from the batteries had died away he had boats from the ships manned and driven through the cannon smoke directly at the corsairs' ships. After brief hand-to-hand fights on their decks they were set on fire and destroyed. Blake wrote, 'The Lord being pleased to favour us with a gentle gale off the sea which cast all the smoke among them and made our work all the more easy, after some hours dispute we set fires on all their ships'. The next day he sailed to Algiers and collected all the British slaves for passage home. He found the Dey considerably chastened for the time being.

Several other punitive squadrons of various navies sailed to the Barbary coast during the next 20 years but without having much effect until 1671 when Sir Edward Spragge burnt the Algerian fleet in Bougie harbour. In consequence the crowd rioted and decapitated the Ago, the Chief Officer, and displayed his head to signify that they wanted peace.

France, which had long been in some kind of alliance with the Moors until late in the 17th century, now adopted a hostile attitude, with some surprising results. In 1683 a squadron sent to discipline Algiers under the command of the Marquis

Top: A painting by Peter Wood of a Barbary corsair attacking a Dutch ship in the mid-17th century.

Above: An engraving by H Robinson of Oliver Cromwell, the first British ruler to order decisive action against the Barbary pirates. *Illustrated London News*

Duquesne, fired 6000 shells into the town and port. It is estimated that 8000 people were killed and many buildings destroyed. The Algerines rose in protest, assassinated the Dey and elected the Captain of the Galleys in his place.

The new Dey sent word to the French admiral that if the bombardment was not stopped at once he would blow every Frenchman in Algiers from his big mortars. The shelling went on and the Dey chose for his first hostage the Vicar Apostolic, a much-loved priest. He was taken to the mole, lashed to the mouth of a mortar and shot towards the French fleet. Yet they carried on firing until their ammunition was finished and they left Algiers. Meanwhile 20 other Frenchmen including the Consul, had been blown from the mortars. Five years later in reply to another bombardment 48 more Frenchmen were blown from mortars or guns.

Into that state of affairs entered the young United States of America. Between 1785 and 1799 the States had been compelled to pay the Dey of Algiers an enormous annual monetary tribute with guns, cannon-balls and jewels in addition. It was so outrageous that Congress ordered the building of a fleet. In 1803 Commodore Edward Peeble sailed to the Mediterranean with the new warships and assaulted Tripoli, forcing the pirates to surrender and accept the American terms.

As a precaution a strict blockade of the coast was kept up for two years, then Tripoli drifted back into its old ways. But the Dey of Algiers went too far by ordering the arrest of all Italians under British protection in Bona and Oran. His orders resulted in the massacre at Bona of 100 unarmed Italians at Mass while 100 more were wounded and 800 robbed and then jailed. In 1816 Admiral Edward Pellew, soon to become Lord Exmouth, was sent to deal with the situation and given a free hand. In company with a squadron of Dutch ships he sailed to Algiers, with one ship, HMS *Prometheus*, sent on ahead to rescue the British consul and his family who were in peril.

The Consul's wife and daughters, disguised as midshipmen, got safely on board but there was also a baby, carried separately, which the naval surgeon doped with an opiate. Hidden in a basket of fruit, it was at the dock gates when it gave a cry. At once the baby, the surgeon, three genuine midshipmen and the boat's crew were taken before the Dey. Three days later the baby was returned to its mother, alone—'a solitary example' as Admiral Pellew bitterly wrote, 'of his humanity'.

Immediately the fleet had arrived the Admiral demanded the release of the prisoners. He received no reply and at once opened fire. By nightfall the main pirate batteries and all ships in the harbour were in flames. The next day 1642 slaves were freed and the Dey was made to apologise publicly to the Consul, who had been imprisoned half-naked and in chains in a condemned cell.

Later, the trade in slaves with its thousands of poor wretches sunk in hopeless apathy, began to get into its stride again but a change was in sight. The French, who had for so many years held an equivocal position with the Barbary pirates, at last decided to ally themselves with Britain, although an attempt by a combined fleet on Algiers came to nothing. So, in 1820, they took matters into their own hands and sent a large fleet with an army of 37,000 troops. They landed and steadily fought their way into Algiers, always with success and under bombardment the fort surrendered and the powder magazine exploded. The Dey was sent off to Naples in a frigate and in turn Tunis was taken in hand; at long last the Barbary coast was tamed.

Algiers

ALGIERS! The very name, in the minds of sea travellers in the Mediterranean up to the 19th century, would have been synonymous with plundering, pillaging, torture and death. Indeed, for centuries Algiers, in common with other North African and Mediterranean ports, harboured a breed of pirates and high seas bandits who harassed any ship which had the misfortune to come within range.

The merchant shipping of all maritime countries suffered at the hands of the Algiers pirates, and various attacks were made on the renegades by organised fleets of specially built ships belonging to the navies of the nations most troubled by the pirates. English, Dutch and French expeditions were sent to loosen the hold of the corsairs. In 1680 the great French commander Duquesne made a strong attack on the Berber fleet at Tripoli which, with Tunis and Algiers, provided a sound base for the pirate expeditions. Duquesne, in spite of his ability, did not really make marked inroads into the Berbers' activities, although he and Claude de Forbin attacked their fleet at Algiers some time afterwards.

Throughout its chequered history Algiers was the site of many lurid incidents and harboured desperate and ferocious characters, the most notorious of which was Khair-ed-Din Barbarossa, a pirate who took Algiers from its Spanish occupiers and perpetrated numerous atrocities.

Perhaps the city's illegal action which most incensed civilised countries was the unmitigated slave traffic in Europeans and Christians during the 17th and 18th centuries. However, matters came to a head in the early 19th century when Admiral Edward Pellew took a small force and successfully bombarded Algiers until the local ruler released hordes of European slaves held there and paid adequate compensation for the booty plundered by Algerian pirates over the years. Thereafter, piracy in that area dwindled considerably and the notorious reputation of the Algerian coast declined with it, although isolated pirates still roamed the seas.

Below: A 50-gun frigate similar to the type employed in the early 19th century to make war on the Barbary pirates. *D Rudkin*

PRIVATEER

Above: Queen Elizabeth I waving from a balcony to Martin Frobisher as he set out in June 1576 in search of the North-West Passage.
Mary Evans Picture Library

Below: An illustration from a Raphael Tuck book depicts the knighting of Frobisher by Lord Howard on board the 'Ark Royal' in 1588.
D Capper Collection

THE JOLLY ROGER, the skull and crossbones flag of the pirate, was not flown by a privateer, although the line between the two classes of seagoing adventurers was thin. The privateer was more respectable, though he might conveniently forget the simple rules of his trade. As the owner of a ship in time of war he could arm her, collect a crew and freely sail away, provided he could show a commission to 'annoy the King's enemies'.

The arrival of peace meant that a privateer saw his livelihood vanish at a stroke. It was then that he might be tempted to relieve other ships of their cargoes whatever their nationalities. But privateering was an ancient calling for English seamen and part of their heritage. It is recorded that King Henry III gave commissions to seafaring folk to attack any enemy ships on condition that the proceeds went into the royal purse.

Another Henry, Bluff King Hal, had words to say in 1544 to the mayors of Newcastle-upon-Tyne, Scarborough and Hull on their slackness in not sending out enough ships. Helping his men-of-war, he said, were 12 or 16 vessels in the west of the country which had gathered more than £10,000 and, he declared, 'It were burdensome that the King should set ships to defend all parts of the realm and keep the narrow seas withal'.

Besides the privateers, there was another category of adventurers—those bearing Letters of Marque, which authorised shipowners who had been robbed in peacetime to seize the value of their goods, by force if necessary, from ships of the robbers' country. Eventually they became confused with privateering and faded away as a separate class. Several other countries supported privateers, notably the French.

One famous British explorer and adventurer was Sir Martin Frobisher, described as 'of great spirit and bould courage and natural hardness of body'. Frobisher was born in Yorkshire and, on the death of his father, he went to his uncle, a merchant-adventurer in London. At the age of 14 he sailed in a disastrous expedition to West Africa which he was lucky to survive. Then for a while he fought as a soldier in Ireland. In 1562 he was at sea again on a voyage to Guinea and on his return he became a privateer captain. His captures included Spanish as well as French vessels and, as England was not yet at war with Spain, he was not popular with the authorities. He then started to have a profitable time with various kinds of dubious seafaring errands, which ended for a time in gaol for taking a London merchant's cargo of wine.

Ever since boyhood, Frobisher had hoped to have the chance of finding the elusive North-West Passage to the Far East and the riches of Cathay. After much planning and scheming, at the age of 37 he saw the dream of his life come true. He had persuaded some friends to finance an expedition as partners and, at long last, on a June day in 1576, he hoisted sail at Blackwall and set off eagerly on the voyage, with a farewell message and wave from the Queen. The expedition was a very small one and had only two 'barks' — little three-masted ships; the *Gabriel* captained by Frobisher, with a crew of 18, and the *Michael*, with 17—and a pinnace manned by four seamen.

The expedition arrived at the Shetlands at the start of an eight-day gale, which whisked the pinnace away with her crew doomed, but Frobisher carried on after the weather improved and sighted the eastern coast of Greenland. They were forced to keep clear of the coast by pack-ice, which proved too much for the *Michael's* captain, who took his ship home. The *Gabriel* went on to reach the coast of Labrador and, several days later, sailing northward, Frobisher found a 'great gutte, bay or passage', which he took to be the division between the continents of Europe and Asia. He gave it his name and sailed up it for 150 miles. Then Eskimos, not too friendly, appeared and he grappled one and heaved him on board, together with his kayak, to act as pilot.

Five of his crew had been carried off by the Eskimos, so, with only 13 left and those worn out, he decided to return to England. First, he sent parties ashore to collect souvenirs. Among the items brought was a piece of black stone. A month afterwards, the *Gabriel* was back in the Thames 'with the great admiration of the people', in the belief that he had found the North-West Passage. When the black stone was examined by experts, verdicts differed; two of them declared it to be iron pyrites and the third found in it a speck of gold-dust. It was enough; Frobisher had seen a land of gold ore.

The immediate result was the merging of the original subscribers in a joint-stock Cathay Company, with Frobisher at the head as 'High Admiral of all seas and waters, land and isles' and all the rest, including Cathay. The Queen actually produced £1000 and lent a splendid ship, the *Aid*.

The North-West Passage was put aside; it was the gold that mattered, waiting to be dug, and on his next voyage Frobisher took 30 miners and refiners. With the *Aid* and two pinnaces, he left the Thames in May of 1577, arriving in Frobisher Strait in July. He brought back 200 tons of the black stone, so pleasing the Cathay Company that they raised money for a large fleet for the next voyage. Queen Elizabeth found well over £3000 as her share and lent two more ships, making a total of 15 to sail with the Captain-General in June of 1578.

But Frobisher Strait gave them no welcome. In an unusually stormy and cold summer, ice floes and bergs caused much damage in the fleet and sank one of the barks. No great quantity of the black rock was loaded before the bitter weather, including blizzards, drove the fleet back to England. There Frobisher met the staggering news that his ore was iron pyrites and utterly worthless. All the effort had been wasted.

He could do little else but resume privateering until, in 1585, he sailed as Drake's vice-admiral to harry the West Indies. Four years later, by then Sir Martin Frobisher, he captured two treasure-ships off the Azores while commanding five of the Queen's vessels. He was on shore attacking a Spanish fort in 1594 when he was mortally wounded and he died later at Plymouth, mourned as being at heart a simple upright man.

Another enthusiast in the search for the North-West Passage was Sir Humphrey Gilbert, courtier, fighting soldier and coloniser. Born in 1539, a Devonian, he was a half-brother of Sir Walter Raleigh. He had many gifts, marred unfortunately by a quick temper that led to fierce rages. He was knighted for bravery some time before he went to sea in 1578. Caught by November gales, he made only a short cruise. It was two years later when he made his second attempt. He persuaded the Queen to grant letters patent of wide scope, giving him authority over any lands not already occupied by Christians. Colonisation was to be his main object.

He could find funds for only four small vessels and a little pinnace and on the second day at sea the largest of his ships deserted and went elsewhere. The others crossed the North Atlantic and made a landfall on the Newfoundland coast and headed South to St Johns. There they found a mixed coterie of fishing craft—Spanish, Portuguese, French and English, 36 of them. Gilbert finally took possession of Newfoundland and established good relations with the fishermen, finding them cheerful and friendly. Soon they were sharing food and frolics for a happy fortnight.

Then two of Gilbert's captains decided that they were too ill to carry on. Considering them not too sick to travel home, he let them go in one of the smaller ships. He himself took command of the pinnace *Squirrel*, small though she was, and refused to take the *Hind*, the larger and safer vessel. He made for Sable Island, off Nova Scotia, to stock up with meat from the wild cattle and pigs that French seamen had left there to breed. But in dense fog the only ship of any size left struck a shoal and rapidly sank. Nearly all her crew were drowned.

The combined effects of the dwindling of the fleet, the shortage of provisions and the approach of winter had such a disheartening effect on the ships' companies that at last Gilbert agreed to turn homeward, but nothing could persuade him to leave the pinnace for the *Hind*. They were north of the Azores in furious weather when the *Hind* surged up alongside Gilbert so that her captain could hail and inquire how he fared. Gilbert's shouted reply was 'We are as near to heaven by sea as by land'. That night, with the sea still wilder, watchers saw the *Squirrel's* lights suddenly go out and they knew they had seen the last of their Captain-General.

Above: An engraving giving another view of Queen Elizabeth bidding farewell to Frobisher. *R Brown*

Below: A portrayal of the death of Sir Humphrey Gilbert in a storm at sea in 1580. *Mary Evans Picture Library*

Below: An engraving of a typical buccaneer of Hispaniola, which today is known as Haiti. *M Mure Collection*

Right: A vivid portrayal of an explosion on board a buccaneer ship. *M Mure Collection*

Facing page top: A painting by M J Barton of 17th-century buccaneers and their ship.

Facing page bottom: Portrait of the most famous buccaneer of all time, Sir Henry Morgan. *M Mure Collection*

Pirates & Sir Henry

THAT MAGIC WORD buccaneer seems to breathe adventure and romance. In reality the Brothers of the Coast, as the buccaneers called themselves, were a loose fraternity of English and French, with a sprinkling of Dutchmen, who had no morals and few inhibitions. Spaniards, afloat and ashore, were their natural prey and since, as a rule, they did not attack ships of their own countries, they were, perhaps, a step above ordinary pirates.

The name of buccaneer, or boucanier as the French had it, originated in Haiti, Hispaniola or San Domingo, as the island has been variously called. The Spaniards who settled there in the 16th century moved to the more promising mainland when Mexico and Peru had been conquered by their countrymen, and they left behind them herds of cattle and pigs which ran wild. In time, they attracted Frenchmen who earned a living by hunting the animals and smoking their flesh over slow fires, making boucan, or smoked meat, and selling it and the hides to visiting ships.

The boucaniers, in their turn driven out of San Domingo by Spaniards, established themselves on the small island of Tortuga, not far away. There, through many vicissitudes they stayed, with Tortuga developing a general market for the needs of French and Dutch ships in return for the piratical loot from captured Spanish vessels.

In spite of repeated attacks by Spaniards, the island's reputation drew many newcomers. The boucaniers proper became swamped by those wanderers who knew little of smoked meat and cared less. What mattered were the boats or ships they borrowed or stole for their forays in their English variant of buccaneers. For a long period Tortuga was their base and their home, a place where a man could live in any way he pleased with no-one to interfere.

Then a still better refuge appeared. In 1655, Admiral Penn and General Venables took Jamaica from the Spaniards and the buccaneers gathered in the haven of Port Royal. Banding together to some extent, they optimistically evolved codes of conduct for behaviour at sea and for the distribution of plunder of all kinds, including human. It was not very long before they had given Port Royal the distinction of being one of the most iniquitous seaports in the known world. There were merged black and white cut-throats, pirates, planters, seamen deserters and escaped gaol-birds. Some time in the 1660s, into that imbroglio came Henry Morgan, destined to be the most noted, or notorious, of them all.

The son of a Welsh yeoman farmer, little is known of Morgan's earlier days, but he was probably about 30 years of age on his arrival at Port Royal, when he promptly became a buccaneer. In 1665 he suddenly sprang to the fore as one of three leaders of an expedition across the isthmus. They marched 300 miles to sack the town of Villa de Rosa but on returning triumphantly they found that Spaniards had seized their ships and were waiting to fight.

Having speedily beaten them off and then chased them, they chose two barques and four canoes and took another town, Rio Carta, by storm. They travelled on by river and road, sacking towns and villages a long distance overland before they turned back, fully satisfied with their haul. Morgan also took part in a less prominent way in several other expeditions on the coast of Honduras, and paddled up the San Juan River on another canoeing trip to sack and burn Granada.

Morgan

Meanwhile, a new Governor of Jamaica, Sir Thomas Modyford, had taken office in 1666. He seems to have had a soft corner in his heart for the buccaneers and a blind eye for their less outrageous behaviour. He actually drew up a 'commission' for a noted buccaneer leader, Captain Edward Mansfield to capture Curaçao. The commission must have been quite a curio.

Sir Thomas seems to have had in mind the old-style Letter of Marque, which was a written authorisation from the Monarch empowering a person who had suffered loss or damage at the hands of a foreign national to obtain redress by force from any ship of the wrongdoer's nation to the amount of the damage. Or alternatively Sir Thomas may have been thinking of the licence or warrant which authorised a civilian to go to sea as a privateer in time of war to attack or seize any ship of the King's enemies. In either case the governor can hardly have had any authority to issue his so-called commission.

At all events, the expedition was a very special one for Morgan, giving him command of a ship for the first time. The buccaneers took Santa Catalina readily enough but afterwards something went awry. Mansfield was taken prisoner by the Spaniards and summarily executed. However, Morgan was elected 'Admiral' in his stead and he acted quickly. He collected together 10 ships with 500 men and sailed with them to Cuba, where he led a landing party to attack the town of Puerto Principe. The inhabitants were taken by surprise and it was speedily captured. Only the payment of a large indemnity saved their homes from being burned to the ground.

Growing bolder after that success, Morgan conceived the idea of taking by surprise in the same way the strongly fortified city of Puerto Bello, as it was reported that plans were afoot there to make an onslaught on Jamaica. The Frenchmen among his buccaneers thought him too ambitious and went elsewhere, but nonetheless he carried on with the remainder of his following. He sailed most of the way to the city and then, anchoring his ships, in the early hours of the morning his men paddled quietly towards it in canoes.

Two of the three forts were quickly taken but the third, in which the governor of the city was setting a fighting example to the garrison, held out for several hours. At last, Morgan set his buccaneers making scaling-ladders so wide that they could be climbed by four or five men abreast. Then came a touch of the real Morgan. He gathered a number of priests and nuns and forced them to carry the ladders up to the walls of the fort, so shielding his own men from the fire of the garrison until they had begun to climb. The governor was killed and the fort fell. At once there began a fierce sacking of the city, with picked inhabitants being tortured to make them tell of hidden treasures.

On his return to Port Royal, Morgan had a warm welcome from Sir Thomas Modyford. It could be that the sight of the booty was enough for Sir Thomas to overlook any question of irregularities in the methods of its collection. Anyhow, Morgan was soon under way with another raid on Maracaibo, which gave him little trouble. Murder, torture and rape once more became the order of the day before a new pile of loot was taken on board the ships.

That time, Morgan was gently admonished by Sir Thomas on his return but even so, he was given a fresh commission to muster a large fleet to harry, sack and burn Spanish shipping and towns and stores. Spaniards had been making a number of attacks on English ships near Jamaica and Sir Thomas thought they should be given a warning.

Hardly anything could have been better to Morgan's taste; he sailed to the Isthmus of Darien, went ashore with a party on the estuary of the Chagres River and attacked and took the Castle of San Lorenzo. Leaving a garrison in the castle to act as a rearguard, he started to paddle up the river with 1800 men and a big fleet of canoes before he had to start marching through the jungle. That march was a terrible experience, not only in

the effort of a small army to force a way through in the tropical heat but still more owing to the Spaniards having taken or destroyed all food. The buccaneers were near utter starvation when, after nine days, they sighted Panama.

In spite of their exhaustion they still had plenty of fight in them. Morgan caught the Spaniards napping outside their forts, although they tried to rout his men by driving a large herd of bulls straight at them. The trick misfired; the terrified bulls stampeded in the wrong direction and charged a line of Spanish cavalry. In the end the Spaniards broke, and the town was Morgan's.

He and his buccaneers stayed there for three weeks, making raids round about in the search for more plunder. When they started to return they took with them 200 pack-mules laden with gold, silver and other valuable loot. On reaching Chagres it was shared out amid a good deal of quarrelling and argument. The general complaint was that they were being cheated out of their fair shares but in the tumult Morgan quietly sailed away in his ship. With him went the lion's share of the booty. His followers were left without food and with no ship at hand, having to console themselves with no more than £10 each. There went the true Morgan of that time. It was not due to him that the marooned men were able somehow to stagger home.

When he arrived at Port Royal as the conquering hero, the Council of Jamaica passed a vote of thanks for his victorious raid but soon the Spanish Government had something else to say. They protested very strongly to Charles II and in April 1672 Morgan was brought home in a ship of the Royal Navy to stand trial for piracy. However, it was too late, Morgan had become such a popular hero that no court would have dared to convict him. Instead, Charles, much attracted, knighted him and sent him back to Port Royal as the deputy governor.

Sir Henry Morgan seems to have turned over a new leaf, carrying out his new duties faithfully. There were no more raids or expeditions for him. As a pillar of the council and a very wealthy planter, he died, much respected, in his bed in 1688 at the age of 53. It was not the ending that might have been foretold for him. He bequeathed all his property to his wife, Mary Elizabeth, his cousin, whom he had married in Jamaica.

Ten years after his death the buccaneers, the Brothers of the Coast, had faded entirely away with their codes of conduct (for what those were worth). They were no longer welcome in a more respectable Jamaica, and in any case there were much improved relations with Spain. Freebooters became mere pirates who might sail across the world to the Red Sea or the coasts of Madagascar or Malabar to ply their trade, the bloodthirsty enemies of all other seafarers for many a day to come.

Top: An engraving of a battle scene after the incident of the stampeding bulls during the taking of Panama from the Spaniards by Henry Morgan's buccaneers in the 17th century.
Mary Evans Picture Library

Above: A 19th-century engraving of Morgan reviewing prisoners after he had captured the Spanish town of Porto Bello.
Mary Evans Picture Library

MUTINY AFLOAT

THE DICTIONARY definition of mutiny is open revolt against constituted authority, especially refusal of five or more members of armed forces to obey the orders of a superior officer. At sea the problem is more acute and potentially more serious than ashore. There have been many mutinies ashore, but a ship at sea is a tightly packed self-contained community, often out of touch with other people for a considerable time, and any upheaval is likely to have much more serious consequences for those concerned. Moreover, others not directly connected with the initial trouble might have to become unwilling participants, because there is no way of retreating from the events.

Mutinies have taken place on merchant ships as well as on military vessels. Conditions on a merchant ship have to be similar to those in the armed forces, with the captain and officers requiring obedience if the ship's functions are to be carried out efficiently and correctly.

Conditions in the armed forces and on civilian ships are now vastly different from what they were less than two centuries ago, when conditions afloat were repugnant, press gangs were used to recruit crews and life for seamen was a round of bullying and torture. It is understandable that under such conditions men were driven to revolt and mutiny.

One of the best-known and well-documented mutinies was that on the *Bounty.* The mutiny and the subsequent happenings made a story which has been coloured by films and fictionalised ac-

Top: A still from the film 'Mutiny on the Bounty' with Trevor Howard as Captain Bligh (left) and Marlon Brando as Fletcher Christian (right). *Courtesy MGM*

Left: An engraving by W H Overend of mutineers hauling down the flag on the 'Royal George' during the rebellion at Spithead.
Cassels History of England (*K Robins Collection*)

counts, but it is obvious from reports at the time that the facts needed little colouring. On December 23, 1787, the *Bounty,* a naval vessel commanded by Lieutenant William Bligh, sailed from Spithead to the South Sea (Pacific) Islands, on behalf of British merchants wanting to transfer breadfruit plants from some islands to others, as part of a scheme for providing cheap food for slaves in transit. The ship touched at Teneriffe on January 5, 1788, and attempted unsuccessfully to round Cape Horn, so the South Atlantic was crossed, the Cape of Good Hope rounded and eventually Tahiti was sighted on October 25, 1788, where the people were friendly and supplied the necessary breadfruit plants.

Conditions on any ship of that day were harsh, but it seems Bligh was a competent seaman, although he had bouts of brutality and could be objectionable to both officers and men. By the prevailing standards he was not considered to be a gentleman. During the voyage Bligh divided the crew into three watches, instead of the usual two, in order to give the men longer unbroken rest periods. The third watch was under Fletcher Christian, who was later made lieutenant.

Bounty left on April 4, 1789, and other islands were visited. Bligh had been to several of the islands 17 years before with Captain Cook and he was known and well received. While off the shores of the Friendly Islands on April 28 Christian and three others entered Bligh's cabin and tied his hands. Other officers had also been secured. The ship's launch was hoisted out and was stocked with food, water and other necessities, including a quadrant and compass. Bligh and other officers and men, totalling 19 in all, were ordered into it and set adrift, leaving 25 on board the *Bounty.*

Not all of those left were willing. The armourer and two carpenters wanted to go, but because of the need of their special skills they were forced to stay. Bligh's later comment on the mutiny was that those concerned wanted to stay with the comforts and women, particularly on the island of Otaheite (Tahiti). That might have been so and subsequent events supported the supposition, but Bligh's own behaviour might also have contributed to the trouble. However, compared with most other mutinies it was a fairly peaceful one. •

The overloaded launch was almost awash and required constant baling. It was rowed to Tofoa, where a few supplies were taken on, but the natives were hostile and one seaman was stoned to death. As a result, no other local islands were visited and the boat had to be lightened by throwing some stores overboard. On absolute minimum rations they went west and eventually reached some islands off New Holland (Australia). They spent six days there, and Bligh described that period as the salvation of his crew. It was then the end of May 1789. From Australia they

Below left: An oil painting by Peter Wood of the famous 'Bounty'.

Left: A 1952 painting by K Dorokhov of the July 1905 mutiny on the Russian battleship 'Potemkin'. *Novosti Press Agency*

Below: A mutiny poster appealing for volunteers.
By Courtesy of Woolwich Central Library (M Muir Collection)

Mutiny at the Nore.

MARINE SOCIETY OFFICE, *June 9, 1797.*

AT a Meeting of the Committee of *Merchants, Ship Owners, Insurers, and other Inhabitants of London*, for the purpose of counteracting the MUTINY now prevailing *at the* NORE,

RESOLVED, That a Gratuity of

TWO GUINEAS

Be given to each *Petty Officer*, and

ONE GUINEA

to each Seaman, to defray their Expences to WOOLWICH, who shall immediately enrol themselves VOLUNTARILY with

COMMODORE SIR ERASMUS GOWER,

at WOOLWICH,

for the Purpose of serving on Board HIS MAJESTY'S SHIPS OF WAR, or GUN BOATS, in the River THAMES, or MEDWAY, until the Suppression of the MUTINY AT THE NORE.

HUGH INGLIS, Esq. Chairman.

made their famous voyage to reach Timor on August 20, a journey of 3600 miles in an open boat lasting almost three months. They were taken to Batavia and home in a Dutch ship. Seven men died, but 12 returned to England.

Bligh was sent out on another voyage for the same purpose and that passed without incident. Captain Edwards was sent in *Pandora* to search for the mutineers and reached Matavia Bay on March 23, 1791. There he was able to take 14 of the mutineers; two others had been murdered. However, on the return voyage *Pandora* was wrecked on the Great Barrier Reef and four of the prisoners were drowned. The other 10 were brought home and court-martialled, and of them, four were acquitted.

That accounted for all but nine of the mutineers, including Fletcher Christian, who sailed *Bounty* away from Otaheite, taking six native men and 12 women. Nothing more was heard of them for 20 years until the American ship *Topaz* under Captain Folger called at Pitcairn Island on May 14, 1809. He was surprised to find people speaking English, and their leader, Alexander Smith, also known as John Adams, was the only survivor of the mutineers of the *Bounty*, the others having been killed by the Otaheitans, who had revolted because of bad treatment. *Bounty* had been deliberately broken up on the island in 1790. Two British ships called in 1840 and confirmed the American findings and reported a population of 40. Pitcairn is still inhabited by descendants of the *Bounty* mutineers.

An earlier mutiny concerned the famous navigator Henry Hudson. In 1607 in a small vessel with only 10 men, he had attempted to find the alleged North West passage around Canada from the Atlantic to the Pacific. He tried again in 1608 and was backed by the Dutch East India Company in 1609. On those trips he had done much exploring, giving his name to the North American river. In 1610 he sailed in the *Discoverie* sponsored by the Muscovy Company, and took some of his previous crewmen, including Henry Greene, whom he had befriended. Greene, aged 22, had no previous experience at sea and was subsequently described as dissolute and self-willed.

Hudson thought he had found the passage when he entered the vast sea now known as Hudson Bay. By then life on board was difficult and there was much dissatisfaction among the crew. Hudson was urged to make for home before becoming iced in, but he demoted two officers, and when the gunner died there was more dissatisfaction when Hudson showed favouritism to Greene in distributing the dead man's effects among the crew. By then Hudson had become an irritable and disappointed man.

Some members of the crew planned to steal a boat and get ashore. They were also discovered hoarding food, as a result of which many of them, including Greene, turned on Hudson. A sick man named Prickett was also involved, but appears to have given only half-hearted support to the mutiny. On Midsummer's Day 1611 the ship's shallop (a small open boat) was cast off with the sick and lame, the carpenter, Hudson and his young son, making a total of nine.

The mutineers went ashore and some were killed by Indians, the remainder then sailed for Ireland. Captain Thomas Button was sent in *Resolution* to look for Hudson and his party, with Prickett as a guide. Nothing was found and Hudson's fate remains a mystery. On July 24, 1618, the last survivors were charged in an Admiralty court but the jury decided in their favour.

The grimness of life in the British Navy at the time of the wars with France was causing much dissatisfaction among seamen. Such feeling came to a head in 1797 when there were large-scale mutinies at Spithead and the Nore. That at Spithead was led by level-headed men who mostly avoided violence and eventually got their wishes by peaceful means, but at the Nore the leaders appear to have been hotheaded and the mutiny was much more violent.

Earl Howe had received several petitions from seamen and, therefore, suspected unrest. Lord Bridport took over from him and on April 15, 1797, he ordered the fleet at Spithead to sail to St Helens. Men on the *Queen Charlotte* manned the fore shrouds instead and cheered. The example was followed by other crews and no ships sailed. Next day four men from each ship met as a committee on *Queen Charlotte* and presented a petition outlining grievances. Valentine Joyce, who was a quartermaster's mate and an educated man from Belfast, was the instigator and protagonist and he was aided by a seaman named Evans who had been a lawyer at Wapping. The Admiralty was given three days to accede to demands, while 16 ships which should have sailed were still anchored at Spithead.

The government, under William Pitt, was afraid of being denounced by parliament if it did not quell the mutiny, so a committee of Lords Commissioners was sent to negotiate. It agreed to give some concessions and returned to meet the cabinet. Next day a meeting of the commissioners and the seamen's committee broke up in disorder. There was consternation in Portsmouth when a red flag was hoisted on *Royal George.* That night the king signed a proclamation pardoning the mutineers if they returned to duty and the seamen's committee advised them to do so. Some ships sailed for St Helens, but the wind was unsuitable for all to get away.

The mood of the men was still uncertain and some crews refused to lift anchors. On Sunday May 7, 1797, the French Fleet was reported ready for sea at Brest, and Lord Bridport signalled anchors to be weighed. None moved. Instead, delegates rowed in boats to the *London,* commanded by Admiral Colpoys. He ordered them away, but men started to climb on board and he ordered the marines to shoot, killing three and injuring five. The crew rushed to the defence and one officer was injured. The situation looked desperate as the mutineers turned a gun on the officers and an officer who shot a man was almost hanged.

The *London* was taken over by the men who arrested the officers, and other ships followed suit. The mutineers intended to try some of the officers; others were ordered off their ships. Captain Bligh of the *Bounty* was among those ordered off. The ships were then sailed around in confusion by the men. The government was also in confusion and Earl Howe was sent to Portsmouth to settle at all costs. He talked for three hours to the mutineers who specified their terms. He agreed and there was an honourable settlement.

Before the mutiny at Spithead was settled similar unrest was being felt by the fleet at the Nore, at Sheerness, where the River Medway joins the Thames Estuary, but there the men were under less control, were generally belligerent and showed contempt for their officers.

On May 10, 1797, the men on *Sandwich,* commanded by Admiral Charles Buckner, refused to weigh anchor. A seamen's committee took over, ordering most officers ashore, and many crews of other ships were persuaded to do the same. By May 20, 10 days after the Spithead mutiny, the mutiny at the Nore involved 20 vessels. The men had made complaints and submitted demands, most of which were similar to those presented at Spithead. Among the complaints about treatment were the unfair distribution of prize money. Richard Parker—believed to be the original 'Nosy Parker'—was made leader but he was a self-important man who misused his forces and eventually antagonised his supporters. He called himself Admiral of the Fleet and held meetings with delegates in Sheerness every day.

Demands were modified and still not met. Popular feeling was moving against the mutineers, and food and water were stopped. The mutineers blockaded the Thames, but could not get many provisions from the ships they stopped. However, despite the war with France, the mutineers made plans to sail away from the country, although they were dissuaded rather neatly by Trinity House lifting all navigation buoys, so ships would almost certainly run aground. Several ships did drift away and on June 15 a total of 14 ships hoisted white flags of surrender. Parker was court-martialled and hanged, there were 12 other death sentences and many others

Left: An engraving of the brutal treatment meted out by the 'Bounty' mutineers to the non-rebellious crew members.
Mary Evans Picture Library

Bottom: An engraving of HMS 'Pandora' in the act of foundering on the Great Barrier Reef while on her way home with some of the 'Bounty' mutineers as prisoners.
Mary Evans Picture Library

Below: Captain Bligh being seized by the mutineers on board the 'Bounty'.
Mary Evans Picture Library

Bottom right: The replica of the 'Bounty', built for the MGM film 'Mutiny on the Bounty'. *Courtesy MGM*

went to prison. However, much better pay and conditions in ships resulted from the mutinies, and terrorism ended.

A brutal mutiny in a small merchant ship occurred only 70 years ago. It took place in the sailing barque *Veronica,* a British ship of 1100 tons under Captain Alexander Shaw, who was deaf. She sailed out of Gulfport, Mississippi, for Montevideo on October 6, 1903, with a mate named MacLeod and a Swedish second mate named Abrahamson. The crew included a Dutchman with the assumed name of Smith, and a German named Rau. Both had smuggled revolvers on board. There were two other Germans, both aged 18, named Monsson and Flohr.

There is little evidence of why the action was taken, but there must have been real or imagined grievances. Whatever the reason, Smith and Rau, supported by Monsson, planned to murder the captain and mate. Towards the end of November Flohr discovered the plot and, although he was afraid, eventually supported it. Rau clubbed MacLeod and threw him overboard, but he was less successful with the captain. He threw a belaying pin at him and fired two erratic shots, but the captain was able to get below, where he was sealed by nailed planks into the navigation room with Abrahamson. After four days they were brought out, and with others were shot and dumped overboard.

The mutineers decided to burn the ship and set course in a boat for Brazil taking with them the terrified cook, named Thomas. A story had been invented and the men drilled in repeating it. They reached Brazil within a week. Captain George Brown of the ship *Brunswick* took them on board and at first believed their story of being castaways, but the stories did not all tally and there was scepticism. Off Teneriffe Thomas broke down and confessed to the captain. They were taken to Liverpool and in prison there Flohr signed a confession. The other three were convicted and sentenced to death. Rau and Smith were executed but Monsson's sentence was commuted to imprisonment because of his youth.

An even more recent mutiny occurred in the Russian Navy in 1905, and it could have been regarded almost as comic opera if it had not been for the brutality of the mutineers' actions. It concerned the cruiser *Kniaz Potemkin Tavrichsky,* known usually as *Potemkin.* She was a 12,500-ton ship with a large complement of men, commanded by Captain Golikov, and was the newest warship in the fleet.

Conditions in the Russian Navy were particularly harsh and Black Sea service in particular was unpopular with both officers and men. Most of the men were illiterate and service at sea was the alternative to starvation ashore. It was also the time of the start of the Russian revolution. In 1903 there had been revolutionary agitation in ships and an attempt at mutiny in Sebastopol in 1904.

On June 14, 1905, when the ship had been ordered to sea for target practice, flyblown meat in the galley passed by the doctor as fit to eat was refused by the men. Complaints were not allowed in the Russian Navy and First Officer Gilyarovsky noticed the refusal to eat and reported it to the captain. The men were called on deck and told they were to eat the food and 12 agreed to do so.

After the captain left Gilyarovsky told the men to stand firm and 30 of them were surrounded by sentries with rifles and bayonets. A tarpaulin was sent for (the sign of an execution) and the sentries were ordered to shoot. Seaman Afansy Matusheshenko, leader of the ship's revolutionary committee, appealed to the sentries not to shoot their friends and the sentries dropped their rifles, which were taken up by others and several officers were shot. Others went overboard hoping to reach other ships. The captain had a plan to blow up the ship, but those he sent to do it were stopped. He went unarmed to talk to the mutineers, but was shot. The doctor who had started it all was thrown overboard.

The revolutionary committee was left in charge of the ship, but did not know how to handle it. Three junior officers were still alive and locked up and a midshipman named Alexiev was put in charge, under the committee's orders. It was planned to make for Odessa, where there had already been many revolts. There were attempts by other ships to capture the *Potemkin,* but they were unsuccessful, probably frustrated by sympathetic crews. Other mutineers actually took over *George the Conqueror* and both ships put to sea.

Odessa did not prove the haven the mutineers expected. After a cool reception there and some involvement with other ships, the mutineers decided to make for Roumania. They got to Constanza on June 19 and at first their reception was friendly. They sailed away but returned on June 24, by which time the future looked uncertain for them and the ringleaders dispersed; many are believed to have got away to various parts of Europe.

Midshipman Alexiev remained on board wi[illegible] about 60 others. Eventually they were tov[illegible]ed back by the Russian battleship *Tchesme* and 57 mutineers were handed over. Three of them received death sentences and the others went to prison.

Captain BLIGH

MUTINY AT SEA makes good cinema box-office and we have two films about Captain Bligh and the mutiny on the *Bounty* in 1788 to prove it. Thanks to the film makers the world has a splendid replica of the original *Bounty* which is on exhibition to the public in Florida, taking a valuable place in the world's growing fleet of replicas of historic ships. At the centre of the cinematic saga is a mythical figure of a cruel sadistic ship's master, flogging his men so mercilessly that the unfortunate crew was eventually driven to mutiny.

In a corner of Lambeth churchyard in London is a big tombstone on which is inscribed, 'Sacred to the memory of William Bligh, Esq., F.R.S., Vice Admiral of the Blue, the celebrated navigator who first transplanted the bread fruit tree from Otaheite to the West Indies, bravely fought the battles of his country and died, beloved, respected and lamented on the 7th day of December, 1817, aged 64.'

Sadly, the picture of him fostered by films has obscured the assessment of his own time. Bligh was a not unusual human type, a man of vision who set himself high standards and who did not suffer gladly men of lesser integrity. There is no doubt that when he was thwarted by the selfishness and baseness of the kind of humanity which comprised ships' crews at the time, he vented a strong temper with a bitter whiplash tongue.

An engraving of Fletcher Christian and the mutineers casting Captain Bligh and his loyal men adrift in the 'Bounty's' lifeboat.
John Freeman & Co

Although the punishment of flogging was very common for all kinds of misdemeanours, both afloat and ashore, Bligh had his men flogged rather less than was common in the 18th-century navy. It is almost impossible for us to realise how filthy, cruel, brutal and cheap life was in 18th-century England. What the press-gang rustled up as ship's crews were the scum of the waterfront. Even volunteers were often criminals running away from a worse fate than life at sea.

When Bligh sailed from the Thames in 1787, his orders were to sail to Otaheite (Tahiti) and transplant breadfruit tree seedlings from there to the West Indies where it was intended that they should provide cheap food for plantation slaves. Insight into the conditions for ships' crews at the time is provided by the fact that on slave ships, the percentage mortality among crews was considerably higher than that among the slaves. Some care was taken to keep the valuable slave cargo alive whereas crews had no monetary value at all.

HMS *Bounty* spent five months at Otaheite while the botanical party did their work of collecting and potting breadfruit tree seedlings. Meanwhile the crew members revelled in a life of sybaritic ease which they had never dreamed of. Willing women kept them in luxury and food and, compared to shipboard life, the connubial joys of life on Otaheite seemed like an earthly paradise. Who would go back to sea? So they went to the length of mutiny to keep their women and luxurious way of life and Bligh, along with 18 loyal officers and men, was cast adrift with some stocks of food. Fletcher Christian and a few mutineers, rightly suspecting that a man of Bligh's calibre would survive, sailed the *Bounty* to Pitcairn Island and burnt her.

Bligh sailed his open boat 3618 miles in 41 days to the Dutch East Indies, one of the epics of ocean navigation, and he managed to keep all but seven men alive through the frightful ordeal. About 18 months later HM frigate *Pandora* captured many of the mutineers who had remained at Otaheite and 10 were later court-martialled in England. Of six found guilty, three were hanged.

In 1792, in the *Providence*, Bligh made a second and successful breadfruit voyage and on the way called at Adventure Bay, Bruni Island, Tasmania, where he was delighted to find that the apple trees planted there during the *Bounty* voyage were flourishing. He did not know it, but he was the man who, indirectly, gave the world the famous Granny Smith apple inasmuch that he planted Australia's first apple tree. In an old churchyard at Ryde, Sydney, overlooking the Parramatta River, an old tombstone commemorates Maria Ann (Granny) Smith who died in 1870. Possibly Bligh walked on the little hill . . .

In the year when Bligh planted that first apple tree on Australian soil, Captain Arthur Phillip sailed the first fleet into Sydney Cove to found the Australian nation. In 1805, having won honour in the navy, Bligh was made first Governor General of New South Wales and with his usual drive, explored energetically but found that, again, his temperament clashed with that of the belligerent settlers. He was at the centre of another mutiny and was virtually a prisoner in his own residence for about two years. He returned to England in 1810.

In assessing Bligh, we must judge him against the background of his time. He was one of the school of scientific navigators inspired by Cook and had been sailing master in Cook's *Resolution*. It says much for their advanced ideas that neither Cook nor Bligh ever lost a man through scurvy, an unbelievable achievement at the time. One can well imagine the irascibility of a man like Bligh on finding ignorant crews refusing to take their scurvy grass or spruce beer—known preventatives of the dread disease.

The *Bounty's* return to the Thames after 175 years was a symbolic one in the shape of the magnificent replica which arrived on September 27, 1962. She was built at the

Above: A model of HMS 'Bounty', built to a scale of 1 : 45 by H D Pearson. *By courtesy of H D Pearson*

Right: The bow of the replica of HMS 'Bounty', in which rotten wood is being replaced, at St Petersburg in Florida. *E C Abranson*

yard of Smith and Rhuland, Lunenburg, Nova Scotia, for the MGM film. A magnificent sea boat, she won the affection of all who sailed in her. As she lay in the Pool of London, not so very far from the silent tombstone in Lambeth churchyard, one could imagine that Vice-Admiral William Bligh would have approved.

SMUGGLING

SMUGGLING HAS NEVER been universally regarded as a real crime. Even today, it is seen as a piece of pardonable wickedness, an adventure in tweaking the nose of authority. To a large extent, such a view is a remnant of days when governments were harsh enough to outrage fair play, remote enough to ignore the effect of their actions, and inefficient enough to allow defiance of the law to flourish.

Serious smuggling in England began in the 14th century, when crippling taxes and export restrictions isolated wool growers from their most profitable market, the cloth-making region in the Scheldt valley of Flanders. With home prices chronically depressed, and bankruptcy threatening more than one hard-pressed wool grower, the business of owling, or wool smuggling, grew up to mitigate the problem. With that, there began an era which lasted until well into the 19th century, when English coasts nearest to Europe came alive with furtive activity on moonless nights. Virtually everything that was taxed was smuggled, and almost everything that was used was taxed.

The taxmen's—and therefore the smugglers'—heyday was, without doubt, the second half of the 18th century, when wars proliferated and dues were levied on a vast scale to pay for them. Many goods were taxed more than once. In 1747, for instance, four subsidies of five per cent each were charged on a large range of items, and in 1759 a fifth subsidy was added. In 1783, corn-distilled spirits carried no fewer than 11 different taxes, and on some goods, such as tea, rum and brandy, the levies doubled or even tripled the original cost.

The smuggling fostered by that situation was tightly organised, minutely planned and, like all undercover ventures, well equipped with euphemisms. A smuggling transaction began when a 'freighter' collected money which a 'venturer' intended to 'invest'. After chartering a vessel, the 'freighter' arranged delivery details with the 'lander'. They included time and place, and a duplicate set of plans in case the Preventive Service intervened and spoiled the original arrangements.

While the 'freighter' was away buying the booty in a foreign port, the 'lander' arranged for a network of signals, to bring the ship to the pre-arranged spot, for transport to carry goods away, and for hiding places in breweries, farms, churches, graveyards, wells, hayricks and any other place where contraband could be stowed.

As the vessel approached the shore, the sharp-eyed 'spotsman' who guided it in would be helped in his tricky task by a fire on a headland or a brief flash from a lantern. One such lantern was the 'spout', which could shine a light out to sea that could not easily be detected from land. Signals could also be 'flinked' by flint and steel angled to catch whatever light the night afforded and blink it out from the shore. While the goods were being brought on to the beach, they and the landing party were protected by 'batmen' with blackened faces, who prowled the area armed with guns or bats made from holly or ash branches.

The success of smuggling—or freetrading

Top: Portrayal of a smuggler being chased by a ship of the Revenue Service. *Mary Evans Picture Library*

Above: An engraving of Louis Mandrin, captain of a gang of French smugglers in the 18th century. *Mary Evans Picture Library*

—operations owed much to the wholesale collusion of the local populace. Money could be earned by flashing a lantern in the right place at the right time, lending a pony, a horse or a cart, making a hidey-hole in a cellar, or by engaging a Preventive Serviceman in conversation at the operative moment. That, and the chance to buy goods they might not otherwise have been able to afford, compensated all but the most faint-hearted for the risks involved.

The risks were not noticeably high while governments were as inefficient and parsimonious as they were in the 18th century. The low pay offered in the Preventive Service, the land-based section of anti-smuggling operations, did not attract men of much integrity, enterprise or incorruptibility. At sea, the ships of the Revenue Service were badly hampered by lack of numbers. In 1703 and for some years afterwards, only eight sloops were provided to mount a watch, day and night, all the year round, on the whole southern coastline from Milford Haven to the Downs. In any case, smuggling luggers were so speedy that, as one frustrated naval commander put it, sending a Revenue cutter to chase them was 'like sending a cow after a hare'.

However, the challenge which the Preventive and Revenue Services presented, despite their disadvantages, was great enough to inspire the smugglers to conceal and protect their contraband in all sorts of cunning ways. Illegal tea chests stowed between a ship's timbers were disguised to look like part of the deck. Two stranded ropes of tobacco coiled into real ropes. Tubs of liquor were tied together, weighted and grappled so that if an emergency arose, they could be thrown overboard and later retrieved.

Violence, naturally, was an inherent ingredient of the undertaking. Smugglers were not averse to killing, crippling or otherwise disposing of their adversaries, and more than one pitched battle took place between freetraders and customs officers in which many men died in the cause of profit. Officialdom, for its part, ran the whole gamut of retribution, threatening smugglers with laws that included the harshest penalties that age of cruelty could devise. In 1741, for example, Mrs Dorothy Rees of Haverfordwest was publicly whipped for two hours for smuggling a flannel petticoat worth $2\frac{1}{2}$ pence. The judge's explicit instructions were that she be flogged 'so effectually that her body be bloody by means of such punishment'.

However, smuggling was not brought under control by such barbarities. Control was achieved, during the 19th century, by more-efficient sea blockading of the smugglers' nests and by stationing men of the new Coastguard Service in houses specially built at strategic points, such as headlands, bays and estuaries. Shorelines were sealed more surely, and the danger of detection grew even greater for the smugglers with the introduction of telegraph and radio communications. Smuggling was not entirely extinguished by such measures, but its most flamboyant and defiant days were certainly over.

Above: A dramatic engraving of smugglers riding the waves on their way to the shore with contraband. *Mary Evans Picture Library*

Below: When the British Coastguard service was inaugurated in 1822 its primary function was to carry on the fight against smuggling previously undertaken variously by the Navy's Coast Blockade, set up a few years earlier, and by the traditional Revenue Cruisers, Preventive Waterguard and Riding Officers, all of which were absorbed in the new service. By about the middle of the 19th century the Coastguard had been given various other duties, including aiding ships in distress around the coast, as depicted in this 1844 drawing of of a Life Brigade rocket-line rescue incident, operating lifeboats and attending beacons, lightships and buoys. *Illustrated London News*

Several of the world's navies maintain sailing ships for training and prestige purposes. This picture of the Portuguese Navy's sail trainer was taken in the English Channel at the start of the Tall Ships Race in 1970. *J Eastland*

7. The World's Navies

THE UNITED STATES OF AMERICA

ON NOVEMBER 16, 1776, the United States brigantine-of-war *Andrew Doria* anchored off Fort Oranje, St Eustatius, in the Dutch West Indies, and for the first time a salute was fired to honour the American flag. At that time, early in the history of the independent United States, the flag was the Grand Union, which took the form of 13 red/white horizontal stripes, with the British pre-1801 Union flag in the upper hoist.

The *Andrew Doria* herself was one of the first vessels of the Continental Navy, which was to prove itself such a thorn in Britain's side through the activities of such commanders as the redoubtable John Paul Jones. After the Peace of Versailles in September 1783, however, financial considerations led to the dispersal of the small US fleet; the last ship, the frigate *Alliance*, was sold out of service in 1785.

The United States remained neutral throughout the French Revolutionary War, but experience soon demonstrated that some naval force was a requirement for national safety. Consequently, in the 1790s, a programme was approved for the construction of a class of powerful frigates. Designed by Joshua Humphrey of Philadelphia, the first three vessels, the *United States*, *Constellation* and *Constitution*, mounted 44 guns and were much more heavily built than their contemporaries in other navies.

In 1812 the United States went to war with Britain over the issues of impressment

Facing page and above: Two views of the US Navy's aircraft carrier 'Wasp' at the NATO naval review in June 1970; the bridge with sides manned and (above) Grumman Tracker anti-submarine aircraft on the flightdeck.
Both A Greenway

Below: The aircraft carrier USS 'Constellation'.
Daily Telegraph Colour Libary

and the right of search by the British of American ships. Already overstretched, however, by the primary requirement to maintain a close blockade of continental Europe, the British Navy was able to spare few ships to meet new commitments and those vessels which did come up against the well-found American frigates were quickly overwhelmed. The British were not helped, either, by a general attitude of complacency, not only on the part of the public but commanders, who for many years had not experienced the kind of determined opposition mounted by the all-volunteer crews of US vessels. Two years of weary and sometimes bloody conflict, with both sides suffering inevitable reverses, showed that there could be no decisive victor. So, in December 1814, the two English-speaking nations thankfully accepted the honourable settlement worked out at Ghent.

The earlier post-war run-down of the US fleet was not repeated; throughout the following half-century, US warships were actively employed in operations against the Barbary states and Mexico, in the suppression of piracy in South American and Chinese waters, and in the suppression of the slave trade. Much police duty was shared with the Royal Navy and on many other occasions unofficial co-operation helped the work of both fleets.

The United States Navy was early in the adoption of steam propulsion. Its first steam warship was laid down in 1814 during the course of the war with Britain. Designed and built by Robert Fulton, the *Demologos* was intended for coastal defence and, with a single-cylinder engine driving a single paddle wheel mounted centrally in a well, was good for a speed of five to six knots. Her paddle wheel being thus effectively protected and with an armament of 20 32-pounder guns, she would have been a formidable opponent for anyone attempting to mount an attack against New York by sea.

No other steam men-of-war were built until the 1830s and 1840s, when a number of paddle frigates and sloops joined the fleet, and, such vessels apart, the United States Navy, like its contemporaries under other flags, remained primarily a sailing navy. By 1859, however, the technological revolution was making itself felt to the extent that in addition to six ships of the line, 11 frigates and about 25 lesser sailing warships, there were seven screw frigates, eight screw sloops and 11 armed paddle steamers. By way of weapons, the ships were armed with shell guns of from eight to 11 inches calibre, with 68-pounder pivot-mounted guns firing solid shot or the older well-tried truck-mounted 32-pounders.

Apart from the protection of American overseas interests, the navy played an important part in the coastal defence of the United States. It was with the latter role in mind that the government was persuaded in 1861 to build a low-freeboard armoured turret ship to the designs of John Ericsson, a Swedish engineer. By that time, however, the Federal north was at war with the dissident Confederate states of the south, who had themselves ordered already the conversion of a cut-down wooden frigate into the armoured screw battery *Merrimac* mounting a mixed armament of smooth-bore 9in and rifled 6in and 7in guns. The Federal turret ship *Monitor,* mounting a pair of 11in Dahlgren guns in a revolving turret, was completed in February 1862. A few weeks later the two vessels met in Hampton Roads in an indecisive action which proved only that contemporary projectiles were of little use against iron armour.

The experience was sufficient, however, to convince the Federal Government that the Monitor type had a future, and orders were being placed for a number of coastal-defence turret ships during the Civil War. In 1864 that concept was taken a stage farther by John Ericsson in the design of the 6000-ton sea-going monitors *Dictator* and *Puritan.* The single turret carried a pair of 15in smooth-bore guns and was protected by 15 inches of laminated iron armour. Unfortunately, the design was not as successful as it might have been because a draught greater than predicted resulted in reduced freeboard and speed.

Ericsson's seagoing monitor type was developed further after the Civil War, when the four vessels of the Miantonomoh class were built. Of composite wood and iron construction, the vessels proved successful within the design limitations of the monitor concept. In fact, the *Miantonomoh,* in the summer months of 1866, successfully undertook the double crossing of the Atlantic to test her sea-keeping qualities.

The monitors apart, the US Navy at the close of the Civil War comprised a number of wooden-hulled screw frigates and corvettes, various gunboats and a variety of mercantile auxiliaries. Funds for the maintenance of the navy were not forthcoming, however, for having settled its internal differences, the nation looked to westward expansion across the North American continent rather than to the sea. Such was the state of affairs in 1881 that the US Navy ranked twelfth among the world's maritime powers; it consisted of only one wooden screw frigate, a number of wooden screw sloops and four iron gunboats! There were about 14 monitors, all laid up in various states of disrepair.

Above: An American submarine in the Grand Harbour at Valletta, Malta. *Tourist Photo Library*

Right: A painting by an unidentified artist of a 19th-century American frigate. *M Pucciarelli*

Below right: A sketch of the action off Cherbourg in June 1864 between the 'Alabama', which is sinking, and the 'Kearsarge'. *Illustrated London News*

Below: the USS 'Claude V Ricketts', a 33-knot guided-missile destroyer completed in 1962, sailing out of the harbour of New York. *US Navy Photo*

A committee appointed to inquire into the affairs of the navy came to the conclusion that orders should be placed immediately for 38 unarmoured cruisers, and 25 torpedo boats of the Herreshoff type for harbour defence. Once again funds were not made available and the navy had to be content with a modest three protected cruisers, named *Chicago, Atlanta* and *Boston*, and the dispatch vessel *Dolphin*. In addition work was restarted on five monitors, nominal rebuilds of post-Civil War vessels, but it was to be 10 years and more before all were commissioned.

The first battleship for the new Navy, the 6300-ton *Texas,* was authorised in 1886. By that time, US resources were able to supply the necessary armour plate, although a design prepared by the Barrow Shipbuilding Co, of Barrow-in-Furness in England, was selected as being best suited to the requirement for a coastal defence ship. The *Texas* mounted a pair of 12in guns, placed in echelon arrangement in single turrets; in service, the arrangement proved unsatisfactory and it was not repeated in later vessels.

The building of three sea-going coastline battleships, to be named *Indiana, Oregon* and *Massachusetts,* was authorised in 1890, and they were designed around a main armament of four 13in guns arranged in twin mountings forward and aft. With a secondary battery of eight 8in guns in twin turrets, in addition to four 6in casemate guns, the ships were considerably over-gunned for their displacement of 10,250 tons, and their low freeboard made them very wet in all but the lightest weather.

Contemporary cruisers, as in other navies, were of the armoured and protected types; the former had a narrow belt of armour to shield their vitals and an arched armoured deck extending the length of the ship, while the protected cruiser was given only a light protective deck.

Like the battleships of the Indiana class, the armoured cruiser *New York* of 1891 suffered through her low freeboard making her very wet forward, but this design defect was overcome in the *Brooklyn,* which followed in 1895, by the addition of a forecastle. The 22-knot vessel mounted eight 8in guns on a displacement of 9200 tons and possessed many features in common with French ships of her date. It was in the *Brooklyn* that the comparative merits of steam and electric turret machinery were evaluated, with the result that electric power was adopted generally in new construction for heavy gun mountings throughout the US Navy.

The make-up of the late 19th century war fleet was completed by the smaller torpedo craft and gunboats, though in the matter of torpedo boat design, the US Navy lagged far behind the navies of western Europe, Russia and Japan. The first such vessel, the 116-ton *Cushing,* had been completed as late as 1890. Thereafter, several boats of the type were built and when the United States went to war with Spain in 1898 the nation had available a small but modern balanced fleet which was to prove more than a match for the scattered Spanish maritime forces.

The fleet then included six coastal defence battleships, of which one, the 6682-ton *Maine,* was destroyed in the incident in Havana Harbour which precipitated the war, two armoured cruisers, 12 smaller protected cruisers and 10 torpedo boats. The half-dozen surviving monitors proved of little value and it was amply demonstrated during the course of the war that the heavily armed coastal defence battleship was no real substitute for the true ocean-going type. As a result, the United States turned to a blue water naval policy in keeping with its post-war overseas commitments, which had been magnified by the newly acquired ex-Spanish territories.

Above: USS 'Proteus', the American Polaris depot ship arriving at Holy Loch, Scotland, in March 1961. *Central Press Photos Ltd*

Right: First US Ensign, the Grand Union. *J Maber*

Far right: The US battleship 'Texas'. *Central Press Photos Ltd*

The first battleships authorised as a result of the new policy were the five vessels of the 15,000-ton Virginia class, completed in 1906-07, which brought the US fleet into line with the pre-dreadnought navies of other nations. Like many of their contemporaries, they were given a main battery of four 12in guns, but once again over-gunning with a secondary battery of eight 8in guns, in addition to twelve 6in guns, impaired their stability and made them rather tender. In the Connecticut class which followed, however, the worst of such faults were overcome and the ships compared very favourably with those under other flags.

The United States Navy acquired its first submarine, USS *Holland* (SS1), from the builder J P Holland in 1900; it was thus early in the field with a relatively successful submersible. Thereafter, the Holland type was developed progressively until, in 1917, the US Navy became responsible for its own submarine design.

A feature which came to distinguish American heavy warships for several years first appeared in 1908-09, when the cage mast was substituted for the heavy military style, in the belief that such a structure would be more resistant to disabling action damage. In practice, however, the cage type of mast proved liable to whip, but it remained in use until the older battleships then in service were taken in hand for reconstruction in the 1920s and 1930s.

Meanwhile, battleship development in the US Navy kept pace with that in the Royal Navy and the construction of two vessels of the Dreadnought type was authorised in 1905. Although smaller and considerably slower than the *Dreadnought* herself, the *South Carolina* and *Michigan* were significant in that they were the first to mount an all-big-gun main armament on the centre line, with the second and third turrets at sufficient height to enable their guns to fire over the first and fourth turrets. This layout of eight 12in guns in four twin mountings permitted an eight-gun broadside, the same as that of HMS *Dreadnought,* and within a few years the so-called super-firing arrangement was adopted for all heavy warships.

The *North Dakota,* launched in 1908, was the first US battleship with steam turbines, but early difficulties in getting engine builders to meet the required specification for that type of machinery resulted in the retention of the reciprocating engine (two shafts) for a number of new ships. At a later date, problems associated with the manufacture of reduction gearing for the high powers involved led to the adoption of a turbo-electric drive on four shafts for the battleship *New Mexico* of 1919, and for the subsequent California and Colorado classes.

In the early years of the present century, the small cruiser force was greatly expanded by the construction of the 10 armoured cruisers of the Pennsylvania and Tennessee classes, nine protected cruisers (Denver and St Louis classes) and three small unarmoured scout cruisers (Chester class). It was from one of the Chester class, USS *Birmingham,* that in 1910 the first successful shipboard aircraft launch was accomplished.

Unlike the British, German and Japanese navies, the US Navy for many years showed little interest in the battlecruiser concept of a lightly armoured fast battleship and not until 1916 were designs prepared for vessels of this type. In the event, the six ships of the Lexington class were not laid down until 1920-21 and construction was not very far advanced when work was suspended in 1922 as a result of the limitations imposed by the Washington Naval Treaty. The United States was permitted, however, to retain the hulls of the *Lexington* and *Saratoga* for subsequent completion as aircraft carriers.

The massive programme of naval and mercantile construction mounted by the United States after her declaration of war against the central powers in 1917 included no fewer than 272 destroyers, mostly of a four-funnel flush-deck design, and a large number of smaller anti-submarine vessels. Few were completed in time to see service in the war for which

they had been intended, but a considerable number survived to play their part in a later war, including 50 of the destroyers which in 1940 were to be transferred to Britain for service with the Royal Navy.

Between the wars, the US fleet was cut back to the strength permitted by the Washington Naval Treaty of 1922, which allowed for parity in numbers of battleships with Britain. During the course of the conference, however, the United States had pressed for and secured an upper limit of 10,000 tons on the size of cruisers and agreement that the maximum calibre of their guns should be 8in. The first two ships in that category were authorised by Congress in December 1924 and were launched about four years later as *Pensacola* and *Salt Lake City.* Armed with ten 8in guns, they were better protected than the early vessels of the British County class, although they suffered from lack of freeboard in heavy weather.

Most other navies turned from the Washington Treaty heavy cruiser to the construction of smaller 6in-gunned vessels in the late 1920s, but the US Navy continued to favour the 8in-gunned type until the mid 1930s, when the Brooklyn class, armed with 15 6in guns, was laid down in reply to the Japanese 6in cruisers of the Mogami class. Thereafter, the delivery of both 8in- and 6in-gunned cruisers continued in parallel until after the end of the Second World War, when cruiser construction came to an end.

Destroyer construction was restarted in 1932 with the Farragut class mounting five 5in guns and eight 21in torpedo tubes. By December 7, 1941, when Pearl Harbour was attacked by the Japanese, the US Navy had in commission 171 destroyers, of which all but 71 were of post-1914-18 design.

It was realised that any future war would probably involve the United States Navy in long-range operations in the Pacific; consequently, efforts were directed to the build-up of a fleet capable of operating well away from fixed forward bases. Techniques for refuelling at sea were perfected, the uses of carrier-borne air power in the strike and defensive roles were exploited and practised, and the concept of a fleet train was developed to provide the combatant fleet with the necessary logistic support.

The assault on Pearl Harbour crippled the US Pacific fleet, but by then, once again, a vast emergency war construction programme was under way and the losses were soon made good by the commissioning of new and rebuilt ships. By virtue of the nationwide shipbuilding effort, the US Navy had in commission in 1945 the largest fleet the world had ever seen, in addition to which a considerable number of ships had been made available under Lease-Lend arrangements for service with the British and Russian navies.

The United States fleet today retains its premier position among the world's navies, although the battleships have gone. However, USS *New Jersey* of 1943 (59,000 tons) was recommissioned in April 1968 for a brief tour of duty off the coast of Vietnam, during which she provided the Army with gunfire support. The striking power of the fleet is now centred on 13 aircraft carriers, including the nuclear-powered *Enterprise* (1961), *Nimitz* (1975) and *Dwight D. Eisenhower* (1977), while the strategic deterrent is deployed by 41 ballistic missile submarines. Several ships of Second World War design still feature in the US Navy List.

Like many of its contemporaries, the US Navy has now turned to gas turbine propulsion for its new-construction destroyers and frigates, respectively of the twin-screw Spruance and the single-screw Oliver Hazard Perry classes, all of which are equipped with two General Electric LM-2500 gas turbines per shaft. The larger fleet vessels now under construction or planned are, however, all nuclear powered, notably the aircraft carrier *Carl Vinson*, the guided missile cruiser *Arkansas* and four missile-armed cruisers of the Modified Virginia class, as is also of course the case with all new-construction submarines.

By the mid-1980s the active combatant surface fleet will be made up almost entirely of second-generation postwar design vessels. In the absence of any further commitment to intervention on the scale of the involvement in Vietnam, such a fleet, albeit reduced in numbers by successive cutbacks in procurement programmes, should be fully capable of looking after all interests of the United States.

As many protectorates of erstwhile empires emerged as fully independent nations, their awareness of the economic importance of coastal waters brought a demand for small ships capable of defending their interests. Here one such is the corvette 'Dorina', one of a pair built in 1972 for the Nigerian Navy by Vosper Thornycroft, a company which specialises in the design and construction of fast small warships. *J Eastland*

Navies of the World
GERMANY

Above: **The German frigate F222 'Augsburg', at the NATO Spithead Review in 1970.** *A Greenway*

This picture: Detail of some of 'Ausburg's' armament and crew. *A Greenway*

GERMANY was the last major European nation to achieve unity after the revolutions which changed the face of the continent in 1848. The several states, dukedoms and free cities had been brought together loosely as the Germanic Confederation in 1815, but apart from those living in the Baltic and North Sea ports, few looked towards the sea and indeed the Confederation itself meant little until 1848, when the King of Prussia took the lead and called the German national assembly together at Frankfurt.

In that same year a nationalist movement in Denmark sought to annexe the German duchies of Schleswig-Holstein, thereby forcing Prussia, in the name of the Confederation, to take steps to protect its shores. Hence the growth of the German Navy stemmed from external pressure resulting in the purchase in 1849 of the wooden paddle steamers *Britannia* and *Acadia,* late of the Cunard Line's Liverpool to Boston trade. Renamed *Barbarossa* and *Erzherzog Johann,* the two vessels, armed as paddle frigates with nine 68-pounder guns apiece, with another paddle frigate, the *Hansa* (ex-American Black Ball liner), and the ex-Danish sailing frigate *Gefion,* taken at Eckernforde in 1849, formed the nucleus of the new German fleet, which wore as its ensign the black over white flag of Prussia.

In June 1866, Prussia went to war with Austria and other German states, bringing about the disintegration of the Confederation and a complete realignment of the central European states. Under the leadership of her chief minister, Otto von Bismarck, Prussia engineered in 1867 the North German Confederation; the new group adopted a new German flag, a horizontal tricolour formed from the Prussian black and white flag and the red and white flag of the old Hanseatic League. The fleet taken over by the new confederation was insignificant by world power standards, but already orders had been placed with British and French shipyards for the construction of a pair of armoured steam frigates (classed as Batterieschiff) which were completed in 1867 as *Kronprinz* (5568 tons) and *Fredrich Carl* (5780 tons) and armed respectively with 32 and 26 72-pounder muzzle-loading guns.

A third ironclad steam frigate, laid down originally for the Turkish government at Blackwall on the Thames to the design of Sir Edward Reed, was acquired while under construction in January 1867 and joined the fleet as *König Wilhelm* in 1869. Although larger than her consorts, her displacement being 9574 tons, she was similarly armed with 33 72-pounder broadside-mounted guns and in general appearance somewhat resembled the central-battery ship *Hercules* of the Royal Navy.

In 1870, rivalry between the Prussian-dominated North German Confederation and the French Empire led to war and the defeat of Napoleon III. Under the leadership of Bismarck, the loosely knit Confederation had achieved a position of predominance in continental European affairs and in January 1871, the creation of the German Empire, with Wilhelm I (of Prussia) as Emperor, was proclaimed at Versailles.

Throughout the time since the settlement of the dispute with Denmark, few calls had been made upon the small German fleet. In 1873, however, anxious to build up a navy in keeping with the nation's role in the affairs of Europe, the German Admiralty drew up a naval programme proposing a fleet of 23 armoured ships, 20 unarmoured cruisers and a proportion-

ate number of lesser craft. In commission at the time were the three ironclads *Kronprinz, Fredrich Carl* and *König Wilhelm,* but already there were under construction at Poplar on the Thames, two central-battery ships, the *Kaiser* and *Deutschland,* designed by Sir Edward Reed and, in German yards, three fully rigged turret ships and a small wooden-hulled armoured corvette, the 3696-ton *Hansa.*

The *Deutschland* was the last major warship to be ordered from a foreign shipyard, but in the matter of design subsequent German vessels followed much the same trends as their British and French counterparts.

In 1878, the *Sachsen,* the first of four 7690-ton mastless barbette ships, was completed by AG Vulcan at Stettin. The main armament comprised six 10.2-inch muzzle loaders, mounted two forward in a pear-shaped barbette and four amidships in a central armoured battery. Like their older consorts, however, they were intended primarily for home defence and were of the shallow draft necessary for service in the Baltic.

The development of the torpedo and doubts about the wisdom of building armoured warships caused the construction of the remaining vessels of the Sachsen class to be considerably delayed, but ultimately it was recognised that the capital ship was the only means of defence against such vessels in an enemy fleet and work was allowed to proceed.

The accession of Kaiser Wilhelm II in 1888 gave renewed impetus to the development of the German war fleet. With his intense interest in imperial and naval affairs, he was an advocate of the need for a deep-water fleet to match Germany's status as a world power.

The first capital ships constructed in line with the new policy were the four 9870-ton battleships of the Brandenburg class, completed in 1893-94 and armed with six 11-inch guns in three twin-barbette mountings. The 11-inch guns in the end mountings were of 40 times calibre length, but those in the amidships mounting were of 35 calibres only which, with the closeness of the guns to the deck and their restricted arcs of fire, rendered their contribution to the ship's total fire-power relatively insignificant.

In the 10,600-ton Kaiser class which followed, a primary armament of four 9.4-inch guns only was provided, although it was supported by a powerful secondary battery of 18 5.9-inch guns. The arrangement was backed up by arguments that, at the probable battle range of the day, the 9.4-inch shell would be capable of penetrating the armour of any known potential enemy ship, while the higher rate of fire compared with larger guns would increase the likelihood of effective hits.

The arguments proved fallacious, however, and demands were made for the build-up of a more powerful fleet with capital ships fully equal to those of other maritime powers. The call for a strong navy was fully supported by Admiral Tirpitz, who saw the need for means to protect Germany's worldwide trade and growing colonial interests. Following his appointment as Minister of Marine in June 1897, Tirpitz pursued an active campaign through the media of the press and the German Navy League to secure the support of the public in his fight for a fixed naval establishment capable of meeting the nation's needs.

The result was the passing in March 1898 of the first Navy Law, which provided for a fleet of 19 battleships, eight armoured coast defence ships and six large and 16 light cruisers. Provision was made for the replacement of battleships and cruisers after 25 and 20 years respectively, a policy which led to the practice whereby new ships were ordered as 'Ersatz . . .', the new ship's own name not being made public officially until she was launched, or possibly even later.

Antagonism between Germany and Britain generated in the wake of the South African War led to further demands for naval expansion and to the passing of the second Navy Law in 1900. It replaced the law of 1898 and made provision for 38 battleships, organised in four battle squad-

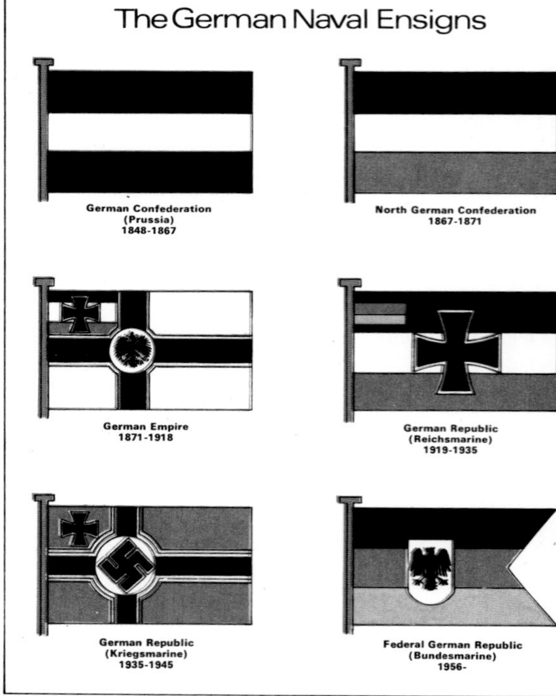

Top left: Painting by W L Wyllie, 'Last of the Scharnhorst and Gneisnau'. *National Maritime Museum London*

Above: Development of the German Naval flags. (Ian Allan Studio). *J M Maber*

Top right: Frigate F224 'Lübeck' of Köln class. *German Embassy, London*

Above right: Engraving of the German Imperial Navy ironclad steam frigate 'Preussen', of the late 19th century. *Mary Evans Picture Library*

rons; 14 large and 38 light cruisers and 96 destroyers.

The first German battleships to compare ship for ship with contemporary construction in the British and other navies were the five vessels of the Braunschweig class (13,200 tons) completed in 1904-05. Armed with four 11-inch guns, in twin mountings forward and aft, and a secondary battery of 14 6.7-inch guns, they were equivalent in most respects to HM ships *Prince of Wales* and *Queen* of equal date. Three sets of triple-expansion machinery developing a total of 16,000ihp gave a speed of 18 knots and set a precedent for the use of a three-shaft configuration in practically all future German battleships.

Post-Navy Law cruisers were developments of the 10,550-ton 19-knot *Fürst Bismarck* of 1897, but not all were as successful as the early vessels of the type. The *Prinz Heinrich, Prinz Adalbert* and the Roon class were poorly protected and saw little service during the 1914-18 war. With the exception of the lone *Blücher,* the most powerful and best protected were the 11,600-ton sisters *Scharnhorst* and *Gneisenau* of 1907-08, but both were destroyed at the Battle of the Falklands on December 8, 1914, when they were brought to action by the British battlecruisers *Invincible* and *Inflexible.*

Much more successful were the light cruisers developed from the design of the 3250-ton Bremen class of 1903-04. A total of 29 had been laid down by the outbreak of war and most saw hard service either with the High Seas Fleet or as commerce raiders in more-distant waters.

When news reached the German Admiralty of the construction of the British battleship *Dreadnought* in 1906, the problem of the design of a similar vessel for the German Navy was tackled with a sense of considerable urgency. The *Dreadnought* commissioned for service in December 1906, but another six months elapsed before the *Rheinland,* the first of four ships of the 18,900-ton Westfalen class, was laid down. The beam of the *Dreadnought* had been kept to 82 feet so that she would be able to make use of existing dry docks.

No such restriction was put in the way of the designer of the Westfalen class; they were about 12 feet shorter than the Dreadnought and had a beam of 89 feet, and proved remarkably steady gun platforms. The main battery comprised 12 11-inch guns in six twin mountings, but the disposition of the mountings allowed a broadside of eight guns only, the same as that of the British vessel. Time precluded the design of turbine machinery and all four were given conventional triple-expansion engines of 22,000ihp driving three shafts. The *Nassau* the first to be completed, joined the fleet in October 1909.

The German Navy took up also the battlecruiser concept from Britain but, in the absence of Sir John Fisher, the German design was not deprived of adequate protection. Consequently, the first of the type, the *Von der Tann,* was completed in 1910 as a fast Westfalen, a little less well protected and mounting eight 11-inch guns only but engined with Parsons turbines of 42,000shp for a speed of $24\frac{1}{2}$ knots. Later developments were the *Moltke* and *Goeben,* but all suffered from a lack of sufficient freeboard forward making them very wet in all but the slightest sea.

The German Navy adopted a three-shaft direct-drive turbine arrangement for the 12-inch gunned Kaiser class battleships, of which five were laid down in 1910. In the case of the *Prinz Regent Luitpold,* however, it was intended that the centre shaft should be driven by a 12,000bhp six-cylinder Germania diesel engine but, in the event, the engine was never installed and the *Prinz Regent Luitpold* remained a two-shaft ship throughout her career.

Throughout the remaining few years leading up to the outbreak of war in 1914, the bulk of the German fleet was concentrated in home waters based mainly upon Kiel and Wilhelmshaven. One capital ship, the battlecruiser *Goeben,* was sent to the Mediterranean, with the light cruiser *Breslau,* on completion of trials in July 1912, but otherwise German representation overseas was limited to a number of cruisers, including Graf von Spee's Pacific squadron.

On the outbreak of war in August 1914, the German fleet numbered 14 dreadnoughts, four battlecruisers and 24 effective pre-dreadnoughts. Under construction or in the final stages of fitting out were three battleships of the 12-inch-gunned König class (a further unit, the *Grosser Kurfürst,* had been completed in July 1914), three 12-inch-gunned battlecruisers of the Derfflinger class and four battleships of the Baden class.

The *Derfflinger, Lutzow* and *Hindenburg* had been laid down in 1912-13 as battlecruiser equivalents of the König class and were armed with eight 12-inch and 14 5.9-inch guns. A four-shaft direct-drive turbine arrangement delivering 63,000shp (*Hindenburg* 72,000shp) gave a design speed of $26\frac{1}{2}$ (27) knots although it was not quite realised in practice. With protection little inferior to contemporary battleships, they were certainly the best conceived battlecruiser design in any navy.

The four ships of the Baden class were laid down in reply to the British Queen Elizabeth class and were similarly armed with eight 15-inch and 16 5.9-inch guns. High speed was not called for, since it was considered that the well-protected German battlecruisers were capable of fulfilling all that was required of the fast wing of the fleet. Thus, the *Baden* and her sisters with a three-shaft turbine installation delivering 52,000shp for 22 knots were in fact closer in concept to the British *Revenge* of similar date.

The first brush with the British occurred in the first few days of the war, when an attempt was made to intercept the *Goeben* and her accompanying cruiser *Breslau.* Knowing Turkey to be sympathetic to the German cause, however, Admiral Souchon made for Constantinople, where eventually the *Goeben* was turned over to the Turks and recommissioned as *Yavuz Sultan Selim.*

More important was the encounter on January 24, 1915, known as the Battle of the Dogger Bank, in which the First Scouting Group comprising the battle-cruisers *Seydlitz* (Rear Admiral Hipper), *Moltke* and *Derfflinger* with the armoured cruiser *Blücher* and light forces were brought to action by Beatty's battle-cruisers. The *Blücher,* a large armoured cruiser of battlecruiser dimensions, but armed with 8.2-inch guns only, took the brunt of the British fire and at 12.10 she rolled over and sank. The main lesson of the Dogger Bank stemmed, however, from an incident in the *Seydlitz*; a 12-inch shell penetrated the upper deck aft and passed through the barbette armour of the rear turret before exploding. Fire spread from the cordite in the loading chamber to the magazine through an open door, thence to an adjacent magazine and up into the next turret. The dead totalled 159 and the after end of the ship was wrecked, but the lesson had been learned and anti-flash protection was worked into all German capital ships before the next major encounter off Jutland (Battle of the Skagerrack) on May 31, 1916.

As the struggle wore on, the German command turned more and more to the submarine and economic pressure in a concerted effort to bring the British to their knees and thus to cripple the Allied war effort. Although not a fleet weapon, the Germans had taken up the development of the submarine in 1906 with a view to its employment in coastal defence. On the outbreak of war the German Navy possessed 38 submarines and, despite their limited range and unreliability, wartime experience soon demonstrated their value in an offensive role against military targets. The strong reliance of the German Navy on the submarine, and the later successful development of auxiliary vessels as commerce raiders, were features that distinguished it from those of other major powers.

Total economic warfare in the form of an unrestricted submarine campaign waged against allied seaborne trade did not start until February 1, 1917, but its initial success was such that work on the majority of surface ships then under construction was cut back in order to concentrate available resources on U-boat assembly. Work on the battleships *Württemburg* and *Sachsen,* the four battlecruisers of the 30,500-ton Mackensen class and the three even larger 15-inch-gunned vessels of the Ersatz Yorck class was brought to a halt, as was also that on several light cruisers.

After Jutland, Scheer had taken the High Seas Fleet on two further sorties, hoping to catch the British unawares, but on both occasions—August 19 and October 19, 1916—the sailing signals were intercepted and the Grand Fleet alerted. After the two abortive thrusts, the fleet kept to its moorings in the Rivers Jade and Elbe while key personnel were drafted to more-pressing duties in the U-boat flotillas. Not surprisingly, morale deteriorated through inactivity, which led to unrest and later to outright mutiny.

The last sortie by the High Seas Fleet was to a prearranged rendezvous with the British Grand Fleet about 40 miles to the east of May Island on November 21, 1918. By noon the German Fleet was at anchor in the Firth of Forth and at sunset on that day the German ensign was hauled down. The war was over, but the fate of the German Fleet remained a problem and in the absence of any inter-allied agreement the ships left the Forth on November 24 for internment in Scapa Flow. There, on June 21, 1919, on receipt of a prearranged signal, the once-proud High Seas Fleet was scuttled. The Imperial German Navy was no more.

Post-war Germany was permitted to retain for coastal defence an assortment of ageing vessels, including the pre-dreadnought battleships *Braunschweig, Elsass, Lothringen, Hessen, Preussen, Hannover, Schlesien* and *Schleswig-Holstein,* and a few cruisers and accompanying flotillas of destroyers and torpedo boats. They formed the nucleus of a new German Navy (Reichsmarine), which adopted as its ensign the black, white and red tricolour charged with a black Iron Cross edged with white.

The Treaty of Versailles limited the displacement of future German capital ships and cruisers to 10,000 tons and 6000 tons respectively, but of more immediate importance was the fact that warship design expertise had been largely dispersed since November 1918. Consequently, the first ship laid down for the new fleet, the 5600-ton *Emden,* was built to a large extent on the lines of the later war-time cruisers. Coal fired and capable of 29 knots, the only important innovation was the introduction of the geared turbine, but that development apart, she was completely conventional with a main armament of eight single 5.9-inch guns in open-backed shields.

In the Köln class which followed, there was, however, a complete break with traditional design represented by the *Emden;* electric welding was extensively employed to keep weight to a minimum and a twin-screw geared turbine/diesel

Left: High speed motor torpedo boat 'Nerz' of the Zobel class. *German Embassy London*

Below Left: Destroyer D187 'Rommel' of the Lütjens class. *German Embassy London*

This picture: A German Navy U boat S192 of type 203. *German Embassy London*

installation combined the high power efficiency of the steam turbine with the economy of a low-powered diesel engine for cruising. The main armament of nine 5.9-inch guns was mounted in triple turrets and, although not permitted at first, two aircraft and a catapult were installed at a later date.

Discussions on battleship design within treaty limits began in 1926 and finally it was decided that the navy's requirements would best be met by a moderately well protected ship, diesel powered to give 26 knots with maximum economy of fuel, and armed with six 11-inch guns in two triple mountings. The first ship was authorised in 1928 and laid down at Kiel as *Ersatz Preussen* on February 5, 1929. The *Deutschland,* as the new ship was named at her launch, outclassed the 'treaty' cruisers of the Washington Conference powers, while her speed put her well out of reach of the majority of capital ships. Classified by the German Navy as Panzerschiff, the type quickly became known throughout the English-speaking world as the Pocket Battleship.

Orders for the *Admiral Scheer* (*Ersatz Lothringen*) and *Admiral Graf Spee* (*Ersatz Braunsweig*) followed in 1931-32 and the *Deutschland* herself was commissioned for service on April 1, 1933. At 11,700 tons, she exceeded the treaty limit by a comfortable margin, but no announcement of the fact was made to the world in general!

In December 1932, the French laid down the first of a pair of fast 26,500-ton battleships, giving the German Navy cause to look for a way round the restrictions of Versailles. British reaction was tested and in June 1935 agreement was reached to the effect that German naval strength should be set at 35 per cent of the equivalent total tonnage in the Royal Navy, and that the size and arming of ships should be in keeping with the treaty limits accepted by Britain and the other 'Washington' powers.

In 1934, preparations were made for the laying down of the third and fourth pocket battleships, but in the event their design was expanded to the nominal 26,000 tons (in actual fact 35,400 tons!) of the *Scharnhorst* and *Gneisenau.* Tactical requirements necessitated a higher speed than the 26 knots of the Deutschland type and in order to meet the demand for 160,000shp ($31\frac{1}{2}$ knots), a three-shaft geared turbine installation was adopted. The triple 11-inch mounting was retained, however, since any change to a larger calibre would have resulted in unacceptable delays in construction, and the sisters were completed with a battery of nine 11-inch guns in two mountings forward and one aft. Protection was extremely good and sub-division well planned, making for a balanced and effective design.

The fact that the *Scharnhorst* and *Gneisenau* were listed officially at a nominal displacement of 26,000 tons and the pocket battleships at 10,000 tons left the German Navy with sufficient margin in hand for the construction of much larger vessels without infringing the agreed limit of 35 per cent of Royal Navy capital ship tonnage (which meant that Germany was allowed 184,000 tons of battleships). Coupled with the fact that other nations were proceeding with the construction of 14-inch, 15-inch or 16-inch armed battleships, it led the German Navy to opt for a nominal 35,000-ton design armed with eight 15-inch guns and to the laying down of two such vessels in 1936.

The two were launched as *Bismarck* and *Tirpitz,* and they were probably better protected than any other battleship afloat and were to present a formidable challenge to Britain, with whom Germany was once again at war before they commissioned for service, in August 1940 and February 1941 respectively. The high speed of the *Scharnhorst* was not called for in the new ships and the weight saved by the provision of lighter machinery was worked into improved underwater protection and internal subdivision. Once again, a three-shaft configuration was adopted with geared turbines developing 138,000shp for 29 knots.

Of the German surface fleet, it was the battleships and the heavy 8-inch-gunned cruisers of the Hipper class that tied down the greater part of the British Home Fleet, preventing its deployment in other theatres of war. Much was achieved by these few ships, but one by one they were picked off by the Royal Navy or the Royal Air Force until finally the last operational capital ship, the 42,900-ton *Tirpitz,* was attacked and destroyed with 12,000lb armour-piercing bombs by Royal Air Force Lancaster bombers as she lay in Tromso Fjord on November 12, 1944. A few months later the Kriegsmarine ceased to exist.

Post-war Germany developed from the ruins as a divided nation but, today, the larger western state is a long-established member of the North Atlantic Treaty Organisation and the small but efficient Federal German Navy (Bundesmarine) plays a full part in the alliance. Three missile-armed destroyers of the Charles F. Adams type and four Fletcher-class destroyers of conventional gun-armed design are of US origin, but other escorts, coastal submarines and mine countermeasures vessels are completely German designed and built, although much of their weapon and direction equipment is of French, Swedish, Dutch, Italian or British origin. There are currently on order six Type 122 CODOG (combined diesel or gas-turbine) frigates, developments of the Netherlands Kortenaer Class but engined with General Electric gas turbines and MTU diesels.

Veteran of numerous actions since her commissioning during the Second World War, and rebuilt to provide further useful life throughout the 1960s, the fleet aircraft carrier HMS 'Victorious' alongside in Portsmouth Dockyard in 1965. *P D Hawke*

Great Britain

The battleship HMS 'Nelson'.
Keystone Press

IN PRE-TUDOR times there was no such vessel as a warship outside the comparatively calm waters of the Mediterranean. In northern waters, in time of war, contemporary merchant ships were employed to carry troops to the coast nearest the scene of hostilities, the only concession to warlike purposes being the erection of fore- and after-castles to serve the needs of defence. Sea battles, such as that off Sluys in 1340, were in fact merely land battles between opposing armies at sea.

The development of the specialised warship and the war fleet dates from Tudor times when ships' hulls were first pierced for guns; finer lines gave the warship greater speed than her cargo-carrying consort and changes initiated by Sir John Hawkins resulted in the type of ship which gave such a good account of itself against the massive but cumbersome galleons of Spain.

No attempt was made, nor was the money available, to establish a standing war fleet until England was involved in war with Holland during Cromwell's Protectorate. That fleet survived the Restoration, however, although corruption and maladministration did much to impair its efficiency until, in 1686, the secretaryship of the Admiralty passed into the capable hands of Samuel Pepys.

The Dutch Wars saw the development of a series of battleships taken to the stage whence there was to be remarkably little change, except for progressive increases in size, throughout the following 200 years. Such were the fighting ships which formed the backbone of the fleet through the long years of the wars with France until the final victory over Bonaparte in 1815.

Of that class of warship, one example remains today, namely, HMS *Victory*, launched in 1765 and now faithfully restored to her Trafalgar condition in dock at Portsmouth. The *Victory* is not in size a typical representative of the wooden battleship genre, however, being one of the small number of 100-gun First Rates, of which there were seldom more than half a dozen in the Navy List at any given time. Such vessels took the part of fleet flagship and provided accommodation for the Commander-in-Chief and his staff.

Smaller than the First Rates were the Second Rates (90 guns), employed as subordinate flagships, the Third Rates (74 guns), which made up the bulk of the squadrons opposing the French, and lastly the Fourth Rates (50 guns). The last-named category fell into disfavour during the later years of the 18th century, being too cramped for efficiency, too weakly armed to engage larger contemporaries and too slow to chase the smaller Fifth and Sixth Rate cruising ships of the frigate type.

The frigates were employed in two primary roles, either as the fleet's advanced scouts, or to protect trade and overseas interests in general. Such vessels did not lie in the line of battle, but in a fleet action would have kept normally to the disengaged flank of the line acting as signal repeating vessels or undertaking the many mundane transport and communications tasks called for by the command.

At the close of the French Wars in 1815, the fleet comprised the following rated vessels:

First Rates	8	(None in commission although the 100-gun *Queen Charlotte* was to recommission before the end of the year).
Second Rates	7	(2 in commission).
Third Rates	94	(45 in commission).
Fourth Rates	9	(7 in commission).
Frigates	176	(142 in commission).

The figures show clearly the preponderance of the Third Rate in the British battle line; it is of interest that by then *Victory* had finished her last commission at sea and was lying 'in ordinary' (in reserve) in Portsmouth Harbour.

Although, after 1815, the fleet was run down rapidly to a peace-time establishment, design work continued. It was under the direction of Sir Robert Seppings, Surveyor of the Navy, who was notable for having devised a system of diagonal bracing and trussing of frame timbers to permit the construction of larger wooden ships with well-protected rounded bows and sterns. A typical battleship of Seppings's period was the 92-gun Second Rate *Nile,* laid down at Devonport in October 1827. Built of wood, she differed from earlier Second Rates in having only two gun decks instead of three. Her rig differed little from that of older ships but her armament was very much heavier, comprised of ten 8-inch shell guns and 82 32-pounders.

As was usually the case in peacetime, the *Nile* spent many years on the stocks and was not launched until the June of 1839; this allowed for weathering of the structure and, since fitting out of a wooden warship was not a lengthy process, meant that a reserve of new ships was available for use in any emergency. After launching, she was laid up at Devonport until 1852, when it was decided to fit her out as a screw steamer. The conversion to steam marked the end of the line-of-battleship era; wooden screw battleships were employed during the Crimean War but only in a bombardment role against fixed fortifications, both in the Crimea and in the Baltic.

In the absence of warlike activity, other than colonial skirmishes, the next quarter-century was marked by a lack of purpose in the design of major warships. Iron had been the subject of trials as a material for warship hulls but had been rejected as being more prone to disabling damage than wood. There matters stood until 1859, when the French pointed the way ahead by the launch of the armoured battleship *La Gloire,* designed by Dupuy de Lôme as an answer to the continuing progress in gun and projectile development. Built of wood on the lines of the screw battleship *Napoleon, La Gloire* was encased by 4¾-inch iron plates from well below the thick waterline to upper deck level and was armed with 34 5-ton guns.

Sceptical at first, the British Admiralty was soon converted and produced an answer in the shape of the 9 210-ton iron-hulled and armoured *Warrior,* launched in 1860. As in her wooden forebears, the original main armament of 34 68-pounder (8-inch) smooth-bore muzzle-loading guns was mounted broadside fashion. Her machinery of 1250hp provided a speed of 14 knots, but she had also full three-masted ship rig as reliance still could not be placed on steam machinery alone. Not only that, the fuel economy of contemporary marine engines was such that 'up funnel, down screw' propulsion was ordered only when the wind did not suffice.

The *Warrior* and her sister ship *Black Prince,* designed by Isaac Watts, were followed by a number of similar broadside ironclads, which put the British fleet once again in a position of undoubted supremacy amongst the naval powers of Europe.

Isaac Watts was succeeded as Chief Constructor in 1863 by Edward Reed, who abandoned at once the broadside concept of vessels designed to lie in a strict line of battle in favour of the 'central battery' ship. The main armament, comprised of a small number of large-calibre guns, was concentrated in a central heavily armoured box, leaving the ends of the ship relatively unprotected. In addition, provision was made for end-on fire, so that ideas for the tactical employment of the battlefleet became in urgent need of revision.

Contemporary with the appearance of the central battery ironclad was the development of the turret ship, springing from Captain Cowper Coles's proposals for a full-ship-rigged low-freeboard vessel with heavy guns mounted in cupolas. In the event, the rallying of public support led to the construction of the ill-fated *Captain* in 1870 and the subsequent loss of Coles's own life with his ship off Finisterre in September 1871.

Although the *Monarch,* a fully rigged turret ship designed with considerably greater freeboard by Edward Reed, proved reasonably satisfactory, it was obvious that revolving turrets requiring clear arcs of fire and a full ship rig were incompatible. Already, mastless turret ships had been built for coastal work and Reed next conceived a sea-going battleship of similar type. The design was modified by his successor as Chief Constructor, Nathaniel Barnaby, and appeared finally in 1873 as the epoch-making *Devastation,* a vessel mounting four 35-ton muzzle-loading guns in a pair of turrets arranged forward and aft of the amidships structure.

Twelve years only had passed since the completion of the *Warrior,* but the fleet comprised such a heterogeneous collection of wooden screw ships, broadside and central-battery ironclads, and turret ships that no-one could really say how they should be employed!

Sir William White became Director of Naval Construction in 1886 and the building of his Royal Sovereign class set a new fashion in armament and protection which was to serve as the model for the Royal Navy for the next 20 years, until the advent of the all-big-gun battleship *Dreadnought* of 1906. Four big guns backed up by a secondary battery of 6-inch guns became the standard, not only in the British fleet but also in the several foreign navies which took their lead from the United Kingdom. The battle fleet was supported by cruisers, employed either on scouting work with the fleet or independently about the many miscellaneous duties in support of the commitments of empire, in exactly the fashion of the earlier years.

One new development in the weapon field had had a profound effect upon the fleet, however; it was the locomotive torpedo discharged from the low-profile torpedo boat. Defence measures against the torpedo included light quick-firing guns and anti-torpedo nets rigged around the ship when at anchor. In due course, the torpedo boat itself was countered with the torpedo-boat destroyer, which became in later years, as the destroyer, the maid of all work of the fleet, fulfilling not only the roles of torpedo boat and its means of destruction, but also hunting submarines, providing anti-aircraft support and deputising on occasion for the gun-armed cruiser.

At the turn of the century, the battle fleet comprised 24 White-designed battleships, plus a miscellaneous collection of modernised ironclads and turret ships dating from the Reed and Barnaby eras. It was still, however, the day of perfection in seamanship and manoeuvre, with little thought given to how such ships should be employed in battle. There were many, with the loss by collision of the battleship *Victoria* still fresh in peoples' minds, who advocated the use of the ram and general opinion among naval officers was that engagements between opposing ships and fleets would be fought out at ranges little greater than those of sailing ship days!

In the early years of the present century, however, the work of Rear Admiral Percy Scott, Admiral Sir Frederic Dreyer, Arthur Pollen and others led to the development of improved training methods. With the introduction of a rudimentary form of gun fire control from a central director mounted high up clear of smoke and funnel gases and the formulation of a set of spotting rules for observing the fall of shot, they resulted in considerable improvements in the accuracy of gunfire at ranges much greater than had been customary hitherto.

The adoption of new tactical rules involving control of gunfire at increased range posed its own problems for the command and, in particular, identification of the fall of shot from a mixed armament gave rise to considerable difficulties; for example, the King Edward VII class of 1905-06 mounted four 12in, four 9.2in

Facing page top: One of the first battleships, the 'Sovereign of the Seas', built in 1637.
National Maritime Museum London

Facing page centre: The 'Rodney' after having been converted into a screw battleship, pictured at Hong Kong in 1870.
P A Vicary (J Maber)

Left: A supplement to the Illustrated London News showing the types of ships making up the British Navy of 1886.
Illustrated London News

Above: The 14,150-ton early battleship, HMS 'Empress of India'.
Rotary Photographic Services (J Maber)

and 10 6in guns. The solution was already to hand, however, in the shape of the single-calibre all-big-gun battleship which had been under consideration by the major naval powers since the Italian Colonel Cuniberti first put forward his ideas in 1903. Sir John Fisher, First Sea Lord, took the vital step by ordering the construction of an 18 110-ton 21-knot battleship propelled by steam turbines; it was to outlcass every other capital ship afloat. Built in great secrecy within the incredibly short time of one year from laying down to sea trials in October 1906, the *Dreadnought*, with an armament of 10 12in guns, rendered the world's battlefleets obsolete at a stroke!

Faced by the build-up of the German fleet, Fisher ensured Britain's lead in the race for naval supremacy by laying down three similar battleships soon after acceptance of the *Dreadnought*, followed by another trio in 1907-08. Yet another three, the *Neptune, Colossus* and *Hercules*, built to a modified design, were laid down in 1909, bringing the total number of dreadnoughts in service or under construction to ten.

In addition to siring the all-big-gun concept for the British fleet, Sir John Fisher was also an advocate of speed as a means of protection, which led him to press for the application of the all-big-gun principle to the lightly protected armoured cruiser. The result was the appearance in March 1908 of the 17 250-ton armoured cruiser *Invincible* and the subsequent coining of the term battlecruiser for the class. Armed with eight 12-in guns and with a maximum service speed of 25 knots, such vessels were intended, as a fast wing of the battle fleet, to seek out and destroy enemy cruisers and to overtake and inflict maximum damage upon a fleeing enemy.

The next development in Dreadnought-type battleship design was the adoption of a 13.5in gun with a lower muzzle velocity, and therefore less subject to barrel wear than the 12in 50-calibre gun fitted in the Colossus class. The *Orion* and her sisters mounted 10 such guns in five centre-line turrets which could be used effectively on either broadside. The King George V class followed; they were similar but had better siting of their fire control arrangement. The group was completed by the delivery of the three battlecruisers of the Lion class.

The final batch armed with 13.5in guns comprised the four battleships of the Iron Duke class and the single battlecruiser *Tiger*, in which the 4in secondary battery was replaced by 12 6in guns to give improved defensive capability against lightly armoured cruisers and smaller torpedo-armed vessels. The design of the *Tiger* had been modified considerably after consideration of Vickers's plans for the Japanese battlecruiser *Kongo*; protection had been improved, engine power increased to 108 000shp for 29 knots and a 6in secondary battery adopted as in the Iron Duke class. Compared with the *Lion*, the layout of the main armament had been vastly improved and in appearance the affinity with the *Kongo* was obvious.

At the outbreak of war in August 1914, the fleet comprised 20 dreadnoughts, eight battlecruisers and no fewer than 37 effective pre-dreadnought battleships. There were in addition 12 battleships and two battlecruisers in course of construction, and another three battleships fitting out for foreign governments which were taken over for RN service. Among the vessels under construction were the five fast battleships of the Queen Elizabeth class, which were intended to act as the fast wing of the fleet in place of weakly protected battlecruisers. (Fisher, raised to the peerage as Baron Fisher, had resigned in January 1910.)

Above: The pre-dreadnought battleship 'Ocean' in the Grand Harbour, Valetta, Malta, in 1905. *J M Maber*

Right: The battlecruiser 'Princess Royal' leaving Barrow for sea trials in 1912. *J M Maber*

Probably the finest battleships in service anywhere at the time, the Queen Elizabeths displaced about 27 500 tons and were the first to be completely oil fired. Provision of machinery of 75 000shp, for a design speed of 25 knots, precluded the installation of the amidships (Q) turret as in the Iron Duke and earlier classes and, because certain foreign navies were planning battleships mounting 14in or 15in guns, it was decided that they should be armed with eight 15in guns in four twin mountings. As in the Iron Duke class, however, the secondary armament comprised 12 (originally 16 in the Queen Elizabeth only, although the plated-over ports aft remained in the other ships too) broadside-mounted 6in guns.

The Queen Elizabeth class played a prominent part in both world wars and saw service in every important theatre from Norway to the East Indies. The many battle honours include Dardenelles, Jutland, Narvik, Calabria, Matapan, Crete, Sicily, Salerno, Normandy, Walcheren, Sabang and Burma. As had been the case since the Dutch Wars, the battleship remained the final arbiter of sea power, although as long as 50 years ago a few men, including Admiral Sir Percy Scott, thought the time would soon come when aircraft would render the armoured capital ship out of date.

The Queen Elizabeths were followed by the slower but similarly armed vessels of the Royal Sovereign class, virtually 15in-gunned versions of the *Iron Duke*. In broad terms, the make-up of the fleet was completed by the scouting cruisers of the Town and Arethusa types and the several flotillas of destroyers intended to act defensively in protecting the fleet against torpedo attack or offensively by the exercise of such attack against the enemy line.

Lord Fisher had returned to the Admiralty in October 1914, still full of enthusiasm for speed and minimal protection in capital-ship design. Further units of the Queen Elizabeth type would have been of greater value to the fleet, but instead, the construction of two additional ships of the Royal Sovereign class was abandoned in favour of building a pair of lightly armoured shallow-draught battlecruisers, to be named *Renown* and *Repulse* and mounting six 15-inch guns apiece. The disastrous loss of three battlecruisers at Jutland, and the fact that by that time Lord Fisher had left the Admiralty, led to a drastic reappraisal of design of such vessels and to the working-in of additional protection during subsequent major refits. Despite the expenditure of many millions of pounds, however, they were never really satisfactory as capital ships until the *Renown* only was completely rebuilt between 1936 and 1939.

In 1915 Intelligence reports giving details of the German Mackensen class battlecruisers (in reality fast battleships) led to a further resurrection of the battlecruiser concept in the Royal Navy and the ordering of four 36,300-ton 32-knot vessels of the Anson class. Armed with eight 15-inch guns, protection was not sacrificed to quite the same extent ordered by Fisher in the case of the *Renown* and *Repulse*, but it was still poor by battleship and German battlecruiser standards. After Jutland the design was recast to incorporate another 5000 tons of protection, bringing the displacement up to 41,200 tons, but it failed to save the *Hood*, the only ship completed of the modified class, from destruction a quarter of a century later when she blew up in action against the German battleship *Bismarck*.

The Washington Treaty of 1922 placed restrictions on the fleets of the signatories, including limits on the size and number of battleships, cruisers, destroyers and aircraft carriers. New-construction capital ships were to be limited to 35,000 tons 'standard displacement' although, exceptionally, Britain was allowed to keep the *Hood*, the only one of the Anson class to be completed.

Four larger 'battlecruisers' to be armed with 16-inch guns had been ordered in 1921, but they were thereupon abandoned, much of the material and weapon equipment being worked into a pair of battle-

ships designed within Treaty limits and laid down in December 1922. The two were completed as *Nelson* and *Rodney* in 1927; they were heavily armed with nine 16-inch guns and extremely well protected; but, on a displacement of only 33,900 tons, something had to be sacrificed and as a result they were rather slow (23 knots) in addition to being difficult to handle. Despite the limitations, both saw hard service throughout the 1939-45 war and the *Nelson* actually carried on as Home Fleet flagship until August 1946, when she joined the Training Squadron. Both were broken up in 1948.

Contemporary cruisers of the County classes were built up to the 10,000-ton Treaty limit, with 8-inch guns (the maximum permitted) and minimal protection. Although much criticised at the time, they proved sea-kindly and were to give a good account of themselves in war service. The Washington conferences had specified a life of 20 years before replacement battleships could be laid down and in 1936 the first orders were placed for ships designed within Treaty limits to take the place of the slow vessels of the R class. In the event, completion of the King George V class was preceded by the outbreak of war; the R-class ships were retained and saw much service on convoy and escort work and in the bombardment role. The five King George V class were at best a compromise within Treaty limits and all saw hard service, at first in northern waters, where they were employed to counter the threat posed by the German fleet, and later in the Pacific. The *Prince of Wales,* of this class, and the *Repulse* were destroyed by Japanese air attack in the early days of the eastern war off the Malay coast.

The manner of the loss of the two ships demonstrated only too clearly that no longer could a fleet operate without adequate air cover; in fact, the day of the battleship was over and with the Battle of Leyte (October 1944), when the formidable air-striking power of the US Navy destroyed the opposing Japanese fleet, the final death knell of the armoured capital ship was sounded.

The ultimate development of the British battleship appeared belatedly in 1946, when the 44,500-ton *Vanguard* was commissioned for service. Armed with a 30-year-old battery of eight 15-inch guns, she was certainly the best British design since the completion of the similarly armed Queen Elizabeth class of an earlier war. Her guns were never fired in anger however, and after several years of showing the flag she was laid up in reserve and finally broken up in 1960.

Cruiser development after the 8-inch-gunned County classes was centred on the smaller 6-inch-armed vessels evolved progressively from the Leander design of 1929. The Apollo, Aurora, Southampton, Belfast and Fiji classes appeared in succession, but from 1938 the need for increased protection against air attack on the fleet resulted in the parallel development of the Dido class with 5.5-inch dual-purpose guns.

The aircraft carrier too was developed into a practical fighting ship between the wars and by 1939 had become accepted as an essential part of the striking force of the fleet. The later development of aircraft in the strike role was fostered by the US and Japanese navies, and at that point the concept of opposing battle fleets passed into history.

In the post-war fleet there still remained considerable nostalgia for the day of the battleship. However, the Korean War again demonstrated the efficacy of carrier-borne aircraft in a strike role while cruisers and destroyers in that theatre were able to provide inshore naval gunfire support. The offensive arm of the Royal Navy from the early 1950s through to the late 1960s was centred on the carrier task force comprising a fleet, or light fleet, carrier screened by destroyers/frigates and supported by replenishment tankers and logistic support vessels of the Royal Fleet Auxiliary service.

The screening role of destroyers of wartime design, of the C, Battle and Weapon classes, passed in the early 1960s to the 5440-ton missile armed 'destroyers' (DLGs) of the County class backed up by the extremely successful Type 12 frigates of the Whitby, Rothesay and Leander classes. Eventually, however, massively increasing costs brought about the demise of the carrier-borne strike force and the abandonment of a global role as the Royal Navy was withdrawn to the NATO perimeter.

So far as frigates and larger surface warships are concerned, steam propulsion has now been abandoned, the current policy being to fit gas turbine machinery of aircraft-derived design adapted for rapid exchange when a propulsion unit is due for overhaul. Mine countermeasures vessels (MCMVs) and minor war vessels are powered by diesel machinery, that in the former craft being of Deltic type.

This then is the pattern for the immediate future; the role of sea power continues to be one of the protection of trade and overseas interests, albeit within a NATO context, while denying an enemy the use of the sea. Today these duties are undertaken by the missile-armed escort, the hunter/killer submarine, the mine countermeasures vessel and the helicopter-borne assault force, but although the ship and the manner of its employment have changed, the purpose remains as it was when Howard, Drake and Frobisher challenged the Spanish in the English Channel.

Ornate poop of the 17th-century French galley 'Reale', the most-decorated vessel in the galley fleet of the day. She was flagship of the General of the Galleys, a post created in the reign of Charles VII and abolished, with the galleys, in 1748. *Maritime Museum Paris*

THE FRENCH NAVY was the creation of Cardinal Richelieu, who came to office as Chief Minister in 1624, determined to make France great and an acknowledged leader in world politics. The aim was to be achieved through the exercise of sea power and Richelieu gave orders for the building of ships and bases and for the undertaking of a detailed survey, the first such in modern times, of the Channel and Atlantic coasts.

Within 12 years, by 1636, France possessed 51 ships, 12 galleys, six fire ships and 12 transports divided between the Atlantic and the Mediterranean (Levant), but at the time of Richelieu's death in 1642 there were no fewer than 63 ships, a number of which had been built in Holland, and 28 galleys, certainly a formidable fleet with which to challenge the navies of Spain, Holland and possibly England.

The ships (vaisseaux) of Richelieu's time ranged from about 200 to 600 tons and in general were more lightly armed than their contemporaries in other navies. The 400-ton *Dauphin*, a 24-gun ship completed at Le Havre in 1638, was typical of French-built vessels; few details of her career are known other than that she served with the fleet until 1662 when she was sold for breaking up. The galleys (galères) were intended primarily, of course, for service in the Mediterranean although in later years a few were based upon Rochefort on the Biscay coast. Galleys were known usually by the names of their commanders and in consequence records tend to be somewhat confusing.

The French navy's baptism of fire was against the Spanish in the later stages of the Thirty Years War, from which struggle France emerged supreme in Europe with, in addition, the foundations laid of an overseas empire. Under Richelieu's successor, Cardinal Mazarin, the French navy was starved of money, however, and after the Thirty Years War the nation itself was torn by internal strife. By 1661, when Jean-Baptiste Colbert took office, the

FRANCE

Above: Model of the French warship 'Royal Louis' displayed in the Maritime Museum, Paris. *Maritime Museum Paris*

This picture: One of the French Navy's small warships, the Aviso 'Le Chamois'. *Courtesy French Embassy London*

fleet had been reduced to 20 ships and six galleys, many of which were unfit for service.

Colbert imported foreign expertise and, in order to ensure a steady supply of men, introduced a system of call-up by rotation, called Inscription Maritime, which was to serve France well until the Revolution brought about a different order of society. The fleet too was rebuilt and when Colbert died in 1683 he left a navy which included 117 ships and 30 galleys. Five years later, France went to war with England over the matter of the English Succession and in 1690 the French gained their first great success when Tourville defeated an Anglo-Dutch fleet off Beachy Head. The allies had their revenge, however, in 1692 when Russell struck at the French off Cape Barfleur and secured a victory which was made complete in the roadstead of La Hogue. Tourville's flagship, the 110-gun *Soleil Royale*, was subsequently destroyed at Cherbourg by Sir Ralph de Lavell.

Throughout the long years of war which marked the 18th century the French navy was frequently starved of money and always overburdened with administration, but all in all it served the country well. In the matter of ship design the French adopted a scientific approach and ship for ship of equal rate, their vessels were markedly superior to those of the Royal Navy, which were designed largely by rule-of-thumb methods blended with the experience of the master shipwrights responsible for their construction.

Many fine French vessels were taken into the Royal Navy during the wars; one of the longest-lived examples was the 74-gun 3rd Rate *Duguay-Trouin*, laid down at Rochefort in 1797 and launched three years later. She served at Trafalgar in October 1805, but was captured a fortnight later at Sir Richard Strachan's action in the Bay of Biscay; after a refit in Plymouth, she was commissioned into the Royal Navy as *Implacable*. After her active career at sea she served as a training ship for many years and then, during the 1939-45 war, as a store hulk. Finally, stripped of everything of value and flying

Left: The French submarines 'Venus' and 'Junon' on a courtesy visit to Palma, Majorca, in April 1966. *A Greenway*

Below left: The escort destroyer 'La Bourdonnais'. *Courtesy French Embassy London*

Bottom left: 'Loire', one of the modern French logistic support vessels. *Courtesy French Embassy London*

Below: The submarine 'Goubet' being hoisted from the water in about 1900. *J Maber*

Below centre: Battleship 'Bouvet' (left) and cruiser 'Galileé' at Villefranche in 1905. *J Maber*

Bottom: French torpedo boat destroyers in the harbour at Oran. *J Maber*

the White Ensign side by side with the French Tricolour, she was scuttled on December 1, 1949, in deep water off the Owers lightship in the English Channel.

After the settlement written into the Treaty of Vienna in June 1815, France was left with a fleet comprising about 50 ships of the line and a number of frigates. At Navarino in 1827 the French fought alongside the British in securing the independence of Greece from Turkish rule. That was the last major action fought under sail alone, for already the steamship was making an impact as a unit of the fleet. In the new development the French were certainly more adventurous than the British and the Algiers expedition of 1830 was accompanied by armed steamers which helped to cover the assault. But they were small vessels and had little direct military value, their main function being to help manoeuvre the cumbrous line-of-battle-ships in and out of harbour.

The application of steam made rapid progress and in 1859 the navy possessed 32 screw ships of the line, with another eight building or converting, and 31 steam frigates; the numbers were greater than the strength of the Royal Navy in both categories. Of the screw 1st Rates, the largest and most modern was the 130-gun *La Bretagne* which had been launched at Brest in February 1855. Equipped with Indret steam engines of 1200 ihp, she was essentially similar to three-decked battleships of contemporary build in the British Navy and, like the latter, was painted black with white strakes in way of the gunports. She spent the greater part of her career based at Brest.

In the meantime, between 1843 and 1845, much experimental work had been undertaken in order to determine a satisfactory scheme for the armouring of warships. Based upon those trials, a leading French constructor, Dupuy de Lôme, produced plans in 1845 for an armoured screw frigate which was to be provided with powerful steam machinery to ensure maximum manoeuvrability; the full sailing rig would be retained solely as auxiliary motive power. Nothing was done to implement the proposals for several years, however, although during the Crimean War the French built a number of armoured floating batteries, the first of which, *Le Tonnante*, was launched at Brest in 1855.

Dupuy de Lôme was appointed Directeur du Material in 1857 and at once applied his talents to the design of the screw battleship *Napoleon*. In the following year the successful design was adapted to that of a wooden-hulled armoured screw frigate and orders were placed for three vessels of the type—the *Gloire* and *Invincible* at Toulon, and the *Normandie* at Cherbourg. The 5617-ton *Gloire* was launched in 1859 and was completed for service as the world's first sea-going armoured ship a few months later. Protected by iron plating $4\frac{3}{4}$ inches thick and armed with 30 50-pounder breech-loading guns, the *Gloire* precipitated a revolution in naval architecture and the ironclad principle was soon adopted by the world's leading navies.

Ironclad development in France followed much the same path as in Britain, although the solutions achieved in successive designs tended to vary somewhat. In 1867 the French Navy introduced the barbette mounting for the 3770-ton wooden-hulled ironclad *Alma*, designed by Dupuy de Lôme and built in the Naval Yard at Lorient. In an attempt to achieve the maximum possible arcs of fire, the barbettes were carried on sponsons projecting well out from the ship's side, but in practice it was found that considerable damage was caused to the vessel's structure and equipment when the guns were fired directly ahead or astern. The same principle was adopted for the 7750-ton battleship of the Océan class, of which *Océan* herself was completed in 1868. The four 10.6-inch breech-loading guns were carried in barbettes at the four corners of a central armoured redoubt, and four 9.5-inch guns were mounted within the redoubt itself, two on each broadside.

For overseas colonial service the French Navy built the large 5500-ton sheathed cruisers *Duquesne* and *Tourville*, both completed in 1876. Once again six guns of 6.3-inch calibre main battery were sponsoned out from the ship's side in order to provide the maximum possible arcs of fire. Like most cruising vessels of their day, they were given a full ship rig; their machinery of 7340ihp gave them a speed under steam alone of nearly 17 knots.

In the meantime, France had been active

in the development of the submarine. As far back as 1863, a 450-ton vessel named *Plongeur* had been launched at Rochefort on behalf of the French Government. Driven by an 80hp compressed-air engine, she was capable of five knots on the surface and could dive to about 40 feet. Once submerged, however, control of longitudinal trim proved impractical for more than a few minutes at a time and although trials were continued for some years, a satisfactory solution eluded her designers and finally, in 1874, the project was abandoned.

Somewhat more satisfactory results were achieved in the 1890s with the electrically driven boats *Gymnote, Gustave Zédé* and *Morse*, but no really practical design was evolved until 1897, when M Laubeuf produced his plans for a 117-ton double-hulled vessel propelled on the surface by 250ihp steam machinery and when submerged by an electric motor. The first boat of Laubeuf type was launched as *Narval* at Cherbourg in 1899 and completed successful trials in the following year. She was armed with four external trainable 18-inch torpedo tubes and at eight knots had a submerged endurance of about three hours, although in the dived condition heat from the machinery and boiler was an ever present problem. *Narval* was classed as submersible, designed primarily to operate on the surface or awash and diving during the final stages of an attack.

The Laubeuf submarine was adopted by the French navy for coastal and fleet work and progressive improvements led to the development of the 398-ton Brumaire (built at Cherbourg), Berthelot (Rochefort) and Ampere (Toulon) classes, in several of which a diesel engine replaced. the steam machinery long favoured for surface propulsion. In war the boats achieved some measure of success but unsuspected design faults prevented full exploitation of their potential.

French armoured ships of the late 19th century were distinguished by their massive tumble-home, heavy military masting and, in many cases, extreme ram bows. Typical of such was the 12,205-ton battleship *Bouvet*, completed at Lorient in 1895. Armed with two 12-inch guns, in single turret mountings forward and aft, a single 11-inch each side amidships and eight 5.5-inch guns, she represented a compromise in the continuing effort to achieve maximum all-round coverage with particular emphasis on an end-on fire capability. The *Bouvet* herself was mined in the Dardanelles on March 18, 1915, and sank in less than three minutes with considerable loss of life.

Among the lesser units of the fleet, early French torpedo boats proved of little value in open waters, even in the Mediterranean and it was not until the advent of the Normand-type destroyers of the Durandal and later classes that the fleet possessed any satisfactory torpedo craft. The first were completed in 1895; they differed from their British counterparts in that the freeboard was less and the upper deck was given a marked turtle-back form over its entire length. All were of about 303 tons displacement and could be relied on for 26 knots in any average sea state.

At the outbreak of war in August 1914 the French fleet comprised two dreadnought battleships of the 12-inch-gunned Courbet class, with another two preparing for service, 19 pre-dreadnought battleships, 19 armoured and four protected cruisers, 81 destroyers and about 50 effective submarines. Much the greater part of the fleet was based in the Mediterranean but in the event its potential was not fully exploited; the main French involvement in the sea war was confined to patrol and escort work, although four of the older battleships did play their part in the Dardenelles campaign of 1915.

The break-up of the German fleet in 1920 brought to France the cruisers *Königsberg* (renamed *Metz*), *Regensburg* (*Strasbourg*), *Stralsund*(*Mulhouse*) and *Kolberg* (*Colmar*); with the ex-Austrian *Novara* (*Thionville*) they helped strengthen the previously inadequate cruising force of the fleet. A number of destroyers and submarines were taken over as well but all had been sold for breaking by the mid-1930s.

France was a party to the Washington naval conferences of 1921-22 but, other than her refusal to consider the outlawing of submarine warfare or to accept any restriction on the numbers of cruisers and destroyers, the decisions had little immediate effect upon the French fleet, which was in any case shackled by financial stringency. Construction of the battleships of the Normandie class was abandoned, with the exception of the *Bearn*, which was redesigned as an aircraft carrier and completed at La Seyne in May 1927. Like the British carrier *Eagle*—another battleship conversion—however, her usefulness was hampered by a maximum speed of only 21½ knots and in war she saw little service other than as an aircraft transport.

Post-war construction started with the laying down in 1922 of the three 6.1-inch-gun cruisers of the Duguay-Trouin class—7250-ton vessels capable of 33 knots but practically devoid of armour protection. In 1924, however, France took a lead from the other Washington Treaty powers and turned to the construction of heavy cruisers mounting 8-inch guns within the

Left: French helicopter carrier 'Jeanne D'Arc' and four destroyers, including 'Chevalier Paul' (D626), 'Casabianca' (D631) and 'Dupetit Thouars' (D625), on a visit to Hamburg in April 1964. *A Greenway*

Below: Page from 'The Illustrated London News' of October 29, 1898, of the French battleship 'Charles Martel' receiving finishing touches at Toulon. *Illustrated London News*

limitation of 10,000 tons standard displacement. Once again, in the case of the *Duquesne* and *Tourville*, protection was minimal, but in the case of the *Algerie*, the final ship of the series which was laid down at Brest in 1931, two knots speed was sacrificed in order to work in a measure of side and deck armour.

It was in the field of fast fleet destroyer (contre-torpeilleur) design that the French Navy really made its name between the wars. The type was first projected in the early 1920s to meet increased French commitments in the Mediterranean; although well armed and capable of sustained high speed, they were given, like contemporary Italian warships, only the minimum fuel stowage to meet envisaged operational needs. Six vessels were laid down in 1922-23 and the first, the *Jaguar*, was completed for service at Lorient in 1926. On a standard displacement of 2126 tons, they mounted five 5.1-inch guns and geared turbines of 50,000shp gave a maximum sea speed of $35\frac{1}{2}$ knots.

Succeeding groups of six vessels each represented a stage in the steady development of the contre-torpeilleur theme which reached its final expression in the design of the Mogador class of the 1932/34 programmes.

Fine vessels of 2884 tons, they were capable of 39 knots, but both the *Mogador* and her sister *Volta* achieved speeds in excess of 43 knots on trials. They were armed with eight 5.5-inch guns in pairs but in service were plagued by the complexity of the mountings and their control arrangements. Construction of the four remaining ships of the Mogador class (1938 programme) was interrupted by the outbreak of war and they were never completed.

In the late 1920s the French battle fleet comprised the ageing 12-inch-gun dreadnoughts *Courbet*, *Océan* and *Paris*, none of which could be considered fit tor first line service, and the *Bretagne*, *Lorraine* and *Provence*, launched in 1913 and mounting a main battery of 10 13.4-inch guns. In 1929, however, Germany announced the laying down of the first of the so-called pocket battleships, a move which led the French to draw up plans for a fast battleship capable of countering any German threat. They resulted in the construction of the 26,500-ton *Dunkerque* and *Strasbourg*, completed in 1937 and 1938 respectively, mounting eight 13-inch guns in a pair of quadruple turrets forward of the main structure. With a speed of $29\frac{1}{2}$ knots and well planned protection, they represented a satisfactory compromise on a limited displacement.

French submarine development between the wars followed conventional lines based upon experience with the Laubeuf type and seized German boats. The massive construction programme involved the laying down between 1925 and 1931 of no fewer than 32 first-class submarines of the 1570-ton Redoutable class, in addition to which a considerable number of second-class boats were built, including 22 vessels of the Diane class. It need only be said that on the outbreak of war in September 1939, the submarine arm totalled 86 boats compared with the 59 at the disposal of the Royal Navy and the 57 German boats in commission.

When the world went to war in 1939 the French navy was certainly a formidable force, although there were deficiencies in the matter of equipment, particularly in the field of anti-submarine warfare. Throughout the 'phoney' war of 1939 and the early months of 1940, however, the fleet co-operated fully with the Royal Navy, but in June 1940 France was forced to bow to the aggressor. A few vessels joined de Gaulle's Free French Force but the remainder of the fleet was more or less immobilised, with an assurance that it would not be allowed to fall into German hands. There followed the disaster at Mers-el-Kebir (Oran) and in November 1942 the final destruction and scuttling of the fleet in Toulon. Thereafter those remaining French warships, scattered in colonial harbours and elsewhere, joined the Allied cause and, backed by British and American vessels transferred on loan, helped pave the way for the victory of 1945.

In 1946 a number of ex-German and ex-Italian warships were acquired and the naval air arm, which had been long neglected between the wars, was given a boost by the transfer on loan, with an option to purchase, of the British light fleet carrier *Colossus*, appropriately renamed *Arromanches*. In 1951 two US light fleet carriers, renamed *Bois Belleau* and *La Fayette*, were transferred under the Mutual Defense Assistance Program and the experience thus gained led the French to embark upon the construction of the 27,300-ton aircraft carriers *Clemenceau* and *Foch*, completed in 1961 and 1963.

The French Navy today comprises a modern and well-balanced fleet which includes, in addition to the aircraft carriers, the helicopter cruiser *Jeanne d'Arc* and the guided missile cruiser *Colbert*, the latter now re-armed with a Masurca SAM system. Two Masurca-armed destroyers (DDG), the 5090-ton *Duquesne* and *Suffren*, are in service, as also are three smaller destroyers of the 4580-ton Tourville class completed between 1974 and 1977. The Tourvilles are armed with Exocet SSM and Malafon anti-submarine missile systems but it is intended that they shall be fitted additionally with the Crotale close-range SAM system when it becomes available. The conventional destroyer arm is represented by the 13 surviving vessels of the well-proved Surcouf class completed between 1953 and 1957, which it is planned to replace with the 3800-ton C70 class CODOG destroyers. The first C70, *Georges Leygues*, was expected to enter service in April 1979. They are armed with Exocet SSM and the US medium-range Tartar SAM systems and are engined with a Rolls-Royce Olympus/SEMT-Pielstick diesel combination.

The post-war rehabilitation of the French fleet has been marked by a desire to retain complete independence in the fields of design, construction and logistic support where ships and their weapon systems are concerned. This 'go-it-alone' policy has been most clearly apparent in the development of a submarine-embarked nuclear deterrent of the Polaris type, which will comprise eventually six nuclear-propelled submarines each armed with 16 ballistic missiles. Four SSBNs, the 7500-ton *Le Redoutable*, *Le Terrible*, *Le Foudroyant* and *L'Indomptable*, all built at Cherbourg, are currently in service. There are in addition serving with the fleet 22 conventional diesel-engined submarines. Under construction at Cherbourg as this is written is the first of a new class of nuclear-powered hunter/killer submarines (SSN).

Although France is not a participating member of NATO, the navy maintains close links with other West-European navies and NATO procedures are employed for fleet work. In addition, joint exercises with the Royal Navy and other forces have enabled the navies concerned to keep abreast of each others' problems.

SPAIN AND THE ARMADA

After throwing off the Moorish yoke and establishing the Spanish American Empire, during the 16th century Spain prospered to become the dominant power in Europe and built up a powerful Mediterranean navy. Spain seized Portugal in 1580, taking over that country's superior shipbuilding experience to develop a great deep-water fleet based on the galleon, consolidating her position of dominance which, despite the débâcle of the mighty Armada that sailed so disastrously against England in 1588, was only gradually whittled away during the 17th century.

Here are illustrated (above) a treasure galleon and escorts of a flota formed to protect her Atlantic trade, from a painting by M Barton, and (left and below) the massed ships of the Armada sailing up the Channel to invade England, and the shattered remnants that escaped destruction. *Both Illustrated London News*

NAVIES OF THE WORLD

JAPAN

This picture: The 35,000-ton Japanese battleship 'Nagato' pictured in 1936 after reconstruction. *Courtesy Lt Cdr Fukui*

Below left: A postcard illustration of a Japanese cruiser capturing a Russian merchant vessel during the Russo-Japanese war. *J Maber*

Below right: Admiral Isoroku Yamamoto c-in-c of the combined Japanese fleet from 1939-45 and planner of the Pearl Harbour attack, pictured here at a New York hotel in 1934. *Imperial War Museum*

JAPANESE CRUISER CAPTURING RUSSIAN MERCHANT VESSEL.

UNTIL THE MID-19th CENTURY, Japan was organised as a medieval feudal society refusing all contact with other nations. Indeed, until 1853 foreigners were rigidly excluded from the Japanese islands, although in earlier years both the Portuguese and the Dutch had established, under severe restrictions, short-lived trading links. Primitive fire-arms and even large guns were manufactured, but the warrior knights (samurai) and their armies wore body armour and used almost exclusively hand weapons. The inhabitants of the islands were forbidden to leave their native land under any circumstances and shipwrecked mariners were subjected to harsh treatment or even put to death. Ultimately, however, pressure from outside brought about a gradual change of ideas and the opening up of the country.

The first contact established by Commodore Perry, of the United States Navy, in 1853 was followed by the Treaty of Kanagawa, which opened the way for American traders through Nagasaki and Hakodate. Within the next 18 months, further treaties were negotiated granting similar privileges to Great Britain, Holland and Russia; Japanese leaders became more outward looking and in due course foreign advisers were brought in to modernise the nation, including its armed forces, financial structure and external relations. An industrial revolution followed and a deep-water merchant marine was established, making necessary some form of naval force for the protection of Japanese maritime interests.

The nominal ruler of the country in the mid-19th century was the Mikado (emperor), but in practice power was vested in the hands of the shogun, the hereditary military commander, and it was in the name of the latter authority that the first Japanese warships were acquired. They included the 140-ton screw gun vessel *Chiyodagata*, launched in July 1862 and the first warship built in Japan, the 1358-ton ironclad ram *Kotetsu* (ex-*Stonewall*) purchased from the United States Government in 1867, and the 1010-ton wooden screw frigate *Fujiyama*, an American-built vessel purchased by the Shogun in 1868.

Internal opposition to the reforms led, however, to unrest, followed early in 1868 by civil war the outcome of which was the re-establishment throughout the country of the authority of the Mikado and the suppression of the shogunate. After the civil war financial difficulties forced a drastic cutback in the funds available for the maintenance of the Imperial Navy, which was reduced in consequence to the three screw vessels mentioned above and four transports.

In 1872 control of Japan's small navy, and responsibility for the naval dockyards at Ishikawajima and Yokosuka, were transferred, from the Ministry of War to the newly formed Navy Department; at the same time European expertise was brought in to advise on the building up of the war fleet. Between 1873 and 1878, six wooden-hulled warships, comprising the screw corvettes *Kaimon* and *Tenryu*, two screw sloops, the gun vessel *Banjo* and the paddle dispatch vessel *Jingei*, were laid down in the Yokosuka Navy Yard under the supervision of French naval architects and engineers. In so far as professional skills were concerned, arrangements were made for the training abroad, mainly in Britain, of naval officers.

The rise of Japan as an international power encouraged the development of the ocean-going navy and in 1875 funds were made available for the construction in Britain of the central-battery ironclad

Fuso—a typical Reed design of 3718 tons with a marked affinity to his *Pallas* built for the Royal Navy a decade earlier—and the small armoured cruisers *Hiei* and *Kongo*.

Ten years later, in 1885, the fleet comprised the armoured ram *Adsuma* (ex-*Kotetsu*), the *Fuso*, three armoured cruisers, the broadside armoured sloop *Ryujo*, five unarmoured cruisers and an assortment of gun vessels and gunboats, with a flotilla of torpedo boats of which the most notable was the Yarrow-built *Kotaka*, a 19-knot vessel of 203 tons carrying six 14-inch torpedo tubes in twin mountings and four one-pounder quick-firing (QF) guns. All in all not an imposing fleet for a nation seeking to become the leading power in the East.

With the passing of the Navy Expansion Bill in 1882, however, the development of the navy had been aligned more closely to the needs of Japanese foreign policy. As a first stage a number of cruisers of French design were laid down, in both French and Japanese shipyards, but it was not until 1893 that any steps were taken towards the acquisition of a battle fleet with which to challenge Chinese rivalry in the Far East in general and over the matter of Korea in particular.

Then orders were placed with English shipbuilders for the construction of a pair of battleships to be named *Fuji* (Elswick) and *Yashima* (Thames Ironworks Co). Displacing 12,450 tons and well protected, they were planned to carry four 12-inch, ten 6-inch and 20 3-pounder guns which, with twin-screw triple-expansion machinery developing 14,000ihp for a contract speed of 18 knots, made a well-balanced design suited to the needs of the Japanese navy. Little progress had been made with their construction, however, before, in August 1894, Japan went to war with China over the Korean issue.

Japan emerged successful from the war with China at a time when the European powers were engaged in bitter rivalry for territorial concessions on the Chinese mainland. Thus was Japan led in 1896 to introduce a Ten Year Naval Expansion Programme, which provided for the construction of four battleships, six cruisers and a number of torpedo craft. The battleships were all built in the United Kingdom and included the 15,140-ton *Mikasa* later to become well known as Vice-Admiral Togo's flagship at the Battle of Tsushima (1905). She was an 18-knot vessel, similar in design to the Royal Navy's Formidable class, and mounted the then conventional four 12-inch guns in twin turrets forward and aft of the superstructure, with a secondary battery of 14 6-inch guns.

Completed at Barrow in March 1902, the *Mikasa* joined the fleet as flagship, in which role she served throughout the Russo-Japanese War. During the night of September 10-11, 1905, however, the *Mikasa* blew up at Sasebo, possibly as the result of a magazine explosion, but she was later refloated and repaired, and today is preserved at Yokosuka as a memorial to Admiral Togo and the Battle of Tsushima.

Destroyer construction under the expansion programme (and the succeeding Second Naval Expansion Programme of March 1897) centred upon Thornycroft and Yarrow designs essentially similar to those built for service with the Royal Navy. The first vessels of the type were the six destroyers of the 307-ton 30-knot Kagero class, practically repeats of the British Angler class and launched by Thornycroft at Chiswick between December 1898 and January 1900, and the six contemporary boats of the 311-ton Yarrow-built (Poplar) Akebono class. Both types mounted one 12-pounder and five 6-pounder guns, with two 18-inch torpedo tubes.

The decisive victory at Tsushima in May 1905 resulted in the addition to the Japanese fleet of a number of surrendered Russian warships, including the battleships *Hizen* (ex-*Retvizan*), *Sagami* (ex-*Peresviet*), *Suwo* (ex-*Pobieda*), *Iwami* (ex-*Orel*) and *Tango* (ex-*Poltava*), four cruisers and three destroyers. Thus, at the close of 1905, the Japanese fleet comprised 11 modern battleships, nine armoured and eight smaller cruisers, about 30 destroyers and a sizeable flotilla of torpedo boats.

The Japanese were hesitant in committing themselves to the adoption of the submarine, which as a type received scant attention until 1902, when a naval mission visited the United States, Britain and France to examine the state of the art. Not until 1904, however, was any move made to acquire submarines; then, as the Russians possessed a number of effective craft, the Japanese turned to the Holland Company of Quincy, USA, with an order for five Holland Type X boats, each of 105 tons and armed with a single 18-inch

Facing page: A painting by Norman Wilkinson of the action between the Japanese and the Russians off Port Arthur in 1904. *Photo D Rudkin*

Top: The Japanese battleship 'Yamato' pictured on trial in October 1941. *Imperial War Museum*

Above: The Japanese ironclad 'Fuso' as depicted in 'The Illustrated London News' of June 16, 1877. *Illustrated London News*

Left: National flag (above) used also as the naval ensign until 1889 and again between 1952 and 1954; (below) the ensign from 1889-1945 and from 1954. *J Maber*

torpedo tube. Two torpedoes were carried.

Experience during the Russo-Japanese War had brought home to the Japanese the advantage to be gained by high speed as a feature of armoured ship design and they were quick to exploit the battlecruiser concept. However, lengthy construction times, resulting from shortage of funds, made the early Japanese-designed vessels of the type—the 14,600-ton *Ibuki* and *Kurama*—obsolete before they were ready for sea.

The same could not be said of the 27,500-ton battlecruiser *Kongo* designed and built by Vickers in England, which was the last major warship to be ordered from a foreign yard. The idea had been to learn from British expertise before ordering the construction of follow-on vessels in Japanese shipyards. In the event, so satisfactory did the design of the *Kongo* prove that the fourth unit of the British Lion class, the 28,500-ton *Tiger,* was redesigned on similar lines. Well protected over her vitals and mounting eight 14-inch and 16 6-inch guns, the *Kongo* was driven by a four-shaft Parsons direct-drive turbine installation developing 64,000shp for a speed of $27\frac{1}{2}$ knots; she was certainly the best-conceived battlecruiser design of that date.

The *Kongo* was delivered in August 1913, by which time orders had been placed with Japanese yards for the construction of three sister ships, the *Hiei* (Yokosuka), *Kirishima* (Mitsubishi) and *Haruna* (Kawasaki). Of contemporary design, and built respectively by the Kure and Yokosuka Navy Yards, were the equivalent battleships *Fuso* and *Yamashiro* (29,330 tons), each mounting 12 14-inch guns and certainly among the most powerful capital ships in the world, although neither so fast nor so well protected as the British Queen Elizabeth class. The fact was, however, that the Japanese had come a long way in little more than 50 years both in the development of a national shipbuilding industry and in the build-up of the premier naval force in the Western Pacific.

Back in 1902, Japan had allied herself with Britain, then the world's leading naval power, and in 1914 she met her treaty obligations, not without self interest in mind, by declaring war against Germany. Apart from convoy work and the dispatch of a destroyer flotilla to the Mediterranean, however, the Japanese navy took little active part in the war. On the other hand, the naval construction programme continued apace throughout, with Japanese naval architects, shipbuilders and engineers by then largely independent of foreign assistance.

Consequently, in 1919, having taken note of British and American experimental work in the operation of aircraft from more-or-less suitably adapted warships and converted liners, the Japanese laid down the world's first aircraft carrier designed as such from the outset. Although small, the 7470-ton *Hosho* was given a full-length flight deck, clear of funnels and other obstructions, and geared turbine machinery of 30,000shp to give a capability of 25 knots. On completion late in 1922, she was turned over to trials and training in anticipation of the entry into service of the fleet carriers *Akagi* and *Amagi,* 26,900-ton vessels converted from the incomplete hulls of a pair of 31-knot battlecruisers.

In 1922, Japan was party to the Washington Naval Treaty which brought about a drastic cutback in the construction programmes of the participating powers; she had hoped for parity with Britain and the United States but was forced to accept a limit of 315,000 tons of capital ships against the 525,000 tons allowed to the Royal and United States Navies. An 81,000-ton restriction on the permitted tonnage of aircraft carriers, not counting those of under 10,000 tons displacement, contributed also to the necessary re-appraisal of the post-war fleet construction programme.

At the same time a unit limit of 10,000 tons 'standard' displacement and 8-inch guns for new-construction cruisers resulted in the laying down of a series of vessels of progressively larger displacement culminating in the 10,940-ton Ashigara class of the 1923 naval programme. Mounting 10 7.9-inch low-angle guns, six 4.7-inch anti-aircraft guns and 12 (4 by 3) 24-inch torpedo tubes, the four ships of the class

Below left: The Japanese submarine RO-58 as completed at Kobe in November 1922.
Imperial War Museum

Below: A painting by Norman Wilkinson of the Japanese battleship 'Asahi'. *Photo D Rudkin*

Bottom: The Japanese submarine chaser No 32 in Tokyo Bay in August 1942.
Imperial War Museum

were the most powerful cruisers afloat and their geared turbine machinery of 130,000shp gave them a speed of $35\frac{1}{2}$ knots. Their protection also was on a massive scale, but like other Japanese-designed warships of the 1920s, embodying the maximum offensive capability on minimum-displacement tonnage, they were somewhat tender and lacking in stability.

The problem of a high centre of gravity and lack of stability was apparent too in the 1923 programme destroyers of the 1750-ton Fubuki class which mounted six 5-inch dual-purpose guns and nine 24-inch torpedo tubes (18 torpedoes were carried). The maximum speed at 50,000shp was 38 knots. In the event, the moment of truth came in March 1934, when the likewise heavily armed 535-ton torpedo boat *Tomodzuru* capsized during exercises in heavy weather off Sasebo bringing about a complete suspension of the cruiser and destroyer construction programmes while designs were recast to reduce topweight and to improve stability. The mishap proved a blessing, however, since the Japanese learned a lesson which was to stand them in good stead during the fast-approaching Pacific war.

The international naval agreements lapsed in 1937, at a time when Japan was involved in disputes and intrigue throughout the Far East. Feeling increasingly more isolated, the pace of rearmament and modernisation of the Japanese fleet was accelerated in the certain knowledge that Japan must fight America. It was the time when the big gun and the battleship were still considered the final arbiters of naval warfare and, being unable to match the economic strength and industrial resources of the United States, the Japanese decided that the answer lay in the construction of a battleship more powerful than any that the US Navy, tied by the limitations of the Panama Canal, might be expected to build.

The result was the adoption of an 18.1-inch gun firing a 3220-pound high-explosive shell, around which was planned the 65,200-ton *Yamato*, a vessel 834 feet long with a designed speed of 27 knots. Final design work was put in hand in 1936 after consideration of a number of preliminary configurations and provision was made for a weapon fit comprising nine 18.1-inch guns in three triple mountings, with 12 6.1-inch low-angle guns, 12 5-inch anti-aircraft guns and no fewer than six aircraft. Two ships, the *Yamato* and *Musashi*, each of 68,200 tons, were authorised under the 1937 Reinforcement Programme and the keel of the first was laid in Kure Navy Yard in November of that year.

Although planned originally to be a four-shaft ship with geared turbines of 75,000shp on two shafts and diesel engines of 60,000bhp driving the other two, design problems with the diesels resulted in a decision in favour of an all-steam turbine installation of 148,000shp giving a maximum speed of 27 knots. Protection was on a scale to resist the impact of an 18-inch projectile and the ship was designed so that a considerable degree of stability would be maintained in a damaged condition. The *Yamato* was launched in August 1940 and was commissioned for service on December 16, 1941, by which time Japan had taken the fatal step posed by her unprovoked attack on the United States Pacific fleet lying at its week-end moorings in Pearl Harbour, Oahu, in the Hawaiian Islands.

In the meantime, the submarine arm of the Imperial Japanese Navy had been built up in step with the expansion of the surface fleet. Post-1914-18 war boats were derived from the very successful British L class (Type L), the Italian Fiat-Laurenti type (Type F) and the French Schneider-Laubeuf type (Type K). Experience with them and with ex-German submarines led to the design of a number of different types of specialised craft, including headquarters (A1), scouting (B1) and attack (C1) submarines, intended to work together as an attack force, plus medium-sized and long-range ocean patrol submarines. The several types were intended to work as part of the fleet, since the Japanese saw little requirement for the use of submarines in the role of commerce destroyers. In the event of war there would be little trade to attack, since the United States were largely self sufficient and the exposed trade route between Australasia and Europe via the Cape was considered too distant. Not until Japan went to war was any attempt made at series construction, but in the event so great were losses that the Japanese submarine arm had little influence upon the course of the Pacific struggle.

Although the battleship continued to hold pride of place in the strike fleet, the role of the aircraft carrier had not been overlooked; in fact the Japanese were well to the forefront in the development of the seaborne air strike force, which was only too ably demonstrated when the First Naval Air Fleet operating from the fleet carriers *Akagi, Kaga, Hiryu, Soryu, Shokaku* and *Zuikaku* struck at Pearl Harbour on December 7, 1941. Japan had staked all in the bid for mastery of the East and the rapid advance southward through the Philippines to Malaya, Java and the Celebes secured the vital raw materials necessary for the furtherance of her aims.

Control of that vast empire soon over-stretched the resources of the fleet, however, and in June 1942 the United States struck back at Midway, where in a bitter air and sea battle the Japanese aircraft carriers *Akagi, Kaga, Soryu* and *Hiryu* were destroyed. The tide had turned and in October 1944 the struggle culminated in Japan attempting a last desperate gamble to stem the American advance in the Leyte Gulf. The remaining strength of the fleet, including the battleships *Yamato* and *Musashi*, was thrown into the battle, but already the day of the big-gun capital ship had passed into history.

Carrier-borne air power decided the issue with little contact between the opposing surface fleets and the Japanese were forced to retreat, having suffered the loss of not only the *Musashi* but also the older battleships *Yamashiro* and *Fuso*, the aircraft carriers *Zuikaku, Chitose, Chiyoda* and *Zuiho*, six heavy cruisers and seven destroyers. Six months later the 68,200-ton *Yamato* was sunk in a vain sortie against the Americans, who had assaulted and taken the island stronghold of Okinawa in the Ryukyu Islands only a few hundred miles from the Japanese heartland.

The Imperial Japanese Navy had been all but destroyed. A few ships, all more or less damaged, remained afloat to be surrendered but in the aftermath of the war they were broken up or scuttled by their captors, with the one exception of the battleship *Nagato*, of 1920, which was expended in the American nuclear bomb tests at Bikini Atoll in July 1946.

In the short term of 80 years the Imperial Japanese Navy had grown from the few ships purchased during the days of the 19th-century Shogunate to become the premier fleet in the western Pacific but, in challenging America and her allies, Japan staked all and lost. The rayed-sun ensign was swept from the seas and by the terms of the surrender signed on board USS *Missouri* in Tokyo Bay on September 2, 1945, the Imperial Japanese Navy ceased to exist. For several years thereafter Japan was not allowed any naval force apart from a fleet of ex-minesweepers and minor war vessels limited to a total of 50,000 tons, which was formed in 1948 to meet essential coastal security and fishery protection requirements.

In October 1952 agreement was reached leading to the creation of a National Safety Agency, of which the Coastal Security Force formed the maritime wing. The vessels concerned wore the national (merchant) flag (a plain red ball on a white field) as an ensign but in 1954 the fleet of ex-American frigates and coastal escorts was restyled the Maritime Self-Defence Force and approval was given for the re-introduction of the rayed-sun flag as the naval ensign.

Today the fleet comprises 46 destroyers and frigates, 16 submarines and a number of corvettes, minesweepers and auxiliaries. Most vessels are of Japanese design and construction but weapons, sensors and aircraft are of American origin, some built under licence in Japan. A new DD122 destroyer design, the construction of the first of which was approved in the 1977 estimates, will be powered on two shafts with a Rolls-Royce Olympus/Tyne gas turbine installation similar to that fitted in ships of the British and Netherlands navies. Further DD122 units are planned but the Maritime Self-Defence Force would be hard pressed if ever it was called upon to protect the maritime communications of the Rising Sun unaided.

SOUTH AMERICA

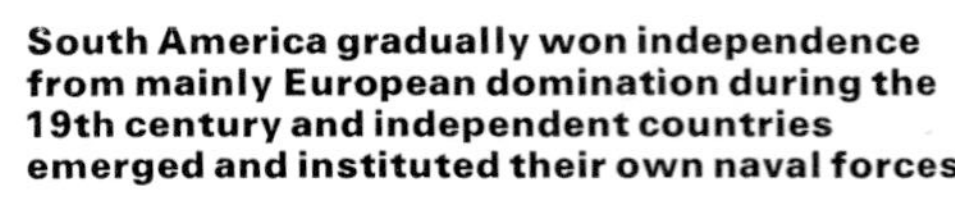

South America gradually won independence from mainly European domination during the 19th century and independent countries emerged and instituted their own naval forces.

Above: The mid-19th-century Thames-built Brazilian river gunboat 'Colombo'.
Illustrated London News

Left: Modern warships of the Chilean Navy at Valparaiso, with the ex-US cruiser 'Prat' in the foreground. *A Greenway*

Below: The cruiser 'Almirante Grau', ex-HMS 'Newfoundland', transferred to the Peruvian Navy in 1959 and pictured here in 1969. The ship was renamed 'Capitan Quiñones' in 1973 and the ex-Dutch cruiser 'De Ruyter' eventually took over the name 'Almirante Grau'. *A Greenway*

NAVIES OF THE WORLD

ITALY

THE VERY early history of Italy is bound up with that of Rome but in later centuries the country came largely under the domination of France, Spain and Austria. After the Napoleonic Wars, Austrian rule was re-established in the northern states of Lombardy and Venice but elsewhere the Papal States and the several minor kingdoms retained their independence from foreign influence and control. Apart from the kingdoms of Sardinia and Naples (the Kingdom of the Two Sicilies) the independent states took little interest in maritime affairs, however, so those two alone acquired naval forces of any con-consequence, although in fact Tuscany and even the Papal States did possess a few minor war vessels.

In 1859 the Sardinian Navy comprised 29 ships, including six steam frigates, while the naval force at the disposal of the King of Naples totalled 98 vessels, including two ships of the line (sail) and 14 steam frigates. In all, it was quite a formidable force when considered in relation to the fact that the interests of the states concerned did not extend beyond the limits of the central Mediterranean basin.

Unification of the Italian states was accomplished in 1861 in the wake of the activities of Cavour and Garibaldi, supported by Victor Emmanuel II of Sardinia-Piedmont, who himself became king of the newly created nation. The several navies were brought together and the first new major warship commissioned for the Royal Italian Navy, a wooden two-decked 64-gun screw battleship of 3669 tons, was named *Re Galantuomo* (Cavalier King) after the popular monarch.

The first armoured ships for the Italian Navy were the 2725-ton central-battery ironclads *Terribile* and *Formidabile* launched at La Seyne, France, in 1861 and armed with eight 7-ton muzzle-loading Armstrong guns. Engined with single expansion machinery of 1100ihp, they were capable of a sea speed of 10 knots but, being small and quite unfit for any line of battle, they were soon re-classified as armoured corvettes.

In June 1866 Italy went to war with Austria, in part over Italian claims to Venezia, and a month later, in need of some swift military success to serve as a bargaining counter in the likely event of an early truce, she attempted an assault against the Austrian island of Lissa in the Adriatic. Lack of organisation on the part of the Italian fleet resulted in a major reverse and the sinking by ramming of the 5700-ton ironclad *Re d'Italia,* flagship of Admiral Count Persano, by the Austrian flagship *Ferdinand Max.* The incident had a profound influence on subsequent iron-clad design throughout Europe, all such vessels and their successors being built with massive rams for the next 40 years although in the event more damage and indeed loss resulted in peacetime incidents than was ever to be achieved by ramming in battle!

In 1888 the Royal Italian Navy included nine modern iron and steel screw battleships, 11 older armoured ships and a

Top: The Italian frigate 'Alpino', showing variable-depth sonar equipment at the stern. *A Greenway*

Above left: The battleship 'Cavour' of 1915, which was rebuilt in the 1930s. *Courtesy the Italian Navy*

Left: A modern Italian frigate, 'Bergomini', with helicopter overhead. *Italian Embassy*

considerable flotilla of cruisers and torpedo craft. In appearance the ships were quite distinct from those of other navies but perhaps the most bizarre in any battlefleet of the day was the six-funnelled *Italia*, a 13,851-ton battleship mounting four 106-ton 17-inch Armstrong guns in pairs on two open-topped turntables placed in echelon amidships within a massive 17-inch compound armoured glacis. In order to meet the requirement for 18 knots service speed, side armour was abandoned altogether and protection was limited to an arched armoured deck with an armoured trunk extending upwards to protect the ammunition hoists. The light bridge structure was carried amidships above the armoured glacis and was surmounted by a single military mast. The *Italia* was built in the Navy Yard at Castellammare di Stabia and entered service in October 1885.

Although battleship construction was confined from the early 1860s to Italian shipyards, the navy turned occasionally to foreign builders for cruising ships and smaller craft. Thus in 1887 an order had been placed with Armstrongs, of Elswick, for the construction of a fast protected cruiser to be named *Piemonte*. Conceived by Philip Watts, she was a development of the Chilean cruiser *Esmeralda* and her design led in turn to that of the Medea and Pearl classes built subsequently for the Royal Navy. She was armed with six 6-inch and six 4.7-inch quick-firing guns and was capable of 22 knots, although being intended for service strictly within Mediterranean waters her coal supply, and hence her operational range, were limited in the extreme. In later years, the characteristics of high speed and limited endurance, with lightness of build and scanty protection, were to typify Italian warship design.

The early torpedo boats were typical vessels of British Yarrow or Thornycroft build, but in the 1880s and 1890s the Italian Navy acquired a number of craft of German (Schichau, Elbing) construction, in addition to which torpedo boats of Thornycroft and Schichau designs were

Top left: Admiral Aubry, who commanded the Italian fleet opposing Turkey in 1911. *Illustrated London News*

Top: Presentation by 'The Illustrated London News' of May 21, 1938, depicting the Fascist Italian Navy as displayed for visiting German dictator Hitler. *Illustrated London News*

Above: The modern Italian missile cruiser 'Andrea Doria'. *Italian Embassy London*

Above right: The submarine 'Mocenigo' about to submerge. *Italian Embassy*

built in Italian shipyards. Destroyer construction started with the none-too-successful *Fulmine*, a 298-ton vessel built by Odero at Sestri Penente and launched in December 1898. The Schichau-built Lampo class followed, but thereafter all but a few craft were of Italian construction, although those built by Pattison (Naples) owed much of their design to Thornycroft influence.

The first Italian submarine of any importance was the 111-ton *Delfino;* she was electrically driven and capable of five knots on the surface but only two knots submerged, and was completed at Spezia in 1892. The *Delfino* was followed by the 175-ton Glauco class, designed by Colonel Cesare Laurenti and built between 1903 and 1909 by the Arsenale di Venezia, which formed the basis for further development culminating in the successful F class of 1915-18. Three vessels of the Laurenti type were built by Scotts on the Clyde for the Royal Navy, but after some brief experience in their operation, the British turned them over to the Italian Navy as S1, S2 and S3.

In the meantime, Colonel Vittorio Cuniberti had been making a name for himself in the matter of the design of capital warships. An advocate of high speed combined with a heavy main battery, his first major contribution to the Italian Navy was the design of the 12,600-ton *Vittorio Emanuele III*, first of its class launched at Castellammare di Stabia in October 1904. With a main armament of two 12-inch guns, a secondary battery of 12 8-inch guns and a maximum service speed of 22 knots, the four ships of the class were in effect the forebears of the battlecruiser concept.

In an article in the 1903 edition of Jane's Fighting Ships, Cuniberti put forward his proposals for a battleship able to inflict maximum damage at long range. It involved the provision of the largest calibre gun and some effective means of gun fire control. The requirement for spotting fall of shot to assist accurate range-laying only confirmed the need for a single-calibre battery; in effect those ideas first reached fruition in the design of HMS *Dreadnought*.

For the Italian Navy, the all-big-gun concept was realised in the 19,200-ton *Dante Alighieri* launched in August 1910. A main battery of 12 12-inch guns in four triple mountings was carried on the centre line, permitting a broadside of 12 guns against the eight of the *Dreadnought* herself. In the matter of machinery, a four-shaft Parsons direct-drive turbine arrangement of 35,350shp gave a speed of 23 knots, again two knots better than that of the *Dreadnought*, but on the other hand protection, although extensive, was light and endurance was limited to that dictated by the confines of the Mediterranean.

The lone *Dante Alighieri* was followed by the three 22,800-ton vessels of the Conte di Cavour class, in which again a centre-line disposition of the main battery was adopted, although the 13 12-inch guns were arranged in a combination of triple and twin turrets.

Italy declared war, initially against Austria only, on May 24, 1915, and brought to the Allied cause a considerable battle fleet well capable of containing the Adriatic-based Austro-Hungarian fleet. In the event, the major vessels of the Italian fleet saw little action during the war and in fact the navy's greatest success was achieved by the 16-ton motor torpedo boat MAS 15, which on June 10, 1918, torpedoed and sank the Austro-Hungarian battleship *Szent Istvan*.

Wartime completions included the battleship *Andrea Doria*, but against that the *Leonardo da Vinci* blew up at her moorings in Taranto harbour with heavy loss of life on August 2, 1916. Apart from capital ships, a number of small cruisers of the scout type were brought into service although, like their larger consorts, they saw little of the enemy.

Little expansion of Italian shipbuilding capacity was achieved during the 1914-18 war and only relatively few destroyers were built, all to designs exhibiting still a marked Thornycroft or Yarrow influence. Typical of the destroyers, and the most numerous, were the dozen 790-ton turbine vessels of the Giuseppe Sirtori and Giuseppe La Masa classes, which differed only in the matter of their respective weapon fits. All were built in the Odero yard at Sestri Ponente and entered service between 1916 and 1919.

The strength of the fleet was augmented in 1920 by the acquisition of a number of ex-enemy warships, including the former German cruisers *Strassburg* (renamed *Taranto*), *Pillau* (*Bari*) and *Graudenz* (*Ancona*), and the ex-Austrian *Helgoland* (*Brindisi*) and *Saida* (*Venezia*), eight destroyers, a number of submarines and several smaller vessels. Most had gone within a few years but two of the cruisers, the *Taranto* and the *Bari*, were rebuilt in 1936-37 for duty as colonial guardships based on Massawa.

The Washington naval treaty limitations of 1922 had little immediate effect upon the Italian Navy but when cruiser construction recommenced in 1924 the opportunity was taken, in common with the other 'treaty' navies, to build up to the limit of 10,000 tons standard displacement and to mount a main battery of 8-inch guns. The first two vessels, named *Trieste* and *Trento*, were launched in 1926 and 1927 respectively, the name of the first reflecting the cession by Austria of the Istrian Peninsula with the port of Trieste to Italy in 1918.

Designed for $35\frac{1}{2}$ knots, they were engined with Parsons geared turbines of 150,000shp driving four shafts; on trials they managed to achieve that speed, but during the war, with much extra equipment, their best appears to have been about 31 knots. Like their British counterparts of the County classes, they carried eight 8-inch guns in four twin mountings. A third Trento, built to a modified design and named *Bolzano*, was completed by Ansaldo at Sestri Ponente in 1933, but in the meantime four somewhat slower and better protected 8-inch armed cruisers of the Zara class had been built under the 1928 to 1930 programmes.

Completion of the *Bolzano* brought the programme of 'treaty' cruiser construction to an end, attention being turned thereafter to a series of 5000-ton 37-knot light cruisers mounting eight 6-inch guns. Known as the Condottieri class, they were named after the mercenary leaders who plagued the Italian city states in the 14th century and like many Italian war (and merchant) ships bearing lengthy proper names they were known usually by their 'surnames' only. Thus the *Raimondo Montecuccoli* was shortened to *Montecuccoli*, while the longest of the lot, the *Luigi di Savoia Duca Degli Abruzzi*, was known briefly as the *Abruzzi*! The vessels were designed as a reply to the French contre-torpeilleurs of the Guépard class which mounted a main battery of 5.5-inch guns. In most cases preliminary trials were run without stores on board, and speeds in excess of 40 knots were achieved.

Destroyer construction started in the 1920s with a series of vessels of basically similar type, built to designs by Pattison of Naples and Odero of Sestri Ponente. All mounted four 4.7-inch guns and were designed for 35-36 knots. They were followed by a series of single-funnelled vessels of progressively increased size and speed, all mounting the basic armament of four 4.7-inch guns and six 21-inch torpedo tubes, culminating in the Soldati class, construction of which started in 1937. Displacing 1715 tons and designed for 39 knots, the Soldati class of destroyers continued to be built until well after Italy's declaration of war in June 1940, although progressive improvement to their weapon fit and strengthening of the later hulls brought the standard displacement up to 1846 tons.

Although there was some expansion of the Italian surface fleet during the years leading up to the 1939-45 war, the primary effort was directed towards the development of the submarine arm. Two main types emerged from the 1920s, the first a series of coastal vessels designed by General Engineer Curio Bernadis which led first to the 12 590-ton boats of the Sirena class completed in 1933-34. They were satisfactory small vessels carrying a single 3.9-inch gun and six 21-inch torpedo tubes (12 torpedoes) and, like the later British U and V classes, were eminently suitable for Mediterranean conditions.

The Sirena class was followed by the 27 boats of the Perla class, which incorporated a number of improvements resulting from experience, and thereafter by the Adua (17 boats) and Acciaio (13) classes. Each succeeding group represented an improvement on its predecessor and the type gave a good account of itself during the war.

Various designers and builders contributed to the larger ocean-going submarines, but they were not built in such large numbers as the coastal boats nor was any standard design produced. In war they were employed mainly in the Atlantic, where they contributed to the German U-boat campaign, and several, notably those of the 1100-ton Guglielmo Marconi class, achieved a considerable measure of success due in part to their high surface speed of 18 knots. All mounted a single 3.9-inch gun and eight 21-inch torpedo tubes, for which 12 torpedoes were carried.

Some of the crew of the guided missile cruiser 'Andrea Doria' pictured on the helicopter deck.
A Greenway

Between 1933 and 1940 the four ageing battleships of the Conte de Cavour and Andrea Doria classes were completely rebuilt and rearmed with new main batteries of 10 12.6 guns apiece. Geared turbines of 75,000shp on two shafts gave them a speed of 26 knots, against their original 22 knots, and on completion they emerged showing little evidence of their past.

At the same time orders were placed for two new battleships to be named *Littorio* and *Vittorio Veneto*, which were laid down at Genoa and Monfalcone respectively. Mounting nine 15-inch, 12 6-inch and 12 3.5-inch AA guns and with a sea speed of 28 knots, they achieved a fine balance between offensive and defensive qualities and proved eminently satisfactory in service. Both commissioned for service in August 1940 but on November 11 that year disaster struck at Taranto, when half the battle fleet was put out of action in the course of a night attack by British carrier-borne Swordfish aircraft. *The Conte di Cavour* and *Littorio* sank in shallow water and the *Caio Duilio*, although still afloat, sustained serious damage.

A third ship of the same successful new class, the *Roma*, was completed before the Armistice, but was sunk by a German glider bomb while she was on her way to surrender to the Allies; the sinking represented the greatest success up to that time for an air-to-surface missile.

Before the 1939-45 war the Italian Navy had looked upon the aircraft carrier as unnecessary in Mediterranean operations, but British successes in that theatre and the obvious mobility of the carrier-borne strike force resulted in a decision to convert the 15-year-old 32,584-ton (gross) *Roma* into Italy's first aircraft carrier. Renamed *Aquila*, she was taken in hand at Genoa for a massive reconstruction, which included re-engining for a speed of 30 knots with geared turbine machinery intended originally for a pair of small Capitani Romani-class cruisers. By September 1943 the vessel was all but ready for sea trials, although she was still without aircraft.

Thereafter the aircraft carrier project was overtaken by events, for on September 3, 1943, an armistice was signed ending Italy's part in the war on the side of the Axis and on September 11 Admiral Cunningham, the British C-in-C was able to signal to the Admiralty in London 'Be pleased to inform their Lordships that the Italian battle fleet now lies at anchor under the guns of the fortress of Malta'. For the Italian Navy the war was over, although some units, caught in northern ports, passed temporarily into German hands, only to be destroyed by Allied bombers or finally scuttled ahead of the Anglo-American advance.

Italy became a republic in 1946 but until the signing of the definitive peace treaty in 1947 control of those warships still in commission was retained by the Allied command. Unlike the other Axis powers, Italy was not deprived of her navy, although a part of the surface fleet was allocated for distribution between Britain, the United States, Russia, France and Greece. In the event Britain and the United States renounced any claim and Italy was left with a small but balanced fleet; any resumption of warship construction was forbidden before 1950. That proviso apart, the use of submarines was banned (a measure of their success!) and most of the existing boats were discarded and sold for breaking-up.

The fleet was augmented in 1951 by the transfer from the United States under the Mutual Defense Assistance Program of a number of destroyers and destroyer escorts, and in 1952 the ban on submarines was ended when approval was given for the reconditioning of the coastal boats *Giada* and *Vortice*, which had been retained in a disarmed state since the peace treaty of five years before. In 1954 the US submarines *Barb* and *Dace* were transferred on loan and renamed *Leonardo da Vinci* and *Enrico Tazzoli*. Italian naval rehabilitation was complete and the nation was enabled to play a full part as a member of the North Atlantic Treaty Organisation.

In 1957 the 20-year-old cruiser *Giuseppe Garibaldi* was taken in hand for conversion to a 'new age' guided-missile cruiser armed with four automatic 5.3-inch dual-purpose guns in twin mountings forward and a double-headed Terrier surface-to-air missile system of US manufacture aft. Ageing the *Garibaldi* might have been, but the use of a suitably sized hull gave the Italian Navy the experience required before embarking on the design of the guided-missile escort cruisers *Andrea Doria* and *Caio Duilio*. These 6500-ton geared turbine-powered vessels mount a Terrier system and eight 3-inch guns and carry also anti-submarine helicopters.

Today the Italian Navy, charged by NATO with assisting in the defence of the organisation's southern flank, comprises three missile-armed cruisers, four missile-armed destroyers, four missile-armed CODOG frigates, 20 other destroyers and escorts and 10 submarines, with a supporting flotilla of minesweepers and auxiliaries. Much of the equipment is of United States manufacture or design but Italian industry is well equipped to cope with other facets of warship design and construction. This is particularly apparent in the design of the 12,000-ton 'aircraft cruiser' *Giuseppe Garibaldi* ordered in December 1977 and to be laid down at Monfalcone in 1980. The hull and twin-shaft machinery layout are of entirely Italian design but the four Fiat/GE LM2500 gas turbines are of US origin built under licence, while the weapon systems and sensors represent a mix of Italian and US design and manufacture. The fact is that in the matter of material, the Italian Navy is modern and currently well equipped for its role in European and NATO affairs but unless funds are allocated for an ongoing programme of new construction the fleet might find itself eventually unable to meet its commitments.

Left: A USSR Navy escort frigate of the Riga class, in the North Sea in 1970. *A Greenway*

Above top to bottom: Russian-built cruiser 'Rurik' of 1894 *(J M Maber)*; **the remarkable circular ironclad (Popoffka) 'Novgorod' of 1875** *(National Maritime Museum London)*; **and the Russian Navy's mine carrier 'Jenissel' as depicticted on a Knight-series postcard in days when the Russians were less touchy about publicity.** *(J M Maber)*

Navies of the world

RUSSIA

PETER THE GREAT (Peter Veliky) ascended to the Russian throne as Czar in his own right in 1689 determined to make Russia a power in the world. At that time the almost land-locked state possessed no outlet to the sea other than the port of Archangel on the inhospitable White Sea coast, where navigation was made impossible by ice for five months of the year. To the north-west, the eastern Baltic states were in Swedish hands and access to the Black Sea in the south was blocked by Turkish dominance in the Ukraine. Peter was wise enough to realise that little could be done to further his policy without the use of warm water ports and the backing of a shipbuilding industry capable of creating a deep water fleet.

Russia had long been at odds with both Swedes and Turks, so, as a beginning, he imported a Venetian admiral and, on the banks of the Don, built a fleet of war galleys with which to blockade the small Turkish-held port of Azof near the river mouth. Azof fell to the besieging Russian forces in 1696; in the event, the port proved of little use to its occupiers, as it was situated at the head of a narrow easily obstructed gulf leading out to the shallow Sea of Azof.

Fired by the minor success, the Czar set out, 'disguised' as Peter Mihailoff, to learn for himself the shipbuilder's art as practised in England and the Netherlands. On his return, he took up arms against Sweden, then under Charles XII, the major power in the Baltic, and after a long struggle, which reached its climax on the bloody field of Poltava, secured for Russia the eastern Baltic provinces of Livonia, Esthonia, Ingria and Karelia. There in 1703, in the midst of the swamps on the banks of the Neva, Peter started work on his seaport and new capital, which he named St Petersburg (now Leningrad).

Russia had reached the sea and beside the new city Peter laid out his naval dockyard where, under the supervision of imported naval architects, the first Russian sea-going fleet was born. The channel from St Petersburg to the Gulf of Finland was comparatively shallow, however, and the complementary naval base and seaward defences were constructed at Kronstadt, on Kotlin Island, about 22 miles to the west. By the middle of 1705, the fleet gathered at Kronstadt totalled nine line-of-battle ships, four brigs and 32 smaller vessels including fireships.

With the assistance of the fleet under the command of General Admiral Apraksin, the Russians next swept the Swedes from the southern shores of Finland and took the port of Abo, thus securing Russian dominance in the Gulf of Finland. Peter, who had served at sea as Vice Admiral Peter Mihailoff in the 60-gun battleship *Svataya Ekaterina,* had learned the meaning of sea power and on his death in 1725 he left an organised fleet, possibly brave rather than efficient but able to exercise command throughout the Baltic.

The Russian fleet played only a minor part in the affairs of the next half-century, by which time the throne was occupied by Catherine the Great (Ekaterina II), under whom the fleet first saw service in foreign waters against the Turks in the Levant. In earlier years a number of Scottish officers, including Admirals Gordon and Saunders, had served with the Russian fleet; Catherine also turned to the British navy, upon which the Russian fleet had been modelled, and induced a considerable number of officers to enter the Russian service. At one stage no less than half the Russian Navy List was made up of officers claiming Anglo-Saxon or Celtic birth.

Above: A selection of contemporary Russian warships from a page of 'The Illustrated London News' dated January 6, 1894. *Illustrated London News*

Right: Drawing from 'The Illustrated London News' of March 5, 1904, showing Russian sailors embarking torpedoes on the 'Czarevitch' just before the outbreak of the Russo-Japanese war. *Illustrated London News*

Far right: Kashin-class destroyer at speed in the Atlantic in 1969. Anti-aircraft-role equipped with twin GOA surface to air missiles. *A Greenway*

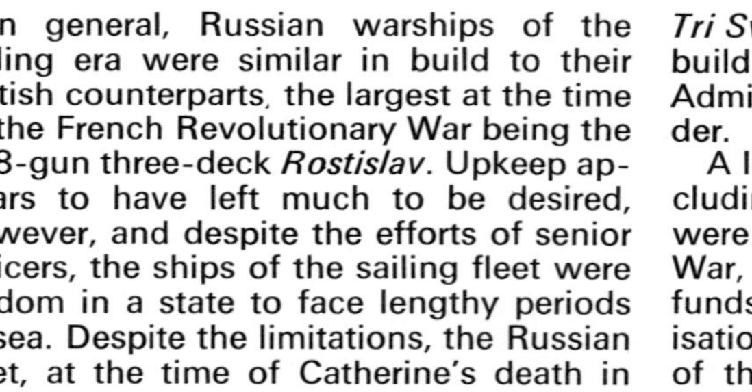

In general, Russian warships of the sailing era were similar in build to their British counterparts, the largest at the time of the French Revolutionary War being the 108-gun three-deck *Rostislav*. Upkeep appears to have left much to be desired, however, and despite the efforts of senior officers, the ships of the sailing fleet were seldom in a state to face lengthy periods at sea. Despite the limitations, the Russian fleet, at the time of Catherine's death in 1796, was second only to the British in material strength.

Following the Congress of Vienna (1815), a series of minor wars brought the Russian fleet to a reasonably high degree of efficiency, although, being built of fir, the active life of the ships seldom exceeded eight years. Thus the powerful fleet 'on paper' could seldom be matched by the number fit for service at sea. In 1853 the navy list included 64 ships of the line and 25 sailing frigates divided between the Baltic and Black Sea fleets but, on Russian admission, only 17 battleships and ten frigates were considered to be fighting fit.

The Russian Navy was slow to adopt steam but in the matter of naval armaments the service was well to the forefront in exploiting new ideas. Shell guns, adopted in 1852, were used effectively in the following year at Sinope, where the Turkish fleet was destroyed in the action which precipitated the Crimean War. The largest vessel present was the 120-gun *Tri Sviatitelia,* a three-decker of traditional build which served as the flagship of Admiral Nahimoff, the Russian commander.

A large number of Russian warships, including many of dubious fighting value, were scuttled in the course of the Crimean War, but once peace had been restored funds were made available for the modernisation of the fleet and for reorganisation of the naval administration. As in other navies, a number of the more modern sailing battleships, of both the Baltic and the Black Sea fleets, were fitted with boilers and low-powered screw engines, sufficient under steam alone for a speed of about six knots. Typical of those vessels was the three-deck 111-gun *Imperator Nikolai I,* launched by the New Admiralty Dockyard at St Petersburg in 1857 and equipped with 600ihp oscillating engines manufactured in England by Humphreys & Tennant. In 1860 the Imperial Navy listed eight such screw battleships, 11 screw frigates, 12 steam corvettes and sundry smaller steamships. There were in addition 12 older sailing battleships but in all probability most of them retained little, if any, value as fighting ships.

In 1860, in the wake of the other European maritime powers, the Russian Navy took the first step towards the acquisition of an ironclad fleet by placing an order with the Thames Iron Works of London for the small iron-hull broadside

armoured frigate *Pervenietz*. Launched towards the end of 1861, she joined the fleet at Kronstadt in August 1863. The *Pervenietz* was followed by a sister, the 3340-ton *Nie Tron Menya*, built to the same drawings by Mitchell & Co at St Petersburg and launched in 1864. The machinery for the later vessel was in fact secondhand, having been first installed in the wooden screw battleship *Konstantin* a decade earlier. Both were distinctive by virtue of prominent ram bows and were rigged as barquentines, although their sailing qualities probably left much to be desired.

Besides building a number of ironclads and small turret ships based on British practice, the Russian Navy took enthusiastically to the American shallow-draught Monitor type for coastal defence in the Baltic. In June 1864, no fewer than ten such vessels were launched, each mounting two smooth-bore 9-inch guns in a central revolving turret. Some years elapsed before all were completed for service.

After the launch at St Petersburg in 1872 of the 9665-ton turret ship *Imperator Peter Veliky*, Russian ironclad battleship development came to a halt for nearly ten years while the navy pursued a new idea—that of the armoured cruiser, envisaged as an iron frigate protected only by an arched armoured deck and a narrow belt on the waterline. The Russian prototype armoured cruiser was named *General Admiral* at her launch in 1873. On a displacement of 4600 tons, she mounted six 8-inch and two 6-inch guns and was protected by a narrow belt of 6-inch iron armour extending the full length of the hull at waterline level. She was given a full ship rig and was capable of 12 knots under steam alone.

In the meantime, with the defence of the shallow Black Sea coast and estuaries in mind, Vice-Admiral A A Popoff took the idea of a broad-beam shallow-draught gunboat to its extreme and designed a circular ironclad. Approval was given for the construction of ten such vessels and the first, named *Novgorod*, was built at St Petersburg, dismantled and taken in sections to Nikolaev on the Black Sea, where she was launched in May 1873. The 2491-ton *Novgorod* mounted two 11-inch guns in a central armoured barbette and was propelled by six horizontal engines, each of 300hp and driving its own screw. She could manage six knots, but in other than slack water directional stability was poor. The low speed proved a handicap and only one other 'Popoffka' was built—the 3550-ton *Vice-Admiral Popoff* launched at Nikolaev in October 1875.

As in other fields of innovation, the Russian Navy was quick to adopt the Whitehead torpedo; in 1881 the Russian was the only fleet using the then large (16-inch) version of the weapon. Early torpedo boats were not very successful, however, and it was not until the navy acquired such vessels as the 64-ton Thornycroft-built *Sokhum* (1883) and the Yarrow-built *Batum* that the torpedo arm merited any real consideration by the command. The early boats were followed by a number of German- (Schichau) and Russian-built craft. Far more noteworthy was the 240-ton *Sokol* completed on the Clyde by Yarrow in 1895. Designed for 29.5 knots, she achieved a world record speed of 30 knots during contractor's sea trials, with engines developing 4039ihp.

Battleship construction was resumed with the *Ekaterina II* and *Tchesma*, launched in 1886 at Nikolaev and Sevastapol respectively for service with the Black Sea fleet. On a displacement of 10,300 tons, they carried six 12-inch guns in three twin mountings within a massive triangular redoubt, two mountings abreast forward and one amidships aft of the main upper deck structure. The secondary battery comprised seven 6-inch guns. In the meantime, construction for service in the Baltic had been concentrated on the armoured cruiser type, including such vessels as the 5796-ton *Vladimir Monomach* (1882), mounting four 8-inch and 12 6-inch guns, and the 7782-ton *Admiral Nahimoff* (1885).

The Russian Navy turned early to the submarine as a means of strengthening the nation's defences. The first such vessel, *Le Diable-Martin*, had been laid down at St Petersburg as far back as 1855 and 20 years later Drzewiecki built two submarines, the second of which was fitted with a primitive periscope. In 1902 the Imperial Navy took delivery of the 60-ton *Petr Kotshka,* an electric battery-driven boat built for service in the Black Sea. By 1906 no fewer than 18 submarines were in service, all but the *Petr Kotshka* being based in the Baltic.

In the space of 200 years, Russia had developed from an almost land-locked inward-looking nation, whose only outlet to the oceans was through Archangel and the White Sea, into an empire embracing territories bordering the Baltic, the Black Sea and the Pacific northward to the Bering Strait. Such were the distances by sea separating its shores, however, that independent fleets had to be maintained, tailored to regional requirements. At the turn of the 19th century, the main fleet was based in the Baltic close to the centre of government at St Petersburg; a smaller fleet, intended primarily for coastal defence in the shallow waters of the Black Sea, was based on Sevastapol in the Crimea. In the Pacific, Russian interests had been served by a small squadron of cruisers and gunboats based on Vladivostok, but after the seizure of Port Arthur in 1898, the Pacific force was strengthened by the addition of battleships as a counter to the threat of Japanese ambitions.

The redeployment of the Russian fleet failed to prevent the disastrous defeat at the hands of the Japanese in 1905; after Tsushima, the Imperial Navy found itself with only a few, mainly obsolescent, ships available for the many tasks required of it. Morale was poor and the situation was not eased by unrest culminating in mutiny in the battleship *Kniaz Potemkin Tavritchesky,* of the Black Sea Fleet. The problems were overcome, however, and reconstruction of the fleet was put in hand as a matter of urgency. The battleships *Andrei Pervosvanni* and *Imperator Pavel I,* under construction at St Petersburg, the *Ievstafi* (State Shipbuilding Yard, Nikolaev) and the *Ioann Zlatoust* (State Shipbuilding Yard, Sevastapol) were altered in the light of experience gained in the war, but it was 1910-11 before they commissioned for service.

All the new ships mounted four 12-inch guns in twin mountings forward and aft and were comparable to the later pre-dreadnought battleships in British and American service. In addition, a number of armoured cruisers were laid down for service with the Baltic fleet, the most outstanding being the 15,000-ton *Rurik* built and engined by Vickers at Barrow, England. Armed with four 10-inch, eight 8-inch and 20 4.7-inch guns, she was well protected and with twin-screw quadruple-expansion machinery developing a total of 20,600hp for 20.5 knots, was probably the best armoured cruiser design developed for any navy.

The destroyer arm of the Imperial Navy comprised a heterogeneous flotilla of boats of British (Yarrow), French (Normand or Forges et Chantiers de la Mediterranée), German (Germania or Schichau) and Russian designs in the Baltic, and others of Yarrow or Laird ancestry in the Black Sea. Between 1912 and 1914, however, orders were placed for 36 boats of Russian construction, evolved from the 1262-ton 36-knot German-designed *Novik* of 1910, mounting four 4.1-inch guns and 12 18-inch torpedo tubes.

The revolution of 1917 resulted in the eclipse of the Russian Navy. The Black Sea fleet was scuttled in June 1918 to prevent its capture by German forces, and allied intervention in the Baltic and the White Sea in 1919-20 resulted in further losses. In February 1918, administration of the navy had been taken over by a Council of Peoples' Commissars for Naval Affairs, but during the immediate post-revolution era there was little available by way of resources to meet either the material or the personnel needs of the fleet. The remaining ships were in urgent need of refit or major repairs and for several years little work had been carried out on vessels under construction. In any event, the Bolshevik government was far too busy with the internal affairs of the nation to spare much thought for the navy and maritime matters.

By 1925, however, conditions had stabilised sufficiently for some thought to be given to the rehabilitation of the potentially serviceable units of the fleet. It included the three Baltic-based dreadnoughts *Oktyabrskaya Revolutsia* (ex-*Gangut*), *Parishskaya Kommuna* (ex-*Sevastapol*) and *Marat* (ex-*Petropavlovsk*), completed in 1914-15 and mounting 12 12-inch guns; the protected cruisers *Komintern* (ex-*Pamiat Merkuria*) and *Aurora*; and 17 destroyers of the *Novik* (renamed *Jacob Sverdlov*) type. There were also about a dozen submarines of the Russian Bubnov and American Holland types. Modernised and refitted, the vessels formed the nucleus of the new Soviet Navy.

The German-designed Novik-class destroyers had proved extremely successful and in the 1930s, the Russians turned once again to foreign expertise for assistance in the design of new ships. The large destroyers of the Leningrad class were inspired by the French contre-torpilleurs of the Le Fantasque class; although they were basically Russian designed, the detailed planning involved a certain amount of French technical advice. In the event, the Leningrad class proved less than satisfactory, being overgunned and poor sea boats. Like the majority of Russian warships, they were fitted for minelaying.

Italian assistance was sought in the design of a new class of cruiser, the first of which was launched as *Kirov* in December 1936. Armed with nine 7.17-inch guns and capable of 35 knots, the *Kirov* was only lightly protected with just a narrow waterline belt of 3-inch armour. Likewise, her endurance was poor compared with that of contemporary British and American cruisers, but set against the short distances involved in the Baltic and Black Sea, range obviously met the Russian naval staff requirement.

In view of the shortcomings of the Leningrad-class destroyers, the Soviet Navy went next to the Italian shipbuilders Odero-Terni-Orlando of Leghorn for a prototype fast destroyer. Delivered without armament in February 1939, the *Tashkent* achieved 44.2 knots on trials and was fitted out at Sevastapol with Russian-manufactured guns of 5.1-inch calibre. Like most Italian-built warships of the period, she proved very lightly built and after a brief career in the Black Sea she was damaged by bombing and subsequently foundered at Novorossisk.

The smaller destroyers of the 1660-ton Gromki (Type VII) class owed their design likewise to Italian influence, but once again poor seakeeping qualities and lightness of build limited their usefulness, particularly in the exacting conditions of the Arctic, where some units were employed on convoy protection. The Silnyi-class (Type VII-U) destroyers, an improved Type VII with the machinery in independent units, followed and altogether 46 vessels (28 Type VII and 18 Type VII-U) were built. The low silhouette of the Silnyi class, with two squat heavily raked funnels, was repeated in later classes and has since become recognised as the classic Soviet destroyer profile.

In 1928, the Russian Navy had salvaged and subsequently recommissioned the former British submarine L55, which had been sunk during operations off Kronstadt in 1919. The vessel was refitted in accordance with Russian ideas and was used as the prototype for a class of about 28 ocean patrol submarines named the L class. They proved particularly successful in service and later improved versions continued to be built for several years. Other submarines of the D, or Dekrabist, class were based on an Italian design and were intended for service in the Black Sea.

The rapid German advance across Russia in 1941 and the early months of 1942 brought all shipbuilding to a halt and, apart from the transfer of a number of obsolescent British and United States warships in 1944, the Soviet Navy had to make do with what it had at the time of the invasion. Much of the wartime service of the navy was in support of the Soviet armies, although in Arctic waters the fleet did co-operate with the other allies to a limited extent in providing protective cover for Russia-bound convoys. After the reversal of German fortunes, the ports were reoccupied by the Soviet Army in 1944 but much reconstruction was necessary before any thought could be given to rebuilding the fleet.

In the immediate post-war period, the Russians learned much concerning German methods of warship construction and the Soviet Navy became independent of the foreign advice upon which designers had relied so heavily in earlier years. In appearance, however, the post-war Sverdlov-class cruisers, the first of which was launched in 1951, still exhibited a marked Italian influence. They were powerful ships, of 15,450 tons displacement, mounting 12 6-inch low-angle guns, 12 3.9-inch anti-aircraft guns and 10 21-inch torpedo tubes, in addition to providing stowage for between 140 and 250 mines. In all, 14 ships of the class were completed by 1960, but it is probable that another four hulls were broken up at Leningrad

Above right: Russian naval ensigns, top to bottom, under Peter the Great, Imperial Russian Navy, Soviet Navy (original), Soviet Navy (from 1935). *J Maber*

Top right: The cruiser 'Czarevitch' at about the turn of the century. *Norsk Sjölartsmuseum Oslo*

Below: Another view of a Riga-class escort frigate in the North Sea in 1970. *A Greenway*

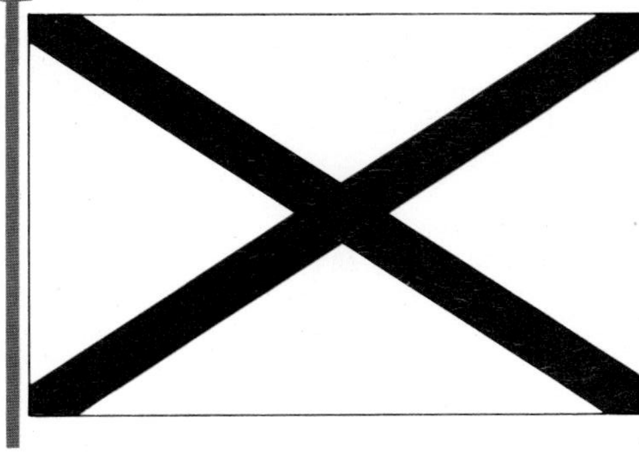

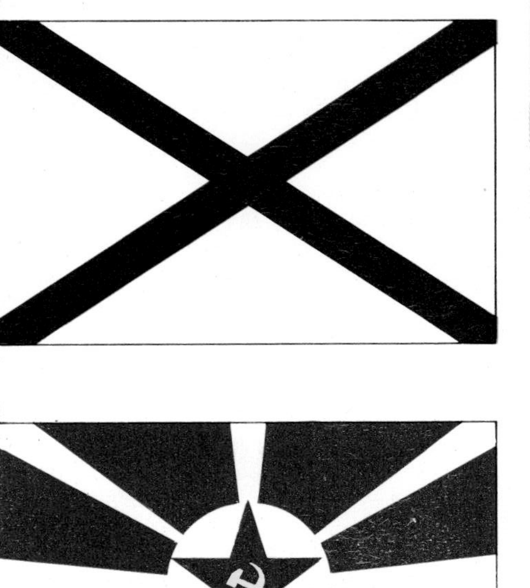

after a change in Soviet naval policy in the 1960s.

At that time, the Soviet Navy's strategic role was primarily defensive and to that end the surface fleet was backed up by a force of more than 400 submarines, many of which were capable of long-range operations against an enemy's commerce. As time passed and experience was gained, however, there came a growing realisation in Soviet governing circles that the fleet was the ideal instrument for the spread of Russian influence among the developing nations. Thus the Soviet Navy turned to a Blue Water policy and the development of an ocean-going fleet capable of lengthy deployment, with its own fleet train of supply and support ships. Soviet leaders, 300 years after Peter the Great had first set the scene, had come to realise the true meaning of sea power.

The results of the change in Russian policy are only too apparent in the advanced design of the 43,000-ton Kiev-class aircraft carriers of which the *Kiev* and the *Minsk* have been completed and commissioned. Apart from a complement of 10 YAK36 (Forger) V/STOL tactical strike/reconnaissance aircraft and around 25 Kemov 25 (Hormone) helicopters, these vessels, with a third possible to be named *Komsomolec*, are armed with a variety of missile systems, anti-submarine torpedoes, close-range guns and weapons.

Far more numerous, however, are the missile-armed cruisers and destroyers which form the nucleus of the Soviet fleets in the Mediterranean and elsewhere. In the absence of official information the several classes are known by their NATO designations. Among the more important in service are the nine ships of the 7500-ton Kresta II-class missile-armed cruisers equipped with SSM, SAM and anti-submarine missile systems in addition to a heavy gun armament, AS torpedoes and a Kemov 25 helicopter. Steam turbine machinery developing 100,000shp gives a speed of 33 knots.

To follow the Kresta II Class, the Soviet Navy embarked on the construction of the 9500-ton gas turbine-engined Kara Class of which at least five units have been identified to date, including the *Nikolaev* which entered fleet service in 1973. These major warships are backed by a variety of missile-armed destroyers of the gas turbine-powered Kashin and Krivaks classes, the steam turbine-powered Kanin, Krupny, Kildin and Kotlin classes and the many older but rearmed vessels.

The Soviet submarine arm comprises about 354 vessels in commission, of which nearly half are nuclear powered, at least 62 of the latter being of the SSBN ballistic missile type. New submarines, of the SSBN and SSN types, are being completed at the rate of about one a month.

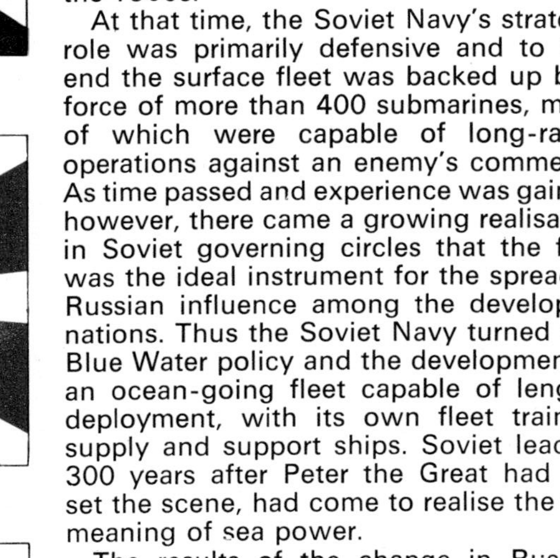

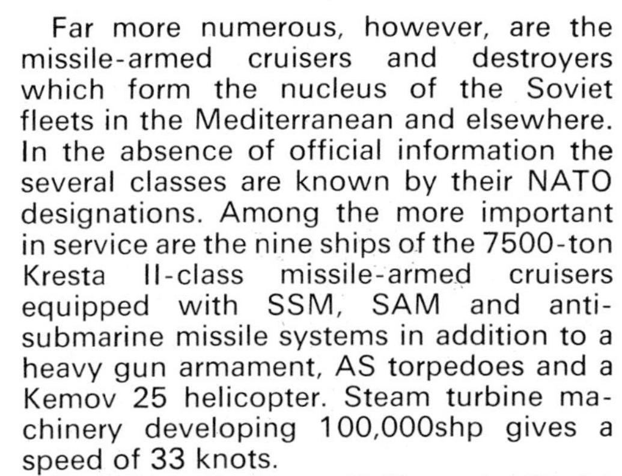

Bulbous bow of the Lubeck-based cargo liner 'Bennekom' alongside at Milwall dock in 1973. *D J Kingston*

8. Commerce and Trade

Hudson's Bay Co Ships

A FEW of the many ships belonging to the world's oldest shipping and trading concern, the Hudson's Bay Company, are featured in these two pages. Hudson's Bay is the oldest active company with a British Royal Charter, and one of the greatest merchant trading companies ever founded.

In the 17th century two French fur traders persuaded Prince Rupert of the Rhine and Charles II that a valuable trade in furs was waiting to be developed from the North American forests with direct access to the waters of Hudson's Bay, rather than by the southern river routes already commandeered by the Dutch and French. Two ships, the *Eaglet* and the *Nonsuch*, sailed for Canada but only the *Nonsuch* made the journey, as the *Eaglet* had to turn back. The cargo of beaver pelts that *Nonsuch* brought back to Britain assured the Royal backers of the venture that it was a success and thereupon King Charles granted a royal charter in 1670.

Side-by-side with trading went exploration and development of Canadian territories and for a time the quest for the North West passage to the Far East was still of importance to the HBC, although it became of less consequence as the company developed its foothold in Canada.

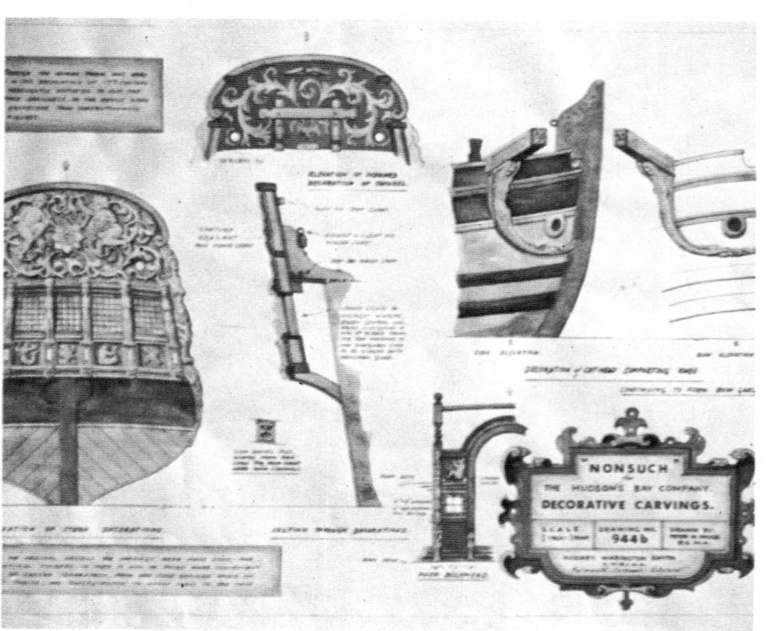

Ships employed by the Hudson's Bay Co to cross the Atlantic varied considerably throughout its long history. The successful ketch, an example of which was *Nonsuch*, was thought to be a useful type because of its size and manoeuvrability. In later years—the 18th century—the company operated brigs, barques and schooners in place of the earlier sloop. Many smaller craft were used for trade, communication and exploration on inland waters and in Hudson Bay itself, including shallops, York boats and canoes.

In 1888 the company acquired its first transatlantic steamer, the barque-rigged ex-whaler *Erik*. In that same year, the steam paddler *Beaver*, which was built in 1834 and was of considerable use to the HBC, the Navy and general explorers, was wrecked at Vancouver harbour entrance. A famous ship which was acquired by the company in the early 20th century was Captain Scott's *Discovery* which took part in the expedition of 1901–4.

There were casualties and heroes among the long line of HBC ships, some fell victim to the severe ice of Arctic waters and were lost such as the *Lady Kindersley* in 1924, the *Baychimo* in 1931, and the *Fort James* in 1937. Two HBC ships, the *Nascopie* and the *Pelican*, claimed the distinction of sinking U-boats in wartime. The days of exploration are over and the ships of the Hudson's Bay Co no longer ply the Atlantic with animal pelts, although the company is still foremost in fur trading today, and memories of its illustrious past live on through the replica of the ketch *Nonsuch*, built for the company at Appledore in Devon, and Scott's *Discovery*, now about to be restored by the British Maritime Trust.

Top: A painting by Peter M Wood of the Hudson's Bay Company pioneer ship 'Nonsuch'.

Centre: A selection of decorative carvings of the 'Nonsuch'. *P M Wood*

Right: A Laurence Dunn painting of the HBC ship 'Baychimo'—the 'will o' the wisp of the Arctic'— adrift with the ice.

Above: Engraving from a February 1849 issue of 'The Illustrated London News' depicting Fort George on the Columbia River, site of the Hudson's Bay Company's establishment.
Illustrated London News

Left: The bow of the replica of 'Nonsuch' at Appledore in Devon in 1968. *P M Wood*

Below: Sailing ships of the Hudson's Bay Co leaving Gravesend in June 1845.
Illustrated London News

THE EAST INDIA

IT WAS all due to spices, those very necessary peppers, cloves, nutmegs, ginger and the rest of the fragrances from the East. The Lord Mayor of London, Sir Stephen Soame, in September 1569 presided over a meeting of worried merchants to discuss the soaring prices. They had come to decide what action they should take in the face of the crippling Dutch monopoly. There and then it was agreed to form a company, the Company of London Merchants trading to the East Indies, and to acquire ships at once.

Although it was to take many years to reach full stature, no-one could have guessed that they had taken the first steps to bring into being a mercantile empire which would last more than 250 years and cover an entire sub-continent, with its own jurisdiction, its own army and above all, its own great fleet.

The aged Queen Elizabeth granted a Charter in December of 1600 to George, Earl of Cumberland, 215 knights, aldermen and merchants with rights in the East Indian seas, renewable after 15 years. Its area was not stinted; it applied to 'all parts and places in Asia, Africa and America between Cape Cod and the Strait of Magellan'.

There were other East India Companies in Europe of varying scope and duration from time to time; they were Russian, French, Danish, Swedish, Scottish and Belgian—and a rival English one until it was merged. One or two of them were competitors to some extent, but none could compete with the Dutch East Indian Company in its firm grip of the spice trade in Indonesia and the Moluccas. They were the first Europeans to arrive as merchants in Java and Sumatra and although there were 15 separate concerns, in 1664 they all merged into a single company which worked hand in glove with the Dutch Government.

Far left: The Danish ship 'Henriette' for the Far East trade passing the Mandarin fort of Bocca Tigris. *Kronborg Museum Denmark*

Below left: The clipper 'Titania'; clippers engaged in the tea trade for a few years before the demise of the British East India Company. *P M Wood*

Left: A model of the 'Slesvig' launched in 1725 and sold to the Danish East India company eight years later. *Naval Museum Copenhagen*

Below: A painting by M J Barton of a typical Dutch East Indiaman.

The Court of Governors of the English Company had not waited for their Charter but had at once bought five ships in the Thames, including a remarkably stout vessel with the odd name of *Malice Scorned*, which was changed to *Red Dragon*. While other vessels of the company were searching in vain for the elusive North-West Passage, she and three smaller ships set off, in 1601, down the Thames with all the bravery of flags and streamers and the blaring of trumpets. They were bound for the East Indies by way of the Cape of Good Hope led by the 'Generall of the Flete', Sir James Lancaster, a successful navigator who gave his name to Lancaster Sound, in the Arctic, with John Davis, who gave his name to Davis Strait in the same area.

COMPANIES

The *Red Dragon* mounted 36 guns and her consorts had 24 guns each. They carried 15 factors, who were to set up trading stations, seven 'volunteer factors', five pursers and a surgeon, with a single parson for all hands. In their holds were iron, lead, tin and cloths as trade goods, with presents for 'Indian princes' valued at £15,000.

On the southward voyage they chased and captured two Portuguese caravels but then scurvy appeared, so that the merchants and factors had to take the helm or climb the mast to take in topsails 'as the common mariners do'. The squadron straggled into Table Bay, where Lancaster took his sick people ashore to recuperate under canvas with fresh fruit and 'bottles of the juice of lemons'.

With some men recovered, he got under way again, sailing first to the Nicobar Islands and then to Sumatra where, to his surprise, he was welcomed by the Dutch factors. At Achen, with much display and parading, Lancaster delighted the native 'King', made terms with him and left two factors to collect cargoes of pepper. Then, sailing on, he captured another Portuguese caravel, one that was so heavily laden that it took six days to tranship her cargo.

452 THE ILLUSTRATED LONDON NEWS Oct. 26, 1867

UNLOADING TEA-SHIPS IN THE EAST INDIA DOCKS.

Above: A page from 'The Illustrated London News' of October 26, 1867, showing the unloading of tea ships in the London East India Docks. *Illustrated London News*

His return to England would have been a triumph but for the deaths of 180 men out of a total of 480 men in the squadron, due almost wholly to the scurvy. It did not deter a second voyage which, although one ship was lost in a storm while homeward bound, made a profit of 100 per cent. On a third voyage in which English ships for the first time traded at Surat, near Bombay, the profit mounted to 234 per cent.

But a change was coming; Amsterdam sent out a Governor-general who made it clear that English factors were encroaching on Dutch trade that had been flourishing for years before they arrived. The factors received such threatening treatment that King James, in 1617, was persuaded to send a punitive force under Sir Thomas Dale who, as a warning, captured a Dutch Indiaman with her cargo of pepper in the crowded port of Batavia. In retaliation, the Dutch Governor sacked two English ships and burnt down an English factory. Matters deteriorated until the massacre, in 1623, of Amboyna, in the Moluccas and the forced withdrawal of Englishmen from Java and Sumatra and the various islands round about.

In 1611, a Captain Saris made a daring voyage with three ships to the almost unknown waters of eastern Japan and at Hirado, near Nagasaki, he set up a factory. After nearly a year he returned to England and reported a profit of 218 per cent on his voyage, but the hostility of the Portuguese missionaries spoilt the prospect of regular trade with Japan for another century. It was much the same story with China and the stream of silks and porcelain, tea and lacquer-ware had to wait. However, in 1612 Captain Best sailed from Gravesend with the *Red Dragon* and the *Hoesander* to Surat, near Bombay where he met four rival Portuguese and beat them in fair fight. Then he proceeded to establish factories and trading posts in the area. It was the beginning of the end for Portuguese expansion in India and the start of an ever-increasing English trade.

At that period, the British East India Company normally had about 30 ships in use. It found that the prospective sellers were in a price-ring, demanding for their ships as much as £45 a ton. The controlling body promptly leased a dock at Deptford and built its own vessels at a cost of not more than £10 a ton. Later, finding honest owners, they were able to hire ships again, adopting a peculiar practice known as 'hereditary bottoms'. Under that contract, as the average East Indiaman lasted for not more than three voyages, the owner, when his ship was worn out, could substitute a new one for her.

The Deptford dock was soon given up and others were dug at Woolwich and Blackwall for repairing and refitting. Attached to the dockyards were a barber-surgeon and his deputy whose chief responsibility it was to see to the health and wellbeing of all the company's servants in ships at anchor or in the dockyards. It entailed trimming the hair of sailors, caulkers, carpenters and labourers once every 40 days at a cost to each man of 2d a month. There is on record a complaint that 'idle fellows under a pretence to be trimmed come into the chirguns house and there lyeth three or four at a tyme an hower together'.

The Indiaman, English and Dutch, was built to look like a warship as far as practicable and she usually had a lower tier of dummy gunports along her sides. The Indian Ocean was notorious for its pirates and for privateers, as well as French and Dutch men-of-war at different periods. They all hoped to capture a fat East Indiaman (the 'fat' referring to the ship's breadth of beam as well probably as to her cargo). The company's blackest year was in 1808 when 10 homeward-bound ships were lost in a fierce storm and a number of others fell into enemy hands, blew up, or caught fire at sea.

A few years earlier the Admiralty, hard pressed for ships, bought 14 Indiamen, gave them more guns and added them to the RN fleet as ships of the line. The company's ships and those of its own private navy, originally named the Bombay Marine, always copied the routine and customs of the Royal Navy, but the captain of an Indiaman was in a class by himself. He was a grand personage indeed, especially in the later days. After making a couple of voyages as a mate, he could purchase his captaincy with a good round sum. Then he would receive a 13-gun salute when he went ashore in India and the guard turned out in his honour.

But they were only symbols; more tangible was the £500 rent for his spacious cabin and roundhouse to some wealthy passenger and the special food, at a price. Yet the main items were the 'indulgencies', his private trading with the $56\frac{1}{2}$ of the 97 tons allowed to captains and officers when outward bound. One captain estimated his total gains in three voyages of 18 months each as upwards of £18,300. More than one landed estate came from those indulgencies.

Passengers, if naval or military or in the service of the company, travelled free, but not their wives or other womenfolk. Their servants' charges were graded according to the rank of their master or mistress and varied from £200 for a general's man down to £70 for a lady's companion or maid. Since the voyage was likely to take at least half a year, it was customary for the passenger of means to send on board enough furniture for his own comfort. He would hope to sell it to the next cabin occupant at the end of the voyage, or alternatively, to buy whatever the previous occupant might have left.

There is the account of the three daughters of a Mr Peter Cherry, who were to join him in India. They were berthed in one-half of the roundhouse and they had brought with them, in addition to other articles, a piano, a harp with candles, three small bureaux and three sofas which were converted at night into couches, a wash-handstand and a foot-tub. Every endeavour was made to protect the ladies from seeing from their window 'nothing so indelicate, indeed so indecent as anything being towed overboard or being hung out to dry'.

Perhaps showing still more optimism was the father who, with his eye set on rajahs or at the least, regimental officers, took out all his six daughters.

They are only small items from the vast story of the conditions on board a splendid great Indiaman in the last few years before the political power of the company ended in 1858. The government of the Indian Empire was absorbed in the British Crown and in 1874, after 268 years, the Honourable East India Company ceased to exist.

OPENING UP THE CHINA TRADE

IN THE LATE 18th century, when East met West in the form of the haughty isolationist Chinese versus the ruthless profit-seeking merchants of Europe, the encounter was the typically violent one of two cultures with not a scrap of mutual understanding between them. Many years later, when Rudyard Kipling wrote that 'East is East and West is West, and never the twain shall meet', he had that example before him to prove his point.

At the root of the conflict lay the complete inability of the Chinese to treat Europeans as anything but barbarian vassals of their Celestial Emperor, and their imposition on merchants who came to trade were of a weight of restriction and indignity that eventually proved unbearable. The foreigners were refused a fixed tariff, were bound by Chinese laws and Chinese law courts which could only be hostile to them, and after 1760 were allowed to trade only through Canton, and only through the officially designated group of middlemen named the Co-hong.

Under Co-hong rules, no foreign ship was allowed to enter Canton unless a Co-hong merchant agreed to serve as security and guarantee that the foreigners would pay all their dues and behave themselves. Conversely, the Co-hong merchants, who numbered between four and 13 at various

Above: Engraving from 'The Illustrated London News' of July 8, 1843, depicting an opium clipper getting under way, with a smuggling boat, oars at the ready, in the foreground. *Illustrated London News*

Below: The East India company steamship 'Nemesis' destroying Chinese war junks in Anson's Bay in January 1841. *Parker Gallery*

times, were the only merchants allowed to sell Chinese tea and silk to foreign traders.

For those dubious favours, the foreigners had to endure continual taunts and insults from the Cantonese who, like their emperor, regarded them as evil foreign devils, and they were forced also to keep the palms of venal officials liberally crossed with silver.

Nevertheless, where there were fortunes to be made, personal irritations and discomforts could be swallowed, at least for a while, and the China market was extremely lucrative, even under such severely limited conditions. By the end of the 18th century the British East India Company's strong well-armed East Indiamen, displacing up to 1500 tons each, were bringing in over 220 tons of tea in their holds on each China-India run. In the other direction, there was a considerable rise in China's imports of British woollens and metals, which stood at a value of £99,113 in 1775 and grew to £590,775 in 1786 and £1,321,813 in 1803.

Pandering to the quirks of the supercilious Chinese could not, however, continue for very long once the foreigners became convinced that they were being excluded from tapping little more than the tip of what they were certain was a colossal commercial iceberg. One market upon which the British cast particularly interested eyes was the north of China, where it was believed that millions of customers awaited British woollens. Before long the Portuguese, the Dutch and the British decided that they wanted front-door treatment; they were tired of doing business through the tradesman's entrance and wanted a proper footing for their commerce, with free trading on the basis of equality and agreed trading ports.

The British also desired an officially acknowledged British ambassador in Peking; to press their suit they sent missions to the Chinese Emperor in 1793 and 1816. The Dutch and Portuguese did likewise, but all were refused in the same arrogant fashion. The answer received by Lord George Macartney, Britain's emissary in 1793, was typical.

'As your Ambassador can see for himself, we possess all things,' the Chinese Emperor Ch'ien-lung informed George III. 'The productions of our Empire are manifold and in great abundance; nor do we stand in the least need of the produce of other countries . . .' The Co-hong system, which the Emperor had permitted 'as a signal mark of favour' was quite sufficient for the purchase of the Chinese tea, silks and porcelain which the 'foreign devils' appeared to crave so much, and to allow foreign trade anywhere apart from Canton would simply encourage 'other nations (to) imitate your evil example and beseech us to present them with a site for trading'.

George III was flabbergasted to discover that Ch'ien-lung regarded him as a lowly vassal, and saw the samples of British manufacture which Macartney had taken to show him as items of tribute. The foreign merchants were furious and frustrated, all the more so because Ch'ien-lung had been quite right to suppose that the Chinese economy was self-sufficient. Between 1792 and 1809, for instance, China exported twice as much as she imported.

However, despite their suppliant status, the British had one supreme advantage they could exploit—the fact that they could offer enormous quantities of opium grown on East India Company land in Bengal to a growing number of Chinese addicts. The idea was first mooted in 1767 at a meeting of the East India Company in Calcutta, but it was not until 1794 that Indian opium began to shift the balance of the China trade in favour of foreigners. In that year, an East India Company opium freighter anchored offshore at Whampoa, 13 miles down river from Canton, and remained there for a year supplying opium to smugglers. That preliminary probe was an encouraging success and in the years that followed the illegal opium trade through Whampoa, and also through Portuguese-leased Macao on the other side of Canton, burgeoned into soaring profits for the traders and a matching rate of addiction among the Chinese.

As more and more Chinese fell under the soporific spell of opium, and more and more officials succumbed to foreign bribes and inducements, the Chinese authorities fumed and fulminated, issuing fierce decrees threatening to annihilate any foreign opium ship by means of 'dragons of war . . . with their fiery discharges'. No-one took any notice, and the opium trade continued unabated. The Chinese war junks were toothless dragons, in any case, for their crews were well aware of the deadly firepower of foreign ships and kept their own craft a safe distance from the scene of opium-smuggling operations.

By 1821, when the opium trade moved from Whampoa and Macao to Lintin Island at the mouth of the Canton River, a well-tried procedure was already established for getting the contraband ashore.

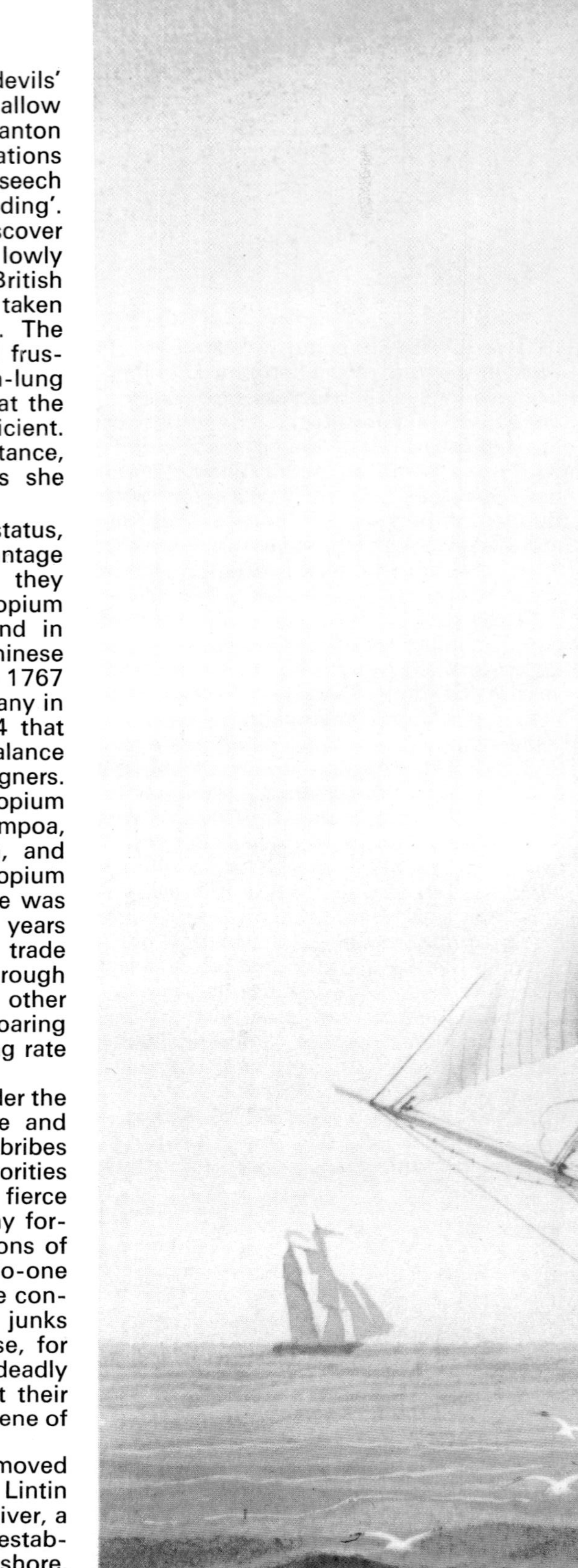

The opium ships offloaded their cargoes on to armed hulks which acted as floating depots, and from which the opium was handed on into the holds of the speedy 'scrambling dragons', the name given to galleys armed with cannon and grappling irons which ferried the opium ashore. Often, they took their cargoes to Canton, 40 miles upriver, where British, French, Dutch and American trading stations were located on a quarter-mile stretch of waterfront to the north of the city. After 1829 the opium runs were refined still further, when speedy manoeuvrable clippers took over the trade and made better time with more certain success against the strong coastal headwinds that blew up the Chinese coast to Canton.

As time went on, the statistics of opium sales rocketed. In 1796, the number of 125lb-140lb opium chests leaving Calcutta, where the East India Company sold them by auction, stood at 1070. By 1835, the year after the company lost its monopoly of the China trade, the number had increased to 12,977. Over roughly the same period, the Calcutta auctions brought the East India Company an average profit of 465 per cent and in 1831, the House of Commons was told that 'the monopoly of opium in Bengal supplies the government with a revenue amounting to £981,293 per annum . . .' That was, of course, in addition to legal British imports into Canton, which in 1834 were valued at £1,345,523.

In money terms, the opium traffic, though officially illegal, was a splendid success. In human terms, opium was ravaging its victims at a horrifying rate; by the early 1840s the number of addicts in China was nearing the 12 million mark. The Chinese Government, frantic to stop the spread of the pernicious habit which was doping and debilitating so many of the emperor's subjects, tried to fight it with propaganda, with executions of opium dealers and with the seizure of a few opium clippers. Such actions proved puny weapons and it was not until 1839 that the anxious authorities discovered the one means which gave them hope of success; it was that rarity among Chinese officials, an unbribable civil servant.

The official in question, the puritanical Lin Tse-hsu, set about his plan to exorcise the opium evil in high-handed forceful fashion. He arrived in Canton on March 10, 1839, and within three months had confiscated 20,283 chests of opium worth £2 million. During the first three weeks of June it was all destroyed by melting it down to a stinking black mass and tipping it into the Canton River. The foreigners in Canton, whom Lin had declared hostages

Far left: Red lacquer throne specially made for the Chinese Emperor Ch'ien-lung (1736-95); it was an example of priceless Chinese treasures shipped out by early traders. *Illustrated London News*

Left: East Indiaman 'Lord Lowther' leaving Prince of Wales Island (Penang), from a painting by W J Huggins. *Parker Gallery*

Above: A painting by M Barton of 'Red Rover', an early opium clipper.

for the opium, were then made hostages for British agreement to stop making opium and to withdraw from the opium trade.

It was at that point that the Chinese first began to realise the true nature of the foreigners they so disdained, for the upshot of Lin's arbitrary actions in Canton, and the outrage they caused in Britain, was war. On June 21, 1840, a force of 20 British warships, carrying 4000 troops, arrived off Macao, sailed up the coast to Chusan Island and plastered the port of Ting-hai to a mass of rubble with broadsides from 15 of its ships. Then, in January 1841, after six months of sporadic fighting during which the British occupied Chusan, the warships began to blast a way up the Canton River, landing raiding parties at intervals to occupy the forts that lined the river banks, and finally bringing Canton within reach of its guns in May. One of the British ships, a powerful paddle-steamer, appropriately *Nemesis*, caused near-panic among Chinese sailors whose archaic junks were in no state to challenge it.

Canton was saved from certain destruction when the British accepted a Chinese bribe of £600,000, but nothing could save the towns in the path of the British advance towards Peking that started in August. Chen-nai and Ningpo were looted; Chepai, south of Shanghai, was set on fire; Shanghai itself fell in June 1842; and Chinkiang in July.

The Chinese were totally helpless before the inexorable show of British armed force, and the grossly one-sided conflict ended with the Treaty of Nanking signed on August 29, 1842. It was the turn of the Chinese to be humiliated. At Nanking the Emperor was forced to allow five 'treaty' ports to be opened at Canton, Amoy, Foochow, Swatow and Shanghai, to cede the island of Hong Kong to the British as a base for protecting their trade, to abolish the Co-hong system, to agree to pay an indemnity of £2 million, and to fix a tariff of five per cent ad valorem. Worse was to come, for other Europeans, perceiving that the British had at long last cracked the barrier of Chinese isolationism, scrambled for pickings. After 1844 the French, the Americans, the Belgians and the Swedes were all granted trading treaties, although a supplementary pact of 1843, the Treaty of the Bogue, reserved 'most favoured nation' treatment for Britain.

Nor did the long-dreaded foreign intrusion end there. By 1849 the British, Americans and French had all been granted consular courts and exclusive settlements for their nationals. By 1850 foreign merchants were operating the trade in tea and silks which, a century before, had been in the hands of little more than a dozen British East India Company supercargo passengers. The opium trade boomed again, soaring from 2000 tons in 1843 towards the 5000-ton mark it reached by 1866. Addiction soared with it, until by the mid-1860s it was reckoned that only one Cantonese out of 10, and only two inhabitants out of 10 in Fukien Province had managed to remain unhooked.

The Chinese, rammed down into such depths of degradation, seethed with fury and resentment; what had formerly been plain straightforward hatred for the foreigner grew into a mood of malevolent loathing. Not unnaturally, it created an unhealthy atmosphere of tension and suspicion which made European merchants feel less and less secure in their gains, and more and more prone to demand greater concessions and further safeguards for their interests.

The camel's back broke over a very paltry straw. On October 8, 1856, Imperial Commissioner Yeh of Canton ordered the seizure of the lorcha—a European-shaped Chinese-rigged vessel—named *Arrow*; she was old and barely serviceable and had long since ceased to appear on Lloyd's Register. The British captain and Chinese crew were flung into prison, where several of them died. The incident was unremarkable in itself, but prodded on by the French, who were outraged over the recent murder of a French priest in Kwangsi, the pugnaciously patriotic British Prime Minister, Lord Palmerston, turned the *Arrow* affair into an insult to the flag and a clamour for vengeance.

When the resultant Anglo-French demands reached the Chinese Emperor, it transpired that the British intended to gain far more than mere compensation for the loss of a near-hulk and the sufferings of its crew. What they wanted was the establishment of foreign legations at the imperial court, extra-territorial rights granting Europeans immunity throughout China, regulation of the opium trade and more treaty ports. It was too much. The Emperor demurred, and the inevitably violent sequel

was the Second Opium War, in which Anglo-French forces bombarded the Taku forts, which guarded the approaches to Peking, destroyed the emperor's Summer Palace and occupied his capital.

When the Emperor finally yielded in 1860, it was on even harsher terms than the ones he had rejected. He was obliged to accept them, and also to agree that Tientsin, the harbour of Pekin, should become a treaty port in order to safeguard access to the foreign legation quarter in the capital. Hong Kong was to be enlarged to include the mainland suburb of Kowloon and the treaty powers extracted a very large indemnity.

The long-term results were that Britons and other foreigners were able to transform China through commercial, moral, technical and religious influences exerted from a privileged protected position. That included, of course, a vigorous flowering of business enterprise in China, with merchants treating the country that was now prostrate before them as a milch-cow, to be milked to the last drop. As a result, the value of opium imports into China rose from 20,946 Hong Kong taels (1754lb of silver) in 1868, to 42,192 HK taels (3533lb) in 1913. Cotton goods rose even more pronouncedly, from values of 18,351 HK taels (1536lb) in 1868 to 110,041 HK taels (9215lb) in 1913. Tea exports from China, worth 33,262 HK taels (2785lb) in 1868, were much the same in 1913, but silk and silk goods rose from a value of 24,544 HK taels (2055lb) to 102,036 HK taels (8545lb).

As trade expanded, Shanghai and Hong Kong, the best of the treaty ports, blossomed as monuments to European effort, on the foundations laid after the First Opium War of 1839-42 as a stepping stone to great commercial lustre.

At Shanghai, where foreign trade opened on November 17, 1843, British imports stood at £500,000 in 1844 and £1,082,207 in 1845. Ten years later, the American firm of Russell & Co pioneered a steamship service between Shanghai and Hong Kong, and in 1862, Russell became managing agents for the newly constituted Shanghai Steam Navigation Company. The new venture helped promote the rise of Hankow to the status of an important inland tea market. Within a few years, Shanghai became the terminal port of the coasting trade and dominated the commerce of the entire 3200-mile Yangtse basin, with the export market in tea and silks and the import market in opium and other European products passing in lucrative quantities through its fine deep-water harbour.

Hong Kong, which also possessed a superb harbour, was converted by its British lessees from a barren unproductive island wasteland into a thriving trading centre, with stone warehouses, jetties, wharves, hotels, a market and a town two miles long which in 1843 had a population of 15,000. Already, Hong Kong had emerged as a rich and busy centre of distribution. In 1844, 20 ships carried over 68,000 tons of British goods from Hong Kong to Shanghai, 96 lorchas totalling 5774 tons took cotton and woollen goods to Canton, and 60 ships of a total of 26,937 tons arrived from Britain loaded with merchandise. After the Second Opium War of 1856-60 Hong Kong became a major ocean junction for steamships and an important focus for banking and mail distribution.

Europeans naturally claimed the cream of the Hong Kong and Shanghai trade, as well as that of Canton, Nanking and other Chinese ports, and a similar monopoly was established at Macao, which the Chinese reluctantly recognised as Portuguese territory in 1887. Towards the end of the century the rapacious Europeans were joined by a new and energetic force in the world, the recently westernised and industrialised Japan. As well as acquiring Western ways and Western methods, the Japanese had also acquired the Western taste for territorial conquest. In 1894 they cast covetous eyes on Korea, which was a semi-vassal state of China, and on August 1 declared war. The conflict was brief and, for the third time in 50 years, it ended in an overwhelming Chinese defeat. By the Treaty of Shimonoseki signed on April 17, 1895, Korea was declared independent—a temporary status as far as the Japanese were concerned—and Japan was awarded Formosa, the Pescadores Islands, the Liaotung peninsula in Manchuria, and the promise of a European-style trading treaty.

Japan's success promoted yet another scramble for yet more pickings among the other foreign powers already established in China, a scramble which approached very close to partition of the country. In 1900, when the maddened Chinese reacted with the hideous barbarities of the anti-foreign Boxer Rebellion, it was already far too late for Imperial China to reverse the irresistible foreign tide. The Boxers gave the foreign devils in Peking 55 days of terror and peril besieged in their legation quarter, but they totally failed to achieve the object which one of their slogans expressed as 'Protect the country! Destroy the foreigners!'

In the event, the foreigners remained, still sheltered by their special status, for more than 40 years. On the other hand, the Imperial China the Boxers knew, disrupted by foreign exploitation and ruined by its own corrupt ineptitude, collapsed in 1912, in less than a quarter of that time. Nearly 40 more years of unrest, anarchy and war ensued before it fell to the Communist People's Republic of China to begin, in 1949, to repair the damage, patch up Chinese pride, and help push East and West apart in ways Kipling never imagined.

Top: Shanghai in 1850; the Bund, or waterfront, of the international settlement as it appeared eight years after the city had opened to foreign trade. *Illustrated London News*

Centre left: The process of welding a coil for a gun in the Shanghai arsenal in 1883 in preparation for possible French/Chinese conflict in Tonking. *Illustrated London News*

Above left: Chinese officers hauling down the British flag on the 'Arrow' after it had been captured on the orders of Imperial Commissioner Yeh of Canton in October 1856. *Cassels History of England (K Robins Collection)*

Above: The opium clipper 'Wild Dayrell', built in Cowes for the Hong Kong firm of Dent & Co. *Illustrated London News*

GUANO &

ETERNALLY COATED with ice and snow, that most savage area of Cape Horn, name of ill omen, is the last rocky outcrop of the South American continent. Only the most hard-bitten of navigators would dare to brave the bitter seas to the south of Tierra del Fuego, the Land of Fire, but once Magellan had made the great discovery of the passage through the strait named after him seafarers began to work their way through it from the Atlantic into the Pacific. They faced 330 tortuous miles of foul winds, cross-currents and many a reef and shoal but some won through, chart or no chart. Among them were several famous names, with Drake's to lead them—Cavendish, Simon des Cordes, Admiral Anson, John Davis, Captain Cook and, in Victorian times, old Joshua Slocum.

Some time in the early days of the 18th century, with the aid of better navigational equipment and well-built ships it became practical to round the Horn in preference to struggling through the Strait of Magellan. A little later, small sturdy barques from the ports of South Wales began to round the Horn carrying coal for Chile. In return they loaded copper ore brought on the backs of llamas from the mines in the hinterland of Peru.

The Welshmen were forerunners, but they were not so very far from the first ships which voyaged to collect guano from the islands on the west coast of South America. The guano trade started in a very small way, but it grew rapidly as shipowners realised how profitable it could become. But guano, though lucrative to owners, was far from being a popular cargo, welcome though it might be to European agriculturalists and their impoverished soils. The deep product of many generations of sea-birds' droppings, it usually had to be hacked out from the rocks of Chilean or Peruvian islands by ships' crews and ferried out to their vessels lying off the coast. In addition to the labour involved with the sacks and at the oars, it had a highly unpleasant habit of spreading a layer of yellow dust over everything and everybody within range.

However unpopular it was, ships of various nationalities and sizes were still entering the guano trade when they were eclipsed by a new type of vessel and a more profitable type of trade—the nitrate clipper. In 1867 the German shipping firm of Ferdinand and Carl Laeisz, father and son, bought half-a-dozen German-built wooden barques based at Valparaiso; it was a portent for the future. The father died but the son carried on, buying good ships to carry nitrate. First he had ordered vessels of 985 tons from a Dutch builder. Then, expanding as no shipping line has never done before or since, he built ships himself and he bought ships, some from Holland and France but most from British yards. One and all, those he bought and those he built were given names beginning with P—*Potosi* and *Pluto*, *Pamir* and *Padua*—and they became famous as the 'Flying Ps'.

The closest parallel to the Laeisz nitrate fleet was the French firm of Antonin Dominique (known as Ant Dom Bordes fils). In 1868 Bordes began buying sailing ships and within a couple of years 13 barques had been acquired from British yards. They were smallish craft, as the nitrate business was then in its infancy and bigger ships had difficulty in filling their holds for the homeward voyage.

Britain at that period was selling and building for sale quite a host of ships to the European mainland and on the death of Bordes senior his sons launched out still more in swelling the fleet and increasing the size of new ships to match the growth of the

Far left: **The five-masted 3784-ton 'France' built in 1890 for the company Ant Dom Bordes & Fils.** *Science Museum London (photo D Rudkin)*

Far left below: The former nitrate carrier, the barque 'Pamir' arriving at Falmouth in October 1949 after a 127-day voyage from Australia. The vessel was lost on an Atlantic voyage in 1957. *Illustrated London News*

Left: Painting by M Barton of nitrate clippers off Valparaiso in Chile.

Below: The Chilean nitrate port of Pisagua, as sketched by Melton Prior. *Illustrated London News*

Bottom: The German five-masted ship 'Preussen'. *C A Lokie*

NITRATE

trade. After they had ordered big iron and steel four-masted barques from English and Scottish shipyards they went further and had a five-master built in Scotland in 1890. Named the *France*, she was square-rigged on all her masts, with a length of 361 feet, a beam of 48 feet nine inches and a tonnage of 3800. Her sail area amounted to 49,000 square feet.

A novel feature to speed cargo handling was the four steam winches for each of the hatches; on one occasion she discharged 5000 tons of coal at the port of Iquique and took on board 5500 tons of nitrate in 11 days. In 1901 she was sailing for Valparaiso with a cargo of Tyne coal when she disappeared. Two months later another vessel sighted her deserted and lying on her beam-ends, being swept by the seas. What had happened in those Cape Horn waters could only be guessed, but she had the reputation of being crank, liable to capsize if carrying too much sail.

The Laiesz brothers also owned a five-masted square-rigged ship, the mighty *Preussen*, which was built in Germany. She was much bigger than the *France*, being 72 feet longer and having a tonnage of 5081, with metal masts and spars and shrouds of wire.

Launched in the year after the *France* was lost, she made 12 voyages to Chile with nitrate and one on charter with case-oil to Japan. One foggy night in October 1910, while sailing down-Channel under full sail, her mate sighted the Newhaven-Dieppe steamer crossing her bows on an inevitable collision course. The *Preussen* was struck out of control but escaped any damage below water. However, a rising wind was reaching gale force and she was drifting dangerously near the Dover cliffs. Her captain dropped the anchors but they dragged. Twelve tugs that came out to help could do nothing and the great ship drove ashore and ended by becoming a total wreck. Fortunately, no lives were lost.

A list compiled of all the nitrate vessels that were lost by misadventure or stress of weather would be a lengthy one indeed and it would by no means be confined to losses at sea. There was case after case of ships being destroyed by fire as they lay at anchor in a west coast roadstead. Nitrate is highly flammable if not packed thoroughly dry, and the ships were largely built of wood in the great days of the trade. Nitrate had another peculiarity, though a more welcome one; it had a lethal effect on rats, mice and other vermin on board—but it was equally harmful to the ship's cat.

The trade had its own special trouble for navigators heading northward along the South American west coast. Many a ship in

trying to make a particular roadstead was carried by wind and current far enough to leeward to double the length of passage. The barque *Lindisfarne*, for instance, when bound for Antofagasta, in northern Chile, from Australia in 1909 was forced to sail north-westward 1300 miles. She was not a solitary sufferer. Only a year previously another barque, the *Hougomont*, also from Australia, left Coquimbo, not far north of Valparaiso, for Tocopilla, which is about the same distance to the south of Iquique. Swept past the anchorage, she was carried 400 miles to the northward. One such voyage was enough for her captain. He threw

Above: Painting by Peter Wood of the French nitrate barque 'Valparaiso'; built at Dunkirk in 1902, she was operating until 1928.

Below: The four-masted barque 'Hougomont' as painted by Peter Wood.

in his hand, tore up his charter and sailed back to Australia.

At the height of the nitrate trade, while the smaller vessels unloaded their coal or other cargoes in the lesser roadsteads up the coast, Valparaiso was a forest of masts; between 40 and 60 clippers are said to have crowded in the port together. In their holds they had brought a variety of goods from cloths to machinery, but generally coal. At their gaffs flew the flags of half-a-dozen or more European nations with Germany, France and Italy well to the fore but with British ships still the largest number.

One of the hazards faced by traders with Chile and Peru was occasional earthquakes, usually followed by tidal waves of varying degrees of violence. The port of Iquique was almost completely destroyed by earthquake, fire and tidal waves in 1866 and again in 1877. In 1873 Valparaiso was severely shaken by an earthquake and two or three ships were wrecked. In the far more violent one of 1906 (the highest intensity ever recorded) much of the town was reduced to rubble, but of the 27 ships in the port—British, German, Italian and a solitary American—not one was damaged.

Nitrate seamen were evidently a fraternity with traditions of their own. The late Basil Lubbock has given a first-hand account of their international 'ceremony of the last bag' that took place in Chilean ports when a vessel was about to sail with a full cargo. As the final sack of nitrate was passed over the rail the youngest lad on board jumped on to it, clinging with one hand and frantically waving his country's flag. His mates heaved him up for everyone to see and then lowered him and the bag out of sight. They lifted and lowered him three times and as he and bag disappeared for the third time he yelled at the top of his voice for three cheers for his ship.

Then quiet for a while, until eight o'clock the same evening, when the ship's bell was struck, followed by the bell of every other vessel in a clanging across the water that might last for a quarter of an hour and could be heard well out to sea. Next, the homeward-bound crew hoisted up a wooden frame holding lights in the form of the Southern Cross. It was the signal for each crew to bellow cheers for the other vessels, one by one, until at last the turn came again of the homeward-bound ship.

Those hearty rites had been developed by sailors, but they were born in sail and they passed with sail. They meant little or nothing to steamship seamen and with the coming of the 1914-18 war they faded away, as the nitrate trade itself faded away, to live on only in the memories of old salts of the Cape Horners.

Clippers on the Tea Routes

Top: One of the Orient Lines clippers. *P & O Line (Richard Sharpe Studios)*

Above: First American clipper to dock in London in 1850, the 'Oriental'. *Mary Evans Picture Library*

TEA HAD BEEN IMPORTED into Britain from China since the days of Charles II, and for a century-and-a-half the lordly East Indiamen carried it around the Cape of Good Hope to England. In times of war, the ships sailed in convoy but a year's reserve of tea was held in London in case the ships should be captured. Thus the tea drunk was always about twelve months old. The Chinese restricted trade to the port of Canton, but after the Anglo-Chinese war of 1839-42, additional ports such as Hong Kong, Foochow, Shanghai and Hankow were opened to trade, the volume of which increased rapidly. The Honourable East India Company had meanwhile lost its trade monopoly, and smaller ships were by then carrying tea.

To increase sales, dealers in England advertised that the 'new teas' had arrived by a certain ship and it was said that they had a better flavour than that kept in stock for a year. Thus a demand grew for fresh tea. The tea was gathered in May and was ready for shipment in June and July, but the problem was that the south-west monsoon was at that season blowing strongly straight up the China Sea, and the ships had to beat down against it before they could pass through Sunda Straits between Java and Sumatra and out into the Indian Ocean. To overcome the difficulty, ships capable of sailing at faster speeds and of beating to windward were attracted to the trade; by the end of the 1840s, a number of ships of about 400 tons had been specifically designed for the purpose.

But in 1849, the British Navigation Acts were repealed, thus permitting ships of any nationality to bring cargoes to Britain, including tea from China. The change coincided with the discovery of gold in California, to supply the needs of which vast numbers of large clippers were built on the east coast of America, and when they had delivered their gold-hungry passengers at San Francisco, they found the tea trade to England was conveniently ready for them. Indeed, their fame had already preceded them, and they were quickly engaged to load tea for London at rates of £6 and £7 per ton, much to the annoyance of the British shipowners, who received about £2 or £3 per ton less.

So began a rivalry which lasted some years, until the fever of the Californian gold rush cooled by 1855. Five years later, the American Civil War removed all competition from that quarter, but competition between British owners continued throughout the next decade.

The principal difference between the British and American ships was size. For instance, the *Oriental,* which was the first American ship to enter the Thames with China tea, was of 1003 tons, double that of the British clippers. But many American clippers that carried tea were much larger, such as the *Challenge* of 2006 tons, *Comet* of 1836 tons, *Sovereign of the Seas* of 2420 tons. They were all built of wood with very few iron structural members in the hull, with the result that the construction became massive to support the strains encountered in such a large vessel. Unfortunately, the ports in China were not accustomed to such big ships and the arrangements for collecting the cargo were only geared to loading small vessels, with the result that delays occurred in filling the big clippers with tea.

Large ships were not necessarily faster than the smaller British ones, especially among the hazards of the China Sea, and there was some consolation to be gained in England from news of the *Oriental's* arrival in December 1850, which showed that the Aberdeen-built ship *John Bunyan* had earlier that same year made a passage of 101 days between Shanghai and London, or only four days longer than the American ship.

It was to Aberdeen shipyards that British owners turned for clippers in the early eighteen-fifties, and it was the yard of Alexander Hall & Sons that turned out some of the fastest ships for the tea trade during that decade. Examination of surviving builder's models shows that *Reindeer* (1848), *Stornoway* (1850), *Chrysolite* (1851), *Cairngorm* (1853,) *Vision* (1854) and *Robin Hood* (1856) were undoubted clippers. All these ships had the Aberdeen clipper bow, which was plainer and less ornate than conventional British practice, but resulted in far greater overhang forward. All were full-rigged ships carrying four or five yards on each mast, and the sails were further extended on each side by the use of studding-sails or stunsails.

The *Cairngorm's* design was not dictated by an owner's requirements but embodied her builder's convictions of what a large clipper should be. It was a bold decision for a builder to construct such a specialised ship on speculation, without first obtaining a firm order, but Alexander Hall & Sons were proved right because, after she was bought by the eminent firm of Jardine, Matheson & Co, she turned out to be one of the fastest British clippers in the tea trade during the 1850s. She cost £15,434, which works out at about £700 less than the original cost of the *Cutty Sark*. *Cairngorm* registered 939 tons new measurement, which meant that she cost £16.43 for every ton. By today's standards, it is an incredibly cheap price for a first-class ship built by superb craftsmen.

Acknowledged as 'Cock of the Walk', the *Cairngorm* made many fast passages, such as her maiden trip of 72 days from Lisbon to Hong Kong in 1853. (She had been obliged to put into Lisbon after being dismasted.) Her fastest homeward passage from China was in 1858-9, when she raced home from Macao to Deal in 91 days.

The American clipper *Comet*, in 1854, sailed from Liverpool to Hong Kong in only 84 days, between dropping one pilot and picking up the other one, and a year later another American ship, the *Eagle Wing*, took $83\frac{1}{2}$ days between her pilots, from Deal to Hong Kong. The design, launching, and sailing of the American clippers was attended with great enthusiasm at their home ports, and the descriptions in the local papers far exceeded anything that the British could read about their own ships. For instance, the *Boston Daily Atlas* ended its description of the *Challenge* in the following manner: 'She is owned by Messrs N L & G Griswold of New York, was built by Wm H Webb, and is commanded by Captain Robert H Waterman. Like the knights of old, who threw their gauntlets down to all comers, her owners send her forth, to challenge the world afloat!'

In the past, the term 'Clipper' was used quite loosely to cover any ship that had made a fast passage, but research today bestows the term only on ships for which plans or models can prove a clipper rating. Such ships had the lines of a yacht and little attention was given to the amount of cargo to be carried, the attainment of high speed at all times being the chief factor. Some of the American clippers had comparatively flat bottoms, in order to gain the required stability for rounding Cape Horn en route to California, but they made up for that by having extremely sharp ends at bow and stern.

British clippers in the tea trade, not having to encounter the big seas of the Roaring Forties, were designed with sharper V-shaped bottoms. American clippers sometimes achieved speeds of 20 and 21 knots, and on several occasions, sailed over 400 miles in the course of 24 hours. The smaller British clippers, with their shorter hulls, did not possess the same potential for speed, yet ships such as *Thermopylae* and *Cutty Sark* could sail at speeds of 17 knots and cover 360 miles in 24 hours.

Other British shipbuilders who specialised in building tea clippers during the 1850s were John Pile of Sunderland, who built the barques *Spirit of the Age* and *Spirit of the North*, and his brother William, who built *Crest of the Wave*, *Spray of the Ocean*, *Kelso* and *Lammermuir*; Benjamin Nicholson of Annan, on the Solway Firth, who built *Annandale*, *Queensberry* and *Shakspere*; and Bilbe and Perry of Rotherhithe, who built *Celestial*, *Lauderdale* and *Wynaud*. It was becoming increasingly rare for deepwater ships of over 500 tons to be built in the south of England after 1850, apart from shipyards on the River Thames.

A number of extremely sharp clippers were constructed entirely of iron for the Australian trade, after gold was found there in 1851; some of those ships later participated in the tea trade, but they were always regarded with suspicion as it was claimed that the tea was damaged in their holds through lack of adequate ventilation. Two such ships, built in 1853, were the *Gauntlet* and *Lord of the Isles* from shipyards on the River Clyde. An engraving of the former published in the *Illustrated London News* described her as 'the most perfect clipper ship ever launched on the Clyde, and she appears more like a yacht of large tonnage than a private merchant ship.' A similar description was given of *Lord of the Isles*, whose fastest passage from China was one of 90 days made in 1858-9 between Shanghai and London or 87 days to passing the Lizard. Many passages were calculated as the elapsed time between losing sight of land and catching sight of it again, or between dropping the pilot and picking up another on arrival.

Although the tea clippers built during the 1860s consistently made shorter passages than those of the previous decade, the majority did not possess any sharper form of hull, and the faster passages must be attributed to the greater experience of the captains and of the shipbuilders. The design of the earlier ships was somewhat experimental in nature, as the building of large clippers was in its infancy. After 1863, design of tea clippers became more stylised as the success of ships built by Robert Steele & Sons asserted itself.

In 1860, there appeared the *Fiery Cross*, designed by the celebrated naval architect William Rennie, and constructed in Liverpool. This ship had a length of 185 feet, a maximum breadth of 31.7 feet and a depth of hold of 19.2 feet and registered 695 tons. She was a beautiful ship and, more important, a fast and successful one, both of which attributes she certainly owed to her first two captains, John Dallas and Richard Robinson. In those days, the first ship to dock in London with the new teas received an extra premium of up to £1 per ton of tea carried, to be divided pro rata among the crew, and *Fiery Cross* won the premium in the years 1861, 1862, 1863 and 1865. No doubt her success influenced ships built in other yards.

The long-established firm of Robert Steele & Sons of Greenock had already produced *Kate Carnie* and *Ellen Rodger*, but it was probable with the *Falcon* launched in 1859 that they first achieved fame with a tea clipper. As a result of the success, they were later able to build such crack ships as *Taeping* (1863), *Ariel* and *Sir Lancelot* (1865) *Titania* (1866), *Lahloo* (1867), and *Kaisow* (1868). Those ships accomplished some of the fastest passages ever made under sail to and from China. In 1866-7, *Ariel* took only 80 days (between

pilots) from London to Hong Kong; in 1869, *Sir Lancelot* was a mere 84 days from Foochow to the Lizard, bound for London; and in 1871, *Titania* took 93 days between the same ports. The ships possessed the advantages found in all fast clippers—a comparatively high speed in light winds and the ability to beat dead to windward in a stiff breeze.

But although so much care and devotion was lavished on the great ships, they still had to produce a satisfactory income for their owners, and the builders were obliged to quote in competition with each other to get orders. The ships built by Steele probably cost no more than £17 or £18 per ton. That would have been for a composite hull, that is to say, an iron framework with external wooden planking—a form of construction that gave extremely long life. Several vessels so constructed still survive. For example, there are the incomparable *Cutty Sark* in dry dock at Greenwich; the *Carrick*, ex *City of Adelaide*, (1864) used as an RNVR club in Glasgow; and the *Ambassador* (1869), now a hulk at Punta Arenas in the Straits of Magellan, with her iron frame intact but most of her planking stripped off by the locals.

Needless to say, there were many races

Above: The sailing ship 'Turakina' speeding past the steamer 'Ruapehu' in 1895 as depicted in a painting by Frank H Mason.
P & O Line (Richard Sharpe Studios)

Below: Said to be the biggest wooden sailing ship ever built, Donald McKay's 'Great Republic' (1853) which was 335ft in length and had a tonnage of over 4500.
Mary Evans Picture Library

between the 'full bloods', as the crack clippers were called but the most celebrated occurred in 1866 between *Fiery Cross*, *Ariel*, *Serica*, *Taeping* and *Taitsing*, which left Foochow in that order at the end of May. Beating down the China Sea, *Fiery Cross* reached Anjer in 20 days, beating the field by one day. *Taitsing*, which had left a day behind the others, gradually closed the gap as they caught the favourable trades in the run down the Indian Ocean to the Cape of Good Hope. The first four all passed Flores in the Azores on the same day, but somehow *Fiery Cross* dropped back in the rush for the English Channel. *Ariel* and *Taeping* logged 14 knots as they ran up the Channel within sight of each other for most of September 5, while *Serica* was out of sight near the French coast. *Ariel* signalled her number off Deal at eight o'clock in the morning of September 6, 98 days $22\frac{1}{2}$ hours after dropping her pilot, and *Taeping* did likewise ten minutes later. The two ships docked later the same day and *Serica* also just managed to get in before the lock gates closed. All England was thrilled with the news, except the dealers who were faced with a sudden glut of tea. In later years, the premium for the first ship home was abandoned.

But there were other splendid clippers which fiercely contested with Robert Steele's ships for the accolade of supremacy. Chief amongst them were the *Maitland* and *Undine,* designed and built at Sunderland by William Pile; the *Taitsing, Spindrift* and *Windhover* produced by Charles Connell at Glasgow; *Norman Court* and *Black Prince* designed by William Rennie; *The Caliph* built by Alexander Hall & Sons at Aberdeen; *Leander* and *Thermopylae* designed by Bernard Waymouth; and the *Cutty Sark* built by Scott & Linton at Dumbarton. The ships themselves were mostly in the 750 to 950 tons range, and so were fairly evenly matched in many cases. All were sailed by skilful captains and handpicked crews of about 30 men.

Many seamen have rated the *Thermopylae* as the fastest all-round British clipper. She was launched in 1868, a year before the Suez Canal was opened, from the Aberdeen yard of Walter Hood & Co, and was of very similar form to *Leander,* which was built the previous year. She registered 948 tons. How lovely she must have looked when making sail in the Downs at the beginning of her maiden passage in November 1868, with her green-painted hull and white masts, her crew sheeting home the snow-white canvas of her new sails as she heeled to the wind. It was the beginning of a momentous voyage, because on each of the three legs she broke the record. From leaving the Lizard to sighting Cape Otway, near Melbourne, it was only 60 days, and the Australian papers marvelled at her speed. Thence, she sailed to Newcastle, New South Wales, to load coal, from where she only took 28 days between pilots, bound for Shanghai. In China, she loaded tea at Foochow, left on July 3, 1869, and was off the Lizard 89 days later. How disappointing for Captain Kemball that his record stood only for 12 days, until *Sir Lancelot* passed the Lizard 84 days from Foochow.

Paul Stevenson records a yarn told by the captain in his book, *By Way of Cape Horn:* 'We were running our easting down . . . when we sighted a vessel astern. It was blowing hard from the nor'west, and the next time I looked, a couple of hours later, there was the ship close on our quarter, and we doing 12 knots. "Holy jiggers", says I to the mate, "there's the Flying Dutchman." "Naw", says he, "it's the *Thermopylae.*" But when she was abeam a little later, she hoisted her name, the *Lothair,* and it's been my opinion ever since that she was making mighty close to 17 knots.'

The *Lothair* was built on the Thames by Walker for Killick, Martin & Co in 1870, and was one of the last composite clippers to be built. After steamers forced the clippers out of the tea trade to London she made some exceptionally fast passages with tea to New York. In the same year that she was launched, two other tea clippers were built on the Thames. They were the *Blackadder* and *Hallowe'en,* both built of iron at Greenwich by Maudslay, Sons & Field. The latter's first three homeward passages from Shanghai were made in 92, 91 and 92 days to London, a most remarkable performance.

John Willis, who owned the two iron ships, had had the *Cutty Sark* built the previous year by a small yard at Dumbarton on the Clyde, and with her he hoped to beat the *Thermopylae.* The two ships had a close race of it in 1872, but *Cutty Sark* had the misfortune to carry away her rudder off the Cape of Good Hope. Nevertheless, she managed to reach London only a week behind. She never made a passage with tea in less than 100 days from China, yet she was capable of high speeds and was given a large spread of canvas with a sharp-bodied hull. It was often the captain who gave a clipper that extra turn of speed, and sometimes he required nerve and daring to keep a thoroughbred clipper under a press of sail day after day.

The clipper captains were a varied bunch; there were the bully-boys, the hell-fire preachers, the pious ones and the strong silent types. To survive, however, they had to have one thing in common – they could drive ships.

The opening of the Suez Canal in 1869 brought the days of the tea clippers to an end, because steamers could make a much quicker passage home with tea through the canal and earn the highest freight rates. The clippers continued racing home until about 1875, but could not afford to load at £1.50 to £2 per ton and so were switched into other trades.

The Cutty Sark was one such ship. She was really built too late for the tea trade, but in the Australian wool trade, under the redoubtable Captain Woodget, she proved fast and almost unbeatable. Her survival and preservation at Greenwich today form a fitting epitaph to the glorious days of the tea clippers.

Impressive bows-on view of the preserved 'Cutty Sark' in her permanent dry dock beside the River Thames at Greenwich in London.
P D Hawkes

New York

NEW YORK has always been a port of superlatives. Even as ships enter the commercial port through the Narrows between Lower New York Bay and the Upper Bay, they are greeted by the world's longest suspension bridge above them. It is the Verrazano Narrows Bridge, opened by the Port Authority of New York and New Jersey in 1964. It is so big that its supporting towers are one-and-five-eighths of an inch out of parallel to allow for the curvature of the earth!

'New York will be a great place', the old wisecrack says, 'when it is finished.' And that is the essence of the Port of New York; it is like a gargantuan galaxy in a perpetual flux of change and movement—movement of people and freight on the waters of the harbour, below them in tunnels under the Hudson and East Rivers, above in the thundering jet aeroplanes or on the elegant bridges which gracefully span the sky in airy arcs, making effortless links between shore and shore, island and island, of the great archipelago which is one of nature's finest harbours.

At the centre of it all is the Port Authority of New York and New Jersey, administering the general management and development of the 1500 square miles of harbour within its official boundaries—a circle of about 25 miles radius centred on Bartholdi's statue of 'Liberty enlightening the world'. The Authority operates from its latest colossus, the twin 1350ft towers of the World Trade Center, a gigantic salute to trade and commerce at the southern end of Manhattan Island, dwarfing even the Empire State Building and seeming to proclaim the vastness of the dominions and undertakings of the Port Authority. In the New York/New Jersey metropolitan area, the world's largest consumer market with a population well over 12 million, it is estimated that one in every four jobs derives directly or indirectly from the activities of the port.

Although the natural harbour is a geographic unity, it is shared by the two states of New York and New Jersey, whose port terminals once fiercely competed so that the entire marine operations were threatened with standstill. Matters were remedied by the formation of a joint port authority in 1921, a public corporation representing the two states equally. Since its formation, the Authority has built piers, docks, bridges, tunnels, bus stations, airports, the World Trade Center and other buildings all representing an investment of about \$3 billion, and at no cost to the general taxpayer.

Nature gave New York a splendid start. With the natural advantages of a tidal range of only $4\frac{1}{2}$ft, enclosed docks are unnecessary. The well-protected waters of the Upper Bay provide a good natural anchorage; the area is practically ice-free and little troubled by fog and the Hudson River connected the harbour to a con-

Top: General view of the Port of New York overlooking Brooklyn and Manhattan Island. *Port Authority of New York & Jersey*

Above: Symbol of New York for millions of travellers, the Statue of Liberty. *J R Batts*

siderable hinterland which was vastly extended by the Erie Canal in the early 19th century. There are deep-water channels linking all the port areas and around the three main islands, namely, Manhattan Island, Staten Island and the southern end of Long Island. Long Island Sound, about 100 miles long, not only gives the port a 'back door' through the Hell Gate but also provides a sheltered route to the southern end of the New England area, an important coasting route still.

Almost the whole of the vast tide of movement of people and freight is guided directly or indirectly by the Port Authority. As well as masterminding one of the world's biggest seaports, it owns and operates four airports, four toll bridges, two tunnels under the Hudson, two heliports, two truck terminals, two bus stations, and a railway line. The majority of the marine terminals are not operated by the Authority although it owns many and built many. Berths are leased to tenants and ancillary services are provided by the Port Authority or the several other agencies which all help to run the port from day to day. Such are the United States Coastguard on Governor's Island, the Marine Administration and the Waterfront Commission of New York Harbour or the United States Army Corps of Engineers, and others.

The Port Authority does own and operate the world's biggest passenger terminal—but it is the bus station on Eighth Avenue! There, from three loading decks, 7500 buses a day operate and about 65 million people use the terminal each year. It has every kind of service, including 40 escalators and its own dentist. From the terminal, many of the buses dive into the Authority's Lincoln Tunnel under the Hudson. Opened in 1937, it has a work force of 350 and each day no fewer than 83,000 vehicles pass through it, making it by far the busiest in the world.

The nearby Manhattan liner piers handle few passengers nowadays compared to the aeroplanes at the Authority's airports. Only about 739,000 sea-borne passengers come to the port each year whereas the port's four airports handle about 38 million people annually. John F Kennedy airport on Long Island handled about 21 million people in 1972. Air cargo, too, is becoming increasingly important; in 1972 about a million tons of air cargo were handled.

A recent major development of the port is the World Trade Center, housing about 50,000 workers and expecting to receive about 80,000 trade and other visitors every day. There, commercial firms and agencies of all kinds are concentrated, and there is computerised data processing of world trade information.

All this emphasises that nowadays a port is much more than ships and the berths for them. The modern concept, exemplified by New York, is of a complete unified transport facility providing smooth exchange between sea, land and air, along with the same smooth passage for the necessary documentation. But ships gave New York birth, for the city is founded on the port, and they come and go at the rate of about one every 28 minutes. There are between 12,000 and 13,000 foreign trade ship movements each year and 5000 to 6000 coastal and inter-coastal movements.

The total of all kinds of water-borne cargo handled in 1970 is said to have been about 174 million tons, making New York the world's second biggest port by the tonnage criterion (Rotterdam is largest with 241.6 million tons). In foreign trade, New York has always been more important as an importing port, an entrepôt. Out of 53 million tons of sea-borne foreign trade in 1971, nearly 48 million tons were import cargo.

The biggest single cargo-handling facility is the Elizabeth Port Terminal in Newark Bay, which handled about 6½ million tons of cargo in 1971 and twice as much in 1972. The majority of cargo there is handled in containers—those standard-size cargo units which have revolutionised major seaports everywhere from about 1965 onwards.

Adjacent Port Newark has 36 ship berths which handle containers, along with a variety of specialised cargoes such as frozen meat, bananas, timber and imported motor-cars. Another form of unitised cargo, largely exploited in New York, is the lighter-aboard-ship, or LASH system; it operates from Port Newark too. Another interesting service operates from Weehawken terminal on the New Jersey side of the Hudson River. There, Seatrain has the New York base for its land bridge service between Europe and the Orient. Instead of taking all cargo by ship via Panama, it is passed by land between New York and Oakland, California. The land bridge route saves ten days on the Europe/Orient service. The company's major ships are gas-turbine driven and carry two spare engines in containers. An engine change can be carried out in eight hours, even at sea.

Ship piers line the Hudson River waterfront on the New Jersey side from Jersey City to George Washington Bridge, although the area was not important until 1847, when the Cunard company built its first New York terminal on that side. On the Manhattan side, traditionally associated with the Atlantic passenger trade, ship berth piers extend from West 57th Street right down the island and round to

Brooklyn Bridge, that pioneer steel cable suspension bridge which filled New York with wonder when it was opened in 1883. The 'Luxury Liner Row' area of the Hudson River waterfront, the Manhattan Piers 86, 88 and 90, was made famous by the 'ocean greyhounds' of the Atlantic. Their era ended with the coming of air travel. The area was rebuilt to handle the very small remaining liner passenger trade and to woo the new luxury passenger ship trade—cruising.

Brooklyn has about four miles of marine terminals extending from Brooklyn Bridge to the quarantine area at the Narrows. They include the Port Authority's Brooklyn, Erie Basin, Columbia Street, Bush Street, and North East Marine Terminals. Conventional break-bulk cargo of all kinds as well as palletised goods and containers are handled. The Staten Island shoreline above the Narrows Bridge has the piers of a Foreign Trade Zone and at Howland

Facing page: A photograph of old New York in the early days of steam.

Top: A drawing published in 'The Illustrated London News' of October 27, 1849, showing the nearly completed 350ft dry dock at the Navy Yard, New York. *Illustrated London News*

Above left: 'Queen Elizabeth 2' at Cunard Pier, New York. *J R Batts*

Left: A Staten Island ferry, operated by the New York City Department of Marine & Aviation. *J R Batts*

Hook there is a big privately owned container port. A similar container facility, Global Terminal at New Jersey, is one of the biggest in the country.

There are other ship terminals and berths, too numerous to list. Those mentioned serve to show how the whole harbour area is being developed.

The first European to come to the harbour was the Florentine navigator Giovanni da Verrazano in the *Dauphine*, sent by Francis I of France in 1524 to seek the fabled North-West Passage to the Orient. When he sailed through the Narrows now spanned by the bridge named after him, Verrazano found himself in 'a most beautiful lake, three leagues in circuit'—Upper New York Bay. The entrance to the Lower Bay from the open Atlantic is an almost casual break in the long sands and reefs of the New Jersey beaches to the south and those of Long Island to the north.

The six miles of water between Sandy Hook and Coney Island *seem* open but they conceal shoals which reach almost to the surface in places. Only at Sandy Hook is there enough natural deep water to give safe passage to big ships and that was the main channel into the harbour until the Ambrose Channel was dredged from the East or 'Fourteen Foot' channel to give 40ft at the beginning of the 20th century. It has since been deepened to give 45ft of depth. When Sandy Hook Channel was the main entrance, around 1800, shifting sands threatened to close the channel—news that rival ports heard with immense pleasure!

The alternative entrance by Long Island Sound and the Hell Gate is beset by six- and seven-knot tides and strewn with rocks. For sailing ships it was a perilous passage, except at slack water. There, in 1904, the excursion steamer *General Slocum* met disaster, burning with a loss of 1000 lives in one of New York's biggest maritime disasters.

Verrazano sailed away without landing and it was Henry Hudson who pushed upstream on the Hudson to Albany in his ship *D'Halve Maen* (*Half Moon*), seeking the North-West Passage for the Dutch in 1609. Next came settlers of the Dutch East India Company, who bought Manhattan Island from the Indians for baubles, bangles and beads worth, perhaps, ten pounds. Their trade in the valued beaver pelts was conducted from New Amsterdam, with its fort where the New York Customs House now stands.

The English sought to break into the trade from 1633 onwards and the resulting conflict with the Dutch was resolved in 1664 when the Dutch Governor, wooden-legged Peter Stuyvesant (the original Peg Leg Pete), had to capitulate to a vastly superior English force. New Amsterdam became New York and very soon afterwards built its first dock. That was the Great Dock, extending from Whitehall Street to Coenties Slip. Almost immediately, the unruly New Yorkers began to build their own private slips and wharves to avoid dock dues!

The 17th century saw the founding of New Jersey in 1666, the port's first pilotage act in 1694 and the growth of several commodity markets in the Lower Manhattan area. Shipbuilding started on the East River waterfront of Lower Manhattan and developed steadily over the next 200 years. The famous East River yards gave to the world pioneer new ideas in ship design and such famous flyers as the China clippers *Rainbow* and *Sea Witch*, the schooner *America*, the California clippers, such as *Swordfish*, which

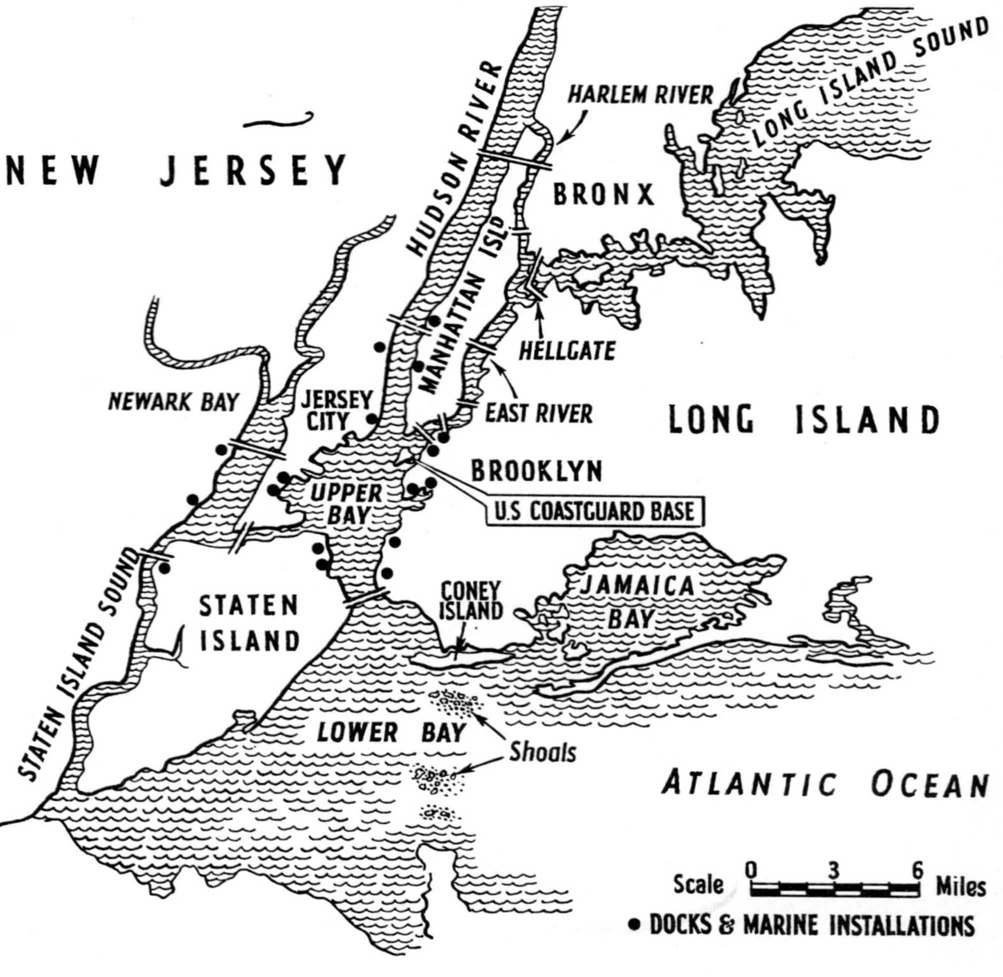

took the fortyniners round the Horn to the goldfields of California, and finally, in 1807, their greatest success of all, Fulton's steamship *Clermont*. Her official name, incidentally, was *North River Steam Boat*. Steaming 150 miles against wind and tide to Albany she finally proved to a sceptical waterfront that steam had a great future. Within two years, she was running regular services on the Hudson and imitators dashed to climb aboard the new marine bandwagon. By 1838, there were regular trans-Atlantic steamer services, following the success of another New York innovation, the regular liner services started by the famous Blackball Line in January, 1818.

In 1694, New York's population was a modest 5000, almost all behind the wooden anti-Indian barricades that stretched right across Lower Manhattan and gave Wall Street its name. Over the next century, the population increased to 33,000 in 1790 and by 1800 reached 60,000.

The most important event of the 18th century was the Revolutionary War of 1775-81 and the recognition of American independence in 1785. Freed from the restrictions of colonial status, New York expanded its trade and scope rapidly. As US shipping increased from 201,562 tons in 1789 to 747,965 in 1795, New York's registered tonnage doubled in five years and trebled in 15. In 1797 it took the lead as the new nation's biggest port. Exports jumped from a value of \$2½ million in 1792 to over \$26 million in 1807. Population reached 96,000 in 1810. The New World was full of zest and limitless promise and its greatest port was on the brink of the half-century of its most phenomenal growth. Innovation, invention and enterprise on the grand scale were its hallmarks then, as now.

It was a port whose leaders, like De Witt Clinton, thought on a big scale, and pushed through the construction of the 363-mile Erie Canal which linked the port, via the Hudson River and Mohawk River valley, to the Mid-West and reduced the cost of transport from Buffalo to New York from \$100 to \$8 dollars a ton. 'Clinton's Ditch' gave a terrific boost to the port. By 1836 the canal and its feeder links to Lakes Ontario and Champlain were sending or receiving 1,310,000 tons of goods via

the port of New York. In 1860 the figure was $4\frac{1}{2}$ million tons.

Population passed the half-million mark in 1850. By then, the wholesale immigration which swelled America's population by $5\frac{1}{2}$ million between 1820 and 1860, was in full swing and by far the greater proportion of the immigrants, about 3,742,000, entered via New York to enact one of the port's greatest human dramas.

By 1870, the booming port seemed to shout for some central control and the New York City Department of Docks was formed. It marked the beginning of organised port development and improvements in navigation channels and marine terminals. Developments in the first half of the 20th century were in essence a refinement of the ideas and technology of the 19th century. The first *Mauretania* held the Blue Riband of the Atlantic for 22 years. Ships got bigger and faster in the 1920s and 1930s, but cargo handling in the world's ports did not change much.

Then came the second world war and an immense stimulus to marine technology from the urgent demands of war efforts. New York yet again found itself up front with the 'mostest'. Over half the American troops sent overseas and more than one-third of war cargo tonnage passed through the port. The Cunard ships *Queen Mary* and *Queen Elizabeth* carried as many as 15,000 men at a time out of New York.

After the war, the industrial revolution concepts—mass production and standardisation—finally came to the world's waterfronts, and were pioneered in New York in the so-called container revolution of the mid-1960s. Today, such streamlined marine terminals as the Elizabeth Port Authority installation on Newark Bay are the modern expression of the transport revolution. There, a couple of dozen men or so with container cranes and container transporters, or straddle carriers, can handle in a day the cargo which, if handled in conventional break-bulk form, would previously have occupied over 100 men for about two weeks.

Thus the expensive part of sea transport's capital equipment—the ship—is kept at sea earning money for a far greater proportion of its working life and labour, which every year gets more and more expensive, is reduced.

Such is the essence of port operations and New York is the quintessence. The rough robust port has always been a leader in the tough world of international trade. From the perspective of history, its past has an air of romance, a patina of grace. But the reality is the present, thrusting and impatient, where time is money and ships, people, aeroplanes, trains, ferries and trucks must always be kept moving.

Facing page above: Map showing the disposition of the many marine installations of the Port of New York.

Facing page below: Cunard's 'Queen Mary' passing under Verrazano Narrows Bridge.
Port Authority of New York & Jersey

Above left: Classic late-20th-century New York maritime scene, with skyscrapers forming a backdrop for the Home Lines cruise ship 'Oceanic'. *A Crisp*

Left: A painting by Henry Reuterdahl of the US Fleet entering New York Harbour.
Courtesy US Naval Academy Museum

Above: An aerial view of the modern port of Lisbon, on the site of the starting point of many of the great voyages of discovery in the 15th and 16th centuries.
Portuguese National Tourist & Trade Information

LISBON

LISBON'S ORIGINS as a city port reach far back into antiquity. Prehistoric idols have been found on the banks of the Tagus estuary, and Phoenicians, Carthaginians, Romans and the Muslim Moors who conquered Iberia in the 8th century AD all knew the splendid natural harbour Lisbon afforded. Muslim nautics encouraged the development of the caravel, backbone of the late 15th-century voyages of ocean exploration which had Lisbon as their starting point.

Lisbon's commanding position on the edge of the western world and close to the gateway of the wealthy Mediterranean had been assured by 14th-century development of Portuguese sea power, maritime commerce and shipbuilding, and two centuries later the port was the recognised European centre for Oriental commerce.

Sadly, Lisbon later fell from grandeur and two centuries of political setback after the earthquake year of 1755 meant that its commercial growth did not properly revive until after 1945. Today, however, Lisbon is a leading world port.

The building of its splendid Salazar Suspension Bridge (1966) prompted valuable development upstream of the bridge, including the busy Alcantara area, centre of the passenger liner service, Santo Amaro and Alcantara docks and Alcantara and Rocha wharves. Altogether, the Port of Lisbon Authority has nearly seven miles of open wharves, with another mile of piers.

Lisbon also contains an oil tanker terminal, a dockyard with three large drydocks, cement, grain and liquified gas handling facilities, and the rapidly developing Santa Apolonia container terminal opened in 1967.

Each year, Lisbon receives over 8000 ships and handles nearly 11 million tons of cargo, 330,000 passengers, 30 million cross-river ferry passengers and a great fishing industry.

Right: Engraving from an original sketch of Singapore in 1857. *Mary Evans Picture Library*

Below: A typically crowded scene in modern Singapore harbour. *Far East Travel Centre*

SINGAPORE

FEW PORTS in the world have ever been so well served by Nature and so favoured by history as Singapore. Only the humble trading town of Byzantium on the Bosphorus which, in the 4th century AD, grew into Constantinople, that glittering monument to Christendom and hub of dazzling commercial prosperity, was similarly placed at a crossroads of the world's great trade routes, and similarly exploited to take advantage of it. In 324 AD, when the Roman Emperor Constantine first set eyes on Byzantium and realised its potential, he was looking at a port which was already doing well enough in a modest minor way.

On January 28, 1819, when Thomas Stamford Raffles, a former clerk of the British East India Company, first set foot on Singapore, it took the optimism of a visionary to see beyond its thick tiger-infested jungle and tangle of mangrove swampland to the great international port it eventually became. Fortunately, the 38-year-old Raffles was just such a visionary, well-equipped with the unique and enigmatic British mixture of pride and compassion, toughness and idealism, energy and romanticism which the demands of empire-building required. His choice of Singapore for a new British trading settlement had an immediate and galvanic effect upon an island which, in the 16th century, had been used by traders from India, China, Siam, Cambodia and Malaya, but which had become nothing but an underpopulated and neglected backwater.

Within ten weeks of his arrival, the scattering of white-sailed Malay kolehs which was all the waters of Singapore harbour normally saw, had been joined by two merchantmen and 100 smaller trading vessels. Within two and a half years, 2889 vessels had entered and cleared the port, representing a combined tonnage of 161,000. Within six years, Singapore was handling trade estimated at £2,610,440 and the 150 inhabitants Raffles had found there in 1819 had grown to more than 10,000. By 1832, population figures had leapt to 22,000 and in that year, 420 fully rigged ships, carrying over £3 million-worth of goods passed through the harbour. In the 1850s, Singapore was handling £5 million-worth of cargo a year. By the end of the 19th century, it was the seventh busiest port in the world, and by 1972, the fourth.

If statistics make the rise of Singapore appear an economic miracle, it was a miracle founded on three hard-headed factors of Oriental life and trade in the early 19th century. The first factor was the stupendous wealth of the trade between

China and India. For the sake of that trade, in which they had a monopoly, British East India Company merchants willingly endured the deliberate humiliations, the 6-per cent tax and the lack of legal protection which the Chinese imposed as the obsequious price of admission.

Even before the 19th century, the China traffic in tea, silks, lacquerware and porcelain was rich enough to make millionaires out of several merchants involved in it. Singapore, situated about 85 miles north of the Equator, was almost exactly half way between India and China and with its sheltered deep-water harbour, which was navigable all year round, it made an ideal port for the landfall which sailing ships had to make during the journey. Furthermore, as an official British possession from 1824, Singapore ensured safety for British ships in waters uncomfortably close to aggressive Dutch rivals in the Netherlands East Indies.

Above: Blue Funnel Line ship being loaded at Singapore.
Ocean Transport & Trading Ltd

Right: The inner harbour at Singapore, for coastal shipping, in 1970. *A Greenway*

The Dutch, who had a monopoly of their own in the trade of the Malay archipelago, conducted their business from behind a great wall of taxes and dues matched for obstructiveness only by the prohibitions, restraints and tolls of the Chinese and Japanese. Free trade, like many other freedoms, was totally unknown in the East at that time, whereas in Britain it was rapidly becoming an integral part of the moral code.

Stamford Raffles allied morality with policy when he made Singapore a free trade port, for he knew that by this means, his greatest single ambition could be realised. 'One free port in these seas,' he wrote, 'must eventually destroy the spell of Dutch monopoly'. He was right.

Raffles provided Singapore with a third assurance of success when he turned it into an oasis of law, order and justice in a desert of oppression. Within the neighbouring Malay states, all the symptoms of decay and decadence were present, including piracy, banditry, slavery, impotent or near-impotent rulers, corruption, exploitation, starvation and crushing poverty. The situation was so hopeless that Malays soon began to crowd into Singapore in an effort to escape from it. There, as the century progressed, they began to enjoy the novel benefits of justice, peace, education, medical care and enough to eat. The Malays were quickly followed by thousands of Chinese, Javanese, Indians, Siamese, Arabs and Armenians who, between them, gave Singapore the cosmopolitan character it still possesses today.

With Singapore an attraction of such magnitude, it is little wonder that it was already the senior partner when, in 1826, it was joined with the two-year old British colony at Malacca and with the settlement at Penang, founded in 1786, to form the Straits Settlements, an outlying presidency of British India. Singapore's trade was then 2.6 times greater than Penang's and 8.7 times greater than Malacca's.

As a town, however, Singapore wore its lustre lightly in those early years and for several decades afterwards. Stamford Raffles and his successors had employed nearly 1000 labourers a day to clear and keep at bay the jungle undergrowth that smothered the entire island. However, despite their constant efforts, until the 1850s Singapore remained a small settlement clinging to the southern rim of the island, with streets no more than muddy pathways, always in danger of flooding, and its houses just simple wooden bungalows.

In a rather primitive setting, European merchants conducted their import-export trade, bringing in goods from Europe, China and India. The Chinese, who quickly came to comprise the overwhelming majority of Singapore's population, acted as their agents, gathering and selling to the Europeans the varied exports of Malaya, Sumatra, Java and other neighbouring areas. Europeans and Chinese played the commercial roles, as merchants and middlemen respectively, at least until the 1920s.

The exports of Singapore comprised an exotic range of wares, including opium, edible seaweed, ebony, camphor and mother-of-pearl from the Celebes; rice, edible birds' nests, gold dust, copra, tin and sandalwood from Java; and beeswax, rhinoceros horn and elephant tusks from Sumatra. In return, Java and Sumatra received iron, raw silk, wheat, salt, tobacco, firearms, cordage and woollens.

Not until the 1860s, by which time there were up to 12 steamers constantly in port, did the practitioners of the burgeoning trade begin to live in matching style. The Europeans moved into handsome brick bungalows set in up to 15 acres of lush colourful garden, with generously matted floors, white-painted walls and silk screen dividers. There, beneath an ever-moving ceiling of punkah fans, which at times did no more than stir the sweatily humid air, they lived the favoured and exclusive life of the pukka sahib. It was complete with armies of servants, leisurely games of cricket and croquet, musical evenings, stifling snobbishness and a horror of mixing socially with other races. Europeans also indulged in grand banquets, consuming vast quantities of food, including mounds of curry and rice, in a manner and with a diligence that would not have shamed the gourmets of Imperial Rome.

Though the richer Singapore Chinese came to it slightly later than the Europeans, as a race they already possessed a much more tasteful way with luxury, and showed it in a natural elegance and style which made their white masters look boorish and crude. In the 1880s, one wealthy Chinese had 'open-worked tracery screens painted in white and pale porcelain colours all over his house . . . with the few solid wall spaces hung with . . . Japanese pictures . . . making the whole house one veiled aerial perspective set with flowers all about the open courts and pathways'. There, he sat 'in azure silk raiment' and amused 'himself and his friends with fishing for fat carp from his windows and feeding them with dozens of slices of bread'.

The profits of Singapore which were later lavished on lush living in this way, were at first, quite rightly, put to use improving Singapore harbour and its facilities. The first ships to sail into the settlement after 1819 anchored opposite the Singapore river, and offloaded their cargoes on to lighters which carried them down to Boat Quay, where a line of bullock carts waited.

To the west, lay another roadstead which was too narrow for square-rigged

sailing ships, but which came into lucrative use after 1845, when the Straits Settlements became part of the Europe-China steamship run operated by the P & O Company. It was New Harbour, later renamed Keppel Harbour after Captain Henry Keppel who, in 1848, had the site surveyed and pronounced it suitable as a coaling station. A coaling station and wharf materialised four years later, when the P & O established both on a nearby headland, Tebing Tinggi. The P & O was only the first of many firms to do so.

In 1859, at a spot west of P & O property, Singapore's first dry dock was built, followed in 1866 by 750ft of wharves built by the Tanjon Pagar Dock Company and capable of berthing four average-sized ships. In 1868, the TPDC opened Victoria dry dock, and by 1870, the shoreline of New Harbour was festooned with four graving docks, more and longer wharves and a line of bunkering piers. With facilities of such calibre, Singapore was in an excellent position to take advantage of the change in the South-East Asian trading picture which followed the opening of the Suez Canal in 1869.

After 1833, when the East India Company lost its monopoly of the China trade, the prosperity of Singapore faltered for a time. There were other factors, too. For sailing ships rounding the Cape of Good Hope—most Europe-to-Asia cargo went that way—the Straits of Malacca were not so convenient a passageway through to the South China Sea as were the Straits of Sunda, 450 miles to the south between Sumatra and Java. Also, Singapore suffered after 1842 from the growing rivalry of Hong Kong, which the British forced the Chinese to cede to them after the First Opium War.

In the years of comparative eclipse, Singapore received a vital consolation prize when the P & O Company responded to the Australian Gold Rush of 1851 by opening a service between the southern continent and the Straits Settlements port. The first vessel to sail the new run, the 700-ton *Chusan*, arrived at Singapore in 1852. The *Chusan* signalled the emergence of Singapore as the major ocean junction for South-East Asia, a position it has never since relinquished. The opening of the Suez Canal 17 years later, confirmed Singapore in the role, and a fresh upsurge of prosperity began, with the 200,000 tons which cleared the port in 1869 rising to over 700,000 in 1872.

By that time, Singapore had acquired new docks, built with the depth of the Suez Canal especially in mind, more miles of wharves and, since 1832, over 75,000 more inhabitants. Between 1871 and 1881, Singapore island absorbed into its meagre area of 209.6 square miles another 42,000 immigrants. Many of them were desperately poor Chinese coolies who harboured a rabid hatred of their British rulers, and expressed it in such pejorative nicknames as 'red-haired barbarian', 'devil' or, for a policeman, 'big dog'.

The resentments these people nursed in their filthy slummy slophouses, where scores swarmed in dozens of cubicles, led to bloody street battles, riots, vicious outbreaks of wanton destruction and more than a few mysterious murders for which members of Chinese secret societies were thought, but rarely proved, to be responsible. Such upheavals naturally brought frightened complaints from Europeans, and it was not uncommon for them to hire armed syces, or grooms, to run beside their horses with lanterns as they made their way home in carriages on dark nights.

Above: A boatbuilding yard on the Kallang River, Singapore. *Far East Travel Centre*

Eruptions of violence, however, proved to be no more than a dark flicker across the bright face of Singapore's ever-increasing affluence. By the late 1880s, when Rudyard Kipling gazed in wonder at 'five solid miles of masts and funnels along the waterfront', Singapore had received yet another lucrative boost in the demands of the new automobile and meat-canning industries for vast quantities of tin and rubber.

By 1900, Singapore was fast becoming the focus of tin and rubber distribution throughout the world, with its own tin-smelting plant on the offshore island of Pulau Brani, and rich rubber plantations about 100 miles up the coast at Malacca. There, the rubber-tapping process invented by Henry Ridley was producing a commercial bonanza which, today, makes rubber the largest single item in Singapore's trade. Rubber was not indigenous to Malaya, having been introduced by the British from Brazil, with the result that Malaya replaced Brazil as the world's prime producer of rubber.

Petroleum and petroleum products come second. The five vast oil refineries now run by international petroleum companies on islands surrounding Singapore operate between them 22 tanker berths; between 1966 and 1971, they produced an average of 28.26 million tons of mineral oil every year. A sixth oil company, Singapore Petroleum, with three berths for bunkering, went into operation during 1973.

The port of Singapore itself, with its prosperous frontage of skyscrapers, lack of beggars and standard of communal cleanliness, phenomenal in Asia, is the source of equally striking statistics. Its area of 950 acres of land and 225 square miles of water is administered by the Port of Singapore Authority, which employs about 12,000 workers.

Singapore's five main gateways lead to Keppel Harbour, which has three miles of wharves, the 60-acre container port at East Lagoon, Telok Ayer Basin, where 2100ft of wharves receive coastal vessels and lighters, the nine-acre Sembawang port, which handles low-value high-volume homogeneous cargoes such as logs and sawn timber, and Jurong bulk-handling port, which has 3000 feet of marginal wharf.

Throughout the vast complex, the traditional trade in tin, rattan, copra, coffee and spices, as well as the newer traffic in machinery and raw materials, is handled by the whole spectrum of modern port equipment, including 232 fork-lift trucks and 25 mobile cranes in Keppel Harbour alone. Berthing and unberthing at Singapore is a 24-hour service, and vessels can be turned round after an average stay alongside of only 39 hours.

More than 38,000 vessels enter and clear the port each year, totalling a net registered tonnage of over 148 million. There has been a 10 per cent per annum increase in cargo handled at Singapore during the 1960s, and a rise of more than 500 per cent over cargo tonnage handled in 1950. In addition, Singapore's 50 shipyards achieved the major feat of doubling their output between 1966 and 1968.

Superlatives have been applied to Singapore ever since Raffles first came to the diamond-shaped island. In the 1970s, superlatives are more appropriate than ever. The independent Republic of Singapore, now the home of about two million people, is among the world's leading oil-refining, blending and distribution centres, a world centre for telecommunications, a vital focus for relaying weather information, the site of an important naval dockyard and possesses the largest and best-serviced harbour within a radius of 1500 miles.

After 1942, from which time Singapore was occupied by the Japanese for three years, it was known by the name of Syonan, 'brilliant south'. Raffles aimed to forge Singapore into a 'great commercial emporium'. Malay tradition has it that around the early 11th century, an invading Sumatran prince named the island Sanskrit Singapura, 'Lion City'. In each case, the descriptions could hardly have proved more accurate.

Right: **The 'Ohio' of 1873, one of the sister ships of 'Pennsylvania', the American Steamship Company's first passenger liner.** *L Dunn Collection*

Below: The American ship 'Paris' (formerly called 'City of Paris') being refloated by tugs after grounding on rocks in May 1899. *L Dunn Collection*

Below right: The US Lines cargo ship 'American Merchant' pictured loading at Hamburg. *L Dunn Collection*

United States Lines

THE UNITED STATES LINES link with maritime history is symbolised by its house flag and its (now seemingly permanent) possession of the North Atlantic speed record, the Blue Riband.

After Brunel's 1340-ton *Great Western* had set a record of 8.2 knots from Bristol to New York in 1838, speed became the paramount factor on the eastward and westward Atlantic passages. With characteristic precocity, the Americans were early challengers; about 24 years before the Civil War of 1861-1865 created the nucleus of a united nation, the subsidised Ocean Steam Navigation Company tried unsuccessfully to break the British Cunard Company's monopoly.

For the next 36 years a tense battle was fought for North Atlantic supremacy between American and British ships. Famous American companies such as Collins and Inman & International followed each other in the struggle against Cunard and White Star. Equally famous ships—the American *Alaska, City of Paris, City of Brussels;* the Cunard *Britannia, Persia, Scotia;* the White Star *Adriatic, Baltic, Britannic, Germanic*—created new records and raised the speeds to more than 18 knots westward and 19 knots eastward. The crossings were reduced to seven days.

In the 1870s and 1880s no one knew about such sophisticated business methods as cost analysis, management by objectives, market research, cash flow, or long-range planning. The experts of the day were sure that the Atlantic trade had no horizons. Despite the acute financial strains, the shipping men reasoned that someone must eventually survive to win the prizes. The lessons of wasteful uneconomic competition were not to be learned for many years. National pride and the prospects of high profits were the spur. However, that instinctive optimism brought failure to all the American challengers, the Inman Line being the last to surrender, in 1892.

The more conservative cautious men, in particular Clement A Griscom, had been watching the early successes and failures. A few years after the Civil War he and some associates formed the American Steamship Company, from which the modern United States Lines directly stems and whose flag it wears.

The company began a steamer service between Philadelphia and Liverpool. Although it was aware of the Blue Riband prestige, its shrewd backers decided that comfort, safety and reliability must be the priorities. Their first vessel, the *Pennsylvania,* sailed on her maiden voyage from Philadelphia to Queenstown (Cobh) and Liverpool in May 1873. Her sister ships, the *Ohio, Indiana,* and *Illinois* made up a regular transatlantic fleet. The four ships were the epitome of safety and advanced design, and were the first to carry liferafts built on modern principles. They were powered by the first compound steam engines to be built in the United States.

Although the ships were faster than many of their rivals, the Blue Riband was not won until the company—which changed its name to American Line—acquired the Inman Line in 1892. For a quarter of a century Inman had fought a brave but gradually losing battle against Cunard and White Star. The British companies survived, although White Star was later to drop out of the speed competition and, later still, to become part of Cunard.

In Inman, the American Line bought fine ships as well as a famous company. Two of them, the *City of Paris* and the *City of New York,* were outstanding vessels by any standards. Clyde-built, each of about 10,600 tons, they had passenger accommodation far superior to that of their rivals. They were the first United States ships on the Atlantic to use twin screws, giving reduced hull vibration and increased power and speed. They also had a series of watertight bulkheads on a scale which later became common to ocean-going liners.

The *City of Paris* had already achieved a notable Blue Riband record by having been the first to log a voyage of six days from Queenstown (Cobh) to New York. By 1893, when their names had been shortened to *Paris* and *New York,* both ships won further Blue Riband honours.

The quest for speed, ruinous to some and expensive for everyone, was imposed by the accompanying publicity. Many of the wealthiest passengers had the snobbish vanity shared by some Jumbo Jet travellers of a later era. But there were people who preferred comfort and luxury to speed, who enjoyed having a day or two longer at sea. The American Line catered for them between New York and Southampton—to which it transferred its main British terminal from Liverpool. The *Paris* and *New York* were the last American vessels to hold the Blue Riband until the US Lines super ship, *United States,* regained it in 1952.

It was a bold decision not to compete for the Blue Riband during the intervening 59 years. The maximum publicity and prestige were obtained by such famous ships as the North German Lloyd *Kaiser Wilhelm der Grosse,* the Cunard *Mauretania*—which held it for 20 years—the North German Lloyd sister ships, *Bremen* and *Europa,* the French Line *Normandie,* and the Cunard *Queen Mary.*

The boldness of the decision can be judged in that during the year after the *Kaiser Wilhelm der Grosse* had won the record, North German Lloyd ships carried 25 per cent of the total transatlantic passengers.

From the end of the 19th century, the American Line and its successor the

United States Lines, was the only company to carry the stars and stripes across the Atlantic. But its reputation for comfort, luxury, and safety was unsurpassed. The *Paris* and *New York* steamed more than 2,000,000 miles, equal to a distance of more than 80 times round the world. They were not, of course, the only ships in the fleet. There were the *St Louis* and the *St Paul,* to be followed through the years by the *Leviathan, President Harding, President Roosevelt,* the *Manhattan* and the *Washington.*

After the 1914-18 war, the American Line suffered from the inevitable shipping slump. It is true that the United States had been in the war for only 19 months, and the company's ships *Paris, New York, St Louis,* and *St Paul* had sailed regularly across the submarine-infested Atlantic with one minor casualty.

However, the shipping depression was universal, although the United States was the first to surmount it. The American Line could soon run out of steam. The four transatlantic vessels were overworked, new shipbuilding costs were prohibitive and income had seriously declined. Nevertheless, expansion and not just continuity was indispensable for survival. The American Government refused the company's offer to buy the ex-German liner *Leviathan,* although she did join the fleet in 1930.

Until then the company could fairly be said to have been conservative, if not unenterprising. But with the end of the 1914-18 war enterprise and action brought its own rewards and made history. The American Line was the first to resume trade with Germany when it reopened its weekly service to Hamburg in December 1919.

Two years later, enterprise turned a loss-making blow into a profitable innovation. Immigration to the United States had always been a cornerstone of American shipping, from the squalid conditions when as many as 900 people were crowded in one steerage to the modest but better third-class accommodation of later years.

Some figures highlight the extent and importance of the immigrant trade. More than 1,700,000 Irish went to America in the 1840s and 1850s. In 1880 there were 250,000 Jews in the United States; by 1924 there were 4,250,000. At the beginning of this century, the immigrant centre at Ellis Island could handle as many as 8000 disembarked people a day. 'In the first two decades of this century,' wrote Alistair Cooke in his book *America,* 'an unbelievable fourteen and a half million immigrants arrived.'

In 1921 there was a major blow when the United States Government cut immigration to about one quarter of the pre-war volume. The third-class business, the hardcore of most transatlantic liners, was virtually destroyed. Reacting swiftly, the American Line converted the deserted quarters and made them available, at third-class rates, to professional people and college students. A whole new public responded to the unique opportunity. Passengers were known as third-class tourist. Later, the name was changed to tourist class, and the system was adopted by every shipping line.

The North Atlantic could provide growth but not expansion. Although the company was to increase its Western Ocean fleet, it sought expansion elsewhere. It reopened the Panama Pacific Line intercoastal service between New York and California via the Panama Canal. There had been one previous, abortive, attempt to begin the Panama Pacific service in 1915, when the *Kroonland's* passage through the Canal had been blocked by a gigantic landslide. That, and the 1914-18 war, had prevented further progress.

The lucrative Far Eastern trade was the next objective. In 1927 the American Line founded the Pioneer Line to operate ships to Australia, India, and the Far East. Four years later, the American Line was incorporated in the United States Line. The Blue Eagle house flag was carried on the new company's ships to begin a new and more important phase. The historic flag, first raised on the *New York* in 1893, still flies from the mastheads today.

With a profitable business to the Pacific and the Far East, the company added the *Leviathian, President Harding,* and *President Roosevelt* to its North Atlantic services. They were acquisitions of existing vessels, but in 1931 plans were made for two custom-built ships. They were to become as famous as any on the Atlantic. The first large passenger vessels to be built in the United States since 1905, and the largest ever built there, the sister ships *Manhattan* and *Washington* were unusual in construction and operation.

The *Manhattan's* keel was laid on December 6, 1930. Incredible though it seems today, she was launched exactly a year later, and nine months after that she left New York on her maiden voyage. When

Facing page top: Another early American Steamship Co vessel, the 'Indiana' of 1873. *L Dunn Collection*

Facing page centre: The 'American Hunter' of US Lines pictured at Le Havre. *L Dunn Collection*

Facing page bottom: The US Lines super ship and Blue Riband holder, the 'United States' entering New York harbour amid a flotilla of tugs. *L Dunn Collection*

'Top: The 'American Hunter' departing from Le Havre. *L Dunn Collection*

Left: 'American Challenger', one of the US Lines' war-built C2 standards. *L Dunn Collection*

the *Washington* was launched in late August, 1932, she was not christened with the traditional champagne but with water from an old spring at Mount Vernon, George Washington's estate on the Potomac River. Rapidly fitted-out, she left on her maiden voyage 10 months later.

Although construction of the ships had been rapid, their operational planning had been long considered. The North Atlantic trade was essentially a super-ship one, with the *Bremen, Europa, Majestic, Berengaria, Aquitania, Olympic, Mauretania* and *Ile de France* competing for the passenger business. Although each was an individual ship, all were cast in a familiar mould.

The United States Lines decided that a quite different mould was required. Its bold tourist experiment having been consistently successful, the company set out to extend what was in effect the economy class. The *Manhattan* and *Washington* each had a tonnage of approximately 24,000, a speed of 22 knots, and accommodation for cabin, tourist, and third-class passengers only. They were truly luxury ships, but with moderate fares. They became the fastest ships of their kind in the world.

But America can seldom ignore a challenge to its pride and prestige. Although the *Manhattan* and the *Washington* were outstandingly successful commercially, the temptation to share in the super-ship reputation could not be resisted. Shortly before the 1939-45 war, the keel of the giant liner *America* was laid. Planned to be the fastest and largest United States ship built up to that time, she was launched in 1940. By then, however, the North Atlantic was a death trap, and her service debut was postponed until after the war, when she and the *Washington* resumed the New York-Europe crossings.

After the war, shipping, like almost everything else, was to face unseen and largely unpredictable changes. If the astute United States Lines executives could have forecast the future, they surely would not have commissioned another big ship—destined, again, to be the biggest and fastest to come from an American yard.

However, plans for the new super liner, the 51,500-ton *United States,* were made soon after the war. When she sailed on her maiden voyage in July 1952, few people realised that the Atlantic passenger trade was doomed. Only a handful of forecasters sounded gloomy warnings and scarcely anyone would face the reality. Nor would most of the people concerned admit that the Atlantic bridge would soon be formed by super jets not super ships, but by the 1950s most liners on the run were beginning to operate below capacity.

On her first voyage, the *United States* set a new eastbound record of three days 12 hours 12 minutes and a new westbound record of three days 10 hours 40 minutes. The legendary mighty *Queen Mary* had been beaten. The Blue Eagle flew with greater pride from the masthead. More than 1600 passengers shared the triumph on each trip. But by 1969, after continuous financial losses, she left the North Atlantic, almost certainly the last ship ever to hold the Blue Riband.

Long before that time, the United States Lines' hunger for expansion and a greater share of world trade had reduced the importance of the North Atlantic passenger business. In the 1950s, new ships and the acquisition of established companies made the United States Lines one of the foremost freighter and cargoliner companies on the Seven Seas. The new vessels included the Challenger Class, the fastest freighters on the North Atlantic trade. They cut two full sailing days from the normal 10-day crossing; advanced cargo-handling equipment and quick-access hatches saved another day on the turnround.

By the end of 1961, the United States Lines owned and operated 52 cargo vessels and the two passenger liners *America* and *United States*. The two liners were plying the North Atlantic in the summer and cruising to Bermuda and the Caribbean in the winter. As the Atlantic passenger trade declined, cruising became a major feature until the *America* was sold in 1964 and the *United States* went out of service five years later.

Growth and expansion had already compensated for the loss of the big passenger business after 86 years. The next phase was to see a different kind of growth and expansion. Three years before the United States retired from the Atlantic, the company was one of the leaders in the greatest revolutions in maritime history – container cargo carrying. One cannot say that it was as profound a revolution as that of iron instead of wooden ships or steam instead of sail. But it was more dramatically immediate and was to change the entire world concept of seaborne cargo.

To appreciate just how immediate the revolution was one must realise that container ships are not converted break-bulk cargo vessels, but are purpose designed and built. Although the company began its container business with converted ships, six years later, in its centenary year, it had a fleet of 16 vessels built as container carriers, plying the company's 15,000 miles of trade routes, providing express service to more than 50 gateways to the world's major marketplaces.

The Far East route takes in New York, Norfolk (Virginia), Baltimore, Long Beach, Oakland, Hawaii, Guam, Hong Kong, Kobe, and Yokohama. The North Atlantic route includes New York, Balitmore, Norfolk (Virginia), Le Havre, Rotterdam, and Felixstowe (England). For the South Atlantic run the ships call at New York, Philadelphia, Savannah, Rotterdam, Liverpool, Bremerhaven, and Greenock. The company has organised a three-continent service so that, for example, one ship can load containers in Britain bound for a whole range of ports extending from New York to Oakland, Hawaii, and the Far East.

The United States Lines has two classes of containerliners, namely, the giant 32,000-ton Lancers and the Leaderships. Lancer-class ships have speeds of 24 knots, a capacity of 1240 containers, a length of 700 feet and a beam of 90 feet. They can cross the North Atlantic in six and a half days. The smaller Leaderships have a speed of more than 20 knots and a capacity of 930 containers.

The new breed of ships is supported by a fleet of feeder vessels, which carry cargoes to markets not served by the containerliners. Their links are worldwide and it would be tedious to name each destination. But the European and Far East feeder services provide a brief summary of the network. There are European services out of London and Hamburg for the North Sea and Baltic ports; out of Liverpool for Dublin and Belfast; out of Le Havre for Portugal and Spain; and in the Far East the link is from Hong Kong to Manila, Keelung, Kaohsiung, Kobe and Pusan.

The whole forms a vast global operation controlled by computers designed to keep track not only of the ships involved but also of the container cargoes. It is claimed that the data produced can pinpoint the position of all containers in transit or in any terminal, and to select onboard location of containers to ensure ship stability and correct unloading sequences. The aim is that cargoes are never lost and administration is reduced to an efficient minimum.

It is a long haul back to the company's founders, just over 100 years ago. The men who began with those first ships – *Pennsylvania, Ohio, Indiana,* and *Illinois* – have little in common with today's sophisticated management and computer control. Except for one thing – the sea.

Below: One of the United States Lines fast container ships the 18,764grt 23-knot 'American Legion', in the early 1970s soon after she entered service. *L Dunn Collection*

ROTTERDAM

A night shot of the busy port of Rotterdam working under artificial light. The pattern of movement of the crane jib lights during the time exposure is interesting. *Bart Hofmeester*

MARCH 9, 1872, and mixed spring weather. On the bank of a waterway a group of people watch a small vessel pass. She is the *Richard Young*, out of Harwich, wearing a line of flags which stand out clear-cut in the keen breeze from the North Sea. A channel has been officially opened and the dignitaries begin to disperse. They include a rather austere man in black, heavily built and with a fringe of beard under his chin. He is Peter Caland. His are the brains behind the waterway, which will save a port. Rotterdam.

This is the Rhine delta, and the Rhine is a strange river. In Switzerland, it starts schizophrenically as two rivers; in Holland, it finishes hysterically as many. Having travelled the length of Germany in a sober and orderly manner, it crosses the Dutch border and divides several times, complicated by the Meuse, which has come up from France and shares the same wide flat valley. Their combined force expends itself in the primary exit of the New Maas. Rotterdam stands about 18 miles up from the mouth.

Nobody knows who settled here first—or even where 'here' was. Sea and land levels change, storms surge and winds battle endlessly. Frail things like coastlines move constantly. Unsurprisingly, therefore, man's earliest traces have been found well off shore. Fishing craft and dredgers have brought up a steady steam of remains, the earliest of which was an auroch-bone pick-head dated at about 7000 BC. Later finds, primarily from old dune heads—or donks, include harpoons and fishhooks, fishtraps and primitive bowls, evidence that man's basic needs—food and dry settlement—have changed but little.

Middens have betrayed the existence of villages, by 2000 BC, whose inhabitants were developing much skill in handicrafts. Knowledge of metals and religious awareness increased and then, in 12 BC, the Romans arrived.

At that time, the Maas entered the sea via a spacious estuary, the Helinium, but this area of non-land, with its damp climate, was not to the taste of the legionaries garrisoned there, as contemporary letters testify. This was the land of the Batavii, subjugated rapidly by the Romans, who took also the land of the Frisii to the north. This marsh, now the Ijsselmeer, was barrier in itself and, by AD 47, the Romans had fallen back to the Oude Rijn; the northern border of a vast empire.

The Romans had numerous garrisons, and ships rapidly proved their value for communication. Indifferent sailors at best, however, they shirked the short sea passage along a treacherous coast from the Helinium to the Oude Rijn mouth. Thus was built the first known major Dutch canal. The general, Corbulo, named it the Fossa Corbulonis and it crept up behind the coastal dunes, past the main outpost at Forum Hadriani.

As the Romans left the area, between 250 and 400 AD, the populace emigrated also, and fell into decay. Not until between 700 and 900 AD was the area resettled, by Frisian and Frankish stock. The Merwede, one of the Rhine's branches, realigned itself in the 13th century, leaving a terrace within a bend. A good site, it became a settlement, based on fishing. Life was precarious, with storm surges bursting up the waterways, ruining crops, so the first engineering works were sluices, or dams, across small waterways. Two thus regulated were the Schie and the Rotte and the terms Schiedam and Rotterdam had appeared by 1270.

Rapid expansion followed, Rotterdam received its charter in 1340. It might well have been favoured with the lowest fordable point on the river. The older communities were bitter rivals; Dordrecht with its staple privileges and Delft, which bought land between the Schie and the Rotte and founded a rival Port, Delfshaven.

Rotterdam still grew steadily. An early map, of 1566, shows two basins, the Kolk and the Steiger, one boasting a crane. The Blaak and Nieuwehaven docks followed by 1600, dealing with ships of about 300 tons burthen and drawing about 10 feet of water. The population was by then 15 000; by 1700, it had quadrupled and the basins numbered nine.

One of the later basins was the Scheepmakershaven, its purpose was shipbuilding. The new industry thrived and was transferred to a larger site around the Zalmhaven. The older site was improved, warehousing added and, as the Boompjes, became the base for the increasingly important short-sea trades. Notable were the ships of the Batavier Line, which still have strong links with London. Besides the UK market, Rotterdam was active with East Indies and Greenland trade, as well as the herring industry. Neighbouring Maassluis and Vlaardingen were sharing in the new prosperity; then problems began.

The great river on which the life of the towns depended carried great quantities of sediment. As the waters slowed in the estuary, their unwelcome cargo was dumped. Longshore drift combined it with beach materials into a curving feature which closed off the river to navigation, to form the famous Hook of Holland.

Instead of only 22 miles, Rotterdam found itself about 59 miles from the sea; twisting narrow-channelled miles around the island of Voorne. Sailing ships with fickle winds experienced days of delay and, as the new route passed conveniently close to Dordrecht, the rival town began to cream off some of the trade. The answer was the Voorne Canal of 1830. Dordrecht was cut out by the new 25-mile approach and access was created for larger ships, drawing up to $16\frac{1}{2}$ feet.

The approach to the new canal was via the Goeree Gat which, capriciously, silted rapidly. Shipping again took the tortuous routes around the islands while plans were re-examined. It was Caland, borrowing an earlier idea of Cruquis, who proposed simply to blast through the Hook; a beautifully drawn map of 1857 showed how advantage was to be taken of a natural dip between the dunes.

The construction of the Willemskade in 1847 and the Westerhaven and Westerkade in 1852 showed that navigation troubles were regarded as only temporary. In 1855, the railway arrived. Bridges were thrown over the river and connection made to the new Koningshaven and appropriately named Spoorweghaven on the south bank.

The go-ahead for Caland's plan was not given until 1866 and it took six years to execute. But the end result was a straight 18-mile lock-free passage to the sea. Oddly, there was but 10 feet of water in the New Waterway and it continually threatened to silt up. Argument and rancour between engineers and backers resulted, the former desperately seeking to find a solution to give the quick return on investment demanded by the latter. The situation eventually was resolved by the development of the self-loading suction dredger, which moved sand rapidly in a water slurry. (Caland had resigned in 1878.)

The Treaty of Mannheim of 1868 granted free navigation rights on the Rhine to neighbouring countries. One effect was to improve Rotterdam's position in inland waterway traffic and increasing transshipment resulted. Private enterprise financed the Binnenhaven and Entrepothaven for the new trade. With developed rail links and standing at the very threshold of the Rhine, the port discharged raw materials from ocean-going ships into barges for the thirsty factories of Europe and eventually accepted the finished products for onward shipment to the export markets of the world, a function which is still vitally important today.

The year 1870 saw 2973 ships aggregating 1 166 305 net tons transitting the New Waterway, still under construction. As the waterway was deepened to 13 feet, the Holland-America Line began a transatlantic service. A series of severe winter gales in 1876 all but closed the canal again, trouble with maintaining depth being continuous until 1881, when the dredger finally won the battle.

A new bulk cargo—grain—began to arrive in such quantities that lines of dolphins were driven into the centre of the dock basins to accommodate the barges engaged in the trade. They are still a feature today. The Wilhelminakade was built in 1885 for both Holland-America and Rotterdam Lloyd vessels. The former company still uses it.

In 1890, the Parkhaven was built on the north bank, but the accent now was on larger basins on the opposite side of the river away from the constrictions of the city. The 75-acre Rijnhaven of 1894 looked small by the standards of the 145-acre Maashaven which followed it; the whole village of Katendrecht disappeared to make room.

By 1900, Rotterdam had overtaken Amsterdam as the first Netherlands port. Rail links were made in 1909 to the St Jobshaven and Schiehaven on the north bank, designed for improved liner services.

Ships need other services and Rotterdam now provided them too; shipbrokers and agents, chandlers and stevedores, storage and transport, repairs and construction. The population was 300 000 and increasing rapidly.

Growth begets growth and bulk handling demands space. The vast 775-acre Waalhaven was started in 1907, but was not ready in 1914, when the war blighted trade. Depression followed, and the project was not completed until 1930. Rotterdam, severely hit by the depression, invested in the future with the liner and barge facilities of the Merwehaven/Ijselhaven complex on the north bank.

A new commodity—oil—became important. In the 1930s at what was then a safe distance from the town, a 1300-acre site between the village of Pernis and the Oude Maas confluence was developed as a refinery for Shell. The project was overtaken by the 1939-45 war. The 'phoney' war ended for the Netherlands here on May 14, 1940. The spring skies were blackened as the almost undefended city had its heart torn out by the Luftwaffe. Occupation followed. It was an interregnum, with little happening. The Maas Tunnel was finished in 1942, giving freer access between the two halves of the wounded city, but there was little traffic.

War ended and a torn Europe needed rebuilding. A mass of seaborne material flowed in, docks being recommissioned rapidly to handle it. The old order had changed and the Netherlands had moved from an agricultural to an industrial economy; industry cried for oil. The first and second Petroleum Harbours were complete and inadequate. They were soon overshadowed in the 1950s by the Botlek project. Incorporating the third Petroleum Harbour, the area was a bastion of oil and its chemical derivative industry. Half the 3200 acres were leased to private firms which could benefit by bulk shipments to their doorstep.

But the old 'three-twelves' tanker had become the 35 000-tonner of the early 1950s and then began to grow at an astronomical rate as the economies of scale were appreciated. Larger ships need

Top left: A postcard from early in the present century showing the 1897 Great Eastern Railway ferry, 'Dresden' in the foreground. *A Lagendijk*

Above: An aerial view of the Maasvlakte, Rotterdam docks. *Bart Hofmeester*

Right: Departure in the sunset of the Holland-Amerika Line's ship, MV 'Nieuw Amsterdam'. *Bart Hofmeester*

Far right: The arrival of a 260,000-ton tanker in Europoort. *Bart Hofmeester*

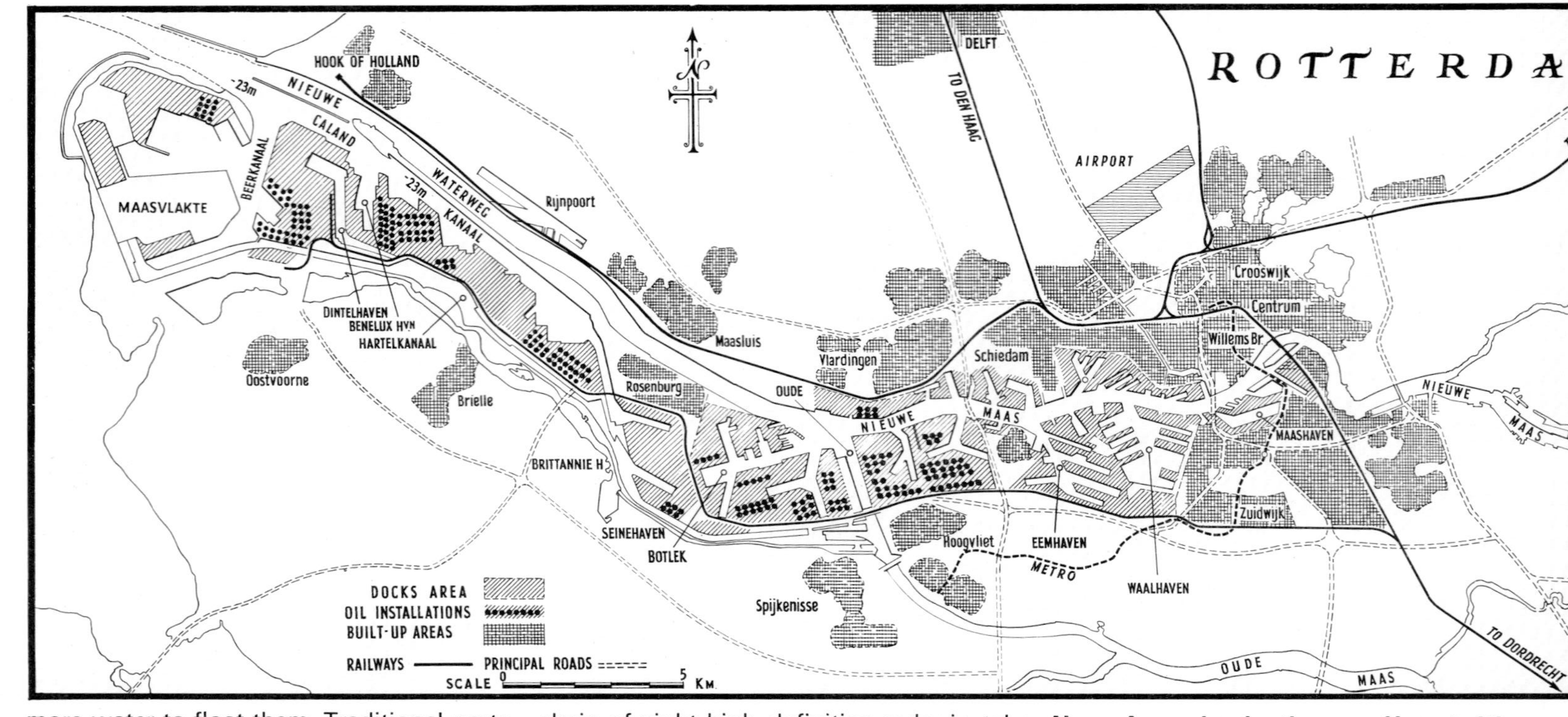

Above: A map showing the general layout of the huge complex of Rotterdam port. Since this map was drawn further installations have been added. *Port of Rotterdam Authority*

more water to float them. Traditional ports were often upstream and had to move down towards the sea. Rotterdam was no exception.

The Botlek was frozen for size and, to cater for the new monsters, a new port area was planned. Termed Europoort—Gateway to Europe, it stretched the rest of the way to the coast. Allowing for advice from the oil companies and surveys of the deep water approaches, much 'crystal-balling' was still entailed when likely sizes of future ships were discussed. The simple maximum parameters taken were 200 000dwt ships needing 62 feet of water. Construction began.

On Rozenburg appeared the new Verolme shipyard, backed by the Britanniehaven. The remaining seven miles to the sea has become a 9000-acre strip full of oil and chemical complexes. Running parallel with the New Waterway is the Caland Canal, giving access to the five major basins of the project. Barge and minor traffic is kept clear of the main channel by virtue of the Hartel Canal, skirting the southern boundary of the zone. Well planted with trees, it provides needed insulation for the land to the south.

Rotterdam had reached the sea, but not its limits. The Hartel Canal construction had altered the tidal flow along the coast and the Westplaat became greatly enlarged. Never ones to waste an opportunity, the harbour authorities instituted experiments to study the effect of full reclamation around the site. It seemed favourable and the Maasvlakte was born.

In a truly massive undertaking, about 5000 acres were won from the sea. The main ally was the suction dredger, which could remove sand from the channel where it was not wanted, pump it along bouyant pipes and spout it up where it could perform a useful purpose. The first step was an enclosing dam. A bank of sand, stabilised by a shingle overlay (dredged from off the English coast) capped by graded stone (from the upper Rhine) and topped off where necessary by 39-ton cubes of concrete delivered by special craft. The space inside was then simply filled as required with sand. Quarter-million ton tankers are now berthed where not long ago was just the scend of the sea. The work continues around them.

Nearly 33 000 sea-going ships were handled in 1971—or nearly 100 per day. Control of such an armada greatly depends upon minute-by-minute reports from a chain of eight high-definition radar installations stretching from the Hook to the Maashaven. The stream of information to masters and pilots is amplified where necessary by helicopter support.

What of the future? Maasvlakte is to be extended southwards and a major roll-on—roll-off port—Rijnpoort—is planned for a north-bank site between the Hook and Maassluis, long associated with the Smit tugs. The environment lobby is working against any further expansion, and the Delta plan has provided better communications southwards, over the new enclosing dikes. Future installations might thus be planted in hitherto peaceful Zeeland; the old city site of Reimerswaal has been suggested, along with Flushing and Terneuzen.

One needs to see the port of Rotterdam to believe it. Emerging from the Rijnhaven with its ranks of timber and general cargo ships, one is immediately in the bustle of the river. A box-like pusher tug with four pairs of barges in front heads purposefully for the raised Willemsbrug. Ore for the Ruhr. They pass the Wilhelminakade with a Holland-America cruise liner and a Dijk loading for the Gulf. Two blasts and one turns downstream. On the Parkkade to starboard, a spanking new cargo liner awaits trials; behind, the Euromast rises from the trees. The Maashaven to port with its great grain silos; between the ventilator towers of the Maas Tunnel; the radar station on the point.

A slight sheer to port as a barge swings out into the stream from the Schiehaven and the Waalhaven entrance is open to port. Dust palls of coal and ore. Grabs, Bulkers, Noise. Slow down while the strange barge-filled shape of a Lash ship moves into the Waalhaven. Hamburg Amerika colours, COMBI LINE emblazoned on her flank.

Shipbuilding to starboard. The green bulk of another Townsend car-ferry lies alongside the Gusto yard at Schiedam. Beyond, Wilton Feijenoord has a cargo liner on the ways. Splashes of bright light from the welders and the din of windy-hammers. The length of the Eemhaven visible to port. Containers. Vast slab-sided ships and boxes everywhere in neat ranks. Yellow side-loaders. Cranes as high as cathedrals. A Japanese flag. Bustle.

Pernis to port and a strong smell of crude. Traffic rushes invisibly below through the new Benelux tunnel. A slight bend to the right and a straight ten-mile run to the sea. Ahead, an 80 000-tonner in ballast, rust streaks down her enormous freeboard. Beneath her Liberian ensign, a screw lazily thrashes the green waters of the Maas. To port, the Botlek. Endless silver towers, tanks and pipes. The opposite side, Vlaardingen and then open farmland beyond the railway. Cloud shadows chase across the flat landscape. A Dutch belfry with angled flagpoles.

Verolme's yard to port with the unbelievable bulk of a 250 000-tonner fitting out. A cargo vessel passes in front. Polish flag? No, it's upside down. She passes, On her quarter, Djakarta—Indonesian. A small coastal tanker follows. Empty, untrimmed, her bows up at a crazy angle.

Maassluis to starboard. Tugs in the inlet; opposite, all is Europoort. Tankers lie quietly at finger piers. Activity is apparently absent from this automated world, but, in the Benelux haven, the big road vehicles are rolling out of the gaping visor door of the North Sea Ferry, just in from the Humber.

Open sea visible ahead. The Hook passenger terminal to starboard and the flame-red funnel of the British Rail night ferry. To port a land of sand. The sun glints off lagoons submitting to the snaking pipes of the dredgers. Massvlakte. The wind perks up and smells fresh. White flecks on the water and the first ship movement as the north breakwater light slips astern.

One looks down on the vast green deck of yet another tanker shipping upstream into the Caland Canal approach. Tugs. The Dutch flag snaps over the last Dutch name. Schouwenbank. Open sea at last, and the land falls away.

CONTAINER & BARGE CARRIERS

PRIOR TO THE 1939-45 war, cargo was shipped either in relatively slow tramps sailing wheresoever inducement offered or by cargo liners working a scheduled service and owned by companies who usually were members of the 'shipping conference' governing that particular trade. Few tramps had a deadweight capacity exceeding 10,000 tons but cargo liners of up to 15,000 tons deadweight were in service under the houseflags of some operators, such as Alfred Holt's Blue Funnel Line and the Glen Line.

There were in addition various specialised cargo vessels catering for the carriage of chilled meat, fruit and other perishables but, irrespective of the nature of the cargo, loading and discharge were in all cases laborious tasks involving much skill and a lengthy turnround in harbour, with the ship incurring a mounting bill for dock dues instead of earning a profit at sea.

In 1945 shipowners were faced with the problem of making good the losses suffered during the previous six years; in the circumstances little consideration could be given to improvements in either ship design or cargo handling methods. Consequently, new ships of the first post-war generation were essentially similar to their pre-war forebears, although speeds in the cargo liner class tended to be somewhat higher than had been usual in the past. Cargo handling gear also showed little advance, although as a result of wartime experience most post-war cargo ships were equipped with a heavy-lift derrick.

Cargo ship design remained practically static in fact until the mid-1950s, when the first vessels of a new generation of faster, and in many cases larger, cargo liners entered service as replacements for pre-war vessels and the wartime so-called standards. Typical of the second-generation fast cargo liners was the 11,463-ton (gross) *Benloyal,* a 20-knot geared turbine steamship completed on the Clyde by Charles Connell & Co for Ben Line Steamers Ltd in January 1959. In appearance she looked decidedly sophisticated alongside her older consorts, while in the matter of equipment, modern aids were enlisted to reduce the demands on manpower. In service, the *Benloyal* worked from European ports with scheduled passage times of 19 days to Singapore and 27 days to Hong Kong.

The problem of lengthy turnround times continued to hamper efficient operation, however. To the shipowner it meant that increasingly expensive ships were being kept idle for much of the time while general cargoes were discharged piecemeal, using methods which had changed little during the previous 50 years. Innovation generally was confined to improved

Left: ACT's container ship 'Australian Endeavour' on her maiden voyage, passing under Sydney's famous bridge.
Associated Container Transport

Above top to bottom: Sequence of pictures illustrating the BACAT (barge aboard catamaran) system; the pictures show 'BACAT 1' in the Pool of London.
All A Greenway

dockside cranes and a limited range of mechanical handling aids.

Manhandling invariably played a major part in the movement of cargo in and out of the ship, particularly within the vessel itself, where the restricted size of hatches prevented maximum use being made of dockside cranage and other facilities. Even for the modern cargo vessel of the 1950s, a month in port at each end of a voyage was not uncommon; all-in-all it served to make for a poor return on the high capital investment represented by the ship itself.

Further erosion of profits resulting from increases in dock dues, insurance premiums and wages brought about the virtual disappearance of the British tramping fleet and caused liner operators also to look to the future with misgiving.

In the United States, however, shipowners were turning already to the use of freight containers, packed at inland depots and carried to the port by road or rail to be loaded aboard purpose-designed or adapted container ships. The freight container had been developed many years earlier by British railways for their short-sea services.

In America, as far back as 1929, Seatrain Lines Inc, of New York, had pioneered a service between New York, Houston (Texas) and Havana carrying railway wagons in cradles aboard specialised ships. The first of them, the 7 648-ton *Seatrain New Orleans,* with accommodation for 95 wagons, was actually built in Britain on the Tyne by Swan, Hunter & Wigham, Richardson Ltd, but later similar ships were products of the Sun Shipbuilding Corporation of Chester, Pennsylvania. In 1959 Seatrain Lines turned to the use of containers designed for loading and discharge on and off the ship in the same manner.

Containerisation involves the packing and emptying—stuffing and stripping—of box-like units, built to internationally agreed measurements and design, generally at depots away from the dock area, and often at the place of production or consumption. The containers are usually the property of the shipowner or the shipper and may be insulated, refrigerated or designed for the carriage of general (break bulk), bulk or tanked cargoes. Once loaded and sealed, they are moved to the port marshalling area for embarkation. The container ship itself is provided with internal cellular and deck stowage for standard-size units and loading involves the use of specialised quayside cranes of 30-45 tons capacity which can handle a unit between dockside and ship in a cycle time of only about three minutes.

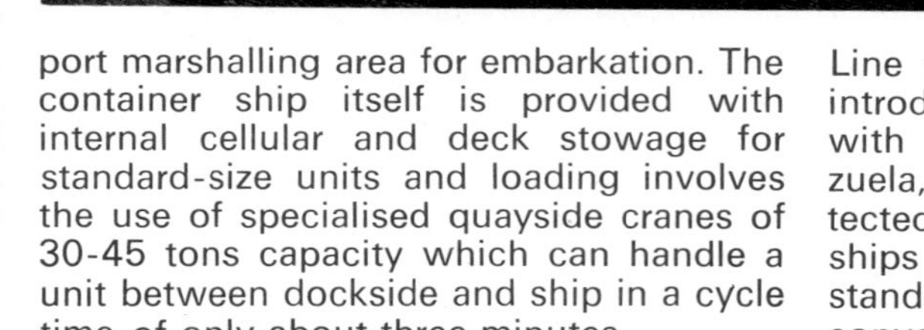

Seatrain Lines Inc has been mentioned already but its move into the deep-sea container business in 1959 came at a time when other American operators were already well established in the field of container transport. Probably the first partial cellular container ships were standard US C2 freighters fitted out in the early 1950s for the US East Coast trade of the Pan-Atlantic Steamship Corporation, now absorbed by Sealand Service Inc. The Matson Navigation Co was also early in the field with a container service between San Francisco and Hawaii, operated initially by the 12,177-dwt *Hawaiian Merchant,* a C2 geared turbine steamship completed in 1945 and converted in 1958.

Other shippers in the United States domestic trade soon turned over to container operation and in 1960 the Grace Line took matters a step further by the introduction of a service linking New York with La Guiara and Maracaibo in Venezuela, the first outside the heavily protected inter-state trade. Once again the ships employed were conversions from the standard C2 cargo type, but in later years conversions from the larger C4 cargo vessels and T2 turbo-electric tankers played their part in the developing container trade.

Huge capital investment was involved in the purchase of containers and the necessary handling equipment, the provision of large clear marshalling areas adjacent to the dockside, and the cost of converting existing conventional ships or building new ones. But the results appeared to justify the cost and container shipment became the accepted practice in the US domestic trades.

Established European shipowners were at first sceptical of the container revolution. It was acknowledged that a 48-hour turnround time would greatly improve the chances of a fair return on capital investment in ships, but difficulties were foreseen in maintaining adequate control over the international movements of large

Above far left: Sponsons and lifting gear of the LASH barge carrier 'Acadia Forest'. *L Dunn*

Above left: The Combi Line's LASH ship 'Bilderdyk' at Rotterdam. *L Dunn Collection*

Left: Sealand Service Inc's converted C2 containership 'Warrior' and a small feeder container vessel at San Juan, Puerto Rico. *A Greenway*

Above: Containership 'ACT 3' at Sydney. *Associated Container Transport*

Below: German cargo liner 'Josef Stewing' and cargo handling by conventional dockside crane at West India Dock, London in 1974. *D J Kingston*

numbers of containers. In addition, many operators were not willing in an uncertain world to commit themselves to heavy capital expenditure in a development which would make their conventional liner fleets redundant. Further, the labour-intensive work of loading and discharging would still need to be provided for, albeit at some inland depot rather than in the ship's hold.

Despite the misgivings of some operators, others were enthusiastic, seeing in particular the attractive economics of a small fleet of large fast ships doing the work of many times their number of conventional cargo liners. In the early 1960s intensive studies were undertaken to examine the feasibility of organising much of North-West Europe's trade into a container network.

As a result, because of the enormous capital outlay involved, in 1965 several leading European shipping companies merged their interests in the formation of three international consortia linked to particular trades. They are the Atlantic Container Line (North Atlantic trade), Associated Container Transportation Ltd (Australasian trade), and Overseas Containers Ltd (Australasian trade). International standards for containers were agreed, orders were placed for the necessary fleets of ships and vehicles and capital was poured into the provision of the necessary port facilities.

Overseas Containers Ltd is a British venture formed by the Ocean Steamship Co, Peninsular & Oriental, the British & Commonwealth Shipping Co and Furness Withy & Co to operate, jointly with Associated Container Transportation Ltd, a weekly service between Tilbury, Fremantle, Melbourne and Sydney. The first vessel for the new fleet, the 27,000grt *Encounter Bay*, registered nominally in the name of the Scottish Shire Line Ltd (a member of the British & Commonwealth group), was delivered by Howaldtswerke-Deutsche Werft early in 1969. (Because of a labour dispute in London she took her maiden sailing to Australia from Rotterdam.)

The *Encounter Bay* was powered by geared turbines of 32,000shp, which provided a service speed of 21 knots. At the time of completion she was the largest container ship afloat, although rapid development of the container trade ensured that the distinction was short lived. She was followed by five sister ships, the last of which, the Clyde-built *Jervis Bay*, was delivered in 1970.

It was in the North Atlantic trade, however, that the most far-reaching changes in the pattern of international commerce were taking place. New international consortia were created and most of the established companies invested heavily in container ships, either conversions or new construction, in order to ensure retention of their own shares of the trade. While several companies were still in the throes of converting to container transport, further developments of even more revolutionary concept were taking place in the United States, where the LASH (Lighter Aboard Ship) system was evolved.

The LASH freighter is essentially a container vessel equipped with its own gantry crane capable of handling and stowing on board loaded purpose-designed lighters (as well as, in some cases, standard containers). The advantage claimed for the LASH system is that vast dockside marshalling areas are not required; the lighters themselves form the terminal transport to and from any convenient site with the necessary depth of water, even far along inland waterways, although the maximum draught of both LASH and Seabee (mentioned later) craft exceeds European limits, occasionally causing problems during the season of low water. A secondary objective in the development was the reduction of port congestion, which was already causing delays of several days awaiting a discharge berth at some ports.

The LASH system was conceived by American LASH Systems Inc, of New Orleans. Delivery of the first vessel, the 43,000 dwt *Acadia Forest,* was accepted from Uraga Heavy Industries of Yokusuka, Japan, in 1969. Registered in the name of the A/S Moslash Shipping Co, Christiansand, Norway, the *Acadia Forest* is chartered to the Central Gulf Steamship Corporation and operates between US Gulf ports, the Thames and Rotterdam. A 26,000bhp diesel engine driving a single screw gives a service speed of 19 knots and the round voyage takes about 30 days.

Stowage is provided in the ship for 73 lighters, each of 370 tons capacity, which are handled in and out by a 510-ton travelling crane spanning the deck on rails extending the length of the vessel's cargo space. The lighters are handled at the rate of one every 15 minutes and are so designed that they can be formed into trains for river navigation in tow. Thus, the cargoes on lighters loaded, say, in upper Rhine ports require no further handling, apart from transfer on and off the mother ship, until they reach their destination, perhaps well inland up the Mississippi. The *Acadia Forest* herself does not carry containers but stowage is provided for liquid cargoes (or ballast) in wing tanks.

On the Pacific, a LASH service is operated between San Francisco, Guam and the Far East by the Pacific Far East Line. The company employs six 26,400-ton vessels designed and built by Avondale Shipyards Inc, of New Orleans. They are 23-knot geared turbine steamships, the first of which, the *Thomas E Cuffe,* was completed in 1971; they provide stowage for 49 lighters handled by a 500-ton rail-mounted crane and 334 standard 20-foot containers. In addition to a lighter crane, the vessels are equipped with a 30-ton gantry for handling containers.

A development of the LASH system is Seabee, conceived by the Lykes Bros Steamship Co, of New Orleans. Three ships of the Seabee type have been built, the first of which, the 20,500grt *Doctor Lykes,* was delivered by the General Dynamics Corporation of Quincy, Massachusetts, in 1972. The three ships and the complementary fleet of 246 barges cost $125 million, a vast investment by any standard and certainly the largest con-

Above: Modern conventional cargo ship with on-board lifting gear, Ben Line's 'Bencruachan', at Royal Albert Dock, London. *A Greenway*

Below: 'ACT 5' berthed for a quick turnround at the PLA's container terminal at Tilbury on the Thames. *Associated Container Transport*

Right: 'ACT 2' on passage with a capacity load over her massive deck space. *Associated Container Transport*

Below right: Stern door and loading bridge of Atlantic Container Line's 'Atlantic Saga'. *L Dunn Collection*

struction programme ever undertaken by a US-flag operator. The development was heavily subsidised by the US Government, no doubt with some thought of military potential. Like the *Acadia Forest*, the Lykes vessels operate between the Mississippi, the Thames and the Rhine, but unlike the LASH system, the entry into service of Seabee required the laying of special moorings.

Each vessel carries 38 barges, which are embarked two at a time through a stern elevator. Tugs position the barges over a submerged platform which is then raised to the required deck level where a transporter runs under each barge, jacks it up off the elevator blocks and moves it into the stowage area. The average cycle time is about 30 minutes and the 38-barge load can be handled in a turnround time of about 13 hours. In addition, each vessel provides stowage for 30,000 tons of liquid cargo.

The *Doctor Lykes, Almira Lykes* and *Tillie Lykes* are engined with geared turbine machinery of 36,000shp driving a single screw to give a service speed of 20 knots; an athwartships bow-thrust unit driven by a 1200hp electric motor is provided to ease the task of mooring. The rear end of the vessels is dominated by a pair of massive sponsons, projecting aft from the true stern, which house the elevator machinery; all-in-all, they present a somewhat bizarre appearance.

Yet another approach to transocean cargo transport has been the development of the roll-on/roll-off (Ro-Ro) vessel from the type introduced originally for the short sea connections making up the North-West European 'home' trade. Such vessels lend themselves in particular to the carriage of export vehicles and loaded trailers and vehicle access to the cargo decks is usually gained over a hinged ramp and doors in the stern or side of the ship.

Typical of the class is the Cunard-registered *Atlantic Causeway* of Atlantic Container Line Ltd; she is 14,946grt turbine steamship completed by Swan Hunter Shipbuilders Ltd in 1969. With a service speed of $23\frac{1}{2}$ knots, she operates between Europe and the United Kingdom and New York or Baltimore carrying vehicles and container cargo. As in the case of the Lykes Seabees, a bow-thrust unit is fitted to assist manoeuvring when docking.

Container ship, LASH, Seabee and Ro-Ro, each represents a different approach to the concept of an integrated transport system; all have their advantages and their limitations, apart from requiring vast capital investment. It is probable, however, that the container system will continue to be the most popular since it lends itself to road, rail or water transport for the terminal connections. By 1976, the container revolution had been extended to India and southern Africa and today there are no major trading routes that are served by only conventional break-bulk vessels.

Even so, conventional freighters and inland freight carriers are unlikely ever to be entirely replaced. Some cargoes, such as pipes and lumber for example, cannot be boxed, and such things as seasonal fruit crops are an embarrassment to container operators. LASH and Seabee operations also would be hampered by ice on inland waterways, and they suffer the further disadvantage that although the parent ships are of high deadweight capacity, a big proportion of the capacity is taken up by the barges themselves.

Royal Research Ships

BRITAIN has traditionally played a leading part in research and exploration, as much or more in surveying and charting the oceans as on land. The pioneer work of HMS *Challenger* during the remarkable voyage of 1872-76 (see pages 104-6) is echoed today by the activities of the Royal Research ships. Research ships with such famous names as *Discovery*, *Challenger* and *Shackleton* are employed in a number of research and survey tasks in the polar regions, to determine and record aspects of marine life and to chart the vast and everchanging polar icecap. The larger vessels often spend as much as 250 days a year at sea, averaging up to 3000 miles a month, and every year British Antarctic Survey sends ships with parties of scientists and their supplies to the established bases in the South Polar region. The Royal Navy also has special ships for patrolling and working in polar waters in support of survey work. The *Endurance* pictured here is a former Danish merchant ship, *Anita Dan*, with strengthened hull for working in ice and she carries two helicopters to extend her range of operation.

Above: The Royal Research ship 'John Biscoe' at Port Stanley, Falkland Isles. *A Morrison*

Below: RRS 'John Biscoe' and HMS 'Endurance' at Storrington, Marguerite Bay, Grahamsland, during the 1970 expedition. *J Newman*

9. Science at Sea

MARINE ARCHAEOLOGY

NAUTICAL ARCHAEOLOGY—the study of ships, harbours, anchorages and man-made sites underwater—is a modern science. It has been developed through the co-operation of divers and archaeologists working side by side seeking to extend research on land into the sea in an endeavour to find out the maximum possible about man and how he lived, whatever the period.

In the past, knowledge of ancient ships has been limited to those discovered in burial mounds or the muddy beds of rivers. Now, the free diver, taking his air supply with him, can work under water carrying all the required tools of his profession—archaeological picks, cameras, air-lift pumps for clearing away the 'soil' from a site, plastic sketch boards and all kinds of measuring and mapping equipment. An established principle in archaeology is that exploration precedes excavation, but unfortunately the rule has not been observed and many valuable sites have been looted by amateurs in search of sunken treasure, although most countries have now introduced strict legislation prohibiting the looting of wrecks or underwater sites.

Under British law, every wreck belongs to someone. Whatever its age, it must be reported to the local receiver of wrecks or Custom House. The law states that a wreck, whether found within or outside territorial limits, must be reported, and if the finder is neither the owner nor operating for the owner, the wreck must be 'delivered' to the receiver of the district. If no claim of ownership is established, the receiver will retain it for one year and, at the expiry of that time, when it becomes vested in the Crown, sell it and make payment of salvage from the proceeds. The receiver has the power to sell wrecks in his custody. The proceeds are then shared between the appropriate government and the salvor.

Above right: The use of a floating crane to lift old mooring chains from the harbour bed. *J Eastland*

Above: A portside gun recovered from Henry VIII's sunken warship the 'Mary Rose', in 1972. *A McKee*

Several organisations have been formed in England to control nautical archaeology, foremost among them being the CNA (Committee for Nautical Archaeology) a voluntary body working under the auspices of the Institute of Archaeology, London University. Its function is to gather information on all aspects of nautical archaeology and to act as an advisory body in matters of policy and in special work. In the Mediterranean practically every wreck discovered has been looted and destroyed by amateurs.

Fortunately it has not happened in British waters. Our sub-aquatic heritage enjoys the protection of less hospitable conditions where extreme competence in diving is required. During the last decade many ships of great historical value have been discovered, recorded and, in some cases, excavated. They include Charles the Second's yacht *Mary,* the Spanish Armada vessels *Santa Maria de la Rosa, Girona, La Trinidad Valencera* and the Dutch East Indiamen *de Liefde, Amsterdam* and *Hollandia.* Henry VIII's battleship *Mary Rose* is the latest and perhaps the most important discovery of all.

In 1901 a group of sponge divers wearing heavy rubber suits and helmets stumbled across the remnants of an ancient ship at a depth of 180ft off the North coast of the Greek island of Antikythera, lying between Kythera and Crete. The ship contained a cargo of objets d'art, including bronze and marble figures and a huge bronze arm which they raised as proof of their discovery. The captain, Demetrios Kondos, was a rough diamond, but he knew the value of such a find and approached the Greek authorities with his news—and the bronze arm. Kondos made a deal with the Greeks. He would divulge the whereabouts of the site on the understanding that he and his divers would excavate the wreck and, no doubt, be paid handsomely for their dangerous work.

The discovery marked the beginning of underwater archaeology as a special study. Archaeology on land or beneath the waves is in essence the application of scientific method to the excavation of ancient objects. It is based on the theory that the historical value of an object depends not so much on the nature of the object itself as on its associations, which only scientific excavations can detect.

But unfortunately, ever since man became interested in digging up his past there have been the casual diggers and plunderers intent on getting something of artistic or commercial value, and there the interest stops. The 'robber' sells the object and it passes from hand to hand until it finds its way to a private collection, or at best to a museum. But by then nobody knows where it was found—or how. It has been torn from its context and can be appraised only as a thing in itself.

So Captain Kondos deserves commendation for his action. He was only human, and humans like finding rare and beautiful things to covet and admire, or sell. He could have made a great fortune, for the salvage expedition, organised by Greek experts, though their methods of excavation were primitive, revealed far more than statues of bronze and marble. Beautiful glass vessels, golden earrings, crew's tableware, storage jars, lamps and a mechanical device consisting of gear wheels, dials and plates which was identified as a complex astronomical computer, gave the discovery and exploration of the site a firm place in the history of underwater archaeology.

Except for the discovery in 1907 of a ship belonging to the Roman dictator Lucius Cornelius Sulla, which was carrying his share of the plunder of Athens consisting of quantities of marble columns and bronze statues, more than three decades were to pass before methods of scientific evaluation were firmly established. It was the Italian archaeologist Professor Lamboglia who developed methodical search techniques and applied his skill on many sites in Mediterranean waters; the most notable was at Albenga, where he was rewarded with a rich collection through which much light has been shed on ancient culture.

The countries surrounding the Mediterranean have given us a great part of our knowledge of prehistoric man. They have been called the cradle of civilisation. Now that the study of archaeology has been taken into the sea, it is fortunate that the Mediterranean is so favourable for divers. In its clear water, scarcely disturbed by the gentle tides, we can see, where the seaweed is thin and scattered, right through to the sandy ocean bed. The number of encrusting animals is limited by the small amount of lime in the rock. All around the coast and into the water there is a chain of ruins and sunken ships marking the points from which, in the days when ships first traded, the sea lanes have run.

From the shores of Majorca, Provence and Corsica in the west to the scattered islands of the Dodecanese in the Aegean Sea, the traders of Egypt, Crete, Phoenicia, Athens, Rome, Carthage and Byzantium lost their ships in storms and battle. During the last 20 years divers have been bringing to the surface broken remains that are piecing together a historical picture of ancient maritime life. It will only be completed if enough wrecks are found with evidence to fix their origin and age.

There are three main approaches to the study of ship wrecks; going under water to the wreck, removing the wreck from the water, and removing the water from the wreck. The first approach, going under water to the wreck, is the only way to study a ship that has lain on the seabed for a thousand years or more.

That is because a wooden ship sunk in coastal waters will almost certainly be broken up on impact with the beach or on rocks, or by the action of waves, tides and currents, resulting in its cargo being scattered over a wide area. Parts of the hull might be found which, by their own sheer weight, have settled deep into the seabed. Even so, further sedimentation settling on the wood might provide a protective covering and even help to preserve the wood. Any archaeological survey would certainly have to be carried out on the seabed.

The dating of an ancient wreck buried in the seabed is not helped by marine growth. The study of undersea fossils shows that the lower forms of marine life—the seaweeds, hydrozoa corals and sponges—have altered little in the course of centuries, and thus will give little information as to the age of a find. Some of them make the archaeologist's work much more difficult as they can eat into the toughest of woods and decompose the hardest of metals, with the help of oxidation. Only earthenware, lead, gold and bronze survive unaltered through thousands of years of immersion in sea water. Even stone and marble are eaten away by mussels. Wood buried in mud or sand retains its shape but becomes as soft as cork when brought to land and it dries out. It warps and shrinks to two-thirds its original size.

The framework of a wreck settled on a hard seabed collapses under the weight of deposits accumulating on it, then the mound of sedimentation covering the wreck flattens gradually until the sea bottom recovers its normal level, showing hardly a trace of the place where the ship sank. In much the same way ancient cities and harbours have disappeared in the sands of time. The graves of many submerged land sites and ships are betrayed only by a fragment of pottery or the projecting neck of an amphora, a hand-carved stone or an area of paving, but they will often evade the eye of even the expert researcher.

Nevertheless, divers using metal detectors and other electronic devices which probe deep into the sand and mud of the seabed have located shipwrecks, town-

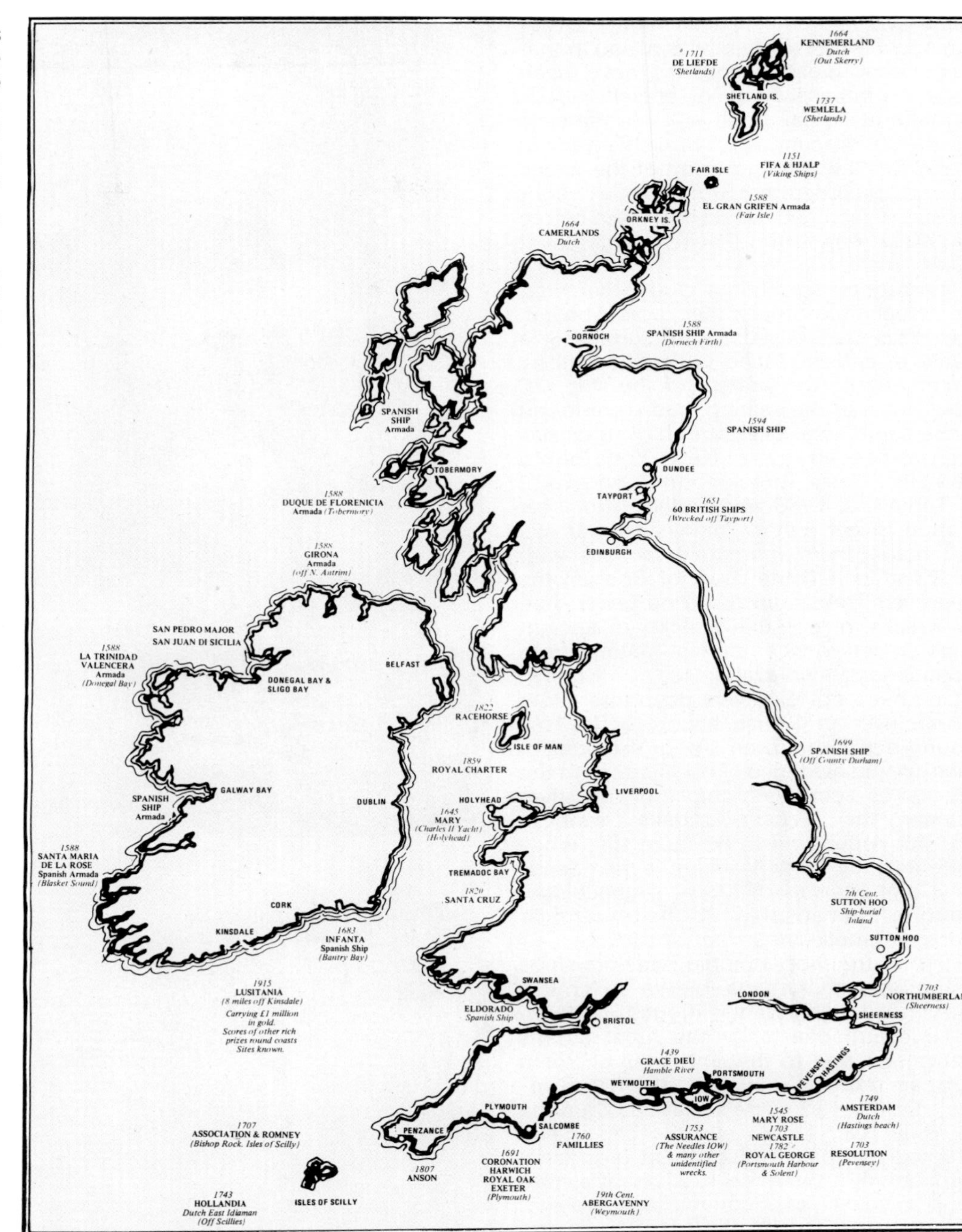

Above: A comprehensive wreck chart of the British Isles. *L Kenyon*

ships and harbours. The lost city of Sybaris in Southern Italy was found in that way. Other great discoveries have been made by intense study of ancient documents in historical archives, as in the case of the 17th-century Swedish warship *Wasa*. But the exact position of the wreck was not recorded, so Stockholm Harbour had to be searched for several years before the *Wasa* was found, lying at a depth of 110ft.

The second method of study, removing the wreck from the water, was applied. The *Wasa* was raised to the surface in a cradle of cables placed under the hull by divers. During the search for the ship, 26 other hulks of the same period were found in the same area. Even that high total has been exceeded by a New York photo journalist, Peter Throckmorton, who went to Turkey in 1958 and sailed with local sponge divers, whose many years at sea had made them intimately familiar with local waters. Off the coast of Bodrum the divers led Throckmorton to no fewer than 30 wrecks, or possible wrecks, of ancient ships, mostly wine carriers dating from Hellenistic to medieval times.

One need not dive very deep into either the archives of British history or the sea around our own coasts, or our estuaries or rivers, to find evidence of our heritage in the wrecks of scores of ships. In the river Thames, the *Serpent,* a galley sunk in AD 852 is believed to be there still, while quite recently Peter Marsden, a member of the Committee for Nautical Archaeology, found a Roman ship in the mud near Mansion House.

Among the most notable finds are ships of the Spanish Armada, blown off course and hurled against our rugged northern and western coasts by the great storms that put an end to the ambitions of Philip of Spain's crusade against the first Elizabeth. Of the 130 vessels that left Corunna on July 12, 1588, exactly half never returned to Spain; 32 of them foundered unrecorded in the oceans, 21 went ashore on the coasts of Scotland and Ireland, six were wrecked off the coast of Europe and the *San Pedro Mayor* came to grief in Bigbury Bay, South Devon, where the country people made 'great pilfering and spoils'. She was said to have been one of the two hospital ships of the Armada. *El Gran Grifen* went ashore on Fair Isle, a little island between Orkney and Shetland.

Several of the ships wrecked on the Irish coast have been identified, the most recent one being the galleass *Girona.* When the storms of October 1588 forced the ship on to the Ulster coast, she carried aboard the combined equipment of five other Armada vessels and the riches of the gentlemen who sailed in them. A Belgian historian and diver, Robert Stenuit, discovered the *Girona* in 1968. After 400 years, deep in the dust of archives he reconstructed the story of the tragedy—the fateful night when a lookout saw breakers ahead, shouted a warning and cut the ropes that retained the anchor, but too late. 'With a terrible grinding even louder than the cracking of storm waves on the jagged coast the ship gutted herself on the rocks, spilling out her cannon, her wealth, and 1300 soldiers, sailors and gentlemen of the realm'. Robert Stenuit and his divers recovered a remarkable haul; guns, anchors, gold, silver plate, hundreds of valuable coins, jewellery of rubies and diamonds and rare navigational instruments.

In 1683 another Spanish ship, the *Infanta,* went down in Bantry Bay, County Cork, and eight years later the *Eldorado* sank off Swansea carrying £80,000 worth

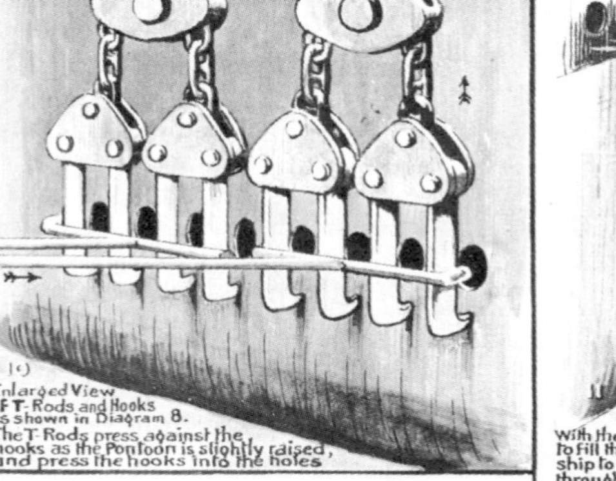

Facing page top: A collection of assorted small items (including stone shot) recovered in a day's dig from the 'Mary Rose' site in September 1972. *A McKee*

Facing page bottom: Sketches from the September 1, 1923, edition of 'The Illustrated London News' showing the proposed Reno System of raising sunken ships through the use of compressed air pontoons and submarine tractors. *Illustrated London News*

Above: More stone shot recovered from the 'Mary Rose' in September 1972. *A McKee*

of gold, of which £13,000 has already been salvaged. In 1699 a third Spanish ship foundered off Seaton Carew, County Durham, with £200,000 on board, £30,000 of which has been recovered. In 1967 the flagship of Admiral Sir Cloudesley Shovell's Mediterranean Fleet, wrecked off the Isles of Scilly in 1707, was found in 100ft of water. She is HMS *Association* and her discovery rates as one of the richest treasure finds in modern history. There is yet one more recent find, the Tudor warship *Mary Rose*, the finest ship in Henry VIII's navy, which sank off Portsmouth in 1545. The next few years might well see the completion of the most exciting project in British archaeology – the excavation and eventual raising of this 440-year-old prize.

Both North and Central America share in the spoils of archaeological and treasure wealth. Twentieth-century sleuthing methods and the love of romance and mystery led Kip Wagner, a Florida construction man, to the Spanish treasure Armada—ten richly laden vessels which were driven on to the Florida Keys 250 years ago. Three million dollars in treasure were recovered in the form of silver pieces of eight, golden doubloons, silver bars and bullion, priceless Chinese porcelain and a gold necklace valued at $50,000.

The third method of study, removing the water from the wreck, was used in surveying two Roman ships sunk in Lake Nemi, 17 miles south-east of Rome. Starting in 1928, the surface of the lake was lowered more than 70ft by enormous pumps which sent the water into another lake lying at a lower level. Four years of pumping elapsed before the ships were exposed to the air. It proved to be one of the greatest discoveries of the century, for not only were they giant craft, nearly 250ft long, but they were obviously built as floating palaces for the nobility of Rome, sumptuously decorated with mosaic and marble flooring over their oak decks, halls embellished with marble columns and bronze statues, heated baths, kitchens and elegant table ware. Study of the ships' construction has been of the greatest value to marine archaeologists. They were able to inspect well-preserved hulls of the Roman period because they had sailed in fresh water free of ship-worm and their hulls were protected by a skin of lead below the water line, similar to most seagoing vessels of the period.

Another means of removing water from a wreck site is by building a coffer dam around the area. A sheet-steel wall is built round the site, forming a sealed box structure, from which the water is pumped, leaving the wreck high and dry. This method was used to excavate the Roman ship found in the mud of the Thames and five Viking ships which were scuttled 900 years ago to block part of the Roskilde Fjord in Denmark against enemy attack. In each case the excavations became dry land operations on which the archaeologists were able to work from gangplanks supported over the fragile wood. After cleaning, the wrecks were mapped photogrammetrically with stereo cameras; all the timbers were tabulated, raised and sealed in plastic bags to prevent them drying out. Then they were transported to laboratories, where the wood was treated with preservatives in preparation for reconstruction prior to museum display.

In the cases mentioned, and in most cases, the water has been removed deliberately to expose the wreck, whose existence was known. Sometimes wrecks are exposed as a kind of byproduct of land reclamation; notable are those of the Zuider Zee/Ijsselmeer, the remains from which have been well displayed in the Netherlands, particularly at the Schockland Museum.

Underwater archaeology is in its infancy. Only those ships which foundered in comparatively shallow water have been surveyed. Even in shallow depths there are many more wrecks to be discovered. But what of the hundreds, perhaps thousands, of ships that sank to depths beyond the capability of conventional divers. Storms and battles must have caused many casualties whose hulks are resting in great depths, some that have settled on rocky seabeds, some that have been enveloped in seabed soil.

Ships lying at greater depths offer exciting prospects for archaeologists in the very near future because the last few years have seen tremendous advances in diving technology—compared with the Aqualung invented 50 years ago—advances which allow a diver to live underwater. Whereas a diver, using Aqualung can stay submerged only as long as his air supply lasts, now, by taking up residence in an underwater 'house' he can live and work on the seabed for many weeks at great depths.

The new form of immersion is called saturation diving. A brief explanation is called for. When an Aqualung diver descends, his body is subjected to pressures that affect the blood to such an extent that a physical procedure called decompressing has to be followed before his blood returns to normal; the diver thus avoids the painful affliction called caisson disease, or the bends. As the diver ascends and the pressure lessens, the frothy bubbles of nitrogen in his blood increase in size, seeking a way out. They eventually do escape as the blood passes through the lungs but it takes a period of time related to diving depth and duration of dive. As an example, a diver working at a depth of 150ft for 30 minutes would have to make decompression stops totalling 40 minutes before he could surface and avoid the bends.

Saturation diving means that a diver can remain under water with his blood totally saturated with nitrogen until such time as he wishes to return to the surface. Then he goes through a prolonged decompression period inside the house in which he has been living. As an example, a diver living at a depth of 150ft for a month would need to be decompressed for 60 hours.

Another invention of great significance to nautical archaeology is the submersible diving vessel which allows its operator and passengers full vision of the seabed while surveying large areas in search of sunken ships. When a shipwreck is found, a house would be lowered alongside and divers would live and work on the site, surveying, excavating and finally controlling the raising of artefacts to the surface.

To date no wrecks of archaeological value have been discovered in depths beyond Aqualung depth capability but, no doubt concentrated study of historical records will reveal such information. One day, perhaps, divers will be living and working 600ft below the surface excavating the French and Spanish warships sunk by Nelson's fleet at Trafalgar.

In the meantime, there are more-modern and very wealthy prizes waiting to be probed by seabed dwellers. For instance, the Italian luxury liner *Andrea Doria* that sank to 300ft after a collision 200 miles off New York in 1956; the *Lusitania* sunk by German submarines in 1915, 350ft down off the South Coast of Ireland; and the *Titanic* which struck an iceberg on her maiden voyage to America in 1912 and is lying a mile down. Great adventure lies ahead for submarine divers who probe the abyss of the oceans.

Above: HMS 'Penelope', used in studies of hull resistance and wake formation in 1970.
MoD (Navy)

Left: Froude's dynamometer of 1871 developed for measurement of ship resistance.
Science Museum London (photo D Rudkin)

Below: A painting in the Science Museum, London, of paddle steamers of the Royal West India Mail Co, built in the 1840s on Scott Russell Wave-line principles, here pictured at anchor in Southampton Water.
Photo D Rudkin

Froude & TANK TESTING

ALTHOUGH EXPERIMENTS were made with small models on tanks and ponds in the 17th and 18th centuries, the testing of scale model hulls as an aid to ship design stems largely from the work of William Froude who in the 1870s investigated the relationship between the behaviour of a model and the full-scale hull in various sea conditions. In an earlier age, the hull design of English ships had been largely a matter of 'rule of thumb' combined with the accumulated experience of the master shipwright concerned. The French, on the other hand, had achieved some success during the 18th century by the application of scientific principles to ship design.

A quest for increased speed at sea and the advent of the iron steamship brought the need for a new approach to the matter of hull design, and the new generation of shipbuilders and civil engineers began to pay attention to the influence of the sea and waves upon the motion of a ship. The necessity was seen also for a hull design which might combine maximum revenue-earning capacity with a minimum power demand for a given service speed, although for a while it was still the 'feel' and intuition of the shipbuilder which decided the issue.

The importance of the waterline form was soon realised, however, and various designers proposed theoretical forms. Probably the best known was the Wave-line principle, developed in the 1840s by J Scott Russell, in accordance with which the greatest breadth of the hull is placed nearer the stern than the bow in the proportion of 4:6. This form of immersed body was calculated to give the greatest speed for a given length on the waterline or in other words, to achieve the least resistance for the length of hull.

Scott Russell attempted to back his theories by experiments with models on the Forth & Clyde Canal, but at that stage no work had been done on the relationship between the behaviour of a scaled-down model and the actual ship in a seaway so that Wave-line still had to be regarded as primarily a theoretical exercise lacking any empirical foundation.

Scott Russell's Wave-line principle was widely accepted by contemporary engineers, among them Isambard Kingdom Brunel who in 1852 sketched his ideas for a giant steamship far exceeding in size any vessel afloat or even dreamed of by mid-19th-century shipwrights. Described by Brunel as the East India Steamship, the idea was for a vessel capable of carrying sufficient coal for the round voyage to Australia—and to make a profit catering for cabin-class passengers, migrants and cargo. Eventually, in December 1853, a contract was placed with J Scott Russell & Company for the construction at Millwall of an iron steamship 680 feet long between perpendiculars, the general design of which was a product of Brunel's fertile brain, although the Wave-line hull was totally Scott Russell.

In 1832 William Froude, then a promising young civil engineer, had joined Brunel's staff working on the construction of the Bristol & Exeter Railway. For the next 14 years Froude worked as a railway engineer, mainly in his native West Country but in 1846 he retired from active civil engineering in order to devote his time and attention to the problem of ship behaviour in a seaway. Thus it came about that in 1856 he was requested by Brunel to investigate, in connection with the building of the *Great Eastern,* the motion of a large ship in waves.

Froude continued his work on the theory of rolling after the completion of the *Great Eastern* and took passage in the vessel in order to qualify his theories by practical observation. His first paper on the subject was presented to the Institution of Naval Architects during the second session of that body in 1862.

As a result of his work on the mechanics of rolling, Froude developed ideas of roll damping by the use of deep bilge keels but it was not until some years later that he was able to demonstrate their effect, at first with models and subsequently in full-scale trials with HM ships *Greyhound* and *Perseus* off Plymouth. He also developed an automatic roll recorder which was used first during the trials of the turret ship *Devastation* in 1873.

At that time the use of models in experimental work was not looked upon with favour by either the Institution of Naval Architects or the British Association; in particular, in the light of his own experience extending over two years, Scott Russell was particularly scathing about the suggestion that the use of scale

Above: A portrait of William Froude, at the Science Museum, London. *Photo D Rudkin*

models could provide reliable data for the design of ships. Froude saw matters in a different light, however, and was of the opinion that the main reason why previous model experiments had proved unsatisfactory was that no relationship had been established between the speed of the model and that of the full-scale ship.

Froude's early comparative experiments on the subject of ship resistance were carried out on the River Dart in 1867 with scale models of differing lengths of the hulls of the screw gunboats *Swan* and *Raven,* which were towed by a steam launch equipped with a sensitive screw log. A form of self-recording dynamometer was used to measure the resistance, but although the trials formed the basis for Froude's later work, the problems involved in obtaining measurements of sufficient accuracy in open water militated against general acceptance of the results.

In September 1869, with the backing of Sir Edward Reed, then Chief Constructor of the Navy, Froude sought Admiralty sanction for a series of experiments with models in a controlled environment to determine the resistance of different hull forms. Eventually his proposals were accepted and in 1870 he was granted the sum of £2000 for the construction of a covered model testing tank on his own land at Chelston Cross near Torquay. At about the same time, however, the Admiralty refused to sanction proposals, fostered jointly by the Institution of Naval Architects and the British Association, for a series of full-scale trials to form a basis for comparison and to be undertaken with naval ships in suitably sheltered deep water such as a Norwegian fjord or one of the sea lochs of the west coast of Scotland.

The Torquay tank, 250 feet long, 33 feet broad and 10 feet deep, was erected in 1871 and was so arranged that the model under test could be drawn through the water by an overhead trolley running on a track the full length of the tank and equipped with a dynamometer to measure the resistance of the model at any given speed. For many years the models were made of a mixture of 95 per cent paraffin wax and five per cent beeswax and stearine. The material was durable and easily worked and was cast to the rough shape required and, when cool, machined to a stepped form in a shaping machine controlled by following the lines of the ship's drawings with a pantograph arrangement. Final finishing to achieve an accurate scale profile was carried out using hand tools. Once afloat the model was ballasted to the correct waterline, trim, metacentric height and centres of buoyancy before being subjected to a series of preliminary tests to ensure that it would rise and fall naturally at the correct running trim.

As an alternative to towing, the models can be made self propelled, the propeller being driven by an electric motor controlled by an operator on the tank carriage travelling at roughly the same speed as the model. Recording equipment registering shaft revolutions, torque and thrust are carried in the model itself.

In recent years the traditional wax mixture has given way to glass-reinforced plastics, although in fact the scale grp hulls are moulded from a paraffin wax master which itself can be modified as required during the investigation of the model hull's characteristics. Being much lighter, the grp hull can carry a greater payload by way of recording equipment than was possible in the case of the heavier wax model.

In the course of his work, Froude developed the hypothesis that the total resistance to motion could be considered the sum of a function of wave formation and skin friction. Likewise he went on to show that the effect of waves upon a model would be similar to the effect on the full-scale hull provided that the speeds of the model and ship were in the ratio of the square roots of their respective lengths. This rule has become known as Froude's Law of Similarity, although in fact it was first proposed by F Reech, Professor of Naval Architecture at Paris in 1852.

In the meantime, pressure for full-scale trials had not abated and although Froude was satisfied that the required data could be derived from model tests, he realised that the former were a necessary complement in order to prove the validity of his work at Torquay. Eventually convinced of the requirement, the Admiralty put the coppered wooden screw sloop *Greyhound* (1260 tons) at his disposal in 1871 and arranged for the iron screw corvette *Active* (3980 tons) to serve as towing vessel.

The trials were carried out in the Solent in good weather and took the form of a series of runs at various trims and displacements, with the *Greyhound* being towed from a 45-foot boom rigged out amidships from the *Active* in order to keep the ship clear of the towing vessel's wake. The results tied in closely with data deduced from model experiments and proved a complete vindication of Froude's methods. The success of the *Greyhound* trials marked a turning point in the acceptance of naval architecture as a science and even that staunchest of former critics, J Scott Russell, was moved to state that '. . . you can take a model as the type of your ship and from the model calculate the performance of your ship'.

From 1872 the Torquay establishment in the grounds of Chelston Cross was known as the Admiralty Experiment Works, but in fact Froude's work was not wholly confined to investigations on behalf of the Admiralty. Indeed, in 1873 trials were run with a model of the Russian circular iron-clad *Novgorod.* The trials proved to Froude's satisfaction that the claims of her sponsors were invalid and that such a design was suited only to a shallow-draught coastal defence monitor for which speed and manoeuvrability would not be important considerations.

Froude's next major investigation involved a study of the wave formation generated by the passage of a hull through water. The experiments were carried out over a wide range of speeds with different lengths of parallel mid-body planks fitted between conventional bow- and stern-

Top: Froude's machine of 1872 developed to shape paraffin-wax models for test.
Science Museum London (photo D Rudkin)

Above: John Scott Russell, originator of the Wave-line theory, from a June 1882 obituary notice in 'The Illustrated London News'.

shaped ends; they proved the link between waterline length and the speed at which a sharp increase in water resistance occurs. He investigated also the transmission of power by propellers and, working on the foundations laid by earlier engineers, formulated the blade element theory of propeller design, which he supported both by model experiments and by related full-scale trials.

The results of Froude's work on propeller design were read to the Institution of Naval Architects in 1878; it proved to be his last appearance before that body for in December 1878, on doctor's orders, he sailed in HMS *Boadicea* to winter in the sun at the Cape. There he contracted dysentery and on May 4, 1879, in Admiralty House, Simonstown, he died, aged 69.

At Torquay William Froude had been assisted by his son Robert Edmund, who then took over his father's work. In 1886 Robert Froude supervised the move of the Admiralty Experiment Works from Chelston Cross to a site adjacent to the Gunboat Yard at Haslar, near Gosport, where it continues today as the Admiralty Marine Technology Establishment.

The present establishment houses two ship tanks, respectively 475 and 886 feet in length, and a large manoeuvring tank 400 feet long by 200 feet wide and 18 feet deep in which artificial sea states can be generated with waves up to a height of 18 inches. The models under test can be towed directly by a rotating arm for measurement of side forces or, in the case of submerged self-propelled submarine models, can be controlled by electromagnetic signals generated on a grid laid out in the bottom of the tank. Surface models are controlled by ordinary radio link.

Other facilities at Haslar include two cavitation tunnels built in the 1940s to study the efficiency improvements in propellers of high-speed coastal craft. The problem of cavitation and its particular association with the small fast-turning propeller had been appreciated for many years, but full-scale direct observation had not been possible before the advent of this type of equipment. The phenomenon is itself the result of the formation of voids along the blade edges, but the work at Haslar led to the design of improved high-speed propellers less prone to cavitation and thus of increased efficiency. There is also a circulating water channel to study water flow over hulls and their appendages.

The policy of the Ministry of Defence today is to encourage the shipbuilding industry, foreign governments and other maritime interests to make use of the facilities and expertise available at Haslar under contract, both for general studies and for the solution of specific problems. Recent examples of the nature of the tasks undertaken have included assistance in the design of a submarine plough for laying power cables on the seabed in coastal waters, investigation of the sea forces acting on the moorings of drilling rigs and the development of improved forms of anchor.

The primary task continues, however, to be the study of ship hull forms in the search for improved efficiency and behaviour at sea. From such work came the development of the Type 12 frigate hull for the Royal Navy, since adopted by other Commonwealth and foreign navies. To date about 78 ships based on the Type 12 hull design have been built for eight navies. The twin-screw steam turbine-driven Leander class of this group is credited with a speed of 30 knots at 30,000shp, or only about three-fifths of the power required for a similar-size 30-knot destroyer of Second World War design and construction.

Above left: A cavitation tunnel at AEW Haslar showing vortices formed at the blade tips of a propeller. *Admiralty Experiment Works*

Above: A sea-keeping model of a Leander-class frigate in the AEW's No 1 ship tank. *AEW*

Below: The original Froude test tank at Torquay in about 1875. *AEW*

Bottom: A rotating-arm machine measuring side forces on a submerged model. *AEW*

The model work on the Type 12 hull was complemented by a series of trials carried out in 1970. The frigate HMS *Penelope* with both propellers removed was towed at speeds up to 23 knots to provide data on hull resistance and wake formation, an exercise which also provided a check on the accuracy of model test information accumulated since the *Greyhound* trials a century earlier.

The work still goes on, not only at Haslar but also at Teddington, where Froude's name is remembered in the William Froude Laboratory that forms part of the National Physical Laboratory, at Dumbarton, Clydebank and other centres in the UK and overseas. Changing requirements and the big increase in the size and speed of bulk carriers, and the huge investment involved in building such ships, has made tank testing more important than ever where commercial operation is concerned, while for naval craft the continuing need for increased efficiency, reduced hull noise and the refinement of hull shape means that tank trials with models have likewise a vital role to play as part of the design process.

William Froude has been gone for just a century but his work goes on. Despite the advent of highly specialised and sophisticated equipment, the basic methods are still those he pioneered in the 1860s and 1870s, when naval architecture was in its infancy as an engineering discipline.

Left: Froude's automatic roll recorder of 1872. *Science Museum London*

Below: A water turbine brake dynamometer to measure the torque of a ship's propeller, of about 1885. *AEW*

DIVING VESSELS

'Underwater men will walk, will ride, will sleep, will talk.' (Mother Shipton, 17th century prophetess)

FOR CENTURIES the seas and oceans of our planet have been treated as hunting grounds for fishermen and highways for ships, but men of vision have long realised that beneath the waves there lies a vast virgin territory as challenging as outer space, and infinitely more rewarding economically. This massive untapped reservoir, supporting a hundred times more food than man can produce on land, and untold mineral wealth, exists in and beneath 330 million cubic miles of water, covering three-fourths of the earth's surface. There can be found more vegetation, more copper, more gold, more iron, more oil—the ocean is relatively inexhaustible, a self-replenishing storehouse of most basic materials needed in modern times, either dissolved in the water or lying fallow in the seabed.

While much is known about even the most inaccessible lands, we are lamentably ignorant about the sea, its behaviour, the life it supports and its fathomless depths. The late President Kennedy 13 years ago asked Congress to double the amount of money the United States Government had been spending on oceanic research. In his appeal he said 'the sea around us represents one of the most important resources. We are just on the threshold of our knowledge of the oceans. Already their military importance, their potential use for weather predictions, for food and minerals are evident. Knowledge of the oceans is more than a matter of curiosity. Our very survival may hinge upon it.'

Much has been accomplished since those words were spoken and 300 million dollars were made available. A third of the award went to the Woods Hole Oceanographic Institute in Massachusetts for the development of underwater research vessels—the prime necessity for marine sciences.

Top left: The Tektite diving vessel being handled by crane aboard an escort ship, with another in reserve on deck.
Daily Telegraph Colour Library

Top right: The Seatask work chamber which conveys divers employed on oil rigs etc to and from the seabed. *Science Museum London*

Above: Artist's conception of the first of six deep submergence rescue vehicles planned by the US Navy. *L Kenyon*

Under the Geneva convention a country has exclusive rights to develop mineral resources of adjacent shelves down to a depth of 200 metres, with development rights beyond that depth, if it has the technical ability to exercise them. At least 30 nations are signatories to the agreement and several of those countries have developed techniques to allow men to live in 'houses' and work beneath the sea without surfacing for weeks at a time, and in depths as great as 1000 feet. The mineral-rich shelves that border the continents (the continental shelves represent 10 per cent of the ocean floor) and some of the ocean bed beyond, lie within this depth. For travelling down to underwater 'houses', and for carrying out oceanographic research, general exploration and experiments, diving vessels of varied designs have been in use for 25 years.

There are two very specific types of diving vessel, both of which operate free of any connection with the surface—the *bathyscaph* and the *research submarine.* (The latter is described later.) A bathyscaph (from the Greek bathy = deep and scaph = boat) is designed for very deep vertical dives with only limited horizontal movement and is constructed on the same principle as a balloon. Just as a balloon uses lighter-than-air gas to make it rise, so the bathyscaph uses lighter-than-water petrol in its float to support the heavy cast-steel sphere in which the crew are enclosed. The relatively fragile hull of the float is not affected by the pressure, because sea water is free to enter through an opening in the bottom when the petrol is compressed. Thus it exerts the same pressure both inside and outside the hull. It need only withstand the ordinary strains of a submarine on the surface. The sphere, on the other hand, is made of cast steel fitted with portholes, and is designed to withstand the pressure of the greatest depths in the oceans.

To make the bathyscaph sink, it is weighted with great quantities of iron pellets, and airlocks are flooded with water. To make it rise, the iron pellets and other ballast, held in place by electro-magnets, are jettisoned by switching off the electric current. The bathyscaph is therefore independent of any kind of external control such as cables, as it carries its own means of sinking and rising.

August Piccard, a Swiss scientist invented the first bathyscaph in 1948. At that time he held the record for the highest ascent in a balloon, and he applied his experience of balloons to deep diving. Professor Piccard first tried out his bathyscaph off the West African coast. He sent it down empty and automatically controlled. On its return its depth meters recorded a sounding of 4600 feet. The vessel was damaged in that test so he built another with the help of his son Jacques. In 1953 they descended several times in the new one, named *Trieste.* Off Naples in the Mediterranean they broke all previous records by reaching a depth of 10,395 feet, more than double the greatest depth previously reached by anyone.

Meanwhile, Commander Cousteau had persuaded the French and Belgian governments to build a bathyscaph, the FNRS 3 (Fonds National de la Recherche Scientifique) which was to incorporate all the latest refinements. It was tested off Toulon by two French naval officers, Commander Houet and Lieutenant Willm. In 1954 they made what was then a record dive of 13,287 feet—$2\frac{1}{2}$ miles—off Dakar in French West Africa.

The dive took more than five hours. They kept in touch with their mother ship above by radio, gave precise details of the bathyscaph's performance and reported seeing a great cavalcade of creatures through the portholes. The beam from the powerful floodlights lit up all kinds of living creatures—jelly fish, squid, cuttlefish, shrimps, giant crabs and glittering plankton.

On the sea floor they saw small fish-like creatures with extended pectoral and tail fins acting as stilts to support them above the very soft mud on which they live. They exist in total darkness and seemed indifferent to the bright floodlights. Perhaps they had no eyes.

The year 1959 saw the beginning of a programme that was to end the following year with a dive to the greatest depth in the oceans of the world. Jacques Piccard and a US Navy lieutenant, Don Walsh, crewed the *Trieste* which had been purchased by the US Navy and substantially rebuilt for the new ultra-deep dives. Their first trial dive was made in November 1959 to a depth of $3\frac{1}{2}$ miles.

Then *Trieste* was towed to an area 200 miles south-west of Guam, in the Pacific, marked on marine charts by a pattern of rings, indicating a sharp drop, named the

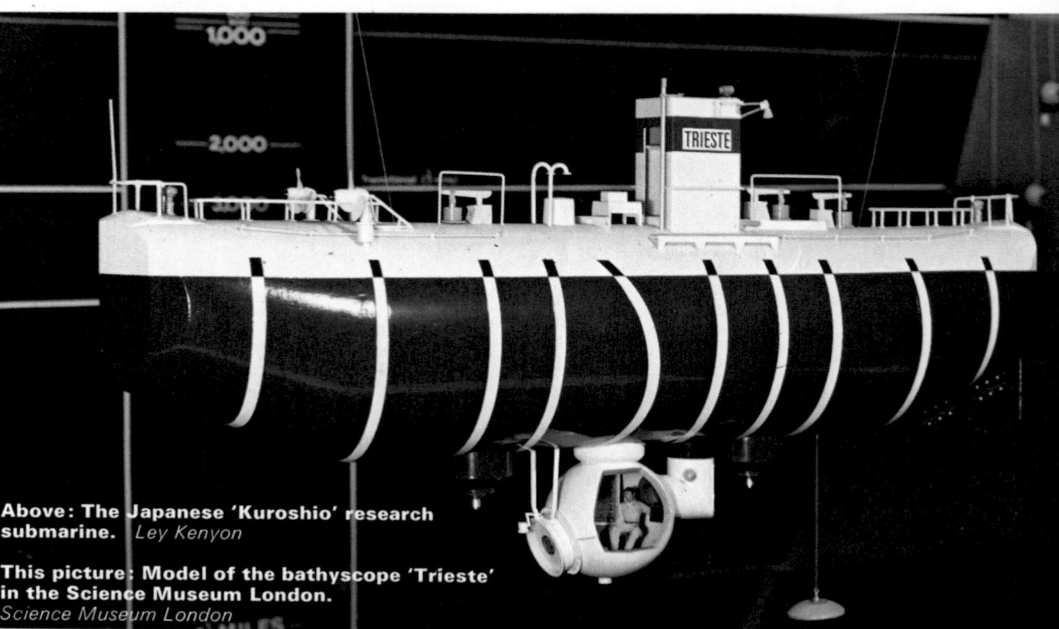

Above: The Japanese 'Kuroshio' research submarine. *Ley Kenyon*

This picture: Model of the bathyscope 'Trieste' in the Science Museum London. *Science Museum London*

Marianas Trench. In December Piccard and Walsh made a second trial dive in the same area into Nero Deep, $4\frac{1}{2}$ miles down. Then on January 23, 1960, the last barrier on earth was passed, and history was made. The two brave men plunged down at a rate of five feet per second into the abyssal trench, named Challenger Deep. Its depth is 35,640 feet, almost seven miles. At that depth the pressure of water on the observation sphere was eight tons per square inch!

Although such record-breaking dives have not been made since 1960, the bathyscaph is by no means a vintage vehicle. It is as significant to oceanography as the rocket is to the exploration of outer space and certainly of greater value in the context of man's desire for knowledge—and survival.

There is no doubt that the superpowers have their priorities wrong. 'In a world which spends more in a single year on research into space than it has done since the beginning of the century on research into the sea is mad'—to quote Sir Frederick Brundrett, and he argues that Britain, a maritime nation, whose life is bound intimately with the sea, must be particularly mad!

Between 1965 and 1970 Britain spent £40 million on space research, and one-twentieth of that amount on marine sciences, distributed in unco-ordinated penny packets. Space research seems highly unlikely to lead to the discovery of any new sources of materials, power or food, while research in the sea will produce all these in vast quantity, before the children being born today have grown up—or died of starvation.

Underwater animal husbandry and marine horticulture must be planned and executed with the same care and forethought that is used on land, applying the scientific advancements that have put food production on its present scale. Farming the sea now seems a practical possibility. An encouraging approach to mariculture is the development of desirable strains of 'domesticated' fish. The cattle on land are far removed from their wild ancestors. Likewise, fish stocks can undoubtedly be bred to have desirable qualities for farming. For example, hybrids derived from crossing plaice with flounders are robust and grow faster than their parents, and produce high-quality meat.

What might well become the greatest pioneering endeavour of the 20th century could see us cultivating undersea 'fish farms', harvesting billions of pounds of fish each year; dredging manganese nodules and other minerals in quantities unobtainable on land; mining industrially important metals such as copper and aluminium; producing electricity by building seabed power stations powered by ocean currents; transporting cargo and people in commercial submarines; refining oil on the seabed; and many other submarine activities related to oceanography, including a matter of imminent concern to the world—pollution.

Such activities would require fleets of diving vessels, ranging from one-man mechanical 'horses' and miniature submersibles for short journeys to large research submarines combining great depth capability, load capacity and horizontal cruising range.

The usefulness of the bathyscaph is very limited, since it is designed for vertical diving with very restricted horizontal manoeuvrability, but it does have potential use in conjunction with mechanical robots and other unmanned devices used for underwater work, which have to be controlled by visual means.

Research submarines, on the other hand are designed for a number of uses which necessitate varied design and construction. There are those that carry men into the sea while they live within in normal atmospheric pressure (they cannot leave their craft underwater) and those that are designed to carry divers who can leave the vessel to swim and work outside at any given depth. The first are used as observation vehicles, sometimes called mesoscaphs, and are fitted with portholes through which scientists can see the object of their research. To collect specimens they have remote-controlled recovery on telechiric arms and floodlights to illuminate the scene. The second kind of vessels are observation vehicles with the extra facility —a pressure chamber in which divers can be 'pressurised' to equal that of their environment, thus enabling them to leave their craft through an airlock, and return in the same way.

The first manned research submarine was built in 1964 by Commander Cousteau. It was named *Denise* and its main purpose was to study fish life and transport divers to an underwater house. Two divers lay on foam-rubber mattresses inside the lens-shaped vessel, from which they could see through portholes. They could stay submerged for 25 hours. *Denise* was propelled by electric batteries and high-pressure pumps which drew in water to expel it again forcibly in jets. It could dive to 1500 feet.

At the same time many countries, especially North America, were experimenting with varied types of vessel, from simple streamlined chambers flooded with sea water (the divers pedal to turn the propeller) to 130-ton craft, called submersibles, that stay submerged for weeks at a time. Two of the most successful heavy submersibles in use today are *Aluminaut* (81 tons) the first true deep-diving boat, which was launched in the early 1960s, and *Ben Franklin* (130 tons) launched in 1969, famous for its fact-finding 'drift', in the Gulf Stream from Florida to Boston, submerged at a depth of 2000 feet. The voyage took 40 days and covered 1500 miles. *Ben Franklin's* designer and captain was Dr Jacques Piccard of bathyscaph fame.

The development of an aluminium submersible began as early as 1942, from the idea of Louis Reynolds, chairman of a large aluminium corporation in Bermuda, to build aluminium undersea ships for warfare and cargo transport. In the early 1950s Reynolds began studying the use of aluminium in surface ships. Some of the findings indicated that the metal would be even more advantageous for submarines because it is buoyant in water, strong for its weight and it does not compress in water. Therefore the deeper the dive, the more buoyant the craft becomes—a feature that provides the ultimate in safe operation. In the late 1950s Reynolds decided thoroughly to explore the feasibility and practicability of an aluminium submarine.

Tests went on for three years before the final design was completed and construction of *Aluminaut* was started in 1962. Two years later she was ready for sea trials, surface and submergence tests and deep dives to 15,000 feet. *Aluminaut* is 50 feet long with an 8ft-diameter hull made up of 11 forged-aluminium cylinders 40 inches long and $6\frac{1}{2}$ inches thick joined together with 400 aluminium bolts. The bow, stern and all superstructures are made of aluminium or light alloys so that the whole craft has an excess buoyancy of 30 per cent—a figure adequate to compensate for dead weight and payload. She is equipped to provide her three-man crew with operating and scientific laboratory facilities for submerged missions lasting up to 36 hours.

Although America is far in advance with diving vessel production (at least six large corporations are building them, including Grumman and Westinghouse, and General Dynamics who built *Aluminaut*), other countries have also become involved. In 1967 Britain launched its first vessel and called it *SURV* (submarine research vehicle). It is mainly used in industrial research work and it has a depth capacity of 10,000 feet. *SURV* is only 11 feet long, completely electrical and propelled by two 4hp motors.

Japan has several craft, including an undersea observation vessel called *Kuroshio*. It weighs 9 tons and is 23 feet long. The Japanese are the most advanced nation in the field of seafood production and *Kuroshio* is particularly equipped with biological and geological apparatus to further that end.

The Soviet Union no doubt has foreseen the importance of deep-sea deployment as an area for an invisible military fleet, not only in the form of conventional submarines but also vessels that can dive ten times deeper. In 1970 they launched a shallow-water sealed laboratory named *Chernomor* (the name of a Russian fairy-tale character inhabiting the Black Sea), which is 26 feet long and carries a crew of four for periods of up to a month. It is more a seabed habitat than a vessel and has to be towed to site behind a tug.

Parallel with the *Chernomor* manned missions is the more sinister work on the production of automatic underwater observatories which are the first of their kind in the world. Their appearance is something like an octopus with hanging tentacles, but the tentacles are in reality cables linking the capsule to a ballasting system. Though they are not true vessels, the deep-water observatories will be capable of moving and hovering over the seabed like unmanned space probes, with two-way radio communication directed by scientists from afar. Such automatic installations transmitting information back to base would be a formidable weapon in future submarine warfare.

All diving craft described so far fall into the category of observation vehicles, in which the crews live in normal atmospheric conditions and cannot leave the craft underwater. By 1956 thoughts were turning towards the development of submarines from which divers could swim and work. Edwin A Link, inventor of the Link pilot trainer, has devoted practically his whole life and unlimited energy to unravelling the wonders of the deep. His ambitious programme named Man in Sea has been directed towards putting a man on the floor of the ocean to live, work and explore.

For several years before 1956, submersible decompression chambers had been used to carry divers to depths far beyond the capability of aqualung divers, where they could leave the chamber by a hatch in the bottom. As the pressure of air in the chamber was equalised at all times with the water outside, water would not enter the chamber, and the diver could return, closing the hatch behind him. Link was not satisfied with a chamber that could only be lowered by cable from a boat. He wanted complete freedom to explore the seabed from an observation vessel and, at any time, put divers into the water. Such ambition created unsolved problems concerning breathing gas and decompression far beyond the facts then known.

At this point a mention must be made of those known facts. Air is a mixture (by volume) of 78 per cent nitrogen and 21 per cent oxygen. Pressure under water increases with depth at a rate of 14.7lb per square inch every 33 feet. When a person undergoes a higher pressure by diving, the partial pressure of nitrogen on the blood is increased and more nitrogen will go into solution in the blood. If a diver stays under for a short time, it is of no great consequence. But if he stays at a given depth long enough for significant absorption to occur he can no longer return quickly to the normal atmospheric pressure at the surface.

Doing so would cause the nitrogen to bubble out his tissue like the effervescence of an uncapped bottle of ginger ale, an affliction called caisson disease, or the bends, which can be fatal. To prevent it, a diver must return to normal pressure slowly enough for the excess nitrogen to pass out of his body through his lungs, in the process called decompressing. The longer he stays at a given depth, the longer he has to decompress, *but only up to the point where the body tissues are saturated with gas.* This important discovery, an unknown fact until the early 1960s, was made by a German scientist Hannes Keller and it has revolutionised diving techniques. The discovery, termed saturation diving, allows a diver to saturate his body with a breathing gas and to stay at his work until it is finished, for days or even weeks. The name Aquanaut has been given to such divers.

Keller also experimented with breathing gases other than air, because of the known fact that the nitrogen in air becomes toxic at depths beyond 200 feet or so, causing a dangerous symptom called nitrogen narcosis. He discovered that helium, a lighter gas than nitrogen, prevented narcosis. Today, helium and oxygen (oxy-helium) is used universally by deep-sea aquanauts. Link's inventive mind produced an idea for a submersible that would allow divers to be pressurised and 'lock out'. The submarine would be compartmented so that a pilot and observer could operate it from a forward compartment, while two divers in the pressurised section could leave and return through a hatch. So *Deep Diver* was built, a complete miniature submersible, self-contained and capable of reaching depths of 1200 feet. *Deep Diver* was launched in 1967, and the diving world looked on as the amazing machine, rather like a helicopter without blades, made test dives to 1200 feet off the coast of Florida, culminating in a series of experiments during which the two divers locked out of the vessel and swam around at the fantastic depth of 700 feet. It was the deepest an American had ever swum in open water.

In 1969 new ground was broken. Link brought forth a design for a second small submersible. Nicknamed the *Bubble Sub*, it featured a transparent acrylic spherical chamber forward for unobstructed 360-degree observation, a great advantage over portholes for marine researchers, and an aluminium-alloy compartment aft for divers to leave and re-enter. The *Bubble Sub* is officially named the Johnson Sea-Link.

Another submarine, the Vickers Oceanics *Pisces*, is a similar type of vehicle which was in the news in August 1973, when for three and a half days millions the world over held their breath for two men trapped on the seabed in the Atlantic off Ireland while they were inspecting a telephone cable at a depth of 1575 feet, far deeper than anyone had previously survived a submarine accident. Men and equipment were rushed to the scene by air and sea from Britain, Canada, Ireland and the USA for the rescue operation, which was completed in a matter of hours.

The oil industry has promoted the most spectacular technological progress in underwater work. There are over 80 drilling and construction sites in the North Sea alone, all of them serviced by underwater

similar to *Pisces*. and Sea-Link.

A company named Comax provides over half of the human deep-diving interventions carried out worldwide for the offshore oil industry. The company works in close conjunction with the diving bell, which is more of a deep-water lift than a vehicle and is used for carrying divers from the surface to the worksite. The bell is a steel enclosure with a sealed hatch at the bottom and is suspended from a carrier cable attached to the top. An umbilical cable supplies it with breathing gases, electricity and hot water from the surface and provides a communication channel.

At present such vessels are being used in connection with such varied projects as diver transport to underwater houses, drilling for oil, laying submarine cables and pipes, collecting geological specimens, studying ocean currents and setting up sonar equipment, archaeological surveys, submarine rescue work and so on.

Diving vessels, however small or large, are expensive to design and build. The Johnson Sea-Link cost £1½ million, *Aluminaut* about the same, and the US Navy's giant DSRV-1 £18 million. Governments of the big powers, faced with the population explosion, know that they could find their food and mineral requirements on the continental shelves, and they know that the cost of extracting it will be high and ever increasing as more and more territory is exploited; but mankind's needs are growing so fast that they cannot be fully met unless men turn to the sea.

Right: 'Pisces III' being winched aboard the parent ship 'Vickers Voyager', *Vickers Ltd*

Below: A drawing depicting an underwater farm of the future. Some of the items in the drawing are in the research stage but most of the principles involved have been tested in the field and proved to be a possibility, while some including the underwater house (bottom left), are in actual use. *Ley Kenyon*

OCEANOGRAPHY

OCEANOGRAPHY is not one science but many. It includes disciplines as diverse as biology, hydrography, geology, chemistry and physics; it does not have any equivalent on land. What gives oceanography its unity and its distinctive character is the hostile environment—the sea—in which the field studies have to be carried out, and the necessary use of floating support-bases—the research vessels.

Oceanography was slow in becoming a science in its own right. The earliest known scientific study of the sea goes back to Aristotle, who described 180 marine species of animals, but it acquired momentum only with the Age of Discovery, with the progress in the arts of navigation and of geography. In the 17th century Robert Boyle was the first to do 'observations and experiments on the saltiness of the sea' (the origin of chemical oceanography) and in the following century Linnaeus founded the modern basis of natural history, including that of the seas; Benjamin Franklin mapped the Gulf Stream; James Cook made soundings down to 200 fathoms in the Pacific; and Alexander von Humboldt described the great current along the Andean shores which bears his name.

In the 19th century, HMS *Beagle* made an epoch-making circumnavigation (1831-36) with Charles Darwin aboard (see pages 100-102). Apart from studying the geology of South America and the land fauna of the Galapagos (which was to lead to his Theory on Evolution), he also described marine life and solved the mystery of the origin of atolls and coral reefs. Handicapped and shore-bound,

Big picture: The 1973 'RRS Challenger' entering Dunstaffnage Bay. *Scottish Marine Biological Assn*

Inset top: Specimens brought up by the Bethnic dredge. *Scottish Marine Biological Assn*

Inset above: The original HMS 'Challenger', shortening sail preparatory to taking soundings. *Institute of Oceanographic Sciences*

Lieutenant Matthew Fontaine Maury USN compiled ship logs and deduced from them the true figure of the marine currents and winds and their seasonal variations. We owe to him the Pilot Charts. At the same time Edward Forbes was pioneering marine biology, but nobody was then thinking in terms of oceanography.

The impetus that brought all the scattered specialities together was the laying of the transatlantic cable; the engineers needed to know what currents would be interfering with their work, what the precise depths were and what sort of animals, if any, lived on the bottom (they might be cable-eaters). Dr Wyville Thomson, professor of natural history at the University of Edinburgh, and Dr W B Carpenter led the first two purely oceanographic expeditions, in the seas near Britain, aboard HMS *Lightning* in 1868 and HMS *Porcupine* in 1869.

Their measurements of temperatures at depth led to the discovery of different water densities and hidden submarine sills; 'living fossils' were dredged up from the abyss. The sea was far more mysterious than expected! As more new questions had been raised than old ones solved, a major scientific expedition was decided on. Funds were voted by the British Parliament and the Royal Navy was to provide the crew and the ship—HMS *Challenger*.

The *Challenger* was a steam corvette 226 feet long overall with a displacement of 2306 tons. She had a 1234hp engine but as her route was to take her far away from any coaling stations and as the coal had to be saved to power the winch, she depended mainly on sails for travelling from station to station; she was fully rigged and crossed royal yards on every mast. After 16 of the ship's 18 guns were taken out the main deck was divided into laboratories, including even a photographic dark room, and into accommodation for the scientific party headed by Dr Wyville Thomson. A special winch was installed on the spar deck with eight miles of hemp warp for dredging and sounding. The sounding weight had a small coring tube attached to it to sample the bottom sediment. Special bottles were carried for sampling water at depth and deep-sea thermometers were part of the

equipment as well as nets, plankton nets and beam trawls.

The *Challenger* left Portsmouth on December 21, 1872, under the command of Captain Nares. She sailed to the South Atlantic, south Indian Ocean, the Tasman and Coral Seas and the China Sea. After a call at Hong Kong she sailed under Captain F Thomson to New Guinea, Japan, across the Pacific, through the Strait of Magellan and towards home. She covered 68,890 miles and completed 362 observation stations which included sounding, dredging, biological sampling, water sampling and analysis and current measurements.

The dredging took hours and was very tedious for the sailors who did not share the scientists' enthusiasm. Yet there was hardly a haul that did not bring to light species new to science. Of radiolaria (planktonic single-celled animals with beautiful lattice shells) alone, 3508 new species were added to the 600 previously known. Overall, 715 new genera and 4417 new species of living things were discovered and the progress in the non-biological fields was on a par. When the *Challenger* sailed into Portsmouth on May 24, 1876, oceanography had come of age. No other single oceanographic expedition has ever brought back such a wealth of new discoveries.

In 1877-86 another trail-blazing voyage took place from the United States. Engineer and naturalist Alexander Agassiz was the chief scientist of the steamer *Blake.* She had an auxiliary schooner rig and sailed the Caribbean Sea, the Gulf of Mexico and the Atlantic off Florida. Agassiz introduced many hardware innovations such as steel warps for dredges and a new dredge design that could not foul. The French got into the oceanographic 'race' in 1880-83 with the naval ships *Travailleur* and *Talisman,* who compared the fauna of the Mediterranean and of the eastern Atlantic.

The US Fish and Fisheries Commission and Agassiz commissioned in 1882 the first research vessel specifically built for the purpose, the USS *Albatross.* She was a large steamer with an auxiliary brigantine rig and an electrical system designed by Thomas Edison. She could dredge and trawl to well over 3000 fathoms. She was a very efficient oceanographic vessel and in one single haul in the Pacific she caught more fish than the *Challenger* had collected during her whole cruise. She had a long career and the sum of her results and samples overshadows even the *Challenger.* The Director of the US Fish and Fisheries Commission, C H Townsend, said, when she was retired in 1925, that 'if ever the American people received the fullest possible value from a government ship, they received it from this one. The benefits to science, the fisheries and commerce springing from her almost continuous investigations are incalculable'.

Agassiz was a rich man who put a lot of his personal fortune into oceanography. Another such man was Prince Albert of Monaco who started in 1885 by using his yacht, the *Hirondelle,* and later the specifically commissioned yachts *Hirondelle II, Princesse Alice* and *Princesse Alice II.* They were all steamers with auxiliary sails. He studied mainly the North Atlantic and the Mediterranean and became particularly interested in the mysterious giant squids. He tried and used many new gear designs, for example nets that could be closed at depth so as to sample only a given stratum, and deep-sea traps using luminous lures.

The same year that *Hirondelle* went on her first scientific cruise, the USS *Tuscarora* was testing a major new technique, namely, piano-wire sounding. Compared to the awkward hemp rope, it speeded up considerably the sounding routine, but the major breakthrough in that field was, of course, the advent of echo-sounding just prior to the 1914-18 war.

The Russians also took part with the circumnavigation by the *Vityaz* (1886-89), during which they took many temperature and salinity measures, in particular in the North Pacific.

In 1893 it was Norway's turn under the leadership of the zoologist, oceanographer, polar explorer and humanitarian Fridtjof Nansen. He had the three-masted motor topsail schooner *Fram* specifically built for polar conditions. She is 117 feet on deck and has a displacement of 800 tons. Her hull is extra thick (up to 30 inches of wood) and it has internal cross-bracings to resist the pressure of ice. Her hull sections were designed so that she would be squeezed out of the ice rather than be crushed by it. From 1893 to 1896 she studied the Arctic icecap drift by getting voluntarily entrapped in it and the voyage is one of the most famous polar expeditions. She made a second voyage under Nansen and in 1910-12 she was the ship used by Roald Amundsen on his South Pole voyage. She is now a museum ship in Oslo.

Germany launched the *National* expedition in 1889 to study the Atlantic plankton. In fact that was when the word plankton was coined to encompass all the forms of drifting sea life as distinct from the nekton, or swimming animals, that are relatively independent of the currents. That expedition was followed by those of the *Valdivia* in the Atlantic and the Indian Oceans. In the meantime the Danes were exploring the Icelandic waters with the

Ingolf and in 1899 the Dutch *Siboga* was surveying the Dutch East Indian waters.

In 1910 the Norwegians, under the leadership of Johan Hjort and financed by Sir John Murray (one of the *Challenger* scientists), investigated in detail the life in the North Atlantic on the *Michael Sars*. That was the first of the systematic investigations which were continued, among others things, by the Carlsberg Brewery-sponsored Danish *Dana* expeditions of 1920-22 and 1928-30 which solved the mystery of the eel migrations.

Britain conducted another major scientific voyage in 1925-27 with the *Discovery,* of Captain Scott fame. Built in 1899 as a polar vessel, she had a chequered career after the return of the British Royal Antarctic Expedition. She is a bark-rigged steamer, 171 feet between perpendiculars and with a 450hp triple-expansion steam engine. Her main purpose as a Royal Research Ship was to study whales. She was joined in 1926 by the RRS *William Scoresby,* which was designed on the lines of a whale catcher.

At that time Germany was staggering under the cost of war reparations, which had to be paid in gold. Sea water was thought to contain an economical concentration of dissolved gold and in 1925 the *Meteor* expedition went 'prospecting'. In fact sea water contained less gold than expected (only four grams per million metric tonnes) and no economical way was found of extracting it. But the *Meteor* did return with a wealth of oceanographic data, including the first continuous echo-sounding profiles of the Atlantic which revealed the unexpected ruggedness of the ocean floor.

Far left: A drawing by Dr Nansen of work to release his ship 'Fram' from polar ice by exploding a mine under her.
Illustrated London News

Left: The American drilling ship 'Glomar Challenger', with a 194ft tower, pictured at Brooklyn, New York. *L Dunn Collection*

Below: The 1962 RRS 'Discovery', equipped for most branches of marine research, has a range of 7500 miles or 30 days.
Institute of Oceanographic Sciences

Right: The US Research vessel 'Argo' pictured in the Gulf of Nicoya, Costa Rica. *E Abranson*

The *Carnegie* (US) discovered mountain ranges in the Pacific in 1929. She was entirely non-magnetic, including her fastenings and engines, because her primary purpose was the measurement of the earth's magnetic field at sea. She met an unfortunate end by explosion aboard.

The RRS *Discovery* was replaced in 1930 by *Discovery II*, which was specially designed for Antarctic oceanography. She was 234 feet long overall and had a 1250hp triple-expansion steam engine and a cruising range of 10,000 miles.

The Woods Hole (Massachusetts) Oceanographic Institution's *Atlantis* was launched in 1931. She is a 142-foot steel ketch with a Bermudian rig and a 400hp engine. She has sailed across all the oceans, logging the equivalent of over 50 circumnavigations. In 1957 she, with *Discovery II*, discovered the counter current which flows below the Gulf Stream. She was retired shortly afterwards.

The 1939-45 war interrupted the big oceanographic expeditions but strategic research resulted in vastly improved technology ranging from radar to underwater acoustics (sonar) and from radio navigation to bathythermographs (continuous vertical temperature profilers). The first big post-war expedition was the Swedish Deep Sea Expedition on the four-masted 259-foot Bermudian schooner *Albatross*, built in 1942 as a sail training vessel. She was chartered for a scientific circumnavigation in 1947-48 and introduced the technique of piston-coring the sea bottom. Piston cores can be over 60 feet long, compared to about 10 feet for gravity coring. The *Albatross* also pioneered the use of marine seismics for the study of sea floor structures.

In 1950 the Danes commissioned the *Galathea*, which specialised in deep-sea biological dredgings. She showed that life exists down to the floor of the deepest trenches. Because of the different time and place requirements of scientists of different specialities the trend was towards specialised deep-sea ships rather than the interdisciplinary cruises of the past. Hence, the US research vessel *Thomas Washington* carried out mainly physical studies, while the research vessels *Argo, Horizon* and *Chain* concentrated on marine geology and geophysics. The well-known *Calypso*, on loan from the French Navy to Dr Cousteau, specialises as a support ship for diving expeditions and underwater habitat experiments.

A new RRS *Challenger* was commissioned in 1950 and, with other ships, she started the real mapping of the ocean floor, at last made possible by the appearance of precision great-depth recorders; topographical features appeared which had been missed by the widely scattered line soundings and by the previous scanty and low-precision echo soundings.

The development of high technology did not mean the demise of sail-assisted research ships. In 1953 the Lamont Geological Observatory (USA) acquired the three-masted schooner *Vema* for bathymetric, geological and geophysical surveys. She was built in 1923, is 202 feet on deck and has a 1000hp engine. However, her rig was soon cut down.

A new era in marine geosciences was heralded in 1961 by the famous Project Mohole with the *Cuss I* (US). A converted 256-foot ex-Navy freight barge, *Cuss I* was a floating drilling rig with a 100-foot tower. She had four huge outboard engines placed on the bows and the quarters to keep her in position relative to transponders dropped on the seabed. The purpose was to drill through the earth's crust. She drilled an experimental hole in 3500 metres of water off Baja, California, but it penetrated only 182 metres of sea-floor sediment.

Also in 1961, *Atlantis II*, 210 feet long overall and 2300dwt, was commissioned to replace her older namesake, and the following year yet another *Discovery* was launched in Britain. She is 261 feet long overall and has a range of 7500 miles or 30 days. She has, like all large modern British research vessels, a bow thruster to improve manoeuvrability at very low speeds. She is designed for multidisciplinary activities.

During the 1960s a revolution occurred in the Earth sciences – the Sea Floor Spreading hypothesis, which supports the older but previously unrecognised Continental Drift theory. The Mohole project was replaced by the Deep Sea Drilling project (DSDP) which proposed not one crust-piercing hole but hundreds of shallower drillings designed to test the hypothesis. In 1968 the specially commissioned drilling ship *Glomar Challenger*, with a 194-foot tower, started a worldwide drilling campaign which eleven years later was still going on. The *Cuss I* technology was improved upon and a method has been devised which allows the drill string to be pulled up in order to change the coring bit and to re-enter the same hole with a fresh bit for further penetration.

The *Glomar Challenger* keeps a fixed station above the seabed relative to a sonar beacon on the bottom, automatically correcting drift with side thrusters and the main propeller. The greatest depth reached as this is written is 1390 metres below the seabed and the deepest drilling site is in 6850 metres of water, in a total of about 500 holes bored. Apart from confirming the Sea Floor Spreading theory, the DSDP has made numerous other scientific discoveries and has found evidence of oil under the deep-sea floor. The technology developed has also some obvious spinoffs of future value.

In the United States the big institutions have recently been replacing older units in their deep-sea fleets with ships of standard design, the Agar class. Such are the research ships *Knorr* and *Melville* operated by the Woods Hole Oceanographic Institution and RV *Colin Star Jordan* of the Scripps Institution of Oceanography. They are 245 feet long overall, of 2075dwt and have a 10,000-mile range. Their propulsion machinery is quite revolutionary; power from a single 2500hp diesel drives two cycloidal propellers, one forward and one aft, which permit thrust to be applied in any direction without the need for a rudder. Cruising speed is only 12.5 knots, but is entirely adequate for oceanographic purposes and the advantage of the system is that it allows total manoeuvrability on station.

Automatic navigation of the ships is achieved through use of an artificial satellite and an onboard computer, which provide a continuously updated digital display of longitude and latitude of remarkable accuracy. The Agar-class ships are multidisciplinary and they can even be converted to drilling ships. Cruises are usually fairly restricted, in the nature of the studies being carried out, but the specialised laboratories and equipments are in modules that can be changed at will to meet the requirements of a specific programme.

In Great Britain the newer large units are the RRS *Shackleton* (200 feet long, 1658dwt), a 1954-built freighter converted in 1971 for Antarctic work mainly as a shore station supply and geophysical vessel; and the RRS *Challenger* (180 feet, 1440dwt) which was launched in 1973 and is primarily intended for biological research.

The trend is for fast and highly versatile ships with the latest sophisticated gear for major deep-sea expeditions, complemented by numerous coastal craft for specific duties. Space has not allowed mention of the specialised fishery research vessels, which also exist in near-shore and distant-waters categories, nor the company-owned geophysical survey ships for oil exploration. There are also many types of research submersibles, some of which are mentioned in the features starting on pages 296 and 305.

Research vessels of all types are highly important to the discovery of the last untapped resources of the earth, and for the exploitation of Man's last frontier – the sea.

FINDING THE LONGITUDE

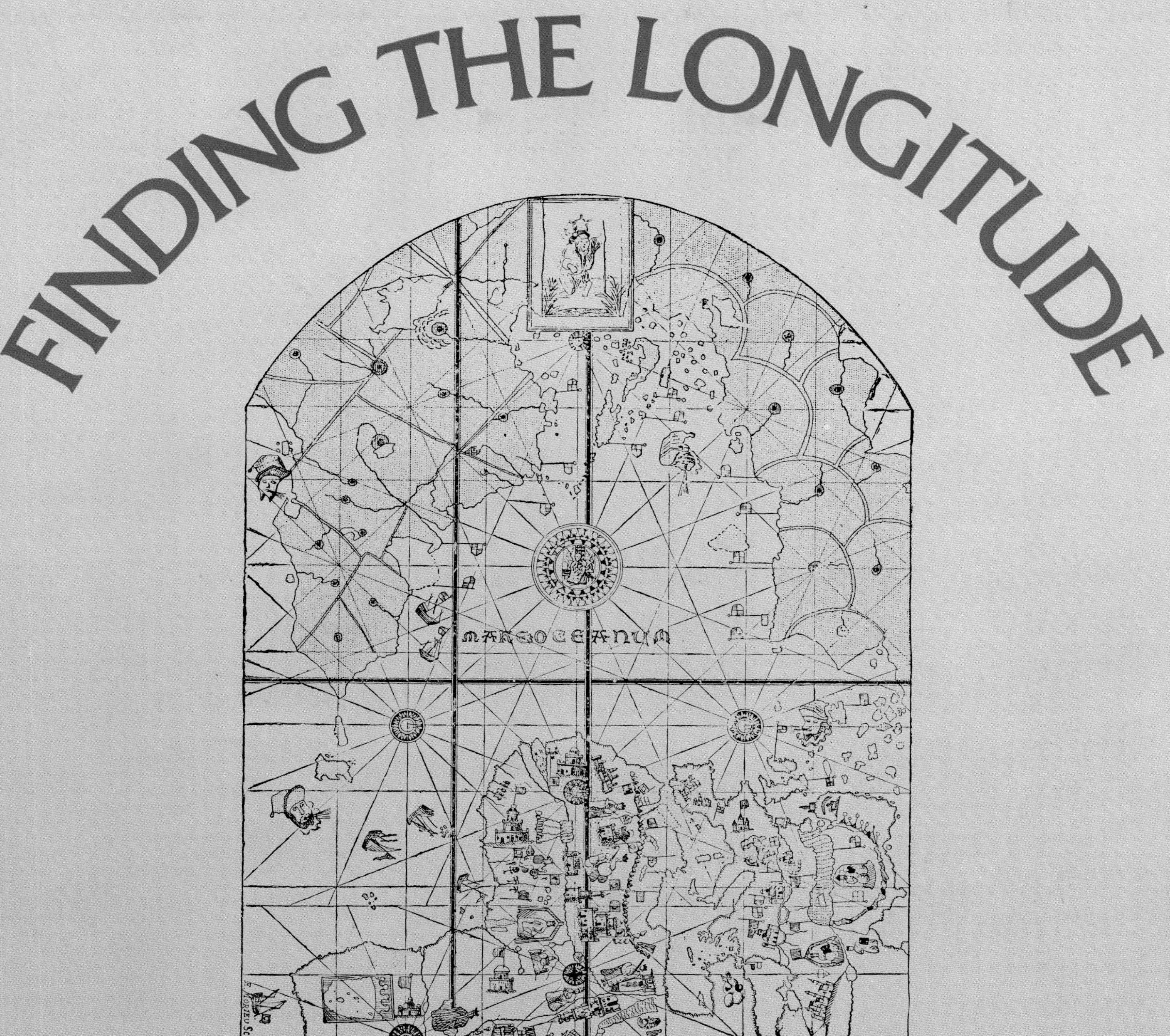

Above: A chart drawn in 1500 by Juan de la Cosa, the pilot who accompanied Columbus on his voyage across the Atlantic.
Illustrated London News

INVENTION, by its very nature, is a frustrating patience-stretching business, and never more so than when the need for discovery is urgent and science has not advanced sufficiently to provide a solution. There were certainly practical impediments in 1530, the year in which the Flemish astronomer and mathematician Gemma Frisius first proposed the use of a time-keeping device for reckoning longitude at sea.

By that time, the age of world-wide maritime exploration was about a century old, and the accumulated experience of hundreds of sailors was revealing a whole new range of taxing problems. Latitude sailing, dead reckoning, the plane chart and other methods and devices which had coped well enough with voyages in European and Mediterranean waters, were proving crucially inadequate when ships came to face mighty ocean currents, daunting ocean distances and long weeks out of sight of land.

Among the most dangerous disadvantages was the inability of mariners to reckon longitude with more than a minimal hope of accuracy once they were out to sea. Reckoning longitude by observing landmarks whose positions were known and charted was a relatively simple matter. Once the land had slipped below the horizon, however, longitude became a thorny problem.

There were two basic methods for use in such circumstances. One relied on observations and reckoning from the positions of stars and planets. The other employed the magnetic compass to read variations from the magnetic poles, which were checked against tables of variations known to exist in specified locations whose longitude was known; the ship's longitude, it was hoped, could be calculated from that. Neither method was entirely satisfactory and even less so was the crude hotchpotch technique of dead reckoning. It based calculations on the course steered and the distance sailed, and modified them with guesses, more or less inspired, regarding leeway, tides, currents, compass variations, allowances for errors of speed and steering and a host of other possible shortcomings.

Reckoning latitude as Christopher Columbus did, by use of a cross-staff and observation of the Pole Star, was a surer business, but without longitude the information gave at best only an approximate idea of a ship's position, the direction of her course and the identity of the next landfall. The uncertainty it all created led to disputes, like the one that occurred on board Columbus's *Nina* early in 1493, when he was returning from his first voyage to the New World.

On February 11, Columbus reckoned that his small fleet was south of the Azores; his second-in-command, Vincenti Pinzon, thought it was 600 miles farther east and approaching Madeira. As it happened, Columbus's opinion was the more correct on that occasion, but one of the reasons he believed his Caribbean discoveries to be part of Asia was his complete ignorance of the longitudes along which they lay.

Such ignorance could be, and often was, fatal to ships and sailors. In 1691, for instance, a fleet of warships mistook the Dodman for Berry Head and was wrecked off Plymouth as a result. About 16 years later, four ships of Admiral Sir Cloudesley Shovell's Gibraltar squadron were wrecked on the Scilly Isles at a time when the reckonings of all but one of his navigators placed the fleet a safe distance west of Ushant; 2000 men died, including the Admiral. In 1711, more ships and more men were lost at the approaches to the St Lawrence River as a consequence of a small error in calculating longitude.

Human incompetence naturally played a

part in most if not all disasters of the kind. But human frailty did not change the fact that inability to reckon longitude formed a serious gap in navigational knowledge, and one which not only involved loss of men, ships and cargoes, but could increase costs, shorten the working lives of ships and create shortages of food and stores on board by keeping vessels at sea longer than would otherwise be necessary.

If it was obvious to Gemma Frisius that the solution he sought was a horological one, it was also obvious that the chronometer he envisaged was a practical impossibility in his day. Such a chronometer would have to be accurate to within three seconds a day if, after a six-week voyage, longitude was to be reckoned to within half a degree. Since one minute of time corresponds to 15 minutes of longitude, a half-degree error meant that in six weeks a chronometer must not lose more than two minutes. In the 16th century, the science of horology was barely 200 years old and the standard of accuracy and stability required of a chronometer was undreamt of even ashore, let alone at sea.

Sea-going timepieces like sand-glasses and portable watches were reliable, at a very rare best, to within three minutes a day, but a more realistic estimate of error was the 15-minute lag of the so-called Nuremberg Egg which Frisius proposed should be adopted for use at sea. Nevertheless, although it was a crude and erratic watch, it did contain in rudimentary form the escape wheel, escapement and escapement-controlling device which are the basic requirements of the modern chronometer. It was, therefore, from the Nuremberg Egg that the nautical chronometer was eventually hatched.

In spotlighting the timepiece as the means by which the longitude problem might be solved, Frisius had also set in motion a diligent search for ways of bringing clocks to the necessary standards. The search, inevitably, fired the imagination of many would-be inventors whose devices were more notable for their ingenuity than for their effectiveness.

'The longitude is now being sought for in Spain by means of clocks . . . constructed in diverse ways,' wrote Alonso de Santa Cruz towards the end of the 16th century. 'Some with wheels, chains and weights of catgut and steel . . . others using sand, as in sandglasses; others with water in place of sand . . . others again with vases or large glasses filled with quicksilver; and some, the most ingenious of all, driven by the force of the wind, which moves a weight and thereby the chain of the clock, or which are moved by the flame of a wick saturated with oil . . .'.

Such early fantasy-bred contraptions were unusable, of course, and even later efforts of more-talented men were not very much more practicable. The great stumbling block at that juncture was the disturbing effect of changing temperatures, notably on the balance spring pioneered on portable watches by Robert Hooke (1635-1703). It was that singular defect that baffled Hooke's brilliant contemporary, the Dutchman Christian Huyghens (1629-1695), and scuttled Huyghens's efforts to construct a viable chronometer. The Huyghens marine clock of 1660 was the first timepiece specifically designed for use at sea. It was driven by a coiled spring, had a verge escapement controlled by a pendulum, three dials showing hours, minutes and seconds, and was set on gimbals to enable it to remain upright at all times.

Sea trials of the machine, made by Major Robert Holmes during a voyage to the west coast of Africa in 1664, seemed

Top: A 25-sided sundial used for navigational purposes in the 17th century, preserved in the Naval Museum at Genova-Pegli.
M Pucciarelli

Above: John Harrison, originator of the first successful chronometers and the winner of the £20,000 prize for determining longitude to within half a degree.
Mary Evans Picture Library

Right: A 14th-century nautical chart now preserved in the state archives in Florence.
M Pucciarelli

Above: An 18th-century sextant and compass; the sextant was used in conjunction with the chronometer to find a ship's position. *Dubrovnik Maritime Museum*

Below: John Harrison's No 1 marine timekeeper of 1737 and, centre foreground, his prize-winning No 4 of 1759. Kendall's copy K1 is on the right and the later K2 once carried by Captain Bligh on the 'Bounty' is on the left. *National Maritime Museum London (Harrison's chronometers are on loan from the Ministry of Defence)*

at first to indicate that at last the long-sought breakthrough had been made. Holmes wrote: 'The Major having called the master and pilots together and caused them to produce their journals and calculations, it was found that those pilots differed from the Major in their reckonings, one of them 80 leagues (240 miles) another about 100 (300 miles) and a third, more; but the Major judging by his pendulum watches that they were only some 30 leagues (90 miles) . . . from the isle of Fuego . . . one of the isles of Cape Verde, and that they might reach it next day . . . they resolved to steer their course thither; and having given order so to do, they got the very next day about noon a sight of the said isle . . .'.

Huyghens was naturally delighted at the apparent vindication of his clock and wrote to a friend in Paris 'I have the more reason to believe that the finding of the longitude will be brought to perfection.' His optimism was premature. Further trials showed that Huyghens's clock was unpredictable and erratic in performance. Only in a completely calm sea, a near-unique state in most ocean sailing, did the clock keep going for any length of time without adjustment and restarting. Such constant wet-nursing was beyond the scope and patience of the average 17th-century seaman, and they naturally became disillusioned with a mechanism which limped along in jerks. After 1674, Huyghens managed to curb the faults to some extent but, like Robert Hooke, he never solved the problem of making the design of his clock springs impervious to temperature effects.

Hooke and Huyghens were two of the more imaginative of the inventors who, in the 17th and 18th centuries, tackled the challenge of creating a reliable chronometer. During those years, when the average watch was correct to within only five minutes a day, the 'discovery of the longitude' and, with it, chronometer construction, became a popular synonym for the impossible. The image was helped along by the failed efforts, some of them inspired, others merely crankish, of men like Gottfried von Leibnitz, the great German mathematician; William Hobbs, a self-styled philosophic mathematician; Henry Sully and Jean-Baptiste Dutertre, both watchmakers; and William Palmer and Stephen Plank, both of whom sought to solve the temperature problem by placing their proposed chronometers near a fire.

Stephen Plank and others were spurred on in their efforts by an announcement made in Britain in 1714 of 'a public reward for such person or persons as shall discover the Longitude.' The Act of Parliament incorporating the offer had been pioneered in the same year in a petition to parliament by 'several Captains of Her Majesty's Ships, Merchants of London and Commanders of Merchantmen,' and the offer varied with the degree of accuracy the winner's design scored at the end of a voyage to the West Indies. Anyone who could devise a method of determining longitude to within one degree would receive £10,000, to within 40 minutes £15,000, and to within half a degree £20,000. The prize remained unawarded for 50 years, but when it was eventually claimed, the winner, John Harrison, took the jackpot.

Harrison, who was born in Yorkshire in 1693, was a self-taught mechanical genius in the very highest traditions of English amateurism. A carpenter and joiner by trade, he studied at night to teach himself mechanics, physics, mathematics and instrument-handling and in 1715, he produced his first grandfather clock. Like most of those made at the time, Harrison's clock featured a simple metal pendulum which expanded in hot weather, making the clock slow down, and contracted in the cold, making the clock speed up.

To obviate the fault, Harrison devised in about 1725 a 'gridiron' pendulum made of two metals, brass and steel. Since brass expands faster than steel, in a proportion of 100 to 62, Harrison reckoned that his bi-metal pendulum had a better chance of staying constant despite temperature changes, and therefore of making the clock to which it was attached a good deal more accurate. Harrison's ingenuity also revealed itself in his 'grasshopper' escapement, a silent and almost frictionless mechanism which needed no oiling.

By 1726 Harrison had incorporated into two time-measuring instruments his bi-metal pendulum and grasshopper escapement; he also fitted a remontoire—a small balancing weight or spring attached to a serrated wheel. Harrison, whose hopes were firmly set on the longitude prize, found his time-keepers, or regulators, as they were called, excitingly reliable; one of them did not lose or gain even a second in a month, and after 14 years' continuous working, Harrison found that its total error amounted to less than half a minute.

In 1728 Harrison went to London to interest the Board of Longitude in his regulator and in his design drawings for a marine clock. Edmund Halley, the Astronomer Royal, who was a member of the board was impressed enough with Harrison's work to refer him to George Graham, the leading British horologist. Graham was just as impressed and lent Harrison about £200 of his own money to help him build a marine time-keeper.

The work took Harrison six years and the result was a large clock with two mainsprings driving a central fusee. The clock was controlled by two 5lb balances equipped with four helical balance springs and connected to each other by wires threaded over brass arcs. The opposing motion of the balances was intended to compensate for the motion of a ship at sea. Harrison also incorporated into the clock modified versions of his grasshopper escapement and bi-metal gridiron pendulum. The machine, which weighed 72lb, was the very first to provide for changes in temperature.

In 1736, that first of Harrison's marine clocks, designated Number One, performed extremely well on a trial voyage to Lisbon in HMS *Centurion* and back to London in HMS *Orford*. As Roger Wills, the *Orford's* master, testified in his certificate: 'When we made the land, the said land, according to my reckoning and others' ought to have been the Start; but, before we knew what land it was, John Harrison declared . . . that, according to his observations with his machine, it ought to be the Lizard—the which, indeed, it was found to be, his observation showing the ship to be more west than my reckoning, above one degree and 26 miles.'

The Board of Longitude was sufficiently encouraged by the results to vote Harrison sums of £500 in 1737 and again in 1741 to refine and develop his design. They supplied Harrison with a further £2500 in £500 lots between 1746 and 1761. By 1761 John Harrison was 68 years old, and the chronometer had obviously become his life's work, for it went through three further designs before he was satisfied enough with Numbers Three and Four for sea trials.

Because of his age, which for those days was considered very advanced, Harrison did not attend the trials. His son William went in his place and on November 18, 1761, he set sail in the trial ship, HMS *Deptford*, bound from Spithead for Portland, Plymouth and Madeira. Land was lost to sight on November 27 and a friendly contest developed between Harrison and the ship's captain, Dudley Digges. Digges placed his trust in the longitude 13°50' west of Greenwich, which he had calculated by dead reckoning, while Harrison maintained that Number Four's reading of 15°19' was the correct one, and that accordingly Madeira would be sighted next day.

Digges bet Harrison five to one that he was wrong – and lost. At six o'clock in the morning of November 28 the lookout sighted Porto Santo, one of the Madeira islands, much to the relief of the crew, whose stock of beer was running low. Harrison predicted the proximity of Desirade Island at 18°20'N 61°06'W with equal accuracy and aplomb and after the *Deptford* docked in Jamaica it was found that his chronometer was only five seconds slow, entailing an error in longitude of 1.25 minutes. It thus qualified for the full £20,000 government prize.

Before parting with that very considerable sum though, the Board of Longitude wanted to make sure that the success of Number Four had not been a fluke and a further trial was ordered. It began on February 14, 1764, when William Harrison sailed once more for Jamaica aboard HMS *Tartar*. The second trial vindicated his father's work completely. When checked against the difference of longitude between Portsmouth and Jamaica of three hours 54 minutes 18.2 seconds, Number Four registered an error of only 38.4 seconds over the seven-week voyage. After William returned to Portsmouth in the *New Elizabeth* the chronometer was found to have gained a mere 54 seconds in 156 days, well within the permitted tolerance of one second per day.

On February 9, 1765, the Board of Longitude passed a unanimous resolution placing on record their opinion that 'the said timekeeper has kept its time with sufficient correctness without losing its longitude on the voyage from Portsmouth to Barbados beyond the nearest limit required by the Act'. The board voted Harrison £7500 to make up the first half of his £20,000 prize. After some wrangling he received the second half in 1773.

Three years later, on March 24, 1776, Harrison – inevitably nicknamed Longitude Harrison – died in London aged 83, having lived long enough to know of the superb efficiency his chronometer reached during Captain James Cook's second voyage to the South Seas (1772-75). The chronometer Cook took with him on that, and on his third voyage (1776-79), was a copy of Harrison's Number Four, made at a cost of £450 by the watchmaker Larcum Kendall. It earned from Cook the tribute: 'Indeed, our error [in longitude] can never be great so long as we have so good a guide as Mr Kendall's watch'.

The original watch, which after nearly a century and a half had solved the longitude problem, was 5.2 inches in diameter with a white enamel dial, black ornamentation and hour and minute hands of blued steel. Harrison found his grasshopper escapement too unwieldy for a machine of small size and Number Four's escapement was a development of the old verge mechanism used in the Nuremberg Egg. The gridiron pendulum devised by Harrison in 1725 was represented by a bimetallic strip, the two metals allowing the effective length of the strip to vary in response to temperature changes.

At that time the chronometer, whose development in England had been paralleled in France by Pierre Le Roy (1718-85) and Fernand Berthoud (1729-1807) was a rare and costly instrument, taking two or three years to construct. Subsequently the work of John Arnold (1736-99) and Thomas Earnshaw (1749-1829) in England, and Fernand's nephew Louis Berthoud (1750-1813) in France, developed techniques to speed up production and lower the cost.

By 1825, when chronometer manufacture formed a major branch of the clock-making trade, they had become general issue to Royal Navy ships. Seamen being by nature among the most conservative and suspicious of men, the innovation was not always welcome and one British admiral refused to allow a chronometer on board his ship on the grounds of its alleged connection with necromancy. Such reactionary attitudes inevitably lapsed with time and by 1880, when they cost about £20 or £30 apiece, chronometers held a virtual monopoly of longitude calculation over their close rival, calculations made from lunar distances.

Luncar calculations, which did not become entirely extinct until about 1909, had had a very long run of almost four centuries and Captain Cook had in fact checked Mr Kendall's watch against such readings. However, lunars, like so many other mathematical methods of reckoning longitude, required an inspired navigator of Cook's calibre to chart an accurate course entirely by their means. Chronometers provided a far less complex as well as a far less error-prone method, and brought longitude calculations within the capability of less conspicuously talented and therefore more numerous seamen.

Below: A considerable reduction in size and complexity is apparent in this picture of No 3 of 1767 compared with No 1 on the previous page. *National Maritime Museum London, on loan from the Ministry of Defence*

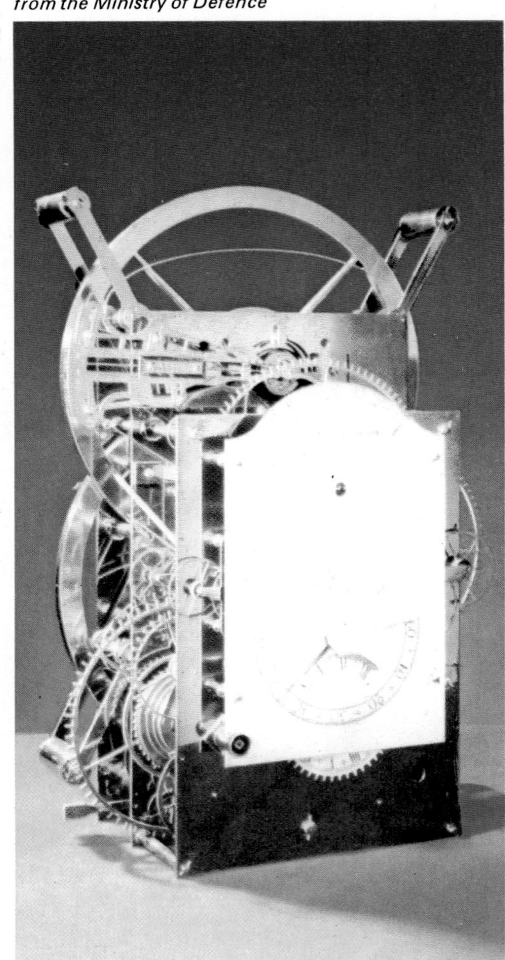

10. Ship Propulsion

A model of 'Charlotte Dundas', the engine of which was designed by William Symington in 1801, making the vessel the first really practical steamboat.
Science Museum London (D Rudkin)

The Steam Piston Engine

THE STEAM ENGINE was first put to practical use in the 18th century as a source for pumping water out of mine shafts, thus solving a problem which had prevented exploitation of deep workings ever since man had first sought to make use of the earth's mineral wealth. Such pumping engines, developed by Newcomen and others, were notoriously extravagant on fuel, however. and it was not until the invention of the separate condenser by James Watt (1736-1819) and his later exploitation of the expansive properties of steam that the steam engine began to look attractive to those interested in water transport. The development of the rotative engine followed and in 1801, William Symington constructed a small single-cylinder double-acting (that is, the steam acted in turn on each side of the piston) engine of 10 nominal horsepower for the stern-wheel steamboat *Charlotte Dundas,* built to the order of Lord Dundas for service on the Forth & Clyde Canal.

At the beginning of the 19th century, the conventional rotative engine comprised a single cylinder with its piston rod connected to a rocking beam pivoted about a central fulcrum. The valve gear controlling the admission of steam to the cylinder and the exhaust therefrom to the condenser was driven off the beam, the free end of which was coupled through the connecting rod to a crankpin on the flywheel. The latter not only helped to govern engine speed but served also to smooth the rotary motion of the driven shaft. Exhaust steam passed to a jet condenser in which a partial vacuum was maintained by an air pump also driven off the beam. The steam was worked thus to less than atmospheric pressure before being condensed by the injection of cold water into the condenser at the end of the piston stroke.

This form of beam engine found almost universal acceptance in the United States both for river transport (other than for stern-wheel craft) and for ocean work, but in Europe it was looked upon with much less favour, because it was bulky and had a high centre of gravity. Such drawbacks led to the development in the United Kingdom of the side-lever engine, in which the heavy overhead beam was replaced by a pair of side beams, one on each side of the engine just above the engine bedplate. Introduced by the Boulton & Watt company about 1814, the side-lever engine became the standard for paddle steamers until the 1860s. In most installations, the engine comprised two cylinders working through individual side levers to two cranks set 90 degrees apart, rather than 180 degrees, on the paddle shaft, so that the engine could start from any stopped position.

Because of its simplicity, the side-lever engine working from a low-pressure boiler retained its popularity for certain services, in particular for the highly manoeuvrable paddle tug, through to the 20th century. A late example is to be seen today in the Neptune Hall of the National Maritime Museum, where the paddle tug *Reliant* of 1907 has been put on exhibition with her twin-cylinder side-lever engine in working trim.

The side-lever engine also had its drawbacks, however, primarily in the matter of weight when relatively high power was a requirement for fast coastal steamers and warships, and many ideas were tried, and some were adopted, in attempts to improve the power/weight ratio. Most of the improvements were based on the elimination of the heavy side levers by mounting the cylinders directly under the paddle shaft. Numerous configurations were tried but few achieved the lasting success of the oscillating engine, first patented by Joseph Maudslay in 1827 and fitted in the Thames steamboat *Endeavour,* which was completed in 1828 for service between London and Richmond.

In the oscillating engine, the cylinder(s) was mounted in trunnions supported by the cast-iron engine frame and the piston rod acted directly on the crank above without the necessity for any intermediate connecting rod. Steam was admitted to and exhausted from the swinging cylinder through valves in the trunnions; the valves were worked by eccentrics on the crankshaft. Improvements to the valve gear introduced by John Penn in 1838 made for a more compact and reliable engine and the type retained a degree of popularity for the smaller paddle steamer until the 1890s.

Typical of small oscillating-engined paddlers towards the end of that period were the sister ships *Edward William* and *Myleta,* completed in 1891 for the South Eastern Railway's Medway ferry service between Port Victoria and Sheerness. As with the side-lever engine, however, the final examples of the oscillating engine were to be found in paddle tugs and probably the last in service in United Kingdom waters was that in the naval tug *Industrious,* completed in 1902 and not sold for breaking up until 1959.

An alternative solution to the requirement for a compact paddle-wheel engine was the diagonal, or inclined, direct-acting engine, in which the cylinder(s) was placed low in the hull at an angle of about 15 degrees to the horizontal so that its axis was aligned with the crankshaft. Transmission to the crank was through the piston rod and connecting rod, the valve gear being worked off eccentrics on the crankshaft. The advantages of the diagonal engine was that much higher steam pressures could be employed than was the case with oscillating machinery and the type retained favour, in compound or triple-expansion form, as long as passenger-carrying paddle steamers continued to be built. One of the last single-cylinder engines of the diagonal configuration was constructed in 1898 for the Clyde steamer *Kenilworth* of the North British Steam Packet Co, but it was not until 1935 that probably the last diagonal (compound) set went into service in the Loch Lomond paddler *Maid of the Loch.*

Although marine engineering as an art had made considerable progress during the first half of the 19th century, the marine engine at the close of that period was still heavy, inefficient and prone to frequent breakdowns. It was capable of fairly satisfactory service at the low speed (rpm) required for paddle-wheel propulsion, but when the ship constructor turned to screw propulsion, means had to be devised to turn the propeller at the comparatively high speed required for its efficient operation. This was achieved by gearing in the form of a rope drive, pitch chains or toothed wheels.

The original machinery of Brunel's *Great Britain,* of 1845, comprised four cylinders inclined in pairs at 33 degrees to the vertical, working by simple expansion on overhanging crank pins at each end of an 18.25ft-diameter drum. Four sets of flat pitch chains connected the drum with another on the propeller shaft to give a speed of 53rpm, compared with the 18rpm of the crankshaft. The four cylinders took steam from the boiler at a pressure of 15 pounds per square inch (psi) and exhausted into condensers placed amidships between the cylinders; the air pumps were driven from the crankpins. The engine indicated about 1500hp, adequate in reasonable weather under steam alone for about nine knots.

Geared engines were built for upwards of a decade, by which time improved engine design and greater precision in manufacture permitted the use of much higher crankshaft speeds than hitherto and enabled the engine to be coupled directly to the propeller.

Early paddle engines with the cylinders mounted vertically below the paddle shaft had been called vertical engines. When that type was adapted to screw propulsion, because the propeller shaft had to be placed low down in the ship, the vertical engine was turned through 180 degrees and built with its cylinders above the crankshaft. That type of vertical inverted engine first appeared in 1846 and formed the basis of all steam reciprocating engine development from that date on.

The two-cylinder inverted vertical simple engine was fitted widely in merchant ships throughout the late 1850s and early 1860s, the installation of the P & O liner *Ceylon* being typical of the many engines of the type. The *Ceylon's* twin-cylinder engine, with pistons acting on cranks at right angles, indicated 2054hp with a boiler pressure of 20psi, sufficient under steam alone of 11 knots.

The problem in warships was somewhat different to that in merchant ships, since the search for economy and efficiency was tempered by the need to keep the machinery below the waterline for reasons of protection. This led to the development of the horizontal screw engine in preference to the vertical configuration and to an exercise in design ingenuity to find ways to accommodate the horizontal piston rod and the connecting rod in the confined space available. Two main types of engine were evolved, the first being the return connecting rod engine, developed in the 1840s and in general use for new construction until about 1876, and the other, the horizontal trunk engine, in which the piston rod was eliminated and the connecting rod attached directly to the piston within a cylindrical trunk.

The broadside ironclad *Valiant* of 1863 was engined with return connecting rod machinery constructed by Maudslay Sons & Field, in which two cylinders of 82in diameter and 48in stroke were supplied with steam at 20lb pressure from six boilers. A pair of jet condensers, each with its own air pump, was arranged opposite the cylinders and the engine indicated about 3560hp. A very forward-looking feature of the installation was a variable-pitch propeller with pitch adjustable between $22\frac{1}{2}$ and $27\frac{1}{2}$ feet.

In the trunk engine the connecting rod was coupled directly to the piston, which carried a large cylindrical trunk extending through the engine covers. The twin-cylinder simple engine in the broadside ironclad *Minotaur* of 1867 had cylinders 112in in diameter by 52in stroke, with 41in-diameter trunks extending from the front and rear of the pistons. The small ends of the connecting rods were secured to gudgeons on the pistons and the big ends worked on balanced cranks set at right angles in the crankshaft. Although compact, however, the trunk engine suffered in the matter of efficiency through the heat loss through the trunks, the heavy reciprocating mass of the trunked pistons and from excessive mechanical wear, but despite the drawbacks the type retained its popularity for a number of years. The last major warship with trunk-type machinery was the mastless ironclad *Devastation,* launched in July 1871 and completed in 1873.

It had long been realised that increased efficiency could be achieved only through the use of higher pressures, thus enabling greater use to be made of the expansive power of steam. Mid-century boilers worked at about 20lb pressure but improvements in construction and the adoption of a cylindrical shell in place of the former box shape permitted the generation of steam at pressures of as much as 60lb per square inch. However, steam at this pressure is at a temperature of 307°F and to expand it within a single cylinder (simple expansion) would entail a considerable range of temperature cycling within the cylinder and consequent loss of thermodynamic efficiency. This fact led, through the work of Alfred Holt and others, to the development of the compound engine in which the steam was expanded in two stages, leading to increased efficiency, reduced weight and lower running costs.

Many argued against the compound

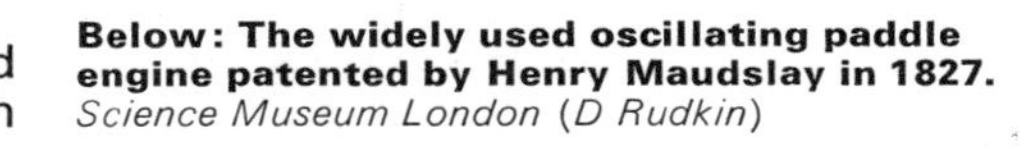

Below: The widely used oscillating paddle engine patented by Henry Maudslay in 1827.
Science Museum London (D Rudkin)

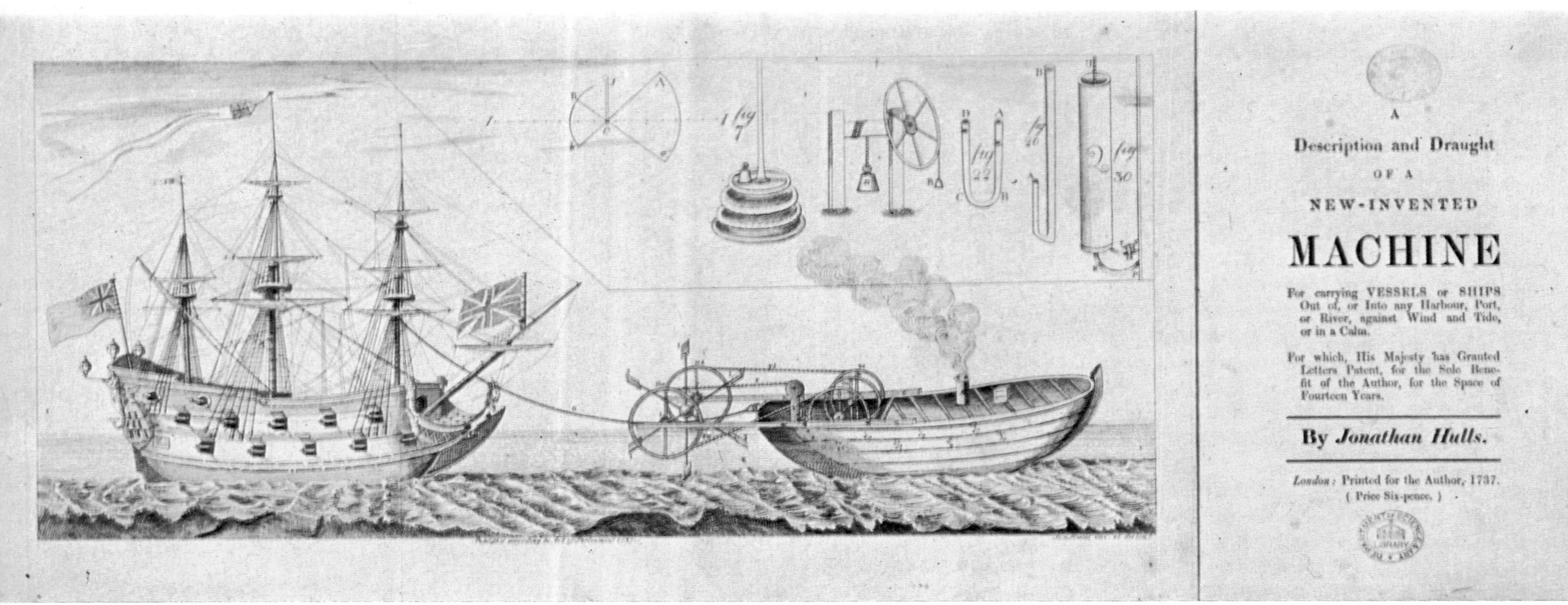

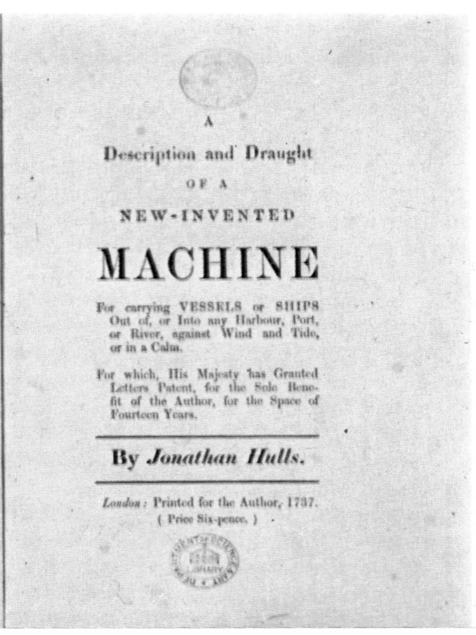

A
Description and Draught
OF A
NEW-INVENTED
MACHINE

For carrying VESSELS or SHIPS Out of, or Into any Harbour, Port, or River, against Wind and Tide, or in a Calm.

For which, His Majesty has Granted Letters Patent, for the Sole Benefit of the Author, for the Space of Fourteen Years.

By *Jonathan Hulls.*

London: Printed for the Author, 1737.
(Price Six-pence.)

Above: A reprint of an illustrated pamphlet published in 1737 by Jonathan Hulls featuring his proposed paddle steamer.
Science Museum London

Left: Henry Warriner's high-pressure non-condensing engine of 1840 as fitted in 1841 to the launch 'Firefly'.
Science Museum London (D Rudkin)

Below left: The massive propulsion machinery of the British steam frigate 'Warrior' of 1861.
Mary Evans Picture Library

engine, however, on the grounds of increased complexity and within the Royal Navy, on the potential danger of high-pressure steam in the wake of damage in action. Indeed, in the twin-screw dispatch vessels *Iris* (1878) and *Mercury* (1879) steam was supplied normally to the four-cylinder compound engines (two high-pressure and two low-pressure cylinders) at 65psi but when clearing for action arrangements were provided to enable the engines to be worked on simple expansion, when boiler pressure was reduced to about 4psi.

The economy of the compound engine was proved, however, and many of the old twin-cylinder vertical inverted engines were converted to compound working. Further increases in boiler pressure during the 1870s led to the development of the triple-expansion engine, which with successive refinements was to serve as the standard power plant for the majority of merchant vessels and warships for the next 30 years and, so far as low-powered ships were concerned, until it was finally displaced by the diesel engine in the 1930s and 1940s. There are in fact still a considerable number of triple-expansion engines at sea today.

Boiler pressures in the 1880s were of the order of 150psi but after the turn of the century pressures of 250lb and even 300lb became commonplace, leading to the construction of some high-powered vessels with quadruple-expansion machinery. In practice, however, little further gain in economy was achieved with the quadruple-expansion engine and the type never became very popular. In many cases, designers, in the quest for higher outputs, turned to multi-cylinder configurations of the triple-expansion engine, frequently with tandem cylinders; the high-pressure cylinders were placed above the low- or intermediate-pressure cylinders, with a common piston rod working on a single crank. Thus, the Cunard twin-screw express liner *Campania*, of 1893, was powered by a pair of 31,000hp five-cylinder triple-expansion engines, each working on three cranks.

The 1890s marked the zenith of the high-power steam reciprocating engine for express liners, major warships and short-sea mail steamships alike. There remained little scope for further development in those applications and in fact an alternative power plant was already to hand. In 1897 Sir Charles Parsons had created a sensation with the performance of his steam turbine-powered yacht *Turbinia* at Spithead, where the fleet was assembled for Queen Victoria's Diamond Jubilee Review.

A representation of the tug-of-war in 1845 between the paddler 'Alecto' (right) and the victorious screw steamer 'Rattler'.
D J Kingston

Below: The 'Mark Twain', a scaled-down replica of a Mississippi stern-wheeler.
D J Kingston

PADDLE VERSUS SCREW

APART FROM the application of muscular power to oars or paddles, the first mechanical means of propelling a ship was the paddle-wheel. Representations from the 6th and 15th centuries show ships with paddle-wheels turned by men or animals. As early as 1817 Londoners could claim that there were actually as many as five paddle boats all driven by steam to be seen puffing along the Thames. But the Scots were well ahead of that by the following year; they had 18 steamers trailing their smoke on the Clyde, there were six others on the Forth and four more on the Tay.

That was not all; in 1814 the *Marjorie* (or *Margery*) steamed south from Scotland to find work on the Thames and in 1816 became the first steam vessel to cross the English Channel. In 1815 the first steam ferry on the Mersey was the *Elizabeth*, which had braved the Irish Sea from the Clyde to start her ferrying between Liverpool and Runcorn.

One and all, those early boats were paddlers, though with more than a little variety. A few had their paddles splashing away at the stern in the style of the later sternwheelers of the Mississippi. Still fewer had twin hulls, linked together in modern catamaran fashion with the engine between them, following the early example of Patrick Miller's boat of 1788. The type that was more generally in use in Britain, however, had a paddle-wheel on each side of the hull. In spite of the usual nautical distaste for new ideas, engines soon began to find their way into quite large ships.

Three vessels using paddles each made a lasting name for themselves within a short period. The *Savannah*, to start with, in 1818 became the first steamship to cross the Atlantic although, truth to tell, she sailed most of the way and used her engine for no more than 80 hours in the course of the 25 days of the voyage. The paddle wheels

Top: A model of the 'City of Paris' of 1865 whose success persuaded Cunard to abandon paddles in favour of the screw propeller.
Science Museum London (D Rudkin)

Above: Model of the 'Savannah' presented to the Science Museum, London, by the Newcomen Society of North America.
Science Museum London (D Rudkin)

could be disconnected and hoisted up on deck when not needed.

Next on the list of firsts was the *Aaron Manby*, which in 1822 became the first iron steamship to cross the Channel from London to Havre. Third, in 1825, the *Enterprise* of 470 tons was the first steamship to voyage from London to Calcutta. Her paddles were described as 'collapsible' presumably because they could readily be stowed in heavy weather.

Another steamer that made a long ocean voyage from Canada to England in 1833 was the PS *Royal William*. Strangely, she made the trip for the sole purpose of finding a buyer. She had been built in Quebec in 1831 with the object of running a packet service between Quebec and Halifax; when the project fell through her owners considered that they would find a surer market for her in Britain.

Outdoing all other vessels in size and completeness, the earliest of Isambard Brunel's trio of mammoth ships, the *Great Western*, began her career in 1838. She just missed the honour of being the first transatlantic steam passenger ship when the much smaller *Sirius* fought her way through stormy seas to reach New York ahead of the *Great Western* on the same day. The *Sirius* had burnt every scrap of coal and practically everything else that could be used as fuel.

An early steam-propelled vessel in the Royal Navy was HMS *Diana*, a steam paddler that served in the first Burmese war of 1825 but little else seems to be known about her. There was also a naval paddler laden with the unfortunate name of *Rhadamanthus*, of 813 tons, which sailed from Plymouth to Barbados in 1832, but the first orthodox paddle-steamer warship appears to have been HMS *Penelope*, launched in 1829 as a 46-gun sailing frigate. She was cut in two in 1843 and lengthened to take an engine of 650 horsepower. The *Terrible* of 1845, a paddle frigate of 21 guns, was designed as a steamship and constructed to carry the heavy armament and machinery.

The screw propeller had been introduced a few years earlier by F P Smith, of Hendon, followed by the Swedish engineer John Ericsson, who had already made his name in England by building a steam locomotive for the Liverpool & Manchester Railway. In order to awaken the Admiralty's interest in the screw, Ericsson in 1837 arranged a demonstration for their Lordships by towing the Admiralty barge with them as passengers from Somerset House to Blackwall and back at a speed of 10 knots with a screw-propelled boat.

Soon afterwards Ericsson left England for the United States, where he became an American citizen of renown. He received from the Admiralty only one-fifth of the £20,000 that had been intended as a reward for the invention of the screw propeller as there was some dispute over patent rights.

By 1843 the propeller had been satisfactorily developed. One caught the eye of Brunel, who had chanced to see it driving a small steamer, the *Archimedes*. He promptly bought the vessel in order to make a series of tests for himself and as a result he altered the partly built hull of the *Great Britain* so that screw propellers could be used instead of the paddle-wheels he had originally planned to use.

Whether or not Ericsson's towing party had influenced matters, the Royal Navy embarked on an extensive programme of trials and experiments to assess the relative effectiveness of paddle and screw, culminating in 1845 in the famous tug-of-war that ended with HM screw-steamer *Rattler* triumphantly running away with the paddler *Alecto*.

Yet even 10 years or so later, from 1853-6, the large British fleet supporting the Allied armies in the Black Sea was an astonishing medley. It included wooden ships entirely dependent on sails, other wooden ships with sails and paddles or screw propellers, and iron ships. Only here and there among the forest of masts, yards and rigging were seen the tall thin funnels of the early steamship in stark contrast.

The British force used in the campaign totalled 10 sailing ships, four paddlers and six screw-propelled vessels, not counting those of six or fewer guns. Among the sailing ships were the *Britannia* of 120 guns, the *Albion* of 91 guns and the *Vengeance* of 84 guns. The 91-gun *Agamemnon*, the flagship of Rear-Admiral Sir E Lyons, was screw-propelled but the *Trafalgar* of 120 guns and the *Bellerophon* and the *London* of 90 guns had sail only.

The French fleet was much smaller but there were a number of very large ships among those with sails only, two of them flagships. In addition there were four paddlers and six vessels with screw propellers.

With such an assortment on its hands, the Admiralty, only two years after the end of the Crimean War, announced that 'sailing ships are unfit for active service'. Surprising and a little premature though the statement might have been, it had become obvious that not only the pure sailer but also the paddler, with or without sails, had been made obsolescent by the screw propeller. The paddle-steamer, quite apart from the question of efficiency, was very vulnerable and the paddles were bound to obstruct the view to some extent.

Improvements in the design of both engine and screw were continually coming forward. In 1874, for instance, triple-expansion engines designed by A C Kirk were first fitted in a sea-going vessel, and high-pressure steam soon followed. The 'battle of the boilers' in Parliament over the adoption of the water-tube boiler was fought and won. Finally, in the 1890s came a major triumph—the steam turbine. Its practical achievement was largely the work of Sir Charles Parsons, who displayed his invention by driving a vessel he named *Turbinia* at a speed of 34 knots in the Naval Review at Spithead in 1897.

Today, the originator of it all, the steam paddler, has practically vanished. In British waters only one ship, the pleasure steamer *Waverley*, may still be seen puffing around the coast and she continues only by grace of the preservation society. It seems almost a touch of ancient history to recall that in 1940 three paddlers were patrolling the Bristol Channel by day and night armed and flying the White Ensign.

The STEAM TURBINE

THE PRINCIPLE OF the reaction steam engine has been known for centuries, reputedly since Hero of Alexandria demonstrated his aeolipyle in the first century BC, but no attempt was made to exploit it in modern times until the last quarter of the 19th century, when engineers in both Europe and the United States developed practical designs.

First in the field was the Hon Sir Charles Parsons (1854-1931), youngest of the six sons of the Earl of Rosse, who patented his parallel-flow reaction turbine in 1884. In his machine, designed to drive an electric generator, the steam was expanded through alternate rows of fixed and moving blades placed at an angle of 45 degrees to the axis of the rotor, but its high speed of 18,000rpm necessarily limited its practical application. As an auxiliary engine driving generators it proved commercially successful, however, and several were fitted in merchant ships and warships of the period.

Sir Charles Parsons had seen from the first that the turbine might be applied to ship propulsion and to that end he turned his attention to the development of a machine comparable with the contemporary reciprocating engine in the matter of economy in the use of steam. He achieved that objective in 1891 with his condensing turbine, in which the steam was expanded well below atmospheric pressure, and in 1894 he formed the Marine Steam Turbine Co Ltd to further its development as a marine engine.

In the meantime, in 1889, the Swedish engineer Carl Gustav de Laval had taken out a patent for an impulse turbine, in which the steam is directed at high velocity through nozzles on to the rotor blades. As in the reaction turbine, the steam is expanded progressively along the length of the rotor, but in the impulse type the successive stages of rotor blading are separated by rows of nozzles which create the required steam velocity. Thereafter, patents were taken out by several other engineers; they included Auguste Rateau, in France, for the design of an impulse turbine in 1896; the American Charles Curtis, also for a turbine of the impulse type in 1896; and Dr H Zoelly, in Germany, for a combined impulse-reaction turbine in 1899.

The first successful development of the marine steam turbine, however, was that of Sir Charles Parsons and the Marine Steam Turbine Co. After testing with models to determine the power required, the first practical full-scale installation was built for the $44\frac{1}{2}$-ton experimental yacht *Turbinia* in 1894. The engine was a radial-flow reaction turbine taking steam at a pressure of 155 pounds per square inch (psi) from a double-ended water-tube boiler (210psi steam drum pressure) and driving a single shaft at 2400rpm. At such a high propeller speed, cavitation, or the formation of voids on the blade surface, resulted in such loss of power that the *Turbinia* could manage only a disappointing 19.75 knots.

The problem was that the turbine could operate efficiently only if the moving blade speed was high, whereas the screw propeller is most efficient at relatively low speeds. Gearing was, of course, the answer but the state of the engineering art at the close of the 19th century had not advanced sufficiently to permit gear cutting of high enough accuracy for the purpose. Consequently, the direct-drive turbine was designed with a large-diameter rotor, to give a reasonably high peripheral blade speed with the lowest possible shaft speed.

Space in the little *Turbinia* was limited, however, and she was rebuilt with a three-shaft arrangement driven by a three-stage parallel-flow turbine set, wherein the steam was expanded progressively through a high-pressure (hp) turbine on the starboard shaft, an intermediate-pressure (ip) turbine on the port shaft and a low-pressure (lp) turbine on the centre shaft. Each shaft was given three propellers, thereby increasing the blade area as much as possible and despite the fact that propeller speed was still extremely high, the *Turbinia* managed an impressive 34.5 knots with the machinery developing 2400 shp.

The rebuilt *Turbinia* was demonstrated to the public on the occasion of Queen Victoria's Diamond Jubilee Review at Spithead in June 1897, when she aston-

Top: Model of the $44\frac{1}{2}$-ton experimental vessel 'Turbinia', the first to be powered by a Parsons steam turbine, which gave a speed of nearly 35 knots. *Science Museum London*

Above: Reproduction of an illustration of 'Turbinia' at speed, from 'The Illustrated London News' of September 10, 1898. *Illustrated London News*

ished all present by her performance. In the same year, the company built the first experimental geared turbine set, which was installed in the 22ft twin-screw launch *Charmian*. The single 10hp turbine worked at about 20,000rpm and was geared to the twin propeller shafts through single helical spur wheels to give a shaft speed of 1400rpm. The speed of the launch was about nine knots.

Having played its part in the development of a practical propulsion turbine, the Marine Steam Turbine Co Ltd was reorganised in 1897 as the Parsons Marine Steam Turbine Co Ltd in order to exploit the commercial potential of the engine. The Admiralty had shown considerable interest already in the development of the steam turbine as an ideal vibration-free power unit for small high-speed craft and in March 1898 an order was placed for the first turbine-engined destroyer. It was the 344-ton *Viper,* which was to be constructed within the limits of the standard 30-knot destroyer hull. The contract called for a speed of 31 knots and the *Viper* was designed with a four-shaft installation and two propellers on each shaft.

On trials in November 1899, the *Viper,* in a one-hour full-power run, averaged 36.58 knots and broke all existing records. A short time afterwards, doubt was raised about the safety of turbine-engined vessels by the loss after breaking in two of the destroyer *Cobra,* which had been built by Armstrong-Whitworth as a private development and purchased by the Admiralty in 1900. However, the subsequent inquiry could find no reason for the accident other than structural failure of the hull due to lack of longitudinal strength.

In 1901 a new company, registered as the Turbine Steamer Syndicate Ltd, was formed on the Clyde for the purpose of operating the world's first commercial turbine steamer, the order for which had been placed by Captain John Williamson with W Denny & Bros of Dumbarton. Completed in June 1901, the *King Edward* was powered on three shafts with one hp turbine, and two lp turbines driving two screws on each of the outer shafts, that is, five screws in all. The design proved a success and similar installations were built for the railway steamer *The Queen* of 1903 and for a number of other Denny-built cross-channel and coastal steamships.

The fitting of two or more screws on a shaft was not repeated, however, since it was found that second or third screws working in already turbulent water contributed little to the overall propulsive effort. Several of the early turbine steamers were extremely long-lived; indeed, the original *King Edward* was not broken up until 1952, after more than 50 years in the Clyde service for which she had been designed.

Turbine propulsion was accepted by the Admiralty for all new-built capital ships, cruisers and destroyers from about 1905, most installations being designed around the Parsons reaction type. The machinery was built under licence from the Parsons company, which provided details of the steam path and blading to suit the power range and machinery configuration envisaged. From an early date, however, the Admiralty showed interest also in the possibilities of impulse turbines of the Curtis type and in 1910 the twin-screw cruiser *Bristol* was engined by John Brown & Co with direct-drive Brown-Curtis turbines of 22,000shp. The great advantage of the impulse turbine over the reaction type was the economy obtainable at low powers and the Brown-Curtis turbine was accepted as a satisfactory alternative to the Parsons turbine until it lost favour after a series of damaging blade failures in the 1920s.

Commercial development followed much the same trend in so far as that the direct-drive turbine quickly became accepted as the most suitable engine for express mail steamships employed on the North Atlantic and short sea routes. Again, early installations were invariably of the Parsons type, such as that in the Cunard intermediate steamer *Carmania* of 1905, which was built with turbine machinery to enable experience to be gained in service alongside her quadruple-expansion-engined sister *Caronia.* Success with *Carmania* led to the adoption of turbine machinery, consisting of a direct-drive triple-expansion

Top: The 10hp geared turbine built by the Parsons Company to power the first geared-turbine vessel, a 22ft launch; the exhibit is on loan by the maker to the Science Museum. *Science Museum London*

Above: A painting of the famous Cunarder 'Queen Elizabeth', built on Clydebank by John Brown & Co and launched in 1938; she was powered by four sets of Parsons reaction geared turbines with a total maximum of 181,700shp. *Science Museum London*

arrangement on four shafts, for the pair of 31,500-ton government-backed express liners ordered in May 1905. They were the *Lusitania* and *Mauretania*; the former entered service in 1907 and, after a relatively leisurely running-in first voyage, amply demonstrated the efficacy of the machinery by taking the Atlantic Blue Riband on her second double crossing at an average speed of 23.99 knots. Subsequently, that particular honour passed to the *Mauretania,* which held the record for no less a period than 22 years.

At that time triple- and quadruple-expansion reciprocating engines were being worked at steam throttle pressures of up to 300psi, but in the steam turbine it was found that the clearances necessary between the working parts resulted in considerable losses at such elevated pressures. Consequently, boiler pressures in early turbine installations were kept to about 200psi. On the other hand, the maintenance of a high vacuum in the condenser enabled the steam to be expanded much more than was possible in the reciprocating engine, where the risk of condensation within the cylinder necessarily limited the degree of expansion. With improvements in condenser and air pump design, a vacuum of 29 inches or more could be maintained, enabling the steam to be worked down to an absolute pressure of less than one pound per square inch.

The turbine has a major limitation in that it is not reversible; thus, with direct-drive turbine machinery, it was necessary to build additional rows of reverse-pitch blading into the machine for use when astern power was required. In practice, the astern turbine was kept small so that astern power was necessarily limited, imposing a considerable restriction on the manoeuvrability of the turbine-engined vessel.

As mentioned above, the necessarily high turbine speed is not compatible with the requirement to keep propeller speed low in order to avoid the effects of cavitation. The direct-drive turbine was thus at best a compromise in which the rotor was of large diameter in order to achieve a high peripheral speed. Since the introduction involved practical difficulties, designers turned their attention to hydraulic and electric transmission to achieve the desired speed reduction.

In Germany much design effort was concentrated on the Föttinger hydraulic transformer, a combination of steam turbine-driven centrifugal pump and secondary water-driven turbine, but in the US turbo-electric drive was for many years the most favoured form of transmission. British engineers concentrated on the development of mechanical gearing of the type pioneered by Sir Charles Parsons in 1894. Single-reduction gearing with a transmission efficiency of about 98.5 per cent compared very favourably with other means of speed reduction and once manufacturing problems had been overcome the geared turbine was generally adopted, for short-sea passenger/cargo liners as well as warships and ocean-going passenger vessels.

In 1909 the Parsons Company re-engined the 22-year-old cargo steamship *Vespasian* with a compound single-reduction geared turbine set which reduced fuel consumption compared with its original machinery by 15 per cent. Two years later Fairfield Shipbuilding & Engineering Company built and equipped the single-reduction geared turbine sisters *Hantonia* and *Normannia* for the Southampton-Havre service of the London & South Western Railway.

Strangely, the direct-drive turbine continued to be favoured for the fast excursion steamers built for the Caledonian Steam Packet Company and the Williamson-Buchanan Company on the Clyde. Hence, the *Glen Sannox* (1925), *Duchess of Montrose* (1930) and *Queen Mary* (1933) were all completed with that form of obviously outdated machinery. Indeed, the last-mentioned, as *Queen Mary II,* is possibly the last direct-drive turbine vessel remaining in service in European waters. On the other hand, the *King George V* of 1926 was powered by a twin-screw single-reduction geared installation taking steam at 550psi from a pair of Yarrow water-tube boilers. The port set comprised a quadruple-expansion arrangement, and the starboard triple-expansion set took in steam from the extra-pressure turbine exhaust on the port set.

Apart from the experimental high-pressure installation in the *King George V* and a 500psi installation in the Thornycroft-built destroyer *Acheron* of 1930, development in the UK during the remaining years before the 1939-45 war centred upon the single-reduction geared turbine set of the Parsons reaction type, with an impulse first stage in the high-pressure turbine and an all-impulse astern turbine, both working at pressures of 300 to 450psi. As it turned out, the practical certainty of war inhibited any major change in turbine or transmission design for warships after 1936 and the well-proved plant installed in new vessels of the 1930s remained virtually unchanged until the early 1950s.

In Germany and the United States, however, very much higher pressures were employed, with varying degrees of success, and their use of double-reduction gearing permitted higher blade speeds, which resulted in higher overall efficiency, particularly at lower output, and reduced weight of machinery.

In British merchant ships, too, the Parsons impulse-reaction turbine remained first choice for the majority of high-power installations, although by then the geared turbine had been largely supplanted by the diesel engine for vessels up to medium powers. In the Cunard liner *Queen Elizabeth,* launched in 1938, a total of 181,700-shp was developed by four independent quadruple-expansion turbine sets connected through single-reduction gearing to four shafts. The astern turbines were incorporated in the second intermediate-pressure and low-pressure casings of each set and steam was supplied at 450psi by 12 Yarrow small-tube boilers.

In France lack of suitable plant and small home demand for marine gearing resulted in the retention of the direct-drive turbine for many years after the adoption of geared machinery by British designers. The handsome express liner *Normandie,* a contemporary of the Cunard Queens, however, had electric transmission, with four sets of Zoelly impulse turbines running at 2430-rpm connected to synchronous alternators supplying current to the four shaft propulsion motors running at 243rpm.

A noticeable fact of naval operational planning during the 1939-45 war was that US warships, in particular destroyers, had considerably greater endurance at cruising speed than their British counterparts. It was due in part to the fact that the overall efficiency of the comparatively simple turbine machinery in the British vessels was at its best at or near full power but fell off considerably at lower cruising outputs. Some ships were fitted with additional cruising turbines or with cruising stages built into high-pressure casings but neither expedient proved very satisfactory in practice.

After the war the problem was put to a committee representing the marine engineering industry and C. A. Parsons Ltd – the land-based turbine manufacturer. An agreement was reached which led to the setting up of the research organisation Pametrada (Parsons and Marine Engineering Turbine Research and Development Association). Facilities for full-scale shore testing of marine engine installations were provided and the work continues today as part of the British Shipbuilding Research Association.

The first practical outcome from Pametrada was the design of an impulse-reaction turbine set for some of the Royal Navy's Daring-class destroyers of 1951-52. Double-reduction gearing enabled designers to take advantage of higher rotor and blade speeds, while an increase in boiler steam-drum pressure to 650psi gave an improvement in overall efficiency. The Pametrada turbine was adopted widely for merchant ships and, among others, the Dutch passenger liner *Statendam* of 1957 was powered by machinery of the type.

The installation in the Shaw, Savill & Albion liner *Southern Cross* of 1955 was typical of its day. It comprised a twin-shaft arrangement with independent compound double-reduction geared turbine sets, each developing 10,000shp at a shaft speed of 120rpm. The high-pressure ahead turbines were of all-reaction design. The high- and low-pressure astern turbines, built into common casings, were of all-impulse design.

Elsewhere, developments of the Rateau and de Laval turbines were favoured but, other than for very low-power installations, the trend throughout the later 1950s and 1960s was towards the internal-combustion engine.

After the large destroyers of the Daring class, in association with the Yarrow and English Electric companies, the Royal Navy developed an integrated installation, named Y-100, for a new class of fast anti-submarine frigates, the first of which, HMS *Torquay,* entered service in July 1956. Double-reduction gearing and careful turbine design resulted in high efficiency at cruising speeds and, apart from detail improvements, machinery of the Y-100 type was employed for all the Type 12-derived frigates, not only for the Royal Navy but also those built for the Australian, Indian, Netherlands, New Zealand and South African navies. Similar machinery was used in the destroyer escorts of the St Laurent and later classes of the Canadian Armed Forces (Maritime) Command.

Today steam turbine machinery is specified only for large crude oil and other bulk carriers, in which operating economics still give it an advantage over the diesel engine and, possibly, the gas turbine. It is likely to remain the case for some years to come, but in naval design the trend is very much in favour of the gas turbine for high-power installations and the diesel engine for smaller ships – with the singular exception, that is, of nuclear-powered ships, particularly submarines, which for the Royal Navy have geared turbines.

For the foreseeable future it seems that further development of the marine steam turbine is likely to be restricted to meeting the requirements of the VLCC (very large cargo carrier) and nuclear-powered vessels. For other classes, from tug to cruise liner, internal-combustion machinery, either reciprocating or gas turbine, now offers designers and operators reduced manning requirements, a smaller maintenance load and ease of unit exchange.

The Diesel Engine

IN 1892 RUDOLF DIESEL lodged his patent for a heat engine based on new working principles. The young German engineer, who had been brought up frugally in Paris, trained in Augsburg and Munich and in the great engineering company of Sulzer Brothers in Switzerland, was concerned at the very low thermal efficiency of the steam engine which, at best, converted only about one tenth of the energy in the fuel burned under its boiler into useful work. In those days, only steam and water power, if available, could be used for the mechanisation of factories.

Diesel set out the reasons for his proposals in the classic work *The theory and design of a rational heat engine* (1893). Evidently his patent was secure, for no-one successfully challenged it in the ensuing years.

The operating principles of the diesel engine are similar to those of the Otto four-stroke petrol engine as fitted in most cars today. There are, however, two very significant differences. The compression ratio is much higher than that of a petrol engine and instead of the descending piston drawing into the cylinder a mixture of air and fuel in the form of a fine mist metered in correct proportions by a carburetter, the diesel engine piston draws into the cylinder a charge of pure air; on the succeeding upward stroke the temperature of the air charge is raised by compression to a point above that of the self-ignition temperature of the fuel. Only then is the fuel admitted to the cylinder in the form of an accurately timed and metered very fine spray.

Ignition of the fuel takes place immediately, followed by complete combustion and a rise of pressure within the cylinder. The pressure acting upon the piston performs the working stroke as the piston descends. The final stage in the cycle of events, after the expanding gases have completed their work at the bottom of the piston stroke, is when the piston rises again, the exhaust valve opens and the waste combustion products are discharged through the exhaust pipe.

Since all the events take place within the engine cylinder there is much less opportunity for the heat (interchangeable with energy) to be lost. Whereas the steam engine wastes a large proportion of its thermal energy by heating the atmosphere with its boiler flue gases and, nearby ponds or rivers by the heat in the exhaust steam, the losses of the diesel engine are confined to that dissipated to the cooling water within the jackets which surround the combustion space and the exhaust gases. The water jackets are necessary to prevent those parts of the cylinder and combustion chamber in contact with the flame from overheating and causing destruction of the lubricating oil film between the cylinder wall and piston.

The diesel engine was certainly radical for those days, since it was able to turn about 34 per cent of the thermal energy in the fuel into useful work, whereas the best steam engines could manage not much better than 10 per cent. Dr Diesel's original ideas were for a compression-ignition engine to burn a charge of finely ground coal dust injected into the cylinder at the top of the piston stroke. However, the resulting ash rapidly abraded the piston rings and cylinder surfaces and that method was abandoned.

Diesel himself never built an engine for sale; manufacture was confined initially to a small number of licensees of which the original eight were MAN (Maschinenbau Augsburg/Nurnberg) and Krupp in Germany, Sulzer in Switzerland, Burmeister & Wain in Denmark, Carels in Belgium, Nobel in Sweden, Werkspoor in Holland and Mirrlees Watson in Scotland. All those firms, or the direct descendants of those who took licences before the turn of the century, are still active in diesel engine manufacture, not only for industrial power and electric generation purposes, as was their original intention, but in most cases predominantly for marine propulsion.

Diesel was not a marine engineer and does not seem ever to have really appreciated the potential of his design for ship propulsion. That was left to others, notably Burmeister & Wain, Sulzer and MAN, who developed the principle in their own individual styles and soon gathered large families of sub-licensees, mainly the engine works associated with shipyards, each building to that particular design.

All the early diesel engines manufactured before the turn of the century followed the same pattern. A cast-iron A-frame incorporating the jacket for each cylinder standing upon a cast-iron bedplate, with a trunk piston and connecting rod, was the basic assembly, to be produced in multiples according to the power required. The high-level camshaft, which operated the inlet and exhaust valves through rockers and without the intervention of push-rods, was generally driven from the crankshaft by a vertical or sloping shaft and bevel or skew gears. The diesel engine of that early design required three more valves than a petrol engine, one for the injection of fuel which was performed by releasing compressed air at high pressure—blast injection—behind the already metered charge of fuel oil, one for admitting starting air and a cylinder pressure release valve. Engines of that type were built all over Europe from 1897 until the middle 1920s and some examples may still be seen at work in pumping stations, where their ready availability made them suitable for handling sudden changes in load.

Apart from a number of examples employed on the Swiss lakes, French canals and Russian rivers, the diesel engine in that form was not seriously applied afloat until about 13 years after Diesel had satisfactorily demonstrated the first engine. The small Italian ship *Romagna* was fitted with a direct-reversing Sulzer engine of the two-stroke-cycle variant which the Swiss engineers preferred in 1909, but she was lost on her maiden voyage due to her cargo shifting and there are no records available.

In 1910 Shell, that great pioneering company, ordered a small coastal tanker, the *Vulcanus,* with a six-cylinder Werkspoor four-stroke engine of 460bhp. After making a few initial voyages in European waters, she was stationed in the East Indies. The attractions of the diesel engine were not immediately realised, for in those

Below: Rudolf Diesel's experimental engine of 1893 which was rebuilt and redesigned before successfully going on trial in 1895; it is now preserved in the MAN works museum at Augsburg. *MAN*

days coal was cheap. It was in manpower that the main advantage lay, for even such a small ship as the *Vulcanus* would have required an engine-room staff of 14 as a steamship, compared with the five she actually carried.

It was the Danish shipbuilding concern Burmeister & Wain which can truly be said to have put the diesel engine on the world's oceans. Ivar Knudsen, a director of the company, had shown a great interest in Dr Diesel's engine and the company signed a licence agreement in 1898 and built a number of single and two-cylinder units of the original design for water-pumping purposes. Knudsen was able to see considerable shortcomings in the engine as it stood for marine propulsion and immediately set about designing and building a directly reversible four-stroke engine of about 1000hp.

Practical support soon came in the form of an order from the East Asiatic Company of Copenhagen for the world's first ocean-going motor-ship. That was the *Selandia*, which sailed from the Danish capital in February 1912 for Bangkok, making a special call in London where she was visited by owners, marine engineers, naval architects and Admiralty officials. Among them was Winston Churchill, who described the ship as 'the most perfect maritime masterpiece of the century'.

The *Selandia* had two eight-cylinder engines of 530mm bore and 730mm piston stroke; each developed an output of 1250ihp at 140rpm; they were very different from those of Dr Diesel's original design. They were of crosshead type and turned at a much slower speed, because they were to be directly coupled to the propellers. The progressive owners believed that with such modern plant a new appearance was also necessary and, as the engines required only exhaust pipes and not boiler uptakes, the traditional funnel was superfluous. Accordingly the *Selandia* and her sister ship *Fiona* were built without funnels, a fashion which was to continue in the company's fleet for about 18 years. The mizen mast served as a funnel to carry off the exhaust gas.

At about the same time a number of designs of big marine diesel engines was being prepared, built and tested by the other licensees, notably MAN, Krupp and Sulzer. Each design had its own characteristics, some of which can be recognised in the respective marques to this day. The three concerns tended to prefer the two-stroke cycle for its simplicity and its potential for higher output per engine. In those designs there were no valves; inlet and exhaust ports were formed in the cylinder liners and were opened and closed by the piston as it moved up and down the bore.

The larger two-stroke engines could not use crankcase compression as do small two-strokes, but required a powered blower of some form to provide the incoming charge of air. The blower took the form of an additional cylinder and piston connected normally to the crankshaft, or a rotary compressor. Because no valves were needed the cylinder head could be of very simple form and, in general, engines so designed were relatively free from the problem of cracked cylinder heads which became a recurrent malady of four-stroke engines.

Better understanding of the practical problems and improved foundry techniques overcame the difficulties and the marine diesel engine became a reliable form of propulsion, gaining steadily in popularity, although for general cargo ships the steam engine and coal fuel still were preferred.

An important British contender in the field of big crosshead diesels is the engineering division of the one-time shipbuilding firm of Doxford in Sunderland. Shortly after the 1914-18 war the Swiss engineer Keller was recruited by the company to establish an engine department. Doxford had hitherto built conventional steam reciprocating engines, and continued to do so sporadically up to the late 1920s. Two single-cylinder prototype diesels were built; the first was of conventional single-acting type but the second employed the opposed-piston layout which has since been used by every Doxford engine. The opposed-piston engine has two pistons working in an open-ended cylinder; the explosion takes place between the pistons and the forces work evenly on them.

In an engine with vertical cylinders the design brings some complication in order to connect the upper piston(s) with the crankshaft in the normal position below the lower piston(s). It also calls for a crankshaft with three throws per cylinder instead of one in a single-acting engine. Although these facts would seem to damn the design from the outset, in fact the Doxford is an exceedingly simple engine and moreover a very light one, since all the combustion forces are carried by steel moving parts and the frame is virtually unstressed. Additionally the inherent balance of the engine makes it possible to design it with relatively few cylinders for a given output. A considerable number of tramp ships built between the wars – the Doxford 'economy' ships – carried 9200 tons of cargo at $10\frac{3}{4}$ knots powered by a Doxford three-cylinder engine burning only $6\frac{3}{4}$ tons of fuel per day.

The era of the passenger motorship began in the mid-1920s with the *Aorangi*, built for the long trans-Pacific haul between Vancouver, Australia and New Zealand. She was followed in 1925 by the *Gripsholm*, a trans-Atlantic liner for the Swedish-America Line, built by Armstrong Whitworth on the Tyne. The feeling in the minds of some designers that it would be imprudent to adopt higher working pressures led to the introduction of the double-acting principle. Essentially, that involved closing the bottom half of the cylinder and making provision for a combustion stroke to take place on the underside of the piston. In the case of the four-stroke engine immense complexity was introduced and the need for heavy maintenance work by operators. For that reason it soon lost favour and had been abandoned by the early 1930s, by which time adequate power could be produced by highly rated single-acting engines.

The double-acting two-stroke engine did survive until after the 1939-45 war, and in fact that type was adopted for the famous German pocket battleships, which had eight double-acting two-stroke engines geared to two propellers, an arrangement that gave them the great range needed for their planned raiding operations. Perhaps the most remarkable double-acting engines ever built were those made by MAN to power a new class of destroyers being built at the end of the war. They had 24 cylinders, arranged in vee form, and produced 48 firing strokes per crankshaft revolution.

Pressure charging was introduced as a means of extracting more power from a given size of engine, since extra air charge could be provided by some form of powered blower. In the 1920s the Swiss engineer Dr Buchi patented his turbocharging system whereby the exhaust gases from the engine were passed through a turbine, where some of the remaining energy in the gases was given up to drive a compressor providing extra air to the cylinders. Careful matching of the exhaust gas turbine to the blower resulted in a substantial increase in output at relatively little extra cost. Working pressures were higher but in most cases designs possessed adequate margins. Today the proportion of marine propulsion diesel engines which are not turbocharged is negligible.

During the period between the wars competition and the depression weeded out the several less effective designs of diesel engine. The process has continued, although at a reduced rate, until there are today only five separate designs of large diesel engine in active production.

The high-performance medium-speed engine, of which the Pielstick type is the most popular, has risen from a position of no prominence to one of major importance. This type of engine first found a place in the car ferry class of ship, where its low profile enabled it to be installed completely below the car deck. It was soon applied to other types of ship, notably cargo liners. It proved easy to install, reliable and, by virtue of its smaller working parts, easier to maintain.

There were, however, more working parts than in the big low-speed engines, and its higher running speed necessitated provision of a reduction gearbox. Engines of this size are now being produced by all the major manufacturers. They are already in service with cylinder outputs that were not generally available from the conventional slow-running engine 20 years ago and it is likely that they will take an increasing share of the world's ship propulsion business in the future.

Except for extremely large tankers and some very fast container ships, the use of diesel engines for merchant ship propulsion is almost universal. At the lower end of the scale are small harbour ferries and tugs which may be powered by the small medium-speed diesel of relatively heavy construction of the so-called automotive conversion; in other words a bus or lorry engine adapted with a reverse and reduction gearbox, thereby becoming a marine engine.

Until fairly recently the application of diesel engines for the propulsion of British naval vessels has been confined to submarines and such light craft as sloops and patrol vessels. In submarines, because a means of travelling on the surface and of charging the batteries had to be provided and petrol engines were clearly out of the question (although the very first submarine did have petrol engines), and in sloops because the diesel engine gave them a long range of action while engaged in unsupported operations. Germany tried hard to introduce large diesel engines to battleships in the 1914-18 war and several huge examples were built and tested by MAN and Krupp between 1912 and 1914.

Similar activity was to be found in the years immediately preceding the 1939-45 war when a series of battleships even larger than the *Bismarck* was planned to have up to 12 engines each. Again the aim was extended range which steam plant could not provide. The Italians also built a powerful prototype battleship diesel at the Fiat works, but that project also was abandoned.

The diesel engine found a modern application in what is known as a CODOG configuration in which it is combined with a gas turbine; the diesel is used to provide long range at cruising speed and the gas turbine is brought in to drive the same shaft when short bursts of very high speed are required. Ships of the type are to be

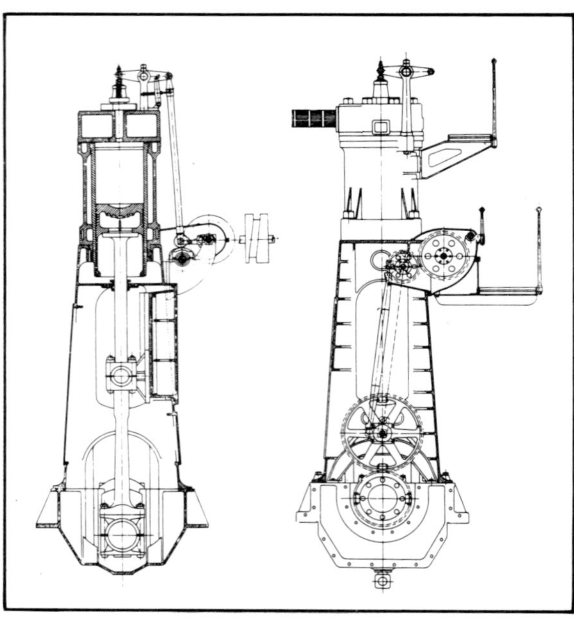

Top: A modern 10-cylinder Eriksberg-Burmeister & Wain engine of remarkable specific power; it develops well over 40,000 hp. *Eriksberg-Burmeister & Wain*

Above left: Cross-section diagrams of the 'Selandia's' engines. *Burmeister & Wain*

Above right: A view into the uncluttered engine room of the 'Selandia', the first ocean-going motor ship in 1912. Each of the eight-cylinder engines produced under 1000 shp. *Burmeister & Wain*

found in several navies, although all-diesel escorts and, more recently, all-gas turbine vessels are also used. The type of naval marine diesel used in these classes is generally a lightweight high-performance unit derived from railway locomotive application, but Germany's famous E-boats employed very handsome 20-cylinder vee-form engines which were in fact developed from a design intended for powering airships.

The greater proportion of the world's shipping today is propelled by diesel engines, and the greater proportion of those on order will be so propelled. Designers are not relaxing their efforts; they have to compete with the steam turbine, which is capable of virtually infinite power, and also the newcomer gas turbine. In addition, and clearly of great significance in view of the fuel situation, the nuclear-propelled merchant ship has been shown to be a possible future contender.

To give scale to 60 years of marine diesel development it is worth noting that the latest big slow-running diesels are designed to produce up to 7000bhp per *cylinder*; each of *Selandia's* eight-cylinder *engines* produced a total of only 1250 ihp, or 900 bhp.

GAS TURBINE

Right: Early Rolls-Royce (Bristol) Olympus gas producer of 27,000 gas hp which in conjunction with a free power turbine provides a powerplant of 22,000 shp. *L Dunn Collection*

Below: The fast patrol boat 'Brave Borderer' powered by gas turbines and capable of 60 knots, pictured off Portsmouth in August 1967. *A Greenway*

INCREASING CONSIDERATION is being given today to the gas turbine as a compact propulsion plant for medium- and high-powered installations; in fact, the Royal Navy's current policy is to fit gas turbines in all surface warships of frigate size and larger. Compared with conventional steam machinery, the modern aircraft-derived gas turbine permits reduced manning coupled with minimal on-board maintenance requirements and ease of unit exchange when a major overhaul is due.

The prospect of increased ship availability has resulted in consideration being given to the advantages of gas turbine propulsion by commercial operators too. In 1971 the 23,100-ton (deadweight) German-built container ship *Euroliner,* a 25-knot twin-screw vessel engined with a pair of Pratt & Whitney FT4 turbines, took her maiden sailing between Bremerhaven, the Clyde and US ports on charter to Seatrain International SA. She is managed, with three sister ships, by J & J Denholm of Glasgow on behalf of the Scarsdale Shipping Co Ltd.

It is probable that attention was first given to the idea of a practical internal-combustion turbine in the early years of the present century. In 1906 M René Armengaud converted a de Laval impulse turbine to operate on compressed air mixed with metered quantities of petroleum vapour, the mixture being fired by means of an incandescent platinum wire igniter. The useful output was about 30hp.

Inevitably, the designer came up against the problem of the high gas temperature which was to prevent any significant advance in practical gas turbine design until the developments in metallurgy engendered by the 1939-45 war. Combustion took place at about 1800 deg C in Armengaud's machine, and the combustion chamber was lined with carborundum. Steam produced in a steam coil within the chamber was mixed with the gas products to bring the turbine inlet temperature down to about 400 deg C.

In addition to the work by Armengaud and others in France, the gas turbine received considerable attention in Germany, where in 1910 Holzwarth designed and built, with the help of Korting Bros and the Brown Boveri company, a vertical constant-volume turbine designed to deliver 1000hp; it was coupled directly to a dc electric generator mounted above the turbine. Instead of the continuous-combustion principle of the Armengaud turbine, ignition in the Holzwarth machine was initiated by a spark generated by a high-tension magneto, and the hot gases were passed to a two-stage Curtis impulse power turbine. Steam generated by otherwise waste heat was used to drive a turbo-compressor supplying the combustion air, absorbing a great part of the theoretical total output, and the useful power amounted only to about 160hp.

Development work came to a halt during the 1914-18 war but it was resumed in 1918 in the wake of interest shown by the Prussian State Railway administration. In the following year an order was placed for a 500bhp unit driving a dc generator. At about the same time consideration was first given to the use of an internal-combustion turbine for marine propulsion and in December 1920 a Holzwarth unit, arranged for mechanical drive through reduction gears instead of electrical drive, was delivered for trials.

Like modern machines, the marine turbine had a number of equally spaced combustion chambers (in its case six) arranged around the horizontal shaft; as in the earlier Holzwarth design, the air compressor was driven by a steam turbine utilising the exhaust gas heat for steam generation. The design of a 500kW internal-combustion turbine of this type for marine propulsion was illustrated and discussed in *The Motor Ship* for May 1922, but at best the machine was regarded only as a possible competitor for the steam turbine.

As it turned out, the complexity of the Holzwarth design and doubts about its material reliability in view of the high temperatures involved militated against any further commercial development of

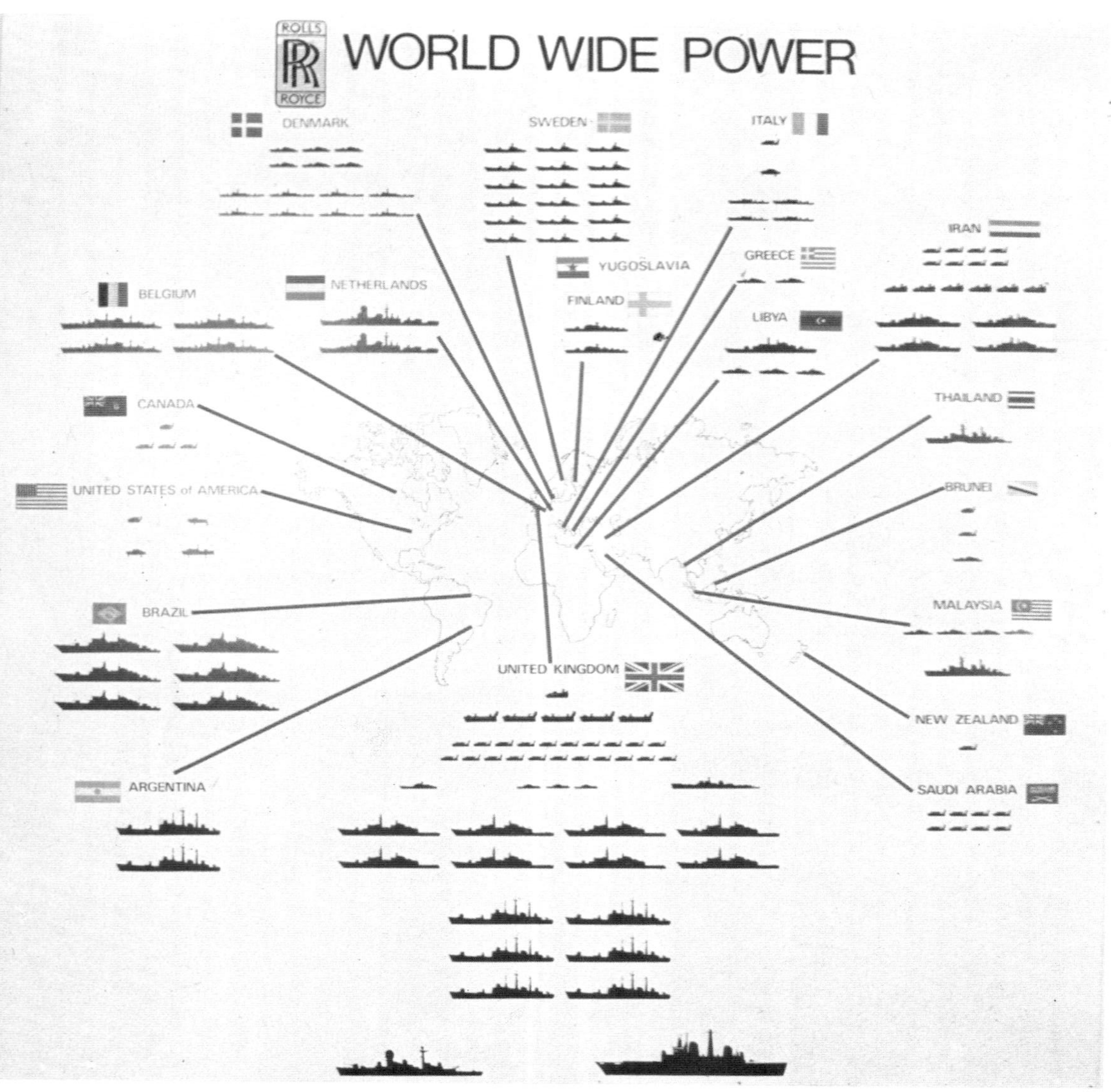

the marine gas turbine for another quarter of a century.

Apart from the lack of suitable materials for use in a high-temperature environment, the early gas turbines also suffered from inefficient compressor design. Between the wars, however, the Parsons Marine Steam Turbine Co in England, and others, devoted considerable effort to the development of axial-flow compressors. In 1938 the Parsons company built an experimental gas turbine employing an engine-driven compressor of the axial-flow type and thus the way was opened for the development of the small gas turbine for auxiliary power drives.

Elsewhere, with the added impetus generated by the impending war, the gas turbine was under development as an aircraft jet engine and in 1941 Sir Frank Whittle produced his first successful aero gas turbine. In the meantime, however, research work continued on the development of what was essentially an internal-combustion version of the marine steam turbine, since advantages were seen in its basic simplicity compared with the diesel engine and the fact that it could be run on a wide range of fuels. Compared with the aircraft gas turbine, such machines were heavy and comparatively slow running but that was considered to be no great drawback; it was expected that engine life to worn-out condition would greatly exceed that of the aircraft jet engine and that on-board maintenance demands would be small.

In Britain, Metropolitan-Vickers Ltd was well to the forefront in the design and development of gas turbines of the marine steam turbine-derived type. In 1951 a 1200hp unit was installed for comparative trials in place of one of the four diesel propulsion engines in the 12,000-ton (deadweight) single-screw diesel-electric tanker *Auris* belonging to the Shell Tanker Co. The gas turbine unit, which burned diesel or the heavier residual fuel oils, proved reliable in service and in March 1952 the *Auris* crossed the Atlantic using only the gas turbine-driven alternator and burning furnace fuel oil. No great problems were encountered and the vessel was able to maintain an average speed of $7\frac{1}{4}$ knots.

In all, the Metrovick machine ran for about 20,000 hours, but in the late 1950s the *Auris* was re-engined with a single geared gas turbine set comprising a low-pressure turbine driving a low-pressure compressor and, through reduction gearing, the main shaft, and a high-pressure turbine driving a high-pressure compressor. The installation proved satisfactory at passage speed but considerable difficulties were encountered when manoeuvring at low engine revolutions. In 1960, however, the *Auris* herself, overtaken by commercial considerations of size and speed, was taken out of service, after which the Shell company virtually abandoned interest in marine gas turbine development.

The *Auris* trials had centred upon gas turbine designs stemming from a steam ancestry, but in the meantime the Admiralty had not been slow in developing a propulsion unit based upon the results of Sir Frank Whittle's pioneer work. The requirement was twofold; first there was a demand for a compact high-power short-life engine of aircraft-derived type for high-speed coastal craft; secondly, in the longer term, there was the need for a boost plant for the surface fleet unit which spends the greater part of its operational time at sea at cruising or lower speeds.

Consequently, in 1943 a contract was placed with Metropolitan-Vickers Ltd for the development of a propulsion gas turbine based on Whittle's F2 aircraft jet engine. It was to have the addition of an output power turbine in the jet pipe and to burn diesel oil rather than the paraffin (kerosene) used in the aircraft plant. Shore trials were completed in April 1946 and in the following year an engine of this type, called the Gatric, was installed in place of the centreline Packard Merlin piston engine in MGB 2009; she was a wartime-built motor gunboat of 115 tons and undertook a successful series of proving trials extending over the following three years. The original gas turbine from MGB 2009, the first vessel to be propelled by gas turbine, is preserved at the Science Museum, London.

The Gatric project proved the suitability of the aircraft-derived engine for the propulsion of high-speed craft and towards

Far left: A chart prepared in 1973 by Rolls-Royce Ltd showing the worldwide application of its marine gas turbines.
Rolls-Royce (1971) Ltd

Centre left: A sectioned model of the gas turbine installation built by the British Thomson-Houston Co Ltd for the 1951 oil tanker 'Auris'.
Science Museum London (photo D Rudkin)

Left: One of the gas turbine-propelled County-class guided missile destroyers HMS 'Devonshire'. *J M Maber*

Below: HMS 'Exmouth', the world's first all-gas turbine frigate pictured in October 1971.
MoD (Navy) Crown copyright

Bottom: The experimental marine gas turbine built in 1947 by Metropolitan-Vickers Electrical Co Ltd of Manchester and fitted to MGB 2009, a triple-screw motor gunboat which was the first sea-going gas turbine vessel.
Science Museum London

the end of 1948 a further contract was placed with Metropolitan-Vickers for the development of a larger gas generator based on the design of the Beryl aircraft turbine. Four of the resulting G2 engines were built for installation in a pair of prototype fast patrol boats named *Bold Pathfinder* and *Bold Pioneer,* built respectively by Vospers Ltd of Portsmouth and J S White & Co of Cowes. Sea trials started late in 1951 but many teething problems were encountered, although much was learned and eventually the G2 engine added considerably to the sum total of experience gained with marine gas turbine propulsion.

In the development of an engine for

larger warships, early work centred on a turbine designed and built by the English Electric Co at Rugby. The EE engine was intended to replace one of the steam sets in the twin-screw turbo-electric frigate *Hotham,* a US-built vessel of the Captains class. In the event, manufacturing difficulties delayed construction and it was not until late in 1951 that the set was ready for shore trials. By that time it was already becoming apparent that there was little future for the type based on steam turbine practice for main propulsion duty and plans for the conversion of the *Hotham* were abandoned.

That was not to say, however, that no future was seen in the long-life turbine as a boost plant, and in fact design work was continued by Metropolitan-Vickers, and subsequently AEI Ltd, in association with the Admiralty, which resulted eventually in the development of the G6, a 7500hp gas turbine for installation as part of combined steam and gas turbine propulsion plants (COSAG) in the new Tribal-class general-purpose frigates and the Seaslug-armed guided missile destroyers of the County class.

In both classes of vessel the gearing is arranged so that the gas turbine drive can be used not only to boost the steam plant for full speed, ahead only, but can also be employed, independently, for manoeuvring both ahead and astern, thus permitting a quick getaway of the ship from cold. Once again limited teething troubles were experienced, but the plant proved itself and pointed the way to the future, although in fact the G6 was the last of the heavy comparatively slow-running and low-powered marine gas turbines derived from the steam age. (Four gas turbines are used in the Countys as well as two steam turbines.)

Gas turbine progress was of course not confined to Britain and in both the United States and France successful plants were developed to the trial installation stage, of both the turbine and an opposed-piston gas generator type. The development of such plant for active fleet units lagged somewhat behind that for the Royal Navy, however, and not until 1966 did the first CODAG (combined diesel and gas turbine) patrol gunboats of the Asheville class commission for service with the US Navy. They are 225-ton two-shaft vessels engined with a pair of Cummins diesels and a single General Electric aircraft-derived LM1500 gas turbine of 13,300shp.

British commercial operators showed little interest in the gas turbine after the withdrawal from service of the Shell tanker *Auris,* but in the United States development continued and in 1967 the cargo ship *Admiral Wm. M. Callaghan* entered service as a commercially operated military transport. The ship is a 7000dwt vessel engined with a pair of Pratt & Whitney aircraft-derived gas generators driving free power turbines geared to the twin propeller shafts. The installation develops a total of 40,000shp for a service speed of 26 knots.

Probably the greatest success story to date in the marine gas turbine field has been its complete suitability as a propulsion plant for fast patrol and other coastal craft. A large proportion of all such craft, of international construction, have been engined with the Rolls-Royce (formerly Bristol) Proteus turbine, a 3500shp unit of which the installation in the Royal Navy's Brave class was typical.

In the two RN vessels (*Brave Borderer* and *Brave Swordsman*) experience totalling many thousands of running hours was accumulated, with a steady increase in the time between engine exchanges for overhaul or repairs. Two similar engines each rated at 4250hp were fitted as the cruise plant in the conversion of the Type 14 frigate *Exmouth* as the Royal Navy's, and indeed the world's, first all-gas turbine major warship recommissioned in 1966.

The primary plant in the *Exmouth* conversion consists of a single Rolls-Royce Olympus unit of 22,500hp, which cannot in fact be utilised at its full output because of limitations of the existing hull design. Similar engines have been fitted, however, in a number of frigates of commercial design built for the Brazilian, Libyan, Iranian, Malaysian and Thai navies by the Vosper Thornycroft, Yarrow and Vickers companies and also as the boost plant in the COSAG guided missile destroyer HMS *Bristol.* The Olympus TMIA gas generator is derived from the aircraft gas turbine employed in the supersonic Concorde, redesigned to burn diesel fuel instead of paraffin and exhausting into a single-stage power turbine driving the gearbox input shaft.

It must be borne in mind, of course, that the operating cycle of the marine gas turbine and its environmental conditions are vastly different from those applying to the aircraft engine. The marine unit must be capable of running continuously at near full power day after day, and the problems of salt and water ingestion necessitate careful design of the intake system. Additionally there is the problem of waste heat disposal which in the equivalent steam plant is transferred to the condenser circulating water and conveniently discharged into the sea.

In the case of the gas turbine plant the hot exhaust gases from the power turbine pass through the uptakes to atmosphere, necessitating careful design and the use of high-cost alloy steels for that part of the system. In early marine installations attemps were made to utilise the waste heat but the weight and size of the heat exchanger, necessarily placed high in the ship, destroyed any advantage that might have been gained, while its presence in the exhaust system resulted in a significant reduction in engine output.

The Royal Navy has now abandoned steam for new-construction surface warships. The new generation of twin-shaft guided missile-armed destroyers (Type 42) and frigates (Type 21) now entering service are engined with an uprated version of the Rolls-Royce Olympus engine for high speed and a marinised version of the Rolls-Royce Tyne for the lower speed range up to a cruising speed of, say, 14 knots. The combined gas *or* gas plant (COGOG) will be employed also in the planned Type 22 frigates. In the new ships the layout of the machinery spaces has been designed for ease of engine exchange so that overhauls and repairs can be planned on a line basis in a purpose-designed workshop on shore.

The Russian Navy too has extensively adopted gas turbine propulsion for the new-generation destroyers of the Kashin and Krivak classes and the many smaller frigates and patrol craft now in service with the fleet.

In the United States Navy for many years the main emphasis for major surface warship propulsion lay with the development of nuclear-fuelled steam plant. Now, however, there are under construction the first units of the missile-armed destroyers of the Spruance class, engined on two shafts with four General Electric LM2500 marine gas turbines each of about 20,000hp. The gas generator design is based on that of the TF39 turbo-fan aircraft engine and, as in the Royal Navy, this type of plant has been adopted because of its compact design, reduced operator and on-board maintenance demands compared with equivalent steam plant, rapid cold start capability and the ease of unit exchange.

Other navies too, including the Netherlands and Belgian, are now committed to the use of gas turbine plant for new-construction surface vessels and it is apparent that there can be no turning back the clock to the days of conventional steam plant.

So far as merchant ship propulsion plant design is concerned, the pace of change has been somewhat slower, since well-proved conventional steam or diesel plant has been readily available to meet the need for a steady power output at a ship's designed service speed and space is not so much at a premium. Today, however, ever mounting running costs lead to demands by operators to cut turnround time in harbour to a minimum, to increase ship availability, and to reduce engine-room complements to a minimum.

Hence the readily exchanged aircraft-derived gas turbine with its high power/weight ratio and minimal on-board maintenance load appears increasingly attractive. No doubt the in-service performance of the *Euroliner* and her Emden-built sisters *Asialiner, Eurofreighter* and *Asiafreighter,* will be watched with interest. If they prove successful other operators in the container and bulk liner trades will soon be turning to the gas turbine as a commercially viable propulsion system.

The big new Baltic ferry *Finnjet* will be an all-gas turbine ship. The high capital cost and short life of the gas turbine might eventually militate against its use over long-haul routes but ferries, with their high speed and short routes, would seem better suited. Engine repair by replacement in only about six hours average could be an added incentive by avoiding over-interruption of tight schedules. So it could be in the increasing fleets of fast ferry ships that the gas turbine will make its big merchant marine breakthrough.

Below: The first large merchant ship to be wholly propelled by gas turbine was the former Liberty ship 'John Sergeant', here pictured near New York. *L Dunn Collection*

NUCLEAR POWER

ALTHOUGH a relatively new concept in the field of marine engineering, the design and operating techniques of steam generation utilising the heat produced in a controlled nuclear reaction are already well established for warships, although it has yet to be shown that such plant can be exploited successfully on a commercial scale. The preliminary empirical work was truly international but the name particularly linked with the first practical reactor was that of Enrico Fermi who, working with a team of American and British scientists in Chicago, constructed his atomic pile which went critical for the first time on December 2, 1942. Ten days later it was run at a power level of 200 watts!

Already, in the United Kingdom, the Maude Committee had forecast in a report entitled *The Use of Uranium as a Source of Power,* published in 1941, that nuclear ship-propulsion would become a practical proposition within a few years. The world was at war, however, and for the time being research was concentrated on the more immediate requirement for a nuclear fission bomb. The weapon was used with devastating effect on Hiroshima and Nagasaki early in August 1945; a few days later, on August 14, the Japanese Government surrendered and the war was over.

Unlike the nuclear bomb, designed to produce a 'big bang' as the result of an uncontrolled chain reaction, the propulsion requirement was for a safe compact reactor to produce heat for use in some form of steam generating plant coupled to conventional steam turbine machinery. The United States, with a wealth of accumulated experience, took the lead and Vice-Admiral Hyman G Rickover was appointed in charge of a US Navy research team. Lack of funds and facilities stifled progress, however, and little was achieved until 1949, when a vote of three million dollars was secured from the funds of the US Bureau of Ships.

It had been envisaged already that the development of a compact nuclear propulsion plant would permit the design of a true submarine, a vessel whose natural element would be beneath the surface rather than on it. The submersible torpedo craft which have featured in the navies of the world for rather more than half a century, although capable of travelling fully submerged for short distances, are still basically air dependent; the capacity of their electric storage batteries is very limited. Thus there was a long-standing incentive for the development of a true submarine, designed for optimum underwater performance without regard for surface behaviour. That was the task set for Admiral Rickover's team.

Already in 1948 the US Atomic Energy Commission, in association with the Navy Department, had awarded a contract to Westinghouse for the construction of a land-based prototype nuclear propulsion plant at Arco in Idaho. Experience with it and other reactors led to the choice of a pressurised water-cooled reactor for the first nuclear submarine, the hull of which was laid down by the Electric Boat Division of the General Dynamics Corporation at Groton, Connecticut, in June 1952.

Reactor design for a marine environment presented far greater problems than

Top: The nuclear-powered aircraft carrier USS 'Enterprise' flanked by the nuclear frigate USS 'Bainbridge' and cruiser USS 'Long Beach'; crewmen on the 'Enterprise' flight deck form Einstein's atomic energy equation. *B P Singer Features*

Above: USS 'Sturgeon', the first of the US Navy's new class of fast nuclear-powered attack submarines, pictured in the Thames River at Groton, Connecticut, after launching. *B P Singer Features*

any faced in the design of land-based installations. The reactor has to be compact and adequately shielded to contain radiation, yet it has to be capable of heat transfer initially to the circulating pressurised water which acts both as a moderator, to slow down the neutrons and thus to sustain the chain reaction, and also as a primary coolant. The primary water circuit includes a steam generator or heat exchanger, whence the heat is transferred to a lower-pressure secondary circuit.

From that point on the geared turbine propulsion machinery is more or less conventional, although working pressures are considerably lower than those employed in modern fossil-fuelled installations. In fact the steam conditions in a nuclear plant are closer to the 'wet' steam practices of half a century ago and in service experience have necessitated the relearning of many long-forgotten lessons discussed at length in the technical press of the time.

The dispersed system, with the steam generator, primary circuit pressuriser and pumps all external to the reactor pressure vessel, is well suited to the military need, however, in that shock and damage resistance are high while reactor control is relatively simple. In addition, the radiation shielding with its attendant weight can be kept to a minimum, which is a particularly important consideration in a submarine with its low reserve of surface buoyancy compared with that of a surface vessel.

Launched as *Nautilus* on January 21, 1954, the world's first nuclear submarine was commissioned into the US Navy in April 1955. Of 3530 tons standard (surface) displacement, she is a twin-screw vessel with a more or less conventional (pre-nuclear) submarine hull form and is capable of a submerged speed in excess of 20 knots. In May 1955 she steamed submerged from New London to San Juan, Puerto Rico, a distance of about 1340 miles, in 84 hours at an average speed of 16 knots. In August 1958 she made the first transit from the Pacific into the Atlantic under the Arctic polar ice in the course of a voyage from Pearl Harbour to Portland, England.

The second US nuclear submarine, the somewhat similar *Seawolf*, was equipped originally with a liquid sodium-cooled reactor (Submarine Intermediate Reactor) developed by the US Atomic Energy Commission; it first went critical on June 25, 1956. The corrosive nature of the sodium-potassium alloy coolant proved an intractable problem, however, and in 1959 the original plant was replaced by a pressurised water reactor similar to that installed in the *Nautilus*.

USS *Skipjack* launched in May 1958 and later nuclear submarines, including the Royal Navy's first such craft, HMS *Dreadnought*, were built to a 'tear-drop' hull configuration with a single screw, giving greatly enhanced underwater characteristics and thus completing the initial development phase of the true submarine.

In the meantime, the USSR had also been active in the development of nuclear propulsion plant, not only for submarines but also to power a large icebreaker for service in the Soviet Arctic. The 16,000-ton vessel, laid down in the Admiralty Yard at Leningrad in 1956 and commissioned for service as the *Lenin* in September 1959, is fitted with three pressurised water reactors providing steam through heat exchangers for four steam turbo-generator sets; they provide power for three dc electric shaft motors driving the three screws. Refuelling is necessary only at intervals of 18 months, an obvious advantage in a ship in service in the Arctic remote from normal bunkering facilities.

The nuclear plant in the *Lenin* was extensively modified in the course of a refit at Leningrad in 1966 and the vessel now requires the use of only two of her three reactors, the third being held in reserve. Each reactor is now housed in a gas-tight containment.

A second nuclear icebreaker, to be named *Arktika* and of 25,000 tons, is now being built at Leningrad and will be fitted with two pressurised water reactors of the modified Lenin type. Mention has been made also of a third vessel to be named *Ledokoly*.

The first British nuclear submarine, HMS *Dreadnought*, which was completed at Barrow in April 1963, was fitted with a US-built pressurised water reactor and propulsion machinery of the type installed in USS *Skipjack*. Later RN fleet submarines of the Valiant, Churchill and Swiftsure classes and the four ballistic missile submarines of the Resolution class have pressurised water reactors of British design. They were developed in association with the Rolls-Royce company after gaining experience with a shore-based prototype installed in the Admiralty Reactor Test Establishment (now HMS *Vulcan*) at Dounreay.

miles. During her first three years' service she carried 848 passengers and 154,000 tons of cargo without incurring any claims on the grounds of nuclear liability.

After the submarine, attention was turned in both Britain and the United States to the application of nuclear power to surface warships and in December 1957 the keel was laid at Quincy, Massachussetts, of the 14,200-ton guided missile-armed cruiser (CGN) *Long Beach*. Powered by two Westinghouse pressurised water reactors, the propulsion machinery develops a total of 80,000shp for a maximum sea speed of about 35 knots. First commissioned in July 1961, the *Long Beach* steamed about 167,000 miles before being taken in hand at Newport News for refit and refuelling in August 1965.

Eight reactors of similar design to those installed in the *Long Beach* were required for the propulsion package in the 75,700-ton nuclear attack aircraft carrier USS *Enterprise*, which commissioned for service on November 25, 1961. Since then the US Navy has taken delivery of four nuclear-powered guided missile frigates (USS *Bainbridge, Truxtun, California* and *South Carolina*) and has completed or under construction three more frigates and three attack carriers named *Nimitz, Dwight D Eisenhower* and *Carl Vinson*. The carriers, of 91,400 tons full-load displacement, are powered by two pressurised water reactors, compared with eight in the

Once the feasibility of nuclear propulsion for warships had been clearly demonstrated, it was not long before consideration was given to its application to merchant ships. In the United Kingdom it took the form of a design study for a nuclear-powered fleet support tanker, but it was the United States which took the lead once again.

In 1958 an order was placed with the New York Shipbuilding Corporation of Camden, New Jersey, for the hull of a 9900-ton 21-knot single-screw passenger/cargo vessel to be powered by a pressurised water reactor with a maximum output of 74 megawatts. The *Savannah* was launched on July 21, 1959, her reactor went critical in March 1962 and after sea trials the vessel was accepted for service on May 1, 1963. The *Savannah* was not intended to be commercially viable although obviously a study of the economics of nuclear plant operation formed a major part of her operational programme.

The nuclear core in the *Savannah's* reactor was replaced after three years operation and in 1970 she was laid up, having steamed in all about 470,000 *Enterprise*, and the nuclear cores are expected to last for at least 13 years, or something in excess of 800,000 miles, before refuelling will be necessary.

It is the fuelling factor which plays such an important part in any decision to 'go nuclear' in ship design. Not only is frequent bunkering unnecessary, but there is no need to make provision for fuel storage or to provide the appropriate ancillary services. Against the advantages must be set the enormous capital outlay, which in the case of the *Truxtun* amounted to 138 million dollars and for the last of the carriers totalled over two thousand million dollars. Moreover, to realise their full potential, nuclear capital ships need nuclear escorts if they are not to be hampered by the fuelling needs of others. With sums of such magnitude to justify, it is understandable that few navies have yet committed themselves to the construction of nuclear-powered surface warships.

In common with current practice elsewhere, pressurised water reactors, of French design, have been installed in the three completed ballistic missile submarines (Le Redoutable class) of the French Force

Below left: The world's first nuclear-powered submarine, the 3530-ton USS 'Nautilus', launched in January 1954.
Barnaby's Picture Library

This picture: HMS 'Dreadnought', the Royal Navy's first nuclear fleet submarine built in 1963. *Ministry of Defence (Navy)*

Below: The American marine reactor trial and development ship 'Savannah', which entered service in May 1963, here being assisted by tugs in New York Harbour. She steamed nearly half a million miles before being laid up in 1970.
L Dunn

de Dissuasion and no doubt are being used also in the two under construction. The French are also building a nuclear-powered helicopter carrier – project PH75 – which is due for completion some time in 1980.

In the United Kingdom the possibilities of nuclear propulsion for merchant ships continued to receive attention throughout the 1960s and a number of design studies were undertaken, but in the absence of any indication that such a system might offer any through-life economic advantage, no provision has yet been made for the construction of such a vessel.

The pressurised water reactor of the type employed in warships, with its highly enriched uranium in a zirconium-fuelled core, offers military advantages by way of compactness and resistance to shock, but running costs are higher than can be tolerated in a merchant ship, while the relative inefficiency of the saturated-steam turbine machinery further militates against economy of operation. The latter problem affected also the economic viability of the *Savannah*, although her reactor core was fuelled by uranium dioxide, with a lower degree of enrichment, in stainless steel.

More recently, in Western Germany, research and development have been concentrated on the design of an integral reactor system more suited to the requirements of a competitive merchantman. The system has a once-through boiler giving some degree of superheat, that is, having the steam generator within the reactor pressure vessel and no external pressurised primary water system.

A reactor of such integral self-pressurised type, with a fuel load of 2.95 tons of uranium dioxide, was installed in the 14,040-ton (deadweight) bulk carrier/research ship *Otto Hahn*, which was launched by Howaldtswerke AG at Kiel in 1964 on behalf of the Gesellschaft fur Kernenergieverwertung in Schiffbau und Schiffahrt (Organisation for the Evaluation of Nuclear Energy in Shipbuilding and Navigation). Preliminary trials were run in the Baltic before the installation of her reactor, but she finally commissioned for service in 1969 and in the course of the next three years steamed about 250,000 miles.

In 1972 the *Otto Hahn* was refuelled with a new core which gave an increase in power density from 33 to 52 kW/litre and a considerable reduction in the overall fuel cycle cost. Like the *Savannah*, the *Otto Hahn* is by no means an economic proposition in commercial service, although her costs include about one million deutschmarks annually on research. In the meantime, as her trials programme continued design studies were put in hand of a nuclear-powered 80,000 shp container ship with a service speed of 27 knots and capable of carrying over two thousand standard 20-foot containers. If current environmental objections can eventually be overcome, perhaps the big containership will become the most likely subject as a pioneering nuclear merchantman.

The Japanese Government decided in 1962 to build a nuclear-powered cargo/research vessel in order to gain experience in propulsion reactor design and construction, operational familiarisation and training. The vessel was laid down in November 1967 and is designed around a pressurised water reactor of the dispersed type (with a pressurised primary system and external steam generator) with a thermal output of 36 megawatts. Launched as *Mutsu*, the ship was completed for trials late in 1974, from which time her history developed into something of a farce. She left harbour for sea trials of the propulsion system, but radiation leaks necessitated a premature shut-down of her reactor, after which a blockade by Japanese fishermen, fearing a repetition of events which occurred a quarter of a century ago, prevented for a time her re-entry into any Japanese port.

The possibilities of the nuclear-powered merchant vessel have been demonstrated, although the state of the art has not yet reached the point where the economics of such a craft can compete successfully with the conventional fossil-fuelled merchantman. However, the gross increases in the price of fossil fuels in the mid-1970s and the feared depletion of world oil reserves could force a reappraisal of the nuclear solution, particularly for the large bulk carrier and container ship. The solution might possibly be in the choice of an alternative form of reactor. The gas-cooled type is of relatively light weight and simple construction and has a high safety factor, it could well be a contender for the future.

In the meantime there are in service with the world's major navies several hundred nuclear-powered submarines and approaching a dozen (all US) surface warships. In addition, the Chinese are believed to have the development of the 23,000-ton nuclear-powered *Zan Than* in progress. In at least one of the civilian applications – the big Soviet icebreakers, in which ability to produce high power for long periods and independence from frequent fuel replenishment are paramount requirements – nuclear reactors appear set to become the preferred form of propulsion. Clearly, the military application is proved, but the true commercial breakthrough is yet to come.

Below: The German nuclear-powered bulk carrier/research ship 'Otto Hahn' at Hamburg. *L Dunn*

Bottom: One of the Royal Navy's four Polaris-armed nuclear-powered submarines, HMS 'Resolution'. *Ministry of Defence (Navy)*

11. Ships at War

Rameses III to Lepanto

TIME GIVES CERTAIN sea battles milestone significance. Among them were the confrontation between the fleets of the Pharaoh Rameses III and the Sea Peoples, would-be conquerors of Egypt (12th century BC), and the Greco-Persian battle of Salamis (480 BC). Rameses III's victory gave Egypt an impregnable reputation for centuries, and Greek triumph at Salâmis left Greece safe from invasion for 1500 years. Similarly, the Mongols, whose armada was 'defeated' (1281) by a kamikaze (divine wind) were the last warlike invaders of Japan for nearly six centuries, and Christian victory at Lepanto (1571) secured Europe for ever from Muslim domination.

All these battles were fought when war at sea was a matter of ramming, boarding and fighting it out on the decks. The technique was pioneered by the spoon-shaped ships of Rameses III which could ride over and sink or overturn an enemy after a collision. By adding bronze lionheads to the bow to take the impact, the first specialised fighting ships were created, with rams above the waterline.

Rameses' fleet surprised the invasion fleet of the Sea Peoples in harbour. The Egyptian rowers twisted and turned their ships to avoid being grappled, while soldiers loosed showers of arrows. At the right moment, the Egyptians rammed their lionheads into the enemy's sides. Victory was complete, and Rameses had a record of it hewn on the walls of his temple at Medinet Habu.

The crisis facing Greece in 480 BC was even more momentous, for the invader, Xerxes of Persia, was already ravaging Attica when the Greek fleet assembled to challenge his 1500 ships at Salamis.

The existence of this fleet was due to Themistocles of Athens who, realising no Greek army could stand against Persian might on land, championed the importance of sea power and persuaded his unwilling hearers to build 200 ships.

After some early desultory clashes, Salamis began in earnest when the main Persian fleet swept down the narrow channel towards the Bay of Alensis, where the Greeks were drawn up. The very sight made the Greeks recoil and draw back. However, the last Greek suddenly shot through a gap in the Persian line and the others, encouraged, charged forward.

The fighting quickly grew ferocious. Ships were rammed, overturned, boarded. Entire crews were slain. However, the outnumbered Greeks gained the upper hand in the dawn-to-dusk contest. The Persians, crammed into the narrow channel, had no space for turning and fouled each other. Ultimately the defeated Persians lost about 200 ships. When the survivors withdrew, Xerxes' army was marooned and his campaign collapsed.

History repeated itself in 1281 when Kublai Khan, Mongol Emperor of China, sent about 4000 junks and, it is said, 300,000 men, to humble Japan. Despite desperate Japanese resistance, the Mongols landed on Kyushu and began forcing their way inland.

The Japanese, helpless, appealed to their gods and divine aid swiftly came. The 'kamikaze', a violent typhoon, suddenly swept over southern Japan and sank or wrecked Kublai's great fleet. Afterwards, like Xerxes' army in Greece, Kublai's force was stranded, gradually worn down and wiped out.

A similar miracle seemed desirable on September 16, 1571, when the fleet of the Holy League (Spain, France, Venice and the Papal States) sailed to confront the Turks in the Mediterranean. The fate of Christian Europe then hung by the slenderest of threads. The Turks, whose invasion of Cyprus (1570) had caused the crisis, had never yet been beaten at sea.

However, soon after the battle began off Lepanto on October 4, the Turkish front line was broken. Their galleys, passing between the six massive 44-gun Christian galleasses, were punishingly bombarded from above. The opposing commanders, the Christian Don John of Austria and the Turkish Ali Pasha, became locked in savage contest after Ali's galley rammed Don John's *Reale*. After a Papal ship rammed the stern of the Turkish galley, every Turk, including Ali Pasha, was killed.

This outcome was being mirrored all over the seaborne battlefield, although Genoese galleys put their own side in danger when they unwisely ran southwards, apparently to avoid being outflanked. By the time Don John and a Spanish admiral plugged the gap, the Turks were fleeing, leaving 30,000 dead, 8000 prisoners and, except for about 40 galleys, virtually their entire fleet. The victorious Holy League suffered 8000 casualties and lost 12 ships.

Left: A gruesome impression of the way the Turks were reputed to have treated Austrian captives at Lepanto. *Mary Evans Picture Library*

Top: Old print showing the Greek triremes in action at the battle for Salamis in 480 BC. *Mary Evans Picture Library*

Right: Two impressions of Kublai Khan's Mongol Armada sent against Japan in 1281 which was destroyed by a typhoon – hailed by the Japanese as a kamikaze, or divine wind. *K Fenwick Collection*

Far right: Rameses III's fleet in battle against the Sea Peoples during the period 1198-1166 BC, as depicted on temple walls at Medinet Habu. *K Fenwick Collection*

THE SPANISH ARMADA

EVER SINCE DAVID felled Goliath, the spectacle of the small audacious venturer, with all the odds against him, successfully challenging the proud and mighty mammoth has had unfailing appeal. It is this appeal which has firmly embedded in English folklore the dramatic and decisive humbling of the Spanish Armada in July and August 1588.

Superficially at least, the David-Goliath analogy seems apt. The force of about 130 galleons, galleasses, merchantmen, carracks and pinnaces with which King Philip II of Spain sought to smash English sea power was certainly massive in size and armament and splendid as a show of strength.

In the face of that formidable fleet, the English initially had ready no more than 64 ships, only 24 of them fighting vessels of any size, when the Armada was sighted off Dodman Point, Cornwall, on July 30.

In the late 16th century, Spain was the dominant power in the world, with a gold- and silver-rich empire in America, from which she sought to exclude all foreigners, and possessions which stretched from the coast of California to the Philippines. It included much of Europe and, most dangerously for England, the Netherlands. It was there that an army under Philip's regent, the Duke of Parma, waited to join the Armada and invade England.

England, by contrast, was a small and overcrowded country, still reeling from years of vicious religious strife, poorly fortified, with limited resources, and materially far from rich. Yet, beneath the modest unpromising façade, there was a strength and power in England and the English which gave both an overwhelming potential. Similarly, the grandeur and glitter of Spain concealed inherent weakness.

Top: An artist's representation of the arrival of the Spanish Armada in the English Channel. *Illustrated London News*

Above: A miniature portrait of Sir Francis Drake. *National Portrait Gallery London*

Psychologically, the Spaniards were burdened with the stiff self-righteous attitude of those who were sure God backed their cause. Just as they assumed that the great Spanish Empire had been bestowed by God as a sign of their worth, they regarded the Armada as an instrument of 'God's obvious design'. Its purpose was to punish the heretic English, who had dared to raid Spanish colonies, sieze Spanish treasure ships and so deny Spain's God-given right to monopolise the New World.

The Spanish attitude was clear in the confident message emblazoned on the Armada's sails—'Arise, Lord, and vindicate your cause,' and it also blinded Philip in his choice of commander. The hapless Duke of Medina Sidonia, on whom the king's choice fell, protested in vain that he was always sick at sea and in any case knew more about gardening than warfare.

The English were far more realistic. They had a hearty hatred of Spanish treachery, and an abhorrence of Spanish Catholicism, but they did not underestimate Spanish power. Lord Howard of Effingham, the English Lord Admiral, called the Armada the greatest fleet the world had ever seen, and the terror which the thought of Spanish conquest inspired in England was very real. The English knew well that only their courage, their wits and their skill stood between them and disaster.

Fortunately, these very qualities had been thoroughly sharpened and tested in the years since 1561, when Queen Elizabeth first made it clear that England would not let Spain exclude her from the riches of America.

If this conflict of views and interests did not explode into war until 1588, the reason was that neither Elizabeth nor Philip had desired it. However, by the time the Spaniards at last lost patience and their long-threatened Armada transpired, a quarter-century of diligent English poaching in America, as well as vigorous experiments in shipbuilding, made the English far more suited than the Spaniards to the exigencies of naval warfare.

The Spaniards viewed war at sea as a floating version of war on land. That was why the Armada's main force of 20 galleons, with timbers four or five feet thick and up to 52 guns apiece, were so high in the stern, so wide in the beam and contained so many more soldiers than sailors;

the ratio was three to one. The idea was to provide a broad lofty platform for deadly volleys of musket-fire and a springboard for grappling and boarding.

The English theory was to fight with sleek easily manoeuvrable ships that relied on longer-range gunpower to sink the enemy from a distance. In the late 1570s and early 1580s, John Hawkins had developed new revolutionary galleons based on that philosophy; when the Armada came, between 14 and 18 of them (the exact number is variously reported) were included in the English force, which totalled nearly 200 sail. Hawkins's ships cut down on the heavy bow and stern castles which made the traditional galleon so top-heavy and awkward to sail. They were slimmer in the waist, longer and more streamlined in shape and more level in the decks. The deep pit in the centre, which had formerly held contingents of reserve troops, was replaced by two decks of heavy guns. In addition, the new design allowed for lighter and more-numerous culverins that could send a 9lb shot streaking over half a mile of water with an accuracy that was frightening by the standards of the time.

By contrast, the Spaniards' gunpower was as unwieldy as their galleons. Their heavy guns could lob a 30lb or 50lb cannon ball over a distance of a quarter of a mile with only a questionable chance of hitting the target. The drastic difference between the ships of the Armada and the new English galleons was no secret to King Philip; neither was the difference in tactics which this implied. However, from his instructions to Medina Sidonia it is clear that the fatal significance of it all did not occur to him.

'You are especially to take notice', the King advised the duke, 'that the enemy's object will be to engage at a distance, on account of the advantage which they have from their artillery and (other) offensive fireworks . . . On the other hand the object of our side should be to close and grapple and engage hand to hand'.

The more level-headed captains who sailed for England when the Armada set out from Lisbon on May 20, 1588, doubted whether they would get the chance to carry out Philip's orders. They had already seen the audacity and daring of their foe in April 1857, when Francis Drake had swooped on Cadiz, destroyed more than 30 of the Armada's ships, looted and burned his way along the Iberian coast and captured a treasure ship worth £114,000 on his way home.

'We are sailing against England', one Spanish captain wrote, 'in the confident hope of a miracle . . . (that might yield) . . . some strange freak of weather . . . or strip . . . the English of their wits'. The latter hope proved particularly vain, as the Spaniards discovered soon after sighting the Lizard, which they reached on July 29 much battered and delayed by bad weather.

Medina Sidonia's instructions were to proceed along the English Channel in strong defensive crescent-shaped formation towards the point off the Flanders coast where the Spanish army from the Netherlands was due to rendezvous with the Armada. To achieve that object the duke needed to gain absolute control of the Channel, which was something the English had no intention of allowing him.

As the Armada made its stately and, for the moment impregnable, progress, the English ships shadowed it, pouncing at intervals to snipe away out of Spanish range, irritating, pin-pricking the Spaniards as a picador does a bull. This particular bull was rattled but refused to be provoked; Medina Sidonia was strict in obeying orders not to give battle but to keep his formation tight and strong.

On the morning of July 31, however, the Armada found itself in a very dangerous position. During the night the flexible and nimble English ships had sidled out of Plymouth on a contrary wind. Brilliant tacking had enabled them to cross the bows of the Spanish ships, work their way westwards and take up a chosen stance well to the windward of the Armada, a feat of seamanship which proved the superiority of Hawkins's new design and gave the English the advantage of position.

The English never lost that advantage and, to the Spaniards' fury, they would not be drawn by Medina Sidonia's next move. The duke ordered his ships to form the battle crescent, with his most powerful galleons at each tip. The English refused to venture between the arms of the deadly trap. Instead, they came near, but not too near, and then swung away, bombarding the Spaniards as they did so.

Twice more, off Portland on August 2 and off the Isle of Wight on August 4, the English attacked at open range, harassing the Armada and peppering the thick Spanish hulls with round shot. But they were firing from a distance that kept them

Below: Engravings by C J Visscher of some of the English ships that fought the Spanish Armada.

clear of the timber-splitting Spanish cannon, which also meant they were unable to damage or delay the Spanish ships.

What damage did occur came about through sheer ill luck. The 46-gun *Rosario* provided pickings for Drake's galleons when she collided with her neighbour, smashed her own bowsprit, lost her foremast and lagged behind the fleet. Then a massive and mysterious explosion ripped open the poop of the *San Salvador*, hurling hundreds of her crew into the sea and littering the Channel with wreckage. But the rest of the Armada sailed on towards Calais, where it anchored off the roads on August 6, slightly scratched, rather ruffled but intact. The English could do no more than emulate them, anchoring watchfully to windward.

It was at Calais Roads on August 7 that Medina Sidonia learned to his despair that bad luck had not only disposed of two of his ships, but of the whole 'Enterprise of England'. Parma's invasion force was trapped in Dunkirk and Nieuwpoort by a double blockade; the English stood guard in the Downs and Dutch rebel 'sea beggars' stood off Flushing. Even if Medina Sidonia had been able to force his way to Parma's rescue his enormous galleons had too much draught to get into harbour.

For the Armada there was no alternative but an ignominious return home. It would be a hazardous one for the way home had to be northwards, through the wild and treacherous North Sea and round the north of the British Isles. The English fleet and the unfavourable wind blocked escape back along the Channel, and to sail eastward risked almost certain suicide on the Zealand banks. That same night the Spaniards found that they were not to be allowed to leave unscarred.

At midnight on August 7-8 the Spaniards saw the flickering of fireships' glow, first dully and then more brightly as eight flaming ships drifted downwind towards them. The sight of those sinister silhouettes outlined in roaring fire, with their cannon spiked and heating up to explosion point, snapped the Spaniards' nerve. They panicked, slashed their cables and swarmed away in a struggling formless mass. None was even scorched for all the fireships missed their target. But they had served their purpose; the strong tight formation which the English sniping had been unable to break was irretrievably gone.

The English ships which attacked the Spanish fleet off Gravelines on August 8 found a badly shaken enemy. For the first time the English had numerical advantage and for the first time they came in close – just far enough away for Spanish grappling irons to fall short but near enough to thunder murderous broadsides into Spanish hulls. Moreover, the Spanish were running short of ammunition whereas the English could replenish easily.

English round shot tore through the high walls of the Spanish ships, spraying splinters and smashing cannon to twisted heaps of metal, and killing so many men that the decks were awash with blood and it ran from hatches and scuppers. Ship after ship fell victim to the point-blank battering by the ships of Lord Howard, Drake, Hawkins and Frobisher and soon the once-proud Armada was a tattered bunch of leaking limping dismasted hulks, though here and there Spaniards who had survived the holocaust dotted their ships' sides, taunting the English to come aboard and fight it out as men had long fought, hand to hand and to the death.

All the while, the crippled Armada was drifting towards shipwreck on the sand bars at Flushing, until at last there came a stroke of mercy. The English broke off the action as the wind became squally and shifted to south-west, allowing the Spanish ships to struggle off the lee shore and steer northwards for deeper water. Their course home to Spain was by then inexorably set, but only 66 survived the long wind-lashed haul around the north of Scotland out into the open Atlantic and back to home waters.

Ships that had escaped destruction by the English were pounded to a mess of debris on spiky rocks, rushed shorewards on mighty Atlantic rollers, or simply sank as shot-torn timbers yielded or strained seams parted. Thousands of Spaniards drowned, succumbed to typhus, dysentery, hunger, exhaustion or melancholy, or died by English or Irish hands as they staggered on to inhospitable shores. Of the 5000 who did reach home in mid-October with the mortified Medina Sidonia two-thirds were dead within a month, and half of the returned ships never put to sea again.

The English, who had followed the fleeing ships for four days, until August 12, when they put into the Firth of Forth, were not at first aware of what they had achieved. September ended before English victory became acknowledged fact. Then Europe realised to its amazement and, depending on Catholic or Protestant sympathies, its disgust or delight, that the might and the pride of Spain had been soundly thrashed.

Defeat bit deep enough to cause the Spaniards to recast their navy in more modern mould, and copy English methods of shipbuilding. Their future treasure fleets were defended from attack by slimmer and more flexible vessels and the treasure itself was carried in speedy frigates rather than lumbering carracks and galleons. The Spaniards learned too that their colonies abroad would be better preserved by fortified walls and batteries of guns than by arrogant injunctions to intruding foreigners.

By defeating the Armada the most intrusive and insolent of those foreigners did not end the danger that Spain posed to them, but the English certainly saved their country, their Protestant religion and their Protestant queen. The tactics that trounced the mighty Armada also proved to be the prototype for all naval engagements up to the Battle of Trafalgar in 1805.

Above all, the week-long battle of the Channel in 1588 gave notice of England's coming of stature as a first-class sea power and, with that, of her dazzling imperial future. By one of the great ironies of history, the wealthy far-flung British Empire which emerged three centuries later was moving towards its zenith in those same years, the 1820s, that saw the Spanish Empire in America crumble and fade away.

Top: Philip II of Spain. *National Portrait Gallery London*

Above: A medal struck in commemoration of the Armada: the Latin inscription translated reads, 'It blew and they were scattered 1588'. *National Maritime Museum London*

Left: A Spanish fleet of pre-Armada carracks and galleons in 1561. *Science Museum London*

Below: Drawing by W. H. Overend depicting action on Howard's flagship, the 'Ark Royal', as she engaged a Spanish ship. *Illustrated London News*

HUNDRED YEARS WAR

'THEY DID THAT WINTER great damage to the realm of England; sometime they came to Dover, Sandwich, Winchelsea, Hastings and Rye and did much sorrow to the Englishmen. They were a great number as 40,000 men'. So wrote Froissart of the start of the Hundred Years War against France in 1337.

Edward III had claimed the throne of France on rather shaky grounds and had been rebuffed. There were also other grounds for his declaration of war. France was threatening English seaborne trade and also had been less than kind to Englishmen in Scotland and in Gascony. However, in spite of everything France was still a splendid country to plunder.

The French King, Philippe VI, had been swift to act. He had unleashed a horde of privateers in the Channel and had followed them up with a large fleet. Taking advantage of the men of the Cinque Ports being engaged on the east coast in their age-old feud with the men of Yarmouth, the French had not only ravaged the ports but had burnt Southampton and Portsmouth. They had caught and sunk a number of ships off the Isle of Wight and had captured two of the King's fine vessels—the *Christofer* and *Edward*, big beamy cogs laden with wool for Flanders.

Rather late, King Edward called on the barons of the Cinque Ports for the 21 ships of the fleet they were bound by their Charter to render. But he took time to collect some other ships at Dartmouth, and those men of the Cinque Ports who were waiting at Winchelsea, and were growing impatient, took matters into their own hard hands. They sailed off to attack shipping in the harbours at Le Tréport and Boulogne, set the latter town on fire and burnt four 'grete shippes' and 19 galleys before sailing home with French captains hanging from their yardarms. It seemed to be enough reprisal for the time being.

Three years later, however, in midsummer of 1340, and after French depredations on the Kent coast, they formed a part of the fleet which Edward commanded in person. Froissart described how he crossed the Channel sitting on the deck of his cog *Thomas* while Sir John Chandos entertained him by singing German songs to the playing of minstrels. The fleet was on its way to a curious battle, although one of much renown. It took place at Sluys in enclosed waters, nearly opposite the Dutch port of Flushing, with the ships so close together that there was little opportunity for manoeuvres or tactics. With the French there were many Genoese as paid allies and the captive *Christofer* and *Edward* had plenty of Genoese crossbowmen on board them as well as in the tops of their own vessels. Small boats filled with stones for dropping on the heads of English boarding-parties are reported to have been lashed up the masts. The English made a special effort in the furious hand-to-hand melée to retake the *Christofer* and *Edward*. Well before the battle was over both of them had been recovered and were fighting on the proper side, with English archers replacing the eliminated crossbowmen.

The Battle of Sluys lasted half a day and at the end of that there was no doubt at all which side had won. As 'an especial act of grace' the King paid a sum of half the cost of the 21 ships provided by the Cinque Ports to show his appreciation of their work.

Edward III wrote from the cog *Thomas* to the Black Prince, 'Very dear son . . . On the Saturday, St John's Day, soon after the hour of noon, in the name of God and trusting in our just quarrel, we entered the said harbour with the tide to attack our said enemies who had assembled their ships in a very strong array and offered a noble defence all that day and the following night, but God with His power and miracle granted us the victory over our enemies for which we thank Him as devoutly as we can. The number of the ships, galleys and large barges of our enemies amounted to 180 and 10 all of which were taken save 24 in all, which fled and some are taken at sea. The men-at-arms and other armed people amounted to 35 thousand of which number by estimate 5000 have escaped and the remainder as we have been given to understand by certain men taken alive are lying dead in a great many places on the coasts of Flanders.'

Right: Engraving of the Battle of La Rochelle of 1372 from Froissart's chronicles.
Macpherson Collection

Bottom: Painting by H Wyllie of Henry V's ship 'Falcon' which is shown carrying his coat of arms on her sail.
Senior Service (K Fenwick Collection)

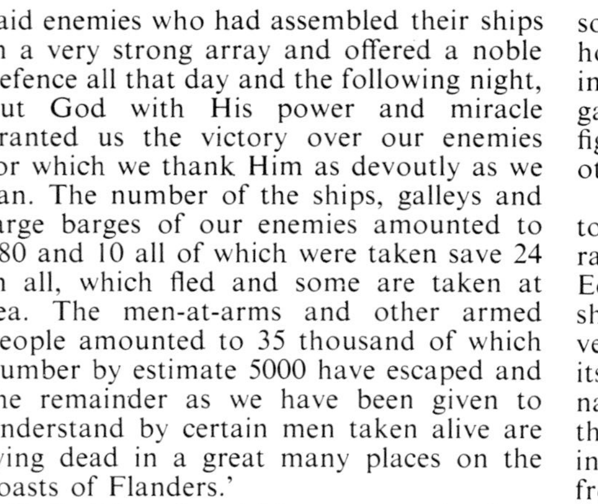

Both Edward and his son were to show their prowess in battle on dry land as well as at sea in the great victory of Crecy that is even more famous than Sluys. In 1350, four years after the name of Crecy had resounded through England and the Black Prince had won his spurs, the cog *Thomas* again carried the King's banner as he sailed to another sea fight. A Spanish fleet with some Genoese vessels in company had sailed up the Channel, capturing English merchantmen and slaying their crews in spite of a truce being in force. They emerged from ports in Flanders where they had done some trading. They were on their way homeward down-Channel when Edward intercepted them off Sandwich with a hastily gathered fleet of 50 ships, which led to the fight known as Les-Espagnols-sur-Mer, otherwise the Battle of Winchelsea.

The smaller English ships shortened sail to draw level and then bore down on them, ramming them with such venom that Edward and the Black Prince each felt his shattered ship sinking under him. In both vessels the broken mast flung the top with its men over the side. Father and son both narrowly escaped with their lives by forcing their way on board the nearest Spaniard, in a fighting company. Stones and missiles from the enemy tops caused many casualties but again the English longbow gained the upper hand as ship after ship was taken, amounting to a total of 17. Night fell and the English anchored, tending the wounded and throwing the miserable Spaniards into the sea '27 ships flying away by night left 17 (to) plunder to the King's pleasure'.

The Hundred Years War actually covered 116 years, although it included two periods of truce, one of them lasting for 10 years. Yet it had little of outstanding nautical interest until Henry V came on the scene.

As one result of his triumph at Agincourt he obviously grasped the importance of

The NAVAL ENGAGEMENT of RICHARD BEAUCHAMP, EARL of WARWICK, with two great FRENCH CARRICKS, in the Reign of HENRY VI.

Left: Impression of a naval engagement between the Earl of Warwick's force and two French carracks in the later period of the Hundred Years War. *Mary Evans Picture Library*

Below: Edward III upon his departure for Flanders as depicted in a 15th-century miniature in the 'Grandes Chroniques de France'. *K Fenwick Collection*

sea power, judging from his enthusiasm for shipbuilding. Two years after Agincourt he owned about 30 vessels, eight of them large carracks, including four captured from the French. There was a general increase in size of ships during his short reign and from the single-masted vessel in general use a two-master was becoming less of a rarity. His *Jesus of the Tower* was of 1000 tons and his *Grâce Dieu*, built in 1418, was 100 feet in length, had one 'great' mast, a mesan or mizen, two bowsprits and six sails with seven bonnets (the sailcloth strips that could be lashed to the foot of a sail to gather more wind).

All those vessels would have been outshone by the *Great Ship* he was having built at Bayonne. At 186 feet long it was so enormous for its time that it is probably fortunate for its potential crew that it was never launched.

When the English at Harfleur were threatened by the French in June 1416, Henry organised a relieving force of 10,000 fighting men and had them ready to sail in August in a large fleet of transports, with his brother the Duke of Bedford in command. The ships arrived in the mouth of the Seine to find a Genoese fleet of nine large carracks and eight long galleys blockading the river. A long hard fight saw the English victorious, with four enemy carracks sunk and five vessels captured. Harfleur was relieved just in time.

For his grand campaign in France in 1417 Henry first ordered the young Earl of Huntingdon to sail with a fleet of 11 ships and sweep the Channel clear of Genoese and French ships that were menacing the crossing. The earl was a worthy choice; he beat off and sometimes captured ships of French, Castilian, Scottish and Genoese origin.

In the meantime Henry had called on the Cinque Ports for their ship service quota, had requisitioned all suitable merchantmen, and added to his own fleet. Altogether the invasion fleet totalled 1500 ships, nearly half of them hired from Holland. They carried across the Channel to the Seine 16,400 fighting troops, from nobles down to archers, as well as hordes of servants, camp followers and artisans of many kinds. Also carried were great stocks of provisions and warlike stores and many horses.

Yet it was a huge waste of effort, of suffering and of lives. Within five years Henry V was dead and not long afterwards Calais, the last foothold in France, was English no longer.

ENGLISH SHIPOWNERS in the latter days of the 17th century were facing ruin. The Dutch had built up the largest fleet in Europe and had spread over a quarter of the globe. A constant irritation to British fishermen and seamen was the huge fishing fleet of two-masted herring busses in their home waters, uncomfortably near to the coast, hauling their nets and protected by men-of-war. Stout allies as the Dutch had been and would be again, monopoly bred arrogance.

On the Dutch side there was anger at the passing of the English Navigation Acts, which were intended to break the monopoly. Also, the captains saw no reason to honour the traditional salute of lowered topsails when their ships were passing up the Channel.

Feelings on both sides were such that it needed only an incident to provoke the First Dutch War. On May 19, 1652, Rear-Admiral Bourne was sheltering with eight ships in the Downs from a stiff breeze when the Dutch Admiral Martin Tromp, who was on his way to escort a convoy from the East, also appeared and took shelter with 42 ships. Tromp had no love for the English. As an eight-year-old he had been captured by an English pirate and had spent two miserable years as a cabin boy.

After the wind had dropped and he was sailing towards Calais, a Dutch captain overhauled him and brought news of trouble in the western Channel between English and Dutch over the question of the salute. Tromp at once altered course just as a British fleet was emerging from Rye harbour. In command was Robert Blake, General-at-Sea and a welcome opponent for the redoubtable Tromp. Short, thick-set and self-contained, Blake was a successful soldier in his fifties rapidly learning to be a successful admiral.

THE DUTCH WARS

He was wearing his flag in the *James*, and Tromp was in the *Brederode*. The ships exchanged broadsides and the *James* took a battering. She had outsailed her consorts and had to fight the head of the Dutch line alone for some time until other ships of the fleet could come to her aid. Nearly surrounded by enemy ships, dismasted and damaged in the hull, with her sailing-master dead and 50 other casualties, she was rescued just in time. Meanwhile Bourne had sailed from the Downs to the sound of guns. He attacked the rear ships, catching them unawares and cutting off two of them. His action decided the fight; after five fierce hours Tromp retired to his own coast, leaving the two ships in Bourne's hands (although one was later recovered by the Dutch) while the *James* was towed into Dover harbour.

Blake sailed north in September to deal with the warships protecting the Dutch herring fleet and had created havoc when Tromp, searching for him with 100 sail, made contact near the Orkneys. But a sudden gale dispersed the Dutch while Blake found shelter in the Shetlands. Tromp's scattered vessels straggled home, having achieved nothing, and Tromp was in disgrace.

His command was taken over by Admiral Cornelius de Witt, who had junior to him Michael de Ruyter, one of the finest of all Dutch fighting admirals. But in the next battle, that of the Kentish Knock, Blake narrowly won the day. Two months later the old war-horse Tromp was in harness again. He escorted a big convoy, outward bound, into the Strait of Dover with 80 warships. Blake had half that number and a large proportion were only armed merchantmen. The battle, fought in November 1652, known as the Battle of the Ness, or Dungeness, left Tromp, so it was said, hoisting a broom at his masthead to announce that he had swept the Channel clear. As for Blake, he made it plain that he wanted no more armed merchantmen under his command.

The battle of the Ness was undeniably a defeat for Blake but when February 1653 came he had his revenge. In one action he met a new kind of engagement. It began when Blake caught an incoming Dutch convoy off Portland and developed into a running fight up the Channel, with Tromp striving manfully to screen the merchantmen from Blake's repeated attacks. It ended with over 50 Dutch merchant ships and men-of-war in English hands or sunk.

Blake had been wounded and when he was recovering, he took charge of 18 ships refitting in the Thames while Deane and Monk, two other Generals-at-Sea, had joint command of the fleet. In June Tromp attacked them near the Gabbard shoal, east of Harwich, when a shot from the Dutch opening broadside cut General Deane in two. Monk flung his cloak over the

Facing page top: A model of a pinnace, a ship type that was prominent in the 17th century and in the Anglo-Dutch conflicts of the time. *Deutsche Museum Munich*

Facing page bottom: From an engraving depicting the Battle of Texel in 1673. *Mary Evans Picture Library*

Left: A Dutch print showing the fleets of Monk and de Ruyter in the English Channel in 1666. *Mary Evans Picture Library*

Top: Painting by Peter Wood of 17th-century Dutch vessels in a breeze, with a fluyt in the foreground. *P M Wood*

Above: An engraving of Robert Blake, General and Admiral of the Parliament Forces. *Illustrated London News*

Above: Admiral Blake defeating the Dutch fleet in 1652. *Mary Evans Picture Library*

body and, for all his lack of experience of sea warfare, carried on the fight until nightfall. On the following day the Dutch were so mauled that some ships, surprisingly for Dutchmen, broke away. Then Blake, hearing the gunfire as the fleets drifted southward, led out his 18 ships for the finishing touch. Tromp himself had a narrow escape when the captains of two English ships with boarding parties actually succeeded in gaining the *Brederode's* upper deck. A lesser man might have surrendered, but not Tromp. He set light to gunpowder and blew the upper deck, the boarders and probably some of his own men, overboard into the sea. He himself had severe burns. The English gained ten prizes.

There was still one final engagement to be fought, although the Dutch had by then lost heart. It was a July battle off Scheveningen, which Monk again won but which cost the Dutch still more. There, the great Admiral Martin Tromp lost his life, fighting to the last at the age of 56. The Dutch had lost the war but Cromwell treated them quite lightly. They had to agree to accept the Navigation Acts which broke their monopoly of trade, to give the salute in the Narrow Seas and to pay compensation for the atrocious massacre at Amboyna but there was little else of importance.

Unfortunately, few Dutchmen appeared eager to carry out all their obligations, especially the awkward little matter of the salute. Then Charles stirred up trouble by sending ships to create havoc with Dutch factors on the Guinea Coast, a curious step, which naturally brought out a Dutch fleet to take reprisals on British factors. In command of that fleet was Michael de Ruyter, who had taken the place of Tromp and was soon to make an undying name for himself.

King Charles had given Holland another cause for irritation by marrying Katherine of Braganza. She brought him a dowry that meant England had to own not only Tangier, which would pose a threat to Dutch trade in the Mediterranean but also Bombay, which gave England a foothold in what the Dutch considered to be their sphere. Already English merchants were nibbling at the seaborne trade both near and far.

The Second Dutch War, which was clearly inevitable, started in the early days of 1665. In June a major battle was fought off Lowestoft between two fleets, each of about 100 ships, with the Lord High Admiral proving his gift for command. He was now Monk, or rather the Duke of Albemarle, since he had been ennobled by Charles at his Restoration. Over a dozen enemy ships were taken in the fighting and as many more were sunk. The Dutch lost particularly heavily in their commanders.

In the next big fight the English fleet was divided between Albemarle and Prince Rupert, as the French were temporarily allied to the Dutch. Rupert, with the smaller detachment was watching their ships. It was Albemarle who bore the brunt of the Four Days Battle, as it was called; one of the bloodiest and most hard-fought encounters in British annals. Heavily outnumbered, on the third day, he was at last retiring towards the Thames estuary when Rupert's ships hove in sight to the south-west. Albemarle turned his shattered fleet and beat to windward through the enemy's line and saved the day.

He could hardly claim a victory when his losses were three times those of the Dutch, but he had lived to fight another day, and fight he did. Seven weeks afterwards he was at sea again and in the St James Day Fight he more than squared the account by losing just one ship to the enemy's 20. That was not all; he followed their retreat to the Texel and sent in Sir Robert Holmes to attack with fireships the shipping in the Vlie and the storesheds in the famous 'Holmes Bonfire', which burned long and most effectively.

But the war was not over even then. With peace negotiations dragging on, the King was persuaded, for the sake of economy, to leave the main fleet laid up in the Medway, at Chatham, instead of making it fit for sea with the coming of spring. The Duke of York gave specific instructions for the fleet's protection, including the stretching of a heavy chain across the river, but his orders, except for that referring to the chain, seem to have been ignored.

Albemarle did his best to alert Charles but his efforts came too late. News came that de Ruyter was off Harwich with a fleet of 100 sail and making for the Thames. At once Albemarle rushed down to Chatham, to be appalled at what he saw. Unmounted guns; cannon-balls of the wrong size; useless forts; and rotting gunpowder. Chatham was practically defenceless. While Albemarle struggled with the chaos, the Dutch entered the Thames, de Ruyter detached three ships and some fireships from the main fleet to sail up the Medway. A landing party broke a bolt in the chain and, free to pass, the fireships burnt three of the finest ships in the Royal Navy. Still worse was the fate of the *Royal Charles*, flagship of Blake and the Duke of York, the very symbol of the restored monarchy. She was ignominiously towed across to Amsterdam, where part of her splendid decorated stern was set up as a permanent memento.

John Evelyn wrote in his diary: 'I went to Chatham and thence to view not onely what Mischiefe the Dutch had done but how triumphantly the whole Fleete lay within the very mouth of the Thames . . . a Dreadful Spectacle as ever English men saw and a dishonour never to be wiped out'.

That astonishing feat of de Ruyter in 1667, marked the end of the Second Dutch War. However, in May 1672, the Third War erupted, with France an ally of England as the result of some dubious dealings between the French King and Charles. Four battles were fought, all of them drawn, with the French taking the part of interested spectators. In one of them, in Sole Bay, a ferocious old-style fight took place between Prince Rupert and de Ruyter, with another off the Texel matching it in courage and tenacity. Eventually, however, naval opinion, backed by the country at large, forced Charles to make peace. But the French continued and the effort of fighting two enemies proved too great even for the valiant Dutch. Exhausted, and with their dykes penetrated by the sea, they were unable to prevent their wealth of trade from falling into English hands, never to be fully regained.

NELSON

ST VINCENT TO TRAFALGAR

HORATIO NELSON, doyen of British naval heroes, was an exception to the rules that genius and arrogance go together, and that to be a successful genius a man has to be somewhat dislikeable. On the contrary, Nelson possessed enormous charm, humanity and an incomparable ability to inspire magnanimous admiration in his superiors, and intense personal devotion in his colleagues and those under his command. So irresistible was he that he managed with impunity to bend the naval rules, disregard orders and flout social conventions with a private life that was scandalous even in an era of debauchery in high places.

For instance, after the battle of Cape St Vincent in 1797, even the cold disciplinarian Sir John Jervis flung his arms round Nelson after Nelson had disregarded orders with the manoeuvre that paved the way to British success.

Again, in 1799, after the Battle of the Nile, Nelson was fortunate to receive only a mild rebuke from the Admiralty for 'having left Minorca exposed to the risk of being attacked without any naval force to protect it'. Completely contrary to orders, Nelson had kept his fleet at Naples ostensibly to prevent that kingdom from falling into the hands of the French. The French, fortunately for Nelson, did not attack undefended Minorca, but it was not so long since a British Admiral, Byng, had been shot for a similar action.

In addition, the consequences of his affaire with Lady Emma Hamilton provided scandal of a calibre that would have sunk the reputation of a man of lesser lustre. For Emma's sake, Nelson commanded his fleet from the Hamilton residence instead of from his flagship for the greater part of 18 months. One serious result was that Nelson left the blockades of Malta and the Levant to others who were unable to prevent Napoleon escaping and returning to France in October 1799.

The Admiralty and society in general were, however, to become accustomed to Nelson's unorthodox behaviour and to be glad of it, for all his great naval victories – St Vincent (1797), the Nile (1798), Copenhagen (1801) and Trafalgar (1805) – were gained by bending the rules. It required considerable moral courage, because the consequence of failure was court martial and disgrace. For Nelson, however, the consequences could hardly have been more fortunate; they included enduring fame, public adulation, a viscountcy and a dukedom (of Bronte), and an annual naval toast on October 21, Trafalgar Day, to his 'immortal memory'.

It was an unlikely destiny for the humbly born and somewhat sickly son of a Norfolk rector, who at 13 years of age, in 1771, began the life at sea for which he evinced an early hatred. Nevertheless, at age 19 Nelson became a lieutenant. The following year he joined the flagship *Bristol* in the West Indies and speedily worked his way up to first lieutenant, then to captain before he was appointed in 1784 to the frigate *Boreas* on the Leeward Isles station.

Five years later France erupted in bloody revolution, thus setting the stage for the 23 years of revolutionary and Napoleonic wars in which Nelson was to make so great a name. The first of these wars began in April 1792 and the following year, Nelson, by then a married man, was in command of the old 64-gun *Agamemnon*, and in hot action in the Mediterranean. From then until 1800 Nelson was in almost continuous active service. In this hectic and hazardous period, he suffered the first of his disfigurements during the fight for Calvi in August 1794. A stray shot flung sand into his face and permanently blinded him in one eye.

In April 1796 Nelson was promoted commodore, and in June he was appointed to the 74-gun *Captain*, the ship in which he first displayed his genius. On February 14, 1797, the Spanish and English fleets came in sight of one another off Cape St Vincent. The Spaniards had 27 ships of the line against the British 15, but the Spanish gunners were not too well trained, which went some way towards evening the odds.

Admiral Sir John Jervis began the fight by cutting through the Spanish line, isolating nine enemy ships. To meet the threat the Spanish Admiral Cordova tried to link up with them by altering course to the north. Shortly before noon, the two fleets began to pass each other on opposite courses. To counter this, Jervis ordered his ships to tack, in succession, to the north, but over half the British fleet had passed to the south of the Spanish before they could do so.

This was Nelson's moment. From his position near the British rear, he saw that the two Spanish sections would soon rejoin. He ignored the Fighting Instruction to maintain allotted stations and, instead, out of turn, he deliberately wore his ship round 180 degrees towards the Spanish van. Most British admirals would have reacted with a peremptory order to resume station, but Jervis realised the value of Nelson's initiative and signalled his rear ship, *Excellent*, to turn also and support Nelson. By 13.30 both British ships were in close action with Cordova's four-decker flagship, the 140-gun *Santissima Trinidad*, which had the vital effect of slowing the Spanish main body for long enough to allow the rest of Jervis's ships to come up with it.

There followed a hotly contested two-hour fight during which four Spanish ships struck their colours before Cordova's two groups finally managed to join. Faced with the

Top: Engraving of Admiral Nelson. *Mary Evans Picture Library*

Above: Four of the decorations awarded to Nelson during his long and distinguished naval career – clockwise from the left: Order of St Ferdinand and of Merit of Naples; Order of the Bath; Turkish Order of the Crescent; Order of St Joachim. *R Westwood*

superior force, Jervis judged it wise to break off action, even though no British ships had suffered worse damage than the *Captain*, which had lost her foremast while crippling the 80-gun *San Nicolas* and the 122-gun *San Jose*. Nelson, who had no fear of commanders-in-chief, subsequently contended that Jervis could have safely taken at least two more vessels. In fact, the premature breaking off cost the British several prizes, including Cordova's flagship.

Cordova, however, had had enough, as was proved the following day when the two fleets were still in sight of each other. Rather than allow Jervis to renew battle, Cordova headed for Cadiz. There his fleet was subsequently blockaded by Jervis, whose fleet therefore played an important part in frustrating France's initial plans for invading Britain.

Nelson was promoted to rear admiral of the Blue, but this initial step on the ladder to glory was closely followed by near disaster. In an attack on Santa Cruz in July 1797, Nelson led his squadron's boats, carrying a landing party of about a thousand seamen and marines, towards the mole, where they were met by such withering fire that only half reached it. British casualties, which ultimately totalled 146 killed and over 100 wounded, included Nelson, whose right elbow was shattered by grapeshot. As a result his arm had to be amputated.

Nine months later, in April 1798, after convalescing in Britain, Nelson hoisted his flag in the 64-gun *Vanguard* and rejoined the fleet off Cadiz. From there, he was ordered into the Mediterranean, where Napoleon was preparing to capture Malta and invade Egypt as stepping stones towards seizing India. Napoleon's fleet, commanded by Admiral Bruey, was anchored in Aboukir Bay off the Egyptian coast near Alexandria. Although ordered by Napoleon to sail into Alexandria, Bruey feared his 13 ships-of-the-line and four frigates would run aground. He hesitated long enough to give Nelson time to muster his 11 available ships. The Battle of the Nile began at 16.30 on August 1, 1798, when five of Nelson's ships passed inside the French van and the rest struck from the seaward side.

Nelson, in *Vanguard*, led the seaward strike. The French van was soon perilously sandwiched between two superior enemy forces, and the unprepared Bruey, taken by surprise, proved no match for Nelson. As the night wore on, the French suffered increasing and crippling damage, ultimately losing 11 ships-of-the-line, two frigates, 1700 dead, 1500 wounded and 3000 men captured. Admiral Bruey was killed just before his ship was rent by explosion at 20.00 on August 1 and sank with all her crew. Nelson's fleet suffered losses including the 74-gun *Bellerophon* and *Majestic*, both badly damaged, and 1000 dead and wounded.

As a result of this stunning victory, Nelson was created Baron Nelson of the Nile and Burnham Thorpe (his birthplace), Napoleon's army was cut off from France and Britain regained control in the Mediterranean.

Nelson took *Vanguard* and two other vessels to Naples for repairs, arriving there on September 22. Afterwards, Nelson intended to establish a blockade of Malta but his plans were abruptly overturned by his encounter with the pulchritudinous Emma, wife of the British minister in Naples.

Nelson also became embroiled in disputes with his new commander-in-chief, Admiral Lord Keith, who succeeded the ailing Jervis (Lord St Vincent) as C-in-C of the British Mediterranean Fleet in June 1799. In July Keith ordered Nelson to send ships to Minorca, which he thought was endangered by the arrival at Toulon of Admiral Bruix, newly escaped from the British blockade of Brest. In the event, the danger did not transpire, but Nelson's insistence on keeping his fleet at Naples, ostensibly to defend it, resulted in tense relations. In February 1800 Nelson pleaded ill-health as an excuse not to carry out Keith's orders 'to prosecute the measures necessary for the reduction of Malta'. After further disputes with Keith, this time over the safe conduct for the Queen of Naples, he was allowed to strike his flag and return to England, where he arrived with the Hamiltons in November.

Nelson's feud with Keith might have resulted in court martial for repeated disobedience, but he was saved from this unsavoury fate by Lord St Vincent, then in command of the Channel fleet, who expressed a strong wish to have Nelson again as his second-in-command. Nelson accepted the appointment. However, no sooner had he hoisted his flag as vice admiral of the Blue than he was detached to sail into the Baltic with Admiral Sir Hyde-Parker as second-in-command of a fleet of eight ships-of-the-line.

They went in response to Russia's decision to join with Napoleon and the King of Denmark in reviving the Armed Neutrality, which presented a serious threat to British maritime trade. The Danes were ready and prepared for a British attack when on April 1, 1801, Nelson, in his flagship the 74-gun *Elephant*, took 12 ships-of-the-line, five frigates and 19 other vessels through the Outer Deep to an anchorage at the southern end of the Middle Ground. Parker, meanwhile, held the rest of his fleet in reserve about six miles to the north. Battle began next morning. Within two hours, by 11.30, the British and Danish fleets were heavily engaged at point blank range. After another 90 minutes Nelson was sufficiently encouraged by the havoc his ships were causing to expect victory.

From his distant flagship, however, Parker saw that three of Nelson's ships had been prevented from supporting their commander. He became so anxious that the outcome would be defeat, for which he would be held responsible, that he hoisted the signal 'Discontinue the Action'. A withdrawal by way of the narrow channel past the enemy forts could be disastrous, and in any case, Nelson had no mind to break off the action. 'I have only one eye', he commented, 'I have a right to be blind sometimes . . .'

The now legendary 'blind eye' gesture was to be fully justified. Soon afterwards, the enemy's fire began to slacken, the Danish flagship blew up and others slipped their cables and were wrecked or fled into Copenhagen Harbour. By 14.30 the battle was virtually over. The bulk of the Danish fleet had been destroyed, with the loss of 1700 killed and wounded and 3500 taken prisoner, against British casualties of only 941. Nelson had won a battle in which, as at the Nile, he had almost annihilated his enemy.

The upshot was that Denmark, and later Russia, withdrew from the pact of Armed Neutrality and the Baltic was made safe water for the British Navy. Nelson was created a viscount, succeeded Parker as commander-in-chief and returned home to the adulation of a nation which idolised him, probably as no commander has been idolised before or since.

About a year after Copenhagen, in March 1802, the Peace of Amiens was signed. However, the lull it provided in the long struggle against Napoleon was brief. With the French apparently preparing to invade Britain, and their troops occupying the Hanoverian lands of the British Royal Family, war was resumed, and in July 1803 Nelson arrived off Toulon to mount a strict blockade. It proved watertight until March

Above: Lady Hamilton, from an anonymous miniature. *Mary Evans Picture Library*

Below: A painting of the action at Copenhagen, with the city in the background, by Nicholas Pocock in 1806. *National Maritime Museum London*

Right: Diagram showing the dispositions and intended movements at Copenhagen. *G Bennett*

Far right above: Vice-Admiral Lord Collingwood, Nelson's second-in-command at the time of Trafalgar. *London Electrotype Agency*

Far right centre: Admiral Lord Nelson.

Far right below: Admiral Sir Hyde Parker, Nelson's commander at Copenhagen, painted when Parker was a captain. *National Maritime Museum London*

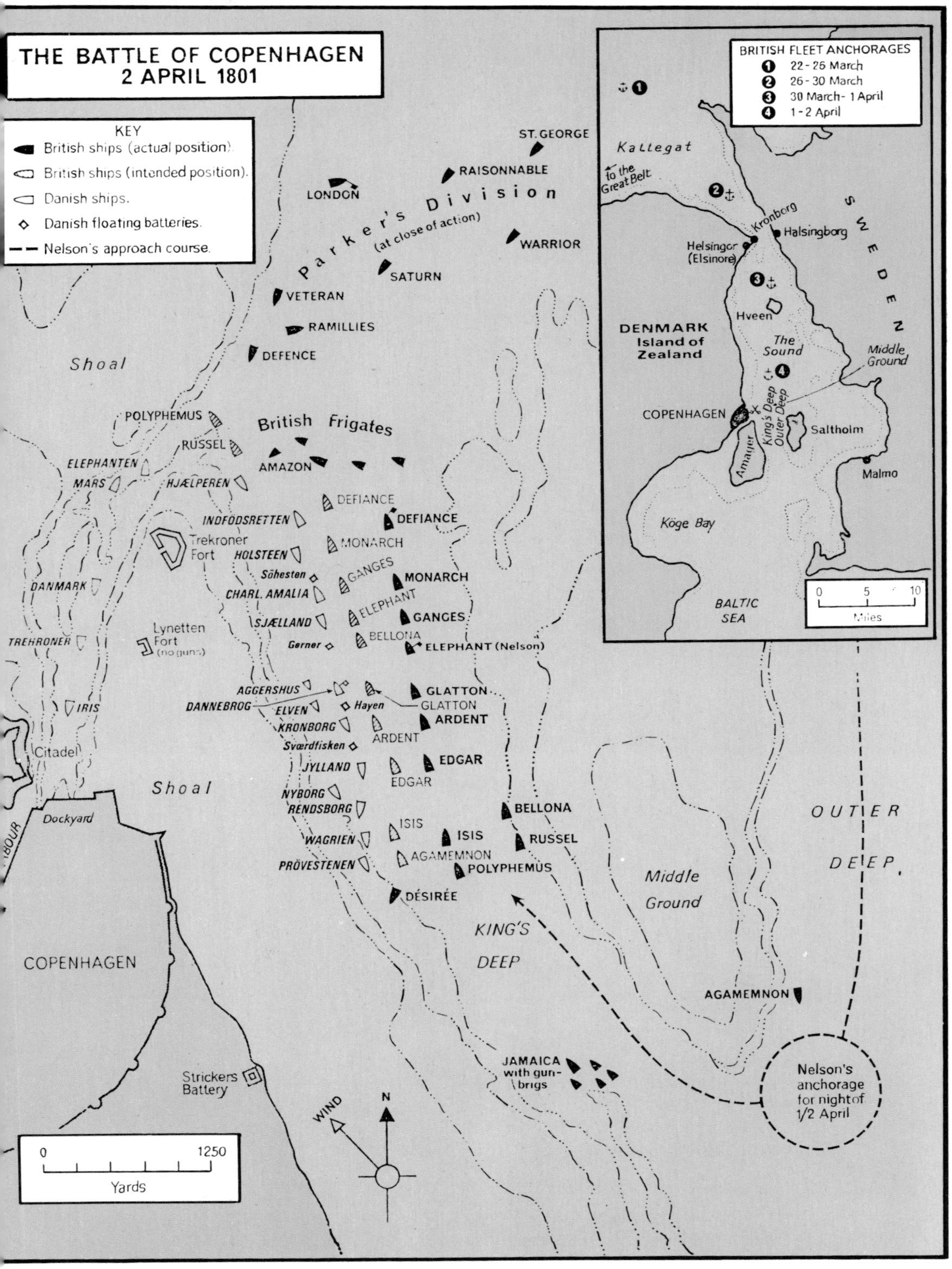
THE BATTLE OF COPENHAGEN
2 APRIL 1801
KEY
British ships (actual position).
British ships (intended position).
Danish ships.
Danish floating batteries.
Nelson's approach course.
BRITISH FLEET ANCHORAGES
1 22 - 25 March
2 26 - 30 March
3 30 March - 1 April
4 1 - 2 April
Kattegat
to the Great Belt
Kronborg
Helsingor (Elsinore)
Halsingborg
SWEDEN
DENMARK Island of Zealand
Hveen
The Sound
Middle Ground
COPENHAGEN
King's Deep
Outer Deep
Amager
Saltholm
Malmo
Köge Bay
BALTIC SEA
0 5 10
Miles
ST. GEORGE
RAISONNABLE
LONDON
Parker's Division
(at close of action)
WARRIOR
SATURN
VETERAN
RAMILLIES
DEFENCE
Shoal
POLYPHEMUS
British Frigates
RUSSEL
AMAZON
ELEPHANTEN
MARS
HJÆLPEREN
DEFIANCE
INDFODSRETTEN
DEFIANCE
Trekroner Fort
HOLSTEEN
MONARCH
Söhesten
GANGES
MONARCH
DANMARK
CHARL. AMALIA
ELEPHANT
SJÆLLAND
GANGES
BELLONA
Lynetten Fort (no guns)
TREHRONER
Gerner
ELEPHANT (Nelson)
AGGERSHUS
GLATTON
DANNEBROG
ELVEN
Hayen
GLATTON
IRIS
KRONBORG
ARDENT
ARDENT
Citadel
Sværdfisken
JYLLAND
EDGAR
EDGAR
Shoal
NYBORG
RENDSBORG
BELLONA
OUTER
Dockyard
ISIS
ISIS
RUSSEL
WAGRIEN
AGAMEMNON
PRÖVESTENEN
POLYPHEMUS
DEEP.
Middle Ground
DÉSIRÉE
KING'S DEEP
COPENHAGEN
AGAMEMNON
JAMAICA with gun-brigs
Nelson's anchorage for night of 1/2 April
Strickers Battery
WIND
N
0 1250
Yards

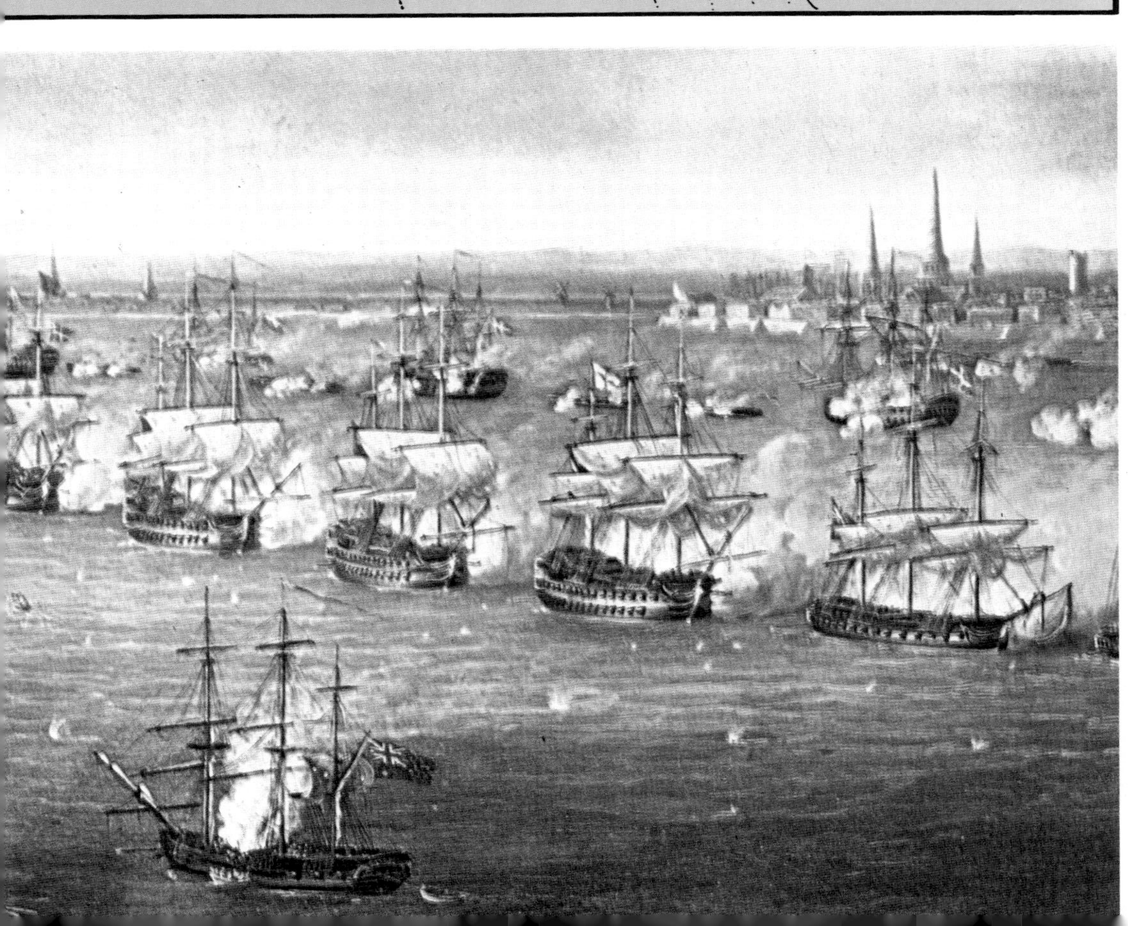

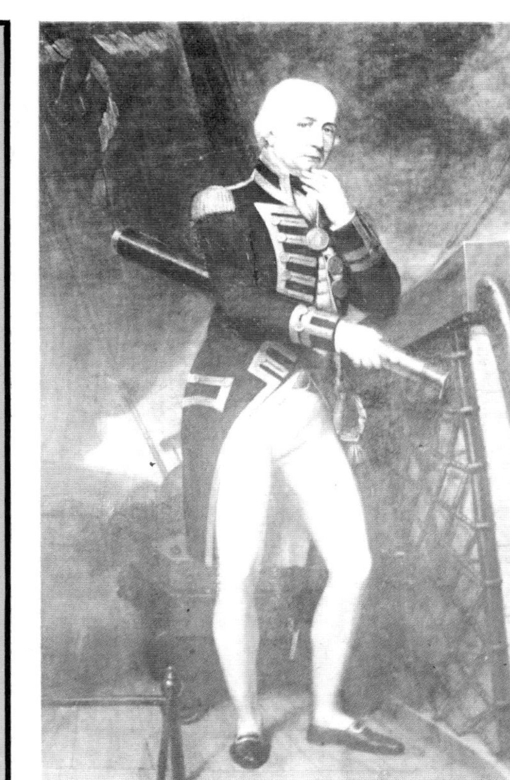

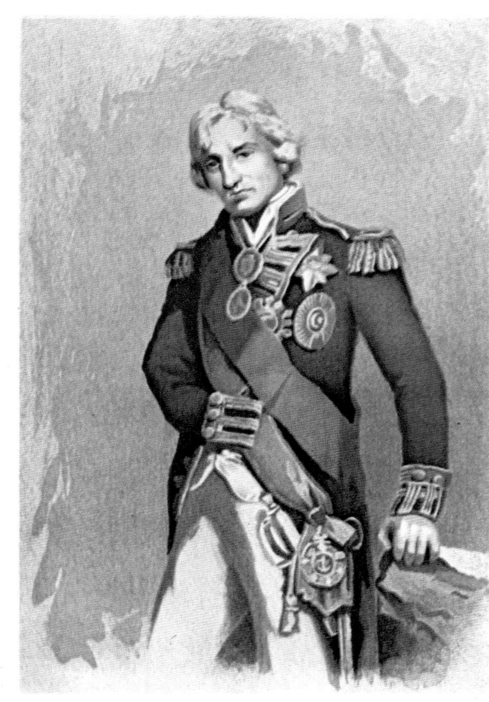

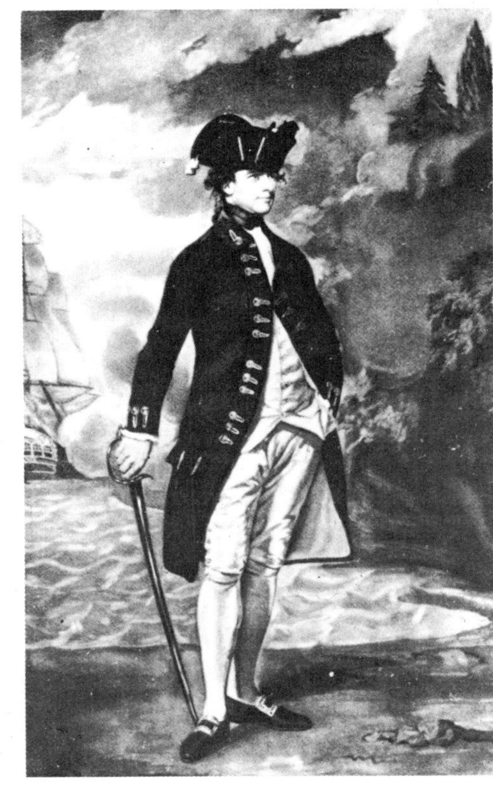

1805, when the French Admiral Villeneuve at last managed to slip out. There followed a transatlantic chase in which Villeneuve tried to draw Nelson away from Europe so that he could safely enter the English Channel. Villeneuve failed and ended up in Cadiz, blockaded by Vice Admiral Collingwood.

As soon as news of Villeneuve's plight came through, Nelson, who had returned briefly to England, arrived in Cadiz (September 28). The hapless Villeneuve was galvanised into action by a threat to relieve him of command and early in October managed to break out and head for the Mediterranean. Nelson's patrol frigates gave the alert and he set off after the elusive French admiral. The French fleet came into sight on the afternoon of October 20.

Both sides were aware that the battle which was soon to ensue would be of conclusive proportions. The Franco-Spanish fleet massed off Cape Trafalgar, on the

Spanish coast, was the larger of the opponents, with 18 French and 15 Spanish ships-of-the-line and five frigates, and a total of 3000 guns. Nelson had 27 ships-of-the-line and four frigates, with 2500 guns. Nelson had already discussed his battle plan in minutest detail with his captains; it closely resembled his tactics at the Nile.

At 11.00 the French and Spanish ships moved northwards in an untidy mass. Nelson, in *Victory*, moved in from the west, with his fleet in two columns, Collingwood, in *Royal Sovereign*, commanding the rear (lee) and Nelson himself the van (weather) division. The well-tried combination of concentration of forces and breaking of the enemy line was again to be used to give the British initial superiority of numbers.

Shortly before noon, Nelson hoisted two signals. The first was 'I intend to push through the end of the enemy's line to prevent them getting into Cadiz'. Then, because the growing swell presaged a storm, when the British fleet would be threatened with a lee shore, Nelson warned 'Prepare to anchor after the close of the day'. Only after that did Nelson amuse the fleet with what has since become the most famous signal in all British naval history, 'England expects that every man will do his duty'.

Collingwood was heading for the enemy line, his target the Spanish 112-gun *Santa Ana*. Nelson was directing his division for the 140-gun *Santissima Trinidad*. A few minutes later *Victory* flew Nelson's last signal; 'Engage the enemy more closely'. Collingwood came within range of the enemy and the French 74-gun *Fougeaux* fired the first broadside of the battle. *Royal Sovereign* passed under *Santa Ana's* stern, into which Collingwood discharged double-shotted broadsides while her starboard guns raked the *Fougeaux*. The remainder of Collingwood's ships likewise sailed into the enemy's rear and by 13.00 all 15 were shrouded in the smoke of a general engagement with 17 of the enemy ships partly separated from Villeneuve's centre. At 14.15 *Santa Ana* struck her colours to *Royal Sovereign*.

While Collingwood's column was thus embroiled, Nelson headed for Villeneuve's flagship *Bucentaure*. Heavily engaged by *Santissima Trinidad* and by *Neptune*, *Redoutable* and by *Bucentaure*, *Victory* sustained serious damage, with her mizen topmast cut in two, her wheel shattered and her sails torn to shreds. By 12.30 *Neptune* and *Redoutable* were so close astern of *Bucentaure* that *Victory's* captain, Hardy, could see no gap through which to steer his ship. He chose *Redoutable*, but as he steered for her *Neptune* veered to starboard, so that *Victory* was able to cut under *Bucentaure's* stern. Firing double- and treble-shotted guns as she passed, Hardy's broadsides killed and wounded nearly 400 French crewmen. *Victory* was raked and mauled from ahead by *Neptune*.

Hardy turned towards *Redoutable* and dropped alongside, one of *Victory's* studding sail booms hooking into the French ship's rigging, carrying both to leeward. *Victory* also used her starboard carronades to clear *Bucentaure's* gangways, but no one countered the Tyrolean sharpshooters in the *Redoutable's* tops, until too late. At 13.15 Nelson, resplendent in his medals, was walking on *Victory's* quarterdeck with Hardy when a fateful musket ball was fired from *Redoutable's* tops. It struck Nelson in the chest and felled him to the deck. 'They have done for me at last', he gasped. A distraught Hardy ordered seamen to carry Nelson below to the cockpit, where the surgeon found the ball had penetrated deep into his chest and had probably lodged in his spine.

Nelson lived for just over one hour more, long enough to know that he had won the Battle of Trafalgar. By the time he died, at 14.30, murmuring 'Thank God I have done my duty', the ships of the French van had broken off the fight and those in the centre and rear were being collected and withdrawn to Cadiz.

Of their 33 ships, the French and Spaniards lost 18, 17 of them prizes in the hands of the British, together with 2600 dead and wounded and 7000 prisoners. No British ships were lost, although half of them were badly damaged. There were 1700 British casualties.

When news of Nelson's death reached London, the nation was thrown into a paroxysm of grief. *The Times* wrote 'If ever there was a man to be praised, wept and honoured by his country, it is Lord Nelson. His three great naval achievements have eclipsed the brilliancy of the most dazzling victories in the annals of British daring'.

This was no fulsome praise, for Nelson's achievement at Trafalgar was of supreme importance and of great future significance. It finally extinguished Napoleon's bids to invade England, totally vanquished Napoleon's navy and established Britain as the world's supreme naval power.

Facing page:

Top: Coloured engraving of part of the action during Nelson's victory over the French at Aboukir Bay in 1798. *Parker Gallery (photo D. Rudkin)*

Left centre: The hero Nelson returning to Portsmouth after his victory at the Battle of the Nile. *Parker Gallery (photo D Rudkin)*

Right centre: Preparation of Nelson's signal 'England expects . . .', from a painting by T Davidson. *National Maritime Museum London*

Bottom: Lady Hamilton welcoming the victors of the Nile on their return from battle, from the picture by Robert Hillingford. *Mary Evans Picture Library*

This page: A painting by Charles Dixon of Nelson's flagship 'Victory' approaching the 'Santisima Trinidad'. *L Dunn Collection*

AMERICA WINS INDEPENDENCE

THE DECLARATION of the American War of Independence in 1776 is often held to have been heralded by the 'Boston tea-party' of four years earlier. But even earlier than that there were outbreaks of force against the clumsy hand and blindness of the British Government, which was coupled with the imposition of taxes and the Colonists' disgust at not being allowed to handle their own affairs.

In 1769 the British armed sloop *Liberty*, which was busily suppressing smuggling, or evasion of taxes, so enraged the people of Newport that they seized and burnt her. Later, in 1772, the captain of the British sloop *Gaspee*, who is described as having an overbearing manner, had the ill luck when chasing a suspected smuggler, outward bound from Newport, to run aground. It was too good an opportunity to miss; boat-loads of men rowed out to her, wounded the captain and set the *Gaspee* on fire.

The Boston tea-party came in 1773. A number of ships had brought cargoes of tea to Boston and some of their captains, finding them unwanted, had sailed back to England. Then the Governor asserted his authority and forbade the other ships to leave until all their tea had been unloaded. They were saved the trouble; about 40 or 50 men dressed as Red Indians scrambled on board the ships and flung the boxes of tea into the sea.

As time went on minor affrays in different ports grew more and more violent and several English naval vessels, chiefly sloops with lieutenants or midshipmen in command, were captured after fights and their guns shared out.

George Washington's first step in nautical matters was to fit out a schooner, the *Hannah*, which sailed from Beverly, Massachusetts, in September 1775 and returned after two days with a couple of English prizes. By the end of the year several other

vessels had been overhauled and manned by the army. Publicly owned vessels included ships fitted out in France and small craft organised by Washington in Massachusetts and later in New York on the lakes and rivers.

The chief asset at first lay in the wealth of privateers in the American states. Until the declaration of war there had normally been quite a large number cruising at sea in the hope of making prizes of French and Spanish ships; as official action against the British hardened their total was greatly augmented. They undoubtedly aided the states to win the war but they were prone to cause trouble with various abuses. All proceeds of their cruises were shared between the crews and the owners, not with the states. It is estimated that more than 2000 men were engaged on privateering and that 550 letters of marque, which gave licences to make reprisals, were issued by Congress.

Since suitable ships for conversion into small warships were very few indeed, there was little difficulty in finding sufficient seamen to man possible vessels. In addition to the fishermen of the Grand Banks and the whalers, there were the crews of merchantmen who had been trading with the West Indian islands.

The idea of what came to be known as the Continental Navy, meaning a combined navy of American states, was broached in 1775 (the same year that the American Marine Corps was brought into being). It led to the building and equipping of a joint American fleet instead of ships of individual states. The Naval Committee of Congress then set up formal prize-courts and ordered matters of discipline, rations and pay, all copied from the Royal Navy.

In November 1775 the committee authorised four merchant vessels for conversion as far as possible into men-of-war. They were visualised as the first of an armed fleet to be composed of five ships of 32 guns and five of 28 guns, and three frigates of 24 guns up to 12-pounders. Also in November, manning was ordered 'with such officers as are proper to man and command'. In the subsequent list, the name appears of a senior lieutenant, the American national hero John Paul Jones. The list is a brief one; it has four first lieutenants, five second lieutenants and three third lieutenants. Surgeons, pursers, midshipmen and other warrant officers are not included.

The states were beginning to receive a great deal of nautical help from France, in spite of some disagreements. There were soon American agents in several French ports, besides a few in Spain and Holland. They actively discussed and dealt with a variety of topics such as prizes, privateers, stores and suppliers, docks and prisoners of war. For a while, however, France did not commit herself to sending material aid; she preferred to bide her time and watch events, always with an eye to England as the arch enemy.

During the course of the war the states themselves had no vessels of appreciable size; Massachusetts had 15 sea-going ships and one galley, Pennsylvania had about 10 ships, 30 boats and galleys, and Virginia from first to last had 72 ships including brigs and schooners, but they were small and weak. Other states had only small craft except Carolina with 15 sea-going vessels. In short the Continental Congress had practically nothing that could be considered a fleet. In 1777, when under a close blockade, only four frigates succeeded in cruising at sea.

Left: An engraving from Penny Magazine of the famous Boston Tea Party.
Mary Evans Picture Library

Top left: George Washington—first President of the United States. *Illustrated London News*

Above: A view of Fort George with the City of New York from the south west in about 1750.
Macpherson Collection National Maritime Museum London

Even so, during the war Britain lost a total of 625 vessels, 38 of them privateers and the rest nearly all merchantmen. The captures were often of great value to the Americans as a source of arms and supplies.

An outstanding exception to the part played by the Colonial Navy was the foray of the redoubtable John Paul Jones. Perhaps because of his mixed seafaring experience he had been sent to France to take up an important command but instead he collected a small squadron with which to harry shipping on the British coasts. He obtained an old French East Indiaman, the *Bonhomme Richard*, overhauled her and mounted extra guns and manned her with a motley crew of Americans, some renegade British seamen who had been prisoners of war, French soldiers and marines and Portuguese sailors. The ships with him, two frigates and a small brig, all had French crews, although the whole squadron flew the flag of the Congress.

Before the end of 1781 Congress reached its lowest ebb in ships. It then had only two frigates, the *Confederacy* and the *Trumball*, the sloop-of-war *Saratoga*, and the two schooners *Alliance* and *Deans* making up the whole of the navy. A 74-gun ship-of-the-line, the *America*, and a frigate, *Bourbon*, still lingered on the stocks, but at that period their navy list showed 22 captains, 39 lieutenants, with 22 marine captains and 12 lieutenants. However, a change was looming. Washington and Rochambeau, having united their armies near New York, were making ready to move either on to New York or against Cornwallis in Virginia.

Another factor was that the gifted French Admiral De Grasse was crossing the Atlantic with his main fleet, at last, to aid the Americans. In anticipation, a British fleet under Admiral Lord Howe, the brother of General Howe on shore, had been dispatched to deal with him. Unfortunately, it was not to be an equal match, nor would it have been even had the two fleets been of exactly the same number. It was notorious that the French ships were larger, stronger and of better design than had come out of English shipyards.

Worse, the British Admiralty was passing through a shameful era of corruption and disarray. The First Lord, the Earl of Sandwich, might have been held responsible but he was only one of many malefactors. At all events at least two, perhaps three, admirals of character would have nothing to do with him. There is a tale of how he at length persuaded Admiral Keppel to take command of the Channel fleet, which had, so he said, 42 ships in all, 35 of them in commission and ready for sea. Keppel went down to Portsmouth and found just 20 ships and of them only six, to use his words, were 'fit for a seaman's eye'.

At that period morale in the fleet was not by any means high and it was under strain after years of almost continuous fighting, at first with the French and then with both Spain and Holland in addition. But when the French admiral appeared off the American coast with a fleet considerably larger than could be mustered under the British flag, Admiral Howe took it in hand without fuss. With involved tactical manoeuvres that bewildered the enemy he cleverly drove them clear of New York and Rhode Island. For the next few years comparative peace reigned at sea.

Then, in 1781, the French Admiral Comte de Grasse appeared with his entire fleet. By that time General Cornwallis was on the shore of the Chesapeake, the great arm of the sea at Yorktown. Although Admiral Howe had gone home, an earlier attempt by a French squadron to enter the Chesapeake had been fought off without much difficulty by the British ships stationed there, but De Grasse was a very different proposition.

On hearing the news of his coming, the British Admiral Graves, at New York, reinforced by ships from the West Indies, sailed to the Chesapeake to protect Cornwallis. He had with him 19 ships, a strong fleet, but to his astonishment he saw moving out of Chesapeake Bay no fewer than 24 enemy ships. In fact he had caught them in no sort of battle order but cluttered up in ragged disarray. However, instead of seizing the opportunity and dashing down upon them, he merely engaged them at long range and barely half his ships came into action at all. De Grasse, having cleared the Bay, remained in indecisive touch with the British for five days and then returned to his anchorage, while Graves tamely returned to New York.

In the following spring Admiral Rodney fought the Battle of the Saints, near Dominica. Fortune favoured him after the British and French fleets had fired their initial broadsides. While they were starting for each other on opposite tacks a sudden shift of wind set the French all aback. It was a golden opportunity, grasped by Rodney, who burst through their line and showed the way to his nearest ships; others ahead and astern saw and copied their admiral, and the French were caught. The Battle of the Saints cost them seven ships of the line and a number of frigates, but no less valuable was its calamitous effect on the French West Indies.

Some historians hold that De Grasse's Battle of the Chesapeake, while insignificant as a battle, was the one final factor in the result of the War of Independence. If that is the case, had it been fought by a Nelson, a Howe, a Rodney or a Hawke, and had both England and Congress been less rigid in their attitudes, the result might well have been different indeed. But General Cornwallis had surrendered at Yorktown and Rodney's victory arrived too late.

Above: John Paul Jones shooting a sailor who had attempted to strike his colours in an engagement. *National Maritime Museum London*

Bottom: General Cornwallis's surrender at Yorktown. *Mary Evans Picture Library*

LANDING OF THE BRITISH DIVISION AT OLD FORT, NEAR SEBASTOPOL.

THE VIEW HERE REPRESENTED IS FROM THE OFF-SHORE SIDE OF THE SHIPS FROM WHICH THE TROOPS DISEMBARKED, AND FORMED LINE ABREAST ON SIGNAL FROM THE AGAMEMNON.

London Published Oct. 4th, 1854, by Read & Co., 10, Johnson's Court, Fleet Street.

NAVIES & THE CRIMEA

THE RUTHLESS destruction by the Russians in 1853 of an entire Turkish squadron at Sinope with great loss of life thrust Britain and France a year later into the Crimean War. The ambitious schemes of Tzar Nicholas, it was thought, had become too great a threat to Europe.

Already a combined British and French fleet had passed through the Dardanelles and had anchored in the Bosphorus to protect Constantinople. They entered the Black Sea in the Spring of 1854 and in March both their countries had declared war. In September, 600 ships carrying 57,000 troops, one-third of them English and two-thirds French, after a stop at Gallipoli and another at Varna on the Bulgarian coast, sailed to find a foothold in the Crimea. Under the guns of the fleet they landed on the sandy beach of Eupatoria, on the western side, and marched round to fight and win the battle of the Alma, opening the way to the citadel of Sebastopol.

While the British seized the bay and port of Balaclava and the French the bay of Kamiesch, the Russians scuttled many of their ships in order to block the huge roadstead on the seaward side of Sebastopol in preparation for a long and bloody siege.

Following what had become customary practice, the British Navy adopted an additional role to help the troops with artillery. In the space of a few days more than 60 guns had been hoisted out of the British warships and brought ashore. They were hauled into position and manned by 1800 seamen formed into a Naval Brigade, with 1500 marines holding the heights above Balaclava.

On October 16, 1854, all was ready for a preliminary bombardment of the southern defences of Sebastopol. The ships of the two navies shelled the forts at the harbour mouth in order to keep them engaged while the main attack was being made on shore. Early the following morning all the artillery opened fire in a ferocious cannonade. But just before the real assault started there came from the French lines a tremendous explosion which silenced their guns; magazines had blown up.

Unaware of what had happened, the British gunners carried on firing without support from the French on shore. But the combined fleets took up their positions to seaward, the sailing vessels being towed by steamships on their farther sides. Five of the big ships composed an inshore squadron to harass the northern defences, including the chief fortress, Fort Constantine, which mounted 100 guns.

Rear-Admiral Sir Edmund Lyons, profiting from previous experience, did his utmost to close well in with his flagship, the *Agamemnon*, but a shoal prevented his getting nearer than 800 yards. There, with HMS *Sanspareil* in support and his other three ships not far away, the remainder of the British and French fleets lay in a line firing some little distance off. Though most of the enemy's projectiles splashed high into the sea, the squadron had to endure the worst of an unending stream of shell-fire and red-hot shot.

Top: Painting in the National Maritime Museum of the British landing near Sebastopol, with the 'Agamemnon' prominent at left centre.
National Maritime Museum London (photo D Rudkin)

Above: Impression of a steam paddle frigate of the type in common use at the time of the Crimean War. *M Muir Collection*

The *Agamemnon's* broadsides were achieving results on the main fort and one lucky shot caused an explosion, followed by a temporary lull, but when the guns restarted one by one she and two other ships were set on fire and had to be towed clear. Rear-Admiral Dundas, away to seaward, sent in two of his ships to their support and at length, late in the afternoon, with 310 casualties and five battered vessels much in need of repairs, the fleet retired.

While the Black Sea Fleet took its part thus in the long siege, another combined fleet sailed in the Baltic. With the naval base of Kronstadt well in mind, the Admiralty had sent Vice-Admiral Sir Charles Napier into the Baltic with a powerful fleet. He had as his flagship a big newly commissioned three-decker, the *Duke of Wellington* of 130 guns, which was propelled by steam. When he sailed from Portsmouth, Napier had been wished God-speed by the Queen and a family party on her yacht *Fairy*.

Napier, once noted for his energy and capability, was then 68 years of age and perhaps his years told. While the Russians kept to the security of Kronstadt, he did little more than patrol and capture an occasional merchantman. When he was joined two weeks later by a French fleet of eight sail-of-the-line and a number of frigates, under the command of Vice-Admiral Deschesmes, the two of them made a good attempt to lure out the Russian fleet from Kronstadt but failed. They agreed that the fortress was too strong for them to attack.

Instead, they reconnoitred another and quite important naval fortress at Sveabourg, also in the Gulf of Finland, and decided that with the aid of troops it could be taken. Admiral Deschesmes asked for and was sent 9000 soldiers and in August a combined land and sea force took fort after fort, ending with the main fortress, which was destroyed and evacuated. The French returned home when ice began to form and were followed some little time later by Napier.

Rear Admiral Dundas in the Black Sea also took his squadron home with the onset of winter. In the following spring he returned and led his ships into the Baltic. With them went gunboats and mortar-ships that had been specially built for the operation.

The admiral of a recently arrived French squadron was quite eager to take part in an attack on Sveabourg, a strongly defended group of five islands which had lately been strengthened by the addition of new batteries. To demonstrate what the gunboats and mortar-ships could do, they were assigned to the first line and soon after they had gone into action the effect showed in rising clouds of smoke; after three hours the buildings on the islands were mostly in flames. Then rocket-boats took over the attack, which was continued until after the coming of daylight. The following night Sveabourg appeared as one continuous sheet of flame and the admirals were content.

Meanwhile, in the Crimea the siege of Sebastopol continued with a series of battles and bombardments, but the final assault had still to come. In order to quicken matters Sir Edmund Lyons determined to occupy the Sea of Azoff and put a stop to the supply of grain to the fortress. Troops were landed and they captured the town of Kerch, while English and French crews destroyed great stocks that were waiting to be smuggled into Sebastopol.

In the Crimea, at Balaclava and other small harbours the numbers of merchant ships must have swelled as time went on to an unforgettable sight. They were always in demand for a variety of duties, from troop transports to victuallers and for moving supplies generally; and there were the wounded – 'We are taking down daily large numbers of sick and wounded and could carry many more if there were ships to carry them', declared the commander of the Ambulance Corps, Major John Grant, speaking from his camp before Sebastopol in June 1855, according to family papers with his descendant Captain Ivar Mackay.

The major was evidently no enthusiastic admirer of either the Royal Navy or the merchant captains. 'There are at the Navy offices plenty of officials. An Admiral, two Captains in the Navy, Lieutenants, Secretaries and Clerks innumerable. They are to be found at their posts at 9 o'clock. The Admiral sits in his office, so do Captain P and Q and Lieuts A, B, C and D and the clerks, all in uniform and spotless linen. They have work to do in their offices – perhaps as much as they can do. There is one man to give the orders for coal, another for water, another for passages. But there is no one to see that the orders are carried out'.

At the beginning of September the allied armies had worked up close to the enemy. Apart from French batteries, 200 British guns were in readiness – double the number which had started the siege the year before. The fleet had provided a big proportion of the guns and 50 were manned by the Naval Brigade and Marines. From a vantage-point mortars were flinging their great bombs into the enemy's works. The final bombardment began on September 5 and continued for two more days before the assault, which routed the Russians. Many of them vanished; they escaped from the south side of Sebastopol by a bridge of boats which had been made in readiness. The great siege which had lasted a year was at an end. It had cost the British 22,000 men, the French 80,000, the Turks 35,000, the Italians 2200 and the Russians 120,000, a total of 259,200 casualties, quite a proportion of them victims of disease and sickness rather than enemy action.

The Royal Navy's casualties had been few except for the Navy Brigade. Between October 1854 and September 1855 nearly 4500 officers, seamen and marines had been landed from the fleet to keep the brigade up to strength. In those 11 months five officers and 95 men had been killed and 38 officers and 487 men were wounded. No fewer than 20 Victoria Crosses had been awarded in the brigade and four others were awarded in the fleet. Among naval winners of the VC was Lieutenant Charles David Lucas 'for having picked up and thrown overboard a live shell from the *Heckla* while the fuse was burning'.

The Battle of Sinope and the Crimean War heralded several major developments in naval warfare. One immediate consequence was that Emperor Napoleon III ordered and had built in 1854 three vessels at first called floating batteries; they were named *Dévastation*, *Lave* and *Tonnante* and were of 1600 tons displacement, low in the water and intended only for coastal use. Being of shallow draught, they were not craft to handle well in a seaway. They were single-screw ships of low power, making at most four knots in tideless waters. They were armoured with $4\frac{1}{2}$-inch-thick plate and carried 16 smooth-bore 50-pounders and a couple of small guns.

Above: Impression of a Russian steamer delivering dispatches for Admiral Dundas under a flag of truce. *Illustrated London News*

The three vessels were sent to the Crimea and on October 17, 1855, they engaged in their first action, shelling Kinburn, the main Russian fort at the entrance to the Dnieper. Closing to within 920-1200 yards range of the fort, they silenced its guns in four hours. The *Dévastation* took 64 hits on her armour and the *Tonnante* suffered 60 but neither was seriously damaged.

Not for the first time in naval history, the British Admiralty followed the French lead quite speedily. They went so far as to order eight floating batteries; *Glatton*, *Meteor*, *Etna*, *Thunder* and *Trusty* were the names of the first batch of five vessels and *Erebus*, *Terror* and *Thunderbolt* formed a second batch. The first group were built of wood with iron patches and were 172 feet long but the last three were iron framed, had plating 4.3 inches thick and were 187 feet long.

From the Crimean vessels were developed, in a lengthy sequence, the great coastal monitors of the 1914-18 war, with their shallow draught, thick armour, heavy guns and no pretensions to speed. They gave good service, particularly in the bombardment of German batteries along the Belgian coast. But they were ships of a highly specialised type whose day has gone and there are scarcely any to be found in the navies of the world today.

SPANISH-AMERICAN WAR

THE YEAR 1898 saw insurrection in Cuba as Nationalists tried to oust Spanish rule. To safeguard American lives and interests, the USS *Maine* was sent to Santiago where she was mysteriously destroyed by a sudden explosion with great loss of life. Anticipating the results of the inquiry—which subsequently did *not* rule out instability in her own explosives—the US Government declared war on Spain.

As America was not a major naval power at that time and its fleet was divided into two by the Panama Isthmus still unsevered by a canal, the disparity in size was not as great as would appear at first sight. Even so, neglected for many years, the Spanish Navy was hopelessly outclassed by the US Navy when war came in April 1898. Spain's one battleship took no part in the fighting, and the best ships that did were four armoured cruisers, of which one—the ex-Italian *Cristobal Colon*—was only partially armed and awaiting new guns that never came. The Americans had five battleships and a strong cruiser force in active commission.

War found the Spanish Pacific Squadron (Admiral Montojo) at Manila with two of its ships under repair and all, as an American officer put it, 'old tubs not fit to be called warships'. The US East Asiatic Squadron (Commodore Dewey) easily destroyed them on May Day 1898 in their anchorage at the Battle of Cavite (or Manila Bay). The Spaniards had 381 casualties, the Americans had eight slightly wounded.

The Spanish Atlantic Squadron (Admiral Cervera), comprising the four cruisers and two torpedo boats, reached Santiago de Cuba only to be blockaded there by four battleships, two cruisers and several smaller ships, under Admiral Sampson. The Spaniards lay behind minefields and were covered by shore batteries. The Americans could not approach to sweep without neutralising the guns, so 16,000 troops were landed to take Santiago. Although their progress was unspectacular, it was sufficient to force the Spanish squadron to sea.

Ordered to sea by Havana on what amounted to a naval 'charge of the Light Brigade', on July 3 the Spaniards left harbour to face the desperate odds against them with the same fiery courage as their comrades at Cavite. The ships' bunkers were nearly empty, but if the coal held out long enough Cervera thought it might be just possible to outpace the battleships and then have a fighting chance against the American cruisers.

The battle was fought very close inshore, with the Spanish ships between the Americans and the land. The two torpedo-boats tried to cause a diversion but before they could get into torpedo range one was sunk and the other became a blazing wreck burning out her life. First to feel the impact of the 13-inch and 12-inch battleship shells and the 8-inch shells of the cruisers was Cervera's flagship *Maria Teresa* (Captain Concas), on fire and sinking when beached 6½ miles from Santiago. Next, the *Almirante*

Above right: The Spanish armoured cruiser 'Vizcaya' at Santiago, photographed from an American battleship. *K Fenwick Collection*

This picture: A painting by Charles de Lacy of the US battleships 'Iowa' and 'Indiana' in action at Santiago. *K Fenwick Collection*

Left: Gun drill on board the 'Vizcaya' before she sailed for Santiago. *K Fenwick Collection*

Left centre: An 1898 photograph of the forecastle of the US battleship 'Iowa' showing a pair of her four 13-inch guns and (right background) two of her 8-inch guns. *K Fenwick Collection*

Bottom: Part of an illustration in the 'Illustrated London News' of May 21, 1898, showing the entrance to the harbour of Havana. *Illustrated London News*

Oquendo (Captain Lazaga), aflame in a dozen places, ran aground and blew up.

With obsolescent and defective guns and old ammunition that had deteriorated in the tropical heat, her coal bunkers on fire and funnels glowing red hot, the *Vizcaya* (Captain Eulate) single-handed fought the battleships *Oregon*, *Texas* and *Iowa* and the cruiser *Brooklyn*, sacrificing herself in the hope of saving her one surviving consort whose speed offered a faint chance of escape. In vain. With boilers hit and belching steam, ammunition readied round the guns burning and exploding, the *Vizcaya* drove ashore and immediately afterwards three violent explosions split her in two.

The solitary *Cristobal Colon* (Captain Moreu) had drawn out of range; but fast steaming had used up her coal and as her speed fell the *Oregon* and *Brooklyn* got into range. The water was too shallow for her to sink and she grounded at the mouth of the River Tarquino, 70 miles from Santiago. Spain lost 500 killed or wounded; the Americans one killed, nine wounded and one accidentally injured.

The United States emerged from the war a colonial and world power requiring a larger navy to maintain her new status and guard the empire she had taken from Spain. But American occupation of the Philippines and other island bases aroused Japanese suspicions and made it certain that some day there would be a headlong collision between the two rising and very ambitious nations.

Battle of the Yalu River

IN THE LATE 19th century, Western technology was more efficiently acquired by the Japanese than by the Chinese, a fact devastatingly proved in 1894 when the new armaments were used in an old quarrel. Sino-Japanese friction over Korea was centuries old. It was renewed in July 1894 when both sides sent troops there after an uprising against the Korean government. War was declared on August 1.

Matters were virtually resolved on September 17, when the British-trained Japanese navy, fighting with remarkable coordination, trapped the Chinese fleet between its two squadrons in the battle of the Yalu River. In the crossfire of the Japanese quick-firing guns, seven out of 12 Chinese ships were devastated.

The battle lasted five hours, until nightfall, when Japanese fear of torpedo boat attack prompted them to break off. The Japanese commander, Vice Admiral Ito, apparently intended to resume by daylight but in the event did not do so. There was no need, for he had achieved his purpose. Their Yalu River victory gave the Japanese command of the Yellow Sea, so denying reinforcements to the Chinese armies in Korea. Without them, the Chinese effort in Korea was doomed and their ultimate defeat became inevitable.

Above left: A Japanese sketch of a Japanese-Chinese engagement during the war of 1894, from the book 'Japan's Fight for Freedom' by H W Wilson. *K Fenwick Collection*

Left: The Japanese cruiser 'Naniwa' attacking the sinking Chinese troopship 'Kowshing', from a Caton-Woodville drawing in 'Japan's Fight for Freedom'. *K Fenwick Collection*

Below: A painting by M J Barton of the Chinese cruiser 'Chih Yuen' attempting to break the Japanese line at Yalu.

THE RUSSO-JAPANESE WAR

TOWARDS THE END of the 19th century Japan, so lately emerged from her medieval past, was rapidly asserting herself as an advancing nation. Already she had gained a modern navy that had been trained by British naval officers and an army taught by Germans. Under Tsar Nicholas II the cumbersome Russian bear had formed a consortium with Germany and France. Then in spite of the defensive compact Britain shared with Japan, Russia had seized Manchuria with the vital naval base of Port Arthur, on the east coast of Korea Bay, to balance her grip on the other strategic harbour of Vladivostok. Now, if she stretched southward into Korea, Japan would lie at her mercy.

After a lengthy period of tension the Japanese took action. They issued an ultimatum and then on February 7, 1904, three days before a declaration of war, their main fleet escorted transports to South Korea and landed troops to seize Seoul. In command of the fleet was Vice-Admiral Togo, who had come to the fore during the war with China. Aged 57, and noted for his determination and courage, he had spent some time in England and had been trained in the *Worcester*. The fleet under his control was at a high pitch of eager efficiency.

Actually Japan was the stronger at sea in the area, having six excellent battleships, six powerful armoured cruisers and a large number of new torpedo-boat destroyers, British designed and many built in England. The battleships carried four 12-inch guns in two barbettes and 6-inch guns behind a thick steel armoured belt. Although they were roughly of the same period as the Russian ships, they had the advantage that all were of similar type while the Russians were a motley mixture of varying strength and gunpower. But time was not on the side of the Japanese. Unlike their enemies, they had no reserve of ships to fall back on; their future relied largely on the guns of the six battleships.

The official view in Moscow of the outcome was expressed by Rear-Admiral Vitgeft, the chief of the Russian Naval staff in the Far East. He announced: 'Our fleet cannot be beaten by the Japanese fleet and so their landing is absolutely impossible whether in the Gulf of Korea or in the Yellow Sea or elsewhere'. The Russian Admiralty made its dispositions accordingly.

The first shots of the war at sea were fired when two Russian vessels, the fast cruiser *Variag* and the sloop *Korietz*, gallantly left a South Korean port to attack the Japanese fleet. The sloop was barely touched but the *Variag* was shelled almost into a wreck,

Left: The badly battered Russian battleship 'Tsarevitch' pictured after the fight off Port Arthur on August 10, 1904. *The Sphere*

Above: A drawing by S Begg of the minelaying operations undertaken by the Russian ship 'Yenesei' in 1904; she was later destroyed by one of her own mines. *Illustrated London News*

Below: The Japanese warship 'Mikasa', Admiral Togo's flagship at the battle of Tsushima, seen here in Sasebo harbour in March 1908.
Courtesy of Lt Cdr Shizuo Fukui (M Muir Collection)

Right: A painting by Norman Wilkinson of the shocking attack by Russian warships on a British fishing fleet in the North Sea in October 1904; the drifter 'Crane' (centre) is sinking while the 'Gull' (foreground) stands by to rescue survivors.
Illustrated London News

Below right: A drawing by H W Koekkoek of Admiral Togo directing the Japanese offensive against Port Arthur from the bridge of the 'Mikasa' in 1904; Togo has been dubbed 'the Japanese Nelson'.
Illustrated London News

with 222 casualties. She herself had fired 425 6-inch and 470 12-pounder shots and approximately 200 shells, without scoring a single hit. Both the vessels were scuttled by their captains rather than have them fall into Japanese hands.

On February 8 the main Russian fleet was lying at anchor outside the harbour of Port Arthur. Most of the destroyers were in the harbour, some of them coaling. The shore batteries were unready for action. All were unaware of the approach of the Japanese fleet. At nightfall Togo sent in destroyers to make a torpedo attack. It was a disorderly affair but it yielded immeasurable results. A total of 18 torpedoes fired caused explosions in two Russian battleships and a heavy cruiser, and shook Russian pride and morale. In exchanges of fire the next day, in which the Russian shore batteries joined, Togo's flagship *Mikasa* was hit and there were casualties on both sides, but the Russians suffering twice as many as the Japanese.

After the first exchanges the Russians at Port Arthur laid very large minefields on the approaches, and lost one of their own minelayers and a cruiser on the mines. Togo tried, not very successfully, to block the narrow harbour entrance with five old merchant ships. In early March Vice-Admiral Makaroff, recently appointed Russian C-in-C Far East, arrived and at once ordered nightly patrols by his destroyers. Several fierce encounters with the Japanese destroyers resulted but with inconclusive results. Makaroff exercised the Port Arthur fleet and witnessed two of the battleships accidentally ram each other, crippling them both.

Meanwhile, the Japanese had mined the Port Arthur approaches and in May Makaroff's flagship *Petropavlovsk* struck one of the mines and sank, taking the admiral, 32 officers and 600 men. One captain wrote sadly of Makaroff: 'With him, all hope of rendering the squadron efficient was buried'. A second battleship, the *Pobieda*, was also mined but remained afloat; the Russians were reduced to three battleships ready for action and two under repair.

At sea in a single day in May Japan lost two battleships by mines and one armoured cruiser by collision, but the Russian Admiral Vitgeft, after starting off with his fleet to take advantage of the losses, had second thoughts. He returned to Port Arthur only to spend the night under continuous attack from torpedo craft.

At last the two fleets met in a general action on August 10. They started on equal terms but the battle was transformed when two 12-inch shells hit Vitgeft's flagship, *Tsarevitch*, killing him and driving the ship out of control. The remaining five battle-

ships broke off the action and managed to reach Port Arthur, but most of the other Russian ships took shelter in neutral ports on various excuses and were interned. That was the last action of the Russian battleships. In the meantime a Japanese military force had made a landing behind Port Arthur but made little headway against the guns of the garrison and the ships until they set up an observation post on the summit of an overlooking hill. At a frightful cost in lives the troops climbed the hill and directed the fire of their 11-inch howitzers on to the Russian defenders. On January 1, 1905, Port Arthur surrendered and the surviving ships were scuttled by their crews.

Based at Vladivostok, a squadron of three cruisers and some torpedo-boats had been harrying Japanese coast and shipping in general. Under the command of Rear-Admiral Jessen they had much success, particularly in July, capturing and sinking Japanese and neutral ships found carrying warlike cargoes. Caught at last by Rear-Admiral Kamimura, commanding four armoured cruisers, they escaped to Vladivostok, with the loss of their oldest and weakest ship, the cruiser *Rurik*. Kamimura had the area heavily mined and left them to their own resources.

Meanwhile, slowly making their way eastward, were the ships of the Russian Baltic fleet, which should have been sent as reinforcements far earlier. Not until October 15 did the first part of the fleet sail from Libau and even then there was no hurry. Vice-Admiral Rojestvensky, who was in command, had a splendid reputation but not for haste. He led seven battleships, two old armoured cruisers, four light cruisers, seven destroyers and a number of auxiliary vessels. They had an inauspicious start. Strangely overtaken by fright, some gunners fired on Norwegian ships in the Skaw and, in daylight one auxiliary attacked a Swedish steamer, a French sailing ship and a German trawler.

At night the Russians steamed through the middle of a British fishing fleet on the Dogger Bank and opened fire, fancying them to be hiding Japanese torpedo-boats. In the panic gunners fired on their own *Aurora* mortally wounding her chaplain, but they also killed a trawlerman and wounded six others as well as sinking a trawler. The British Government just avoided declaring war on Russia and ordered British cruisers to escort Rojestvensky's ships as far as Tangier.

Rojestvensky disregarded international law regarding the stay of warships in neutral ports. The specified limit was 24 hours, but he stayed for three months or so on the coast of Madagascar. There, a telegraphed message from his government asking for his views on the outlook elicited the reply, 'I have not the slightest prospect of recovering command of the sea with the force under my orders'. His government then sent to join him a scratch mixed squadron of old and small ships of little fighting value commanded by Rear-Admiral Nebogatoff.

Of the several possible routes to Vladivostok, Rojestvensky chose the Straits of Korea. Wireless signals warned Admiral Togo of his coming and at 04.30 on May 27 his ships were sighted from a scouting cruiser. By about two o'clock that afternoon the two fleets were in contact at the start of the Battle of Tsushima, in which the Russian Fleet was annihilated by superior Japanese ships, weapons and command, and the course of history in the Far East for the next half-century was determined.

Tsushima is also notable for having been the last clearcut naval victory until the 1939–45 war and the only one that involved pre-dreadnought battleships (eight Russian and four Japanese); it was also the first in which radio communication and destroyers were used. Aspects of the action that attracted naval interest included the major role played by armoured cruisers, the general ineffectiveness of the secondary 6-inch armament in battleships, and that neither side had attempted to use the ram (which was still a feature of most warships) and that that anachronism could at last be abolished.

Top: A Japanese postcard depicting the third blockade fleet at Port Arthur. *L Dunn*

Above left: Facsimile of a coloured sketch by a Japanese war artist showing the firing of a gun on a warship during the Russo/Japanese conflict. *M Muir Collection*

Left: A photograph taken from the book entitled 'With Togo' by Seppings Wright, showing the Armstrong gun on a Japanese cruiser. *Seppings Wright*

The First World War

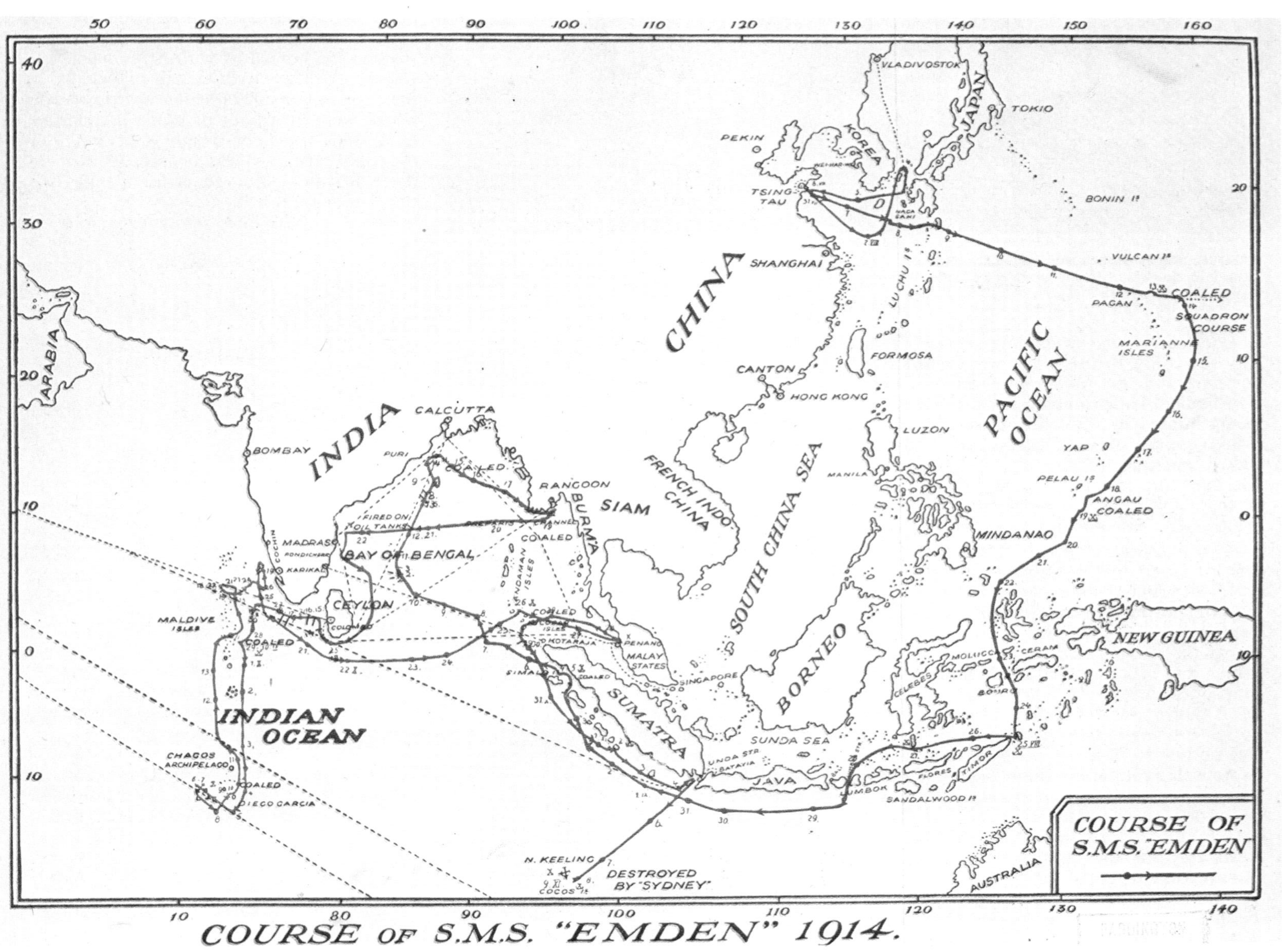

A map of the course followed by the 'Emden' in 1914 as presented in the book 'Emden' by Prince Franz Joseph.
By courtesy of Prince Franz Joseph

THE ROYAL NAVY'S prime function in the First World War was the time-honoured one of guarding against the invasion of the British Isles by maintaining control of the North Sea. Its secondary duties, with ships spread across the globe, were the protection of friendly shipping, the destruction of the enemy, the stopping of his seaborne supplies, the safeguarding of British troops in transit and the shelling of enemy batteries and installations along the Belgian coast, giving invaluable aid to the Allies and culminating in 1918 in the epic raid at Zeebrugge.

The Zeebrugge raid, forerunner of the many commando strikes against the European coast in the Second World War, earned an early and characteristically ringing tribute, from Winston Churchill. He called it 'The finest feat of arms in the Great War and an episode unsurpassed in the history of the Royal Navy'. The raid which earned such an accolade was designed to deprive the Germans of Ostend and Zeebrugge, the ports at which two canals reached the sea from Bruges, where three flotillas of German torpedo boats and about 30 U-boats were based.

After two abortive starts, the raid finally got under way on the afternoon of April 22, 1918. The action which ensued witnessed gallantry of the highest calibre and tragic loss of life, made all the more poignant bv the fact that the Zeebrugge raid was only partially successful and the Ostend raid not at all. Nevertheless, a submarine and three blockships were sunk against Zeebrugge lock gates and the landing parties inflicted much damage.

An important, if less tangible casualty, was German morale. It was ebbing very low at the time and in the context of naval war had never been appreciable. This was understandable, for there were not many sources of proper pride for the German Navy in the 1914-18 war. Unlike the Royal Navy, with its lustrous history and Senior Service confidence, the Germans lacked the guidance of naval traditions. Despite a fleet of well-designed ships, and well-trained officers and men, the Navy took second place in German national regard to the Army and had no developed naval war staff behind it. It suffered the further handicap of having no direct access to the open sea, other than the narrow English Channel or the passage between Norway and the Scottish coast, and the disadvantage that German naval policy was primarily defensive, while the British was offensive. This was not to say that the German Navy lacked its successes. On the contrary it administered, on occasion, some severe shocks and frights to its opponents. For instance, German U-boats posed a nearly fatal threat and the exploits of the commerce raider *Emden* became an adventure epic of the war at sea.

The light cruiser *Emden* belonged to Admiral Graf von Spee's East Asiatic Squadron, originally based on Tsingtau, in the German concession of Kiachau in China. When Japan seemed likely to enter the war on the Allied side, von Spee had to leave Tsingtau and since Germany had no dependable coaling stations, he split up his squadron of eight cruisers and two armed merchantmen. The latter were quickly caught by British ships, while six cruisers sailed separately to rendezvous in the Pacific. That left *Emden* and *Königsberg*, both of which made for the Indian Ocean and embarked on bouts of commerce raiding.

The *Königsberg*, commanded by Captain Looff, spent a fruitful week on the trade routes off Aden, where he first captured and later, on August 6, sank the 6000-ton SS *City of Winchester*. Then, lacking other prey, he turned his ship south for an anchorage in the delta of the Rufiji River. In mid-September *Königsberg* sailed to Zanzibar, where it surprised and sank the *Pegasus* before returning to the Rufiji delta.

Above: Super dreadnoughts of the British Navy in double column headed by 'Iron Duke' and 'Marlborough'. *Illustrated London News*

Looff hoped to remain concealed from any searching British ship in the mangrove swamps while the *Königsberg*'s engines were overhauled. Unfortunately for Looff, he was being hunted by the light cruiser *Chatham*, whose captain, S. R. Drury-Lowe, had collected enough information to locate the German ship inside the creek and he sealed it there by sinking a blockship at the entrance. The rest was not so simple.

Two attempts to get at *Königsberg* from the air failed in December 1914 and April 1915, although the blockade was strengthened after wireless messages had been intercepted between *Königsberg* and the *Kronborg*, the former British steamer *Rubens* which had been interned in Hamburg at the start of the war and had arrived at the island of Aldabra, in the Indian Ocean, hoping to serve *Königsberg* as a coaling ship during her raiding forays.

As well as stiffening the blockade, Drury-Lowe proposed also to put two 1260-ton monitors up the Rufiji River in a direct attack on the German ship, but had to wait until July for the monitors to reach East Africa from Britain.

The two monitors needed two attempts before they finally succeeded in sinking *Königsberg*. Hammered from less than 1000 yards and fighting back vigorously, the cruiser suffered an explosion on board at 13.15 on July 14. Fire broke out and, at length, spotter aircraft overhead reported 'Target destroyed'. Looff, who was injured, abandoned ship and with other survivors escaped into the surrounding jungle. The *Kronborg*, née *Rubens*, had already come to grief on April 14; she was chased by the British cruiser *Hyacinth* and was later found abandoned in Manza Bay. Her captain and crew also escaped into the bush.

While the protracted siege of *Königsberg* took place, Captain von Muller in *Emden* had set up a phenomenal record. In 70 days during the latter part of 1914 *Emden* claimed no fewer than 23 Allied ships. She started in the Bay of Bengal, where she sank or captured eight merchant vessels (September 10 to 14) and renewed her coal stores from some of them. The intrusion caused such alarm that vessels trading in the bay were held in port and all traffic stopped on the Colombo-Singapore route. Before she was finally trapped and driven ashore by the Australian light cruiser *Sydney*, near the Cocos Islands on November 9 *Emden* eluded her frantic hunters for eight weeks, to claim six ships near Ceylon and a Russian cruiser and French destroyer at Penang, and to bombard Madras.

Eight days before von Muller and *Emden* succumbed, his commander, Admiral von Spee, with five cruisers, encountered four cruisers of the British West Indies Squadron under Rear Admiral Cradock at Coronel, off the Chilean coast. Von Spee's ships had done some mild commerce raiding in the Pacific and at Pernambuco before being driven back through the Magellan Straits by the threatening presence of British and French warships.

At 18.18 on November 1, 1914, despite the inferiority of his force, Cradock decided to engage von Spee. Disaster ensued. At 19.00 hours, when the British ships were silhouetted against the afterglow of the sunset, von Spee closed to 12,000 yards and his armoured cruisers *Scharnhorst* and *Gneisenau* began pounding Cradock's armoured cruisers *Good Hope* and *Monmouth* to such devastating effect that within 45 minutes both were ablaze. The *Good Hope*, Cradock's flagship, blew up at 19.50 and *Monmouth* was later sunk by one of the German light cruisers. The other two British ships escaped in the darkness.

Despite von Spee's victory, the first serious British naval defeat for over a century, the German admiral was ordered home, since cruiser warfare by then was thought by the Germans to offer few prospects of success. However, von Spee delayed a full month before rounding Cape Horn, and then interrupted his Atlantic voyage to raid the Falkland Islands. There the Royal Navy exacted its revenge. Thinking the Falklands undefended, von Spee attacked Stanley Harbour on December 8. He was challenged by two fast 17,250-ton dreadnought battlecruisers, *Inflexible* and *Invincible*, which had been specially dispatched to the South Atlantic to reinforce British naval strength there.

The two battlecruisers opened fire at about 16,000 yards and, after ordering three light cruisers to escape, Graf Spee confronted the holocaust with *Scharnhorst* and *Gneisenau*. They were struck repeatedly by the 12-inch guns of *Inflexible* and *Invincible*, which were firing out of range of the German ships, both of which were sunk. Of the light cruisers which were chased by three British armoured cruisers only one, the *Dresden*, got away.

Three months later *Inflexible* and *Invincible* were engaged in a far less successful, in fact tragic, endeavour. In company with the 15-inch-gunned *Queen Elizabeth* and 14 pre-dreadnoughts and French battleships, *Inflexible* was shelling the Turkish forts in the Dardanelles in the hope of sailing up to Constantinople if all went well. It went ill. There were three bombardments between March 2 and 8, each hampered by shortage of ammunition and lack of accurate spotting and none doing any serious damage. In a further bombardment on March 18 answering Turkish fire set *Inflexible's* forebridge ablaze and the *Agamemnon* was hit 12 times in under 30 minutes.

A momentary slackening of Turkish fire encouraged Allied minesweepers to enter the Narrows and start clearing a 900 yard-wide channel through the minefield. Reserve battleships, following behind, came to appalling grief. Just after 14.00 the French pre-dreadnought *Buvet* blew up in Erenkoy Bay and disappeared in a cloud of steam and smoke, taking nearly 600 men with her. Two hours later both *Inflexible* and *Irre-*

Above: The German heavy cruiser 'Blücher' which was caught and sunk by Admiral Beatty's battlecruisers in the North Sea. *L Dunn Collection*

Right: Action at the Battle of Jutland on May 31, 1916, taken from a painting by W L Wyllie RA. *By courtesy of the United Services Club*

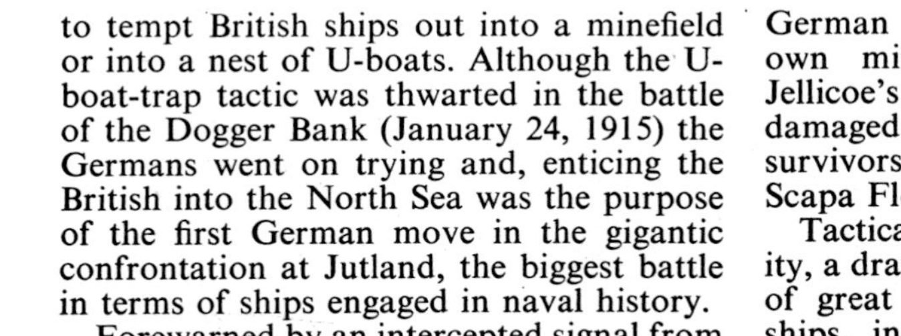

sistible struck mines and the Allied action had to be terminated.

It was then decided that before mine-sweeping could take place, troops would have to land to capture and neutralise Turkish artillery positions. The enormous blunder of pitting warships against fortresses in an attempt at invasion by naval forces alone was therefore followed by the tragedy of the Gallipoli land expedition, which cost the Allies 252,000 casualties.

The lack of success achieved by their own naval tactics, with cruiser commerce raiders, had by then prompted the Germans to try other methods. Already in November and December 1914 there was a series of hit-and-run raids on the English coast, which did much damage and killed over 100 people. Apparently the object of the slaughter was to tempt British ships out into a minefield or into a nest of U-boats. Although the U-boat-trap tactic was thwarted in the battle of the Dogger Bank (January 24, 1915) the Germans went on trying and, enticing the British into the North Sea was the purpose of the first German move in the gigantic confrontation at Jutland, the biggest battle in terms of ships engaged in naval history.

Forewarned by an intercepted signal from the German commander, Admiral Scheer, the British Grand Fleet, under Admiral Jellicoe, made for the Skagerrak to bar the Germans' path. As the German High Seas Fleet left harbour at 02.20 on May 31, 1916, first shots were being exchanged by the advanced cruisers of both sides. In the series of turns, counter turns, chases, torpedo attacks and gun actions which followed, the German fleet was nearly trapped inside a converging arc. However, between 18.35 and dusk Scheer executed a series of 180-degree turns which took his fleet snaking out of the trap and fleeing for its home ports.

Knowing that the British force was being rushed to block his way, Scheer hammered to safety in a ferocious night battle fought so closely that it involved several collisions. Eventually Scheer got clear and the surviving German ships reached safety behind their own minefields. Nothing remained for Jellicoe's Grand Fleet but to search for damaged German vessels and any British survivors, before returning to Rosyth and Scapa Flow.

Tactically Jutland was that naval curiosity, a drawn battle. In this last of a long line of great fleet actions the British lost 14 ships, including three battlecruisers – all victims of magazine explosions – and 6090 dead, and the Germans 11 ships and 2550 dead. Nevertheless, Jutland convinced the Germans that they could not overcome the Royal Navy in formal confrontation. For the later years of the war, therefore, they pinned their chief hopes on their U-boats.

The U-boats came whisker-close to striking a fatal blow and the effect on Allied morale of an unseen enemy attacking out of the deep blue sea was truly a chilling one. The first chill had been experienced when three British Bacchante-class cruisers, *Hogue Cressy* and *Aboukir*, were torpedoed off the Dutch coast and sunk with the loss of 1459 men (September 22, 1914). The sinkings were a profound shock and nullified the belief of British naval opinion that trade routes could be adequately protected by patrolling warships.

Several of the protecting ships were former passenger liners converted into armed merchant cruisers. Although none was a match for a regular warship, they could face enemy auxiliary cruisers on reasonably equal terms. Armed merchant cruisers were therefore used as part of the distant blockade developed by November 1914 to control neutral shipping and prevent vital supplies of raw materials reaching Germany.

It had to be distant, because submarines and mine warfare had rendered close blockade impossible. Such duties were also arduous and tedious and, in stormy northern waters, frequently dangerous. The patrol line between the Orkneys, Iceland and Norway had originally been policed by the 10th Cruiser Squadron, but its ageing Edgar-class vessels proved unequal to the task and they were soon replaced by an assortment of armed merchant cruisers with better sea-keeping qualities.

However, as the U-boats moved farther and farther afield, the task of protection became increasingly difficult, and increasingly unsuccessful. Even before unrestricted submarine warfare began on January 31, 1917, British shipping was suffering alarmingly and afterwards the situation grew worse and the total of destroyed merchantmen mounted so greatly that the Germans were soon confidently predicting that Britain would soon be starved out.

It was no groundless boast. No fewer than 800 ships totalling nearly two million tons were sunk between February and the end of April 1917. With this sort of war being waged, the Admiralty was forced to look harder at its defensive measures. The Admiralty already had its Q-ships, small decoy vessels of the coastal trader type with concealed guns, which, after an unsuccessful start in 1914, had made quite a mark on the war against the U-boats. What the Q-ships did was to play the part of a slovenly coaster inviting attack by a surface submarine, and then unexpectedly answering it with gunfire.

However, closer and more-direct defence was imperative. The situation was that 100 German U-boats had sunk about 1360 ships by the end of 1916, and the thousands of surface antisubmarine craft, 70 airships and a huge number of patrolling seaplanes and flying-boats had, in reply, sunk a mere four U-boats. What was more, there were still sufficient surface raiders about to endanger the regular trade routes. With the failure of the Admiralty's first remedy, a huge increase in the patrol system, the only recourse was to readopt the old convoy system. In addition, merchant ships were armed with guns.

There were problems with providing sufficiently powerful escorts for convoys, particularly as the best candidates, destroyers, were in short supply. However, the 10th Cruiser Squadron, with its long experience of sea patrolling, was able to provide particularly valuable escort, and by November 1917 the convoy system was operating both homeward and outward and in the Mediterranean. Success was immediate. Losses in convoy were only one-tenth of those among independently sailing ships and escorts were inflicting heavy losses on the U-boats.

There was, of course, a backlash, for with the introduction of convoys no ships in or near British home waters were safe from unexpected attack, not even hospital ships, which succumbed in appalling numbers. Such was the slaughter that the still determinedly neutral Americans grew increasingly restive, an understandable reaction since American ships and lives were being destroyed. This was no sudden upsurge of emotion. Such response had been boiling up ever since May 7, 1915, with the sinking of the *Lusitania*, which was carrying 188 American citizens at the time. The torpedoing of *Lusitania* by a U-boat 12 miles off the Irish coast became an international emotional *cause célebre*, producing melodramatic accusations about German 'blood lust' and 'moral leprosy'.

The fact was, however, that *Lusitania* was no innocent passenger ship, but little short of a floating arsenal carrying about 11 tons of explosives among her cargo. The wave of righteous anger took no account of this, and two years later the depredations of the U-boats revived emotions and led the United States to declare war. The entry of a fresh, and mammoth, force into the struggle against them doomed Germany and her allies, and the war ended 19 months later.

On November 21, 1918, 10 days after the Armistice was declared, the German Grand Fleet steamed out into the North Sea, formed into long columns of over 30 capital ships and cruisers each and, accompanied by ships of the Royal Navy, sailed into the Firth of Forth to surrender. Next day, after they had been disarmed, the German ships were transferred to Scapa Flow. They were a pathetic company, with their grey paint streaked with rust, their commander Admiral von Reuter all too anxious to co-operate with the victorious British, and some of their crews discontented to the edge of mutiny.

This dejected force, however, had the last bitter laugh, on June 21, 1919, eight days before the retributive Treaty of Versailles was signed. Just before 11.00, when guarding British warships were away on exercise, the rusting German vessels anchored north of Flotta Island began to sink, one by one, scuttled by their caretaker crews. It was a squalid end, and, as Adolf Hitler later put it, did 'not redound to the credit of the German Navy'. However, with the Allies at Versailles preparing to carve up the German fleet among themselves, de Reuter felt there was no honourable alternative. 'It was unthinkable', he said, 'to surrender defenceless ships to the enemy'.

Above: Wounded received on HMS 'Castor' after the Battle of Jutland, from a painting by Ian Gordon. *Imperial War Museum London*

Below: A dramatic painting by Charles Dixon of the battle-scarred HMS 'Vindictive' returning from Zeebrugge in 1918. *The Sphere*

The Second World War: Europe

THE 'PHONEY WAR' which stalled hostilities on land in the first seven months of the Second World War never applied at sea. On the contrary, the sea war sprang to instant violent life. On the first day, September 3, 1939, German E-boats were in action in the Baltic and the passenger liner *Athenia* succumbed to U-boat attack in the Atlantic.

The menace of the U-boats was augmented by the presence of German surface raiders; late in August two of them, the pocket battleships *Deutschland* and *Admiral Graf Spee*, were on station in the Atlantic ready to start marauding in an area of lifeline significance. The Atlantic convoys from America carried supplies of food, arms, ammunition, fuel and other items crucial to Britain's war effort and survival.

That was why British victory in the Battle of the River Plate had emotional as well as material importance. For the destruction of *Admiral Graf Spee* as a result of that battle demonstrated that German pocket battleships were mortal despite their unique standing as vessels more powerful than any cruiser afloat, and faster than any existing potential enemy ship, except for three British battlecruisers.

The pocket battleships or *panzerschiff* (armoured ships) were produced in response to the 10,000-ton limit on the size of German vessels imposed under the Treaty of Versailles (1919). However, while keeping to these limits, the Germans provided the *panzerschiff* with high speed (26 knots) and six 11-inch guns. The result was a powerful marauder of massively destructive potential. Proof that the recipe worked was awesomely demonstrated when *Graf Spee* disposed of nine merchant ships totalling 50,089 tons in the South Atlantic and Indian Oceans.

Encouraged by such fruitful pickings, *Graf Spee's* commander, Captain Langsdorff, headed for the River Plate vicinity, the hub of the South Atlantic trade routes. There, he thought, a marauding fox among the Atlantic chickens could have the pick of prizes. Instead, early on December 13, 1939, *Graf Spee* encountered Force 9 – the British cruisers *Exeter*, armed with 8-inch guns, and the 6-inch-gunned *Achilles* and *Ajax*. The *Graf Spee* opened fire on *Exeter* at 06.20 and in the ensuing running battle, the German was seriously hit so many times that Langsdorff decided to make for Montevideo, where the worst of the damage might be made good.

Under international convention, warships could remain in neutral ports only for sufficient time to repair damage affecting seaworthiness. Consequently, *Graf Spee* was allowed three days for essential repairs, but during the respite strong British forces gathered outside Montevideo for the ultimate kill. So, realising escape was impossible, Langsdorff scuttled *Graf Spee* in the Plate Estuary at 19.10 on December 17.

However, despite the end of *Graf Spee* and *Deutschland's* limited success in the North Atlantic, the ocean held enormous perils for Allied convoys, almost to the end of the war. It was significant that the Royal Navy Patrol Service, whose craft acted as convoy escorts, minesweepers and rooters-out of U-boats, lost more vessels than any other section of the Royal Navy. Crewed mainly by Royal Naval Reserve fishermen, who were dubbed 'Harry Tate's Navy', the Patrol Service's mixed assortment of trawlers, drifters and whalers were constantly in the thickest of the war at sea, all over the world from India to the icy seas of the Arctic.

The occupation of Denmark and Norway gave the German Navy and Air Force the haven of the fjords and airfields from which to attack Allied shipping in the Atlantic and Arctic. The German invasion on April 9 was a model of meticulous planning, surprise and swift accomplishment. Consequently, Captain Warburton-Lee, in the destroyer *Hardy*, with her sisters *Hunter*, *Havoc*, *Hotspur* and *Hostile*, ordered to Narvik to ensure no enemy troops landed there, arrived at around 16.00 hours on April 9, 1940, to discover at least six German destroyers already in Ofotfjord.

Warburton-Lee was not, however, deterred. At 01.00 hours on April 10, in thick snow and mist, his flotilla slipped into Ofotfjord and towards Narvik. At 04.30, the white silence of the Norwegian dawn was shattered by broadsides and seven torpedoes from *Hardy*. Strikes from *Hunter* and *Havoc* followed and within an hour two of the 10 German destroyers in Narvik were devastated. Tragedy followed triumph when, on the way back along Ofotfjord, the little force encountered two German warships, which sank *Hunter* and *Hardy* and cost Warburton-Lee his life. Three days later the battleship *Warspite* arrived with nine destroyers, to sink the remaining eight German destroyers in the second Battle of Narvik.

This success had felicitous consequences, for without those 10 destroyers, the Kriegsmarine had little hope of fending off the

Below: A painting by C E Turner of a 1942 convoy off Malta being saluted by the Royal Navy, with destroyer HMS 'Ashanti', flagship of Rear Admiral H M Burrough, in the foregound. *Illustrated London News*

Royal Navy in the projected invasion of Britain. Combined with the RAF's Battle of Britain victory, the Narvik battles preserved the British from the fate which overwhelmed western Europe in May and June 1940.

This deliverance was, of course, far from certain when, as the stunning power of German blitzkrieg smothered French resistance, the British Expeditionary Force had to be evacuated from Dunkirk. The heroic exodus in which nearly 350,000 troops were saved by a mass of 'little ships' and ships of the Royal Navy, was certainly a naval, if not a military, triumph. One of its more positive aspects was the escape of French seamen who joined the Free French naval forces, later to fight alongside the Royal Navy.

Unfortunately, only a few days after Dunkirk this benefit was marred by one of the great naval tragedies of the war – the attack by Force H of the Royal Navy on the French Atlantic Squadron at Mers-el-Kebir. The task, dubbed 'a filthy job' by Admiral Sir James Somerville, the Force H commander, sprang from Anglo-American concern that the defeated, divided French would be unable to prevent the enemy requisitioning their navy; the fourth largest in the world. The British managed to secure units of the French fleet in Plymouth, Portsmouth, Alexandria and Dakar, although nothing could be done about the four 8-inch cruisers at Toulon, in collaborationist Vichy territory. This left a magnificent prize at Mers-el-Kebir in the French colony of Algeria – the Atlantic Squadron, which accounted for one-fifth of the entire French fleet.

To gain this prize, Force H embarked on Operation Catapult, arriving off Mers-el-Kebir early on July 3, 1940. Somerville then gave Admiral Gensoul, commander of the French Atlantic Squadron, the choice of joining the British, sailing under British control to a British port or making for the West Indies. The choices had a sting, for if Gensoul refused them all, Somerville had orders to fire on his ships to prevent their falling into enemy hands.

The stubborn pompous Gensoul, abetted by the anglophobic Admiral Darlan, refused to co-operate or negotiate. Consequently Somerville had to open fire and in the holocaust of 15-inch shells that howled down on Mers-el-Kebir the battlecruiser *Dunkerque* was crippled, the battleship *Provence* and the destroyer *Mogador* were sunk and 1297 French sailors were killed and 351 injured.

A factor in this grievous event was the entry of Italy into the war, on June 10, 1940. The Italian Navy was one of the most modern and superbly equipped in the world, a pristine and powerful monster which could not, of course, be ignored. Only later did it transpire that its heart and spirit in no way matched its image. The fact was that the Italians went in mortal fear of the Royal Navy and its supposed supremacy, and that fear was enhanced by a remarkable attack against their ships berthed at the important naval base of Taranto on November 11, 1940.

When six Italian battleships, nine cruisers and numerous destroyers were detected by RAF reconnaissance berthed at Taranto, Admiral Sir Andrew Cunningham, C-in-C of the British Mediterranean Fleet, put into effect a long-cherished plan – a carrier-borne air strike. On the night of November 11 21 Swordfish torpedo bombers were launched from the deck of the carrier *Illustrious* 180 miles from Taranto. The Swordfish eluded Taranto's sophisticated early warning system to loose their 18-inch torpedoes, 11 of which destroyed half the Italian fleet in the harbour and wrecked installations, including the seaplane base.

Four months later, the fear inculcated at Taranto made Admiral Iachino, the Italian C-in-C, find one excuse after another not to bring his fleet out in support of the German invasion of Greece. Eventually, however, after the Germans had promised air cover, Iachino grudgingly sailed from Naples at 21.00 on March 26 and headed for the Straits of Messina.

German promises of air cover soon proved spurious and, to Iachino's chagrin, the Italian force was observed by British reconnaissance planes. Unknown to Iachino, one British fleet under Admiral Cunningham had sailed from Alexandria at 19.00 on March 27 and another under Vice Admiral Pridham-Wippell had left Piraeus.

At 11.00 on March 28 Iachino, in the 35,000-ton battleship *Vittorio Veneto* came within sight of Pridham-Wippell and fired a salvo, which the British avoided by making smoke, turning south-east and stepping up speed to 30 knots. The *Vittorio Veneto* gave chase, but at 11.27 eight aircraft from Cunningham's carrier *Formidable* appeared overhead and released torpedoes. Iachino at once broke off and steamed away westwards and homewards.

Cunningham set off in pursuit, hoping to use his air arm to halt the fleeing prey. Cunningham partly succeeded but at 19.30, just as the sun was setting, the Italian cruiser *Pola* was stopped by an aerial torpedo which struck her amidships. Fifty minutes later, Iachino learned what had happened, detailed two cruisers and four destroyers to go back to *Pola's* aid and so provided Cunningham with the sitting target he had been longing for all day. At 22.23, near Cape Matapan, Cunningham's ships came upon *Pola* and her rescuers. The ensuing night action was fought at point blank range, for which the Italians were totally unequipped. Five of their vessels were destroyed and about 2400 of their crews killed. Another 900 were rescued from a sea littered with bodies and wreckage, to become prisoners.

Meanwhile, on top of the problems of protecting Atlantic shipping from the depredations of the U-boat 'wolfpacks', the German attack on Russia in June 1941 saddled the British Navy and Air Force with further huge burdens and the merchant fleets with additional grievous losses. Despite earlier Soviet opportunism in making its pact with the Axis, Britain (and still-neutral America) felt bound to aid Russia. She was short of every type of modern military material and the only practical route to get supplies to her in time for any effective use was by sea through the primitive Arctic ports of Murmansk and Archangel.

The story of the Russian convoys, the first of a long series of which set off from Iceland in August 1941, is one of epic heroism in the face of every type of hazard experienced in a form more concentrated than ever elsewhere. To the natural hazards of summers of perpetual daylight denying respite of night-time concealment and winters of unremitting ice and blizzards were added the constant attack from aircraft, surface raiders and submarines entrenched along the northern European coasts. Even after American entry into the war and the depletion of German forces to the Eastern Front, it was not until early 1944, when escort carriers could at last be spared to provide effective air cover, that the Russian run was other than an extremely hazardous undertaking.

Back in the Mediterranean, the night-fighting capabilities of the British so devastatingly demonstrated at Matapan prompted the Italians to steam away with alacrity on December 17, 1941, after a British force

escorting a supply ship on a fuel run to Malta sighted an Italian fleet on a similar mission near the Gulf of Sirte in Libya. In this encounter, known as the First Battle of Sirte, the Italians fired one shot and quickly retired.

The Second Battle of Sirte, three months later, was a far hotter contest. On March 22, 1942, a convoy carrying 26,000 tons of supplies to beleaguered Malta and escorted by a fleet under Rear Admiral Vian, traversed the waters between Cyrenaica and Crete known colloquially as Bomb Alley because of the many merciless aerial batterings which British ships had endured there. At 09.00, when the last covering fighter had had to leave the convoy, Vian knew that a mighty Italian force, vastly superior to his own, was already closing in.

However, when the Italians came in sight at 14.27 Vian embarked on a tactic that evened the odds, using smoke to keep the Italians at their distance. Fighting in or near smoke, as Vian well knew, was something the Italians disliked as much as fighting by night. He ordered his ships to fire through the smoke and, after a brief long-range gun duel, the Italians hastily veered away. At 16.30, however, they reappeared with reinforcements mustering a total broadside of 24,000 pounds, as against less than 6000 pounds of the British. The British, fortunately, monopolised the weather gauge and used the strong south-easterly wind to spread another bank of smoke between themselves and the Italians.

The Italians, fearing that the smoke might conceal undetectable British torpedoes, attempted time and again to circumvent the smokescreen. Then, at 17.50, the main Italian force was sighted only 14,000 yards from three British destroyers, which plunged

Top: The first British naval action in Narvik Harbour on April 10, 1940, as portrayed in a painting by G H Davis that appeared in the 'Illustrated London News' as a double-page spread in April 1940. *Illustrated London News*

Above: A drawing by Montague Dawson of French warships under fire from the British fleet. *The Sphere*

Left: End of the 'Admiral Graf Spee' after she had been blown up by her own crew off Montevideo.

into the attack and from 6000 yards loosed a barrage of gunfire and torpedoes.

The Italians managed to draw ahead, but at 18.00 were confronted by two more British destroyers which loomed out of the smoke and fired torpedoes at the battleship *Littorio* from 13,000 yards. At once, the Italians backed off. At 18.40, four destroyers came surging towards *Littorio* at 28 knots all forward guns thundering, then fired 25 torpedoes at 5000 yards. Though all missed, the Italians were rattled enough to retire and make off north-westwards at a spirited pace.

Nevertheless, they had delayed the British convoy long enough for it to be still at sea after sun-up on March 23, long after the safest time for entering Malta – just before dawn. Consequently, German bombers, which had pounded the convoy for most of the previous day with little success, gained a fresh opportunity to cripple or destroy it. One merchantman was sunk before it could reach Malta, and although the other three managed to struggle into harbour, one was sunk at her berth by enemy bombers on March 29 and the other two were seriously damaged. In all, only 5000 tons of the 26,000 tons of the convoy's cargo reached Malta.

Such tales of courage and tragedy and achievement gained at forbidding price were a standard feature of the gargantuan struggle to supply Malta. The island was, of course, crucially placed to control the Mediterranean supply routes, and particularly those which succoured the forces fighting in North Africa after 1941.

The Italian Reggia Aeronautica predictably bungled its attempts to overcome Malta. In total contrast, however, the Luftwaffe's Fliegerkorps persistently hammered British sea communications in the area, starting on January 10, 1941, with a shattering attack on the carrier *Illustrious* while she was escorting a supply and ammunition convoy from Gibraltar to Greece.

After April, roles were reversed. When the Fliegerkorps left to participate in the fight for Greece and Crete, British aircraft pounded convoys supplying the Axis forces in North Africa. The lull also allowed Malta to be restocked to last until May 1942, which was fortunate, since late 1941 saw a succession of disasters. On November 12 the carrier *Ark Royal* was torpedoed by a German U-boat and, despite efforts to keep her afloat, sank 50 miles out while being towed to Gibraltar. It was a depressing end for a famous ship, which had made her mark in some of the most significant and epic actions of the war, including Norway, Mers-el-Kebir, the River Plate and the destruction of the *Bismarck* (1941).

Equally depressing, the battleships *Barham*, *Queen Elizabeth* and *Valiant* were eliminated by U-boat or human torpedo attack, and a cruiser squadron fell foul of a minefield. The Axis air forces took advantage and battered Malta with 4927 sorties and over 6700 tons of bombs. By the end of April 1942, despite Spitfire reinforcements flown in from carriers, Malta's air defences were almost non-existent, and the submarines, the only Royal Navy units still operating from the island, had to leave.

The valiant efforts made to fight convoys through in February and March, when the second Sirte battle crippled the attempt, were similarly plagued by ferocious air attacks and by May 10, 1942, Field Marshal Kesselring confidently reported to Berlin that 'the neutralisation of Malta is complete'. He was wrong. The same day 60 carrier-borne Spitfires reached Malta and stormed into action to inflict the first of a number of sharp defeats on the enemy. The peak of Malta's ordeal by bomb was past and when the bulk of German air strength was transferred to Libya to assist Rommel's offensive there, the intensity of the attack fell dramatically.

Nevertheless, the ordeal of the Malta convoys was far from over. In mid-June 1942, despite a heavy escort, the ships of operations Harpoon from Gibraltar and Vigorous from the eastern Mediterranean were ferociously pounded and the ships of Vigorous had to retire. Of the Harpoon's freighters only two, carrying 15,000 tons of supplies, reached Malta.

The colossal cost of Vigorous and Harpoon led to the re-establishment in July of Malta's submarine base. The submarines played an important part in denying Rommel supplies and contributed largely to his defeat at El Alamein (October–November 1942), but starvation on Malta was still so much a possibility that a further supply convoy was planned for August.

This was the even more tragic and costly Operation Pedestal which involved a convoy of 13 fast freighters and the large fuel tanker *Ohio*, and extremely heavy air and sea protection. The convoy's protection sufficed to bring it to within 24 hours sailing of Malta with only the loss of the carrier *Eagle*, a destroyer and one freighter. However, the protecting carriers and battleships could not accompany the convoy through the restricted waters of the Sicilian Channel. The melancholy result was a night of destruction in which enemy submarines, surface craft, bombers and torpedo planes reduced the convoy to a mere six ships by dawn on August 13. Two more freighters succumbed to air attack that day, and it was only by superhuman effort that the damaged *Ohio* managed to crawl slowly into Malta, carrying 10,000 tons of precious fuel oil and paraffin.

Happily, though, the need for further sacrifice and loss on convoys such as Pedestal was soon removed by the Eighth Army's victory at Alamein. It foreshadowed the end of the Axis war effort in North Africa, which collapsed in May 1943.

The final collapse and defeat of Germany two years later, was inaugurated by Operation Overlord, the Normandy invasion, on D-Day, June 6, 1944. A crucial part in supplying the invasion forces was played by the Mulberry artificial harbour. Mulberry was a substitute for French ports so strongly fortified and defended by the Germans that there was doubt whether they could be captured and used for supply purposes. The artificial substitute was designed to enclose an area about two miles long, one mile wide and six storeys high, and featured a line of blockships, flexible roadways, huge linked concrete caissons and floating booms (bombardons) to shield the Mulberry from the wind and sea. Despite their colossal size, the construction of two Mulberries in areas around the British coast was kept completely secret from the Germans.

Mulberry A (St Laurent Beach) was, however, wrecked by temperamental Channel weather, and it was through a strengthened and augmented Mulberry B (Arromanches Beach) that supplies were landed during the two months after D-Day. On a typical July day 11,000 tons of stores were unloaded. At the same time PLUTO (pipe line under the ocean) ran from a tanker terminal in Britain to pump vital oil to the invading forces, and nothing the Luftwaffe or the Kriegsmarine could do interrupted the tide of stores which supplied what was to become the force that liberated Europe.

Below: Detail of a painting by Leslie Cole of tanks being loaded on board ship bound for Russia in World War II.
Imperial War Museum London (photo D Rudkin)

The Second World War: The Far East

A painting by Norman Wilkinson of the action at Pearl Harbor.
National Maritime Museum London

AMERICAN SHOCK and chagrin at the Japanese sneak attack on Pearl Harbor on December 7, 1941, derived as much from amazement that such a long distance air-borne strike was possible, as it did from the devastation caused and the treachery displayed. To naval minds devoted to the battleship as the prime instrument of naval warfare, it was virtually incomprehensible that 423 aircraft should take off from carrier decks in the vastnesses of the Pacific and mount an attack such as that suffered by the US Pacific Fleet. However, carrier-borne naval warfare quickly came to characterise the Second World War in the Pacific. Major naval engagements at the Coral Sea (May 1942), Midway (June 1942) and Leyte Gulf (October 1944), all involved aircraft in the prime roles and changed the face of naval warfare for ever. Conventional warships of both sides rarely came within sight or range of an enemy ship and the battleship's big guns were as useless as popguns. The aircraft carrier had assumed the mantle of the capital ship.

As an introduction to this new age, Pearl Harbor was a set-piece example of its kind. In deepest secrecy, the Japanese task force of 30 vessels, including six aircraft carriers, sneaked 3000 miles across the Pacific to its attack position 200 miles off Oahu. At dawn on December 7 the first wave of 185 Kate torpedo bombers, Val dive bombers and Zero fighters took off, and headed towards a target peopled by personnel entirely ignorant of impending catastrophe.

Euphoria was rudely shattered at 07.55, when the Japanese roared in over their target and Vals tore down upon the American airfields where, for safety against sabotage, aircraft were lined up wing-tip to wing-tip. The result was a scene of splintered ruin and raging fire. Simultaneously, Kates swooped in a shallow dive towards the long sweep of vessels in Battleship Row. Their torpedoes split open five battleships of which one, the 32,000-ton *Arizona*, blew up in a mass of fragments when an armour piercing shell penetrated her forward magazine. *Arizona* sank with over 1000 men trapped inescapably below her decks.

For over an hour the Japanese bombed and strafed the docks, the harbour and the airfields, finally leaving the scene of mangled vessels, smashed aircraft, wrecked buildings, fire, smoke and slaughter at 09.55.

For the loss, to spirited if tardy American AA fire, of 29 aircraft and 100 pilots, the Japanese had wrought appalling damage; four battleships and a minelayer were sunk, and four battleships, three light cruisers, three destroyers and a repair ship were badly damaged and 92 Navy and 96 Army aircraft were destroyed. The Pearl Harbor airfields and shore installations were virtually laid waste and over 3500 people were killed or injured. By great good fortune the main fuel store escaped and the aircraft carriers based at Pearl were at sea at the time of the attack, otherwise the Pacific war would certainly

The Japanese cruiser 'Morgami' with her superstructure and turrets badly damaged after attack by US planes.
Department of the Navy Washington

have taken a very different course.

The Americans, humiliated and infused with the desire for revenge, were pitchforked out of their isolationism and declared war. The elated Japanese, for their part, fell almost universal victim to 'victory disease'. Now, they presumed, there was no one to bar the spread over the Pacific of the Greater South-East Asia Co Prosperity Sphere, the wholesale snapping up and milking of territories for the succour of the Japanese home islands.

At first this seemed a reasonable presumption. In the wake of Pearl Harbor and other attacks the same day, Japanese landing forces swept across the Pacific to create, by February 1942, a new empire covering most of South-East Asia and one-third of the Pacific. The supremacy of the Japanese, and of the aircraft carrier, was underlined on December 10, 1941, by the sinking from the air of HMS *Prince of Wales* and *Repulse*, and by the thrashing the Japanese dealt on February 27, 1942, to an Allied naval force in the Battle of the Java Sea.

The Allies, commanded by the Dutch Rear Admiral Doorman, were handicapped from the start. The crews of two heavy and two light cruisers and 10 destroyers from the American, British, Australian and Dutch navies had had practically no co-ordination training. Worse, they lacked common signal books and codes for communication, and air cover for protection.

The task of this heterogeneous fleet was to thwart Japanese landings in Indonesia. Battle proper was preluded by a preliminary bout on February 14, in which the Allied force miraculously escaped an eight-hour aerial barrage, a clash on February 18 which lost Doorman a destroyer and a cruiser badly damaged, and eight days later, a fruitless search for a Japanese convoy of heavily escorted transports reported to be making for Sourabaya. Doorman had almost given up when, just after 15.30 on February 27, a more accurate report took him heading north-west for the convoy's position off the Javanese north coast.

At 16.12, in calm weather with maximum visibility, the Allied fleet sighted three columns of Japanese cruisers and destroyers coming in fast from the north-west. At 16.16, the 8-inch cruisers of both sides opened fire at 28,000 yards. Doorman, realising that his present course would give the enemy the advantage of 'crossing the T', hauled round to the west, parallel to the enemy, at 25 knots. Despite a Japanese 8-inch shell hit on Doorman's flagship, the light cruiser *De Ruyter* (it failed to explode), the range was too long to allow truly effective gun action, and 43 Long Lance torpedoes launched by Japanese destroyers failed to reach their targets for the same reason.

Then bad luck intervened for the Allies. At 17.08, an 8-inch shell put six of the cruiser *Exeter's* boilers out of action, drastically cutting her speed. The *Exeter's* captain had to haul clear of the Allied line, which at that juncture was angled away from the line of Japanese torpedo attack. The *Exeter's* 90-degree turn to port combined with smoke obscuring *De Ruyter* to convince other Allied ships' captains that Doorman was leading his line round to port. They made the turn, converting the line into an ideal torpedo target. Miraculously, only one torpedo scored a hit, on the *Kortenaer*, which blew up and sank. The Allied force, however, was confused and temporarily slowed to 15 knots and at that point the Japanese decided to close for the kill.

In the next confused minutes, over a battle area shrouded in smoke, both sides pot-shot at fleetingly glimpsed targets. Doorman lost the *Electra* which, after hitting *Jintsu*, was stopped by damage in the boiler room and had to be sunk by gunfire at 18.00.

Doorman was still determined to attack the Japanese transports, though with his lack of search aircraft he could not discover that they were, in fact, only 30 miles to the north. Doorman had no option but to hunt for them in the darkness of the tropical night. However, he failed in all attempts to work round the enemy's cruisers and get at the troop convoy. Ultimately, his efforts cost him his life. At around 22.50, both *De Ruyter* and *Java* were hit by Long Lance torpedoes, and neither Doorman nor the ships' captains survived.

The Battle of the Java Sea provided the Japanese with a decisive victory, in which they sank half the Allied force without losing a single ship. Moreover, their troop convoy was never at risk, and the battle's aftermath, in which *Exeter* and two destroyers were sunk, eliminated Allied naval power in the East Indies. Ten days later, on March 9, the Allied forces on Java surrendered.

Little wonder that the Japanese grew bolder and more arrogant than ever, striking as far west as Ceylon (Sri Lanka) and the Indian Ocean (April 1942) and towards Port Moresby and Australia in the south-east (May 1942).

Now, however, the flaw in the attack on Pearl Harbor – the escape of the aircraft carriers – began to make itself evident. This fortunate coincidence, whose import was immediately recognised by Admiral Yamamoto, creator of the Pearl strike, left the

Americans with a vital nucleus of carrier power to bridge the gap until their huge war potential got into top gear. Once it did, they were able to build up mighty carrier power and the Japanese first felt its searing breath in the Battle of the Coral Sea (May 3-8, 1942), the first naval battle fought entirely by carrier aircraft, and one which left the Americans with a strategic if not a material victory. The Japanese southeastern advance was halted as a result.

The following month, at Midway, the Japanese experienced Nemesis, losing half their carrier power, 250 aircraft and dozens of irreplaceable pilots. Yamamoto had intended the invasion of Midway Island to round off the work of Pearl Harbor and punch American sea power out of the Pacific. Midway guarded the approaches to North America and was therefore a target the Americans were bound to make maximum efforts to defend. To bring them to this showdown, Yamamoto gathered the entire Japanese main fleet – four carriers with 270 aircraft, two battleships, three cruisers and 12 destroyers. Against this, the US Navy could send to sea only three carriers with 230 aircraft, six cruisers and nine destroyers.

However, they had the great advantage of Midway's naval base and air force, and the inestimable one of having cracked the Japanese naval codes. By this means the American commander, Admiral Nimitz, learned in advance the name of the target and the dispositions of the Japanese fleet.

As the Japanese approached Midway early on June 3 the first American strikes, by aircraft from Midway, were costly, ineffective and failed to prevent Vice Admiral Nagumo's carriers from flying off 108 Vals, Kates and Zeros for the purpose of destroying Midway's defences. The island's facilities suffered heavy damage, prompting great jubilation on board the Japanese ships.

There was more jubilation after anti-aircraft fire and defending Zeros countered the unexpected appearance at 09.20 of Devastator torpedo bombers and escorting Wildcats from the US carriers *Enterprise* and *Hornet*, which had returned to the main battle area from the morale-building Doolittle raid on Tokyo in April 1942. The Zeros shot down almost every one of the slow unwieldy Devastators as they came in low to drop torpedoes. Not one found a target on the sharply manoeuvring Japanese carriers below. The Zeros repeated their success against 12 of *Yorktown's* Devastators, only four of which survived.

Once again there was jubilation but this time it was short lived. At 10.24 dive bombers from *Yorktown* suddenly appeared and screamed down on the Japanese carriers. Four direct hits on *Kaga* plunged through the flimsy flight deck to the hangars below. Two hits on *Akagi* and three on *Soryu* fired fuel systems and tanks, and exploded stocks of bombs and torpedoes.

The fourth Japanese carrier, *Hiryu*, had become detached from the others during the frenzied manoeuvring to avoid torpedo attacks. While her sisters were being destroyed, 18 Val dive bombers and six Zeros had taken off from *Hiryu* and had only to follow the retiring American planes to be led to *Yorktown*. Eight Vals broke through to score three bomb hits and at 14.00 a second strike of 10 torpedo planes and six fighters from *Hiryu* slammed two torpedo hits into *Yorktown*. The crew abandoned ship.

The *Hiryu* soon tasted American revenge. A strike by 24 dive bombers from *Enterprise* and 16 from *Hornet* swooped at 17.00. The *Enterprise* planes scored four direct hits which shattered *Hiryu* and set her ablaze.

Though both sides had further losses to suffer, the Battle of Midway was virtually over. When the distraught Yamamoto learned of the destruction of his four carriers, he broke off and ordered his fleet into full retreat.

Midway, key sea battle of the Pacific war, permanently robbed Japan of the strategic initiative, for their war capacity was never able to make up the losses of ships, aircraft and experienced crews suffered there, or later. This fatal drawback was punishingly demonstrated after November 1942 when, starting at Guadalcanal in the Solomons, the Americans began island-hopping their victorious way across the Pacific to close in on Japan itself by 1945.

It was no easy progress, however. In one island stronghold after another the Japanese resisted with savage fanaticism, and at sea the suicidal tenor of their warfare was demonstrated, in October 1944, in the conflagratory showdown of the Battles of Leyte Gulf. It was a drama in four violent acts, fought in the Sibuyan Sea (October 23-24), and in the Surigao Straits on the 25th.

The Japanese were attempting, vainly, to stop the American invasion of the Philippines, and when news arrived of the first American landings at Leyte (October 20) the entire Japanese fleet put to sea. Battle began in the Sibuyan Sea on October 23, when US submarines sank three heavy cruisers of Vice Admiral Kurita's First Striking Force A. Alerted by this event, three American carrier groups launched strikes with about 260 planes early on October 24.

Seeking vengeance for the destruction of the aircraft carrier *Princeton* by Japanese planes from Luzon that morning, the Americans obtained bomb and torpedo hits on the battleships *Yamato* and *Nagato*, and sank *Musashi* with numerous torpedo and bomb hits. The Americans lost 30 planes, but as an indication of the way the war was shaping the *Princeton* turned out to be the last of the five US carriers sunk by the Japanese. By 15.00, the intensity of US air strikes persuaded Kurita, who had no fighter protection, to reverse course and 'retire temporarily from the zone of enemy air attack'.

That night, the Japanese First Striking Force C and Second Striking Force headed into the Surigao Strait. Alerted by shadowing planes, six American battleships deployed at the eastern end of the strait, with cruisers disposed near by and destroyers patrolling the entrance. After an ineffective American PT-boat attack at 02.00 on October 25, and torpedo hits by US destroyers which sank four Japanese, the Surigao battle ignited at 03.50, when the main American fleet opened fire on three approaching enemy ships. Though all but overwhelmed, they reacted gamely, firing on three American cruisers and launching torpedoes. The 14-inch battleship *Yamashiro* hit a destroyer, but succumbed to attack itself and turned west, ablaze from bow to stern. The pulverising American gunfire and a torpedo strike against *Yamashiro* at 6200 yards convinced the Japanese that escape was vital. In the attempt, *Yamashiro* was struck again by two torpedoes and rolled over and sank. Another battleship victim was the *Mogami*, which was disabled.

The Second Strike Force, not realising that Force C had been destroyed, entered Surigao Strait, to be met by the American PT137 which torpedoed the cruiser *Abukuma*. The Japanese commander, Vice Admiral Shima reversed course to await developments, only to have his flagship *Nachi* run down by the limping *Mogami*, which suffered further damage from the guns of three American cruisers. The *Mogami* was sunk at 08.45 by a Japanese destroyer.

Kurita had slipped through Surigao Strait shortly after midnight on October 24-25 and was not spotted until 06.45, when he was only 20 miles from Leyte Gulf. At 06.48 the *Yamato* inaugurated the battle of Samar by opening fire at 37,000 yards. The northernmost of the Seventh Fleet's escort carriers flew off every available strike plane, then steamed away south. By 07.06 Kurita was closing with disconcerting rapidity and the volume and accuracy of Japanese fire increased. Then a rain squall and a smoke screen hid the Americans for the next half hour, while Kurita ordered 'General Chase'. It was a cardinal mistake; by the time the Americans emerged from cover, Kurita was no longer in control of a coherent force.

American destroyers closed the Japanese to under 10,000 yards and opened torpedo fire that compelled even the mighty *Yamato* to reverse course. Three other Japanese ships were hit, and one sunk. Two American

Left: A drawing by W G Whitaker of the 'Langley' sinking under air attack off Java.
The Sphere

US Navy Dauntless dive bombers stand by to take off for a mission against the Japanese on Marcus Island in the western Pacific.
Keystone Press

destroyers were lost. At 07.43, while still firing on the enemy, Kurita's ships were being attacked by planes from all 18 of the Seventh Fleet's escort carriers. Two hours of bombs, torpedoes and machine-gun fire forced the Japanese capital ships to make frequent evasive alterations of course, so that they could only close the range slowly on the escort carriers heading southwards. Nonetheless, the Japanese succeeded in sinking *Gambier Bay* and damaging *Kalinin Bay*. Two Japanese were lost before their cruisers gave up the chase and turned away. Kurita had miscalculated the speed of the retiring Americans. He credited them with an impossible 30 knots and concluded they could not be overtaken.

After further attacks by 70 American planes, in which the battleship *Nagato* and the *Tone* were hit, Kurita had had enough and ordered withdrawal. Ironically, he was unaware that during the morning, aid was being provided him by first kamikaze suicide attacks, which damaged two American carriers and sank another, the *St Lo*. Kurita lost three 8-inch cruisers at Samar to the Americans' two escort carriers and three destroyers. Both sides had several ships badly damaged, and suffered heavy casualties.

Off Cape Engano, an hour before Kurita's withdrawal, carrier aircraft of the Third Fleet under Vice Admiral Halsey were bearing down on Vice Admiral Ozawa's carrier force of six carriers, three cruisers and nine destroyers. They sank the carrier *Chitose* and a destroyer, and damaged Ozawa's flagship *Zuikaku*, which afterwards succumbed to three torpedoes launched by a second airborne strike. The American aircraft, totalling 527 planes, delivered four more strikes by 19.00 hours. In sum, their sorties sank four Japanese carriers and one destroyer but, mainly because of Japanese AA fire, barely scratched Ozawa's two battleship carriers, his three cruisers or eight of his destroyers.

Determined to have all his capital ships available to sink by gunfire such of Ozawa's force as remained afloat, Halsey did not detach Task Force 34 to block Kurita's escape from Samar. Kurita therefore managed to slip through the strait, and in fact, despite attacks during his withdrawal that day and the next, October 26, several Japanese ships got clean away.

There was subsequent criticism of Halsey's handling of the Third Fleet, which he threw into the battle almost in entirety, leaving the San Bernardino Strait unguarded at the start of the Cape Engano battle. This, however, was a small grumble compared to Halsey's achievement. He destroyed almost all that remained of Japan's carrier forces, a vital contribution to total Japanese losses at Leyte, which amounted to four aircraft carriers, three battleships, six heavy cruisers, four light cruisers, 11 destroyers, 150 aircraft and 10,000 dead. To achieve this, the US Navy suffered the loss of one light and two escort carriers, three destroyers, 100 aircraft and 1500 dead.

The cumulative effect of the Leyte battles was to extinguish the Japanese Navy as a coherent fighting force so that, though Leyte did not end the Pacific war, it pointed the Americans and their Allies towards their ultimate victory by leaving them undisputed masters of the ocean.

12. Sea Travel

SEA TRAVEL IN THE MIDDLE AGES

Left, top to bottom: Woodcuts of a pilgrim galley at Rhodes; the stern of a 1486 ship; and the port of Modon, all taken from the book 'Breydenbach's Travels'.
All courtesy Science Museum London

DURING the 13th, 14th and 15th centuries many pilgrims made the journey from French and Italian ports down the Mediterranean to the Holy Land. A German pilgrim, Bernard von Breydenbach, wrote the story of a journey he made in 1485; 12 editions of the narrative, all illustrated with woodcuts, were published between 1486 and 1522.

Breydenbach and two companions left Oppenheim, near Mainz, on April 25, 1485, and travelled to Venice, where they joined others who wished to make the pilgrimage to Jerusalem. After much bargaining Breydenbach, in accordance with the customs of the time, made a contract with Augustino Contarini, a galley master, for the sea passage at a charge of 42 ducats, one half to be paid at Venice and the other on arrival at Jaffa.

The terms of the contract laid down that the master was to provide arms for 80 men for the defence of the pilgrims; the galley was not to stay more than two or three days at any port of call unless departure was delayed by weather; meals were to be provided twice a day and were to consist of good bread, good wine, fresh meat and other victuals; if any of the passengers were to die their belongings were to be passed to their heirs, and if any should die before reaching Jaffa half the deceased's passage money was to be returned; and that an interpreter when needed was to be provided by the master.

The party sailed from Venice on June 1 and after calls at Parenzo, Corfu, Rhodes and Cyprus arrived at Jaffa on June 30, having suffered a stormy passage that prevented calling at some other intended ports. After visiting Jerusalem, Bethlehem and Mount Sinai, the party journeyed to Cairo and thence by boat down the Nile to Alexandria, where a contract for the return voyage to Europe was made with a Venetian galley master. Leaving Alexandria on November 15, the galley called at Modon, in Greece, on December 14 and arrived at Venice on January 8.

The large volume of pilgrim traffic in the Middle Ages led several port authorities to form regulations to help intending passengers. The port of Marseilles restricted the number of passengers according to ship tonnage. Venetian ships had to have iron marks nailed to their hulls; during the first seven years of its life a ship could be laden to 2½ feet above the mark lowest in the water but after that age it could be loaded to only two feet above the mark.

Trading was carried on by a ship's master and by its owner, crew and the passengers. The practice caused so much overcrowding of deck and cabin space that in the 13th century Venice limited merchants, sailors and knights to one chest each and servants were not allowed to take goods. On embarking, each passenger's name was recorded by the escrivain, an officer equivalent to the modern purser. Richer passengers were accommodated in the more comfortable and less crowded summer or after castles, but the ordinary passenger was allocated a space six feet by two feet on the lower deck, where he slept with his head towards the outside and his feet to the middle, leaving a centre gangway which was usually filled with bundles and chests containing the pilgrim's goods.

Felix Faber, a Dominican Father, who made two voyages from Venice to the Holy Land between 1480 and 1485, describes the allocation of space and something of the life aboard a Venetian galley. The cabin at the bows was used for spare sails and ropes, and the highest deck of the after castle was reserved for the helmsman with his charts and nautical instruments. A cabin in the after castle was assigned to any noblewoman who might be travelling.

Access to the lower deck, where the ordinary pilgrims slept, was by a ladder through a hatchway. The crew and passengers slept on straw mattresses laid on the deck; during the day bedding was hung from a hook in the ship's side. Sick pilgrims would sometimes be spared the awful stench of the lower deck and found places elsewhere.

Each morning the passengers were served a measure of malvoisie, a wine from Candia which was considered an antidote to seasickness. Meals were announced by trumpet call and the wealthy ate in their cabins or at tables near the mainmast. Ordinary passengers ate from tables set in the after part of the vessel. Despite the terms of contract the food was usually very bad. Bread lasted only a few days and then hard biscuits were served. Salted meat had to serve, except when one of the animals usually carried was killed, washed down with musty water or sour wine.

On pilgrim ships three religious services were held each day, at daybreak, at eight o'clock in the morning and in the evening. The pilgrims generally passed the rest of the time reading or playing (forbidden) dice or card games. There was no regard for hygiene and the death rate usually rose rapidly within a few days of a vessel leaving port and fever and disease claimed more victims than storms. Even so, pilgrims who went by sea from Marseilles or Venice could generally be more certain of reaching the Holy Land than any who undertook the long trip overland.

THE PADDLE STEAMER

Top: The General Steam Navigation Company's 600-ton sail/paddle steamer 'John Bull', in 1835. *P&O Line (Richard Sharpe Studios)*

Above: 'New World', one of the Hudson River steamers in 1861. *Mary Evans Picture Library*

THE WIND, harnessed by sail, has provided the power to drive ships since the earliest times and by the 18th century, ships of considerable size were sailing the oceans of the world, and all of the major nations had their sailing warships carrying large numbers of men and guns. However, another power was being developed. In 1698 Thomas Savery had produced a practical steam pumping engine—the so-called Fire Engine; Newcomen followed with a better one in 1705, and by 1781 James Watt had perfected the first rotative steam engine, which could be adapted to the propulsion of many things, including ships.

It was the time of the Napoleonic wars and much commercial development of steamships in Europe did not have effect until the wars were finished. The engineer William Symington designed the engines of two experimental steam paddle boats on the Forth and Clyde Canal. One was a success and is recorded as travelling at seven miles per hour in 1789. The governor of the canal company, Lord Dundas, commissioned him to build a steam tug driven by a stern paddle wheel. Named *Charlotte Dundas,* in 1802, she towed two laden 70-ton barges 192 miles against a head wind in six hours. However, the proprietors decided there was too much damage to the banks and the tug was abandoned. It was not until 1856 that steam lighters came into general use on the canal.

In the United States, untroubled by the war, Robert Fulton, of Irish parentage, produced the 133ft paddle steamer, the *Clermont,* in 1807. Fulton was not so much an original inventor as a man capable of assessing other people's ideas, so that he could amalgamate the good ones and discard the bad ones. His first steamer was a success, and was followed by many more to be used on the rivers and off the coast of the north-eastern United States.

In Britain, in 1812, an amateur enthusiast named Henry Bell had a 43ft paddle steamer, named the *Comet,* built by John Wood & Co at Port Glasgow. This little ship carried passengers on the Clyde and is believed to have been the first steam-driven craft to carry a paying load in Europe. The Clyde became an important paddle steamer building area and is one of the places where paddle steamers are still used.

The early paddle steamers were used mainly in sheltered waters, on canals and rivers, rather than on the open sea. There was a mistrust of the new means of propulsion, particularly by naval authorities. There was also the need to use a lot of space to carry coal as fuel, which could not then be used for cargo. This meant that steam and sail were used together in vessels intended for long voyages.

The first ship to use steam across the Atlantic was the American *Savannah* in 1819, but that can hardly be claimed a crossing under steam, because during most of the voyage her machinery was stopped and her paddles were removed. She did the bulk of the voyage under sail only (29 days crossing, with only 80 hours under steam). By 1827 the Dutch had a British-built steamship, called the *Curacao,* making regular crossings of the Atlantic to the Dutch colonies in the West Indies. Another early paddle steamer to cross the Atlantic under steam was the *Royal William,* which crossed from Canada to England in 1833.

The potential of paddle steamers was now being realised. Hull shapes had originally been the same as for sail, and sail as an alternative means of propulsion was still carried. For a pure steamship, performance was much better with finer bows and slender lines. Sailing ships had rather bluff bows running off finer towards the stern.

Ships of increasing size were built to cross the Atlantic. They, like all the earlier ones, were of wooden construction, with a pair of paddle boxes or sponsons amidships. Some internal framing might have been iron, but wood was still the only covering used. By the standards of those days the ships were large, although by modern standards they were quite small. Early purpose-built Atlantic paddle steamers were the *Great Western* of 1778 tons, built in 1837 and designed by that versatile engineer Isambard Kingdom Brunel to 'extend his Great Western Railway', and the *President* of 2366 tons, built in 1839.

Steamship lines were being formed and the advantages of having fleets of identical ships were realised. The Cunard company, of trans-Atlantic fame, started its services with the paddle steamer *Britannia* and three sister ships in 1840. A year later there was a fleet of 14 similar ships, each of 1285 tons, crossing to the West Indies under the flag of the Royal Mail Steam Packet Company. Shortly afterward the P & O Line had a fleet of paddle steamers in the Indian Ocean.

The first threat to both wooden construction and the use of paddle wheels came with the launching of the *Great Britain* (designed by Brunel), which was built in 1843 of iron and driven by a screw propeller. This did not mean the immediate death of paddles or wooden construction, but the change had to be accepted as progress. Many fleet operators changed to the new methods of construction and propulsion and many paddle steamers changed over to screw. The famous old *Great Britain* has now been returned to the Bristol dock where she was built, from the Falkland Islands where she lay beached as a hulk for many years.

The *Great Britain* was 3448 tons and was the biggest ship in the world in 1843, but in 1858 came the *Great Eastern*, also by Brunel, a paddle steamer of the then fantastic size of 18,914 tons and a length of 692ft. She had five funnels and six masts. It was intended that she should carry 3000 passengers and 6000 tons of cargo to Colombo, Ceylon, via the Cape of Good Hope. She never did. There were hitches and accidents during launching, and the costs involved then ruined her owners. New owners put the ship on to the Atlantic trade, for which she was never intended and she was a failure there. The ship spent eight years successfully cable-laying, but after 31 years she was broken up at Liverpool. Although the *Great Eastern* provided an unhappy story, there was much about her design and construction that became standard practice in later ships. Brunel's death and the first trials of the *Great Eastern* coincided.

The only satisfactory fuel available in the early days of steam was coal. The conversion of the heat from burning coal to boil water and generate steam, which then drove pistons, reciprocating to turn a shaft and drive paddles, was not very efficient with early boilers and engines. The low efficiency necessitated carrying a considerable amount of coal, and explained why sail was carried as well, to conserve fuel. An example was the P & O *Hindostan* of 2017 tons, built in 1842. The ship was fully rigged on three masts and had two funnels. She had to carry 500 tons of coal, which limited cargo capacity to 200 tons.

Steamships without sail were first used for the short sea crossing to France and for coastal trade, where there was no need to carry enormous quantities of coal. Some of the first cross-Channel steamers were owned by the railway companies. They were smart in their lines and well finished, setting a standard for subsequent paddle-driven pleasure craft. Typical of the period were the twin steamers *Paris* and *Rouen*, 250ft long, with a moulded beam of 29ft and 55ft over the paddle boxes. They were built in anticipation of the heavy traffic for the 1889 Paris Exhibition. The two funnels and masts all raked aft at the same angle. Sailing ships had been steered from aft. Changes in position came gradually and the new Channel ferries were steered from the forward end of the promenade deck, although a bridge as known today was not used.

By building a paddle steamer long and narrow, quite high speeds could be achieved. The Dover-Calais crossing has always been something of a challenge. It still is today, with Channel ferries proud of their two-hour crossings. In 1876, the slim long paddle steamer *Calais-Douvres*, looking smart with light-coloured funnels and paddle boxes, with two slender raking masts, was able to maintain 14 knots on the crossing. *Brittany* and *Normandy* were built on the Clyde by Fairfield in 1882 and achieved $17\frac{1}{2}$ knots, crossing from Newhaven. They used higher boiler pressures, but also had more efficient paddles, with blades that feathered.

Early steam engines were single-cylinder and much of the power of the steam was wasted. Around 1860 the compound engine was introduced, which made for better use of steam and therefore economy in the use of fuel. In a compound engine, the expanded steam exhausted from the first cylinder is admitted at a lower pressure into another cylinder to gain additional power from the still-expanding steam. A further development added a third cylinder, to make the more-efficient triple-expansion engine which soon became general.

Although the heyday of paddle steamers was during the period when wood was the normal shipbuilding material, iron was used when that became acceptable. While iron had many advantages, including a long life (the *Great Britain* is still remarkably sound), it was very heavy. Steel began to take the place of iron and could provide strength with lighter plates. A light hull can be driven with less power, so nearly all paddle steamers which have survived and are in use today are steel ships.

Paddle steamers, built as tugs, did a useful job towing sailing ships in and out of port. Paddles can have an advantage over a screw propeller in increased manoeuvrability. With each paddle wheel driven by a separate engine, it would be possible almost to turn within a ship's own length, with one wheel turning forward and the other reversed. Many tugs, as well as some pleasure steamers, had a rudder at the bow as well as the stern for finer control of turning.

A typical harbour tug, the 126ft *Aid*, was almost symmetrical in side view, with two funnels and no masts. She was built at Preston in 1889 and served at Ramsgate until going into war service in 1915.

Of course, a large number of paddle tugs served on the Thames and the last in use was the *Iona*, which left the river in 1920 after 44 years of service there and was not scrapped until 1928. She was 121ft long, with a beam of 21ft. Normally based at Poplar, much of her work was helping liners in and out of dock, or towing alongside windjammers, but she was also chartered for pleasure trips.

Above: The Cologne Dusseldorf Steamship Co paddle steamer 'Frieden' at Bacharach on the Rhine on August 20 1964. *B Stephenson*

Far left: The parent engine of early steam navigation, William Symington's design of 1788. *Mary Evans Picture Library*

Left: A paddle steamer packed with passengers at Buochs on the lake of Lucerne, Switzerland, in September 1970. *J Winkley*

Right top to bottom: The paddle ship 'Hjejlen', built in 1861, pictured here on the Silkeborg Lakes in Denmark. *J R Batts*

The American paddle steamer 'Savannah'—the first to use steam during an Atlantic crossing. *Tourist Photo Library*

A close-up of the paddle of the Lucerne steamer 'Wilhelm Tell', in September 1970. *J Winkley*

The 'Tattershall Castle' on the New Holland Pier — Hull ferry service. *C J Gammell*

Far right above: A paddle steamer at Montreux on the Lake of Geneva, in August 1970. *D J Kingston*

Far right below: The 'Mark Twain', a replica of a Mississippi paddle steamer, at Disneyland, California, in November 1972. *D J Kingston*

Some paddle tugs have survived and even the Royal Navy found a use for them, and, indeed, continues to employ some turbo-electric paddle tugs for warship handling.

Paddle steamers introduced Londoners to the pleasures of day trips to the sea. The name *Eagle* has been associated with Thames paddle steamers from the early days, the first in 1824 being a peculiarly rigged sail-cum-paddle steamer trading to Ramsgate; in 1856 came the second *Eagle,* which had discarded sail, was 200ft long and had a speed of $14\frac{1}{4}$ knots. She was licensed to carry 466 passengers and kept up a popular passenger service for thirty years.

Other *Eagles* followed. The 275ft *Golden Eagle* of 1909 also gave war service as a troop ship, carrying over half a million men without incident. The last of the series was the *Royal Eagle,* 290ft long and launched in 1932.

Probably the most famous Thames paddle steamer was the *Royal Sovereign.* She came after the earlier *Koh-i-Noor,* which was 310ft and had a promenade deck almost the entire length and width of the ship. She was a great success when she went into service from London to Clacton in 1892. She was broken up in 1918. The *Royal Sovereign* was almost a sister ship, in service in 1893 and carrying four million passengers during her life of 32 years. Both ships had lowering masts and the funnels withdrew through the deck to pass under London bridges. Maintaining the old tradition, the paddle steamer *Caledonia* remains on the Thames to this day, having been converted into a pub on the London Embankment.

Sea-going paddle steamers still in use in the 1970s on the Clyde, besides their use for day cruises, served as passenger tenders to liners. Another fleet, Campbell's steamers, operated in the Bristol Channel. Up to the last war, a larger number of these smart little White Funnel Fleet ships were based on Bristol and Cardiff and plied between the piers of holiday resorts and out to Lundy, as well as operating from south coast resorts. The annual trips to deliver to and from a ship's southern summer base were cruises much sought after by enthusiasts.

Apart from war service in other ways, many paddle steamers were used in the evacuation from Dunkirk, and not all survived. One reason why paddle steamers were preferred in such places as the Bristol Channel is their comparatively shallow draught. A screw-driven vessel has to be given a certain depth to allow the propeller to operate efficiently. A paddle-driven vessel of the same size can perform successfully in shallower water. With a

tidal range of 40ft or so in the Bristol Channel, the shallow paddle steamer can make the most of each tide, getting into the end of a pier in the minimum amount of water and creeping up the Avon to Bristol before the tide had made enough water for any other ship.

The principles of both paddles and screws were known before steam power became possible for ships. No doubt man's familiarity with water mills influenced his choice of paddles as the first attempt at power propulsion. There is also the comparatively slow speed of turning of a steam engine, which generates considerable torque, but at quite low revolutions per minute—certainly when compared with the rpm of the internal-combustion engine more common today. This slow-turning power plant could be coupled directly to the shaft of paddle wheels, or would need only simple gearing.

Unless a propeller is very large it needs to turn very fast if it is to work efficiently, so for a propeller of reasonable size to be driven at a suitable speed by a steam engine would call for more complicated gearing. Of course, screw propeller design for the purpose was new and had to be tackled from first principles, so the simpler idea of paddles was more attractive, and it was not until about 40 years after paddle steamers had come into use that screw propellers became serious competitors. Another thing in favour of paddles was their fairly easy addition to existing sailing ships, while screw propulsion would involve major alterations.

Although the majority of paddle steamers have a pair of paddles at the sides somewhere near amidships, another method uses a stern paddle (sternwheeler). The pioneer tug, *Charlotte Dundas,* used a stern paddle. For canal work, it has the advantage of not increasing the beam of the boat. Compared with screw propulsion, it has the further advantage of being little affected by debris and it does not need much draught. Because of the advantages, enthusiastic amateurs have used stern paddles on modern canal craft. Some have even coupled them to steam power. More recently, paddles have been fitted between the split hull of catamaran-type vessels, with disappointing results.

Many of Fulton's paddle-driven river boats had side wheels, but there were others with stern wheels. In particular, on the mighty Mississippi with its many shallows and sand bars, steamers had to have extremely shallow draught. The type of passenger steamboat which evolved had many decks which braced the hull, while cargo-carrying craft had to be trussed in the length, with ropes over posts to prevent the hull hogging out of shape. Whether side or stern wheels, the paddles were of considerable size.

In the heyday of the Mississippi river boats, in the latter half of the 19th century, the boats were upwards of 100ft long, some as much as 300ft, and equipped as lavishly as the finest hotels. 'An engine on a raft with $11,000-worth of jigsaw around it' was one description. Tall twin smoke stacks, for the wood-burning furnaces, were usually forward side by side. Because of fire hazard and frequency of snagging their bottoms on submerged treestumps, many of the hundreds of these lavish pleasure boats had extremely short lives, some as little as five years. Mark Twain has immortalised these boats. The most famous, the *Robert E Lee,* is remembered in song. The *Delta Queen* is a modern traditional-style stern-wheeler which still takes passengers cruising on the river.

CRUISING IN

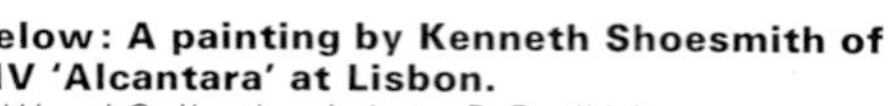
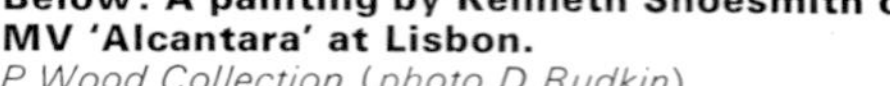

Above: An impression by Kenneth D Shoesmith of SS 'Empress of Britain'. *L Dunn*

Right: A Science Museum model of the 1927 liner 'Arandora Star'. *D J Kingston*

Below: A painting by Kenneth Shoesmith of MV 'Alcantara' at Lisbon.
P Wood Collection (photo D Rudkin)

THE THIRTIES

PLEASURE CRUISING; those are the words that once brought a picture of far-away places, of a hot sun and the answer to many a secret dream. It was a dream that became a reality in the 1920s when that kind of holiday was first brought within the reach of many.

The first shipping company to organise sight-seeing tours or cruises was the Peninsular and Orient Steam Navigation Company—the P & O Line. In 1840 the company arranged tours in the Mediterranean from Gibraltar and Malta to Athens and the Middle East.

To publicise its new cruises the P & O Company gave the novelist William Thackeray a free cruise in 1844. Thackeray sailed to Gibraltar via Lisbon and then on to Malta, Constantinople, Jaffa and Alexandria, with land excursions to Jerusalem, Cairo and the Pyramids. After his return Thackeray was very complimentary about what he called 'a delightful excursion' and recommended 'all persons who have the time and means' to make a similar trip.

Further developments took place during the last decade of the 19th century, when Albert Ballin, Director-General of the Hamburg-America Line, arranged for certain vessels to be used as 'cruising yachts'. In the succeeding years Hamburg-America liners, which were not fully employed on the Atlantic routes, were used for pleasure cruising, a practice which continued until the outbreak of war in 1914.

In the 1920s the idea of spending a holiday at sea spread very rapidly. Many people who, until then, had looked on sea travel as being the privilege of the wealthy, had begun to realise that voyages were within their grasp. 'Cruising clothes' appeared in shop windows; sun-bathing outfits, backless evening dresses and baggage, at a price for every pocket, as indeed were the prices of the new cruises, from the luxury first class down to the newly-named tourist class accommodated on the lower decks. Steerage, the original name, had acquired too many unpleasant connotations for its continued use in the new floating hotels. Many of the famous steamship companies, including the Royal Mail Line, White Star Line, Blue Star Line, Hamburg-South America Line and the P & O Line, were vying with each other for the custom of a new and growing clientele with liners devoted to pleasure cruising, all offering much the same type of voyage; the rivalry lay in the amenities they provided as they competed in the lavishness of decor and meals.

Above: Postcard representation of the 10,138-ton 'City of Nagpur' owned by Ellerman Lines and periodically employed on Wilson Line cruises in the 1930s. *L Dunn*

Top right: The Harrison Line passenger cargo liner 'Ingoma' which operated popular cruises to the West Indies. *L Dunn Collection*

Above right: Blue Funnel Line passenger/cargo ship 'Patroclus' which operated six-day cruises from Glasgow for £7 first-class in the 1930s. *L Dunn*

Right: A corner of the dining saloon of MV 'Britannic' from a White Star Line brochure of 1932. *L Dunn Collection*

The *Orford*, of the Orient Line, spent July and August running cruises to and from the western Mediterranean for £12 tourist and £21 first class. The sister ships *Orontes* and *Orcades* of the same line, were limited to the first class only and they sailed from April to September into the eastern Mediterranean at fares from about £23 upwards.

There were a great many attractive cruises at similar low prices. The Norwegian fjords, for instance, could be visited, or the northern capitals, in 13-day cruises each at a cost of £21. But undoubtedly it was the warmer climes and the sun that so excited the bulk of holiday-makers from the north. The *Homeric*, 34,350 tons, of the White Star Line, undertook nine cruises of 14 days' duration in 1933; at the same time a 14-day spring cruise in the Royal Mail Lines *Atlantis* to the Atlantic Islands cost from £25.

Several shipping companies, in addition to running short-distance pleasure cruises, catered for the passenger who wanted to travel in comfort just for a change of scene, or to recoup after illness, or simply for the pleasure of a long ocean voyage. The Union Steam Ship Company of New Zealand offered two ways to sail to and from New Zealand and Australia; going by one route and returning by the other.

The British India Steam Navigation Company advertised no fewer than 10 ways round the world at charges between £149 and £271. The P & O Company offered a luxurious holiday round the world and home again at a cost of only £149.

With the increased popular demand for cruises some vessels were specially fitted and converted for the purpose. For instance the Blue Star Line's *Arandora Star* launched in 1927, later known as the 'Queen of cruising liners', was originally fitted for the passenger and refrigerated-meat trade between London and South America. However, in 1929 she was altered to a first-class cruise liner with accommodation for passengers on the main, upper bridge and upper promenade decks. Two- and three-room suites with private bathrooms were available. One of her glories was the Louis Quatorze dining room on the upper deck, measuring 85 by 68 feet. She was luxury indeed, with a garden lounge, a very wide promenade deck and many up-to-date contrivances.

After 10 years of cruising the *Arandora Star* left Southampton on what was to be her last winter cruise in January 1939. The islands of Madeira and Trinidad, the Windward and Leeward Islands, Cuba, Puerto Rico, Florida and the Cayman Islands were visited before the liner returned to Southampton on March 16, 1939. In July 1940 the *Arandora Star* was torpedoed and sunk in the Atlantic by a German submarine.

The famous *Empress of Britain*, built by John Brown & Co at Clydebank in 1930 for the Canadian Pacific Line, was used for the Southampton-Quebec service in the summer and for world cruises in the winter. At the time of her completion she was the largest liner built in Great Britain after the 1914-18 war; she had 10 decks, and the hull was subdivided by 14 watertight bulkheads, the doors of which were hydraulically

Left: Grace Line's cruise ship 'Santa Rosa' at Curacao, from the company's travel brochure of the 1930s. *L Dunn Collection*

Below: A painting by Peter Wood of the P&O liner 'Strathnaver' cruising in the 1930s; the cutter 'Falcon' is in the foreground. *Photo D Rudkin*

Bottom left: The passenger liner 'Atlantis' in a Norwegian fjord as depicted in a painting by Kenneth Shoesmith. *P Wood Collection (photo D Rudkin)*

controlled from the bridge. Cabin accommodation on a luxurious scale was provided for 465 first-class, 260 tourist and 470 third-class passengers.

The *Empress of Britain* was 760 feet long overall and 42,348 tons gross register; her Parsons single-reduction turbines driving four propellers gave a speed of 24 knots. The three funnels were 35 feet in diameter and 68 feet in height. Flood-lit at night, with the blue line round her hull and a green waterline, the white-painted ship must have been an unforgettable sight. The *Empress of Britain* was sunk by enemy action off the Irish coast on October 28, 1940.

After the end of the 1939-45 war the popularity of the holiday cruise was revived and many fine ships were used regularly for cruising. Even the great super-liners *Queen Mary*, *Queen Elizabeth* and *France* were used as cruise ships. In the early 1970s the P & O Line operated the largest cruising fleet in the world and eight of the company's finest vessels were scheduled to make a total of 31 cruises in 1972. By the late 1970s, scheduled liner services had become virtually extinct and sea-cruising was the only activity in which the once-ubiquitous great passenger ship still engaged.

The Blue Riband Liners

THE OCCASION when the expression 'Blue Riband of the North Atlantic' was first coined appears not to have been recorded; certainly it seems to have come into common use only after the 1914-18 war. The term Blue Riband is particularly apt, however, and the Oxford Dictionary quotes in that context a definition, in use since 1848, which reads, 'The greatest distinction, the first place or prize'. It qualifies the honour in so far as the North Atlantic ferry is concerned although, in fact, the Blue Riband carried no prize or material recognition other than the attendant publicity.

It is a matter of history, however, that in 1935 an American citizen, Mr H K Hales, did present an imposing trophy, but the idea of such tangible recognition was not welcomed by certain leading shipping companies. In August 1936, when the Cunard-White Star liner *Queen Mary* took the record from the French *Normandie*, her owners refused to accept the award. In July 1952 the record passed finally to the 53,329-ton liner *United States* of the United States Lines with an average speed of 35.39 knots eastbound and 34.51 knots for the homeward passage. Now, the regular North Atlantic ocean ferry has itself passed into history and the likelihood of there being another contender for the honour is indeed remote.

The first crossing of the North Atlantic by a steamship whose owners intended anything by way of a regular service was that of the 703-ton wooden paddle steamer *Sirius*, which arrived in New York from London via Cork on April 23, 1838, after a passage of 18 days 10 hours from Cork (2961 miles). Within a few hours, however, the performance was eclipsed by Brunel's steamship *Great Western*, which secured alongside Pike Street Wharf later that same day having covered the 3223 miles from Avonmouth in 15 days 10½ hours.

In November 1838, the British Admiralty, then responsible for the carriage of British mails overseas, invited tenders for a mail steamship service between an English port and Halifax with a through connection to New York. Proposals were submitted by the British & American Steam Navigation Co, operators of the diminutive *Sirius*, and the Great Western Steamship Co, but in the event a contract, valued at £50,000 per annum, was awarded to the British & North American Royal Mail Steam Packet Co (later to become the Cunard Steamship Co Ltd) as the result of an agreement dated May 4, 1839. Cunard undertook to provide a regular service, fortnightly during eight months of the year and otherwise monthly, between Liverpool, Halifax and Boston (rather than New York) employing three 800-ton wooden paddle steamers. Later, it was decided to build four considerably larger vessels to ensure maximum availability, and the annual subvention was increased to £60,000.

The first of the quartet in service on the Boston route was the 1135-ton paddler *Britannia* which left Liverpool with 63 passengers on July 4, 1840, but not until 1847 did Cunard appear on the premier New York route. By that time, rival (unsubsidised) concerns having dropped out one by one, Cunard was in a position to command the bulk of the first-class traffic; in 1848, the company's reputation was enhanced when the 1834-ton *Europa* recorded a time of 11 days 3 hours for the 3047 miles separating Liverpool from New York. Like her several consorts, the *Europa* was a wooden paddle steamer with twin simple side-lever engines of 1400 ihp and a speed of about 10 knots. Of course, steamers of the day were usually barque or barquentine-rigged with a full outfit of sails, which would account partly for the *Europa's* record passage at an average speed of 11.52 knots.

In October 1845, the US Government invited tenders for the carriage of mails between the United States and Europe and eventually a contract was awarded to the New York & Liverpool United States

Top: Cunarder RMS 'Queen Mary' passing Spithead in July 1967. *A Greenway*

Above: 'Lusitania', of 1907, which captured the record on her second voyage; she was torpedoed and sunk during the 1914-18 war (May 7, 1915) with the loss of 1198 lives. *J Maber*

Mail Steamship Co, usually known as the Collins Line, which undertook to provide a fortnightly steamer service between those ports during eight months of the year, and monthly during winter. The subsidy of $385,000 per annum was to run for 10 years and eventually, after several changes of plan, orders were placed for the construction of four wooden paddle steamers to be named *Arctic, Atlantic, Baltic* and *Pacific.*

At 2860 tons each, the vessels were the largest afloat, except for Brunel's iron steamship *Great Britain.* Their accommodation, originally for 200 first-class passengers only, was far more luxurious than that of the Cunard ships. Among the amenities provided there were steam heating, fitted bathrooms, a smoking room and a barber's shop. Like most other early ocean paddle steamers, they were driven by simple twin-cylinder side-lever machinery, in their case of 2000ihp. In the event, additional government money had to be injected before the quartet could be completed but in April 1850, the *Atlantic* took the first sailing from New York to Liverpool and, despite damage to a paddle caused by ice, completed the passage in 13 days.

The advent of the Collins Line marked the beginning of the first real struggle for steam supremacy on the North Atlantic and in July 1850, the *Atlantic* took the eastbound record with a time of 10 days 8½ hours. By that time, the value of the attendant publicity was acknowledged and in the following October, Cunard fought back with an eastbound passage of 10 days seven hours by the 2226 ton paddler *Asia.* Westbound, however, Collins took all the honours and the *Baltic's* passage in August 1851 of nine days 18 hours was to stand untouched for a full 10 years.

Despite the apparent success of the Collins Line, which in 1851 carried three passengers for every two travelling by Cunard, the company failed to generate a profit and, notwithstanding further injections of government capital, the line foundered finally in 1858, a demise helped no doubt by the adverse publicity stemming from the loss of the *Pacific* without trace in January 1856.

In May 1856, the eastbound record was taken by Cunard's iron paddle steamer *Persia,* a handsome clipper-stemmed brig-rigged vessel of 3300 tons with a service speed of 13 knots. During later passages, the *Persia* improved on her own time but in the absence of any sustained competition there was little incentive for any radical change in the pattern of the service. The last of the great mail paddle steamers, the 3871-ton *Scotia,* established records in both directions, in December 1863 (eastbound) and July 1866 (westbound) but her success marked the end of an era.

The early mail contracts had insisted upon the use of paddle steamers but that requirement apart, Cunard had not paid sufficient attention to the several unsubsidised fleets of screw steamships by then making a name for themselves on the North Atlantic. Operators such as the Inman, Guion and Hamburg American Lines had come to the North Atlantic primarily in the migrant trade, but their ships were well found and usually provided for a number of first- and second-class, in addition to steerage passengers. In course of time, such companies put emphasis more on the first-class traffic and to the construction of ships fully equal to the best of the subsidised mail steamers. Thus it came about that on her second eastbound crossing in December 1869, the 3081-ton Inman liner *City of Brussels* broke all previous records and destroyed Cunard supremacy with a passage between New York and Queenstown at an average speed of 14.66 knots.

The credit attaching to a record run led to a tacit agreement between the companies concerned that the recognised departure points should be Sandy Hook off New York and Queenstown (now Cobh) in Ireland. In later years, however, with the increasing use of south coast and European ports, vessels headed for the Channel were timed to either Eddystone or Cherbourg until finally, in the 1930s, the American Ambrose light and English Bishop's Rock lighthouse became the accepted departure points.

A new challenger appeared in 1870 in the guise of the White Star Line, which set out to achieve new standards of comfort and reliability on the North Atlantic. Orders were placed with Harland & Wolff of Belfast for four iron compound-engined screw steamers with a designed service speed of 14 knots. Speed and superior passenger accommodation were the prime aims and, despite early teething troubles in the *Oceanic* (1871), the quartet quickly settled down. In the meantime, two somewhat larger vessels had been laid down and it was the first of the later pair, the 3888-ton *Adriatic,* which secured the westbound record for the White Star Line in May 1872 at an average speed of 14.52 knots. Eight months later, the *Baltic* crossed eastbound from New York at 15.09 knots.

The battle then began in real earnest. The Inman Line was determined to regain the premier position and ordered from

Facing page above: White Star Line's 'Celtic' of 1892, later renamed 'Amerika'. *Nautical Photo Agency (J Maber)*

Facing page below: A 1911 postcard featuring the 'Mauretania', which held the record for 22 years from November 1907. *A D Deayton collection*

Above: Illustration from 'The Illustrated London News' of March 6, 1869, depicting an Atlantic race between the 'Russia' and the 'City of Paris'. *Illustrated London News*

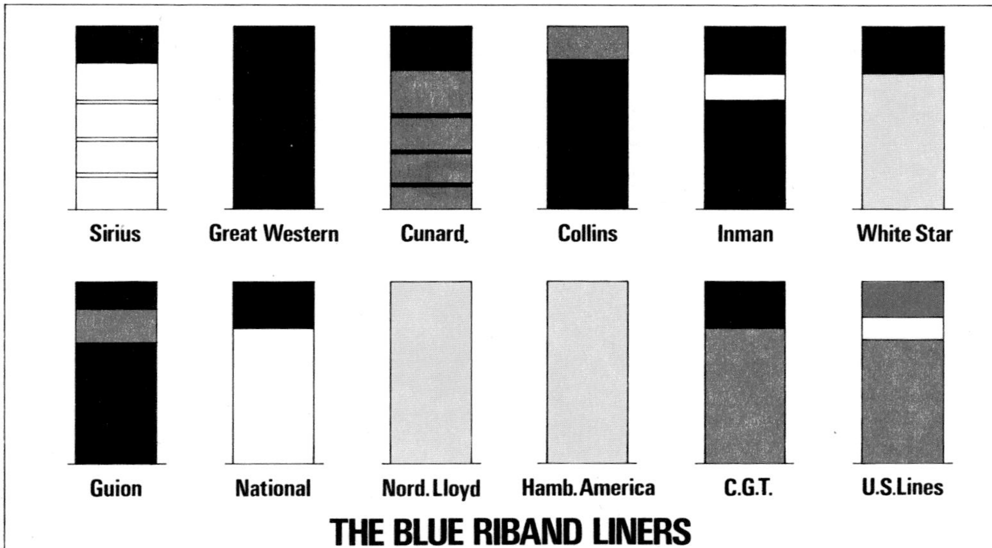

THE BLUE RIBAND LINERS

Caird's on the Clyde a 5500-ton 15-knot express liner to be named *City of Berlin.* The ship had the greatest length/beam ratio of any Atlantic liner ever built at 11:1. She was commissioned in April 1875 and in September/October of that year regained the record for Inman in both directions with average speeds of 15.21 knots westbound and 15.37 knots eastbound.

Despite the fact that five of the White Star's six ships were sufficient to maintain a weekly service between Liverpool and New York, pride and a desire to regain first place prompted the company to order two 5000-ton 15-knot improved versions of the *Oceanic,* which were completed in 1874-75 as the *Britannic* and *Germanic.* They were two-funnelled barquentine-rigged steamships of the build that even then was becoming recognised as typical of Harland & Wolff. So, the *City of Berlin's* record was short lived, for after a mere four months the *Germanic* retrieved the eastbound record for the White Star Line by a comfortable margin with an average speed of 15.79 knots. The *Britannic* followed with the westbound record in November 1876 with a passage from Queenstown in seven days 13 hours (15.43 knots).

The Inman and White Star Lines were not the only North Atlantic operators to seek fame in the early 1870s. In 1871, the Liverpool & Great Western Steamship Co (Guion Line) placed orders with Palmer's of Hebburn for the construction of a pair of 4300-ton compound-engine steamships with the avowed intention of securing the record. The *Montana* and *Dakota* were given 100psi water-tube boilers which proved utter disasters; they had to be fitted with boilers of lower pressure before their long-delayed entry into service. Undeterred by the experience, Guion went ahead with new plans and ordered a 5150-ton vessel to be named *Arizona* from John Elder & Co on the Clyde. That time, the outcome was left in no doubt and in July 1879 the *Arizona* wrested the eastbound record from the White Star liner *Britannia* with an average of 15.96 knots.

The success of the *Arizona* encouraged the Guion Line to build a consort, the 6900-ton *Alaska,* which entered service in November 1881 and soon proved herself equally satisfactory by taking the record in both directions, for the first time at average speeds of more than 16 knots. Both the *Arizona* and the *Alaska* proved expensive to run and it was decided that the only way to ensure profitability was to build a third comparable vessel to make possible regular weekly express sailings from Liverpool. Surprisingly, the 7400-ton *Oregon,* completed for service in October 1883, was built of iron rather than the by then readily available steel, but the new liner proved a flier, taking the record outwards and homewards at speeds in excess of 18 knots. By that time, however, the Guion Line was overstretched financially and within a few months the record-breaking *Oregon* was sold to Cunard, which thus fortuitously regained the North Atlantic prize after a lapse of 15 years.

In the meantime, yet another contender for the record flourished briefly, encouraged no doubt by the Guion Line's ephemeral success. The National Line's 5528-ton single-screw steamship *America,* an impressive looking schooner-rigged vessel with two tall elliptical funnels and a clipper stem, entered service in May 1884 and achieved immediate fame by breaking the record in both directions—only to be overshadowed within two months by the *Oregon*!

The *Oregon* was purchased by Cunard as a consort for the 7718-ton sisters *Umbria* and *Etruria,* completed in 1884-85, but her career under her new flag was brief, for within two years she was lost in collision near Fire Island off New York. The *Umbria* and *Etruria* shared the record for a couple of years but in 1889 the Inman Line, which had become the Inman & International Steamship Co and American controlled, reappeared to take the honours in both directions with the elegant three-funnelled clipper-stemmed sisters *City of New York* and *City of Paris.* The White Star Line also made a brief comeback with the 9950-ton sisters *Majestic* and *Teutonic* in 1889, but thereafter, the company abandoned the construction of record breakers in favour of medium-powered vessels of extreme size and solid comfort.

With the completion of the 12,950-ton

steel twin-screw sisters *Campania* and *Lucania* in 1893, the Cunard Line returned to the top. Equally magnificent in appearance and in the opulence of their appointments, they were driven at 21 knots by five-cylinder triple-expansion engines of 31,000ihp and proved reliable and consistent performers. The *Lucania* retained an edge over her sister in the matter of speed, but each took the record in turn and, with age, the performance of both improved, occasional crossings being made at more than 22 knots.

Apart from the short-lived supremacy of the Collins Line, the Blue Riband had been a completely British affair, although in fact the Inman & International record breakers of 1889 were American inspired and financed. The passage time between Queenstown and New York had been reduced to $5\frac{1}{2}$ days and, once again, Cunard held the coveted honour with a weekly service by the *Campania, Lucania, Umbria* and *Etruria*.

Towards the end of the century, the Bremen-based Norddeutscher Lloyd company determined to secure for itself a greater proportion of the lucrative North Atlantic ferry traffic and in particular to attract more custom from among the American and British public. To that end, an order was placed for a 14,350-ton twin-screw steamship which entered service in November 1897 as the *Kaiser Wilhelm der Grosse.* Capable of 22 knots, she was of strikingly individual appearance, with four funnels arranged in separate pairs and two pole masts. The new ship took the eastbound record at an average of 22.35 knots between Sandy Hook and the Needles on her third voyage and quickly followed that success with the westbound record in March of the following year.

The other great German North Atlantic company, the Hamburg American Line, followed with an order to Vulkan of Stettin for the 16,600-ton *Deutschland,* a vessel of somewhat similar appearance to the *Kaiser Wilhelm der Grosse* with four funnels in two separate pairs. Completed in 1900, the *Deutschland* fulfilled her owners' expectations by wresting the record from the NDL, but she proved expensive to maintain and suffered from severe vibration. So, after one brief and none-too-satisfactory experience, Hamburg American withdrew from the race and, like the White Star Line, sought public custom through size and comfort.

The Norddeutscher Lloyd built two further ships, the *Kronprinz Wilhelm* (1901) and the 19,350-ton *Kaiser Wilhelm II* (1903), both of which took westbound and eastbound records in turn. The machinery arrangement in the latter vessel was of particular interest in that she had four sets of quadruple-expansion engines, two to each shaft, sited in separate engine rooms.

In 1902, the British Government appointed a committee to look into the question of building two large fast vessels suitable for rapid conversion into armed merchant cruisers. In due course, agreement was reached with the Cunard Company and in the light of the report of a technical committee it was decided that the vessels should be powered by Parsons direct-drive turbine machinery. Orders were placed in May 1905 for the construction of the two express steamships the first of which, the 31,550-ton *Lusitania,* was delivered by John Brown & Co in September 1907. A graceful vessel, with four evenly spaced funnels and two pole masts, she marked the beginning of a new era in design for the Atlantic ferry and on her second voyage recaptured the Blue Riband for Cunard with record passages in both directions. Her sister, the famed *Mauretania,* built on the Tyne, entered service in November 1907 and after a certain amount of give and take between the two, the *Mauretania* settled down as slightly the faster, averaging over 25 knots.

Passage times were then under five days and it was apparent that any further reduction could only be bought at considerable expense. Thus the *Mauretania,* which first gained the eastbound record in November 1907 with a crossing at 23.69 knots, retained the honour for the following 22 years! In point of fact, the *Mauretania* matured with age and con-

tinually bettered her own times until August 1929, when, in a magnificent attempt to better the time of the NDL *Bremen*, she crossed from the Ambrose light to Eddystone at an average of 27.22 knots.

National pride brought Germany back to the competition with the construction of the Norddeutscher Lloyd quadruple-screw geared-turbine steamers *Bremen* (1929-51) and *Europa* (1930-49), which were, in fact, the first vessels to challenge the *Mauretania's* long tenure. Completion of the *Europa* was delayed by fire but the *Bremen* took her maiden sailing in July 1929 and crossed in record time from Cherbourg at an average of 27.83 knots. Eastbound, she made sure of her claim to the Blue Riband by crossing at 27.92 knots. The Norddeutscher Lloyd hold on the record was threatened briefly in August 1933, when the 51,062-ton Italian liner *Rex* crossed from Gibraltar at 28.92 knots, but that fast one-way passage on a fair weather route was not repeated. Hence, the achievement did not qualify for the Blue Riband, which needed record double crossings.

In May 1930, Cunard announced plans for an 80,000-ton 29-knot geared-turbine liner, the first of two for the weekly service from Southampton as replacements for the company's ageing trio, *Mauretania, Berengaria* and *Aquitania.* Yard No 534 was ordered from John Brown & Co on the Clyde and her keel was laid in December 1930, but a year later work was suspended in the wake of the world-wide depression. In the meantime, the French Line (Compagnie Generale Transatlantique), with similar plans in mind, had ordered an 80,000-ton quadruple-screw turbo-electric vessel, which was launched as *Normandie* in October 1932. Work on No 534 was resumed with government assistance in April 1934 after agreement to a merger of Cunard and White Star interests and the vessel was launched as *Queen Mary* on September 26 following.

Delivered to the French Line in May 1935, the *Normandie* left Le Havre on the 29th of the month and, during her first round voyage to New York, broke all existing records with an average of 29.98 knots outwards and 30.35 knots in the homeward direction. The *Queen Mary* followed a year later and although Cunard stated that it was not their intention to indulge in record-breaking attempts, she did, in due course, bring the honour back to the house-flag under which the diminutive *Britannia* had first crossed the Atlantic nearly a century before. The *Queen Mary* consolidated her position in August 1938 with crossings at 30.99 knots eastbound and 31.69 knots westbound, but in fact the two vessels were very evenly matched and the French Line made no further attempt to regain the Blue Riband before war intervened in September 1939.

To all intents and purposes, the race was over, since there was no longer any commercial benefit to be gained by higher speed which could be bought only at prohibitive cost, and which might reduce passage times at the most by a few hours. Commercial considerations notwithstanding, however, there was one record breaker still to come, namely the *United States* (1952-53), designed as a fast transport to meet US Navy Department requirements and sold on completion to United States Lines for the sum of £32 million, having cost an estimated £77 million to build. The *United States* took her first sailing from New York on July 3, 1952, and covered the 2942 miles from the Ambrose light to Bishop's Rock in three days 10 hours 40 minutes at an average speed of 35.59 knots. She returned at 34.51 knots and thus made sure of the record for the foreseeable future.

Today, even the *United States* has been taken out of service and the North Atlantic ferry passenger is whisked by jet to New York without sight or sound of the sea. Occasional summer seasonal sailings are offered by Cunard, the French Line and Hapag-Lloyd (the Norddeutscher Lloyd and the Hamburg American Line having merged their interests) but few today can connect those names with the aura and public interest once generated by any reference to the Blue Riband of the North Atlantic.

Far left: A Raphael Tuck postcard showing the 'Laurentic' of 1908; she was powered by a combination of reciprocating and turbine engines. *A D Deayton collection*

Left: Reproduction of a double-page picture of Brunel's massive 'Great Eastern' from 'The Illustrated London News' of November 7, 1857. The ship was not designed for the Atlantic trade and spent only a short and troubled time in it. *Illustrated London News*

Below left: Cunard forebear's—British & North American Royal Mail Steam Packet Company—'Britannia' of 1840, which made a first crossing on July 4 that year at an average speed of 10 knots. *Science Museum London*

Below: White Star Line's 'Germanic' of 1875, before alteration in 1895; she was later renamed 'Ottawa' and then 'Guldjemal'. *Nautical Photo Agency (J Maber)*

Right: Postcard showing the 'Etruria' of 1885 at Liverpool around the turn of the century. *J Maber*

Traditional Passenger Liners

MUCH HAS BEEN WRITTEN about the express liners of the North Atlantic ferry, but those fast vessels were not typical of their genre since they provided luxurious accommodation for a privileged minority while affording the absolute basic necessities for hundreds or even thousands of migrants in primitive steerage conditions. In addition, passage times of only a week or less were not conducive to the generation of the kind of communal spirit that developed aboard vessels trading to India, Australasia and the Far East. Apart from the voyage lasting perhaps six weeks, or even more, the numbers of passengers were comparatively small, usually first and second class (tourist in modern times) only.

An amusing comment in that connection is that in 1880 the P&O line went so far as to insert in London newspapers the statement that 'The Peninsular & Oriental Company steamers under contract for the Australian Mail Service do not carry Third Class or Steerage passengers'.

Before the 1914-18 war, migrants were catered for primarily by the provision of temporary accommodation erected in the 'tween-deck spaces of dry cargo vessels which readily found cargoes for loading homewards to United Kingdom or other West-European ports. Certain companies in the Australian trade, such as Lund's Blue Anchor Line (later the P&O Branch Line Service) and the Aberdeen Line, did provide permanent berthing for third-class passengers, however, and between the wars a number of lines built comfortable specialised vessels for the migrant trade; among them were numbered the 13,850-ton sisters of the Australian Commonwealth Line's Moreton Bay class and the contemporary 13,000-ton quintette of the P&O Branch Line's Ballarat class.

The traditional passenger liner, on the other hand, catered for businessmen, diplomatic and colonial officials, military personnel and the like, and their wives and servants, the servants usually occupying the second-class accommodation. Numbers of passengers varied considerably from a few dozen to perhaps 400 in the first class, with approximately half those numbers travelling second class.

In addition to passengers and the mails, the vessels provided considerable cargo stowage, either for goods of an expensive or attractive nature or for perishables requiring a quick passage such as frozen or chilled meat and dairy products from Australia, New Zealand and the River Plate, fruit from South Africa and tea from India and China. Regular travellers returning home for their periodical leave came to know the ships and the several companies' officers and servants well, leading to the generation of numerous legends. One of the best known is that associated with the P&O concerning the origin of the term Posh, which is reputed to have derived from Port Out, Starboard Home when selecting a cabin in order to escape the worst rigours of the sun during the Red Sea passage.

Until the mid-19th century travellers voyaged under sail, those taking up appointments in the Indian sub-continent being afforded passage in vessels of the Honourable East India Company's own fleet. The demand for regular mail services, backed by large subsidies, boosted the development of the ocean steamship, however, and the 1840s were marked by the growth of a steam network linking much of the world. It was the age which saw the founding of many of the great names in the mercantile shipping world, such as the African Steamship Co (later to come under the management of Elder, Dempster & Co), the Peninsular & Oriental Steam Navigation Co, the Royal Mail Steam Packet Co, the Pacific Steam Navigation Co and the Pacific Mail Steamship Co, to name but a few. The puny steamships relied upon sail as much as upon their inefficient machinery, which was subject to frequent breakdowns, but they did establish a pattern of services capable of meeting the needs of commerce, the military and government service.

Typical of early vessels were the Peninsular & Oriental sisters *Madras* and *Bombay*, completed by Tod & McGregor on the Clyde in 1852 for the company's Southampton to Constantinople service. Iron-hulled screw vessels of 1185 gross tons apiece, they provided accommodation for 80 first-class passengers only and after a year in the Levant trade were transferred to the short-lived Singapore to Melbourne and Sydney branch. Historically they were important since they were the first screw steamers built for a subsidised mail service, the Admiralty having insisted in earlier contracts upon the employment of paddle steamers.

With the opening of the Suez Canal in November 1869, through working to India, Australia and the Far East became possible, although it should be noted that auxiliary screw sailing vessels had maintained some sort of direct service round the Cape of Good Hope for a number of years. Few such hybrids achieved any great success, although the Liverpool & Australian Navigation Co's 3443-ton steamship *Great Britain* (now being painstakingly restored in the dock in Bristol wherein she was built a century and a quarter ago) must surely count as an exception.

Iron continued in use as the usual

Facing page: A painting by C E Turner of the Orient Line ship, RMS 'Orion', en route between England and Australia.
J Sandilands Collection

Left: Postcard of the Orient Royal Mail ship SS 'Ortona' leaving Marseilles.
J M Maber

Below left: Illustration from a Holland-America Line calendar depicting the SS 'Statendam'. *L Dunn Collection*

Below: The wintergarden lounge in the Hamburg-Amerika Line ship 'Kaiserin Auguste Victoria' as depicted on a 1907 postcard.
L Dunn Collection

material for ships' hulls throughout the 1870s, but the uneconomic simple machinery of the early liners was replaced first by twin-cylinder inverted compound machinery and subsequently by the ubiquitous triple-expansion engine which, apart from a steady increase in boiler pressure, was to undergo remarkably little change until it was finally abandoned for passenger and passenger/cargo liners in the 1930s. Steel replaced iron in the 1880s; one of the first steel-built ocean liners was the P&OSN Co's 3372-ton screw steamer *Ravenna* completed by Wm Denny & Co for the company's Australian and Eastern services in 1880. Accommodation was provided for 102 first-class and 32 second-class passengers; another sign of the changing times was that she and her iron-hulled sisters *Rohilla* and *Rosetta*, were the last liners built to P&O order with the first-class accommodation aft over the screw.

The main UK-based competitor of the P&O in the Australian trade at that time was the Orient Line, whose steel-built *Austral* (5524 tons), completed in December 1881, far surpassed her contemporaries in the rival fleet. Her maiden voyage attracted little attention, but her second voyage was marred by a series of mishaps which started with an assortment of engine defects during the passage from London to the Cape, where she was detained for a week by a smallpox epidemic ashore. More engine trouble followed and at one stage she was reduced to maintaining steerage way under sail alone until repairs could be completed.

The ultimate misfortune for *Austral* occurred while she was coaling in Sydney at the end of the outward passage, when she developed a list, flooded through the coaling ports and settled to the bottom on

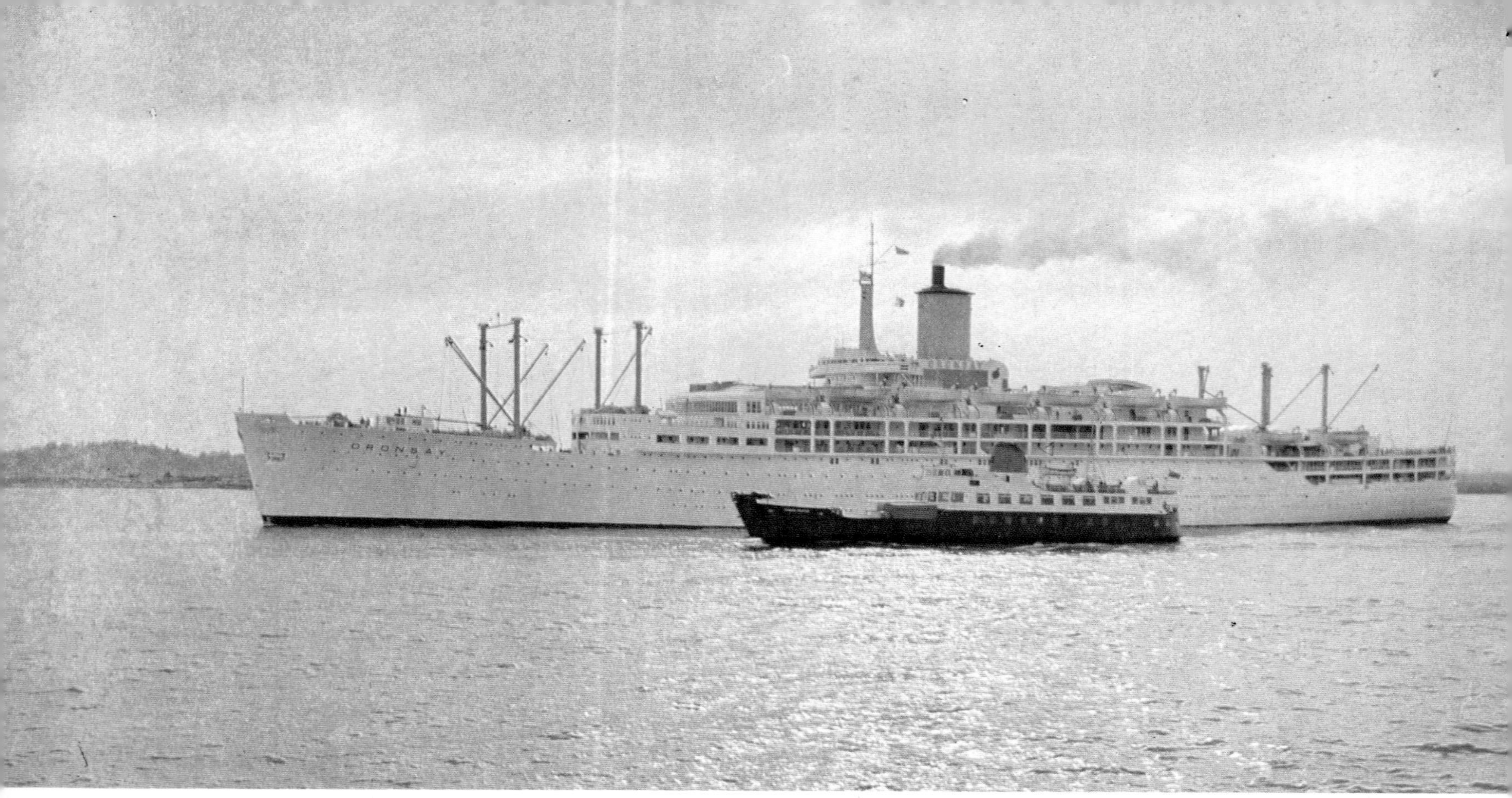

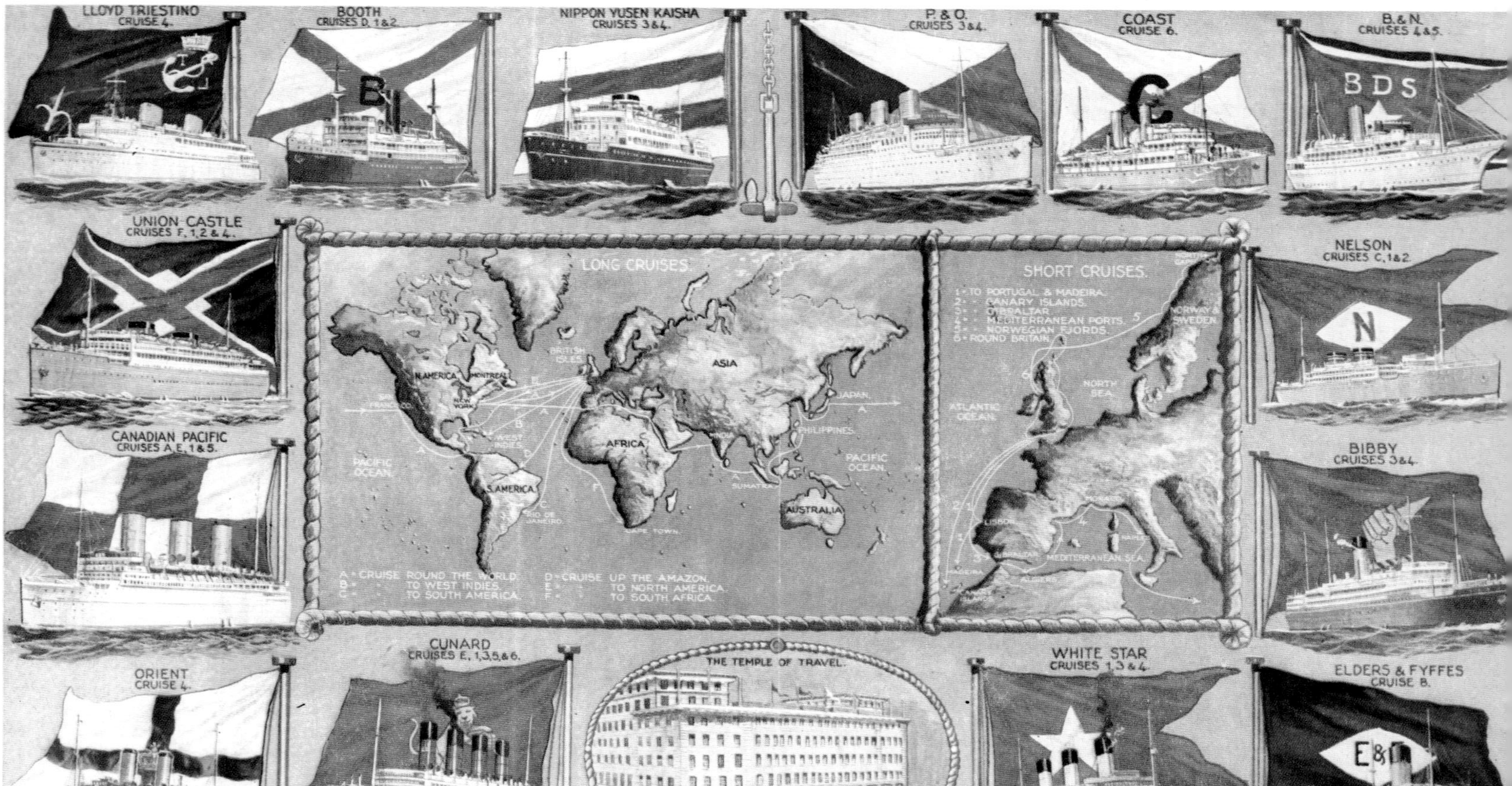
LLOYD TRIESTINO
CRUISE 4.
BOOTH
CRUISES D, 1 & 2.
NIPPON YUSEN KAISHA
CRUISES 3 & 4.
P. & O.
CRUISES 3 & 4.
COAST
CRUISE 6.
B. & N.
CRUISES 4 & 5.
BDS
UNION CASTLE
CRUISES F, 1, 2 & 4.
LONG CRUISES.
N. AMERICA
MONTREAL
NEW YORK
BRITISH ISLES
WEST INDIES
ASIA
JAPAN
PHILIPPINES
AFRICA
S. AMERICA
RIO DE JANEIRO
CAPE TOWN
SUMATRA
AUSTRALIA
PACIFIC OCEAN
PACIFIC OCEAN
A - CRUISE ROUND THE WORLD.
B - " TO WEST INDIES.
C - " TO SOUTH AMERICA.
D - CRUISE UP THE AMAZON.
E - " TO NORTH AMERICA.
F - " TO SOUTH AFRICA.
SHORT CRUISES.
1 - TO PORTUGAL & MADEIRA.
2 - " CANARY ISLANDS.
3 - " GIBRALTAR.
4 - " MEDITERRANEAN PORTS.
5 - " NORWEGIAN FJORDS.
6 - ROUND BRITAIN.
NORWAY & SWEDEN
NORTH SEA
ATLANTIC OCEAN
MEDITERRANEAN SEA
NELSON
CRUISES C, 1 & 2.
N
CANADIAN PACIFIC
CRUISES A, E, 1 & 5.
BIBBY
CRUISES 3 & 4.
ORIENT
CRUISE 4.
CUNARD
CRUISES E, 1, 3, 5 & 6.
THE TEMPLE OF TRAVEL.
THOMAS COOK & SONS HEADQUARTERS, LONDON.
WHITE STAR
CRUISES 1, 3 & 4.
ELDERS & FYFFES
CRUISE B.
E&F

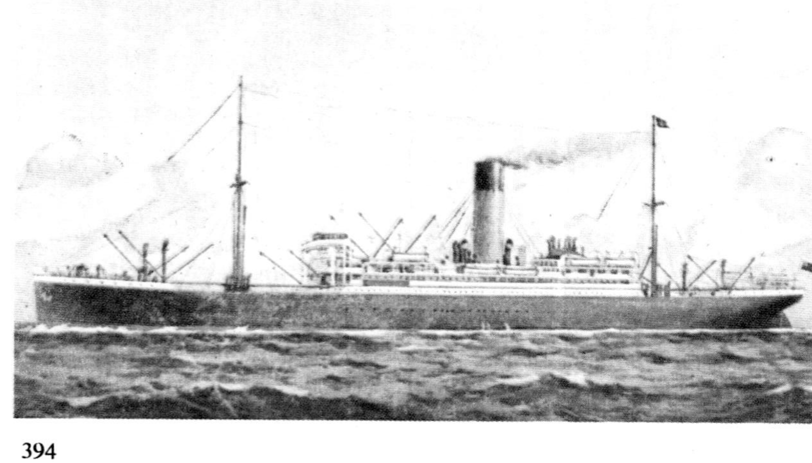

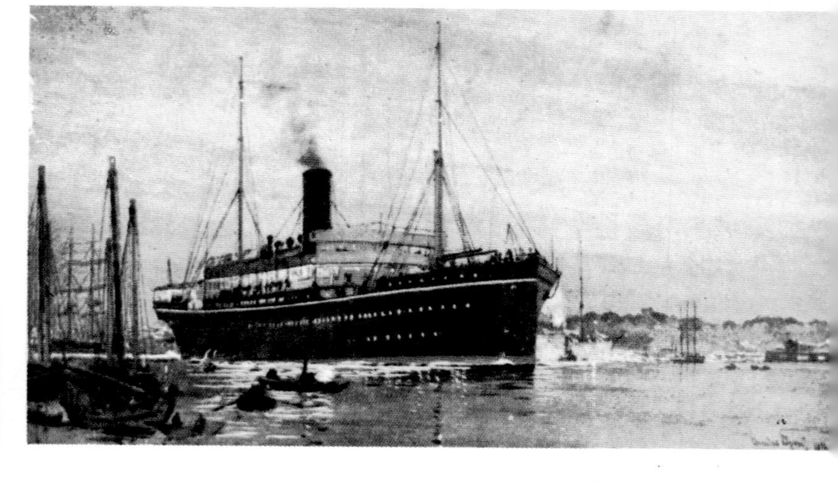

an even keel! Refloated and refitted, she resumed service to Australia in November 1884 after a series of voyages in the Liverpool to New York trade on charter to the Anchor Line. Fortunately there was no recurrence of the earlier troubles and she served under the Orient houseflag until 1902, when she was sold for breaking at Genoa.

The Orient Line surpassed even its own earlier efforts with the entry into service in November 1891 of the magnificent 18-knot twin-screw steamship *Ophir* (6184 tons). With the machinery sited between the boiler rooms, she looked somewhat unusual with her very widely spaced funnels, but in service she proved extremely popular. Like her contemporary, the Union Line steamship *Scot,* however, she was notoriously heavy on fuel; with only limited cargo stowage, she proved completely uneconomic in service, although record-breaking did create publicity and she worked to capacity in the high season, being laid up off Southend when trade was slack.

Such prestigious vessels were not typical of their time, however, for it was the many small slower but equally comfortable vessels which catered for the greater part of the global passenger traffic. Before the 1914-18 war large fleets were built up under the houseflags of such old-established concerns as the British India Steam Navigation Co, trading to Persian Gulf ports, India, Queensland (via the Torres Strait) and East Africa; the Booth Steamship Co, working from Liverpool to Madeira, Para and thence 1000 miles up the Amazon to Manaos; the Anchor Line, trading to Bombay; and Henderson's British & Burmese Steam Navigation Co which, with the Liverpool-based Bibby Line, catered for traffic to Ceylon and Rangoon.

The British India M class, completed between 1913 and 1922, ran in all to 17 vessels of which the first pair, the *Malda* and *Manora* built on the Clyde by Barclay, Curle & Co, each provided accommodation for 43 first-class and 25 second-class passengers. Of 7900 tons, they were engined with triple-expansion machinery driving screws for a service speed of 13 knots. The *Malda* and three vessels of the subsequent Mashobra class became war losses, all in 1917, but the remaining ships and their later geared turbine consorts worked the company's East African and Indian services for many years. It was not until 1954 that the last survivors of the class, the *Modasa, Matiana* and *Mulbera,* were withdrawn from service and sold for breaking. The later vessels started out with accommodation for 127 first-class and 41 second-class passengers, but second class was abolished in the 1930s.

The name of Paddy Henderson's Glasgow-based British & Burmese Steam Navigation Co will always be associated with William Denny & Co, of Dumbarton, builders of the company's passenger fleet. Sturdy single-screw vessels capable of about 13-14 knots, they provided solid comfort for first-class passengers only and worked out from Glasgow with calls at Liverpool and Naples to Port Said, Port Sudan and Rangoon. As in the case of most lines operating via the Mediterranean to the East, the call at Naples (subsequently replaced by Marseilles), enabled travellers to cut short the sea voyage by crossing overland by train.

The design of the company's steamers changed little over the years and apart from the fact that they were turbine engined and were given semi-cruiser sterns, the final pair, named *Prome* and *Salween* and completed in 1937 and 1938 respectively, were essentially copies of their predecessors of 25 years before. Those smart little vessels with their plain black hulls and single funnels, each provided accommodation for about 150 passengers and were designed for a service speed of 14 knots. Both were taken up for government service during the 1939-45 war, the *Prome* as a mine transport and the *Salween* as a troopship. They survived and, refitted with reduced accommodation for 76 passengers, returned to service under the Henderson houseflag until 1962, when they were withdrawn and sold for breaking.

An interesting sidelight on the history of the Henderson Line and the Burma trade was that the company controlled the Irrawaddy Flotilla Co, itself the economic lifeline of Burma which linked Rangoon, Mandalay and other towns by scheduled services along the great rivers and served also as a feeder for Henderson's ocean steamers. The independence of Burma and the nationalisation of the Flotilla Co in 1948 was followed by a rapid decline in the Burma trade, however, and in 1952 control of the Henderson Line was acquired by Elder Dempster Lines, which diverted the greater part of the fleet to the West African trade.

The aftermath of the 1939-45 war brought a considerable demand for tonnage in the traditional passenger liner class and many such vessels were built in United Kingdom shipyards, not only for the British register but also for owners in France, Portugal, India and Argentina among others. Those for UK owners included a quartette of diesel-driven City-class vessels for the Bucknall South African service of Ellerman Lines, each of which provided accommodation for 104 first-class passengers. The 13,363-ton *City of Port Elizabeth* took the first sailing from the Thames for the Cape, Durban, Lourenço Marques and Beira on January 10, 1953, and with the completion of her three sisters the company was able to offer four weekly sailings on a route which, apart from wartime interruptions, had remained unchanged since the 1890s. Intermediate sailings by cargo liners providing accommodation for 12 first-class passengers, however, enabled the frequency of the service to be doubled to give fortnightly departures from London.

The largest post-war fleet was that built for the Australian and Eastern services of the Peninsular & Oriental and the associated Orient Line. The 28,164-ton twin-screw steamship *Orcades,* completed in 1948, reduced the passage time between London and Melbourne from the pre-war 36 days to 26 days and introduced an accelerated service to be operated eventually by six ships. They were the *Himalaya, Arcadia* and *Iberia* of the P&O and the *Orcades, Oronsay* and *Orsova* of the Orient Line. Although essentially similar in internal arrangements and machinery, the Orient vessels were of radically different appearance, with vertical funnel and mast grouped with the bridge in a single structure, and the hull painted the distinctive corn colour adopted originally for the company's new-construction ships in 1935.

Immediate post-war developments in the field of air transport had little effect on the passenger business of the established shipping lines. The network of services disrupted by six years of war was rebuilt and until the late 1950s liners sailed with full complements of passengers both outward and homeward. During off-peak periods some of the larger vessels were diverted to cruising but all in all the liner operators enjoyed a boom period which fully justified investment in new construction. In 1956 there were no fewer than 137 ocean-going passenger vessels, other than those carrying 12 or fewer passengers, registered in the names of United Kingdom operators alone.

The advent of the big jets and the escalating cost of travel by sea in the early 1960s damped down the demand for passage, however, and in particular the businessman, to whom time represents money, turned increasingly to the speed and convenience of air travel. As the decade advanced the increasing frequency of scheduled services by air made further inroads into profitability and, with the cost of replacement tonnage rising rapidly, liner operators began to cut back their fleets. Many vessels, including ships of post-war construction, were sold to Greek or other overseas buyers enjoying lower operating costs, frequently for re-registration under the convenience flags of Panama or Liberia. Others, if not sold for breaking in the United Kingdom, joined the one-way procession to breakers in Spain, Hong Kong or Taiwan.

By the early 1970s, with one exception as far as United Kingdom-based operators were concerned, regular scheduled services by sea had become a thing of the past. Infrequent services to West Africa, the River Plate, New Zealand and the West Indies operated by three or fewer vessels, with sailings by 'twelves', offered an alternative to travel by air and indeed some preferred to take passage in one direction by sea if only to relax after an intensive business tour. For many vessels, cruising became the normal mode of employment and indeed certain operators turned their fleets over entirely to leisure travel.

The news early in 1974 that the 14,083-ton *Aureol* was to be withdrawn from Elder Dempster's West African trade marked a further reduction in the UK-registered ocean passenger fleet. Thereafter, only on the route to the Cape was a regular service still maintained, with weekly sailings from Southampton each Friday operated jointly by the Union Mail Steamship Company and the South African Marine Corporation (Safmarine). The route continued to be worked by seven ships, but one by one these vessels were withdrawn from service and on September 2, 1977, the 32,697-ton SA *Vaal,* formerly the *Transvaal Castle,* took the last sailing from Southampton to the Cape.

The Peninsular & Oriental and Cunard still offer occasional sailings on their traditional routes and seasonal services are worked, among others, by Fred Olsen to Madeira and the Canary Islands; the 4851-ton *Dwarka,* operated by P & O Strath Services and now 32 years old, still maintains the British link between Bombay, Karachi and Arabian Gulf ports, but these minor services apart there is now little alternative to the aeroplane as a mode of overseas travel.

Top left: Another popular P&O ship, the 'Oronsay'. *A Crisp*

Above left: Double-page spread from 'The Illustrated London News' of April 23, 1932, featuring typical ships and flags of the most prominent steamship companies of the time. *Illustrated London News*

Far left: The Blue Funnel Line ship TSS 'Nestor' of 14,628 tons. *J M Maber*

Left: The 7000-ton P&O ship SS 'Nore' at Yokohama. *J M Maber*

Queen Elizabeth 2

CUNARD LINE'S *Queen Elizabeth 2* is a natural successor to the other two great Cunard 'Queens', the *Queen Mary* and the earlier *Queen Elizabeth.* Since her service life started in 1969 the *QE2*, as she is colloquially known, has proved worthy of the title queen, and is as popular as a cruise ship in winter months as she is an 'Atlantic Greyhound' during the summer. In fact, the design of the ship was formulated to adapt to either role, with passenger accommodation arranged to be readily converted from single- to two-class operation.

QE2's programme is geared to modern travel trends and to make maximum use of her versatility. In fact, many of her itineraries, especially the cruises, link up with air services so that passengers can make the best of both forms of travel. All the ingredients of a luxury liner are present in the *QE2* – swimming pools, numerous sumptuous public and entertainment rooms and spaces and spacious passenger accommodation.

Queen Elizabeth 2 is the biggest passenger liner still in service at 65,863grt and 963 feet long, and much the fastest at 28½ knots, and accommodates about 2000 passengers. She was the 49th Cunarder built by the John Brown yard on Clydebank since the company completed the *Jura* in 1852. Although the latest Cunard Queen reflects the great progress made in ship design and propulsion since the earlier Queens were laid down, she has sacrificed none of the grace and majesty of the many great Cunarders that preceded her.

Top left: An aerial view of 'QE2' steaming up the Channel. *R Adshead*

Inset: The tourist class Midships Bar aboard 'QE2'. *A Crisp*

This picture: Another view of the 'QE2' in the Channel in 1972. *R Adshead*

13. Dangers and Disasters

An engraving depicting the breaking up of the 'Halsewell' on the rocks of St Alban's Head.
National Maritime Museum London

THE WRECK OF THE HALSEWELL

THE SAILING SHIP *Halsewell* was an East Indiaman, built for sturdiness rather than speed. The commander matched the ship. Captain Richard Pierce, a veteran officer, was distinguished for his resilience and determination. His ship left the East India Docks on November 16, 1785, stopped at Gravesend to complete her cargo and entered the Downs, that portion of the English Channel which lies off the Kentish coast, on New Year's Day 1786.

The weather changed mood rapidly. A favourable breeze was followed by a dead calm. Then a sharp southerly sprang up and, on the evening of January 3 the captain decided to come to anchor. The weather worsened during the night and, by dawn, a gale-force blast threatened to drive the ship on to the shore. Ordering the cables to be cut, Captain Pierce ran out to sea. Hour after hour the *Halsewell* ploughed through rolling waves, running before the wind under press of sail. Much water was shipped on the main deck. Then an examination of the hull revealed a leak. By the time it was discovered, the water in the hold was already five feet deep.

All available hands were set to the pumps. At first it seemed that the task was hopeless and the captain, willing to try every expedient, ordered the main and mizen masts to be cut away; five men were washed overboard in getting the masts clear.

By mid-morning of the 4th the weather had begun to improve; the wind died down; the water in the hold was brought under control; the clouds and mist disappeared. In the distance the outline of Berry Head could be seen. Captain Pierce ordered his crew to rig up jury-masts and, with as much canvas as he could spread, made for the safety of Portsmouth Harbour. Before he could attain his goal, however, the weather had turned once more and wind and sea began again to buffet and toss the luckless passengers and crew of the *Halsewell*. Pierce turned and turned about repeatedly but found himself unable to make safe headway in any direction for more than a few minutes. Towards evening he decided to make for the shelter of Studland Point. By eleven o'clock the skies had begun to clear and with horror the captain and crew made out the craggy promontory of St Alban's Head.

Realising at once the danger of the situation, Pierce tried to prevent his crippled ship from being drawn towards the rocky coast which would assuredly complete its destruction. Taking in sail, he let go the small bower and sheet anchors, but they were unable to hold the ship and inexorably the *Halsewell* drove inshore.

It was by then nearly two in the morning and, in his round-house on the main deck, the captain and his officers held a hurried conference to decide how they might save the passengers. But, even as they spoke, the vessel struck. Cruelly cast from rock to rock by a raging sea the *Halsewell* swiftly bilged and began to keel over, broadside on to the shore, and it was as inhospitable a strip of coastline as one could expect to find anywhere along the English Channel, with massive cliffs screening the shore from the sight of those inland and preventing any possibility of speedy rescue.

While most of the soldiers and sailors, following the orders of the second mate, swam and scrambled towards the shore as best they could, the passengers and officers crammed together in the remains of the round-house, hoping that the ship would hold together until morning light made their rescue possible. They lit candles and lamps in the hope of attracting attention, but the hope was vain, as the towering cliffs cut off all sight of their perilous situation.

A number of the seamen who managed to swim ashore did eventually manage, by some superhuman effort, to scale the heights and rouse the inhabitants of nearby cottages. But, hours before they had done so, the *Halsewell* had finally broken and its wretched complement of human souls had met their fate. Of the 240 men, women and children who had sailed with Captain Pierce from Gravesend only 74 survived. The captain, whose every resource and endeavour had failed to save his vessel, went down with his ship and with him perished both his daughters, who were among the passengers on that hapless voyage.

SHOVELL'S SQUADRON

Top: An engraving of the ill-fated Admiral Sir Cloudesley Shovell.
Mary Evans Picture Library

Above: Model of a bomb ketch similar to the type used in Shovell's attack on Toulon.
Marine Museum Lisbon

IN AN AGE when a military life was still considered superior to one afloat in the Navy, Admiral Sir Cloudesley Shovell did much to alter that long-held opinion with his dashing energy and successful exploits. He was an intrepid commander who inspired his men to accomplish great tasks, and he showed exceptional skill in the attempt to capture Toulon in 1707, where his resource at handling combined operations was seen at its best. Winston Churchill wrote of him as the Duke of Marlborough's 'trusted naval leader' and as 'Britain's finest Admiral', so his death by drowning later the same year, on his way home from Toulon, was a great tragedy for his country.

A local history of the Scillies by Robert Heath was published in 1750 under the title *Account of the Islands of Scilly,* and the following account of the disaster is taken from it.

'Sir Cloudesly Shovel, a Native of Morson, near Clay, in Norfolk, after arriving to high Honours in the Service of his Country, was lost near these islands, upon the Gilston Rock, returning from Thoulon, October 22, 1707, and not upon the Bishop and Clarks, as by some have been represented. It was thick foggy weather when the Whole Fleet in Company, coming (as they thought) near the Land, agreed to lye-to, in the Afternoon; but Sir Cloudesly, in the *Association,* ordering Sail to be made, first struck in the Night, and sunk immediately. Several Persons of Distinction being on Board, at that Time, were lost; particularly the Lady Shovel's two Sons by her former Husband, Sir John Narborough, with about eight hundred Men. The *Eagle,* Capt Hancock Commander, underwent the same Fate. The *Rumney* and *Firebrand* also struck and were lost; but the two Captains and twenty-five of their Men were saved. The other Men of War in Company escaped by having timely Notice.'

The spelling of that day was not noted for its accuracy and it was at the village of Morston near Cley (sometimes pronounced Cly) that he lived at the Manor House. To this day, the villagers either farm the land or wrest a living from the sea. Sir Cloudesley was born a few miles inland at Cockthorpe in 1650, but must have spent his boyhood aboard the deep-water ships which then entered the havens of Blakeney and Cley, before the harbour began to silt up. He was a cousin of Admiral Sir John Narborough, which was another reason why he went to sea.

Sir Cloudesley Shovell had a distinguished naval career. He began his service in the wars against the Dutch and in 1676, when a lieutenant, was in command of the boats which burned four piratical galleys at Tripoli. For that action he had petitioned King Charles II and received a medal worth £100, but later recipients, such as captains of the ships, received medals worth only £50 or £60. Four years later, Shovell was in command of the 4th Rate *Sapphire,* and from 1681 to 1686 he had another 4th Rate, the *James Galley,* and much of that time was spent in the Mediterranean. In 1687 he got command of the 3rd Rate *Anne* and a year later of the *Dover;* but within a further 12 months he was captain of the 3rd Rate *Edgar* at the battle of Bantry Bay against the French, for which he was knighted.

In 1690 he was appointed Rear-Admiral of the Blue, but missed the Battle of Beachy Head when he escorted William III to Ireland. Two years later, at the battle of Barfleur, he was Vice-Admiral of the Red, under the command of Russell, when he broke through the French line. Although the French managed to extricate themselves from a precarious situation, 15 of their ships were later burned. He must have served with distinction because he was continuously employed as a flag officer.

In 1696 he was appointed Admiral of the Blue and in 1701 was promoted to the White squadron. Three years later, as second-in-command to Sir George Rooke, he entered the Mediterranean to harass the French. In July, an attack was launched on Gibraltar by land and sea and the place fell on August 4. Only nine days later, the French fleet gave battle off Malaga, and Shovell led the English van in line abreast. When about to administer the coup de grâce against the French ships opposing him, he drew off his squadron to support the crumbling English centre, by which action the line was preserved, and for which he was highly praised.

It was considered a masterpiece and done strictly in accordance with the fighting instructions. Nevertheless, the French were able to withdraw and Louis XIV claimed a victory, with the result that Rooke's enemies succeeded in depriving him of his command. Actually, by the action Rooke defended his capture of Gibraltar, as informed circles realised. To fill the vacancy, Sir Cloudesley was appointed Commander-in-Chief, although he remained Admiral of the White.

The post of Rear-Admiral of England had been conferred on him in January 1704. It carried an annual stipend and the appointment was considered a favour from the Monarch. Although a fairly new post, a connection can be traced back to the rank of Lord High Admiral and the assistants he required.

In 1705, as the War of the Spanish Succession dragged on, the allies determined to place the Archduke Charles on the Spanish throne and Sir Cloudesley was in command of the fleet which conveyed the Earl of Peterborough and a strong force to Barcelona. The port was eventually captured and the following year Madrid was entered, thus bringing to a close the 'Year of Victory'.

The year 1707 was not so successful and the allies were defeated in Spain. The main attack against France was to be made in the south that year, while the Duke of Marlborough merely remained on the defensive in the north. Accordingly, Prince Eugene marched from Italy along the Riviera to attack Toulon, and he was supported by Shovell with the strong English fleet. The French sank about 20 of their own warships for the protection of the port and the allied fleet did some

Below left: **A view of 18th-century Gibraltar and the bay showing the new fortifications.** *M Pucciarelli*

Below right: A portrait of Sir George Rooke, Vice Admiral of England and Shovell's superior in the Mediterranean in 1704. *Mary Evans Picture Library*

Below centre: A portrayal of the loss of the 'Association', from a Raphael Tuck book. *Courtesy Mrs D Capper*

Bottom: Cutaway drawing of a naval ship of 104 guns. *M Pucciarelli*

damage to the harbour and shipping, but the land attack on Toulon failed, and the Imperial army retreated back to Italy. Accordingly, the English fleet sailed for home, calling in at Gibraltar on the way.

Sir Cloudesley Shovell flew his flag in the 2nd Rate *Association* of 96 guns (incidentally the only ship ever to carry the name in the Royal Navy). She was built in Portsmouth Dockyard in 1697 and had a length on the keel of 165 feet and a breadth of 45½ feet, giving a tonnage of 1459 burthen. She would have carried a crew of 600 to 700 men, crammed together like sardines in her hull. She must have closely resembled the *St George*, whose model is now in the Henry Huddleston Collection at the United States Naval Institute at Annapolis. The proportions of the hull are heavy, with a short length in proportion to breadth.

The foremast is stepped right up in the bows and there is a high-steeved bowsprit, with a topmast at its outer end. The fore and main masts could set courses, topsails and topgallants. A long lateen yard on the mizen set the mizen course with a square topsail and topgallant above. The gunports on the poop and upper deck were encircled with wreaths; guns were also carried on two lower decks. There was an elaborate figurehead and an even more richly garnished stern and flanking quarter galleries.

Such a ship must have been difficult to manoeuvre, as we think of it today, and would have required time to answer the helm. She must have made a lot of leeway when sailing close-hauled and a sailor accustomed to modern ocean racing techniques would have found the gear very strange and clumsy. The larger ships were really intended as floating gun platforms, although improvements were always being made.

There were altogether 15 men-of-war in the squadron which sailed from Gibraltar, with six smaller craft, but they had a stormy passage to the 'chops of the channel' and had relied on dead reckoning for days before the admiral ordered them to heave-to early in the afternoon of October 22, 1707. So confused was the fleet, that all the captains were ordered aboard the flagship for a conference to decide just where they were. It might sound ludicrous today for an entire fleet to be ignorant of its position, but the science of navigation was much more primitive then with little to assist the master except his own shrewdness and experience.

The men assembled in the rocking cabin of the *Association* would have vividly recalled how other fleets had been in dire peril at the mouth of the Channel. In 1673, Sir John Narborough's squadron from Cadiz found itself among the rock-strewn waters around the Scillies, and was lucky not to be entirely lost. Narborough observed on that occasion that 'our being northerly more than expectation is by the current that do constantly set northerly; the soundings also deceived men in their depth and ground'. Ten years later, Lord Dartmouth and his squadron from Tangier did not know whether they were nearing the coast of France or the rocks of the Scilly Islands, and sometimes the Navy sent out small cruisers to intercept homeward-bound fleets and guide them to safety.

Aboard the *Association*, all the captains, with one exception, maintained they were off Ushant, a French island at the western extremity of the rugged Brittany coast. The man who disagreed was the master of the *Lenox*, of which Sir William Jumper was captain. In his opinion, the fleet was but three hours' sail to the west of the Scillies. As the Scillies are about 110 miles NNW of Ushant, the discrepancy was great, but all the others contended that the fleet was off the French coast, and so Sir Cloudesley accepted the verdict of the majority.

While he sailed on with the main body, the *Lenox*, *La Valeur* and the fireship *Phoenix* were detached from the fleet with orders to sail direct for Falmouth. The three ships, thinking they were already in the English Channel, steered a northerly course but, as the weather deteriorated and the wind increased, altered course to ESE and then found themselves surrounded by rocks. *Lenox* and *La Valeur* wore ship and got clear, but *Phoenix* stranded on rocks near Samson Island, and it was a few days before she was got off.

Unaware of their true position, which

the master of the *Lenox* had correctly surmised, the fleet stood bravely on in the gathering dusk, with the flagship leading. It was a dirty night with rain and a confused sea when, just after nine o'clock and an hour before high water, the vanguard drove on to the rocks of the Gilstone Reef which were lying just submerged off the south-western edge of the numerous rocks and islands forming the Scillies. Also in the van were the 3rd-Rate *Eagle*, 70 guns, the 4th-Rate *Romney*, 50 guns, and the fireship *Firebrand*. The first two foundered with the flagship but the latter got off only to sink soon after. The rest of the fleet managed to claw their way to safety, probably alerted by the three guns fired from the flagship after she struck.

Accompanying the fleet was the yacht *Isabella* of 105 tons, armed with eight 3-pounders, and Captain Reddall gives a graphic description of the scene in his logbook. 'At 8 at night saw ye light of Scilly bearing SE by S distant per judgement about 4 miles. We took it to be one of our Admiral's lights; we steered after it till we perceived it to be a fixed light, it being very thick dark rainey wether. We perceived ye rocks on both sides of us; we being so very near to them we immediately wore our yacht and layed our head to ye westward, crowding all ye sail we could to weather ye rocks under our lea. We filled full and full and by God's Mercy got clear of them all for which Deliverance God's Holy Name be praised'.

The captain of the 80-gun ship *Torbay*, which was one of those that escaped, wrote in his journal what was really the understatement of the year. 'We were much to ye northward of what was expected and likewise much to the eastward'.

The number of lives lost has been given variously as between 1500 and 2000; unless there were soldiers on board the lower figure would seem to be the more accurate, if one totals up the number of crew normally assigned to each of the ships lost. There were few survivors; the chaplain of the *Association* had gone to another ship to administer the sacrament to a dying man and so was saved; the *Romney's* quartermaster, 'a lusty fat man', reached the shore alive but was badly hurt by the rocks; out of the *Firebrand* the captain and 17 men were saved in a boat and five more got ashore on pieces of wreckage.

The body of Sir Cloudesley Shovell was washed ashore on the eastern side of St Mary's at Porthellick Cove, a distance of eight or nine miles from where his ship went down. As the stern of the admiral's barge was washed ashore close by, as well as his private chest and his pet greyhound, and also the bodies of Captain Loades of the *Association*, the admiral's two stepsons and the son of the Bishop of Winchester, it is thought he might have tried to reach safety in a boat, which is a likely enough assumption. What happened to the admiral has been much embroidered by legend and the many fanciful tales woven around the incident.

A letter written nine days after the disaster says that some fishermen who were searching the shore took a tin box from the pocket of one of the floating corpses and found in it an admiral's commission, and upon examination found that the body was Sir Cloudesley's.

An account written two years later states that he was found on the shore with his shirt stripped off, by two women who confessed to the deed. By order of his chaplain, Henry Penneck, he was buried four yards from the beach, but his old friend Mr Paxton, purser of the *Arundel*, had him dug up for a decent Christian burial. The purser recognised him by a black mole under his left ear and by other marks, and he was uninjured except for a small cut on his face. Two rings were missing from one of the fingers of his left hand, although the impressions were still there; one was an emerald, later restored by a priest after the thief made a death-bed confession; the other, a silver ring with a clasped blue stone was never recovered and is said to be still in the possession of a Scillonian.

The story that he was found alive on the beach and was killed by a woman who then cut off his finger to get the rings is proved fanciful. No missing finger is mentioned by anyone who saw his body, nor by the Plymouth surgeon who embalmed him for a fee of £50. The admiral was conveyed to Plymouth aboard the 54-gun ship *Salisbury*, which had been lying in the roads, and from there the body was taken to London where he was buried in Westminster Abbey.

A fantastic story still persists that the admiral ordered a man to be hung from the yardarm of the flagship on the very afternoon of the disaster, because he voiced an opinion that the fleet was in the vicinity of the Scillies, whereas everyone else maintained that it was off the coast of France. The Scilly Islanders seem to have invented the episode as if seeking some reason to explain why the admiral lost his life, saying that Divine judgment meted out justice to him for his inhuman act. They also claimed that grass refused to grow on the spot where his body was temporarily buried. But such legends grew up a century or more later and have been elaborated during long winter nights, when gales stir the imagination.

In 1967 divers began to bring to the surface some of the treasures scattered on the seabed where the *Association* had foundered, but because of the strong currents none of the hull has survived. Indeed, divers have often been obliged to secure themselves to prevent the currents carrying them away. Rumour has it that between £1 million and £3 million was carried in the flagship, and many gold and silver coins have been recovered. Three expeditions vied with each other to recover objects and five bronze cannon were brought to the surface that first year. Two were auctioned at Sotheby's in 1969 for £3000 each. They were heavily ornamented and one had a length of nine feet nine inches and a bore of six inches. On Trafalgar Day that year one of the 3-ton guns that was sold fired six trial shots in the grounds of a shooting school at Northwood, Middlesex.

Other relics are a six-foot-high Royal coat of arms supported by a lion and unicorn which is now on the wall of the Penzance courtroom. It and the encrusted guns, silver plate, coins and other metal objects such as anchors and cannon balls are the only tangible remnants of the once-proud ships that piled up on the treacherous rocks about 270 years ago, but the men who handled them are gone for ever.

Right: An artist's impression of the disaster that struck the 'Lady Hobart' in June 1803.
K Fenwick Collection

At one o'clock in the morning of Monday June 27, 1803, while on passage for England, the packet-brig 'Lady Hobart' hit an iceberg north of the Grand Banks of Newfoundland and began to sink. In a strong gale and heavy sea, a cutter and a jolly boat were launched and all passengers (including three women, one of whom, Mrs Fellowes, was wife of the captain) and crew got aboard them, though both boats were overloaded virtually down to the gunwales.

In desperately cramped conditions, in constant danger from being swamped and with tiny rations of ship's biscuits and some wine, rum and water, they sailed and rowed in appalling weather until July 4 when, except for one man who went mad and jumped overboard, they were rescued within sight of Newfoundland, about 350 miles from where the brig went down.

TITANIC

THE UNSINKABLE SHIP

THE SENIOR MASTER of the White Star Line in 1912 was the bearded Captain Edward Smith. Aged 59, he had served the company for nearly 40 years. Twelve months earlier he had been appointed to command the new trans-Atlantic liner *Olympic*. Now he had been transferred to the newer and even larger *Titanic* of 46,328 tons. On April 1 he took the 882ft-long ship out of the Belfast yard of her builders, Harland and Wolff, and headed for Southampton at her maximum speed of 25 knots.

She was a ship of which Captain Smith could well be proud. Her passenger quarters were more elaborately fitted out, more luxuriously furnished, than the *Olympic's*. In the dining saloon 'the *Olympic* didn't have a carpet, but in the *Titanic* you sank in it up to your knees'. More important, she had a double bottom and was sub-divided by 15 transverse bulkheads. So the size of her major watertight compartments was such that she should remain afloat even though any two of them were flooded, and no one could envisage a maritime accident that would do greater damage than that. Indeed, the *Titanic* was labelled 'unsinkable' in the public mind and in the mind of her Master. That was not, however, the reason why she carried boats for only half her complement of passengers and crew. The Board of Trade's current regulations required no more.

One week after the *Titanic's* arrival at Southampton, at noon on April 10, 1912, Captain Smith gave the order to slip for her maiden voyage. Steaming out through Spithead, he set a course for Cherbourg, where he called for passengers from France. Next day the liner entered Queenstown (now Cobh), Ireland, for passengers and mail. When she took her final departure for New York she carried 1316 passengers and a crew of 891, in all 2207 souls.

The passengers were of many nationalities, though British and American predominated. ***Who's Who*** and the ***Social Register*** were well represented. The former included Mr Bruce Ismay, managing director of the White Star Line, and Mr Thomas Andrews, managing director of Harland and Wolff, professionally interested in the ship's success on behalf of the owners and builders respectively. The third-class passengers were mostly immigrants from Ireland. The ship also carried freight, the value of which made up for what it lacked in bulk; there was, for example, a priceless copy of the ***Rubaiyat*** of Omar Khayyám.

Top right: Captain E J Smith, Master of the 'Titanic'. *Illustrated London News*

Right: The elegant reading and writing room on board the 'Titanic', now at the bottom of the Atlantic. *Illustrated London News*

A portrayal of the sinking of the 'Titanic', now in the Museum of Posts and Telecommunications in Rome. *Mauro Pucciarelli*

Throughout April 12, 13 and 14, the *Titanic* steamed westwards at high speed. By midnight on the 14-15, she was about 300 miles south-east of Newfoundland. Captain Smith was not out to break records, indeed Bruce Ismay had agreed that an arrival on the 17th would be more convenient than one late on the previous night. So, on the morning of the 15th, people in Britain believed that in 48 hours' time the unsinkable ship would receive the customary firefloat and siren welcome from the people of New York, and a new jewel would scintillate in Britannia's crown.

But, before that triumph could be claimed, on the morning of the 16th, the silence of British breakfast-tables was shattered by this brief announcement in *The Times:* 'An ocean disaster, unprecedented in history, has happened in the Atlantic. The White Star liner *Titanic,* carrying nearly 3000 people, has been lost near Cape Race, and there is grave reason to fear that less than 700 of the 2358 passengers have been saved.' Next day *The Times* added: 'The news of the sinking of the *Titanic* is confirmed. It is practically beyond doubt that 868 passengers, consisting mainly of women and children, represent all that are alive of the 3196 human beings who set out on the voyage. It is a catastrophe without parallel in the annals of shipping.'

What caused the disaster, so momentous that President Taft and King George V exchanged messages of sympathy on behalf of their respective countries? On Sunday, April 14, the weather was cold but calm.

From 09.00, the liner's radio intercepted ice reports from other ships, from the *Caronia*, the *Baltic*, the *Amerika*, and the *Californian*. There were icebergs in the area through which the *Titanic* would pass. But none was sighted from the liner's bridge. Perhaps for that reason, perhaps because Captain Smith was reluctant to believe reports indicating ice farther south than was to be expected at that time of the year, he did not slacken speed when darkness fell, even though the temperature fell from 43deg F at 19.00 to 33deg F at 21.00.

The accident occurred at 20 minutes to midnight, when most of the passengers had gone to their cabins, leaving only a few in the smoking-room and third-class saloon. Half a minute before 23.40 the crows-nest lookout reported to the bridge; 'Iceberg right ahead'. First Officer William Murdoch glimpsed the glistening white shape through the darkness and ordered, 'Hard-a-starboard', followed by, 'Full astern' (old-style helm orders). But he was too late to avoid the iceberg; as the *Titanic's* bow swung to port it scraped down her starboard side.

The grinding noise brought Captain Smith on to the bridge as Murdoch rang down, 'Stop engines'. He saw nothing; nonetheless he acted on the First Officer's report by ordering, 'Close emergency doors'. Then he sent Fourth Officer Boxhall to arrange for soundings to be taken in the hold. But Carpenter Hutchinson reached the bridge before Boxhall could leave it. 'Sir,' was his breathless report, she's making water fast.'

Many of the passengers were unaware that anything unusual had occurred, so slight was the shudder when she struck. One or two thought it worthwhile to go out on deck for a moment, but if they glimpsed the berg they thought nothing of it. The *Titanic* seemed as solid and safe as had been advertised. However, it was a different story down below. The firemen in the foremost boiler-room had heard a deafening crash and had just enough time to escape into the next boiler-room before the inrushing sea overwhelmed them. They could not stay there for long because it, too, was flooding. Fortunately the next boiler-room aft, No 4, was dry. There, the firemen were troubled only by the avalanche of coal brought from the bunkers by the collision.

Although the ship by then lay stopped, the passengers had no sense of an emergency. Those that questioned stewards received a reassuring reply; she would only be delayed a few hours. In reality water was entering, not two main compartments, but all four forward of the foremost boiler-room which, with No 5, made a total of six. The berg, acting like a giant tin-opener, had sliced a gash in the *Titanic's* starboard bow a full 300ft long, a third of her length.

Captain Smith realised quickly enough that his ship was seriously damaged. He told Bruce Ismay so when he climbed to the bridge. Then, summoning Thomas Andrews, the builders' representative, he went below to see the damage for himself. The *Titanic* had a noticeable list by the time they returned to the bridge, and Andrews had learned enough to tell Smith that she must sink. The flooding could not be confined to the six compartments that were holed. As they filled and the ship trimmed by the bow, the incoming sea would flood over the transverse bulkheads into compartments farther aft, because the bulkheads extended only up to D or E decks.

At 00.05, 25 minutes after the accident, Captain Smith called all his officers and gave the order to uncover the boats. But he delayed another ten minutes before ordering his radio officer to send out the distress call.

While the *Titanic's* seamen cleared away her 16 lifeboats, eight on each side, her stewards went from cabin to cabin instructing the passengers to put on warm clothing and to take their lifebelts up on deck with them. There they waited quietly while the boats were swung out and lowered to boat deck level, when First Officer Murdoch on the starboard side and Second Officer Lightoller to port, ordered them to be filled with women and children. Only a few men attempted to defy the traditional order, although it separated many a husband and wife and divided fathers from children. But there were wives who refused to go alone, and other women who still could not believe that the *Titanic* would sink. So, around 00.30, Murdoch and Lightoller allowed some men into the boats.

Not until then were the third-class passengers allowed up to the boat decks from their own accommodation forward. The *Titanic's* considerable trim by the bows made it difficult for them to climb the ladders, which explains the disparity in the proportion of women who survived from the different classes, 217 out of 236 first and second, but only 81 out of 179 third, and all children but one from the first and second classes but only 23 out of 76 third.

Captain Smith had not yet given the order to put the boats into the water. Knowing their limited capacity, knowing, too, that no-one could survive for more than a few minutes in a near-to-freezing sea, he was anxiously awaiting news that another ship, close enough to reach her before she sank, had heard the *Titanic's* distress calls. Several had already answered; the ss *Frankfurt* at 00.18, then the *Mount Temple*, the *Virginian*, the *Burma* and the *Olympic*. But all were 150 to 500 miles away—ten hours or more steaming distance—and the *Titanic* could not last that long. But 00.25 brought a more-promising reply from Captain Arthur Rostron; the *Carpathia*, of the Cunard Line, was only 60 miles away. She had altered course and increased to her maximum speed of 14 knots, which meant that she would reach the *Titanic* in four hours' time.

However, long before that, at 00.45, Captain Smith realised that, with his ship so much down by the bows, he could no longer delay lowering boats. Andrews had calculated that the liner would only remain afloat for another hour. First, however, Murdoch and Lightoller had renewed efforts to overcome the reluctance of many passengers to fill the boats. For that reason, as well as a shortage of seamen to handle them, it took a long time to get them all away. Not until 02.05 were the four collapsible canvas boats launched.

A survivor described the scene: 'The sea was as calm as a pond, just a gentle heave as the boat dippled up and down in the swell. It was an ideal night except for the bitter cold. In the distance the *Titanic* looked enormous. Every porthole and saloon was blazing with light. It was impossible to think that anything could be wrong with such a leviathan were it not for the ominous tilt downwards in the bows, where the water was by now up to the lowest row of portholes.'

Andrews did not go in the boats. He was last seen in the smoking-room, stunned by the disaster that had overwhelmed the ship he had built. But Bruce Ismay found a place, and his survival was to add fuel to the fierce fires of criticism that later assailed his company, when he had little option but to resign his post and withdraw from public life.

The liner's crew, with the exception of the seamen detailed to go in the boats, stayed on board. Some, with the balance of the passengers, watched as they pulled away into the darkness. Others remained at their stations, especially in the engine-rooms and unflooded boiler-rooms, maintaining steam for lights and pumps until the rising waters drove them on deck. In the radio room Operator Phillips and his assistant, Bride, urged the *Olympic*, the *Frankfurt*, and the *Carpathia* to hurry, hurry . . . until at 02.10 their transmitter power failed, which was after Captain Smith had ordered, 'Abandon ship. Every man for himself'.

An eye-witness described the final curtain to the tragedy: 'At about two o'clock we observed her settling very rapidly with the bows and bridge completely under water. She slowly tilted straight on end with the stern vertically upwards. The lights in the cabins and saloons died out, flashed once more, then went out altogether. At the same time the machinery roared down through the vessel with a groaning rattle that could have been heard for miles. It was not quite the end. To our amazement she remained in that upright position for five minutes. We watched at least 150 feet of the *Titanic* towering above the sea, black against the sky. Then, with a quick dive, she disappeared. Our eyes had looked for the last time on the gigantic vessel which had set out from Southampton. Then there fell on our ears the cries of hundreds of our fellow beings struggling in the icy water, crying for help which we knew could not be answered.'

It was 02.40. Captain Smith remained to the last on the bridge of his great command and was not seen again.

Less than an hour later, at 03.20, the survivors, the 393 women and children, 119 male passengers and 139 crew who had been lowered in the boats, together with those who had subsequently been picked up, sighted the *Carpathia* coming to their rescue. At 04.10, she rescued the first boatload, at 08.30 the last. Before that she was joined by the *Californian*, of which more will be said later. At 08.40, the two ships, doing all they could to succour 705 survivors of the greatest of all peace-time sea disasters, set course for New York, where they arrived on April 21.

Why was the *Titanic* lost? In days when there was neither radar nor an ice patrol to the south of Newfoundland, Captain Smith continued steaming at high speed, despite ice warnings from other ships and despite a fall in temperature which presaged ice. But responsibility for the large loss of life, due to the limited capacity of the *Titanic's* boats, rests with the Board of Trade and the whole shipping world. The former lacked the strength to require more boats to be carried, for want of public interest when the tide of popular opinion against government interference ran strong, while the latter opposed equipping their ships with anything that did not make a positive contribution to their profits.

Three steps were soon taken to reduce the possibility of a recurrence of such a disaster. British Board of Trade regulations, and other nations' equivalent rules, were amended to require ships to carry boats or rafts for their whole complement. An International Ice Patrol was established, charged with keeping ice in the north-west Atlantic under observation and broadcasting warnings to shipping, so that vessels could be routed clear of danger. And, for ships that did not carry sufficient radio operators to maintain a 24-hour watch, an automatic alarm was devised, which responded to a distress call by ringing a bell on a ship's bridge.

So did good come out of evil. Yet over this great tragedy there remains one unsolved mystery. Half-an-hour after the collision, by the time he realised that his ship was doomed, Captain Smith's hopes of an early rescue were raised by the sight of a ship's lights to the south. Since no vessel so close answered his radio call, he tried signalling by morse light. When that produced no reply he began firing rockets. But even that had no result; that ship just steamed slowly away, or so it seemed by the way her lights disappeared below the horizon.

The two inquiries held into the disaster—one by Lord Mersey in London, the other in New York—did not hesitate to identify the vessel as the 6000-ton Leyland liner *Californian,* bound from London to Boston. She was lying stopped because of the ice danger, and was not keeping a radio watch between midnight and 04.00 because she carried only a single operator. Her officer of the watch saw rockets and reported them to his captain, Stanley Lord. But Lord did nothing until, as already mentioned, his radio operator resumed watch and learned that the *Titanic* had sunk. Then he hastened to her rescue. For failing to respond to the rockets, when his ship was only an hour's steaming distance from the stricken vessel, Lord was censured.

There are many who believe that it was an injustice. They argue that rockets were not then a recognised distress signal, that Lord was not justified in hazarding his ship by steaming through ice just to discover why some unknown vessel was putting up a firework display in the middle of the night. They argue, too, that the *Californian* was not the ship whose lights Captain Smith saw from the *Titanic's* bridge, that the *Californian* was considerably farther away, and that between her and the *Titanic* there was another vessel which should have succoured the stricken vessel.

Those who hold this view could be right. But, and it is a sizeable 'but', how strange that the supposed other vessel has never been identified. And even if Lord did not deserve censure, he cannot be entirely acquitted of failing to steam to the *Titanic's* help earlier than he did. A wiser captain, on seeing rockets fired in mid-Atlantic for no obvious reason, would have ordered his radio operator to reset watch to see whether anything more could be learned.

A braver man would have accepted the ice hazard and started to steam towards those rockets, and the lights of the ship from which they were being fired, which showed that she was a liner. Even if there was another ship nearer to the *Titanic,* and even if the *Californian* was about 20 miles away instead of the 10 claimed by those who inquired into the disaster, Lord might have reached her before she sank, and might have rescued more than those who got away in the few boats which the *Titanic* carried.

Be that as it may, it is only fair to mention that Stanley Lord, after briefly protesting his innocence, decided that his career would best be furthered by dignified silence. And since he continued to be employed in command of various ships during and after the 1914-18 war until he reached the age of retirement, he was wise to do so. Not until he was an old man, and had been vilified by the book and the film *A Night to Remember,* did he allow a campaign to be launched to clear his name. The Government has been asked to hold a fresh inquiry, but, understandably, to no avail.

Like King Charles I and Admiral Byng, Stanley Lord is now dead. No rational person now supposes that there would be any value in ordering a fresh trial of a Monarch who tried to tax his people against their will, or of a seaman who lost a battle, because it is thought they were unjustly executed. Stanley Lord was, after all, at worst guilty only of an unhappy error of judgment such as many another in the same position might have made. There is no sea captain who does not, on learning of some mistake made by another of his profession, say to himself, 'There but for the grace of God go I'.

Top: A sectional view of the main passenger staircases and possible escape routes aboard 'Titanic'. *The Sphere*

Above: 'Carpathia', the ship which answered 'Titanic's' SOS and rescued some of the 705 survivors of the disaster. *Illustrated London News*

Above: A painting by M J Barton of HMS 'Calliope' being buffeted by wind and sea during the Samoa Hurricane of 1889.

Samoa Hurricane

THE SAMOA HURRICANE of March 1889 stands out as one of the worst maritime disasters of all time. A considerable number of American, German and British warships and merchant ships were overwhelmed by a hurricane, despite being in a protected anchorage, and only one warship and a small schooner survived. The warship which escaped was HMS *Calliope*, the only British warship present, and her escape has become an epic of seamanship and bravery.

Apia Harbour is a fine natural harbour in Samoa, half a mile wide at the mouth and about three-quarters of a mile long. It is formed by the estuary of the Vaisigano River but its sides are bounded by coral reefs. It was regarded as a good anchorage in the hurricane season on account of its holding ground and the protection by the reefs outside.

Samoa began to attract attention as European traders began to penetrate the South Pacific in the middle of the 19th century. A British consulate was established in 1847, the Americans followed in 1853, and the Germans established their interests in 1861. Trade in copra flourished despite endemic warfare between native factions in the islands. American interests in Samoan affairs was particularly noticeable, and in 1872 Commodore Richard Meade in the USS *Narragansett* negotiated the exclusive right for the United States to use Pago Pago as a naval station.

The British Government kept a wary eye on that development, but their indignation was sufficient to persuade Washington to repudiate an attempt to annexe Samoa. In the spring of 1877 the American Commercial Agent had to be reprimanded for over-reaching himself, but the continual fighting among the natives of Samoa made such ideas attractive to the European commercial interests, if only to give them a quiet and profitable life. The British, who already controlled Fiji, tried to avoid involvement but the Germans resented the Americans' steady expansion of their commerce.

Inevitably the European Powers took sides in an attempt to stabilise the situation. The Germans supported a chief called Tamasese, while the Americans and British supported Malietoa. No sooner had the Germans deposed Malietoa than the Americans threw their weight behind his successor, a chief called Mataafa. Throughout 1887 and 1888 a civil war raged, with armed bands roaming all over the island. By early 1889 the situation was so tense that the German and American governments had sent warships to protect their interests. To ensure that British interests were not overlooked the corvette *Calliope* was ordered to remain in the area.

When HMS *Calliope* first arrived at Apia in February 1889 she relieved HMS *Royalist* and found the German corvettes *Olga* and *Adler*, and the American corvette *Nipsic*. All seemed quiet; the presence of the warships seemed to overawe the local chiefs. Mataafa's men even brought provisions down to the beach for sale to the sailors. The British and Americans passed the time by teaching one another cricket and baseball, but Captain Kane of the *Calliope* refused to allow general shore leave to anyone below the rank of 1st-class petty officer. The ban was not for discipline but because of the unhealthy climate; the American and German sailors were badly affected by fever and dysentery in a short while.

On February 10 the German corvette *Eber* arrived from New Zealand, followed a fortnight later by the USS *Vandalia*. To show how seriously the Americans were taking the crisis they sent Rear-Admiral J A Kimberly in the frigate *Trenton* on March 11. The line-up of warships was then: British, *Calliope*, corvette launched 1884; American, *Trenton*, wooden frigate launched 1876, *Vandalia*, corvette launched 1874 and *Nipsic*, gunboat launched 1879;

and German, *Eber*, gunboat launched 1887, *Olga*, corvette launched 1880 and *Adler*, gunboat launched 1883.

All the warships mentioned combined steam and sail, with sail power to assist their somewhat uneconomical steam engines, but they were quite capable of running under steam alone. Their speeds were nominally 10 to 14 knots, but in practice only the *Trenton* and *Calliope* could manage 14 knots; the *Eber* was good for 12 knots but the others could make only seven knots, too little for really bad weather.

As the *Calliope* was shortly to play such an important role it is not out of place to give a more full description of her. She was a steel- and iron-hulled corvette of the Comus class, useful unarmoured cruisers designed for work on foreign stations in the unending police work carried out by the Royal Navy in the 19th century. She was powered by tandem reciprocating engines driving a single propeller, but to conserve coal on long voyages she had a full ship rig. With tropical service in mind her hull was sheathed and coppered, which meant that she would not accumulate marine growths and so lose speed. When under sail alone her funnel would be lowered and the screw propeller raised to reduce drag. Although she only displaced 2765 tons (full load), the displacement of a modern destroyer or frigate, she carried a heavy armament of four sponsoned 6-inch breech-loading guns and 12 5-inch guns.

HMS *Calliope* was launched on June 24, 1884, at Portsmouth Dockyard by Lady Phipps Hornby, wife of the commander-in-chief. She commissioned on January 25, 1887, for the China Station; her commissioning was unusual in that she was still in dry dock as work on her propeller had not been finished. She left England on February 26 for China, but in September 1887 she received orders to transfer to the Australian Station temporarily as the unrest in Samoa required the presence of British ships.

The weather had not been good, and between February 10 and 14 three ships had been wrecked in Apia, but the locals assured the naval officers that the hurricane season was over. In any case Apia was a safe anchorage with good holding ground. A gale on March 7-8 caused little damage, and although the usual precautions were taken little thought was given to a report of bad weather on Thursday, March 15, 1889. The barometer was falling and it began to rain heavily, but there was no sign of wind. The barometer continued to fall until at two o'clock in the afternoon it reached 29.11.

The *Calliope* and the other warships struck their lower yards and topmasts, and got up steam as a normal precaution, but still the locals insisted that the signs heralded nothing but a heavy rainstorm. What nobody realised was that the rain had swollen the Vaisigano River to a roaring flood which was steadily washing away the layer of mud and shingle which formed the holding ground. Once the debris and mud on the harbour bottom was washed away there was nothing but hard coral or old rotten coral left, the one too hard and the other too soft to hold an anchor.

During the afternoon of Thursday, the wind came up from the north-east, and soon reached gale force. By daylight the wind was blowing a full hurricane, and found the *Calliope* with dragged anchors and close to the reef. The German gunboat *Eber* had already sunk, leaving only five survivors. The anchorage was crowded with shipping, making it difficult for Captain Kane to avoid hitting other ships. He had the reefs to worry about as well, and green seas were breaking over the *Calliope's* topgallant forecastle. The captain of the *Adler* gave up hope of trying to get free and slipped cables at the right moment, allowing her to drive sideways up on the reef. In that way she avoided sinking in deep water, and although 20 of her crew were drowned the rest remained safe until rescued two days later.

To the frightened men on board the *Calliope* the situation was getting worse by the hour. By 08.00 on Friday March 16 heavy seas were breaking beyond the reefs. The *Vandalia* was dragging down on the British corvette, the *Olga* was close on her starboard quarter, and to port was the reef. The port cable parted and the *Calliope* swung against the *Vandalia's* stern with a great crash, but fortunately she lost only her jibboom and bowsprit fastenings. Next the *Olga* came up on her starboard side and nearly rammed her, but *Calliope's* foreyard acted as a fender, and although it was severly damaged it kept the *Olga* clear.

By then the *Calliope* was within a few feet of the reef and Captain Kane decided that the best course was to make a run for the open sea. The alternative was to beach the ship on a sandy patch, and that was later achieved by the *Olga*, but Kane knew that his ship's machinery was in good condition and so he chose the bolder course. The staff engineer was asked to raise every pound of steam possible, and Kane ordered the remaining cable to be slipped (the sheet anchor had already been slipped as it had hampered movement).

Slowly the *Calliope* gathered way and pulled her bows round towards the sea. All the while the hurricane shrieked and howled in the rigging and gigantic seas broke over her bows. Lying right in the fairway was the doomed *Trenton*, the flagship of Admiral Kimberly. Although the fastest of the American squadron, the *Trenton* was ill-equipped to face the hurricane; she had shipped an enormous amount of water through her hawsepipes and was too waterlogged to move. The Americans thought that the *Calliope* had no chance of survival, but nevertheless the *Trenton's* sailors gave three cheers for the British ship as she passed under her stern. Kane took the *Calliope* so close that her foreyard nearly fouled the *Trenton's* quarter-boat, but the next moment she was clear and heading for the gap in the reefs. Everything rested on the state of her machinery now, for if her two tandem reciprocating engines broke down she would be swept back into the fatal anchorage.

There is no doubt that *Calliope's* engines saved her, for they ran at full power from 09.30 until 20.00. The wind increased in force during the afternoon, and the ship could only make one knot against it. Apia is surrounded by reefs, and Captain Kane had no idea of how close he was to them. But after 20.00 the wind began to slacken and it was possible at last to reduce speed. But it was not until noon the next day (Saturday March 17) that the wind could be described as 'reducing to an ordinary gale'. That modest line from Kane's official report is mute testimony to the appalling ferocity of the Samoa Hurricane, which his ship had escaped as if by a miracle.

The sun appeared briefly in the afternoon, allowing Kane to get a sight of land to confirm that he was clear of the coastal reefs. The *Calliope* had been carried so far away from Apia by the ferocity of the hurricane that it took her the whole night and the following day to get back and he re-entered Apia Harbour on March 19, three days since he had escaped from the harbour. However fearful Captain Kane and his ship's company might have been during those days they had no doubt that their gamble had been worthwhile. What greeted their eyes on the *Calliope's* return was a desolate anchorage, filled only with wrecks.

The *Vandalia* was under water, with only her nettings and masts showing. The *Trenton's* main deck was submerged and the *Adler* was high and dry on the reef. The *Olga* and *Nipsic* were above water but firmly aground on the sand. Of the *Eber* there was no sign, and 15 merchant ships were either sunk or wrecked. Of all the ships in Apia Harbour five days before only one small schooner was still afloat to greet HMS *Calliope.*

The fate of the other warships varied. As we have seen, the *Eber* was an early casualty; she had foundered with the loss of 73 of her crew at about 05.30 on the Friday morning. The *Adler* had managed to perch herself on the reef, and had avoided the same fate. Similarly the *Olga* and *Nipsic* had put themselves firmly ashore quite early on, and had lost only seven men between them. The *Vandalia* sank not long after the escape of the *Calliope,* but her captain had ordered all his men into the rigging to give them a chance of survival. Unfortunately the *Trenton* was then driven down on to the wreck of the *Vandalia* and most of the men in the rigging were drowned, including the

captain. The *Trenton* slipped her last cable just as the *Calliope* had done, but she promptly collided with the *Olga.* The water flooding through her hawsepipes put out the boiler-fires and so she was quite helpless. She drifted on to the reef, but all her men stood to their stations and as a result only one drowned.

HMS *Calliope* had not escaped without serious damage. She lost three anchors and three boats as well as her foreyard and spars. With no anchor buoys left and only one anchor, Captain Kane was reluctant to linger at Apia, and after taking on 150 tons of coal he left for Sydney. The *Olga* and *Nipsic* were eventually refloated and repaired by their respective navies, but the *Adler, Trenton* and *Vandalia* were total losses. The Americans sent out a salvage party to strip both ships of all fittings but the Germans left the hull of the *Adler* on the reef to act as a memorial, and she remains there to this day.

The best feature of the disaster was the way in which the Samoans went to the aid of the warships. All fighting ashore stopped immediately and both sides did all they could to save lives. Chief Mataafa sent 300 of his men down to the beach to start rescue work, and High Chief Seumanutafa took the first boat out to the *Trenton.* Nor did the harmony end there, for the disaster seems to have had a sobering effect on the protagonists. The conference held in Berlin reached a conclusion more rapidly than had been thought possible. Under an agreement signed on June 14, 1889, Samoa was guaranteed its autonomy under the protection of the European Powers and the United States. Chief Malietoa was reinstated as King, and reigned peacefully until his death in 1898.

The subsequent history of Samoa was not so simple. In 1899 the island was partitioned between Germany and the United States, with the United States annexing its portion outright and Germany granted a protectorate. The German protectorate was transferred to New Zealand after the 1914-18 war, and New Zealand has recently granted independence to its subjects. The United States, on the other hand, retains its annexed portion of Samoa as a remaining example of colonialism.

HMS *Calliope* returned to England and when she docked at Portsmouth on April 9, 1889, she was given a great welcome. She had steamed 76,814 miles, and had spent 528 days at sea out of a total of 1191 in the entire commission. The days of the rigged corvette were numbered, and she finally paid off in January 1905 preparatory to being sold for scrap. She was reprieved, however, and served as a Royal Navy Volunteer Reserve drillship on the Tyne for many years. She was finally sold in 1951.

A special Calliope Medal was struck by the Marquis de Leuville; a gold medal was given to Captain Kane, but his officers and men received a white-metal copy. Queen Victoria sent a message of condolence to President Harrison. In the United States Secretary of the Navy Benjamin F Tracy, told Rear-Admiral Kimberly that he and Congress were satisfied that the ships at Apia had done their duty with courage, fidelity and sound judgment. Congress then awarded a year's pay to all the survivors by way of compensation.

The Samoa Hurricane remains one of the best-known natural disasters in the history of the sea. Despite the fact that the loss of life and ships was comparatively light, it has passed into the annals of the sea as an event of major importance. The feat of the *Calliope* in clawing her way out to sea from that death-trap excites the senses just as it did 85 years ago.

The Royal Navy of the 1880s might not appear very progressive by later standards but the seamanship of Henry Coey Kane was not untypical of the Victorian Navy. Bred to a lifetime of seamanship and shiphandling, both officers and men of the Royal Navy were renowned for their skill and quick thinking. In the 50 years between the Crimean War and the *Dreadnought* of 1904 only 16 British men-o'-war were lost by shipwreck, collision or fire. (Although a high average by present-day standards, it was low in an age when losses of sailing merchant ships were staggeringly high). The *Calliope's* achievement at Samoa does much to explain that record.

Bottom left: Sketch showing part of the town of Apia with the shore in front of the American Consulate strewn with wreckage.
Illustrated London News

Below: The German gunboat 'Adler' of 1883, one of the numerous warships at Apia wrecked by the hurricane.
Illustrated London News

Bottom: An impression of HMS 'Calliope' passing USS 'Trenton' in the mountainous seas that wrecked Apia Harbour and most of the ships there. *K Fenwick Collection*

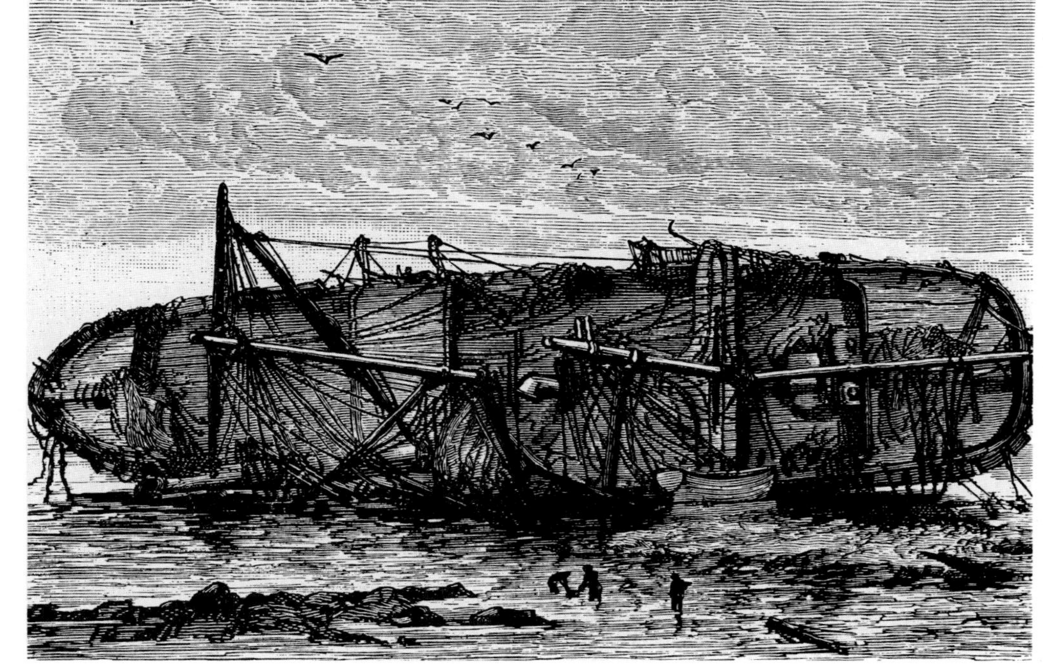

Above left: The cruiser HMS 'Juno' which was ordered from Queenstown to escort 'Lusitania' through the danger zone off the Irish coast. *L Dunn*

Above: A picture from 'The Sphere' of May 15, 1915, of two trawlers which helped in the rescue work. *London Electrotype Agency*

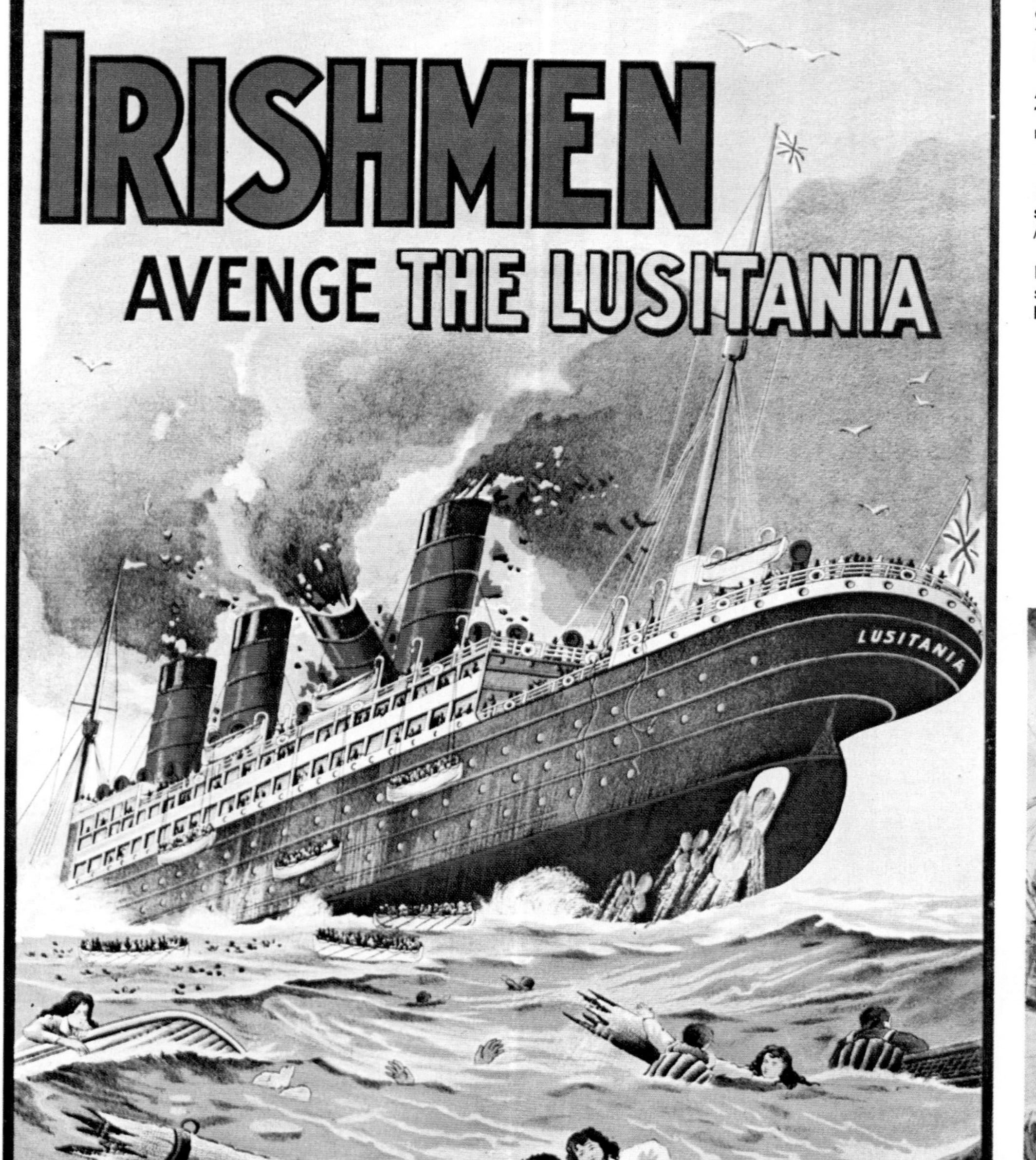

Left: A recruiting poster issued after the sinking of the 'Lusitania'.
Imperial War Museum London (photo D Rudkin)

Below: Passengers on board 'Lusitania' spotting the approaching torpedo seconds before it struck the ship. *The Sphere*

Left: A drawing by Montague Black of 'Lusitania's' arrival at New York after making a record Atlantic crossing in just under five days. *Illustrated London News*

Below left: A postcard representation of Cunard's 'Lusitania', once the pride of their fleet and sunk by a U-boat in 1915. *A Wood*

Below: The German transatlantic record holder 'Kaiser Wilhelm II' which lost the record to the 'Lusitania' in 1907. *L Dunn*

THE LUSITANIA

THE LOSS of the 32,500-ton Cunarder *Lusitania,* torpedoed and sunk 12 miles south of the Old Head of Kinsale, Ireland, on May 7, 1915, was one of the causes of the mental trauma that resulted from the 1914-18 war. That catastrophic conflict, the first to engulf all Europe for a century, pitchforked a whole generation out of their view of war as a glorious gentlemanly venture into appalled awareness of its bestiality and sordid futility. Millions who embarked on the struggle in a mood of bellicose jubilation survived it in bitter disillusionment and horrified disgust.

If the tragic end of the *Lusitania* helped to promote the painful metamorphosis, her beginnings, equally, typified the pre-war age of unashamed superlatives and grandiose assumptions. In 1906, when the *Lusitania* was launched at John Brown's Clydebank shipyard, one shipbuilding magazine named the occasion as a matter 'transcending in interest every event of the kind for many years, if not in the entire annals of shipbuilding on the Clyde'. The phrases 'epoch-making' and 'triumph of naval architecture' were liberally used and long before the new ship sailed from Liverpool on her maiden voyage to New York on September 7, 1907, she was already widely regarded as the most magnificent ship in the world. The excited enthusiastic crowd of 200,000 who saw her off certainly seemed to think so.

The *Lusitania's* overall statistics were indeed impressive. With her four funnels, four screws and measuring 165 feet from waterline to aerial tips, she carried 1800 officers and crew and had accommodation for over 2000 passengers. She was the tallest ship afloat and also among the most powerful. *Lusitania's* four direct-action Parson steam turbine engines provided enough thrust to make her a strong contender in the race to dominate the transatlantic passenger trade. Snatching that dominance from the Germans had, in fact, been Cunard's main reason for building her.

The *Lusitania,* however, had been designed to meet the challenge of war as well as the challenge of peace. Like many other liners of the time, she was built with British Admiralty requirements in mind that ships should incorporate features to allow for their wartime conversion to armed auxiliary cruisers. In *Lusitania's* case, the requirements explained why her below-deck arrangement closely resembled that of a warship; her engines and 25 boilers, her steering gear, fuel controls and other important machinery were all situated below the waterline.

The awesomely powerful machinery—75 per cent more powerful than that of any previous Cunarder—combined with the soaring magnificence of her exterior to produce an instant glamour image. The image was enhanced on her second voyage in October 1907, when she captured the coveted Blue Riband of the Atlantic from the German record-holder *Kaiser Wilhelm II.* On that occasion, *Lusitania* crossed from Queenstown to New York in four days 19 hours 52 minutes at an average speed of 25.88 knots.

Compared to the lustrous *Lusitania,* the submarine had a very ignominious reputation. It was widely regarded as a maritime troglodyte, grubbing about in dastardly fashion beneath the surface of the sea. In Royal Navy circles, submarines were generally seen as crankish contraptions which no civilised nation would be caddish enough to use in war. That blithe attitude was reflected in the fact that the 73 submarines possessed by the RN in 1907 had dwindled by 1914 to 61, of which only 17 were fit to operate outside coastal waters. Their main purpose was defensive and, it was widely supposed, their attack capabilities were minimal.

The Germans had a far more realistic concept of the submarine's potential in war; they possessed 21 fully operational U-boats, all of them capable of far longer range than the British Admiralty imagined. To the Admiralty way of thinking, the only means by which German U-boats could get to the Irish Sea was by forcing a way through the English Channel. The truth was that the U-boats were capable of circumnavigating the British Isles.

Perhaps because of the misconception, the Channel was assiduously mined and patrolled while southern Ireland, the junction for ships sailing the vital Atlantic routes, was left in a highly vulnerable state. Vice-Admiral Sir Henry Coke, in overall command of the Atlantic approach area, had at his disposal a derisory defence force of four torpedo-boats and four units of the Auxiliary Patrol. The patrols, each consisting of one armed yacht, four motor fishing boats and one motor boat, possessed five wireless sets between them and nothing more deadly than one 12-pounder gun.

Official smugness and lethargy, which had permitted such totally inadequate precautions, received a rude shake-up on September 22, 1914, seven weeks after

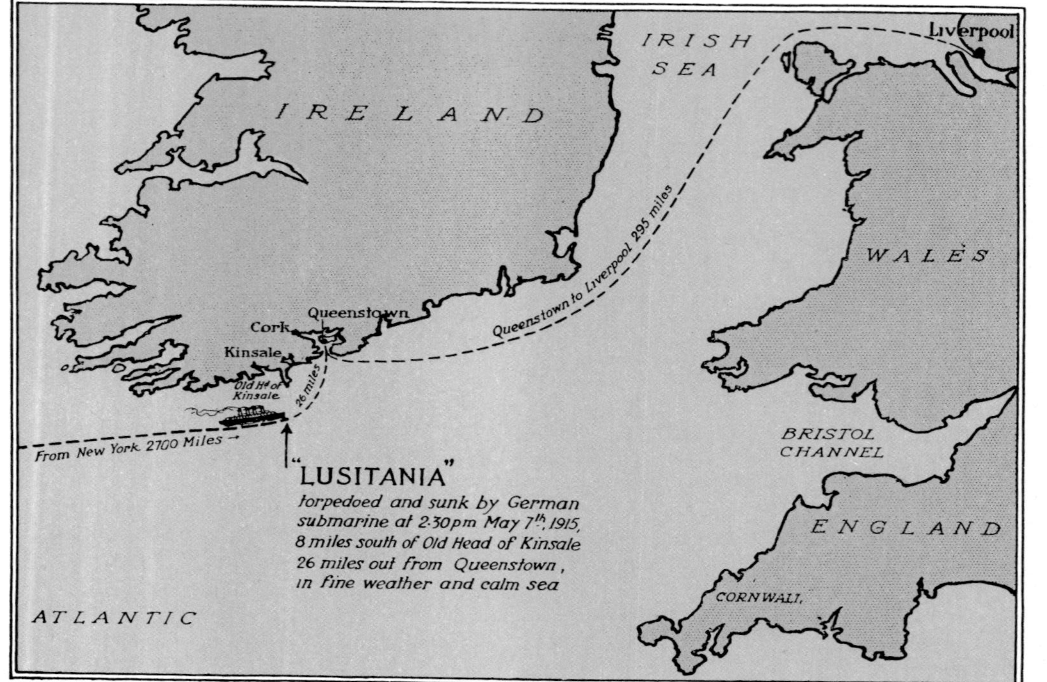

"LUSITANIA"
torpedoed and sunk by German submarine at 2.30pm May 7th 1915, 8 miles south of Old Head of Kinsale 26 miles out from Queenstown, in fine weather and calm sea

the outbreak of war. Early that morning, off the Dutch coast, three Bacchante-class cruisers, *Aboukir, Hogue* and *Cressey* were torpedoed and sunk with the loss of 1459 lives. In October, in a resultant mood of outraged fury and embarrassment, the Admiralty ordered British merchant ships to defy the Cruiser Rules and attack U-boats on sight or ram them, and to treat captured submarine crews not as prisoners of war, but as felons. The following month, the British designated the North Sea a war zone and announced that they would blockade it. The Germans retaliated in February 1915 with an even more extensive war zone and blockade—of all British and Irish coastal waters—and announced unrestricted submarine warfare.

Then an unprecedented ferocity entered the war at sea. In February and March German U-boats sank 26 merchant vessels, 16 of them without warning. Twice the *Lusitania* was perilously close to the scene. On February 20 two merchant ships only 10 miles away from her were sunk by the U-30 and on February 21 U-20 torpedoed a nearby cargo vessel.

By that time *Lusitania* was no longer among the Admiralty's fleet of wartime auxiliary cruisers; in September 1914 Cunard had been advised that the ship would not be used in that capacity. Nevertheless, a wartime role had been allotted to the ship as a carrier of munitions and other war material from the United States; she was regularly used in that role and only one of her monthly wartime voyages was made with no munitions on board.

The obvious hazards and dubious legality of such work, and the nearby disasters of February 1915, proved to be more than the *Lusitania's* master, Captain Dow, was able to countenance. On March 8, after arriving in Liverpool with 10,000 gallons of American diesel oil as cargo, Dow refused to sail again if the ship carried war materials as well as passengers. Cunard relieved Dow of his command and replaced him with the stolid and less sensitive William Thomas Turner. On April 17 Turner took the *Lusitania* out of Liverpool and crossed the Atlantic without incident.

The great ship docked at New York on April 24, just as concern there over the U-boat offensive and its effects was reaching emotional heights. Most concerned were a group of German-Americans, led by newspaper editor George Vierick, who feared that the escalation of the war at sea might force the United States to enter the conflict on the British side. The death of the American citizen Leon Thresher, who was among the victims of the liner *Falaba,* torpedoed by the U-28 on March 28, produced headlines of lurid fury in the American press and Vierick contemplated with horror what might happen if a German submarine should sink a large liner with a large American contingent among its passengers.

With the concurrence of Franz von Papen, military attache to the German Embassy in Washington, the German-Americans decided to publish a notice on April 23, warning United States citizens of the great risks they ran by crossing the Atlantic in a ship flying the flag of Great Britain or one of Britain's allies.

At that juncture, the next big passenger liner due to leave for Europe was the *Lusitania,* a fact that considerably increased German-American anxieties. The ship's resplendent reputation, the public's cocksure confidence that she could outpace any submarine ever built, the notion that the great Cunarder was somehow too sacrosanct to be harmed, all tended to dilute the warning's urgency.

The euphoria was all the more dangerous because, among more innocent food cargoes, *Lusitania's* holds were loaded with 74 barrels of oil and six million rounds of ammunition, including 1248 cases of shrapnel shells and 4927 boxes of cartridges, totalling a weight of explosives amounting to nearly 11 tons. If the ship was not a floating arsenal when she set sail shortly after noon on May 1, she was something perilously close to it. Moreover, she carried among the 2160 passengers enough prominent Americans to give the German-Americans nightmares. Among the 188 United States citizens on board were the millionaire Alfred Vanderbilt, the famous theatrical producer Carl Frohman and a number of well-known socialites.

While the *Lusitania* was nosing her way out into the Atlantic, the German submarine U-30 was creating such havoc in British home waters that the Admiralty became convinced that the area was alive with a whole pack of marauders. U-30 sank no fewer than six vessels in three days before being relieved on May 4 by the U-20, commanded by Kapitan-Leutnant Walter von Schwieger. At nine o'clock next morning U-20 was sighted north-west of Fastnet and the Admiralty stopped the departure from Devonport of the battleship

Top far left: The battleship HMS 'Orion', which was allocated as part of the escort protection for 'Lusitania' as she approached Britain en route from New York in 1915. *L Dunn*

Centre far left: Map indicating the spot off the British coast where 'Lusitania' was torpedoed and sunk. *The Sphere*

Left: A drawing by D Macpherson of the 'Lusitania' sinking, with rescuers aiding the survivors. *The Sphere*

Above: The bulk of 'Lusitania' dwarfing other shipping in New York Harbour as she left for Britain. *The Sphere*

Above: The damaged Norwegian oil-tank steamer 'Belridge' with a hole similar in size to that torn in the side of 'Lusitania' by the German torpedo. *Illustrated London News*

Orion and the recall of the *Colossus* from the North Atlantic. In addition, the escort and protection cruiser *Juno* was ordered to leave Fastnet and return to Queenstown. In Queenstown Vice-Admiral Coke was instructed to 'do his best' to protect *Lusitania*, which Captain Turner was by then bringing in towards Fastnet at 20 knots.

Coke's best was painfully inadequate, handicapped as he was by his Admiralty brief. He was not allowed to send specific warnings about dangers in definite areas; instead signals of 'a general and negative nature' had to be sent implying that 'certain areas were unsafe'. Consequently, on May 5 Coke did not warn the *Lusitania* of the day's developments and Captain Turner's plans for rendezvous with the *Juno* and a home run to Liverpool along the Irish coast made no allowance for them.

At 14.00 next day, May 6, U-20 cleared Fastnet and set course for a route along the Irish coast that would keep the submarine 20 miles offshore. That was precisely the route and distance chosen by Captain Turner for *Lusitania's* passage through the same area next morning. While the liner closed unwittingly on the sinister rendezvous, Schwieger and U-20 notched up several successes, destroying the sailing schooner *Earl of Lathom* and the Harrison Line steamers *Candidate* and *Centurion*.

By the evening of May 6, U-20's activities at last spurred Vice-Admiral Coke to warn Captain Turner directly. At 19.50 he received Coke's signal 'Submarines active off the south coast of Ireland'. Already, at noon, Turner had learned through a general Admiralty warning of the presence of submarines off Fastnet, but the precautions he was able to take were limited. He could not alter course without Admiralty permission, and if he cleared Fastnet too far out, he might miss the link-up with the *Juno*, which he still supposed would take place. The most Turner could do was to slow his ship down, extend the clearance distance for Fastnet to 25 miles, have the 48 lifeboats prepared and post double look-outs.

The *Lusitania* entered the war zone next morning in thick fog. Visibility was down to 30 yards as her siren bayed out over the water to denote her arrival to *Juno*, which was at that moment 100 miles to the east, heading for Queenstown. Straight ahead, 120 miles distant, Schwieger was debating whether or not to return home because the fog was hampering his hunting. At 11.00 he half decided to leave when he sighted motor boats patrolling outside Queenstown Harbour. Finally he resolved to wait an hour and again spy out the prospects through his periscope.

While U-20 was lurking about almost within sight of his headquarters at Queenstown, Vice-Admiral Coke was making frantic attempts to persuade the Admiralty, without success, to allow him to divert *Lusitania*. Not only had U-20 been sighted four times in two hours, but at 11.00 Coke was informed of the fate of the *Candidate* and *Centurion*. Simultaneously, he received an Admiralty warning of submarines active in the southern Irish Channel, 20 miles south of Coningbeg lightship. The news was 28 hours out of date, but Coke, his anxiety greatly increased by the pile-up of alarm, had a coded message sent to the *Lusitania*. Captain Turner later maintained that that message, which took some time to decode, ordered him to divert to Queenstown. At 12.15 he ordered a change of course to head for the harbour there.

Five minutes later and 40 miles away, Schwieger brought U-20 to the surface and moved off at full throttle in the direction of Fastnet. Behind him, the *Juno* was steaming towards Queenstown across a sunlit and by then fog-free sea, having throbbed over the submerged U-20 at noon. At 13.20, after an hour's speeding, Schwieger spotted *Lusitania's* four massive funnels on the starboard bow 14 miles ahead. Immediately, U-20 dived and Schwieger set a course that would bring him into perfect alignment for a flank shot if his quarry took a starboard turn and positioned herself parallel with the Irish coast. At 13.35, in the last of a series of tragic coincidences, Turner ordered precisely that change of course so as to bring his ship into Queenstown. At 14.10, having hurtled at high speed to gain an up-front position, Schwieger loosed a torpedo from a range of 675 yards. The missile foamed through the water and slammed into the liner's starboard side just forward of the bridge.

The explosion roared up out of the sea, sending a shudder through the whole ship. Water surged into the starboard coal bunkers and within 10 seconds the *Lusitania* had slumped into a 15-degree list. Then, a second and even mightier detonation, possibly caused by exploding munitions in the cargo, rumbled up from below and burst over the decks. Dust-filled smoke shot hot and choking out of the ventilators. The stern reared up as the ship's bows plunged below the surface and by 14.15 the foredeck was completely awash. Eight minutes later, the list had increased to 25 degrees. The propellers broke surface and revolved impotently in the air while the bows balanced momentarily on the granite seabed 320 feet below.

The rush for the lifeboats, which were suspended eight feet above the top deck, 68 feet above the water, culminated in near-panic when it was seen that on both sides of the ship, the list had swung them into an almost unlaunchable position. The crew managed to get only six lifeboats safely into the water, together with some of the 26 collapsibles. No 2 lifeboat, crammed full with passengers, crashed into the sloping deck as soon as the snubbing chain was knocked free and splintered down on top of a fully loaded collapsible. The two craft slewed down the deck locked in grisly partnership, pushing passengers along their path and squashing them as they collided with the superstructure of the bridge.

Lifeboat No 14 was half lowered when it bucked on the davits as the liner's bows struck bottom. It plummeted down on top of the wreckage of lifeboat No 12, which had crashed into the water after spilling its passengers into the sea. No 18 lifeboat met the same fate as No 2, scything a gory passage through a mass of struggling, screaming, shoving passengers and crushing at least 30 of them to death.

The sea surrounding the stricken Cunarder was soon festooned with corpses, planks of splintered wood, swimming survivors and a scattering of floating Moses baskets in which uncomprehending infants kicked and cried. The baskets were swamped by the turbulence set up when the ship's No 3 boiler exploded in a massive upsurge of steam, shearing off No 3 funnel. Giant clouds of smoke enshrouded the whole vessel, and beneath the enveloping blanket the *Lusitania* finally sank at 14.28, with what one survivor called 'a terrible moan'. When the smoke cleared away, she had vanished.

Shortly afterwards the first bedraggled survivors reached shore on the Irish coast and searchers began combing the beaches for bodies. For an 'ordinary' body Cunard offered the finder £1, and for an American £2; the top prize of £1000 was reserved for the discoverer of the body of Alfred Vanderbilt. Out of 1201 victims, the bodies of only 144 were recovered.

The convulsion of rage and recrimination caused by the loss of the *Lusitania*, in which 114 Americans died, more than justified German-American fears. The outcry scaled hysterical heights and produced newspaper comments like 'The Kaiser has proclaimed himself an enemy of the human race' and 'blood lust has toppled reason from its throne'. Germans were luridly described as 'the nation of the black hand and the bloody heart' and Germany as 'a moral and international leper'. On July 17 the court of inquiry added an official voice to the uproar by bringing in a verdict of 'wholesale and wilful murder' against Kaiser Wilhelm and the German Government.

The outcry naturally drowned out more reasoned commentators, some of whom sadly realised that total war could not be less than totally savage, while others believed that the cargo of munitions had made the liner fair game for attack. Others suspected, not without reason, that the British might have deliberately sacrificed the *Lusitania* in order to embroil America in the war. In any case, the United States was embroiled, but not until April 1917. The various opinions, in their turn, put several other 'culprits' in the firing line of accusation. Among them were Captain Turner, the British Government, the Admiralty and its First Lord Winston Churchill, the Cunard Company, the *Lusitania's* officers and, for allowing the ship to sail carrying munitions, the Customs Officer at New York and the American President Woodrow Wilson.

Public affection for great ocean-going liners, and particularly for Cunard liners, was then extremely strong. Today, in a world sated with technological wizardry, the response might not be quite the same, but even in this more blasé climate the name *Lusitania* is still an emotive one. That most tragic of the great Cunarders is still synonymous with martyrdom at sea, still a monument to the malignity of war and still cited as a poignant example of how fatal bad faith, bad luck and bad judgment can be.

THETIS

Above: The submarine 'Thetis' about to leave her builder's yard for acceptance trials in June 1939. *Illustrated London News*

THE BRITISH SUBMARINE *Thetis* was launched from Cammell Laird's Birkenhead yard in December 1936. Displacing 1090 tons, she was 269 feet long, and armed with 10 21-inch torpedo tubes and one 4-inch gun. On the surface her best speed was 16 knots, submerged it was nine. First commissioned on March 4, 1939, with a crew of five officers and 59 ratings under the command of Lieutenant-Commander G H Bolus, she was required to carry out trials before being accepted by the Admiralty.

The trials culminated on June 1, when at 10.00 the *Thetis* sailed for her first dive in Liverpool Bay, with as many as 103 on board. The additions to her normal crew included Captain H P Oram, commanding the flotilla which the *Thetis* was due to join, Engineer Captain S Jackson and other submarine officers, several Admiralty officials and various employees of Cammell Laird. She carried 131 sets of Davis Submerged Escape Apparatus (DSEA) divided between her six watertight compartments.

The Liverpool tug *Grebecock,* which was chartered to attend the *Thetis,* proceeded to sea ahead of her. Commanded by Mr A E Godfrey, she carried Lieutenant R E Coltart as naval liaison officer. Her duties were to take superfluous personnel off the *Thetis* before she dived, and to ensure that no surface vessel approached her while she was at periscope depth.

The tug and submarine met at noon by the Bar Light vessel, where Bolus signalled Godfrey to follow at nine knots. The weather was fine and the sea calm when, just before 13.30, both vessels reached a position 38 miles out from Liverpool, 15 miles north of Great Orme Head, Llandudno. There Bolus hailed Godfrey, saying he would not be disembarking anybody, that the tug should take station half a mile on the *Thetis's* port quarter, and that the diving course would be 310 degrees. Then, at 13.40, Bolus sent a signal to Flag Officer Submarines (FOSM) at Fort Blockhouse, Gosport, saying that the *Thetis* was diving for three hours, and gave the order to flood main ballast tanks.

For the next 50 minutes, Coltart, on board the *Grebecock,* watched the *Thetis* trying to dive. Bolus must have been having trouble with his boat's trim. Then, quite suddenly, the *Thetis* disappeared, and Coltart waited for her to surface; she was due to come up to check trim after her initial dive, then to dive again to periscope depth before finally going down to 60 feet and firing smoke candles. But to his increasing concern she did none of those things, so that at 16.45 he signalled FOSM indicating his anxiety. The signal was delayed in reaching Fort Blockhouse until after 18.00. Well before that, the Chief of Staff to FOSM, Captain I A Macintyre (FOSM himself was away sick), had begun to worry because no surfacing signal had been received. But since a transmission delay was always possible, he did no more for the moment than instruct Fort Blockhouse to try to establish communication with the *Thetis* by radio, and to inquire whether the Admiralty or C-in-C Plymouth had any news.

What, in the meantime, had been happening on board the *Thetis?* When flooding her main ballast tanks failed to take her down, Bolus judged her trim to be light. For the first dive of a new boat, there was nothing unusual in that. So Lieutenant H Chapman ordered the auxiliary tanks to be flooded, but the *Thetis's* conning tower still remained above water.

Chapman's trim calculations had assumed Nos 5 and 6 torpedo tubes to be flooded, representing a torpedo load. The possibility existed that, by some misunderstanding, the tubes had not been flooded before the *Thetis* left her builder's yard that morning. Lieutenant F Woods, who was in the forward compartment, decided to test the possibility by opening the cocks of both tubes. They were shown to be empty, and to confirm it he decided to open all the rear (torpedo loading) doors. First, however, he checked the indicators showing the positions of the bow (torpedo firing) caps; they were closed. Then, beginning with No 1 tube, he first tried the test cock, then opened the rear door. Nos 1 to 4 were proved dry. No 5's cock emitted nothing, so he opened its rear door. As soon as that was freed, it was swung open by a flood of water under pressure, 21 inches in diameter, pouring into the submarine.

Woods immediately realised that the tube must be open to the sea and supposed it to be fractured, so he made no attempt to close the door. He phoned the control room, 'We're flooding fast through number five tube. Blow main ballast'. Then he ordered the forward compartment to be evacuated. That done, Woods and his men tried to close the watertight door in the bulkhead dividing the tube space from the next compartment aft. But they could not clip it because one of the butterfly nuts was jammed. And, with the *Thetis* down by the bows under the weight of water in the forward compartment, they could not clear it before the flood reached the coaming of the door. So Woods ordered a further evacuation; all climbed through No 2 bulkhead, then closed and secured its watertight door.

Meanwhile, Bolus was doing all he could to surface the *Thetis,* by blowing main ballast and going full astern on the electric motors with hydroplanes hard to rise. But that failed because her bows were stuck in the mud at a depth of 160 feet. A conference between Bolus, Woods and Oram then revealed that, when the pointers of the bow cap indicators were set to 'shut', they did not all point the same way, so that Woods had misread them. No 5 bow cap was open—and its operating gear was in the flooded compartment. Quickly appreciating the danger of his boat's position, Bolus stopped blowing tanks; he knew the importance of husbanding compressed air. The *Thetis's* stern then sank until she was nearly level on the bottom, after which Bolus ordered the forward indicator buoy to be released before planning to send an officer wearing DSEA into the forward compartment, by way of the forward escape chamber, to close No 5 tube's rear door.

Unfortunately, before the escape chamber could be flooded completely to allow Chapman to pass through it, he almost fainted, due to breathing oxygen under pressure. Woods and Torpedo Gunner's Mate Mitchell then volunteered to make a joint try. That time Mitchell fainted. Second Coxswain Smithers volunteered for the third attempt, but he was also overcome, and the idea was abandoned.

The time then was 19.00, and much was happening on the surface. Although the *Thetis's* surfacing signal should have reached Fort Blockhouse by 17.05, Captain Macintyre had been unwilling to initiate emergency procedure, chiefly because he had as yet heard nothing from the *Grebecock.* But Coltart's (already mentioned) message, when it arrived at 18.15, triggered action. By 18.22 the destroyer *Brazen* in the Irish Sea had received orders to proceed to the *Thetis's* last reported position. Two submarines with underwater signalling equipment, the salvage

THE FIRST PHOTOGRAPH EVER TAKEN INSIDE A SUBMARINE.

OVERHEAD is the commanding officer's platform, and the steering-wheel. To the right is the inside tiller-wheel and below it the driving-wheel to deflect the rudders. In the middle background is the flywheel, and behind it are the submarine's engines. On the left is the indicator which shows the depth beneath the surface and the vessel's deflection from the horizontal. The question of escape from sunken submarines is seriously engaging the attention of engineers, and also that of communication with the surface. The presence of a disabled boat can be revealed by the detachable buoy connected with the vessel by a reel of wire. It also establishes telephone connection. This apparatus is now being fitted to the U.S. submarine *Plunger.*

vessel *Vigilant,* a minesweeping flotilla, HMS *Tedworth,* the Navy's deep diving vessel, and the First Anti-Submarine Flotilla and Sixth Destroyer Flotilla, then at Portland, were also ordered to the scene. So, too, were aircraft from various airfields. Finally, at 22.00, Macintyre left Portsmouth in the destroyer *Winchelsea.*

The *Brazen* sighted the *Grebecock* at 21.00 and began searching around her estimated position of the *Thetis.* Shortly afterwards an RAF flight from Abbotsinch sighted the submarine's marker buoy about seven miles away. Unfortunately their leader signalled its position incorrectly so that throughout the night the *Brazen* was unable to find the buoy.

During those hours Bolus concluded that the *Thetis* could not be brought up without help from the surface. He decided that, as soon as the submarine had been located by rescue craft, one or more officers or men should be sent to the surface by way of the after escape chamber, to ask for a high-pressure air pipe to be connected to the submarine to blow out the flood water. Towards dawn, by jettisoning fuel and moving fresh water

from tanks aft, Bolus raised the submarine's stern to bring the after escape chamber near to the surface. By 07.00 the *Thetis* had assumed an angle of 34 degrees down by the bows. However, conditions within the submarine had seriously deteriorated; with two compartments flooded and a double crew on board, the available air would not support life much beyond 15.00 that afternoon and escape was becoming a matter of urgency unless salvage could be rapid. But as yet there was no indication that any craft had reached the scene; anyone who went to the surface would be risking his life by drowning.

Oram and Woods accepted the risk; between them they had all the knowledge of the *Thetis* needed for rescue craft to take speedy action. Wearing DSEA the two officers left the *Thetis* through the after escape chamber just after 08.00. They had only 20 feet to go to reach the surface. One hour earlier Lieutenant-Commander Mills in the *Brazen* had decided to search to the north and east of his position during the night with the result that at 07.50 he sighted the submarine's stern showing above the surface. He promptly lowered two whalers to save anyone who might come to the surface, thereby rescuing Oram and Woods.

There was some delay aboard the *Thetis* before anyone else could be sent up. Water draining from the escape chamber caused a short circuit in the motor room, and an electrical fire had to be extinguished and the resulting smoke dispelled, before Chapman ordered two of the *Thetis's* ratings and two of Cammell Laird's employees into the escape chamber. It was then flooded, but after that those watching through its window could see no sign that the four men were opening the escape hatch. So the chamber was drained again and the door opened. Its occupants had to be pulled out; three were already dead and one managed to gasp, before he lapsed into unconsciousness, that the hatch was jammed.

Bolus vetoed further attempts at sending four men into the chamber. Instead, he sent in one of his ratings, Leading Stoker Arnold, and one of Cammell Laird's men, Mr Frank Shaw. They also had difficulty with the hatch and suffered nausea and dizziness, but just before 10.00 they reached the surface. A few moments later they were hauled into the *Brazen's* waiting whaler.

By that time the *Vigilant* had arrived on the scene. As soon as her Captain Hart had been told about Bolus's plan, he radioed for oxy-acetylene cutting gear, a portable air compressor, and divers. At 10.40, the Sixth Destroyer Flotilla arrived. Having conferred with Oram, Mills, and Hart, Captain R S G Nicholson of the *Somali*, the senior officer, concluded that, in the time available before the remaining air in the submarine became too foul to breathe, it was impossible for everyone in her to make their way to the surface by the escape chamber. It was therefore decided to connect the destroyer's armoured air

Facing page top: A picture from 'The Illustrated London News' of November 1906 showing the first photograph ever taken inside a submarine. *Illustrated London News*

Bottom centre group: A series of pictures of the attempt on June 2 to raise 'Thetis', showing 'Vigilant' with tow-rope attached to the stern of the submarine, and two pictures of the eventual raising and lifting ashore on November 23, 1939.
All Barnaby's Picture Library

Above: A method mooted by Sea Salvage Co in 1912 of raising a sunken submarine, prompted by the loss of the A3.
Illustrated London News

Left: The Davis deep-sea observation chamber evolved by Siebe Gorman & Co in the early 1930s. *Illustrated London News*

Above: HM Submarine 'Thunderbolt', as 'Thetis' was renamed, probably soon after commissioning early in 1941.
Barnaby's Picture Library

Right: Raising submarine 'Artemis' which sank by the quay at HMS 'Dolphin' in July 1971. *J Eastland*

Far right: Drawings from 'The Illustrated London News' of January 21, 1950, showing methods of escape from sunken submarines.
Illustrated London News

HOW ESCAPE IS MADE FROM A DISABLED SUBMARINE: TWO METHODS BY WHICH MEN, WEARING THE DAVIS ESCAPE APPARAT
LEAVE BY THE ESCAPE HATCHES—(MAIN PICTURE) THE FIXED CHAMBER; (INSET, TOP LEFT) THE TWILL COLLAPSIBLE TU

hose, used for charging torpedoes with compressed air, to the submarine's gun recuperator, and thus supply the *Thetis* with fresh air. As soon as the rising tide allowed, the *Vigilant's* diver went down. But, in the half-hour available to him, he was unable to do the job. It would be 17.30 before he could try again at low water. And that would be two and a half hours after all life on board the *Thetis* would be extinct.

Meanwhile, around noon, the *Vigilant* passed a wire hawser round the *Thetis's* stern to prevent it sinking. Two tugs and the *Vigilant* subsequently took the strain and by 13.30 the *Thetis* was visibly higher out of the water. Because there had been no sign of anybody else escaping, Hart's purpose was to bring one of the after manholes sufficiently far above water for it to be opened. From a precarious perch on the steeply slanting hull, Wreckmaster Brock managed to remove an outer manhole cover. But, at 14.40, before he could unscrew the inner one, the *Thetis* suddenly pivoted round on her mud-embedded stem, and sank.

Since the tug *Crosby* then arrived with oxy-acetylene cutting gear, it was decided to use that to gain access and allow escape from the submarine. Once again the *Vigilant* and two tugs took the strain on the wire around the *Thetis's* stern, bringing it up far enough to start cutting. But before that could begin, the submarine heeled over until the wire parted, and the *Thetis* again sank below the sea. For a short time her stern stayed only a few feet below the surface, long enough for the *Vigilant* to make one vain attempt to pass another wire. Then she went to the bottom, to the despair of all who watched.

Meanwhile, within the *Thetis*, preparations had been made for another pair of men to leave. Unfortunately, because everyone on board was suffering from a shortage of oxygen, the proper drill was not carried out; the escape hatch, which had been opened by Arnold and Shaw, was not properly closed. So when Lieutenant W A Poland and another of Cammell Laird's men tried to escape from the flooded chamber, they found the hatch foul, and before it could be drained down to pull them back into the boat, Poland collapsed and died. When the Cammell Laird man explained the difficulty, Bolus selected two more to make the attempt, but they too failed to move the hatch.

It was then getting cold inside the submarine, so Bolus called everybody together for warmth at the after end—30 in the steering compartment and nearly 70 in the engine room. There they listened to the sounds of Brock's vain attempt to remove the manhole cover. There was still enough life in them for two to try the escape chamber again when the submarine suddenly swung round on her stem. But someone opened its door into the engine room while the flood valve was open, and the sea poured in. Within a few minutes, all within the submarine died, either by drowning or by carbon-dioxide poisoning under pressure of the incoming water. And under its weight the *Thetis* canted, parting the *Vigilant's* second wire, and sank to the bottom.

The *Winchelsea*, with Captain Macintyre onboard, reached the scene at 17.20. At 20.30 another salvage vessel, the *Salvor*, arrived, and a little later Mr Thomas McKenzie, the salvage expert, with seven of his diving staff from Scapa Flow. At 00.25 on June 3, the next slack water, the senior of them went down to check by hammering on the hull whether anyone was still alive. He found the *Thetis* lying on an even keel, with a list of 30 degrees, but his signals received no reply. Then came the *Tedworth* from Greenock with two 'camels'. And at 16.00, low water, several of the Navy's divers went down, as well as Mr McKenzie's men, but only to confirm what had been known since around midnight about the sunken submarine.

During the forenoon the Commander-in-Chief Plymouth reached Liverpool Bay. From his own experience of submarines, he realised, after conferring with all concerned, that there could be no hope of further survivors. So diving was suspended, and at 16.10, about 48 hours after the accident, Whitehall issued the tragic announcement, 'The Admiralty regrets that hope of saving lives in the *Thetis* must be abandoned'. Only four of the *Thetis's* trial complement of 103 had survived one of the most tragic disasters in British submarine history. To those who died Oram paid the tribute, 'I would like to make known the excellent behaviour of all the men on board. I saw no sign of panic at any time. I heard men talking and joking until the foul air caused them to keep quiet; and they showed a quiet bravery which is a memory which will live with me for ever'.

Mr Justice Bucknill's subsequent inquiry referred to 'the many mischances which almost conspired to lose the *Thetis* in a sea of troubles'. There was the Cammell Laird employee who, after coating the inside of No 5 torpedo tube with bitumastic, failed to ensure that the test cock was clear of the preservative. There was the Admiralty inspector who failed to check it. Lieutenant Woods, having tried the test cock and supposed that the tube was dry, failed to use the rimer provided to ensure that the hole was not blocked with bitumastic or some other obstruction before he opened the rear door. Finally, and most disastrous of all, there was the open bow cap. The Tribunal dismissed the possibility that the *Thetis* had left Birkenhead in that condition; it had been opened 'not many minutes before the accident'. But no-one was able to say why, or by whom, and the events remain among the sea's inexplicable mysteries.

LOSS OF THE Princess Victoria

NATURE has always been a very volatile factor in human life, and the sea has always been the most fractious of her children. In the winter of 1952-3, when the two of them combined to beleaguer and batter the British Isles and northern Europe with gales, snow, sleet and rainstorms, mountainous seas, tearing winds and floods, living memory was stretched to the limit to recall any situation quite as perilous.

In that context the British Railways 2694-ton car ferry *Princess Victoria* found the Irish Sea—never the most tranquil of runs—in an even more evil mood than usual when Captain James Ferguson took her out of Stranraer at 07.45 on January 31, 1953. The *Princess Victoria* had 125 passengers, 49 crew and 44 tons of cargo on board as she nosed her way down Loch Ryan towards the North Channel on her 35-mile voyage to Larne, Northern Ireland.

The sheltered waters of the loch provided some protection for the first half-hour or so, but the relative immunity was brief, for in the North Channel, north-westerly winds were gusting up to 80mph. Almost as soon as the ferry turned westwards into the channel, a Force 11 gale came shrieking down upon her, hurling the ship from side to side on a convulsed surface of gigantic waves.

The *Princess Victoria* was a stout vessel, launched in 1947 and equipped with Sulzer diesel engines, but in that paroxysm of storm and sea she could make only slow progress. Nevertheless, the ferry ploughed on for over an hour before an extra large sea overtook and pooped her, thundering down on the steel stern doors which led to the car deck. The doors snapped inwards and the sea surged through, distorting the starboard sections and twisting the stanchions, preventing them from being closed properly. One heavy sea after another, swamping in after the first freak wave, burst open both sides, shifted the cargo and swung the ship over into a 10-degree starboard list.

The list increased minute by minute and Captain Ferguson decided to use *Princess Victoria's* bow rudder to steer her back to Loch Ryan stern first, that being thought less hazardous in the conditions than attempting to turn about. However, the ship was pitching so violently that crew-members attempting to release the rudder's lock-pin were in great danger of being swept off the forecastle and the idea was abandoned. A tow by tug then seemed the only hope of returning safely to port, and at 09.46 Captain Ferguson sent out the distress signal, 'Hove to off Loch Ryan. Vessel not under command. Urgent assistance of tug required'.

The storm that was whipping up and

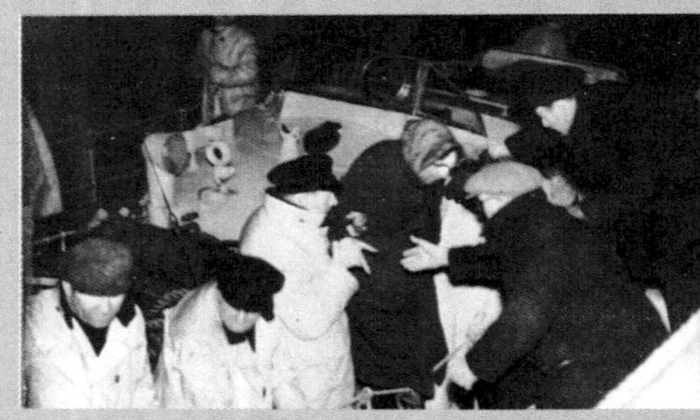

Top: The British Railways 2694-ton car ferry 'Princess Victoria' in the Irish Sea.
Ian Allan Library

Above: A survivor from the sunken ferry being landed in Ireland on February 1, 1953.
Press Association

down the coast had imprisoned the two nearest tugs in Douglas Bay, Isle of Man, and so the 1700-ton destroyer HMS *Contest* was ordered out of Rothesay to the *Princess Victoria's* aid. The destroyer was on her way when at 10.32 Captain Ferguson put out a frantic SOS. At that juncture the ferry was drifting southwards only six miles off the Scottish coast and water which had started to filter began to pour into her lounge through a fireproof door forward of the car deck.

At 10.45 the passengers were issued with lifejackets and struggled up to B deck, the assembly point, with the help of lifelines; without them, they would most certainly have gone sliding into the boiling sea. At 10.54 the ferry's radio operator, David Broadfoot, began sending out a stream of messages, ending eventually with 'SOS. Estimated position now five miles east of Copeland entrance Belfast Lough.' Safety in Belfast Lough was relatively near by then because the sea and wind had driven the ship across and a little beyond the North Channel. No tug or rescue vessel came out from Belfast, however, and the *Contest* was still nowhere to be seen. In fact, at 12.44 the destroyer had radioed the dismal news that she had had to reduce speed in heavy seas and could not reach the *Princess Victoria* until 13.30.

Before that time, at 13.15, Captain Ferguson gave the order to abandon ship. A blinding blizzard was raging round the ferry and her list had increased to 45 degrees. The starboard lifeboats were mere inches from the water, and the port boats were poised perilously high and could not be lowered because of the list. Nevertheless, women and children were put into port boat No 4. The falls were released in the hope that it would float clear when the ship capsized, but a huge wave came sheering along the side of the ship, smashed the 26ft wooden lifeboat against the hull and toppled everyone on board into the water. At 14.00 before any of the other port boats could be launched, the *Princess Victoria* foundered. She capsized slowly so that several people were able to step into the No 6 port boat from the hull, and the boat floated clear.

Moments earlier, while the ferry was still wallowing in her last agonies, rafts had been thrown overboard and several men had jumped into the maelstrom to take their chance of reaching them. Some of the women, however, were too rigid with fear to emulate them and they were still on board when the ship rolled over. With a horrible scraping and tearing, a fully loaded lifeboat was dragged across the keel as the hull cleared the surface. The upturned ferry floated momentarily and about 50 people dotted along the hull clawed wildly to gain a handhold.

Most failed and slithered down into the water. Their choking gurgling cries for help reached the rafts, but men who had managed to reach safety there could neither see nor rescue them. Of the 177 people on board the *Princess Victoria*, only 44 were rescued alive. The remainder perished from drowning or exposure. Captain Ferguson went down with his ship in valiant style, with one hand clinging to the rail of the bridge and the other raised in salute.

Ships trying to reach the stricken ferry were greatly hampered by her rapid drift, which made her position hard to estimate. The later SOS messages also gave faulty positions; the *Contest* at least went to a wrong location.

At 14.50 the British coaster *Orchy* arrived at the scene to find that the ferry had disappeared, leaving behind a scattering of wreckage and oil, three lifeboats and some rafts. About 33 of the survivors were in the lifeboats, most of them in boat No 6, which had been floated away from the sinking ferry as she poised upside down in the water. When HMS *Contest* finally arrived she retrieved eight men from the water, while the trawler *Eastcoats* picked up one man and six bodies. The remaining two survivors, both men, were taken on board the Portpatrick lifeboat.

The resultant inquiry into the disaster, which met between March 1 and May 9, placed major blame on the malevolent weather, but worrying details were also revealed about the generally unseaworthy condition of the lost ferry. Chief among them was the inadequacy of the stern doors, which had suffered damage two years previously; their failure to withstand the onslaught of the seas led to one of the most shocking and tragic sea disasters recent years have seen.

The Wahine

The ferry 'Wahine' pictured on trials in the mid 1960s. L Dunn

COOK STRAIT between the North and South Islands of New Zealand is more of a gap than anyone unfamiliar with the country might suspect. The nearest points are about 20 miles apart, but the distance between suitable places for ferry terminals is considerably more and the shortest, from Picton to Wellington, takes several hours for a car ferry. Another, primarily a coastal passage, from Lyttelton Harbour, adjacent to the city of Christchurch in the South Island, normally takes about 12 hours to Wellington.

It was from Lyttelton that the *Wahine* (pronounced Wa-hee-nee) left for an overnight run to Wellington at 20.45 on April 9, 1968. She was one of the ferries belonging to the Union Steam Ship Company of Wellington, and for her size of 488ft by 71ft (8944 gross tons) was one of the best car ferries afloat. She had been launched in Scotland in December 1965 and arrived in Wellington on July 24, 1966. She loaded from the stern and garaged vehicles centrally, with some accommodated, through use of a ramp, above the main car deck. On the trip concerned she was not fully loaded. There were 71 passenger vehicles on board, with 48 of them on the upper deck, and the others on the lower deck, shared with commercial vehicles. The ferry was under-booked by about 300 passengers. There were 569 adult passengers and 41 children, and a crew of 125.

The ship was well appointed, with cabins for all who wanted them, and the usual passenger rooms and facilities. High winds are fairly common and, although the ship was stabilised and the winds at departure were only about 15 knots behind the ship, many travellers sought their beds early, in the hope of getting to sleep before they had a chance to feel sick. All the signs were that this would be a routine voyage, and they expected to wake in time to go ashore in Wellington at seven o'clock next morning.

Captain Robertson had been with the line for 30 of his 41 years at sea and had been captain of several of the Union Company ships for 16 years. He had taken over command of the *Wahine* in October 1966. That morning, after the ship had berthed, he had watched the crew at lifeboat drill, in which all the ship's eight boats had been lowered and circled the ship before being hoisted on board. In less than a day they were to put their drill into life-and-death practice.

Cook Strait is the centre of an area subject to high winds and to the effect of earthquakes. Wellington Harbour is a large natural harbour to the east of the narrowest part of the strait, with a considerable area of sheltered water and broad entrance that might be considered ideal for the use of any shipping, except that in the entrance is Barrett Reef—a bank of rocks which break the surface and are buoyed, with the lighted Barrett Buoy marking them at the seaward end. The Barrett Reef reduces the width of the main channel to about three-quarters of a mile—ample in normal conditions.

However, high winds and strong tidal current complicate navigation in the area. Gale and storm conditions are quite common. Ships take pilots, but the captains of the ferries are qualified to pilot their own craft in and out of Wellington. The regularity and safety of the ferries had been established for over 80 years. Although in the roughest weather ferries might be delayed, the certainty of their running whatever the conditions had been accepted by the people of Wellington. The certainty that everything would be all right was, to a certain extent, to be the cause of emergency action not being taken as quickly as it might have been.

April is autumn in the Southern Hemisphere and, although many of the passengers were businessmen making routine crossings, others were holidaymakers, either travelling with their own cars or with organised parties. Many were elderly.

The ship carried one radio operator, Robert Lyver. While travelling north he heard an SOS from a Japanese ship and the response of other ships near her. He also heard the weather forecast, which included a storm warning, with winds up to 100mph at North Cape (the extremity of North Island), but for Cook Strait the warning was for winds northerly at 40 to 55 knots next morning, with rain and poor visibility. The information was passed to the captain at 20.15pm and was the last positive weather information received on the ship. Lyver was off duty during the night.

By midnight the wind from the south had increased to 25 knots and the ship was making steady progress with an easy motion. The cyclone to the north was hitting the eastern coast of the North Island. A weather forecast at 03.00 (not heard on the *Wahine*) predicted gale force and above in Cook Strait. The storm built up over Wellington about 04.00. The storm centre was moving south into Cook Strait much quicker than the forecasters anticipated. Chief Officer Luly took over watch at 04.00. He did not know that by then winds were lifting roofs in Wellington and during his watch the ship would be in serious trouble. By 05.00 the ship was in the strait. Lyver had come back on duty and contacted the harbour pilot station. He was told that if conditions made it necessary, a tug would be available to help berthing.

By 06.00 the *Wahine* was approaching the area of the strait south of the entrance to Wellington Harbour and Luly noted the Baring Head light about five miles to starboard. He ordered reduced engine revolutions to aid steering in the following sea. Captain Robertson came on to the bridge after a night below. The ship's normal docking time was 07.00, but she was expected to be a little late. Passengers were getting up and preparing for arrival, although some with uncertain stomachs were staying in bed as long as possible. Regular travellers knew the motion should ease once the ship had passed between the Heads.

In normal conditions boatswain George Hampson would have gone forward to prepare the anchors and mooring lines and would have stayed in the bow. Instead, he went to the garage deck to help secure an articulated vehicle, loaded with coke, that was in danger of turning over.

The onset of disaster was sudden. The ship began to sheer to port as much as 30 degrees towards the Barrett Reef, and the helmsman was unable to correct it, despite the captain ordering full ahead to help steering. Although the radar had been working satisfactorily, it began to give trouble about 06.00, so the location of the rocks could not be checked. Captain Robertson ordered full astern on the starboard engine in an attempt to pull the bow round. At that moment a huge sea hit the port side of the ship. Captain Robertson and others claim they were thrown the full width of the 74ft bridge without touching anything. His thoughts were that they were rushing straight for Barrett Reef at 16 knots and he estimated they would hit in $1\frac{1}{2}$ minutes. He tried to pull the ship round and head for open sea.

The first witnesses ashore were Stuart Young and his wife, who had seen the ferries come in and out for many years. It was at 06.30 that they recognised the *Wahine* apparently entering normally despite the weather. Ten minutes later they were surprised to see her on the western side of the reef and apparently coming ashore. They rang the police, who sent cars to the shore. By then the ship was no longer visible.

At about the same time the lookout, Alvyn Finlayson, thought he saw a house. The captain was handling the ship by instinct. Chief Officer Luly spotted the light of the Barret Reef buoy ahead. They were too late to get clear. The ship closed on the rocks and started to grind on them.

Most of the passengers were unaware of the drama outside. Many were still in their bunks. Tea and breakfasts were being served. The engines were stopped by the damage, as the bottom plating was torn out. Many sick passengers at first enjoyed the near-stillness after their rough passage.

Lyver informed Wellington of the grounding. Alarm bells were sounded and passengers were told to go to their cabins. The captain sent Luly and Hampson forward to let go the anchors. The two had to crawl to the bow, but they finally got there and went through the procedure of preparing to let go the anchors. The brake refused to grip under the strain and both cables ran to their full extent. At 07.02 Wellington radio sent out an SOS on behalf of the ship. The first response came from the *Waikare,* of the same company, then off the South Island and making for Wellington. All shore services were alerted.

The nearest shore point was the suburb of Seatoun on the west side of the harbour. An army camp there went into action preparing food for survivors. The harbour

tug *Tapuhi* took on extra towing wire and set out to help. The 80ft pilot launch *Tiakina* was also on its way. Meanwhile the *Wahine* was dragging her anchors and bumping along the reef.

Chief Officer Luly inspected damage and found the stern doors still tight. All the bottom of the ship was flooded, some of it nearly up to the garage deck. She was rolling but recovering to vertical and the captain decided not to pump, as it might affect stability. The ship dragged clear of the end of the reef but, still drifting and swinging to her anchors, she barely cleared the point at Breaker Bay. The captain radioed he expected to go ashore there, but the ship cleared the point and continued to drift.

Passengers were at muster stations, mostly waiting quietly. Stewards provided coffee. The ship was on emergency lighting as daylight was weak and grey. Most passengers were unaware of what was happening and some did not appreciate the seriousness of it. A group of cricketers played cards and bemoaned missing their first match.

By 09.15 the ship was drifting in clear water and apparently in no immediate danger. The tug and pilot boat were opposite Steeple Beacon. Their captains felt it would be unsafe to go further down the harbour. Shore radio gave no hint of imminent danger to the *Wahine*. The storm reached its maximum about 09.00 and many shore services were busy dealing with damaged buildings, fleeing residents and similar problems in gusts over 100 knots.

When the weather appeared to be moderating, around 11.00, the *Tapuhi* tug tried to get a line on board and pull the *Wahine* into the more-sheltered water of Worser Bay. Using a rocket and line they got a cable on board, but an enormous sea tossed the tug so violently that the cable snapped. With no power on the winches, men on the *Wahine* were trying to haul in anchor cable by hand.

The *Tapuhi* was only a harbour tug not intended for salvage work, but in the shelter of Worser Bay she prepared a second cable. Meanwhile the *Tiakini* succeeded in getting close enough for the deputy harbourmaster, Captain Galloway, to jump to a ladder and get aboard the *Wahine.* That was about 12.30. Water was rising in the ship, but the chief officer thought she would remain stable. He radioed ashore for pumps, which were taken on board the *Arihina,* another pilot launch.

Passengers were becoming bored. They were given food and drink. Some even wrote letters. An observant music teacher noted that the ship rolled one way and not the other and deduced it could be getting unstable. (That was not necessarily so, as there was strong wind and sea on the same side.) By 13.00 a list became more pronounced. At 12.45 the deputy harbourmaster had noticed the ship was floating

Above: A painting by Peter Wood showing the 'Wahine' battling in the storm off Wellington on April 10, 1968.

Left: The sheltered waters of Wellington Harbour in November 1969. *D J Kingston*

much lower aft. By then the tug with its second line ready made several approaches, but had no success.

The exceptionally high tide had turned and was running out. The effect was to swing the ship, which by 13.15 was listing about 25 degrees. It gave some shelter on the starboard side and the order was given to abandon ship, from that side.

The passengers were plunged from comparative comfort to the reality of the situation and the need to go into the sea or a lifeboat. The four lifeboats on the starboard side were made ready for loading and liferafts were also prepared. By radio the tug was told to abandon attempting to tow and to save lives, and other craft were called to help. One of the four starboard lifeboats had an engine. The others were propelled by their crew working levers to drive a propeller. Because of the list boats were swinging several feet away from the sides, but passengers were persuaded to jump or were flung into them.

Many went into the sea and many of the children were carried by crewmen as they jumped into the sea. The officers cleared the ship before themselves abandoning it. Meanwhile ashore there was an appeal for craft to go to the rescue. Fortunately, the weather was moderating, but seas do not go down quickly after a storm, and conditions were unsuitable for any but large or specialised craft. A surf rescue boat under oars was able to save many people and two inflatable rescue craft picked up many more. Other harbour and commercial craft took part.

The first private boat on the scene was a small power boat skippered by Jim Toulis, who reported how crewmen in the water directed him to those in most need. The second private boat on the scene was a launch called the *Cuda*. Captain Robertson and Captain Galloway were dragged into it and they asked to pass close to the *Wahine* to make sure no-one was on board. By then she was at an acute angle and as they passed, she rolled on to her side, resting on the bottom, with part of her hull still above water.

Three lifeboats got ashore, either towed or under their own manual power, but the motor boat capsized and accounted for many of the lives lost. Many of those in the water and on liferafts were swept ashore in places where there was no-one to help and had to walk or crawl to safety, but in other places emergency help was well organised. Altogether the final figure of dead was 51, 43 of them over the age of 40. Seven of them were Australians and all the others were New Zealanders. There were 684 survivors.

At an inquiry four months later the court ruled that the prime cause of the *Wahine's* loss was 'that the ship, struck by the worst-ever storm in New Zealand, sheered off course in zero visibility, went out of effective human control and struck Barrett Reef, sustaining serious underwater damage. Immediate cause of the ultimate capsize was free surface water on the vehicle deck.' There were some criticisms, particularly of the harbourmaster, but the court ruled 'that no cause has been shown why the certificates of the ship's master, chief officer and chief engineer should be cancelled or suspended.'

Some of the cars and other things on board were salvaged soon after the sinking, but the problem of dealing with the half-submerged wreck and restoring her attracted many suggested solutions, none of which proved feasible. The position of the *Wahine* did not offer much obstruction or hazard to shipping using the harbour, but she lay for several years and was then cut into pieces which were lifted and removed separately. Disposal of the wreck was not completed until the end of 1973.

Below: The 'Wahine' listing badly in Wellington Harbour with the tug 'Tapuhi' on the right of the picture ready to pick up survivors. *Associated Press*

THE TORREY CANYON

Above: **Twin columns of black smoke rising into the sky from the 'Torrey Canyon' after the vessel was bombed.** *Press Association Ltd*

CONSERVATIONIST and pollution experts for some time had viewed with alarm the increase in size of oil tankers and could only theorise on the effect of one of the huge craft being wrecked and spilling its cargo on the sea. On Saturday, March 18, 1967, the inevitable eventually happened and the authorities were presented with the first practical example of such a mishap, when the fully loaded giant tanker *Torrey Canyon* went aground on the Seven Stones rocks, between Land's End and the Isles of Scilly, menacing south-west England and northern France.

The problem was only mastered after the complete loss of the ship, the expenditure of a considerable amount of money and the employment of thousands of people, spread over about six weeks. One result was an international move to take action to make similar disasters less likely.

Torrey Canyon was built in America in 1959 by the Newport News Shipbuilding and Dry Dock Company and then had a deadweight of 65 920 tons (the weight the ship is designed to carry). She was named after an American oil field. In 1965, the Sasebo Heavy Industries Company, in Japan, cut the ship in two and added a centre section, increasing the deadweight to 118 285 tons. The ship was then 974ft long and 125ft wide. Her maximum draught was 51ft and her two steam turbines generated 25 000 shaft horsepower driving a single propeller to give a speed of 17 knots. A full load of crude oil converted to petrol would keep over 54 000 cars running for a year. Such was the ship and its load stranded on the Seven Stones.

Like many other ships, the *Torrey Canyon* sailed under a flag of convenience and was owned by a Liberian company, the Barracuda Tanker Corporation, registered in Bermuda. Her captain (Pastrengo Rugiati) and crew were Italian, mostly from Genoa. She had loaded oil in the Persian Gulf and was on her way to the British Petroleum Company's depot at Milford Haven. The ship had been aground once before, at the entrance to Los Angeles harbour in 1965, but had been pulled off by tugs. The *Torrey Canyon* was 100A1 at Lloyds, meaning that she was built to the highest classification.

The Seven Stones are a collection of rocks forming a reef close to or breaking the surface, seven miles north-east of St Martins in the Isles of Scilly and 15 miles west of Land's End. They are marked by a lightship—the present one, with a lantern visible for 11 miles, has been on station there since 1958 and is held by a four-ton anchor, the largest in the Trinity House service. This gives a clue to the roughness of possible conditions, although on the day of the stranding, conditions were quite mild, with a wind of 15 knots and visibility of eight miles.

At 09.10 on that Saturday, the man on watch on the lightship saw the *Torrey Canyon* approaching. Warning rockets were fired. Code flags JD were hoisted (meaning 'You are standing into danger'). Then the lightship crew could see the ship was aground. High water had been a couple of hours earlier and the tide was then ebbing.

On board the *Torrey Canyon*, the captain was awake and talking to Second Officer Fontana until about 02.30, when he wrote instructions for First Officer Silvano Bonfiglio, who would take over the watch at 04.00. The ship was travelling at full speed. By 06.30, Bonfiglio had picked up the Scillies on radar. He then altered course to head for the Bishop Rock Lighthouse, at the south-western limits of the Isles of Scilly, then about 24 miles or $1\frac{1}{2}$ hours away. When he told the captain of this he was admonished. He had expected to take the ship outside the Scillies. Instead, the captain intended to pass to the east of the islands.

There was, of course, plenty of room east of the Scillies. Captain Rugiati had been through the main channel between Land's End and the Seven Stones 16 times as first officer of the *Homeric*. He had not previously been between the Seven Stones and the Scillies. When he arrived on the bridge of the *Torrey Canyon* about 07.00, the ship was already back on a course to take her east of the Scillies and west of the Seven Stones. Bonfiglio went off watch at 08.00. The captain was then on the bridge. There was a helmsman, Biagio Scotto di Carlom, and the inexperienced third officer, Alfonso Coccio. Coccio plotted the position of the ship at 08.12 and 08.18, using points visible on the Isles of Scilly. There was only 30 minutes' sailing time to the Seven Stones. Coccio got another fix at 08.25.

Two fishing vessels were sighted. They were the *Mater Christi* and *Cité d'Arvor*—French craft plucking crayfish and lobsters off the Seven Stones reefs.

By 08.38, when Coccio took another bearing, Captain Rugiati realised that the fix was grossly inaccurate. He told Coccio then to take bearings on the lightship.

By 08.40, when the new fix was plotted, the ship was only 2.8 miles from South Stone, the nearest of the Seven Stones. The captain personally altered course to true north. Another bearing by Coccio showed less than one mile to the nearest rock. The helmsman was ordered to put the wheel over to port. Nothing happened. After a short period of searching for the reason, it was realised that the wheel was disconnected due to a lever operating the automatic control equipment not being in the manual position. That was rectified and the ship started to turn, but it was too late. At a speed of 15.75 knots she slammed into Pollard Rock at 08.50.

The crews of the fishing vessels watched in amazement. They knew the Seven Stones rocks thoroughly. They saw oil gush up as the bottom of the ship ripped open. Guy Follic of the *Mater Christi* took his boat to within 50 yards of the ship and saw men running up and down. He called Land's End radio and was the first to report the grounding.

At 08.51, a helicopter took off from Penzance on the regular passenger service to the Scillies. By 09.00, the tanker was sighted and the pilots smelled oil. They thought the tanker had stopped, but did not learn she was aground until they landed at St Mary's. On the return flight they saw the French fishing boats and the *Torrey Canyon* in an unnatural position, and the oil leaking.

An SOS sent through Land's End radio brought several ships in the vicinity racing towards the disaster. It also brought the Dutch salvage tug *Utrecht*. For such a tug, a wreck meant work, and she happened to be nearby in Mount's Bay (Penzance). The Scillies lifeboat from St Mary's was called out and was asked to stand by, as there was no immediate danger. By 09.23, the crude oil slick was already one mile long down tide and spreading rapidly.

Command Headquarters, Naval Forces, Plymouth, realised there was an unusual problem facing them. From previous experience of smaller spills of oil, they knew that the only effective way to treat an oil spill was by the use of detergent, although it killed some marine life. Without treatment, the thick crude oil floated on the surface and would pile up on beaches. foul birds and not disperse. A naval tug and a minesweeper put to sea on Sunday, carrying 4500 gallons of detergent. Lieutenant Michael Clark was lowered from a helicopter on to the deck of the *Torrey Canyon.* He reported 10 of the 18 oil tanks ruptured.

Meanwhile, Captain Rugiati had signed a contract with the owners of the *Utrecht,* giving them the right to salvage the vessel. The contract was on a no-cure no-pay basis, as is usual for salvage, being a gamble that could produce an enormous award or leave the salvors to pay the costs if unsuccessful.

The lifeboat stood by all night. The weather turned rougher and the forecast for Sunday was that winds from the north-west would increase to gale force. The ship crunched and scraped on the rocks during the night. As the sea began to be whipped up menacingly, 14 of the least essential members of the crew were taken off by the lifeboat, with a considerable amount of personal luggage of all the crew.

Utrecht made the first attempt to tow off the ship stern first and snapped a 5in steel cable. Captain Rugiati was pressed to have more men taken off. He realised that there was a possibility of the ship catching fire and gave the remaining men the option; all but three (and some salvage men) were taken off. The original 14 had been transferred by the lifeboat to another ship. In the deteriorating conditions, Matt Lethbridge managed to get some of the men one at a time on to his lifeboat, but the final nine were lifted off by helicopter.

By Sunday night it was estimated that 20 000 tons of oil had escaped and was floating as a black mass 18 miles long and three miles wide. It was blowing to the south, but the wind was expected to back to the west, which would turn the oil on to the Cornish coast. It was optimistically estimated that the oil could be dispersed in a fortnight and the government voted half a million pounds for the job 'without prejudice as to who finally pays'.

The British government had to decide what was to be done with the *Torrey Canyon* and something like 100 000 tons of oil still in her. She might be emptied, salvaged or blown up. With the possibility of an explosion, transferring the cargo to another tanker was considered too hazardous because of the difficulty of getting a big enough vessel into shoal water. Blowing up also was out of the question because it would have released large quantities of oil still in the holds.

The Dutch salvage experts were allowed to make the attempt at towing the ship away, but they soon realised that the job was too big for them and asked for the help of the British government. After examining the ship, Peter Flett, the Admiralty's salvage expert, decided that it would be impossible to float and salvage the ship, so the government salvage service could not help. During the Dutch salvage attempts a man named Stal was killed in a mysterious explosion on board. That was

Right: The 'Torrey Canyon' broken in two on the Seven Stones reef off Land's End, Cornwall. *Press Association Ltd*

Below: The first oil leaks coming from 'Torrey Canyon'. *Thomson Newspapers Ltd*

Below right: Another shot of the black smoke coming from the bombed 'Torrey Canyon' off Land's End. *Press Association Ltd*

on Tuesday, March 21. All the remaining men were taken off. The oil slick was said in some reports to cover 35 miles by 20 miles.

During Wednesday and Thursday, March 22 and 23, little was done at the ship, but naval and other ships were spraying the oil with detergents in an attempt to disperse it before it reached land. The wind had still not backed, as expected, to the west, so Cornwall was still clear. By Friday (Good Friday) 43 large spraying vessels were at work and others were being made ready.

On Saturday, March 25, the edge of the oil slick, then estimated as covering 260 square miles, reached Sennen Cove, near Land's End, and was soon piling up in great black balls on many beaches. Troops and volunteers tackled the menace, mainly with detergent, or merely by carrying it away and burying it.

Meanwhile, at the *Torrey Canyon*, the Dutch salvage company was having another try. By then the wind was more westerly and gusting to gale force. Tugs had succeeded in pivoting the ship on a rock, but four tugs heaved at the ship without success on the Sunday. She was, of course, impaled on the rocks, and would have had to be lightened considerably for the attempt to have had any change of success. She broke in two and, later, the forward section broke again. By Thursday, March 28, the Dutch salvage firm Wijsmuller admitted defeat and ended its salvage contract. By then oil had reached the Cornish coast all the way round from Newquay to the Lizard.

Although there was no hope of moving the ship, there was still a considerable amount of oil on board, and the authorities had to decide how to deal with the further menace. The Royal Navy considered that the oil compartments would have to be ruptured and the oil set on fire if it was to be prevented from adding to the pollution. To achieve that end it was planned to drop 1000lb high-explosive bombs. It was recognised that there was a risk of the oil on the sea catching fire over a wide area; because of the possible danger a helicopter crew stood by to take men off the Longships lighthouse if necessary, 14 miles away. The Seven Stones lightship was towed from the area. It was also recognised that if the plan went wrong and the ship sank instead of catching fire, oil could leak to the surface for years.

However, it was decided that the risk had to be taken. Twin-jet Buccaneer aircraft were used, making bombing runs at an altitude of 2500ft. The first aircraft dropped two bombs, making a near miss. The second aircraft hit the stern half of the tanker, which burst into flames. Others followed, and soon the whole of the tanker was burning. James Summerlee, the BEA helicopter pilot on the Scillies run, who had first flown over the *Torrey Canyon* when she stranded, described the plume of smoke as 'like an atomic explosion'.

The first bombs were followed by tanks of paraffin, to encourage the fire, dropped by Hunter jet fighters, and then more bombs were dropped. Within two hours 36,000lb of high explosive and 5400 gallons of paraffin were dropped but within half an hour of the last drop the fire had gone out. A helicopter returned with oxygenated bricks, which had seemed effective in starting oil fires during experiments. They started the leaking oil burning but the fire again soon faded.

Although it had been a marvellous show and had all the appearance of a success, Wednesday morning, March 29, showed the slick still there and oil still leaking, with little sign of any effect of the fire. After reconnaissance helicopters had been over bombing had been resumed, with rockets and napalm in addition to the high-explosive bombs and paraffin. Fires started again and smoke billowed from the hull, but despite many direct hits no fires were of very long duration.

On Thursday, March 30, bombing attacks were resumed, with little resulting fire. It was announced that it was believed that all oil in the ship had been destroyed. She was left to the sea and the parts soon sank. A derrick remained above the water for a short time but that also soon disappeared.

That was the end of the *Torrey Canyon*, but not the end of the problem it had caused. Workers ashore had managed to clear many beaches. News of the oil and sensational stories in the press had sometimes given people elsewhere an unbalanced picture of the state of Cornwall. It was quite a blow to the tourist trade and there were many holiday cancellations that year.

Fishermen were also affected. Newlyn is the busiest Cornish fishing port. Its men and ships had been engaged in spraying detergent, and the men began to think that their trade was finished. However, when the trawler *Pioneer* was used for four days of fishing, with a scientist on board, there was a good catch and the fish were normal. Fishing could be resumed.

The fish were unaffected, but not so the birds. Enormous numbers of birds died. Oiled birds could not swim or fly. Many volunteers worked to clean birds and the RSPCA was active in setting up bird hospitals and organising the work. But, after all the effort, only a very tiny proportion of the oiled birds survived. One estimate of the number of birds killed put it at at least 25,000, and possibly three times as many – all from one accident.

Spraying at sea had only minimal success and oil slicks were floating in the English Channel. On the British coast progress was being made, but only by the expenditure of considerable amounts of labour and money. On the other side of the Channel there was a feeling that it was not their problem and on April 4 *Paris-Presse* announced that wind and current patterns showed that the Brittany/Normandy coast would not be affected. But three days later an oil slick reached Guernsey and, with the wind westerly, there was a possibility of it reaching Normandy. Booms were prepared to protect oyster beds, and stocks of sawdust and detergent were built up at Cherbourg. The wind turned north-easterly and the oil did not touch Normandy. Instead, it was driven on the unprepared Brittany coast and was affecting a 90-mile stretch by April 11, with a build-up of oil generally worse than in Cornwall.

The French were slower at dealing with the oil. There was a feeling against detergent, as it was believed to affect shellfish, and much of the Brittany coast is famous for oysters and other shellfish. So not so much detergent was used. Booms were tried with some success and, at sea, it was found that chalk and sawdust caused the oil to sink. Much of the early work was locally organised but by April 15 troops were sent in large numbers and the problem became a national one. Oil slicks were floating around in the open sea for some time and a change in the wind drove more on to Cornish beaches by April 26, but by then the organisation was able to cope successfully.

Captain Rugiati and his crew had been returned to Genoa. While the British and French authorities were fighting the effect of the stranding of the *Torrey Canyon*, representatives of the owners and insurers had to start trying to find out why the ship went aground. The Liberian Government set up a court of enquiry with three Americans in charge and on May 3 they published their report putting all the blame on Captain Rugiati.

Above left: The charred and blackened remains of 'Torrey Canyon' after the bombing.
Thompson Newspapers Ltd

Left: The stranded tanker after breaking her back on the Seven Stones rocks.
Keystone Press

14. Safety at Sea

LIGHTHOUSES & LIGHTSHIPS

TODAY, more than 60 000 navigational lights, with their sophisticated lighting and reflector systems, radio beacons and sound signals for use in fog, signpost the world's waterways. They do it so effectively that the most hazard-strewn channel can be navigated safely, but such a high standard of security is comparatively recent.

Less than 150 years ago, an average 550 ships were being wrecked every year on British coasts alone, all too many of them on the jagged gale-swept reefs of the Cornwall and Devon coast. This was not only the sinister graveyard of countless sailors; the seas that hammered down so furiously upon it also smashed the first of several famous lighthouses built on its most perilous point.

Henry Winstanley's Eddystone lighthouse, made of timber and first lit in 1698, was swept away to mere crumbs of wreckage in a cataclysmic storm only four years later. Winstanley, who perished with his lighthouse, was an artist rather than an engineer and had made it an extremely elaborate affair, a microcosm of a country house with its gilded bedchamber, carved and decorated stateroom and fine gallery surrounded by a classic balustrade. Yet, for all its outward glamour, the first Eddystone was basically no different from the first-ever lighthouse, the Pharos at Alexandria, a 400-foot tower completed in 280 BC; both were nothing more than tall structures with a fire burning on top.

The Romans, although indifferent seamen, built many lighthouses of the cresset type; the remains of one still exists at Dover.

Until the late 18th century, lighthouses still displayed light no more penetrating than that given by wood or coal fires burning in braziers or a battery of candles enclosed within a lantern. Illuminants did not begin to grow more illuminating until 1784, when the Swiss engineer Aimé Argand invented the first practicable oil-burner. It burned oil in a circular hollow wick fanned by a current of air.

The more-brilliant light that beamed from the world's lighthouses after the advent of oil grew even more intense after 1901, with Arthur Kitson's burner, in which vaporised oil and air created gas light three times brighter than lamps of the Argand type. In the improved version devised by David Hood in 1921, Kitson's burner is still employed in lighthouses where the use of electricity is impracticable.

Electricity actually made a rather hesitant entrance on to the lighthouse scene. The first electric light was at the South Foreland lighthouse in December 1858. It was an experimental installation of about 1500 candle-power and the apparatus did not come into full service until June 1862. The electric carbon lamps installed at Dungeness lighthouse in 1862 proved too powerful for the lens system there, and it was not until the early 1920s that high-power filament lamps began to come into widespread use. In Britain, the first lighthouse to be so equipped was at South Foreland, where a 4-kilowatt lamp was installed in 1922.

Candle-power thus leapt up to thousands and, since 1922, to millions, as beams of higher and higher intensity, such as from Xenon high-pressure arc lamps and Mercury arc lamps, have been sent spearing out over greater and greater distances. The 600 000 candle-power light of the world's

Facing page top: The Sumburgh Head lighthouse guarding the notorious Sumburgh Roost meeting of the Atlantic Ocean and the North Sea. *G Daniels*

Facing page below: The Europo Point lighthouse, Gibraltar. *J Eastland*

This page:
Top: The lighthouse at Portland Bill, Dorset; a responsibility of Trinity House. *A Greenway*

Left, upper centre: A drawing by Fleming Williams of a Trinity House relief steamer trying unsuccessfully to approach a lightship in a gale in 1907. *Illustrated London News*

Left, lower centre: A Trinity House Lanby buoy which replaced the Owers light vessel. *A Greenway*

Bottom: The 'Calshot Spit' lightship anchored between the Isle of Wight and Calshot on the mainland. *D J Kingston*

tallest lighthouse—a 348ft tower near Yokohama in Japan—has a visibility range, for instance, of twenty miles.

The Yokohama tower is made of steel, a relative newcomer as a material for lighthouse building. Just as naked flame was the sole light source for so many centuries, so one material—stone—has held a long, long monopoly of lighthouse structure. The traditional lighthouse, and virtually the only type until the present century, was a solid column of masonry sited either on shore or on the dangerous rocks and reefs it guarded.

In 1759, John Smeaton, a civil engineer, added ingenuity to the great innate strength of stone by dovetailing, one into the other, the 1493 blocks that went to make the third Eddystone lighthouse. It stood for over 120 years. Smeaton's method of construction, and the developments that sprang from it, made a lighthouse into a straight wall strong enough to break the force of the sea and throw it back, and not surprisingly, it established a standard for the building of wave-swept masonry structures the world over.

The absence of solid rock foundations, such as the red granitoid gneiss of Eddystone or the stern black porphyry of Heaux de Bréhat on the Brittany coast, once settled automatically the choice between building a lighthouse or mooring a lightship; until fairly recently, the latter was employed where it was impossible to build the former. Of the two, the lightship was the less satisfactory, for it was relatively expensive to maintain and could shift position on its necessarily slack cable.

The revolutionary method used in 1838 in the building of Maplin lighthouse—screwing iron piles into sand—heralded today's general decline of the lightship. Ironically enough, it did so in precisely the same area, the Thames estuary, where the world's first lightship, *Nore*, was moored in 1732. For at Maplin, it proved possible to erect a lighthouse on what had formerly been totally insecure foundations. Maplin, which stood until 1932, was the prototype for lighthouses like the open-steelwork template structure erected in 1961 at Buzzard's Bay, Massachusetts, where four steel-pipe legs were driven down to bedrock at 268ft below low water mark.

Buzzard's Bay was among several similar lighthouses specifically intended by the Americans to be replacements for lightships. The same idea was in the minds of the Swedes when, in 1930, they embarked on a plan to replace with permanent towers the light-vessels which encroaching ice forced them to withdraw in the winter months.

The Swedish method was to use an ingenious adaptation of the caisson, a cylinder designed to be sunk into place as a lighthouse foundation, first pioneered in 1881 by the Germans on the Rotersand in the Weser estuary. The Swedes developed the concrete caisson, designed to be floated into position, and in the late 1950s, produced the telescopic caisson set, in which an inner cylinder was raised up from an outer one to form a light tower.

The ready-made lighthouse, pulled rabbit-like from a pharological top hat, is the latest means of marking out the hostile treacherous fringes of the world's land masses. They fulfil a need that has existed ever since Man first went to sea, and will continue to exist as long as he ventures upon it.

The Lifeboat Service

Above: The crew of an Inshore Rescue launch pictured battling against bad weather. *J Eastland*

Right: A sketch from the November 27, 1875, edition of 'The Graphic' showing the trial of a new life-saving vessel at Blackwall. *Illustrated London News*

Facing page; below left: A 17ft rigid-hulled Dory Inshore Rescue boat powered by twin 40hp outboards which has a top speed of 30 knots. *J Eastland*

Facing page, below right: A painting by G H Davis showing a motor lifeboat of a type equipped with a life-saving net, searchlight and cabin space for 50.

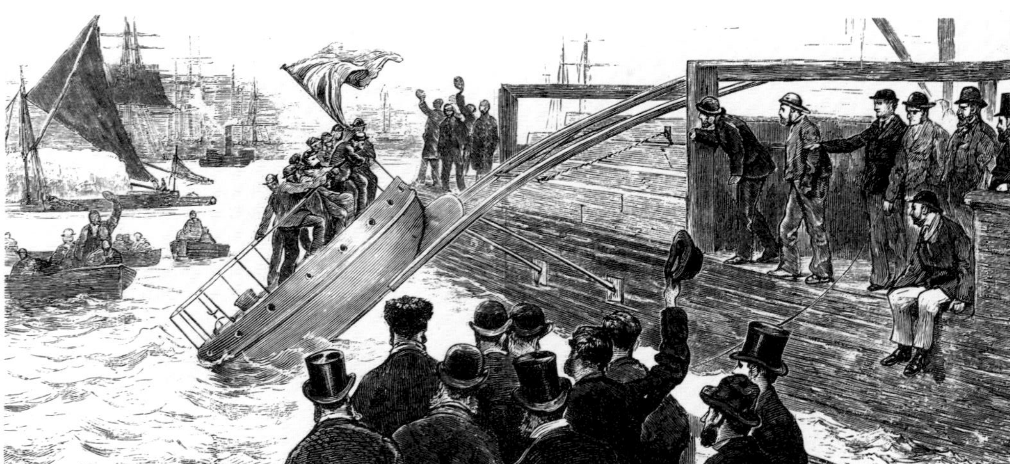

A COUPLE OF HOLIDAYMAKERS are cut off by the tide on a sandbank. Two men run down the beach carrying and dragging an inflatable boat. They are quickly afloat, an outboard motor starts up and within only a few minutes of the warning being given, the couple concerned are picked up and brought ashore. This might seem a far cry from what most people regard as the traditional job for a lifeboat, but it is a modern concept and an extension of the activities of the Royal National Life-Boat Institution today.

Earning a living from the sea has always been a hazardous occupation, whether the sailor was cruising the oceans or using a boat to fish close inshore. For most of recorded history there has been little provision for the rescue of mariners in distress. Around many coasts of the world there is still no rescue service. Some are remote and there might be no warning of coastal hazards. In such places and in the open ocean a seafarer in trouble might have to depend on his own resources or those provided by other craft in the vicinity.

Of course, with the modern miracle of radio and the high speed of aircraft, no-one need be quite so remote from help as he was only 50 years ago. However, it is not on the high seas that seamen expect trouble. It is when they are 'within soundings' and near the coast in bad weather that they more usually need help. Even in these days of powerful engines and electronic aids, a ship can get into difficulties and come to grief, so that the crew are at risk of their lives and outside help has to be called. In the days when a ship's only power came from the wind, the risk of being driven ashore or on to rocks was considerably greater.

Salvage has to be distinguished from life-saving. If outside help can save or recover a ship in distress, that is salvage and those who perform the service are entitled to an award from the owners. Saving life is a different matter. Sometimes the two may be linked, but no true seaman would expect to be rewarded for saving life. It always has been an unwritten law of the sea that help would be given to save mariners in distress, and it would be given priority over other considerations. Witness today how ships and aircraft abandon whatever else they are doing and respond to an SOS call.

There are tales of wreckers who enticed ships on to rocks by waving lanterns, but no seaman would deliberately go towards a light because it was there. He would be more likely to regard it as a warning to keep away. No doubt many people profited from what they could get from wrecks, but that does not mean they contrived the wrecking.

It is probable that in some places longshoremen relied as much on wrecks and salvage as they did on fishing for a living. Boatmen of Deal and Walmer once made a considerable income from salvaging parts of ships and their cargoes from the treacherous Goodwin Sands. Additionally, they were always ready to save lives, and there are records of livesaving there from 1616. Although progress has made the Goodwin Sands less hazardous and the possibility of salvage rare, plenty of local men are still willing to man the Deal lifeboat in any conditions of weather and sea.

Early rescues were in boats intended for other purposes. One of those exploits, involving Grace Darling, had a marked effect on the planning of a proper lifeboat service around the British Isles. On September 6, 1838, when Grace Darling was 22, she was with her father at the Longstone Lighthouse on the Farne Islands, when an increasingly strong wind got up from SSE. They lashed their only boat, a coble, and made preparations for an exceptionally high tide.

During the night the new steamer *Forfarshire*, on her normal passage from Hull to Dundee, had boiler trouble. The wind had backed to the north and reached gale force. Captain Humble decided to make for the shelter of the Inner Farne. He misjudged his course. The ship struck one of the Harker rocks and soon broke in two. Grace saw the wreck from her window in the lighthouse. She and her father rowed about one mile to the steamer. Grace alone rowed back with some survivors, leaving her father to help on the wreck. Two of the survivors then rowed back and rescued her father and the remaining survivors.

Those are the plain facts. For some days nothing much happened, then Grace was proclaimed a heroine. The public went wild. According to her father's log, it was only one of many rescues carried out and regarded by him almost as routine, but one result of the almost hysterical reaction of the public to his daughter's part in a rescue was an aroused interest in the provision of lifeboats around the British coast. Grace did not live much longer. She died four years later at the age of only 26 years.

The first lifeboat station was set up in the 18th century at Bamburgh, about a century before Grace Darling was born there. It came about because Baron Crewe, who was Bishop of Durham, died in 1721 and left the means of setting up the Crewe Trust at Bamburgh Castle. There is no record of what boats were used, but in 1786 a London coachbuilder, named Lionel Lukin, had been experimenting with ways to make a boat 'unimergible'. He applied his idea to a coble, which served at Bamburgh for many years.

In 1729 the Newcastle ship *Adventurer* was wrecked at the mouth of the Tyne. Seeing the crew drown without being able to help prompted a local social club to offer a prize for the best design of a lifeboat. William Wouldhave, the parish clerk of South Shields, was given only half the prize because some of the committee thought his design could be improved. The modified design was passed to a local boatbuilder, named Greathead. The resultant boat, which was the first boat to be built specifically as a lifeboat, was called the *Original*. She was launched in 1790 and remained in service for 40 years.

Greathead built 30 similar lifeboats, which were 30ft long and propelled by six pairs of oars. They had rising ends, cork along the gunwales and cork buoyancy built in. The boats were paid for by private charities and administered locally.

All that was still long before the setting up of a national lifeboat organisation. In 1823 Sir William Hillary published an appeal from the Isle of Man, setting out in detail how a 'National Institution for the Preservation of Lives and Property from Shipwreck' should be set up. The following year he interested Thomas Wilson, a London MP, in the project. Wilson called a meeting and on March 4, 1824, the National Institution for the Preservation of Life from Shipwreck was set up. Thirty years later its name became the Royal National Life-Boat Institution.

It was and remains a voluntary body, and even 13 years after its foundation its income was only £250. There was a period from 1854 to 1869 when government money was accepted because of serious financial difficulties. At all other times, including today when the annual turnover is between two and three million pounds, the Institution runs as a voluntary body dependent on contributions, collections, bequests and similar gifts.

In the days before mechanical power, in the conditions in which a lifeboat was needed, sailing would have been difficult or impossible, so the same man who had to help at the wreck might have had to row there and back. Crews were—as today—volunteers, mostly local fishermen. With the best craft available, being the crew of the lifeboat could be a dangerous occupation.

In December 1886 the barque *Mexico* of Hamburg went aground in a WNW gale off Southport. The Southport lifeboat crew were called out and the boat was taken by horses 3½ miles along the sands. With the lifeboat near the ship a heavy sea struck it and capsized it. Two men, out of the 15 crew, survived and were washed ashore with it two hours later. The St Annes lifeboat also had been called out. She started under oars, then made sail. What happened to her is not clear, but all her 14 crew died. The Lytham lifeboat, also called out, was a new boat on her first mission. She succeeded in getting the barque crew off and taking them ashore, but 27 lifeboatmen died that night.

One reaction to the disaster was the giving of a considerable amount of money to the Institution. Lifeboats were paraded through the streets, probably originating the idea of the annual lifeboat flag day, which now gives members of the public an opportunity to show their appreciation of the lifeboat service.

Of course, lifeboats were steadily improving, but to stimulate progress the Institution held a competition in 1850. One result was really a combination of ideas that resulted in the self-righting lifeboat. It had the raised buoyant ends which, to most people, still distinguishes a lifeboat from other sorts of craft.

For a long time self-righting was regarded as an essential property of a lifeboat, but in 1887 George L Watson, a famous yacht designer, was appointed consulting naval architect. He had a considerable influence on lifeboat design. He was of the opinion that self-righting, although necessary for smaller boats, was holding back the design of large craft. The Watson 43ft sailing boat, which was not self-righting, became one of the standard boats of the Institution.

A story of the days of pulling lifeboats showing the sense of service of those involved and the achievement of the almost impossible concerns the taking of the Lynmouth lifeboat overland to Porlock on January 12, 1899. Anyone who has travelled in that area will know that the route consisted of a mile up the 1-in-4½ gradient of Countisbury Hill, about 10 miles across Exmoor and then down the 1-in-4 Porlock Hill. A farmer provided upwards of a dozen horses and, with the help of many men and women, the boat on its carriage was heaved up Countisbury Hill.

In the full force of a gale, the lifeboat crew and 20 helpers went on in the dark with only the light from lanterns. At one place too narrow for the carriage, the boat was drawn a mile on skids, which had to be constantly lifted and moved forward. Getting down Porlock Hill was managed safely, but at the bottom trees had to be felled and some cottages partly demolished.

Eventually reaching the beach, the lifeboat was launched after 10½ hours overland and the crew went afloat immediately to the help of the *Forrest Hall*,

a fully rigged ship of 1900 tons, which had sent out a distress call nearly 24 hours before. They were able to help a tug, which had also arrived, and the ship was taken to Barry.

The first steam lifeboat was the 50ft *Duke of Northumberland,* which used a water-jet propulsion. She remained in service at several stations for 33 years and saved 295 lives. Others were built and the last was withdrawn from service in 1928. Most of them had propellers and had to be kept moored afloat. There was one major disaster in 1900, when a steam lifeboat capsized, with the loss of eight of her crew.

The first internal-combustion engine, fuelled by petrol, was fitted to a lifeboat in 1904. Thereafter they were fitted to all lifeboats, first as auxiliary to sail, then as the primary source of power. The switch to diesel engines was started in the lifeboat at Yarmouth, Isle of Wight, in 1932 and quickly became standard for all new lifeboat construction.

A lifeboat can be launched by running down a slipway or by slipping her moorings in harbour in suitable situations. But in many places in the early days the boat had to be taken over a beach for launching, for which borrowed horses might be used, and many horses and men were drowned. Largely as a result of the rapid development of internal-combustion engines in tractors during the 1914-18 war, launching tractors were introduced in 1920. The last recorded launch by horses was at Wells, Norfolk, in 1934.

Other developments included the introduction of radio. The first lifeboat equipped with a transmitter and receiver was at Rosslare Harbour in 1927. A problem in the early stages was that only telegraphy was used, with Morse code instead of speech, and full-time trained operators had to be employed, but by 1929 two-way telephony had reached the stage where a part-time operator could cope. Nowadays radio plays an important part in rescue operations, including communication with helicopters and other aircraft.

A lifeboat is such a complex and expensive craft that financial consideration dictates the achievement of as long a life as possible. Consequently, progress and the adoption of new ideas might sometimes seem slow. For example, there are still lifeboats with petrol engines, and the last sailing lifeboat was in service at New Quay in Cardiganshire until 1948. A modern 52ft lifeboat with two 60hp diesel engines is a very large investment for a

Above: The launch of a new lifeboat at Blackpool, as depicted in the October 10, 1885, edition of 'The Graphic'. *Illustrated London News*

Right: The awkward and uncomfortable way a lifeboat was launched circa 1875. *Illustrated London News*

Far right below: The German lifeboat 'Adolf Bermpohl' off the coast of Heligoland in June 1968. *A Greenway*

charitable body and might have to last for 30 years.

After the Fraserburgh disaster in 1970, when all but one of the crew of *The Duchess of Kent* were lost after capsizing while out on a rescue call, the Institution has prepared many modifications, including the possible return of self-righting qualities. The Watson 46ft 9in type, of which the Fraserburgh boat was an example, was given a self-righting air bag on the after cabin top, which has been found able to right a boat in six seconds. The new Rother class is self-righting. It also has radar and a covered steering position, and looks more like a motor cruiser than a traditional lifeboat.

In Britain it has been the practice to have lifeboats which were mostly kept ashore and launched rapidly; in the United States lifeboats have been normally kept afloat. The American craft, operated by the US Coast Guard, put more accent on speed and were always of very different appearance from the British craft. The British service never regarded speed as very important. Most calls for help would be comparatively close, often resulting from the ship in distress having been too close to the shore. Sea-keeping qualities were more important than speed in the lifeboat. Modern lifeboats of traditional British type do about 9 knots.

The US lifeboats had a much greater coastline to protect and individual boats might have to travel long distances. Consequently, higher speeds were desirable to save time. British boats have nearly all been built of wood, but many recent US Coast Guard boats are of steel. The rescue services of both countries are investigating and using glass-reinforced plastics, but complete building in the new synthetic material is not yet fully accepted.

In 1964 a 44ft 13-knot US Coast Guard steel lifeboat was brought to Britain for experiment, and six very similar craft have been built here. The Institution also started building more-traditional boats in steel. The 48ft 6in Solent class, introduced in 1969, is based on the older Oakley boat of the same length. Self-righting in the new class comes only from the reserve buoyancy provided by the rather large enclosed superstructure, that is, without the transfer of water ballast that was usual in earlier self-righting boats.

There are now larger lifeboats, such as the steel 71ft Clyde-class boat, one of which is kept afloat at Clovelly at the entrance to the Bristol Channel. It has twin 230hp diesel motors and is capable of 11 knots. It carries an inshore rescue boat capable of 20 knots for use in shallow waters.

Inshore rescue is a comparatively recent responsibility of the British lifeboat service. Now some stations have had their traditional lifeboats moved elsewhere and have only inshore craft. In 1972 the 113 inshore lifeboats in service saved more lives than conventional boats. Inflatable inshore rescue craft were introduced in 1962, to be followed in 1968 by glassfibre-hulled McLachlan 18ft ragged-chine boats with twin diesel or petrol motors and speeds of 20 knots.

There has been considerable development going on in the design of inflatables and semi-inflatables, with rigid V bottoms surrounded by inflatable tubes. The Institution backed experiments with such craft at the Atlantic College and one result has been the introduction into service of the rigid-bottomed Atlantic 21, fitted with two 40hp outboard motors, which can travel at 28 knots. Experiments continue with jet propulsion of shallow-draught craft for use in surf—a reversion to the method in the first powered lifeboat.

Today the key man in the local organisation of the RNLI is the honorary secretary of the Station branch committee. He decides if the boat is to be launched. At sea the coxswain is in command. At most lifeboat stations there is one paid full-time man. Other members of the crew are volunteers, who get nominal payments and have to be called in various ways if there is an emergency. Modern power boats need smaller crews, which might number five or seven men. A recent report showed an active fleet of 138 lifeboats around the coast of Great Britain and Ireland, with a reserve fleet of 30 boats. The inshore rescue fleet had 113 boats on station, with 28 in reserve.

The British lifeboat service has given a lead to the rest of the world, and many bodies elsewhere have followed its lead in keeping free from government finance and control, and much advice and help continue to be given to other services. During the East Pakistan disaster in 1970, inshore rescue craft were taken to help in rescue and to train local people.

The Royal National Life-Boat Institution is likely to continue its voluntary work for a long time. It works successfully with many official bodies, such as the Coastguard service and the Royal Air Force, but when life is at risk, bureaucracy is cut across and all unite in the one aim of immediate succour to those in peril.

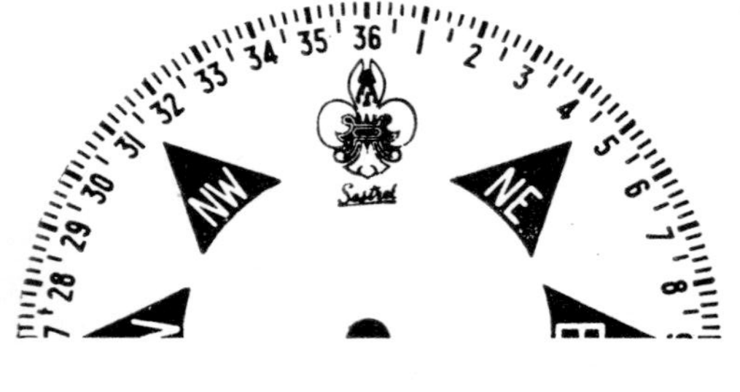

Compasses

THE INVENTION of the compass has been ascribed to the Chinese, although, as there was little if any communication between the several ancient civilisations, it is probable that an appreciation of the properties of the magnetised needle was born independently in various maritime societies during the first millenium AD. There is evidence in Scandinavian records that the mariner's compass as a practical navigational aid was probably developed in northern Europe between the years 868 and 1100 AD.

In its earliest form the compass consisted merely of a suspended bar of lodestone, a magnetic oxide of iron found in China, Bengal, Arabia and (of lower quality) in Germany, Scandinavia and the west of England. Presumably its use stemmed from the realisation that its directional properties could be related to the bearing of some celestial body, in particular in the northern seas to the Pole Star which occupied an apparently fixed position in the heavens. The crude use of lodestone was soon overtaken by the technique of magnetising an iron needle, a process that could be repeated as necessary to restore its north-seeking property.

The early crude method of floating the needle, supported by a piece of cork or straw, on water was soon replaced by mounting it on a pivot. The compass card, eight to ten inches in diameter and marked with the 32 points, to which the needle was affixed, came next, possibly in the 15th century and certainly in the 16th; also by the 16th century the complete compass was being mounted on pivots in a wooden box fitted with a glass lid, so that it was protected from the elements. The whole assembly was supported in brass gimbals so that it might remain level irrespective of pitching and rolling movements of the ship.

It was soon realised that although in Mediterranean waters the compass indicated something close to the true north, elsewhere it was subject to differing amounts of error, called compass variation. In Britain and France, variation was allowed for by offsetting the needle half a point to the eastward of the meridian line of the card, but as ships moved elsewhere it led to considerable navigational errors. Moreover, the design and manufacture of the compasses themselves were crude until the middle of the 18th century when Dr Gowan Knight applied himself to the task of designing a compass on well-engineered scientific principles.

Knight's compass was adopted as standard for the Royal Navy and served well until the advent of iron-hulled ships in the mid-19th century. Already it had been appreciated that substantial masses of iron, such as guns and stanchions, had a marked effect on the accuracy of the compass and that the anomaly was itself subject to change with alteration of course. The error, or deviation, formed the subject of an investigation by Matthew Flinders, who devised means to correct the compass by the use of vertical soft iron bars usually placed abaft the bowl.

An iron hull made matters worse but the work of the Astronomer Royal, Sir George Airey, produced an answer in the form of a mass of soft iron placed on each side of the compass which was itself placed high up in the ship as far removed as possible from the effects of the iron structure. The modern magnetic compass derives from the work of Sir William Thompson (Lord Kelvin), 1824-1907, who assimilated that of Flinders and Airey and produced a well-engineered instrument, the design of which has changed little during the past hundred years.

The early years of the present century brought new developments which made complete reliance on the magnetic compass unnecessary. The principle of the gyroscope and the laws of precession had long been known and it could be shown mathematically that a suitably constrained gyroscope would precess until the axis of spin lay horizontal in the plane of the earth's axis. Hence, unlike the magnetic compass, it would indicate true north. Practical development of the theory led to the design of the gyro compass, the first seaworthy version of which was produced by the German firm Hermann Anschütz in 1908. The Anschütz compass was later modified and further developed by the Arma Corporation of the USA and was installed in a number of British warships.

In the meantime Elmer A Sperry in the US had developed another design of gyro compass which was easier to manufacture and much bigger, and hence potentially more accurate, than the German one. The Sperry design employed a rotor weighing 52lb which was driven electrically at 6000rpm. It was adopted by the British Admiralty and for 50 years the Sperry design and developments from it have served as the standard gyro compass in HM ships.

A third type, designed by S G Brown in England, first appeared in 1916 and has since been employed extensively in both merchant ships and warships. In addition to the basic fact that the gyro compass is not affected by either the earth's or the ship's magnetic fields, there is also the advantage that the transmission to remote repeater compass heads is easily arranged.

A recent development is the Ship's Inertial Navigation System (SINS) derived from equipment produced in the 1950s for use in ballistic missiles; as well as an indication of true north, and hence ship's heading, the system shows ship's position in latitude and longitude and its speed over the ground. The use of SINS is confined mainly to major warships, other vessels being fitted with modern versions of Anschütz, Sperry, Arma or Brown gyro compasses with the necessary repeaters to meet all navigational needs.

The magnetic compass continues to be fitted in many small craft, although for larger vessels it is now regarded as an anachronism. No doubt new developments will ease further the task of the ship's navigator, but in the meantime the gyro compass is an accurate and reliable instrument capable of presenting course data wherever required, and of being integrated with automatic navigational equipment.

Above: The C3 compass card (left) which is marked every 5° and with cardinal points only; the C1 card (right) is marked every 2° and is an alternative to the C3. *Henry Browne & Son Ltd*

Right: 18th-century navigating instruments displayed in the Maritime Museum at Dubrovnik. *Dubrovnik Maritime Museum*

Below: 18th-century Chinese navigational instruments. *M Pucciarelli*

MARINE COMMUNICATIONS

THE NEED has always existed for devices to expand human activities beyond the bounds of human limitations. One such device was the wheel, another the ship, and another some sort of method for conveying messages or instructions further than the human voice could carry or the human ear could hear.

Before the days of complex telecommunications, that method was usually by flag, and it is likely that in their earliest form, flags were simply handy pieces of material or complete garments, and the use of sails to make signals was common up to the 17th century. One of the earliest flag signals at sea is said to have been given before the battle of Salamis in about 480 BC, when the Greek commander Themistocles ordered a red cloak to be tied to an oar and hoisted aloft as a sign to his fleet to attack.

Such basic or pre-arranged signals were all that were possible at that time, and for many centuries afterwards, for literacy was a luxury confined to scholars and monks. And without literacy, a detailed flag code system would have been incomprehensible. In that context, it is significant that the first such system was not compiled until the late 18th century, when the ability to read and write was becoming more widespread, and the medieval notion was fading that such skills were unworthy of fighting men and a sign of the non-combatant weakling.

The ten-number system published then had additional 'Preparative', 'Yes' and 'No' flags, a substitute flag to avoid carrying duplicates and code book to explain the meaning of the various flag arrangements. The two signal books, outlining the numeral system, which were produced by Admirals Lord Howe and Kempenfelt in 1782 and 1790, were later supplemented by the marine vocabulary drawn up by Sir Home Popham. It consisted of a dictionary

Above: A crew member using a signalling lamp on the Italian sail training ship, 'Amerigo Vespucci'. *M Pucciarelli*

Left: A plaque showing painted signal flags and letters inside the wheelhouse of the paddle steamer 'Ryde'. *J Eastland*

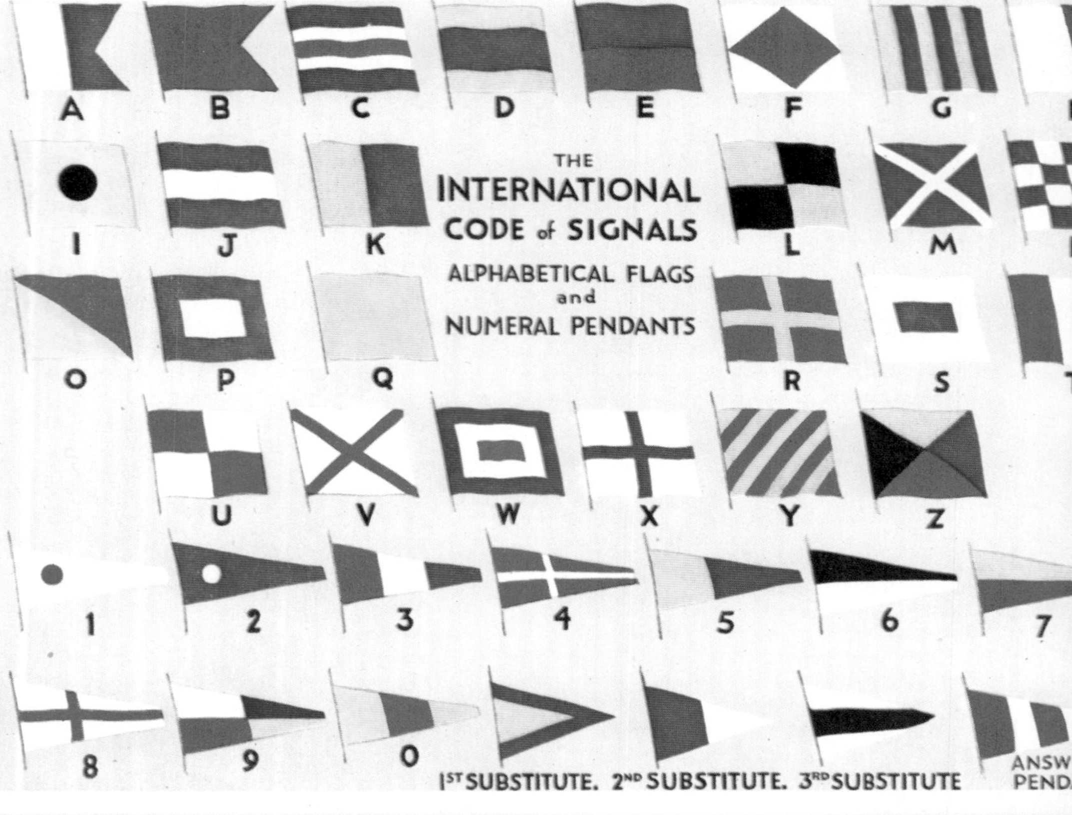

Above: The Trafalgar signal as displayed on the rigging of the preserved ship HMS 'Victory'.
P D Hawkes

Above right: The International code of signals showing alphabetical flags.
Shipping Wonders of the World

Right: The arrest of the notorious murderer Dr Crippen, demonstrating the successful use of wireless communication at sea.
Illustrated London News

Facing page: A colourful collection of 18th century nautical flags. *M Pucciarelli*

KEY TO INTERNATIONAL CODE OF SIGNALS

- **A** Undergoing speed trial
- **B** I am taking in or unloading explosives
- **C** Yes (affirmative)
- **D** Keep clear of me—I am manoeuvring with difficulty
- **E** I am altering course to starboard
- **F** I am disabled—communicate with me
- **G** I require a pilot
- **H** I have a pilot on board
- **I** I am altering course to port
- **J** I am going to send a message by semaphore
- **K** You should stop your vessel instantly
- **L** You should stop. I have something important to communicate
- **M** I have a doctor on board
- **N** No (negative)
- **O** Man overboard
- **P** Blue Peter—at sea / At sea—your lights are out
- **Q** My vessel is healthy. I request free pratique
- **R** The way is off my ship
- **S** Engines are going astern
- **T** Do not pass ahead of me
- **U** You are standing into danger
- **V** I require assistance
- **W** I require medical assistance
- **X** Stop carrying out your intention and watch for my signals
- **Y** I am carrying mails
- **Z** Used to address or call shore stations

in which certain groups of flags were assigned to each word. The Howe-Popham flag code was used at Trafalgar by Nelson to make, in 12 hoists, the most famous flag signal in the history of the British Navy.

Popham had provided in his vocabulary for the first word, *England* (253), but not for Nelson's choice as the second, confides. Nelson substituted *Expects* (269), and was able to use the vocabulary for *That* (863) *Every* (261) *Man* (471) *Will* (958) *Do* (220) *His* (370); curiously, Popham had omitted to include the last word of the message, for which there was no convenient substitute, and so *Duty* had to be spelled out letter by letter as 4, 21, 19 and 24.

About 20 minutes after Nelson's signal was completed, another, ready-made, signal was hoisted—No 16, 'Engage the enemy more closely'.

Signalling shorthand of that kind was vital in battle and in situations of danger or emergency. Five centuries before Trafalgar, English warships would fly a flag at half-mast to call captains into council, and hoist it to the masthead to indicate to the fleet that the enemy was in sight. In the 16th century, Sir Walter Raleigh sent similarly brief or urgent messages by lowering and immediately re-hoisting one or more sails on his ship.

Today, speed and simplicity are still crucial for warning or distress signals, and the combined numerical and alphabetical International Code enables them to be more specific. There are, for instance, two-flag hoists for *Want Immediate Assistance* (CB), *You Are Standing Into Danger* (JD), or *You Should Stop Your Vessel Instantly* (SO) With one-, two,- or three-flag hoists, the most common and most important are the single flags; least important, but of course most numerous, are the three-flag hoists. Four-flag groups are usually ship's names or 'numbers', used for reporting identity to signal stations and so on.

Alphabetical flags, when flown singly, may indicate a vessel on speed-trial (A), or one that is unloading or loading explosives (B). The signal O indicates *Man Overboard,* and GW indicates the additional request *Please Take Action To Pick Him Up.* The famous 'Blue Peter'—flag P—announces that a ship is about to sail.

Because it is obviously dangerous and could be fatal to presuppose good visibility at sea when sending urgent signals, there are several arrangements which require no 'reading', but rely simply on the position or condition of flags and other devices. Flying an ensign upside down is a well-known distress signal, but even that can be misinterpreted or not fully understood when visibility is impaired, or the flags are streaming towards or away from the observer. More immediately clear is the flag with a ball hoisted above or below it, or a wheft (a flag bound in the middle).

Such signals, of course, are internationally understood, unlike early flag code signals which were deliberately designed for secrecy. The code books carried by Royal Navy vessels were, in fact, weighted so that if the ship was in danger of capture by an enemy, the books would sink

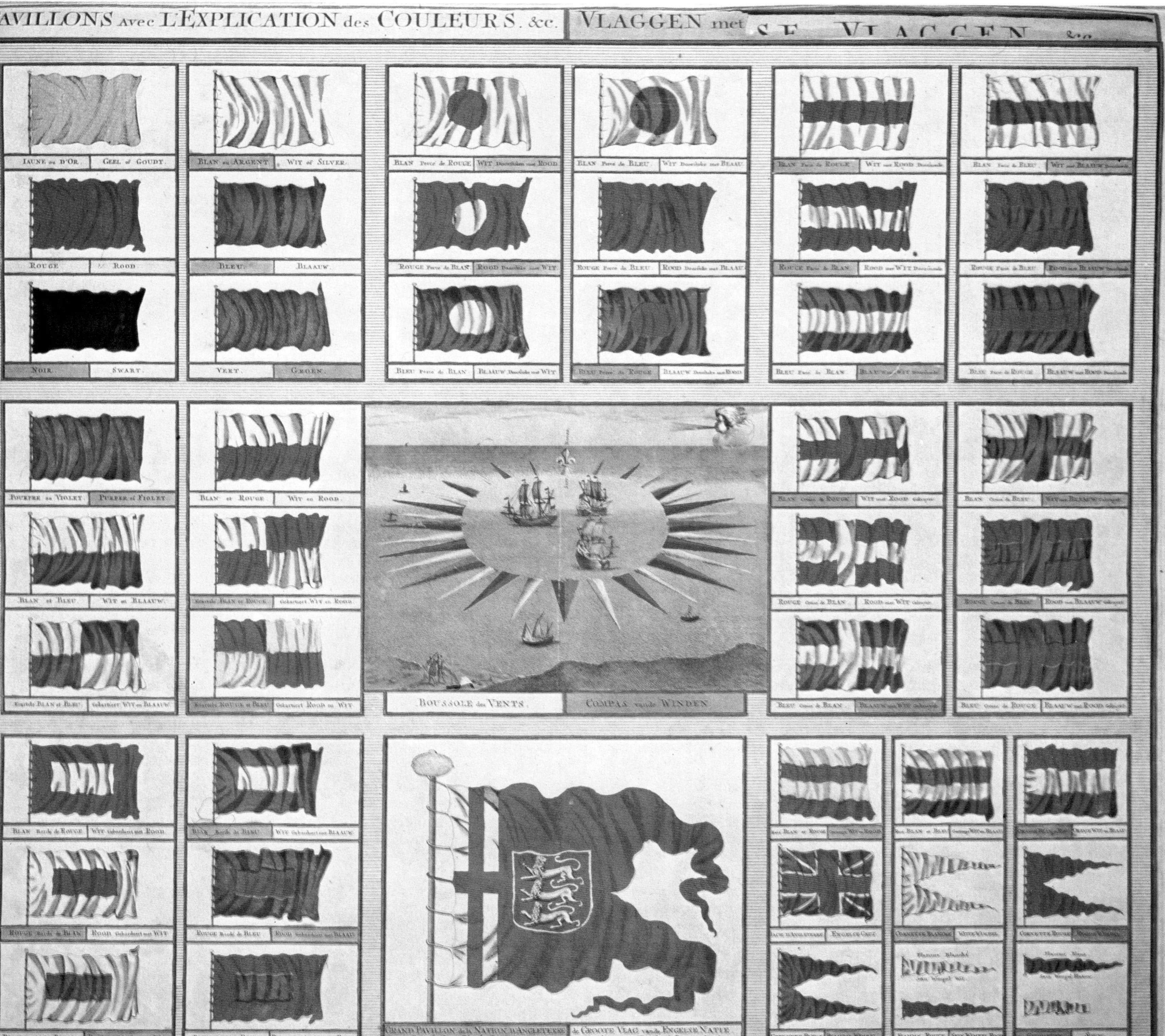

immediately they were thrown into the sea.

In 1817, the secrecy ingredient was removed from the naval flag code when Captain Frederick Marryat converted it for use by merchant shipping, removing those signals designed to give orders for battle and introducing new ones more in keeping with the requirements of commerce. By 1857, Marryat's code had begun to prove too limited in the number of different hoists it allowed. The Board of Trade therefore substituted for it the first international code of flag signals, and the first one to use alphabetical rather than numerical flags.

The new code consisted of a Code and Answering Pendant and 18 flags, from which the five vowels had been omitted in the cause of international amity; it was feared that, inadvertently or deliberately, foreign swear words might be hoisted and perhaps spark off international incidents. Unfortunately, the lack of vowels also limited the new code's scope, for it did not allow for spelling out words and names not covered in the code. A revised code introduced in 1901 repaired the omission, but it, too, eventually proved inadequate for the number of hoists needed. The code was enlarged again in 1927 and once more in 1948, when the number of flags was brought up to 78.

Flashing light signals and the sophisticated electronics of today might make communication by flag seem rather primitive. However, more than one 'sparks', faced with a foreigner at the other end of the transmission, has been glad enough of the international flag code to make conversation possible; and more than one ship, isolated at sea by a technical breakdown or a faulty power line, has been grateful for its signal flags and a brisk sea wind to fly them by.

Late 20th-century people, spoiled by science and pampered by so many different sorts of communications facilities, have to perform mental gymnastics to envisage the loneliness, suspense and enforced patience of the past, when communications were slow, crude and severely limited. Until the second half of the 19th century, not to see or hear was not to know; what was happening out of earshot and beyond eye-range did not exist for any practical purpose, and many of the dangers of seafaring were the dangers of isolation.

Over short distances, in daylight and in reasonable conditions, signalling by flags gave a basic, but sufficiently articulate, sort of intercourse between ships. Night-time and storms, however, considerably reduced even those limited facilities. In the absence of electric beams to pierce the featureless blackness of night hours at sea, light signals between ships depended on the power and range of candles in horn lanterns. Sound signals that would travel any feasible distance could be provided only by ships' guns, which were fired in unison to avoid confusion of sound.

Seamen coped with the handicaps with a fair amount of ingenuity, combining light and sound to transmit various set messages and orders. In the late 18th century, for instance, an admiral gave orders for his fleet to unmoor and ride short by hanging out three lights one above the other in the main topmast shrouds, and by firing two guns. Receipt of the orders was acknowledged by answering guns fired on the flagships and by a light hung in the mizen shrouds of other vessels in the fleet.

One light hung in the main topmast shrouds and the firing of a gun comprised the admiral's orders to weigh anchor. One gun fired with no alteration of existing lights indicated that the admiral intended to change course. In perilous situations, the combined light and sound night signals included a suitable element of emergency. A ship sailing into danger had to blaze out the fact by showing as many lights as possible, and by firing a gun. A ship in which two lights of equal height were hung, and which fired its guns repeatedly was broadcasting the news that it had sprung a leak. When the guns stopped firing, this meant that another ship had come to the rescue.

A strange ship approaching a fleet was treated with understandable caution, and standing orders were that such a vessel should not be allowed to pass through the fleet. Conditions, naturally, did not always make it easy invariably to carry out such orders, and a strong sea wind could also prevent the verbal communication which the ship nearest to the stranger was supposed to establish. The ship therefore had to fall back on the continual firing of a gun and the display of a number of lights. This was a warning to the admiral of the fleet, which the guns of his ship would then acknowledge.

Other combinations of lanterns and guns enabled an admiral to order his fleet to veer, to moor, to lower yards and topmasts, to hoist them again, to lie short or a-hull or to make sail once more. The system could not, however, do more than transmit the routine signals required to keep a fleet sailing in good order, with extra arrangements for some known emergencies. For unforeseen dangers or a sudden crisis, the seamen had to rely largely on his own enterprise and instinct, and on that curious sixth sense that develops in those who deal with the elements face to face.

It was small protection, even for ships which sailed with the safety of numbers and the comfort of company to ensure some sort of rescue when necessary. The lone ship, of course, was in particular peril at a time when there was no proper means of signalling for help at sea. If such a vessel got into difficulties, it was almost inevitably doomed unless by a fortunate and not very frequent coincidence, another ship happened to be near enough at the time. Even in the late 19th century, a disaster at sea became known only when a ship failed to arrive in port. At one dismal period, a loss of 2000 ships a year was recorded, a statistic that implied the deaths of thousands of men who might have been saved had better communications existed.

The key to those better communications was electric power, the subject of many experiments from the early nineteenth century onwards. The first feasible means of electric signalling did not arise until 1844, when the American artist and inventor Samuel B Morse demonstrated his electric telegraph. Combined with the dot-and-dash code Morse had devised in 1838, it offered a far more flexible and far-reaching means of communication than had ever existed before.

The Morse code, the most successful of all such signalling systems, was particularly versatile, since it could be transmitted not only by sound, but by vision. The shutter on a heliograph, which used sunlight reflected on to two adjustable mirrors, could be manipulated to transmit the long 'dashes' and short 'dots' of which the Morse code was composed. In 1867, in fact, heliograph signalling was adopted by the British Navy. After 1869, when Thomas Edison produced the first practical electric light bulb, it also became possible to use electric lamps to flash Morse code messages in almost any conditions.

As time went on, the peculiar noise-making qualities that could be produced both by electricity and compressed air gradually brought about a whole new generation of sound signals—the wailing siren, the baleful fog signal, and the diaphone which rounds off its piercing blare with a characteristic grunt and can transmit sound over a distance of nine miles.

The new signalling methods were heralding the end of those long centuries when men were marooned by distance and imprisoned by time and were forced to suffer whatever the elements had to offer in silence and solitude. The elements were, in fact, being turned from masters into servants, for in many ways by the end of the 19th century, scientists were harnessing natural powers for positive purposes. Particularly notable among those natural powers were the electromagnetic or wireless waves, whose existence in the atmosphere was first proved by the German physicist Heinrich Hertz in experiments between 1885 and 1889.

The sound of bells ringing has always been a sound of some importance, either as a warning or as a message of joyful news. The bell which rang in 1894 in a downstairs room of a luxurious villa near Bologna in Italy was of the second variety, for it heralded a revolution in worldwide communications that was to expand human capabilities far beyond human limitations.

The impulse that made the bell ring came from the attic, two floors up, where 20-year old Guglielmo Marconi had built a crude radio transmitter. The success of young Marconi's experiments to harness wireless waves—an achievement then being eagerly pursued by amateur and professional scientists the world over—was a practical complement to the work of the British physicist James Clerk Maxwell and the German physicist Heinrich Hertz. Between 1885 and 1889, Hertz had proved the existence of the natural wireless waves in space first postulated by Maxwell in 1864. Marconi's work also gave a new and sophisticated slant to the system of electric telegraphy which had been in use since the 1850s for transmitting messages, most often in Morse code.

Like so many inventors before and after him, Marconi had to struggle to get his ideas accepted. However, the struggle in his case was comparatively slight because his device for transmitting messages to places out of sight and beyond hearing had so many obvious advantages, particularly for communication at sea. There, for centuries, a ship that encountered difficulties was alone in its plight unless it happened to be near another vessel that could mount a rescue operation. When Marconi demonstrated how messages could be sent across the Bristol Channel (1897), the English Channel (1899) and the Atlantic Ocean (1901), it was clear that a miracle method had arrived which could save lives, ships and valuable cargoes whose safety had once been almost completely at the mercy of the volatile sea.

Top: A typical modern naval signalling lamp and signal flag locker. *A Greenway*

Above: The late Professor Morse, American author of the electric telegraph, pictured in 'The Illustrated London News' of May 4, 1872, shortly after his death. *Illustrated London News*

Above right: The wireless-telegraphy room of an Atlantic liner of the early 20th century, similar to that aboard 'Titanic'. *Illustrated London News*

Right: Night signals by lights and flares: 1: Steam vessel under way 2: Steam vessel towing 3: Vessel not under command 4: Vessel repairing or laying cables 5: Pilot vessel on station 6: Steam trawler under way 7: Vessel aground 8: Open boat, fishing gear extended 9: Vessel attracting attention 10: Thames dredger at work 11: Steam pilot vessel at anchor 12: Light vessel off proper station 13: Vessel marking a Thames wreck 14: Ships at anchor 15: Vessel being overtaken.

Marconi was still experimenting and demonstrating when the first radio shore stations were built and the first ships to carry radio were being equipped. Over one hundred shore stations were in existence by 1901, with more being constructed, and about 200 ships had had radio installed.

The first radio room to be built into a British ship was little more than a tiny airless shack, the size of a small cupboard. The ship in question was the *Lake Champlain,* and the radio operators who had to work in the makeshift cabin were obliged to leave the door open in order to get enough light and air. A fair part of the minimal floor space was occupied by the accumulators, and the rest of the equipment consisted of a transmitter-receiver housed in an old wooden box, a cell-charger screwed to the wall and a cumbersome somewhat ancient Morse keyboard.

It took a certain amount of physical strength and endurance to operate the keyboard.'The maximum speed we could handle was about ten words a minute,' one early wireless operator once recalled; 'We suffered mostly from strain in the arm, as the key worked like a pump . . . and if we went faster, the thing failed to function.'

The 'thing' however, soon proved a great life-saver, for not only was there a distinct drop in the number of accidents at sea, but those that did occur were not invariably disastrous. Between 1901 and 1910, only nine people died out of the six million who travelled across the Atlantic Ocean. Three or four decades before, about 2000 ships and an average of 3000 seamen were being lost every year; with the resignation of helplessness, such losses were accepted without undue surprise.

Naturally, not every shipowner, nor every seaman, was converted to acceptance of radio on ships, and not all those who did accept it realised just how vital it was to take full advantage of the protection it offered. Reluctance was partly due to economics, natural conservatism, and smugness and partly to that odd quirk in human nature which gives a precaution its proper due only after its absence or failure has proved fatal.

In the case of radio at sea, the disaster which proved the point was the sinking of the *Titanic* in April 1912, with the loss of 1470 out of the 2200 persons on board. The liner *California,* which was only 20 miles away and might have saved many of the victims, had only one radio operator and he was off watch during the fateful hours.

As a result of the *Titanic* calamity, the first International Convention for Safety at Sea, which met in London in 1913, outlined rules which included the carrying of enough radio operators to maintain a 24-hour service. In the same year, it became illegal for a deep-sea ship carrying 50 persons or more to be without wireless. Today, ships of 500 tons and more are obliged to carry some form of radio communication.

The uses of radio on board ship have, naturally, evolved beyond the sending of Morse code signals, and the call for help beyond the simple SOS or the voice crying 'M'aidez!' Those internationally understood distress calls are still widely used, of course, and it is also possible for radio signals from one ship to activate automatic alarms in another. The unique advantage of radio is, however, that it enables communications to be made by voice. As a direct result, diagnoses have been made from one ship to another in the case of sickness, and in one or two cases, emergency operations have been performed by proxy, as it were.

Time signals, news bulletins, weather forecasts and other important information are transmitted by shore stations for the benefit of shipping, and ships which encounter adverse conditions can reciprocate by warning the stations and other vessels at sea. The role played by ships and radio is, of course, crucial in the business of weather forecasting; in fact, the forecasts are largely formulated from reports radioed by ships at sea.

The impact of radio upon seafaring life has revealed itself, too, in the advance it has produced in navigational aids. They include radar—radio detection and ranging—by which a ship may be guided blind in poor visibility or fog, direction-finders to help keep the vessel on course, and echo sounders to check on the depth of water beneath the keel, or in the case of fishing vessels, to detect shoals of fish.

The Mariner's Telescope

THE PRINCIPLE of the telescope was described by Roger Bacon of Oxford in about the year 1250, but as a practical optical instrument it dates probably from 1608 when, among others, Zacharias Jansen of Middleburg in Holland constructed his first working model. Galileo of Padua, when visiting Venice in May 1609, heard of a Belgian instrument and on his return to Padua constructed his own telescope with a convex lens at one end of a lead tube and a concave lens at the other. He gradually improved upon the design and in 1610 constructed a telescope with a magnification of 33 diameters which he used in his discovery of the satellites of the planet Jupiter.

Those early telescopes produced an inverted image but that was of little consequence for astronomical observation and in fact the modern astronomical instrument, which is used primarily for photographic work, likewise gives an inverted image. For terrestrial use the addition of a third lens between the objective and the eyepiece was necessary in order to produce the desired erect image, although it does, of course, considerably restrict the field of vision.

The marine draw-type telescope constructed on this principle came into use in the late 17th century, but poor lenses and the consequent effects of spherical and chromatic aberration made necessary a long focal length and hence a long instrument. Lightweight materials were used for portability, the body being usually of wood and the draw tubes of papier maché vellum with ivory fittings. Typical of that early generation is one in the National Maritime Museum, constructed in 1690 with five gilt tooled vellum draw tubes, which when opened fully is about five feet in length.

In 1729, Chester Moreton Hall discovered that the use of an eyepiece lens formed by cementing together crown glass convex and flint glass concave elements dramatically reduced the effects of chromatic aberration, but the advantages of the achromatic lens were little publicised and it was not until 1757 that its use was exploited on a commercial scale by John Dolland of London.

A much reduced focal length resulted in an instrument about 20 to 24 inches long constructed with a wooden body, frequently leather covered, and brass draw tubes. Being strong, the Dolland telescope was much used at sea and until 1790 Dolland and his son, Peter, enjoyed a virtual monopoly in the manufacture of telescopes for the British service.

Further improvement in the form of an achromatic objective was introduced by Dolland in 1760 and one example of this type on display at Greenwich was possibly owned by Lord Howe, victor of the Glorious First of June in 1794. A similar instrument, used at Trafalgar by Captain T M Hardy, Nelson's flag captain in HMS *Victory*, can be seen in the Royal Naval Museum in Portsmouth.

Development in the 19th century was confined to detail although improved methods of assembly eased considerably the problems of cleaning and repair of not only telescopes but optical instruments in general. Costs were reduced and a steady demand enabled manufacturers to market a standard range of telescopes to suit all prospective buyers. In the 1880s E Walton of Gosport, across the harbour from Portsmouth, was advertising a standard pattern brass Officer of the Watch model for sale to budding naval officers, while for those able to afford only a cheaper product the Cadet model would appear to have been the best buy.

The telescope body was leather covered and, once acquired, the instrument was usually decorated with some form of sennit work in order to give vent to an expression of individuality. More expensive instruments were made of German silver and one Admiralty prize telescope awarded to Mr W R Napier, of HMS *Britannia*, in December 1892, and now on display at Greenwich, is of silvered brass and fully sennit bound. Magnification was of the order of 12 to 15 diameters.

A much larger telescope to be found on the flag deck in HM ships until the late 1950s was the so-called cruiser telescope, a pivot-mounted instrument about four feet long with a magnification of 50 or 60 diameters. However, development of ship-to-ship voice communication has practically eliminated the need for instant recognition of distant flag signals and visual call signs, and the use of semaphore has long since been abandoned.

Today the telescope is little used at sea, having been superseded for all practical purposes by prismatic binoculars, which are steadier, more compact and permit a much larger field of vision. Such an instrument was in fact patented by the Frenchman A A Boulanger in 1859 but binoculars found little favour among seamen until the turn of the century. By that time Ernest Abbé had evolved a design in which the prisms were positioned with the object glasses wider apart than the eyepieces, which enhanced the stereoscopic effect. It remains essentially the type of instrument in general use at the present time, later developments being concerned with improvements in the optical system and details such as methods of focusing to suit the needs of users.

In the meantime, the telescope continues to fulfil a ceremonial need as a badge of office for the Officer of the Day aboard HM ships in harbour.

Below: A mariner's telescope for day and night viewing by Spencer Browning of Liverpool. *Parker Gallery*

Bottom: A Dolland telescope used by Nelson, photographed with the admiral's famous walking-stick used at Naples. *Illustrated London News*

Radar aids Port Control

WHEN RUDYARD KIPLING, that great neglected poet of the merchant seaman, wrote:

'O, the mutter overside, when the port fog holds us tied,
And the sirens hoot their dread,
When foot by foot we creep o'er the hueless viewless deep
To the sob of the questing lead!'

he was, as always, presenting a true picture of life at sea at the turn of the century. Fog has always been the mariner's most treacherous enemy, distorting sounds, hiding leading marks, buoys and, of course, other ships at anchor and under way. One of the most important items of the pilot's creed was that it was the action of a prudent mariner to anchor if, having run the distance from the last known position, the next mark was not sighted.

An Elbe pilot, writing of pilotage 50 years ago, states 'The ships were mostly furnished with a magnetic compass and an echo-sounder was a great technical advance. During fog, all the ships dropped the anchor, and only some small passenger ships in the traffic between Hamburg and England tried to proceed. As old pilots report, they often grounded in the river several times during such a voyage. But most of the ships rode at anchor, and the sleep of the pilot was disturbed only by the ringing of the anchor bells. I believe it was a beautiful time . . .'

Those leisurely days when safety meant safety and not 'an acceptable risk' have departed, never to return until the world regains its sanity in a revised scale of values. Never before in the history of shipping has money been so closely equated with time, and never has port time been so expensive a purchase for the ship operator. Every minute of delay incurred by one of today's monster ships is closely scrutinised and valid reasons must be produced for the above-expectation port time of that call.

If there is no valid reason and the delay is one of an unnecessary series, then the port responsible could be waving good-bye to a very lucrative trade. The old breed of shipowner with a loyalty to a particular port has now almost vanished, to be replaced by multi-national combines and property speculators who manipulate their ships not as a service but as a means to a quick profit. 'There is no attribute of fog which physically holds a ship back,' said a speaker at a recent conference, 'so why cannot a ship go as quickly in fog as in clear weather?'

Leaving aside the moral and legal requirements for ships to proceed in such a manner as not to endanger other navigators, the shipowner holds the purse strings, and the question has to be answered. Banishing port delays is not only a matter of keeping up speeds safely in fog, but also a matter in all weather states of using port facilities to the best advantage. It is useless to have a queue of ships forming at an entrance lock and taking them in order of random arrival if

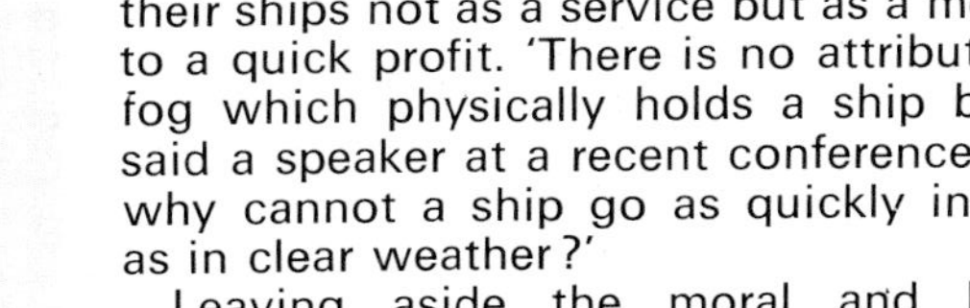

Top: A fine night shot of the radar control tower overlooking the port of Havre. *L Dunn*

Above centre: The Clan Line cargo liner 'Argyllshire' passing the Port of Southampton radar station in June 1973. *A Greenway*

Left: The Port of Southampton Operation Centre at 37 Berth, Eastern Docks. *A Greenway*

Top: The Port of Liverpool's new radar station now in operation at the Royal Seaforth Dock. *The Mersey Docks and Harbour Company*

Above centre: Personnel at work in the radar room of the Port of Liverpool's radar station. *The Mersey Docks and Harbour Company*

Above: The port operations HQ at Sheerness on the Medway showing the 25ft Decca harbour radar aerial. *Decca Radar Ltd (L Dunn Collection)*

Facing page above: Diagrammatic drawings by G H Davis from an August 1948 edition of 'The Illustrated London News' showing the first Liverpool harbour radar station. *Illustrated London News*

Facing page below: A pilot boat coming alongside off Harwich in June 1971. *A Greenway*

the tide is going to fall too far for the large container ship at the tail of the queue to cross the sill. Obviously, she must be given precedence, and some form of control over the wishes of individual shipmasters to be first must be exercised by the harbourmaster if confusion and delays are not to proliferate.

Perhaps one of the most efficient forms of control was the convoy system used in the Suez Canal. Two convoys left each end of the canal every day, and there was a strict deadline time for the acceptance of ships on the next transit. The vessels were marshalled by the Canal Authority with the 'benzines' (dangerous or low-flashpoint cargoes) at the rear, followed only by known 'lame ducks,' usually with a tug in compulsory attendance. The canal pilots made sure that the prescribed order of entry was maintained.

Signal stations were placed at intervals along the banks, and from those the pilot was informed of the interval between his own ship and the next ahead, the maintenance of which was vital if the control programme was to be carried out. Other orders could be relayed visually to the ships in convoy, and times adjusted so that the northbound and southbound convoys passed each other in the Bitter Lakes or the New Cut with minimum loss of time. Radar was used only to cover the Suez Bay and Port Said sea pilot stations.

A control system, the first to use air traffic control procedures in the marine environment, was opened in 1969 to cover shipping movements in the North American River St Lawrence. A computer is programmed with ship details through direct radio link and 24 reporting stations. The river is covered for 400 miles. Ships are indicated electronically on a 33-foot wall chart from which the traffic controllers—each in direct contact with the ships in his sector—can take in the traffic situation at a glance. The St Lawrence system is first cousin to the Suez Canal scheme, with a radar station at Quebec covering Sept Iles to Montreal Harbour.

The Port of Liverpool has to control enclosed docks entered by locks and there are also the locks at the entrance to the Manchester Ship Canal. There are shipyards, oil terminals, coaster berths, ferries; a busy estuary which, in the second half of the 20th century, caters for far more traffic with conflicting movement patterns than even our fathers thought possible. In July 1948 the Mersey Docks and Harbour Board correctly assessed future trends, and became the first port in the world to install shore-based surveillance radar, using equipment specifically designed for the purpose.

It was not in fact the first instance of shore-based radar being used to assist shipping. In the previous year, a radar station had been set up to guide the cross-Mersey commuter ferries through other traffic using the river in fog, the radar information being passed to the ferries by short-range radio-telephone. No doubt, experience gained with that limited installation was of benefit to the MD & HB when it built its first radar station at Gladstone Dock to cover 13 miles of the approach channel. Bearing and range discrimination in the new shore radar was marginally better than that in the marine radar, and the operators were able to gain much useful information from their six radar displays.

However, information in a radar station is of no use unless it can be disseminated to the ships under way in the coverage area. It is of no use, either, if each echo appearing on the screen cannot be identified and 'given a name', which means 100-per cent efficient radio-communication between shipping and radar station; a state we have not reached, even today. In 1948 very few ships were fitted with VHF radio-telephone; Liverpool pilots boarded with their equipment in a haversack over their shoulders. But the system worked. Shipmasters, pilots, owners and port authority were all optimistic, yet conscious that much still needed to be done, especially in the field of communications with small non-piloted non-fitted and unco-operative ships. The problem unfortunately, still remains a quarter of a century later, especially with amenity craft.

In those days, Southampton was dubbed Britain's Premier Passenger Port. Scheduled arrival times and departures of the transatlantic and cruise liners were crucial, or boat train timetables were disrupted, bringing delays and chaos to other parts of the railway system. The proposal of a major oil company to establish a nine-berth terminal between docks and sea caused the Chamber of Shipping to urge the port to adopt a system of control to prevent conflicting movements of ships using the oil terminal and the docks.

Once more the stumbling block was communications. The shipowner was not prepared to pay for his ships to be fitted with VHF which could, under a Control of Movement Order, be the means of delaying his ship at the behest of a harbourmaster! In fact, when the Port of Southampton Radar and Operations Station opened at Calshot Castle after more than five years of intensive discussion, only *four* ships were fitted with the equipment to make use of the system!

Then came what has been termed the 'Navigation Explosion'. More and more ships were crowding the trade routes and ports of the world. One writer in 1969 thought that the greatest hazard was no longer that of navigating accurately from departure to landfall, but of avoiding collision on the way! More ships fitted increasingly sophisticated radar for collision avoidance and coastal navigation. The penny then dropped that VHF radio-telephone was an integral part of the equipment required for safe and expeditious navigation, although some shipowners still refused to equip their ships.

It might be thought that the increase in the number of ship-borne radar sets and VHF radio-telephones diminished the necessity for a shore-based radar system. It is perhaps true for pilotage purposes when ships are in the navigational charge of a licensed pilot and the ship's radar is functioning well. However, even the best-maintained of radar sets occasionally blows a fuse or suffers other derangement, and then those on the bridge are back to the Mark I eyeball and the pilot's creed!

In such a situation, the pilot still has his unrivalled knowledge of the district to assist his navigation, but he must reduce speed because he has no idea where other ships are. He can hear fog signals, but knows not whence they come nor whither they go. The ship's place in the organised traffic pattern would be lost, leading to frustration and the possibility of needless risk-taking. Port radar, provided that identification procedures are followed by all ships in the coverage area, can provide the pilot with all the information he needs to proceed in safety and in his proper sequence.

Standard ship's radar has one great disadvantage. It shows the movement of other ships *relative* to the movement of the observer's own ship, which remains

A NEW AID TO NAVIGATION: THE LIVERPOOL HARBOUR RADAR STATION—THE FIRST OF ITS KIND IN THE WORLD.

THE "ALL-SEEING EYE" OF RADAR AS AN AID TO NAVIGATION: HOW THE NEW LIVERPOOL HARBOUR INSTALLATION FUNCTIONS IN FOG AND DARKNESS EXPLAINED IN A SERIES OF DIAGRAMS.

stationary at the centre of the PPI, the plan/position indicator. Time is required to obtain the necessary number of observations to solve the triangle of velocities and to obtain the true movements of the other ship. In pilotage waters there is often a multitude of targets and neither the time nor the personnel to maintain a plot on board. Worst and most dangerous of all, course changes do not show up immediately, but require a plotting interval to become apparent.

Developments in electronics and computer techniques have made possible a new generation of shipborne radars with a collision avoidance capability. These radars can solve triangle of velocities problems and tell the watch officer not only thc true course and speed of menacing targets, but also the result of any avoiding action he might take.

Shore radar, being stationary, sees all movements as true in direction and speed. Violations of local speed and traffic regulations can be spotted instantly; approaching ships can be warned of potentially dangerous situations such as yachts converging irresponsibly on to a narrow dredged channel. There is the other great advantage of shore radar; it can see the whole district of coverage, enlarging it at will on to one of the several displays to scrutinise a particular area of interest.

From that point it is only a short step to the next improvement – coupling the radar to a small computer. Provided that the programming is done by experts, and pilots have a big role to play in that, all possible queries can be answered at the touch of a button. Again, and it cannot be too often stressed, adequate VHF facilities must exist if the information is to be given to the right person, the man on the ship's bridge.

Traffic control was seen at first as an emasculation of the master's powers over the conduct of his ship. But even where full control is exercised, he still has a choice. He can either enter the control area and be subject to the instructions of the operations officer confirmed by his pilot, or he can choose to remain outside the control area until conditions improve for less stringent control to be exercised.

There are, of course, as many control schemes and operational procedures as there are ports. In Britain, for example, pilots, despite their obvious qualifications and experience, are not usually involved in the shore radar stations, although the Harwich pilots provide their own very efficient port information and radar service. In Germany, radar stations are operated in clear weather by civil servants, but pilots are brought in when visibility closes in to 1.7 nautical miles.

One of the arguments against having pilots to man the radar stations is that they tend to identify themselves too closely with the man on the bridge, and offer information slanted to what they, as pilots, would do in similar circumstances. This argument has not been borne out abroad, and information given by pilot-operators is purely factual. Pilots are, in fact, unique in knowing just what information is required by their colleague at a particular time. They also will probably have experience of handling the vessel in their colleague's charge.

There are also various methods of using shore radar, from surveillance to ensure that ships comply with the control pattern to the system akin to block signalling on the railways, which is used on the New Waterway on the approach to Rotterdam. There, ships are passed from one radar station to the next in a chain of seven; no

CUMULUS

Left: The Euromast and control tower overlooking the New Waterway at Rotterdam. *D J Kingston*

Below left: The Finnish cargo vessel 'Araguaya' in the New Waterway at Rotterdam as seen from the Euromast in June 1962. *A Greenway*

Below: Another view of the New Waterway at Rotterdam from the Euromast. *D J Kingston*

Right: The Central Operations Room of the Thames Navigation Service in the early 1970s. *Port of London Authority*

Below right: A southbound convoy passing the El Kantara signal station on the Suez canal in December 1964. *A Greenway*

Bottom right: The Deccaspot system of surveillance as seen on the radar scanner at Milford Haven. *Decca Radar Ltd*

vessels are allowed to move in the coverage area without shore agreement and new entries are prohibited once saturation level of traffic is reached.

The Port of Southampton was faced recently with the necessity to move its Port Operations and Port Radar Station from Henry VIII's old shore defence castle at Calshot to a new station at the Eastern Dock's 37 Berth. Extra coverage was obtained by siting an additional scanner at Hythe and placing the Calshot scanner atop the new Coastguard tower on the Spit. The most modern equipment was installed, the radar being coupled to a small computer fed with all the information required in a modern port specialising in quick turn-rounds of container ships. However, the Port of Southampton took one further step, and bought a bag of Deccaspots.

Deccaspots are small highly accurate markers which appear on the radar PPI; they are generated independently of the radar equipment by means of geographical co-ordinates which are fed into the computer, and so are free from drift. At Southampton the Deccaspots are one cable (about 600 feet) apart, with distinctive markers at turning points and every five cables. They are approximately at the centre of the deep-water channel, but are always referred to as the Radar Reference Line, distances being given along or from the line. To be told that an approaching ship is on the same side of the Radar Reference Line is an immediate danger signal.

Once again, despite all the sophisticated radar and computers, the vital link is good communications and co-operation. Without them, identification is frustrated and the passing of complete information impossible. If all ships participate properly, everyone proceeds with safety, order and dispatch . . . but it requires only one unco-operative master, of even the smallest vessel, to reduce all the operations officer's plans to waste paper! For that reason, the Port of Southampton maintains a patrol launch under the orders of the operations officer. The patrol officer can go alongside a yacht or other vessel and verbally convey control instructions to the person in charge – and also identify the vessel for the port radar.

Not all ports need a sophisticated system such as those employed in Southampton or Liverpool. A simple system will suffice for a small port needing only to ensure one-way traffic in a narrow entrance. It needs an expert to decide which system is right for which port, and it also needs an expert to decide where the radar aerial is to be sited to prevent loss of targets in shadow areas. The last-named problem faced Liverpool Port Radar when the new container terminal produced a large and unacceptable shadow area. The new radar station was therefore built at the north-western corner of the Royal Seaforth Dock, the scanner being 84 feet above MLWS (mean low water spring tides).

British radar leads the world in this specialised field. Shore-based radar is being installed in more and more of the world's busy ports and in today's congested port and estuarial traffic conditions the master must accept a small diminution of his power over the movements of his ship.

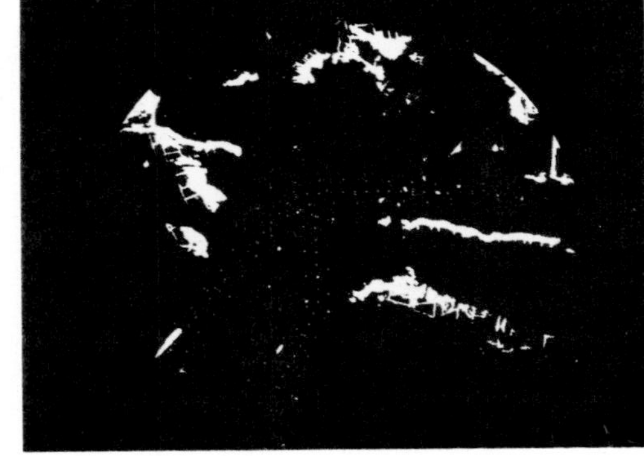

He must accept that traffic routes and separation zones are here to stay for the safety of all users, just as the Coastguard surveillance radar at St Margaret's Bay is here to stay to track down those masters who, from selfishness, ignorance or incompetence, violate the lane discipline of the Dover Strait. A recent survey has shown that lane discipline in a traffic separation scheme improves when it is known that radar surveillance has been instituted, so an increase in the number of Coastguard radar stations can be expected, especially in focal areas for large tankers using the new oil terminals in the far north of the British Isles.

The ship's master must accept the control of movement orders from the harbourmaster – indeed the law provides penalties for non-compliance – if his pilot advises him that such actions will not hazard his ship. By subordinating the interests of his own ship to the common good of all navigators in the area the safe navigation and timely arrival of all is secured.

Marine Insurance

INSURANCE as we know it today began at sea, and the reasons were both simple and obvious; whatever the perils of plague, war, fire and brigandage which had to be faced on land in centuries past, they were vastly outmatched by the perils of the sea, where every moment afloat was a moment of potential danger.

Ships, valuable cargoes and lives could be lost in sudden storms that would rip a vessel to pieces or wreck it on some hostile shore. Above all, pirates could pounce on a lone ship miles out at sea, and carry off both cargo and crew.

Although scientifically based life assurance did not emerge until the 18th century, when Edmund Halley produced the first life expectation tables, sailors had been insuring their lives for many years, mainly against the risk of being captured by Turks or corsairs and sold into slavery. The early insurances, normally taken out for the duration of one voyage only, were envisaged as a source of ransom money.

The risks against which early sailors insured themselves did not become really widespread until the 13th century. By that time, the eight hundred years of chaos which had ravaged Europe after the fall of the Roman Empire had evolved into more-settled more-peaceful times, making possible the commercial expansion of Italian Lombard city states like Venice, Genoa and Florence.

The expansion was rapid, with whole families of Lombard merchants making fortunes from trade in the wool, cloth and metals of north-west Europe and the spices, silks and luxuries of the East. Consequently, more merchant ships carrying more-valuable cargo on more-frequent voyages were facing the perils of the sea, and merchants began once more to use insurance methods once favoured by the ancient Greeks and Romans.

One was the partnership, in which several merchants joined together to finance a particular mercantile venture. Another was the nautical loan, with the moneylenders receiving their money back, with interest, on safe arrival of ship and cargo.

Neither practice, of course, was pure insurance as we now know it, except that both provided some sort of protection against risk. Recognisable marine insurance policies did not appear until about 1350, and even then protection was provided by a mixture of methods. For instance, the business records of one prosperous Lombard merchant of the late 14th century, Francesco di Marco Datini of Prato, near Florence, included 300 deeds of partnership as well as 400 insurance policies. Datini's records show that in the year 1384, he underwrote the risks on wool, silk, cloth, fustian and malmsey wine at rates varying from three to eight per cent.

Merchants like Datini operated in a rather militant religious atmosphere, and great care had to be taken not to contravene—or appear to contravene—the laws forbidding Christians to practise usury. Because of that, the moneylending nature of nautical loans was often disguised by the notaries who drew up the contracts; instead of charging interest, which was illegal, the nautical moneylender earmarked for himself a share of the profits of the voyage.

In time, though, the insurance element in nautical loans and deeds of partnership became more frankly acknowledged for what it was. Both fell into disuse as separate mercantile practices and became, simply, aspects of marine insurance.

The Ordinances regarding insurance which were codified in Florence in 1523 do not differ substantially from the principles behind modern marine insurance. The perils insured against were listed as 'of the sea, fire, jettison, reprisals or robberies of friends or foes and all other causes, perils, tempests, disasters, impediments and misfortunes, even such as cannot be thought of, that might happen . . .' The various ideas about marine insurance were brought to London by Florentine and other Lombard merchants in the early 14th century; Lombard Street was named after them.

For more than two centuries insurance business was discussed in a casual informal way, still largely typical of the City of London despite modern organisation. They made their transactions standing on the cobblestone of Lombard Street and did not move indoors until 1568, when Sir Thomas Gresham, financial adviser to Elizabeth I, opened the Royal Exchange, near Cornhill. There, insurers became known as underwriters from the practice of writing their names under their promises to compensate the insured for ships or cargoes lost at sea.

Above: The underwriting room at Lloyd's in the 1970s. *Lloyd's of London*

Left: Detail of a sketch depicting Edward Lloyd's coffee house where the great insurance business was started. *Lloyd's of London*

By that time the great voyages of discovery had opened up, great new trading areas and the expansion generated new volumes of marine insurance, and necessarily started the process of formalisation of the business. In fact the traditional straightforward person to person arrangements were no longer adequate to cover the volume of business.

Many of those early transactions were made over an informal dish of coffee in one of the two thousand London coffee houses that had sprung up since the first was opened in 1652. One particular house, situated conveniently near the Thames, became a favourite meeting place of sailors, merchants and underwriters after it was opened by Edward Lloyd in 1688. The popularity stemmed from the service provided by Lloyd, which included writing materials and the latest shipping intelligence brought in by runners from the Thames-side waterfront as well as coffee.

Out of those simple beginnings grew the great insurance market Lloyds of London, whose Marine Insurance Policy first adopted in 1799 is still used, with only minor amendments, in all marine insurance policies issued today.

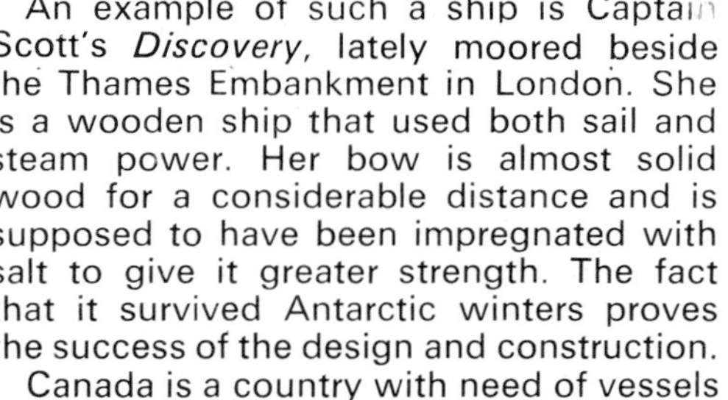

THE ICEBREAKER

WHEN MAN RELIED on the wind or his own muscles to move boats and ships, those who voyaged in higher latitudes had to accept the fact that their activities were stopped when the seas and waterways froze. It was not until the coming of steam power that man was able to think about ways of forcing his way through ice at sea. Until then a ship might be frozen up in port for many months, and if caught in the ice at sea it might be crushed. If that did happen the crew most likely died from the cold or starvation.

During the period of canal fever in the middle of the 19th century attempts were made to keep frozen navigations open to traffic by horse-drawn barges and narrow boats. A boat equipped with reinforcing iron plates around the bows and with rails at each side would carry a team of men who rocked the boat with a see-saw motion while horses plodded along the towpath. The method worked, and similar icebreakers continued on the canals into the days of steam and internal-combustion engine power. It made a passage only as wide as the boat (not much more than 7ft) and there are records of canal children running on the ice alongside their floating homes.

An icebreaker for use at sea is a vessel designed to clear a way through ice to provide a path for other craft, particularly merchant ships. Of course, some ships have been given some or all of the attributes of icebreakers so they can clear their own way. Craft intended for polar exploration are examples. Besides massive construction, they were given a bow form that allowed them to ride on to the ice and crush it, and they were shaped so that if they became trapped the pressure of the ice would lift rather than crush them.

Above: Icebreaking cargo ship 'Kaisa Dan' of the J Lauritzen line, at Fowey, Cornwall, in April 1974. *A Greenway*

Right: Ancestor of all big Russian icebreakers, the 'Ermak', built on the Tyne, pictured here on an early-20th-century postcard.
L Dunn Collection

An example of such a ship is Captain Scott's *Discovery*, lately moored beside the Thames Embankment in London. She is a wooden ship that used both sail and steam power. Her bow is almost solid wood for a considerable distance and is supposed to have been impregnated with salt to give it greater strength. The fact that it survived Antarctic winters proves the success of the design and construction.

Canada is a country with need of vessels to keep service open through ice. Such a craft was the Arctic supply vessel *C. D. Howe*, which made its maiden voyage in 1950. The *C. D. Howe's* duties involve an annual cruise into northern waters looking after Eskimos and weather stations, besides gathering hydrographic and topographical information. The *C. D. Howe*, which was one of the first of such vessels to carry a helicopter for prospecting the state of the ice, has been within 900 miles of the North Pole.

Denmark, with her association with Greenland, has long had need of ships that could continue service in iced conditions, and the Copenhagen company J Lauritzen has been running ships into northern waters for 30 years. They had been strengthened ships, but not icebreakers. The underwater detail of a strengthened hull differs considerably from that of a full icebreaker hull, and the latter would hardly be economic for a commercial craft.

In 1952 Lauritzen had built the *Kista Dan,* an 800-ton 185ft ship designed as an icebreaker that would carry passengers and cargo; she incorporated several new ideas. There were an ice horn and fins around the variable-pitch propeller to protect it from lumps of ice. There were full engine controls at the bridge and at the high lookout position on the foremast. Early criticism that such an expensive ship could not be operated successfully was proved wrong and Lauritzen followed it in 1956 with the 1600-ton *Magga Dan;* she could carry 35 passengers in comfort and had engines of 4500hp. The lookout position was reached by steps inside the foremast. Both ships have served as Greenland freighters and on expeditions. Captain Hans Christian Petersen, of the *Kista Dan,* said she would roll even in the placid waters of the Suez Canal, but

Top left: Scene from the Russian icebreaker 'Moskva' as she opens the way for merchant ships along the northern sea route.

Left: Danish (Lauritzen) ship 'Perla Dan' on ice work for a British Antarctic survey.
Mrs M Morrison

Above: Charles Dixon drawing for a February 1904 issue of 'The Graphic' commemorating the last journey of the Lake Baikal icebreaking ferry before the ice closed in and Trans-Siberian Railway passengers took to sledges over the lake section for the winter.
Illustrated London News

Top right: 'Kista Dan', first of J Lauritzen's modern icebreaking cargo-passenger ships, photographed on trials in 1952.
L Dunn Collection (*Hauersler*)

Above right: The mighty nuclear-powered Russian icebreaker 'Lenin'.

otherwise was a great success. The ability to make a controlled roll is an attribute of a good icebreaker, so she can avoid being trapped by ice pressing at the sides.

The countries with the greatest need to keep the seas open for their shipping include Canada, Denmark, Finland, Russia, Sweden and the USA, but the first practicable icebreaker was built in 1871 at Hamburg. With the coming of coal-fired steam engines the way was opened to ingenious designers to build ships to force their way through ice and keep paths open for more normal shipping.

Although iron and steel craft could be made much stronger than wooden craft, metal lacks the flexibility of wood, so in extreme conditions, when the pressure of ice might crush a metal hull, a wooden one might spring sufficiently under the impact and survive. With the increases in power available today and greater knowledge of steel construction, most new icebreakers are of Arctic grades of steel (less prone to low-temperature brittleness), but there are still wooden icebreakers in existence. In many cases their great age indicates the durability of the material and the effectiveness of the constructional methods.

To a certain extent an icebreaker cuts into the ice, but it relies mostly on forcing the heavy bows on to the ice and breaking it up by its sheer weight. The ship drops into the water again and the process is repeated. Early icebreakers often had rather rounded bulbous bows and in the years up to the mid-1920s forms were tried with varying degrees of slope under the bow to enable the ship to slide on to the ice under the thrust of the propellers aft. A slope of only about 30 degrees to the horizontal proved effective, although some bows had a more conventional pointed stem below the ramp just forward of the keel.

One problem with icebreaking by crushing is that quite sizable pieces of ice are left floating in the opened up water. To clear the ice lumps icebreakers have been fitted with bow propellers, used not so much for propulsion as to draw the broken ice aft. It works successfully for comparatively thin ice, but propellers cannot be expected to stand up to work in thick Arctic ice and the largest icebreakers intended for such conditions do not have them.

Typical of the moderate-sized icebreaker with bow propellers is the Finnish *Karhu*, built in 1957 and intended to help shipping through comparatively narrow and shallow waters. She is 243ft long, 57ft beam and 19ft draught. With a displacement of 3370 tons and with 7500shp to drive her, she has two stern and two bow propellers. All four propellers can be controlled from the bridge, wheelhouse and aft bridge, giving the man in command direct control and avoiding the delays inevitable with the need to signal the engine-room.

The *Karhu* has two heeling tanks and 100 tons of water can be pumped from one to the other in 90 seconds—a modernised version of the men rocking the horse-drawn canal boat—to break ice and free the ship if the ice started to grip the hull.

The uninviting frozen seas around the north of the Soviet Union have made a challenge to navigators. There was much trade into Russian Arctic waters both from the Norwegian and the Far Eastern ends, with ships reaching considerable distances and penetrating river estuaries in favourable conditions, but none was able to make the complete through passage. The Russians attempted to establish a freight-carrying service right through, with the merchant ships assisted by large ice-breakers. A fleet of eight icebreakers was built, but in the first attempt in 1937 to take a convoy through seven of the eight were frozen in with the 20 ships they were escorting.

Russia persisted and in 1939 the ice-breakers successfully led through a group of dredgers and tugs. In 1940 the Russian-built icebreaker *Josef Stalin*, 11,000 tons, 10,000hp, made a run through in both directions, the first vessel ever to do so. She carried three aircraft which could be launched by catapult for surveying the state of the ice ahead. Examples of the more massive craft needed to perform ice breaking duties in Arctic conditions where power and weight are the factors needed to crush very thick ice are the Russian 15,000-ton ships of the Moscow class. They are 400ft long, of 80ft beam and 34ft draught, and are pushed by 22,000hp.

Because of her situation Russia has had to concern herself with large icebreakers and they naturally arouse a lot of interest. For most maritime nations that suffer from iced seas, however, smaller craft are more suitable for use in the harbours, estuaries and immediate coastal areas that have to be kept clear. Russia can suffer from ice on any of her coastlines, on the Arctic Ocean, the Baltic and the Black Sea, and in the Far East, while the Scandinavian countries suffer similarly, but mostly in comparatively shallow waters. All have a great many icebreakers.

Typical are Swedish craft where some fishing cutter types have been used as inshore minesweepers. Driven by diesel motors, they are of 100 tons, 62ft long and of 19ft beam and only $4\frac{1}{2}$ft draught, so they can deal with ice in waters as shallow as fishing and other craft are likely to reach. For coastal work the Arkö class are typical. They are wooden icebreakers of 260 tons, 131ft by 23ft by 23ft and 8ft draught. Sweden also used smaller motor launch-type icebreakers for harbours and confined waters.

By their nature icebreakers are of substantial construction and therefore able to stand up to war conditions. As the majority of icebreakers are controlled by a country's navy, many of them have a double purpose and can be fitted with guns. The high power needed for ice breaking can also be used to give the craft a good speed in clear water, although the low length/breadth ratio and bluff form normally militate against high speed de-pite high power. Even so, the Swedish Arkö-class minesweepers can carry two guns and achieve a speed of 14.5 knots.

Russia's varied fleet of icebreakers for use around her various coasts are mostly under 350ft and 2000 tons, and some very much smaller. Like the ships of many other nations that need icebreakers, some of the craft have achieved ages of upwards of 50 years. Great strength has to be built in, contributing to a long life, although in some cases craft which have outlived their usefulness in other spheres have been strengthened and adapted to the role of icebreaking in less arduous conditions. Coal-fired boilers seem to have persisted in icebreakers longer than in most other craft.

Coal firing has continued, for example, in Russian icebreakers, in the country which has brought the most modern source of power to icebreaking. The USSR has the nuclear-powered icebreaker *Lenin*. In 100 years of icebreaker development, the *Lenin* represents the peak of progress in reducing the impediment of ice to shipping in sub-zero conditions.

The *Lenin* has three reactors, two of which are normally in use and the third is in reserve. Although fuel and associated equipment for nuclear power take up little space, there has to be a heavy protective casing, and the nuclear machinery weighs 3000 tons. Heat generated in the reactors is used to drive steam turbines which can develop 44,000hp—twice the power of the only slightly smaller Moscow class and enough to make most other icebreakers seem puny.

The *Lenin*, 439ft long and 88ft beam, is designed to break her way through ice 8ft thick at a steady two knots; in ice-free waters she can reach 18 knots. She, and an even larger nuclear icebreaker currently under construction in Russia, appear to point the way to navigation of almost any waters, whatever the state of ice. And apart from sheer size and power, the difficulties and hazards of making passage through ice are considerably reduced by using heavily notched stems designed to permit two icebreakers to push in tandem, and the now common air-bubbling equipment which prevents parted ice from closing in on the hull. A scouting helicopter is of great value also in prospecting the most favourable course ahead.

Below: The Argentine icebreaker 'General San Martin' in the Weddell Sea in 1973. *J Newman*

Bottom: Another of the Lauritzen icebreaking cargo-passenger ships, 'Magga Dan' *L Dunn*

WEATHER SHIPS

LIKE MANY scientific activities, the patient and unspectacular, but at times dangerous, work of the weather ships is very much a 'back-room' element in modern life, conducted far away from the public eye, but invaluable, all the same, to the public good.

Weather ships are a natural development in a world which, in all practical senses, has had no frontiers since travel and communications became international. The need for such special ships arose not from nautical considerations, but from the requirements of trans-ocean air travel.

Even as recently as 1939, crossing the Atlantic by air was a rare thrill for the fortunate few, rather as the motor car was confined in its early years to the role of rich man's plaything. As with the car, the novelty of trans-ocean flight tended to camouflage the element it inevitably contained of venturing into the unknown and exploring new and as yet untested capabilities.

The need for greater and more detailed weather information, as required for the safety of air travel, made clear the limitations of the system that then existed. Weather information had been provided by voluntary observers on merchant ships, and while valuable, their observations were necessarily restricted. The details they were able to give concerned only surface conditions, not conditions in the upper atmosphere; moreover, a moving vessel could only rarely be in the right place at the right time for the meteorologists who relied on them.

First steps towards providing stations for more regular observations were made just before the 1939-45 war broke out and virtually cleared civilian and private cargo flights from the skies. In 1939, the French were operating a stationary meteorological ship, the *Carimare*, in the North Atlantic. The *Carimare* transmitted observations of weather on the surface and in the upper atmosphere. The Germans had their counterpart in the *Ostmark* weather ship, which operated in the South Atlântic and provided observations that helped guide pilots flying the air routes to South America.

When war came, weather ships automatically became a military matter. One positive consequence of hostilities was an acceleration of scientific and technical trends, the weather ship service included. During the war, greater numbers of aircraft than ever before began to fly the Atlantic from America to Europe; the hefty Liberator, which shuttled war material across the ocean, was perhaps the best known of them, but mostly they were aircraft being ferried across to the European war from American factories.

At that time, merchant ships could no longer perform their traditional weather observation tasks. They dared not radio information at sea, in case it revealed their position to marauding submarines. To deal with the situation and provide weather information for the great airborne armada, the Allied navies set up a chain of weather ship, mostly corvettes, to take the place and perform the former functions of the merchant ships.

After the war ended in 1945, it became clear that merchant ship weather observations alone were not going to be sufficient for the volume of trans-Atlantic air traffic which the post-war years were likely to bring. On the joint initiative of the World Meteorological Organisation and the International Civil Aviation Organisation, an international conference was held in London in 1946; as a result, 13 ocean weather stations were established. Since then, the number of stations has been reduced so that, at the end of 1973, the signatories to the weather ships agreement were operating eight Atlantic stations, two of which were scheduled to cease operations by the end of June 1974. The reduction in numbers has no doubt been made possible by the contribution now made by satellite surveillance, coupled with improved accuracy of forecasting and storm radar on aircraft.

Top left: Ocean Weather Station 'Weather Monitor', showing winch house bridge and main radar antenna.
Courtesy Controllers of HMSO

Top right: Launching a radio-sonde balloon from the after-deck of OWS 'Weather Reporter'. *Courtesy Controllers of HMSO*

Above: A full view of OWS 'Weather Reporter'. *Courtesy Controllers of HMSO*

The stations all require at least two ships for continuous manning, and all work in waters that are more than 1000 fathoms deep. That means, of course, that anchoring is out of the question, and the ocean weather ship has to be under way continuously. The lonely ocean outposts do more than simply spot the weather; they provide a variety of services, including air-sea rescue facilities for aircraft and shipping, and navigational guidance and communication relay facilities for aircraft. Oceanographical, ornithological and other scientific work also features among the activities on a weather ship.

Because of their remote locations, fishing from the weather ships can produce some fascinating results; one day's fishing from one ship once produced 33 unidentified specimens, and on another vessel, three sharks were caught in two days.

Every hour, day and night, weather ships make surface observations concerning, among other details, wind direction and force, visibility, barometric pressure, air and sea temperatures, cloud height, type and cover, and the direction, period and height of waves.

In addition, the upper winds are checked every six hours, and every 12 hours a 7ft-diameter hydrogen balloon equipped with a miniature transmitter and capable of rising at about 1100ft per minute is released to check temperature, humidity and pressure of the upper atmosphere. As the balloon rises the weather ship's radar, beamed on to a radar target attached to the balloon, provides data for the meteorologist's calculations of wind speed and direction. Only the very roughest weather and sea conditions normally prevent the release of the balloons or the recording of the information they transmit up to heights of around 80,000 feet, at which height atmospheric pressure has reduced to the extent that the balloon bursts.

The various observations made are transformed into a special international 'figure' code, which is the lingua franca of the meteorological world. Meteorologists use the figure codes from the weather ships', merchant ships' and other observations to construct weather maps of surface conditions and upper air conditions. The maps then form the basis of bulletins which alert ships, aircraft and the general public to the existing weather conditions in any part of the world and any changes likely to occur within the next 12 to 24 hours.

The work is a striking example of how harmoniously people of different nationalities are able to co-operate for mutual advantage. The ocean weather scheme brings together 20 different nations in a common activity which exemplifies science at its most obviously beneficial and human nature at its most concordant.

THE AMVER SYSTEM

THE NAME AMVER is derived from Automated Mutual-assistance VEssel Rescue. Operated by the United States Coast Guard, it is a system for providing aid in any emergency at sea by co-ordination of search and rescue efforts. A ship participates in the system by completing a questionnaire providing the ship's radio watch schedule, available medical and communication facilities, and other useful information. The information is stored in AMVER's computer and can be very quickly researched in an emergency.

A merchant vessel participating in the system leaving port on a voyage of 24 or more hours radios a coded message to the AMVER Centre on Governor's Island in New York Harbour, giving the ship's name, position, course, speed, destination, estimated time of arrival and the route it is proposed to take. While under way she continues to forward periodic position reports, thus enabling the plot to be kept accurate.

The messages can be sent free of charge through any of the approximately 70 co-operating radio stations around the globe. Over 300,000 such messages are processed each year from more than 6000 ships. They make up a voluntary world-wide merchant vessel plotting system designed to aid in emergency or distress by predicting the location of ships that are in a position to help.

Should the master of a vessel require assistance of any kind, including medical advice or aid, he could cable Coast Guard, New York, giving the name of his vessel, its position and other necessary details. From the plot AMVER would be able to give the master the names and positions of ships in his vicinity able to render the necessary assistance.

If, in the case of a request for urgent medical aid, there were no ships with a doctor aboard in the immediate vicinity, the Coast Guard controller would obtain a local doctor's diagnosis and recommendations and relay them to the requesting ship. As well as medical aid, the system enables a wide variety of services to be rendered, covering such hazards as accident, wreck, fire, iceberg, man overboard—in fact, simply any peril of the sea. In the past, the life or death of mariners in distress has often hinged on pure chance—the sheer luck that help was near and could be summoned in time. By keeping a constant electronic watch AMVER reduces the uncertainty.

Although AMVER is now a global service, it all started with a modest hand-calculated plot of shipping limited to the Coast Guard's Atlantic Ocean area of responsibility. As the quantity of participating shipping increased hand plotting proved inadequate and a computer was brought into use in 1958.

With plotting automated it became possible to extend the area within which ships could be tracked, in 1960 eastward to longitude 15°W, but limited still to the North Atlantic (the letter A in AMVER then stood for Atlantic). In 1963 it was extended to the Greenwich meridian, and the following year still farther eastward to the North Sea, the Mediterranean and the South Atlantic areas.

Merchant vessel captains realised the increased measure of security provided by the system and it was their requests that stimulated the initial plan to serve ocean areas not strictly the responsibility of the United States. Computer technology developed and electronic equipment was updated in 1965, enabling AMVER's coverage to be extended to the North and South Pacific areas. The equipment is programmed to plot all offshore voyages of longer than 24 hours of all ships capable of submitting the periodic position reports to maintain plot accuracy.

The computer produces a surface picture (SURPIC) listing vessels in any area of a given emergency, which is available to any rescue centre throughout the world. The SURPIC tells how best each ship can be contacted, whether it carries a doctor and so on, according to the nature of the emergency.

Top: A watchkeeper (right) keypunching vessel data onto computer cards while a colleague checks the cards for accuracy. *Official US Coast Guard photo*

Below: The 'Don Jose Figueras', stricken by fire on a routine passage, was aided by two vessels which appeared on an AMVER SURPIC. *US Coast Guard photo*

A brief look at some of the emergencies dealt with by AMVER will help to illustrate its comprehensive service. Aboard a Liverpool-bound freighter in the South Pacific there is a smell of smouldering cargo. Investigation locates a fire in a cargo hold. While crew are rushed to deal with the blaze an officer is asking whether other ships are near enough to assist if the fire gets out of control. A message to AMVER Centre gets the information quickly.

The pilot of an airliner on a flight across the South Atlantic discovers one of his engines is on fire and must be shut down. If it becomes necessary to ditch his aircraft he will want to come down near a vessel which could quickly rescue the passengers and crew. A pull on the emergency fire control handle, and then a look at a list of the ships located along his route provided to him by AMVER before he took off tells him what he needs to know.

Seven crew members of the 140-foot schooner *Tina Maria* disabled in a North Atlantic storm have good reason to testify to the value of AMVER. The captain radioed the Coast Guard that the storm-tossed craft would not stay afloat much longer. AMVER was able to get a message to the SS *President Jackson* (through an improvised rig as her own radio aerial had been destroyed by the gale) and the *Jackson's* master was able to arrange a hazardous nine-minute evacuation. Miraculously, all seven were taken aboard before the schooner went down.

The Philippine freighter *Don Jose Figueras* caught fire in the North Atlantic and four hours after the vessel's call for help she was listing 25 degrees. The fire raged out of control in two holds and was spreading quickly to a third. The Coast Guard had tried to drop fire-fighting equipment without success. Two vessels, the *Ogishima Maru* and *Cuba Maru*, were contacted through the system and went to help. When the *Don Jose Figueras* had to be abandoned the 42 crew members and a dog were transferred safely to the waiting *Cuba Maru*.

Non-participating vessels can also benefit from the AMVER service. On December 4, 1973, the US Coast Guard cutter *Alert* intercepted a distress call from an unidentified vessel. The call said water was coming into the holds and gave a vague position but failed to state either its name or call sign. *Alert* asked for a SURPIC of vessels in the area, set course for the vessel's approximate location and radioed asking ships in the area to keep a lookout.

Having heard the broadcast, within minutes two merchant ships, the *Gypsum Queen* and the *Robert L D*, were steaming to the scene. The sinking vessel was finally located and identified as the ore carrier *Aegis Duty*. One ill crewman was evacuated by a Coast Guard helicopter, and two hours later the *Robert L D* arrived and took off the remaining 19 survivors from lifeboats. Shortly afterwards the Coast Guard vessel *Unimak* reached the scene; the survivors were transferred to her and taken to Governor's Island, New York.

AMVER is open to all vessels on a voluntary basis, regardless of nationality and at no charge to ships or shipowners. The system offers a rapid and efficient means of providing distress assistance – the purpose to which the officers and men stationed at AMVER Centre, under the United States Coast Guard, are dedicated.

The Publishers and the Editor are indebted for this feature to Arch Laughton, author of the article of which this text is an abstract, and the Editor of Port of London, *in which the article appeared.*

15. Pomp and Circumstance

Royal Reviews at Spithead

Top: A painting of the Royal Yacht HMS 'Victoria & Albert'. *Barnaby's Picture Library*

Centre: The Naval Review at Spithead in 1855 as depicted in a print published in Queen Victoria's Diamond Jubilee year, 1897. *Barnaby's Picture Library*

Above: A postcard representation of the Royal Yacht steaming through the Fleet dressed overall. *Barnaby's Picture Library*

SPITHEAD IS the arm of the sea, about eight miles long by three miles wide, which separates the eastern end of the Isle of Wight from the English mainland. To the Royal Navy, it is best known for its channel past the Spit Sand, which leads into Portsmouth dockyard. To merchant navies, it is as well known as the way to the great trans-ocean liner port of Southampton. To historians, it is, perhaps, best recalled for the great mutiny in the British Fleet in 1797. And to many thousands of erstwhile sailors and soldiers, it is remembered as the anchorage from which a whole armada of ships and craft carried an Allied army to the Normandy beachhead in 1944.

But to a much larger number than all of them, Spithead recalls the great Royal Reviews of the Fleet, for which it has provided an ideal setting. Here is a safe anchorage which can take as many as six long lines of warships between two shores —Southsea, Portsmouth, Gosport, Alverstoke and Lee-on-Solent to the north, and from Bembridge by way of Ryde to Cowes on the south—which serve as grandstands for all who wish to see the Royal Yacht, flying the Sovereign's Standard, leading a stately procession around the anchored ships-of-war.

The early Reviews were impromptu affairs, one of the first having been staged in 1512. The chronicler Holinshed tells us how Henry VIII, who sired the first British warships, 'having a desire to see his Navy together, rode to Portsmouth', where he assembled his captains and then, having treated them to a banquet, had himself rowed round the anchored ships. But the next British Sovereign to show interest in the Fleet, Elizabeth I, preferred to inspect it in the Thames, off the Royal Dockyards of Deptford and Woolwich. It was there that she knighted Francis Drake when he returned after circumnavigating the globe.

James I went once to Spithead, to see the ships which had carried his son Charles and his favourite, Buckingham, on a fool's mission to Spain. Charles I, who had a great love for ships, and who built one of the largest warships ever to grace the Royal Navy, the famous *Sovereign of the Seas*, went down to Portsmouth in the summer of 1627, to visit the fleet which, under Lord High Admiral Buckingham, was destined for La Rochelle in a vain attempt to help the Huguenots in their struggle against the French Crown. Accompanied by a large retinue, he began by boarding the *Victory*. There he inspected guns, ropes and stores, before being carried to the *Rainbow*, and then to the *Triumph*. On board the *Triumph*, he had a lengthy 'dinner which passed away with as much mirth as Sir Robert Deall, the Fool Archie, and the Duke's musicians could make. Afterwards he went on board the *Warspite*, the *Repulse* and the *Vanguard*, and thence ashore'.

Charles II, who gave the name Royal Navy to what Cromwell had turned into the People's Ships, instead of being the Sovereign's personal property, loved them as he loved everything to do with the sea. He went often to look at them from one of his yachts, of which the Dutch gave him his first at his restoration, named *Mary*. The following year he had another, the *Katherine*. Both were about 100 tons burthen. And in due course he and his brother James, Duke of York, had no fewer than 25 more similar small vessels built for their own pleasure.

Although he was at Portsmouth in 1661, Charles II did not have an opportunity to inspect the Fleet until 1665, when it was mobilising for the second Dutch War. But he saw it again when it returned to Spithead after its first battle, off Lowestoft. And when the third Dutch War was brewing, in the summer of 1671, he not only reviewed his Fleet at Spithead, but went to sea with it and was caught in an easterly gale, so that he had to land in Torbay.

On May 3 in the following year, a squadron of unaccustomed allies, the French, arrived to join the British ships at Spithead. So on that occasion, Charles II went down to review a combined Anglo-French Fleet, which must have been a splendid sight, since it numbered nearly 100 ships, mounting 6000 guns and manned by 24,000 men, under the command of the King's brother, the Duke of York. Unfortunately, it was not followed by a famous victory; the hostile fleets met off Solebay, where the French squadron sailed in one direction while the two English squadrons sailed in another. The Dutch Admiral De Ruyter made the most of it, setting on fire the *Royal James*, the flagship of the Earl of Sandwich, who had to transfer to another ship, in which process his boat capsized and he was drowned. Otherwise the encounter ended all-square, but might perhaps be counted one of the finest achievements of that over-rated weapon the fireship.

After the war was over, Charles II went again to Spithead, accompanied by the great Samuel Pepys, chiefly to visit Sir John Narbrough's flagship. And he was at Spithead yet again, in June 1675, chiefly to see the launching of a new *Royal James* at Portsmouth Dockyard. On that occasion, he decided to sail round from the Thames in a small sixth-rate, the *Greyhound*, taking with him a whole squadron of yachts. When Pepys arrived at Portsmouth by road on June 29, he was alarmed to find no sign of the *Greyhound*. Fortunately, the yacht *Anne* sailed in the next day, carrying James, Duke of York, and a cargo of bedraggled courtiers, with news that the *Greyhound*, after a stormy voyage, had managed to land the King on the Isle of Wight, soaked to the skin, famished with hunger, but unbowed; he reached Portsmouth on July 2.

Charles II was so delighted with the new *Royal James* that he knighted her architect, Anthony Deane. Afterwards he re-embarked in the *Harwick*, a far more adequate vessel than the *Greyhound*, and was carried back to London without further adventures.

Charles was succeeded by his brother James II, who had on two occasions commanded the English fleet in action with the Dutch and who had, for the first 13 years of his brother's reign, been Lord High Admiral. But instead of inspecting his ships at Spithead, he spent most of his short reign alienating his subjects by trying to make them Roman Catholics. Nonetheless, he did not altogether neglect his Fleet, which he inspected at least once at Spithead, in 1687.

With the coming of William and Mary, England found herself again at war with France. And as early as April 1689, the English Navy, under Admiral Herbert, had to defend Ireland from a French fleet dispatched by Louis to support the exiled James II. The two fleets met in Bantry Bay in an indecisive action, after which Herbert returned to Spithead. When he heard the news, William hurried down to Portsmouth and, boarding Herbert's flagship, congratulated all the officers on a great victory (though he knew it was not), because he had to keep up the morale of the Fleet. Moreover, he created Herbert Earl of Torrington, knighted two of his captains, and gave ten shillings to every seaman.

William next went to Spithead for a more worthy occasion, to see his Fleet after the twin battles of Barfleur and La Hogue had been won, when he conferred a knighthood on Admiral Rooke.

Queen Anne's connection with the Royal Navy was never very close, though for a short time, in 1708, she was Lord High Admiral, after her husband, Prince George of Denmark, had occupied that office from 1702. It was much the same with her successor, George I, who could not speak English, and had little interest in anything beyond his beloved Hanover. Nor was his son George II much better, being no English-speaker and in most ways a foreigner. Neither, so far as we know, visited Spithead.

It was otherwise with George III. During his long reign, he visited Portsmouth and Spithead many times, the first for what is now accepted as the first formal Royal Review. On arrival at Portsmouth in June 1773, he was saluted by a 'triple discharge of cannon', and proceeded to the dockyard where admirals and captains were assembled, each with his barge, to escort him to Spithead. The ships were those that had fought the French in the Seven Years War, and the King made a formal tour around them in his barge.

He came again five years later, this time bringing his Queen, to see his ships shortly before France joined Britain's American colonies in their fight for independence. There was another visit in 1794, after Lord Howe's victory at The Glorious First of June, when Midshipman Dillon wrote that;

> 'The King and Queen went on board the *Queen Charlotte*. To the noble and gallant Admiral Lord Howe, His Majesty presented a diamond-hilted sword of the value of 3000 guineas: also a gold chain to be worn round the neck. The Royal party dined on board with his Lordship. It was whispered that the King intended investing him with the Order of the Garter. However, rumours led me to believe that political prejudices restrained the Royal will. After dinner the Royal party returned on shore. They were saluted and cheered by the whole Fleet, both coming and going. The two next senior Admirals, Graves and Hood, were created Irish peers: the four Rear-Admirals, baronets. All the Flag Officers received gold chains similar to that given to Lord Howe, and the Captains received medals. Pensions were settled on all that were wounded. The senior lieutenants of all the ships-of-the-line that were in action received the rank of commander.'

Early in the next century, George III became insane and his place was taken by the Prince Regent who, both before he came to the throne as George IV and afterwards, showed great interest in Spithead and the ships anchored there. He paid his first official visit in August 1803 and, after cruising round on his own yacht

Top: Aerial view of His Majesty's Yacht, 'Victoria & Albert', passing between lines of battleships during the 1937 Spithead Review.
Barnaby's Picture Library

Above: An aerial view of Queen Elizabeth II's 1953 Coronation Naval Review.
Barnaby's Picture Library

for three weeks, returned for a full-scale review on September 14. Thereafter the exigencies of the Napoleonic War cramped his style. He had to wait until 1814 for a Review to celebrate the Treaty of Paris, and to show the Allied Sovereigns 'the tremendous naval armaments which had swept from the ocean the fleets of France and Spain and secured to Britain the domain of the sea'. Fifteen ships of the line and 31 frigates were present. Six years later he returned in triumph as King, when he held what amounted to the first Coronation Review.

The Sailor Prince William's love for the sea extended, on occasions, to hoisting his flag onboard a ship at Spithead and taking a squadron to sea in the Channel without informing the Admiralty, much to Their Lordships' irritation. He was, nonetheless, created Lord High Admiral in 1827, an office that had long been in abeyance. And as such, he made an early visit to his Fleet at Spithead, when his ship had the novel experience of being taken in tow by one of the first steam vessels, the *Lightning*, which, against the wind, 'brought her into the harbour in a beautiful manner amidst the cheers of thousands of most respectable people assembled on the lines and beaches'.

Three months later he was at Spithead again, once more inspecting the Fleet. He went back a third time after another three months, to inspect Admiral Codrington's fleet on its victorious return from the battle of Navarino

After he came to the throne, William IV often frequented Portsmouth and Spithead but never for a formal Review. However, with the accession of Queen Victoria, Royal Reviews became regular institutions. She was very conscious of the Navy's importance and greatly attached to many of its officers. And a Royal Review was the best way of showing other countries the might of Britain, and how rash it would be to challenge her, under the guise of ceremony and polite entertainment. There was also another motive. With the growing power of the press and the larger number of people who not only paid taxes, but had votes, their views had to be considered. And a touch of pageantry was an admirable way of letting them see that money spent on the Navy was well spent.

In 1842 Queen Victoria, with Prince Albert, held a 'Grand Naval Review', They inspected the *St Vincent*, and the new three-decker *Queen*, where Victoria endeared herself to the men by drinking a basin of grog, and liking it.

But times were changing. When the Queen inspected the Experimental Squadron in 1845, she used her new yacht *Victoria and Albert*, first of two paddlers to bear the name. And that was the last Royal Review of a fleet comprised only of sailing ships. The Crimean War was responsible for two Reviews, one before it in 1853 and one after it in 1856. For the latter, no fewer than 254 ships gathered at Spithead and the Fleet had taken on a very mixed appearance. A few of the bigger ships were screw-propelled and among the smaller craft many were driven by screw or paddle. The Queen, the whole of the Royal Family, the Board of Admiralty and the Commanders-in-Chief of the Black Sea and Baltic Fleets embarked in the new Royal Yacht *Victoria and Albert* (2) and spent a long day at Spithead. From its anchorage in two lines, the Fleet weighed in succession and passed the Royal Yacht to make a sham attack on Southsea Castle.

In 1867, the Sultan of Turkey visited the Queen, and a Review was held in his honour. On that occasion, the Fleet was divided into two squadrons, one of wood and one of ironclads. The latter included 12 of what later would have been termed battleships, the most famous being the *Warrior*, a steam-powered armoured frigate with $4\frac{1}{2}$-in armour and capable of $14\frac{1}{2}$ knots, though carrying a full set of masts and yards. The wooden squadron comprised a hotch-potch of new and old — mostly old — ships-of-the-line and frigates. In all, 74 ships were present, but in power they would have vanquished the 250 at the previous Review.

Six years later the Shah of Persia came to Britain, and the Fleet was again reviewed, again forming a very mixed bag of ships. Then there was a big Review in 1886 on the occasion of the Colonial and Indian Exhibition. But that of July 1887 was even bigger, to mark the Queen's Golden Jubilee. All the large ships then were of iron, and armoured, the biggest being the *Inflexible*, of 12,000 tons, with armour 24in thick. There were also numerous of the then recently introduced torpedo-carrying boats.

Ten years later came the Diamond Jubilee Review, when whole classes of all-but identical steel battleships displacing nearly 15,000 tons, and mounting breech-loading guns, anchored at Spithead. But it was not the monsters which stole the limelight; all eyes were turned on a tiny pioneer vessel, the *Turbinia*, the world's first turbine-propelled ship, which tore along the lines, uninvited, with the then incredible speed of 34 knots. The Fleet at that Review was the first at which foreign

Below: Ships at the 1937 Naval Review lit up at night. *Barnaby's Picture Library*

Bottom: HMS 'Surprise' passing HMS 'Superb' at Queen Elizabeth's Coronation Review in 1953. *Barnaby's Picture Library*

Right: Another aerial photograph of the 1953 Coronation Review. *Controller of HMSO MoD (Navy Department)*

Right below: Manning the yards on board HMS 'Minotaur' during the Jubilee Naval Review, as depicted on the cover of the July 30, 1887, edition of 'The Graphic'. *Illustrated London News*

men-of-war represented other navies. The British contingent included 21 battleships, 37 cruisers and many smaller craft, totalling 165 ships.

In January 1901, Victoria died at Osborne in the Isle of Wight, and when the day came for her body to be taken to Windsor for burial, the whole of the Channel Fleet and the Reserve Fleet were moored in one line from Cowes to Spithead, as the old Queen steamed slowly past them in HM Yacht *Alberta*.

The new King Edward VII's Coronation Review took place at Spithead on August 16, 1902. On that occasion, the Royal Yachts, led by the Trinity House yacht *Irene,* were headed by the screw-driven *Victoria and Albert* (3) whom many alive today will remember well. In 1905, to celebrate the *Entente Cordiale,* the French Fleet came to Spithead to visit their British brothers, and the King reviewed both from this new Royal Yacht.

George V held a Coronation Review in the summer of 1911, the first to include Jacky Fisher's turbine-driven dreadnought battleships and battlecruisers. But it was in July 1914 that Spithead saw the greatest naval pageant of all time. It was not just another Review; it was a full-scale test mobilisation, to commission the ships of the Second and Third Fleets to join the First Fleet. The King reviewed the long lines of grey-painted warships of every kind, headed by no fewer than 59 battleships, a tremendous spectacle of implacable power. But after the King had led his Fleets to sea for exercises in the Channel, they did not disperse, as had been planned. At Sarajevo, the fuse had been lit of an explosion that was to engulf nations, the assassination of the heir to the Austro-Hungarian throne. So the Fleet proceeded to its war stations, most of it to form

Jellicoe's Grand Fleet at Scapa Flow.

Between the two world wars there were Royal Reviews at Spithead in 1924 and for George VI's Coronation in 1937, both of which reflected the changing pattern in war at sea, since the latter included as many as five aircraft carriers.

After the 1939-45 war, came Queen Elizabeth II's Coronation Review in 1953, when the discerning spectator could see how the cumulative experience of two great wars had influenced naval design. In particular there was only one battleship present, the recently completed *Vanguard.* All the other big names were aircraft carriers. This time Her Majesty steamed through the lines on board the dispatch vessel *Surprise* because the old *Victoria and Albert* (3) had gone to the scrap heap after the war and the splendid new *Britannia* was not yet ready.

That was not the last review by Queen Elizabeth II, as she reviewed the ships of the Royal Navy and many other nations on the occasion of her Silver Jubilee, and in the traditional Sovereign's office of Lord High Admiral, in 1978.

This time she found the fleet greatly changed – much smaller, with submarines powered by atomic reactors, and many ships by gas turbines, and armed with guided missiles.

But although ships and weapons have changed so much since the first formal review, tradition lives on. The ships are still manned as the Sovereign passes, a Royal Salute is fired as in 1773, and after dark the Fleet is 'all lit-up'. Now, all switches are closed simultaneously and electric bulbs outline the ships. Then, when *Barfleur's* bell struck two strokes, every gunport was opened to show a burst of light. So, *plus ça change, plus c'est la même chose.*

Left: USS 'Kansas', one of the ships of the battle squadron led by the flagship USS 'Connecticut'. *L Dunn*

CRUISE OF THE GREAT WHITE FLEET

ON DECEMBER 16, 1907, the Battle Fleet of the United States, headed by the fleet flagship *Connecticut* and belching black smoke from the uptakes of its many coal-fired boilers, sailed out into the Atlantic from Hampton Roads, Virginia, passing in review order before Theodore Roosevelt who had embarked in the presidential yacht *Mayflower*.

It was a powerful armada, painted in the white-and-buff livery of an earlier age and under the command of Rear-Admiral Robley D Evans, USN, comprised four battle squadrons, each of four ships (USS *Connecticut*, *Kansas*, *Louisiana* and *Vermont; Alabama*, *Illinois*, *Kearsage* and *Kentucky; Georgia*, *New Jersey*, *Rhode Island* and *Virginia; Maine*, *Minnesota*, *Missouri* and *Ohio*), a flotilla of destroyers, the destroyer tender *Arethusa*, the repair ship *Panther*, two supply ships and the small dispatch vessel *Yankton*.

The original plan had been conceived as a cruise from the Atlantic coast round into the Pacific to show the flag, but shortly after the departure of the Great White Fleet it was disclosed that the force would continue around the world, across the Pacific to New Zealand, Australia and Japan and thence homeward via the Suez Canal and the Mediterranean. Nothing on such a scale had been attempted by way of a peacetime exercise before and it was indeed to be a stern test of organisation on the part of the command and those responsible for logistic support.

After calling at Port of Spain, Trinidad, where a traditional Christmas was celebrated, the fleet spent nine days at anchor in the magnificent harbour of Rio de Janeiro before heading south to the bleak inhospitable Magellan Strait and the Chilean port of Punta Arenas, the southernmost town in the world.

Valparaiso, Callao (Peru) and Magdelena Bay (Mexico) were visited in turn, followed by a month devoted to half-yearly gunnery firings and target practice interspersed with fleet and squadron sporting activities, and thence in mid-April to US west coast ports where the social round was interrupted by calls at navy yards for essential maintenance and docking. By that time Rear-Admiral Evans, plagued with rheumatism and stomach trouble, had handed over command of the fleet to Rear-Admiral Charles S Sperry, USN.

The destroyers were detached on the west coast while the defect-ridden battleship *Alabama* and the *Maine*, never an economical steamer, were replaced by the *Nebraska* and *Wisconsin*. Then on July 7, 1908, the refitted fleet, with white hulls, buff funnels and brasswork gleaming, passed out through San Francisco's Golden Gate en route across the Pacific to Honolulu, Pago Pago (Samoa), Auckland (New Zealand) and Australian ports, where the ships' companies were afforded a particularly enthusiastic reception.

After a call at Yokohama, where the visit did much to ease the existing tension between Japan and the United States, the fleet returned south via Amoy, while one of the battle squadrons visited Manila, capital of the Philippine Islands, then only recently transferred to United States jurisdiction. The greater part of November 1908 was spent exercising in Philippine waters, in order to ensure that the true function of a war fleet was not forgotten, and then south again across the South China Sea and through the Malacca Strait into the Indian Ocean.

After a call at Colombo in Ceylon, the fleet passed the Straits of Bab el Mandeb into the Red Sea and, after a brief delay caused by the grounding in the Suez Canal of the battleship *Georgia*, entered the Mediterranean, where the squadrons split up for three weeks showing the flag in a dozen North African and European ports. While they were there the town of Messina was devastated by an earthquake and teams were sent in from the battleships *Connecticut* and *Illinois* and the supply ship *Culgoa* to help with the relief work.

Eventually the fleet reassembled at Gibraltar and on February 18, 1909, George Washington's birthday, it was welcomed back by President Roosevelt at another full-scale review in Hampton Roads. The armada, manned by 14,000 men, had steamed about 42,250 miles around the world in 14 months, consuming in all 430,000 tons of coal. It had been worked up to a peak of efficiency and in no small way the United States of America had demonstrated its right to a say in world affairs.

The gleaming white paint, the brasswork and the ornate gilt bow scrolls and badges were of the past, however, for the international horizon was indeed set for a storm. One by one the ships were taken in hand for refits from which they emerged in the drab grey of a navy prepared for war. The cruise of the Great White Fleet had been a demonstration of power for peace but it represented the end of an era; the United States had now to be ready to protect its interests by sea, and eventually to go to war. A short ten years after the ceremonial departure from Hampton Roads the United States fleet went to war in support of the Western Allies.

Above: The Union Flag flying from the jackstaff of a modern warship. *A Greenway*

Right: A selection of international signal flags. *A Greenway*

Below right: The Royal Standard of the British monarch, flown at sea at the end of the 17th century. *M Pucciarelli*

SEA FLAGS

THE USE OF FLAGS at sea stems from the need for some symbol which might serve as a rallying signal and in the heat of battle as a means of recognition. Themistocles at the Battle of Salamis in the 5th century BC is reputed to have used a red cloak hoisted on an oar to rally the Greek fleet in the face of the Persians under Xerxes, by whom they were outnumbered four to one. As it turned out, that use of a flag-like device as a symbol of leadership was followed by a resounding victory over the Persian fleet.

The Roman vexillum hung from a horizontal crossbar at the head of a staff was a later example of the use of a flag for a military purpose and was a sea flag only in the sense that soldiers went to sea to do their fighting. The Saracens also employed their own version, which like the modern flag was attached by one side to the staff. In northern Europe the Danish Raven flag in the 9th century was probably one of the first to be displayed in that manner.

In the east the Chinese spread the use of the flag, again hung from a staff by one side. The almost universal adoption of the flag throughout Europe as a means of recognition stemmed, however, from the long series of wars known as the Crusades; likewise, it is from the heraldry of those medieval wars that many of today's national flags have inherited in one form or another the use of the Christian cross.

By late Tudor times Europe had become largely a continent of nations and free states, with a thriving maritime trade conducted by the newly founded chartered companies or private individuals, all employing vessels sailing under some form of distinctive national flag. It was in the 17th

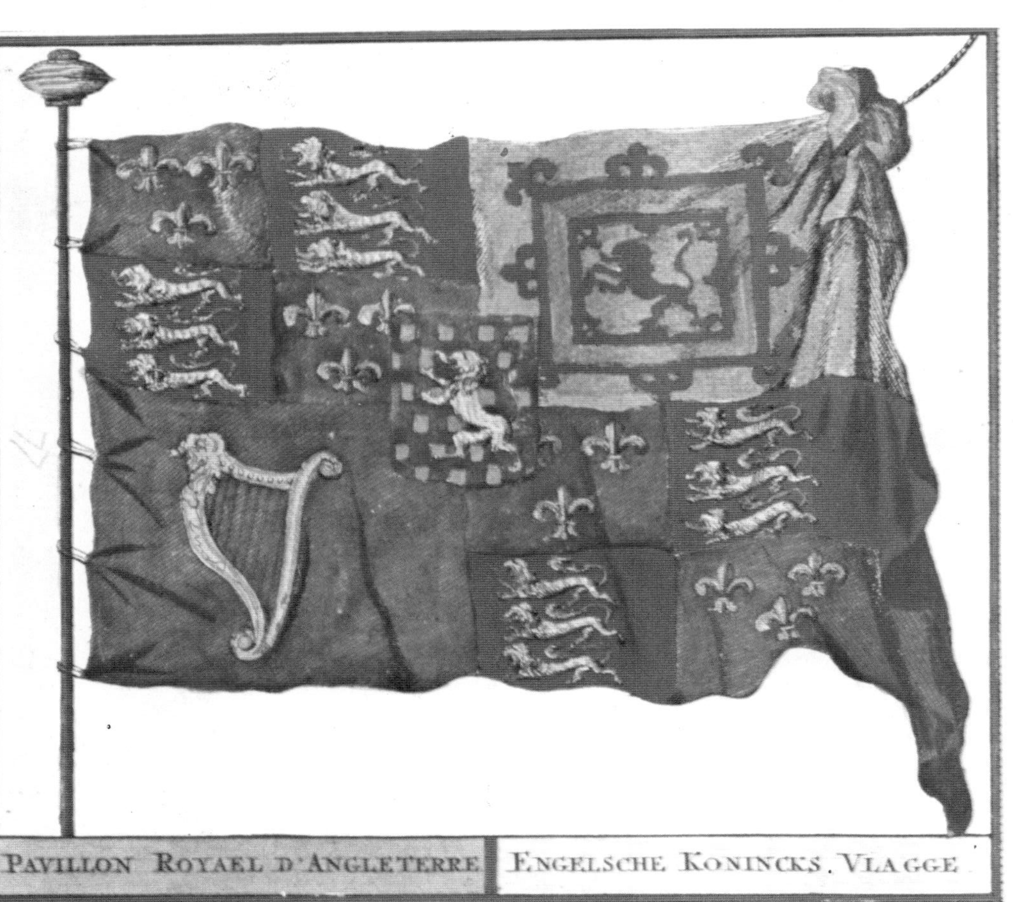

century, however, that the use of formal designs, to identify both warships and trading vessels, became generally accepted. The first British Union Flag combining the St George's cross of England with the Scottish saltire was introduced in 1606, but an order in 1634 restricted its use at sea to 'our Navie Royall . . .'

Merchantmen and other privately owned vessels were to use flags bearing the St George's or St Andrew's cross as appropriate. Those flags were flown at the mainmast head, and in addition it was customary to fly an ensign at the stern; although in the early 17th century the ensigns worn by English vessels had no official significance, various designs, usually incorporating the cross of St George in the upper hoist or canton and dating from Elizabethan days, were in general use.

The first red ensign, a red flag with the cross of St George in the upper hoist, appeared in 1621 and within a few years there appeared also blue and white ensigns which were used freely by merchant ships sailing to foreign ports. By a proclamation of 1674, however, merchantmen were ordered to wear the cross of St George at the masthead and forward on the spritsail topmast, and the red ensign at the stern. The red ensign was also worn by warships not attached to a particular squadron, although in their case it was employed in association with the union

Above: Various yacht ensigns, from top to bottom; Finland, Sweden and the United States. *A Greenway*

Top right: The flag of the 'Bucentaure', the 18th-century Venetian state barge. *M Pucciarelli*

Above right: The West German flag on the bows of FGNS 'Lindau' at Portsmouth in August 1974. *D J Kingston*

Right: Danish national flag seen on the stern of a Danish frigate at Princes Dock in Glasgow in 1968. *A D Deayton*

flag, worn both at the mainmast head and forward as a jack. For Scottish vessels, the St George's cross was replaced by the saltire of St Andrew. The practice of wearing a jack at sea was abandoned with the disappearance in later years of the spritsail mast.

When organised as a fleet, naval vessels were grouped in three squadrons, in order of precedence, the red (centre), white (van) and blue (rear) squadrons; individual ships wore ensigns of the appropriate squadronal colour. That form of organisation involved also the necessity of flags to identify the several degrees of command both within the fleet and the individual squadrons. Thus the practice of wearing the union at the mainmast head, as provided for in the order of 1634, was revised and in its place admirals' flagships of the white and blue squadrons hoisted a plain flag of the appropriate colour.

There was, however, no Admiral of the Red until 1805 and the fleet commander, if the Lord High Admiral, before 1702, flew the royal standard and thereafter a red flag bearing a yellow fouled anchor (known later as the Admiralty flag). An admiral, other than the Lord High Admiral, in command of a fleet continued to fly the union flag, worn as hitherto at the mainmast head by the fleet flagship. Vice-admirals and rear-admirals flew plain flags of the requisite colour at the fore-top and mizen-top respectively, while private ships of the three squadrons were distinguished by a commission pendant, again of the squadronal colour and with a St George's cross in the hoist.

The next major change came in 1707, after the establishment of a joint Anglo-Scottish parliament, when the union replaced the cross of St George (and in Scotland the saltire of St Andrew) in the ensigns worn by naval and merchant vessels. In addition the white flag flown by flag officers of the white squadron was replaced, at the suggestion of the officers of the fleet, by a white flag bearing a broad St George's cross, while an alternative form of white ensign appeared with a cross of St George in the fly in order to avoid the possibility of confusion with the French colours, then a white flag bearing the gold lilies and royal arms of the old regime.

The union flag was modified in 1801 in the wake of the formation of the United Kingdom by the addition of the red saltire of Ireland, in which form it continues in use today. The several British ensigns were of course altered in step with political development but the rules for their use at sea remained unchanged. Rules notwithstanding, to avoid confusion, Nelson ordered at the outset of the action off Trafalgar on October 21, 1805, that the British fleet should fight under the white (St George's Cross) ensign, although his second-in-command on that occasion, Cuthbert Collingwood, held the rank of Vice Admiral of the Blue. His flagship, the 100-gun *Royal Sovereign*, did in fact open the action with the combined Franco-Spanish fleet under the blue ensign.

The organisation of the fleet into red, white and blue squadrons was retained until 1864 but thereafter the White Ensign was adopted as the distinctive flag of the Royal Navy. Merchant ships and other non-public vessels retained their right to the use of the Red Ensign in line with the declaration of 1674, which was confirmed by the Merchant Shipping Act of 1894. The use of the Blue Ensign was restricted by the order of 1864 to craft employed in the public service, but its use has since been accorded to those merchant vessels under the command of an officer holding a commission in the Royal Naval Reserve and with a proportion of the crew, officers and ratings, members of the reserve. The grant of the privilege is by Ministry of Defence (formerly Admiralty) Warrant and it is not unusual to see vessels belonging to the prominent liner companies, such as Cunard and the Peninsular & Oriental, sailing under the Blue Ensign.

Today, a British warship wears the White Ensign, at the ensign staff aft in harbour and usually from the mainmast gaff at sea, with the commission pendant, white with the cross of St George in the hoist, from the masthead or some convenient site clear of radar and other antennae. The Union Flag is worn forward at the jack staff in harbour but at sea it is worn as a jack only when the ship is dressed with masthead ensigns on ceremonial occasions or in the presence of the sovereign.

Flagships wear the flag appropriate to the rank of the senior officer embarked in lieu of the commission pendant; the designs of these distinctive flags is similar to those adopted generally in 1864 when the squadronal colours were abolished. Minor changes were made in 1889 when sail had more or less given way to steam and few ships had more than two masts so that ease of recognition as opposed to position assumed greater importance. These flags continue in use today and on the rare occasions when an Admiral of the Fleet is embarked, the Union Flag is worn at the main or only masthead—electronic equipment permitting! The Union Flag is worn also at the masthead in harbour if a court martial is assembled on board.

The Royal Standard is worn by a ship when the sovereign is embarked; in the case of the royal yacht, which has three masts, it is flown at the mainmast head. On such occasions the fouled anchor flag of the Lord High Admiral is worn by the yacht at the foremast head. That ancient flag had become the flag of the Admiralty Board when the office of Lord High Admiral was taken over by the 'Lords Commissioner for Executing the Office of . . .' On the formation of the unified Ministry of Defence in 1964 the ancient office and function passed into history; the title of Lord High Admiral and the right to the use of the flag were taken over by the sovereign. At the mizen masthead the royal yacht wears the Union Flag.

From 1864, mercantile auxiliaries attached to the fleet wore the Blue Ensign, defaced in the case of the Victualling Department by crossed fouled anchors in the fly, but around the turn of the century replaced for all civilian-manned auxiliaries by a Blue Ensign bearing a horizontal yellow anchor without cable. In 1911, on the formation of the Royal Fleet Auxiliary Service, the latter flag was adopted as its ensign, with a square jack of the same

Top left: The Royal Yacht 'Britannia' wearing the Admiralty flag at the foremast, the Royal Standard at mainmast and Union flag at mizenmast. *A Greenway*

Centre left: The RFA ensign (since altered), which is basically a Blue Ensign, flying from the signal mast of RFA 'Lyness' in 1969, with the Pilot flag on the right and the ship's code flag on the left. *A Greenway*

Above left: The White Ensign, which may be worn by yachts belonging to the Royal Yacht Squadron, seen here worn by 'Golden Beaver' in August 1963. *A Greenway*

Left: The Red Ensign at the stern of a British Rail steamer in Portsmouth. *A Greenway*

design. In 1970 the anchor in the RFA flags became vertical, but the original design continues in use as the ensign of the Port Auxiliary Service which operates the navy's fleet of harbour service tugs and tenders.

One other organisation apart from the Royal Navy is entitled to the use of the White Ensign, the privilege having been granted to the Royal Yacht Squadron by Admiralty Warrant in 1829. Several other United Kingdom and colonial yacht clubs are entitled, however, to the use of a defaced Blue or Red Ensign, the granting of such a privilege being vested today in the Ministry of Defence (Navy). Exceptionally some yacht clubs in independent and former British Commonwealth territories retain the right to the use of such a flag, including among others the Royal St George Yacht Club of Dun Laoghaire, Eire.

Various government departments and other public bodies are entitled to the use of a defaced Blue Ensign bearing some device such as the portcullis in gold surmounted by the royal crown featured on the flag of HM Customs, which is employed both afloat as an ensign by HM Customs vessels and craft and over the Custom House ashore. Similarly British consular officers afloat in foreign ports use the Blue Ensign charged with the Royal Arms.

In accordance with an Admiralty circular promulgated in January 1866, vessels other than warships belonging to colonial governments were granted the right to wear the Blue Ensign charged with the badge of the colony concerned. Colonial warships wore the White Ensign, a right which passed to the various dominion navies when independent status within the empire or commonwealth was achieved by the territories concerned. In harbour the vessels were distinguished by the defaced Blue Ensign worn as a jack. Merchant vessels were similarly identified by the use of a defaced Red Ensign.

Since the 1939-45 war, however, the growing demand for an independent national identity in the several dominions and the loosening of the bonds of empire has resulted in the abandonment in most cases of the Union Flag-derived ensigns and jacks and their replacement by designs of local significance, such as the red and white maple leaf flag of Canada. Australia in 1967 and New Zealand in 1968 also abandoned the St George's cross White Ensign, although in both cases new white flags charged with their respective representations of the Southern Cross Constellation retain the Union Flag in the canton. In both Australia and New Zealand the use of the defaced Blue Ensign as a national flag and jack, and the defaced Red Ensign as a merchant flag, continues unchanged.

Despite the adoption of distinctive national designs, the maritime flags of several of the commonwealth states retain links with the British-based designs formerly employed. For example, Indian warships wear a St George's cross White Ensign with the Indian national flag in the canton, while merchant vessels of India, Pakistan and Ceylon all fly their own versions of the Red Ensign. Although no longer associated with the commonwealth, Burma also retains its maritime link in the form of a local version of the St George's cross White Ensign worn by Burmese warships.

No other nation enjoys such a proliferation of maritime flag designs as the United Kingdom; every government department and agency claiming any remote connection with the sea has a right to the use of an appropriate flag and ensign, usually a defaced Blue Ensign, although exceptionally the flag of the Commissioners of Northern Lights, the lighthouse authority for Scotland and the Isle of Man, is white with the old pre-1801 Union in the canton and a blue lighthouse in the fly. Trinity House, which is responsible for lighthouses, light vessels and buoyage around the coasts of England and Wales, uses the Red Ensign charged with its own badge in the fly. Trinity House vessels in harbour wear a jack of the same badge design derived from the Arms of the corporation which themselves date from 1573.

Merchant ships usually fly a house flag, not necessarily that of the owner; it is customary for chartered vessels to display that of the charterer, sometimes in addition to that of the owner. The design of houseflags in their infinite variety forms a subject of study on its own and it is sufficient to say here that some of the older flags still in use reflect the early history of the companies concerned. A case in point is the flag of the Peninsular & Oriental Steam Navigation Company; it links the red and yellow of Spain with the blue and white of royalist Portugal, the countries served by the original Peninsular SN Co, which received its Royal Charter in 1837.

There is no legal precedent for the wearing of a jack other than a Red (or Blue) Ensign by merchant ships, but certain liner companies use a square version of their respective houseflags as a jack and, exceptionally, Lamport & Holt's vessels wear a flag bearing the Arms of the City of Liverpool as a jack when in harbour. The white-bordered Union Flag or 'pilot jack' is sometimes employed as a jack but again its use as such lacks official sanction, although in 1949 the Admiralty '... saw no reason why they should discourage the practice.'

A number of maritime nations including Canada, France, the Netherlands, Portugal and the United States make no distinction between their respective mercantile flags and naval ensigns. However, in the case of America distinctive ensigns are authorised for use by vessels of the US Coast Guard, the US Customs Service and by yachts registered with certain clubs. Other navies, those of Argentina and Spain for instance, use an ensign similar in design to the national or mercantile flag with the addition of a distinctive coat of arms or badge. War vessels of the Scandinavian countries and Iceland are distinguished by versions of their respective national flags with a forked fly, a shape which probably had its origin in a form of the Danish flag (the Dannebrog) known to have been in use as early as the year 1400.

When in foreign ports it is customary as a courtesy for merchant vessels to fly, usually at the starboard forward yard arm or foremast head, the mercantile or national flag of the country being visited, termed a courtesy flag. The correct flag for foreign-registered vessels in British ports is the Red Ensign although frequently, through ignorance, the Union Flag is displayed.

Misuse of British flags afloat can lead to heavy penalties, although of course deliberate abuse or intent to deceive would need to be proved. A case in point occurred in 1882 when the steamer *Dotterel* of the City of Cork Steamship Co (formerly the St George Steam Packet Co) was ordered at Basra to stop using as a houseflag the plain cross of St George, the flying of which afloat was restricted to admirals in the Royal Navy. Eventually a compromise was achieved by the addition of a blue star in the centre of the flag.

The maritime history of the world since the time of the Norman conquest of England is reflected to a large extent in the design and usage of sea flags; today, as in the past, changes of style and design in the wake of political and other developments continue to reflect the passage of events. The process can never be complete but the story thus far is well documented and worthy of study by professional and layman alike.

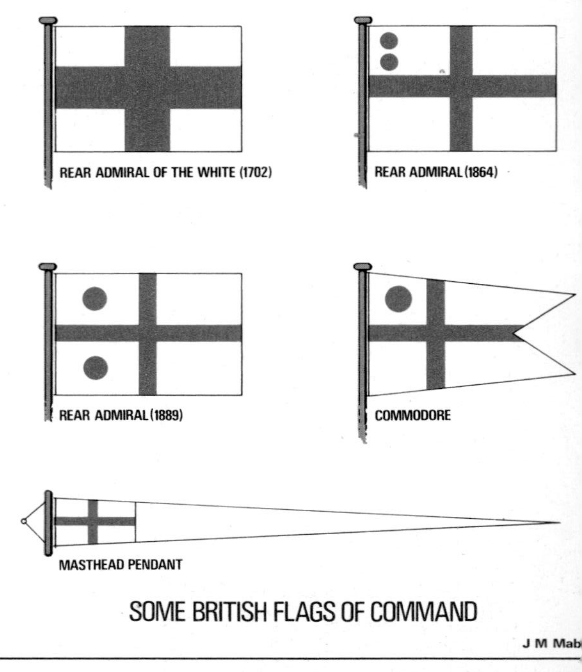

J M Mab

Above: House flag and charterer's flag on the yard of a Naess bulk carrier. *A Greenway*

Facing page: Prominent hind figurehead of the replica of Sir Francis Drake's 100-ton ship 'Golden Hind' (previously 'Pelican') in which he sailed round the world between 1577 and 1580, appropriating considerable treasure from Spanish ships on the way. The replica 'Golden Hind' was built in an English yard to the order of a group of San Francisco businessmen to commemorate Drake's visit to San Francisco Bay in 1579. *J Winkley*

Figureheads

THE ORIGIN OF figureheads lies beyond history, but recent customs in some parts of the world and prehistoric carvings in others provide clues. The beginning was magical and later religious, as was head-hunting. Possession of a human head gave one power over the dead man's spirit and until very recently in some parts of Borneo rice fields were guarded from harm by the enslaved spirits of unfortunate enemies whose heads, impaled on posts, stood in the fields.

Rock carvings about 6000 years old have been found in Nubia showing canoes with bulls' skulls on the stems, evidently to give strength to the frail craft, as a bull was the ancient symbol of strength. In war a victorious tribe returned with enemy heads on its spears and after a successful canoe raid the heads would be carried on the stems. Indeed, as late as 1718 Lieutenant Robert Maynard, RN, after defeating and killing the notorious and particularly bloodthirsty pirate Edward Teach (Blackbeard), returned to Bath Town, North Carolina, with Teach's head nailed to the bowsprit of his sloop, the *Ranger*. The head was then set up on a pole ashore as a warning to other pirates, just as the heads of malefactors were exposed at Temple Bar or on Old London Bridge.

Cretan ships of about 2000 BC had fish figures on the very high stem or stern post (which end went first is debatable) and Egyptian river boats often had lotus-bud terminations at stem and stern; funeral barges had statues of the hunting god Horus; and fighting ships of 1190 BC had a lion's head on a prolongation of the keel which was used for ramming. The ships of their enemies at that time had birds' heads on both stem and sternpost.

Archaic Greek ships in drawings on pottery have stags' antlers on the bows, to give them swiftness, and Phoenician merchant ships were easily recognised by the horses' heads on their stems. Ancient ships of the Mediterranean world and the Far East, when they had no figurehead, had eyes painted on both sides of the bows so that the ship could see her way. Still found in many parts of the world today, they probably derive from the ancient Egyptian Sacred Eye of Ra which appears in tomb carvings of sea-going ships as early as 2700 BC.

Ships of classical Greece often had warriors' helmets as terminations of the stems, and at others animals or mythical figures. Roman merchantmen merely had carved and painted panels on each side of the stem, their main guardian at the stern being the cheniscus, the figure of a goose, thought to be particularly lucky for sailors,

Above right: Preserved figurehead from the ship "Supply' at Chatham on the Medway. *R Westwood*

Right: Carved rudderhead from a Danish ship of 1700. *Kronborg Museum Denmark*

Above far right: The patriotic figure of Britannia. *R Westwood*

Far right: Elaborately carved and gilded lion figurehead of a 90-gun ship, circa 1706. *Science Museum London (K. Fenwick)*

for 'they swim on top of the water and sink not'. Roman war galleys were elaborately provided with figureheads of bronze to reduce damage to the bows when ramming. In addition to the ram (often representing a fierce animal's head) there would be projecting swords or heads above it to protect the wooden stem. There was also a sacred bust or statue of the god or goddess into whose care the vessel was entrusted. The ships were topped by a carved or painted picture, sometimes carried on a pole, to identify the individual galley; a tree, a mountain, animal or any other suitable subject. The figureheads of ships taken in battle were often lodged in the temples dedicated to the gods who were credited with having bestowed the victory.

When a Greek ship entered port her figurehead was removed and taken ashore to salute the local deity, and there were special altars to stranger gods for sacrifices on behalf of the figureheads and their ships, wherever they came from.

Many centuries later, in Iceland, ships of the Viking period wishing to enter port had to take down their dragon or serpent heads lest they alarm the spirits of the place with their 'gaping heads and yawning snouts'. The reason is made clear.by passages in the *Egissaga*, written in Iceland in the early 13th century but dealing with events of the mid-10th century. The magic mentioned was being practised on land, but longships' heads were only a more permanent way of bringing curses and ill-fortune on the enemy. Briefly, an Icelandic chieftain fixed a horse's head on the top of a post and whichever way he turned it the guardian spirits of the land fled in terror and curses descended upon the country. Another instance dealt with a carving of a human head which, when set up on a post planted in the body of a sacrificed horse, was turned towards the enemy's home and brought bad luck to it. The connection with a horse strangely echoes the horse figureheads of ancient Phoenicia.

Norman ships carried on the Viking tradition but the heads shown in the Bayeux Tapestry seem intended to represent real as well as mythical beasts, including lions. It is curious how the lion recurs through thousands of years as a favourite subject for figureheads. In the Middle Ages, when a ship was prepared for war service her figurehead had to be removed to make way for the forward platform which, in time, became permanent as the forecastle. Then, when the forecastle became the carrack head, projecting far ahead of the stem, figureheads vanished and for a while were replaced by badges with coats of arms on the bows below the carrack head. However, that did not satisfy mariners, so a beak was added jutting well out in front of the forecastle and terminated by a small head, usually of an animal or reptile.

In Henry VIII's Navy only some carracks had those features, the others having a small head on the forecastle. It was not until the galleon reached perfection in Elizabeth's reign that the English began to mount figureheads at the end of the beakhead which had developed from the spur. Usually they had no connection with the ship's name and the queen's ships favoured the supporters of the Tudor Arms, the lion and the dragon of Wales. An exception was in the *White Bear*; when she was rebuilt in 1598 she was given Jupiter and his eagle. Very occasionally a tiger or a unicorn was used.

During the 17th and 18th centuries the lion was so generally used, in foreign as well as in English ships, that the figurehead —whatever its subject—was called the

lion. Throughout the 17th century the main difference between English and Dutch lion figureheads was that the former were gilded and the latter were painted red. The French rarely used the lion, even when their ships were built in Holland. Their taste ran to classical mythology, such as Neptune with his seahorses, tritons, mermaids (French mermaids had two fish tails, one in place of each leg), or the reigning monarch. In the 18th century figures of Greek and Roman heroes were frequent, and the images of living royal personages were used for important ships. French figureheads were generally of higher aesthetic value than those of other nations, although in the late 17th century Grinling Gibbons did some superb work for the English Navy.

Spanish ships favoured lion heads until well into the 18th century. Then they occasionally used royal portraits, and towards the end of the century there was an outburst of figures of saints, even the entire Holy Trinity for the four-decker *Santisima Trinidad* (1769-1805).

In England the lion was no longer used for the most important ships. Thus the *Prince Royal* (1610-1666), the finest ship of James I's fleet, had a mounted figure of St George riding down the dragon, and Charles I's masterpiece, the *Sovereign of the Seas* (1637-1696), had a mounted figure of King Edgar trampling seven kings. When the triumphant Cromwell had the *Naseby* (1655-1673) built he copied the *Sovereign of the Seas* figurehead, but with great tactlessness had himself represented on horseback riding over the bodies of an Englishman, a Scotsman, an Irishman, a Frenchman, a Spaniard and a Dutchman, while the figure of Fame held a laurel wreath with the words 'God With Us'.

At the Restoration it was removed and hung from a gibbet, and then burnt on Coronation Day. Mr Pepys was annoyed because the new figure of Neptune cost £100 and he thought that people would soon have forgotten that the old one represented Cromwell and would have accepted it. The ship was renamed *Royal Charles*, but she was taken by the Dutch in their 1667 raid on the Medway and carried off to Holland, where relics of her are still preserved.

The Admiralty decreed in 1703 that all figureheads in future would be lions, but from the start the rule was broken for particular ships, so other subjects continued to be used, much as before. Even after the order was cancelled in 1727 the lion still remained the usual subject, including a period when Chinese lions were fashionable.

Owners of merchant ships with beakhead bows, similar to men-of-war, made

Above right: Modern figurehead on the Fred Olsen cargo ship 'Baghdad' pictured at London's West India Dock in the early 1970s. *Fred Olsen Line*

Right: Figurehead by Grinling Gibbons, one of the noted English figurehead designers. *R Westwood*

an effort to provide suitable figureheads, but they were expensive and most of the smaller merchantmen had vertical stems anyway which were unsuited to the fitting of figureheads. Many of the smaller classes, both naval and merchant, with suitable bows, had fiddleheads and billetheads. They were curled terminations like a violin, the former turned inwards and the latter outwards from the ship.

Figureheads were occasionally gilded or painted entirely white, but were usually in natural colours. Unless the captain could afford to buy suitable paints, colours issued for other purposes might have had to be used. Lower-deck taste ran towards gaudy colour schemes, especially for female heads. The facial colouring was reputed to be inspired by the make-up worn by seaport prostitutes. One frigate captain was so ashamed of the way his men had painted the figurehead that he dug deeply into his own pocket and had it gilded, to the great pride of all hands. Later, on the South American station, the men, bored by prolonged cruising, began to quarrel among themselves. Summoning them to the quarter deck, the captain announced, 'Now, my lads, if this is not put an end to and hearty goodwill restored, by the Lord Harry I'll paint your figurehead black and put the ship into mourning!' That terrible threat ended the trouble.

Since figureheads were the personification of a ship, sailors lavished loving care upon them. Parts liable to damage, such as arms, were unshipped at sea, and to make repair easier they were never all in one piece.

The *Royal George* (1756-1782) had a mounted figure of George II and when, in 1778, the fleet had to retreat before a vastly superior Franco-Spanish force, a bosun's mate tied his hammock over its head, lest the figure see a British fleet retreating. At the Glorious First of June 1794, the *Brunswick's* head, representing the Duke, had its hat shot away and a deputation came aft, under very heavy fire, and asked Captain Harvey (he was already twice wounded and would soon receive a third and mortal wound) to give them his cocked hat for the Duke. He did, and the carpenter nailed it to the figure's head. The ship's honour being thus saved, the deputation went back to their posts and sank their opponent, the *Vengeur.*

When the *Atlas*, launched in February 1782, was being masted for service it was found that the globe of the world the figure was supporting was too high and prevented the shipping of the bowsprit. The top was therefore sawn off and it was noticed that the American Colonies had gone. In March the Tory government fell and was replaced by a Whig administration composed of politicians sympathetic to the Americans, who ordered the British forces to stop fighting the colonists. By then the tide had turned and prospects of final victory were bright, but the new government made peace and granted independence to the future United States. Coincidences of that kind are not uncommon in the history of figureheads, and it all added to the mystique surrounding them.

One of the most curious figureheads borne by a ship of the Royal Navy was that of the 18-gun sloop-of-war *Termagant* (1796-1819), which had a double head with a woman on one side and a man on the other. The woman was equipped with a real broom and was belabouring the man, all painted in appropriate colours, including a bleeding nose. In its own way, it must have looked quite impressive, but it was unusual for such a small ship. In 1796 an attempt was made to abolish figureheads

Above: Figurehead of the Royal Danish yacht 'Falster' of 1742. *Naval Museum Copenhagen, Denmark*

Below: Preserved figurehead of 'Nymphe' at Chatham. *R Westwood*

Above: Ferocious-looking head from HMS 'Warrior', a 3rd Rate warship of 1781, displayed in the Victory Museum, Portsmouth. *R Westwood*

Above right: Wax figurehead models (from left to right) from the 1825 frigate 'Havfruen', 1822 frigate 'Rota' and the brig-of-war of 1819 'St Croix'. *Naval Museum Copenhagen, Denmark*

Right: Figurehead of 'Le Soleil Royal' of 1669. *Bibliothèque Nationale Paris (K. Fenwick)*

Far right: Drawing of a figurehead of a line-of-battle ship from the 1815 edition of Falconer's Dictionary. *K Fenwick*

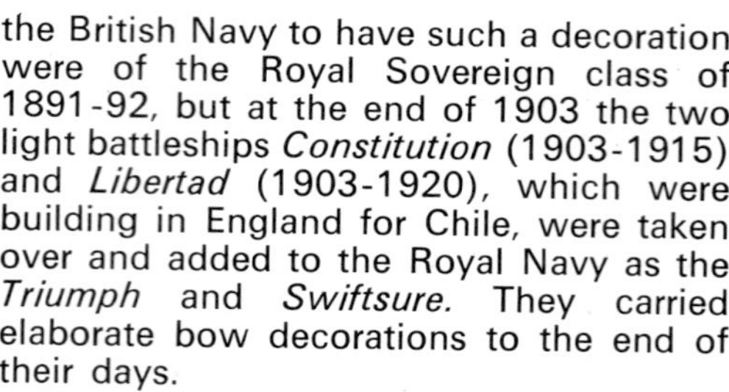

and replace them with scrolls. Because of unpopularity the order was never enforced; instead ships such as frigates and lower rates were permitted only busts and whole figures were reserved for ships of the line.

In France an attempt to abolish figureheads had been made in 1785 and an escutcheon with the fleur-de-lys was ordered, but figures crept back, and during the Revolution some very unusual ones appeared. The frigate *Carmagnole* (1793-1800) had a guillotine, and the *Ca Ira* (formerly *La Couronne*) of 1749-1795, when she took her new name got a new figurehead—the lanterne of the Place de Grève from which many people were hanged during the Terror. Other renamed ships were given the busts of revolutionary leaders. The classicism fashionable under Napoleon brought back many figures from Greek and Roman history or mythology.

Pegasus was popular in clipper ship days, for the flying horse suggested the speed on which they prided themselves. Other clippers had portraits of the owner's family or of characters from literature, oriental subjects, or heroes of the wars in India. The most famous merchant ship figurehead is the witch in Burns's *Tam o' Shanter*, carried by the *Cutty Sark* of 1869.

Figureheads lingered on in warships as long as their bows provided suitable mounts. Those of the first two iron-built ironclads, the *Warrior* of 1860 and *Black Prince* (1861-1923) were especially fine and still survive; but the advent of ram bows caused figureheads to be replaced by escutcheons and supporting decorations. Some were very elaborate, especially in German warships built in the 1880s and 1890s. The last battleships built for the British Navy to have such a decoration were of the Royal Sovereign class of 1891-92, but at the end of 1903 the two light battleships *Constitution* (1903-1915) and *Libertad* (1903-1920), which were building in England for Chile, were taken over and added to the Royal Navy as the *Triumph* and *Swiftsure*. They carried elaborate bow decorations to the end of their days.

The favourite Chilean escutcheon bore the Lone Star, while the National Arms, or other national symbols, were usual in various navies. The Chinese decoration was the dragon, and the Japanese used their national flower, the chrysanthemum, until far into the 20th century. Most US sailing warships had billetheads but especially important ships were given figureheads. The three super-frigates, *Constitution* of 1797, *President* (1800-1817) and *United States* (1797-1866) had, respectively, Hercules, George Washington and the Goddess of Liberty. In 1807 the *Constitution's* Hercules was replaced by Neptune, then in 1812 by a billethead, but in 1833 she received a portrait of President Andrew Jackson. Political opponents sawed it off one night and it was a year before it was replaced. Finally she returned to a billethead.

At the turn of the present century US midshipmen touched their caps every time they passed the figurehead of the Indian chief Tecumseh in the grounds of the Naval Academy at Annapolis. It had belonged to the 74-gun ship *Delaware* (1817-1861) and there was a tradition that midshipmen who did not salute it would fail in their examinations. The custom has long since died out and been forgotten by later generations of midshipmen.

American pre-dreadnought battleships had a decoration supporting a Stars and Stripes shield, but the *Massachusetts* (1893-1920) was presented by her namestate with a life-size bronze statue of Winged Victory with the inscription 'With Duty Done is Honour Won'. It was fixed to the fore turret, between the pair of 13-inch guns. In some navies the decorations were abolished and the stem left plain; instead there was an escutcheon on each side of the bow. The Germans were especially fond of that form and continued it for their major warships right through the days of Hitler's Navy.

Figureheads and escutcheons have long gone from the British Navy, yet the need for something personal to the ship remains. It was found, unofficially at first, in badges with an individual crest for each ship. They were carried on the gun tampions, but with the coming of missile armament they are now worn in a prominent place on board, accompanied by the ship's motto and scrolls with the battle honours of the name across the centuries. It is a naval version of the military custom of wearing each regiment's battle honours on its Colours. A fitting conclusion to the long history of naval figureheads.

Similarly with some merchantmen, tradition, modified to suit modern conditions, lingers on. The common use of the soft-nosed bow since the 1939-45 war has permitted owners frequently to repeat company insignia on bows and funnel, which can be a useful guide to the true owner of a ship whose funnel bears the colours of a charterer. Not all modern bow designs are company-orientated. For example, Orient liner motifs are inspired by individual ships' names and Ellerman Citys bear the escutcheon of the city after which each is named. Some, notably those on Fred Olsen ships' bows, are just attractive creations intrinsically.

the America's Cup

Above: **The 210-ton yacht 'Sappho' which helped to retain the America's Cup in 1871, from a painting in the Naval Museum at Genova-Pegli.** *M Pucciarelli*

Left: The original cup winner 'America' starting a race at Cowes, from 'The Illustrated London News' of August 30, 1851.

IN 1851 THE AMERICAN 102ft twin-masted schooner *America,* with 5263 square feet of sail, was sailed across the Atlantic to take part in a race organised by the Royal Yacht Squadron around the Isle of Wight. The prize was a 100-guinea cup. Sailed on August 22 of that year, the 53-mile event with 18 entrants was won by the *America* and the cup was taken back to America. In 1857 the syndicate which owned the schooner presented the cup to the New York Yacht Club, who renamed it the America's Cup and offered it for international competition. *America* had a varied career, including taking part in the Civil War, and she was not broken up until 1945.

Maybe, if the New York YC commodore had sent his *Maria* and won the race, the cup would not have been named after her and the event would have been forgotten, but the name America seemed to give a special aura and the New York YC has been saddled with the organisation of the competition to this day.

Challenges have been numerous, but in the 22 attempts to win it from the United States up to 1974, not one has been successful. There are a few rules and they have been altered over the years, but it has always been customary for the races to be held in the home waters of the defenders. Consequently they have all taken place in the vicinity of New York.

The America's Cup races have caught the fancy of the general public as well as of devotees of sailing. They have attracted owners who have spent fortunes building craft to challenge and defend. To produce the high-class racing machines required, an almost bottomless purse has to be taken for granted. Challenges are by clubs, although individual owners or syndicates foot the bill. As might be expected, most challengers, including the early ones, have come from the British Isles, but other countries have played an increasing part in recent years.

The cup was taken to America in 1851, but it was not until 1870 that America was first called on to defend it. The challenge came from the Royal Thames Yacht Club. Adhering to the rule that the challenger should first cross the Atlantic on her own bottom, the 108ft schooner *Cambria,* owned by James Ashbury raced across, narrowly defeating James Gordon Bennet's schooner *Dauntless.* In the race for the cup *Cambria* joined a mixed fleet of 23 sloops and schooners. It was a handicap event and *Cambria* finished 8th, but was 10th on corrected time.

The following year James Ashbury was

back again with the 126ft schooner *Livonia*, on behalf of the Royal Harwich Yacht Club. On that occasion the cup was defended by a single boat—a practice followed ever since. Actually the Americans had four boats to choose from, and they used *Columbia* for light weather races and *Sappho* when heavy weather was expected. *Livonia* won two of the first three races against *Columbia*, but *Sappho* took over and won the remaining two of a series of five.

In 1876 the Royal Canadian Yacht Club challenged from Toronto with *Countess of Dufferin* against John S Dickerson's schooner *Madelaine*. She was unsuccessful, but in that series the original, and by then venerable, *America* accompanied the two yachts around the course and actually beat the *Countess* by 20 minutes, and was only seven minutes behind the winner.

In those days opinion was divided between a spread-out comparatively low rig, as exemplified by the schooner, and the taller single-masted sloop or cutter rig. The single-masted rig suffered from the complexity of rigging needed to keep a tall mast aloft. It is not until much more recent years that technical knowledge has improved to the stage where the known greater efficiency of the sloop rig could be exploited without the masses of rigging spoiling all the aerodynamic advantages.

Although found today mainly in sailing dinghies, centreboards were favoured for much larger yachts in the latter half of the 19th century. Often, quite massive centreboards were used to provide keel surface, sometimes retracting into a shallow fixed keel. Both yachts in the 1876 series had centreboards.

In 1881 there was another challenge from Canada when the Bay of Quince Yacht Club had the 70ft centreboard sloop *Atalanta* towed by mule to New York via the Erie Canal. She was a 'skimming dish' type, having a shallow-draught hull and most of the necessary depth to grip the water provided by a centreboard; in other words, very fast but not a seaworthy hull. The cup was defended by the more conventional 67ft *Mischief*, which won, but the Americans realised they were up against a type of boat that might eventually beat them, and one that did not fit what they had in mind for competing yachts. The deed of gift was changed so that only an ocean-going yacht could compete and it had to arrive for the match under sail on its own bottom.

It was not until 1885 that the Royal Yacht Squadron challenged with two yachts; Sir Richard Sutton's cutter *Genesta* (displacing 141 tons and carrying 7150 square feet of sail) and Lieutenant William Henn's cutter *Galatea*. In fact, only *Genesta* raced that year. The series was troubled by lack of wind and spectator interference—something which has become more of a problem in recent years. In one race *Genesta* could have won by a sail-over as the defender, *Puritan* (displacing 105 tons and carrying 7982 square feet of sail), had fouled and was disqualified, but Sir Richard sportingly refused. *Puritan* retained the cup.

In 1886 Lieutenant Henn crossed the Atlantic with his *Galatea*, but was then representing the Royal Northern Yacht Club instead of the RYS. *Galatea* was a narrow 'plank-on-edge' racer, of the type considered fastest at the time. General Paine had built a beamy centreboard defender named *Mayflower* (displacing 110 tons and carrying 8600 square feet of sail) and she won by comfortable margins.

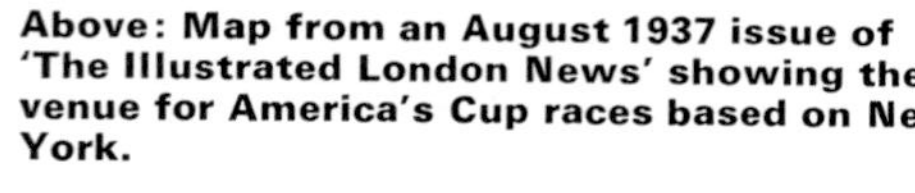

Above: **Map from an August 1937 issue of 'The Illustrated London News' showing the venue for America's Cup races based on New York.**

Below, left to right: A line-up of America's Cup contenders, 'American Eagle', 'Weatherly', 'Endeavour II', 'Columbia' and 'Sceptre', and 'Kurrewa V'.
All Beken of Cowes Ltd

Scotland came into it in 1887 with *Thistle,* designed by George L Watson and owned by James Bell representing the Royal Clyde Yacht Club. The match was won easily by *Volunteer,* Edward Burgess-designed and owned by General Paine. The series finished with a lot of hard feeling and distrust on both sides.

The New York Yacht Club altered the deed of gift so that various leading dimensions of a challenger should be announced 10 months in advance. The Royal Yacht Squadron objected to the requirement and eventually it was modified so that only the length need be announced.

It was not until 1893 that there was another challenge, when Lord Dunraven entered the 92ft sloop *Valkyrie II.* She was a Watson design, and Edward Burgess was no longer alive to take up the challenge. Instead Nathanael G Herreschoff had come on the scene and he designed the 124ft bronze sloop *Vigilant* as defender. She was owned by a New York syndicate and won three straight races. Displacements were getting lower and sail areas were increasing; both yachts were under 100 tons, but carried over 10,000 square feet of sail.

Lord Dunraven renewed the challenge in 1895 with a *Valkyrie III,* which was met by a Herreschoff *Defender.* Sail areas had become yet greater; both had around 13,000 square feet on displacements of about 100 tons. In two races Lord Dunraven accused the defenders of breaking the rules and fouling. He withdrew after the third race had started because of spectator crowding. The objections were looked into by New York Yacht Club officers, who ruled that the earl was wrong on all counts.

The British name mostly associated with the America's Cup is Sir Thomas Lipton. With the support of the Royal Ulster Yacht Club he made five unsuccessful challenges. As with earlier contenders, those were the days when yachts were sailed by professional crews and owners did little more than pay the bills. If they sailed, it was as passengers. Sir Thomas Lipton, despite sinking a fortune in attempts to wrest the cup from America, knew little about sailing and left the building and sailing of his yachts to experts.

Lipton's yachts were all named *Shamrock* and had Will Fife of Fairlea as designer of the first, Watson for the second and Fife again for the third. Then came Charles E. Nicholson who designed *Shamrock IV* and *V.* The challenges were in 1899, 1903, 1905 and 1914 (delayed until 1920 because of the war) and then there was a gap until 1930. Three defenders were designed by Nathanael G Herreschoff. He designed a second *Columbia* for 1899 and 1901, *Reliance* for 1905 and *Resolute* for 1920. By 1930 Herreschoff had retired and the defender for that year was designed by W Starling Burgess, son of Edward Burgess of earlier fame, and owned by a syndicate headed by Harold S Vanderbilt.

As was customary, all of the later yachts were gaff cutters. Overall lengths were around 130ft with displacements increasing over the years from 102 tons to about 140 tons for *Shamrock III* and *Reliance.* Sail areas were about 13,000 square feet, but *Reliance* went up to just over 16,000 square feet—an enormous area of canvas. After that it was agreed that smaller yachts would be used. On the waterline both *Resolute* and *Shamrock V* were 75ft, with displacements under 100 tons.

Like the earlier events in the series, the races up to 1920 were sailed out of New York Harbour. By 1930 conditions there were such that the venue had to be moved farther north around the coast to Newport, Rhode Island. The first four of Lipton's matches totalled 18 races and he lost all except one, in which *Resolute* was withdrawn because of rigging trouble.

Up to that stage the contending yachts had differences and there had to be handicapping. By 1930 J-class yachts had come in. They were the largest of the internationally recognised racing yachts, built to a rather involved formula which took into account hull dimensions and sail area as well as other factors, so although yachts were not identical, in theory two yachts of similar rating should have similar abilities.

It was agreed in 1930 that *Shamrock V* and the defender *Enterprise* should be built to the highest rating of the J-class rule and would race without handicap. Both were about 120ft overall and had about 7500 square feet of sail in Bermudan cutter rigs. *Enterprise* won four races by much narrower margins than the Americans had managed in most earlier matches. *Shamrock V* was withdrawn from another race when the main halliard parted.

In 1934 there were two more J-class yachts racing. T O M Sopwith, famous as an aircraft designer, challenged with the Nicholson-designed steel *Endeavour* and the backing of the Royal Yacht Squadron. *Endeavour* suffered from a strike for higher wages by her professional crew. Faced with an ultimatum, two-thirds of them stayed home and their places were taken by amateurs. The total crew was 31. The defender, designed by Burgess and named *Rainbow,* had Vanderbilt as skipper. Britain came nearer than she had done before to winning the cup, by winning two of the first four races, but *Rainbow* went on to win the rest of the seven in the match. They were the first yachts in the series to abandon jib topsails and use genoas.

The Sopwith/Nicholson team crossed the Atlantic again in 1937 to challenge with *Endeavour II.* Vanderbilt brought in another famous designer, Olin Stephens, to join Burgess and they produced *Ranger. Ranger* turned out to be the fastest J-class yacht ever; she won four races in a row and set a new course record.

The 1939-45 war halted America's Cup racing and brought an end to the very expensive J class. No-one was likely to be able to afford such massive racing machines again, so the New York Yacht Club had to think again and had the deed of gift altered in 1956. The J-class yachts had waterlines upwards of 65ft; The rules were altered to allow 45ft waterlines. It was also agreed that contenders need no longer arrive under sail on their own bottoms.

The changes opened the way for yachts conforming to the 12-metre rule, which, as with the J class, uses a formula involving many measurements (metric) and the result must not exceed 12 metres. The 12-metre boats race each other without handicap. Rigs are Bermudan sloops with very tall masts.

In 1958 there was a challenge under the new rules, from the Royal Yacht Squadron with a 12-metre yacht named *Sceptre,* designed by David Boyd. The defender was *Columbia*—an old name for a new boat—designed by Stephens. *Columbia* ran away from *Sceptre* in three races. Compared with the earlier racers the new contenders were much more modest yachts, but still large by present-day standards. Both were about 69ft long, displaced about 26 tons and carried 1800

square feet of sail—not much more than one-tenth of that carried by *Reliance*.

Apart from the early challenge from Canada, the America's Cup races had really been between the USA and Britain, but in 1962 Australia came into the picture. There was nothing in the rules to prevent any country challenging, but until then the feeling among most world yachtsmen was that no-one could come up to the standards of Britain and the United States.

The Royal Sydney Yacht Club challenged with *Gretel* designed by Alan Payne. The crew was headed by Sir Frank Packer and Jock Sturrock. *Weatherly*, designed by Phil Rhodes, owned by Henry Mercer and skippered by Bus Mosbacher, defended. Both were 12-metre yachts and obviously closely matched. *Gretel* lost the first race, but won the second by 57 seconds. She lost the third race and was only 26 seconds behind in the fourth race—the closest finish in any America's Cup race. *Weatherly* won a further race and retained the cup.

In 1964 Peter Scott went over from Britain with *Sovereign*, designed by David Boyd, and was easily beaten by the Olin Stephens *Constellation*. Both sides had selection races before the event. *Sovereign* was able to beat the almost identical *Kurrewa* and *Constellation* was selected to defend after races against *American Eagle*.

The Royal Sydney Yacht Club challenged again in 1967 with *Dame Pattie*, named after the Australian Prime Minister's wife. The boat was designed by Warwick Hood, who had been an assistant to Alan Payne, the designer of the previous Australian challenger. Tested against *Gretel* she proved very fast, but was unable to come near the American *Intrepid*, another yacht by Olin Stephens.

Intrepid was used again as defender in 1970 (the centenary of the start of the series), but she had many modifications, including a new stern section to the hull. Alan Payne had designed a new *Gretel II* for an Australian challenge. There was a French challenge from Baron Bich (of Bic ballpoint pens). but his *France* could not stand up to *Gretel II* in eliminating races. In the first race *Intrepid's* five-minute win was largely accounted for by the time *Gretel II* had needed to rescue a man overboard. In the second race the Australains came in first, but were disqualified because of a foul on the start line. *Intrepid* won the third and fourth races. The Australians won the fifth, slow, race.

In 1974 there were challenges from Australia and France. America built two defenders, *Mariner* and *Courageous*, while

Top left: 1885 British contender, the 80-ton cutter yacht 'Genesta'.
Illustrated London News

Top centre: Peter Scott's 1964 yacht 'Sovereign' which lost to 'Constellation'.
Beken of Cowes Ltd

Above: The 1974 French contender 'France' which was defeated in preliminaries by the Australian 'Southern Cross' and so did not compete with the American holder. *R Fisher*

Left: An ILN 1937 reproduction of a Frank Mason painting of 'Endeavour I' being sighted by the 'Cheyenne' after the yacht had broken adrift in a hurricane and sailed the Atlantic alone. *Illustrated London News*

Top right: The two 1974 possible American defenders 'Courageous' and 'Intrepid'; 'Courageous' was selected and held the cup.
R Fisher

Right: The unsuccessful French contender in 1974 under sail. *R Fisher*

Intrepid was given rejuvenating treatment. *Mariner* soon proved unsuccessful, while the old *Intrepid* started by consistently beating *Courageous,* but major changes to the latter and her crew brought her into the lead and the job of defending.

Alan Bond, an Australian, had the *Southern Cross* built. At first she had difficulty in beating the old *Gretel II,* but improvements to *Southern Cross* increased her speed and she set out to challenge, with Jim Hardy at the helm. She first had to meet the French challenger, *France,* to decide which country should challenge America. *Southern Cross* easily beat *France* in four races.

On the record of performance of the competing yachts before the series started, Australia appeared to stand a very good chance of beating the defender, but it was not to be. In the first race, with a fleet of 750 large spectator craft and a course patrolled by coastguard craft, *Courageous* finished just under five minutes ahead of *Southern Cross.* In that and the second race there were protests from both yachts. In the second race the Australian yacht was only seconds behind the American yacht for much of the distance, but *Courageous* finished just over one minute in the lead.

An attempt to run the third race was frustrated by fog—on Friday September 13. A second attempt at the third race was beaten by the time limit of $5\frac{1}{2}$ hours. Because of lack of wind, time ran out when *Courageous,* in the lead, was still $4\frac{1}{2}$ miles from the finish.

At the third attempt at the third race, on Monday September 16, *Courageous* won by over five minutes. On Tuesday in a light breeze *Courageous* finished over seven minutes ahead of *Southern* Cross, to complete the successful defence of the cup once more. There was no need to sail any more of the maximum of seven races to get a decision.

Since the races started in 1870 there have been 22 matches, but in those challengers have only won seven individual races. In more recent years since 1937, there have only been two individual races won by challengers. Building and racing such yachts has become an increasingly expensive pastime. Time will tell if there will be more challengers, but the urge to wrest the cup from the New York Yacht Club is still great.